WITHDRAWN

HARVARD LIBRARY

WITHDRAWN

Also in the Variorum Collected Studies Series:

NELSON H. MINNICH
The Catholic Reformation: Council, Churchmen, Controversies

LOUIS-JACQUES BATAILLON
La prédication au XIIIe siècle en France et Italie

JOHN W. O'MALLEY
Religious Culture in the Sixteenth Century

PETER A. LINEHAN
Past and Present in Medieval Spain

JEAN RICHARD
Croisades et Etats latins d'Orient

JEAN-PIERRE DEVROEY
Etudes sur le grand domaine carolingien

ALFRED SOMAN
Sorcellerie et justice criminelle: Le Parlement de Paris (16e-18e siècles)

PAUL GRENDLER
Culture and Censorship in Late Renaissance Italy and France

C.R. CHENEY
The English Church and Its Laws, 12th-14th Centuries

C.R. CHENEY
The Papacy and England, 12th-14th Centuries

ANTOINE DONDAINE
Les hérésies et l'Inquisition, XIIe-XIIIe siècles

ROBERT SOMERVILLE
Papacy, Councils and Canon Law in the 11th-12th Centuries

JEAN BECQUET
Vie canoniale en France aux Xe-XIIe siècles

E. WILLIAM MONTER
Enforcing Morality in Early Modern Europe

HENRY KAMEN
Crisis and Change in Early Modern Spain

The Fifth Lateran Council (1512-17)

Depiction of the Eighth Session (1513) of Lateran V

I.B. DE GARGIIS, *Oratio in octava sessione Lateranensis Concilii...*,
Romae: Marcelo Silber, n.d.

Nelson H. Minnich

The Fifth Lateran Council (1512–17)

Studies on its Membership, Diplomacy and Proposals for Reform

VARIORUM

This edition copyright © 1993 by Nelson H. Minnich.

Published by VARIORUM
    Ashgate Publishing Limited
    Gower House, Croft Road,
    Aldershot, Hampshire GU11 3HR
    Great Britain

    Ashgate Publishing Company
    Old Post Road
    Brookfield, Vermont 05036
    USA

BX
830
.1512
.M56
1993

ISBN 0-86078-349-9

A CIP catalogue record for this book is available from the
British Library and the US Library of Congress

The paper used in this publication meets the minimum requirements of
    American National Standard for Information Sciences
— Permanence of Paper for Printed Library Materials, ANSI Z39.48-1984.

Printed by   Galliard (Printers) Ltd
             Great Yarmouth, Norfolk
             Great Britain

COLLECTED STUDIES SERIES CS392

CONTENTS

Acknowledgements   vi
Preface   vii–viii

PARTICIPANTS

I   The Participants at the Fifth Lateran Council   157–206
Archivum Historiae Pontificiae 12 (1974)

DIPLOMACY

II   The Healing of the Pisan Schism (1511–13)   59–192
(With New Appendices)   193*–197*
Annuarium Historiae Conciliorum 16 (1984)

III   The 'Protestatio' of Alberto Pio (1513)   261–289
Società, politica e cultura a Carpi ai tempi di Alberto III Pio: Atti del Convegno Internazionale (Carpi, 19–21 Maggio (1978), ed. Rino Avesani et al. (Medioevo e Umanesimo 46), Vol. 1. Padova: Studio Bibliografico Antenore, 1981

REFORM

IV   Concepts of Reform Proposed at the Fifth
Lateran Council   163–251
(With New Appendices)   252*–253*
Archivum Historiae Pontificiae 7 (1969)

V   The Proposals for an Episcopal College
at Lateran V   213–232
Ecclesia Militans. Studien zur Konzilien- und Reformationsgeschichte, Remigius Bäumer zum 70. Geburtstag gewidmet, ed. Walter Brandmüller, Herbert Immenkötter and Erwin Iserloh, Band I. Paderborn: Ferdinand Schöningh, 1988

Index   1–8

This volume contains viii + 342 pages

ACKNOWLEDGEMENTS

Grateful acknowledgement is made to the following publishers for permission to reproduce in this volume articles originally published by them: Editrice Pontificia Università Gregoriana, Piazza della Pilotta 35, I–00187 Rome, Italy (I, IV); Verlag Ferdinand Schöningh, Jühenplatz am Rathaus, Postfach 2540, D–4790 Paderborn, Germany (II, V); Studio Bibliografico Antenore, Via G. Rusca 15, I–35100 Padova, Italy (III).

PUBLISHER'S NOTE

The articles in this volume, as in all others in the Collected Studies Series, have not been given a new, continuous pagination. In order to avoid confusion, and to facilitate their use where these same studies have been referred to elsewhere, the original pagination has been maintained wherever possible.

Each article has been given a Roman number in order of appearance, as listed in the Contents. This number is repeated on each page and quoted in the index entries.

PREFACE

At the international conference held at the beginning of September 1963 that commemorated the fourth centenary of the close of the Council of Trent, Hubert Jedin is reported to have lamented the paucity of studies on the Fifth Lateran Council (1512-17), the council that preceded Trent and in various ways shaped some of its procedures and decrees. Responding to his call for new research, Heiko A. Oberman offered in the spring term of 1966 a seminar on Catholicism from Lateran V to Trent in the Harvard Divinity School. When I enrolled as a transfer-student in this seminar, Professor Oberman directed me to work on Lateran V. I soon became fascinated with this Council that was called to reform the Church on the very eve of the Reformation, and the paper I wrote was later expanded into my master's thesis at Boston College under the direction of Samuel J. Miller. With encouragement from John W. O'Malley, S.J., and Burkhart Schneider, S.J., I revised a section of this thesis and published it in 1969 as a study of how Lateran V envisioned reform (here Study IV). While working with the original printings of the conciliar speeches and decrees, I came upon two woodcut depictions of its sessions which became the subjects of two collaborative studies with the art historian Heinrich W. Pfeiffer, S.J., that appeared in *Archivum Historiae Pontificiae* 8 (1970) and 19 (1981). The woodcut that adorned De Gargiis' speech of 1513 is reprinted here as the frontispiece of this volume.

Convinced that the Fifth Lateran Council offered numerous opportunies for original research, I decided to write my doctoral dissertation in the History Department at Harvard University under Myron P. Gilmore on a central theme of the Council, episcopal reform. As an aid to locating relevant documents, I tried to determine who attended the Council. The more I worked on a list of participants, the clearer it became that the commonly accepted charges that the Council was poorly attended and that its membership was almost exclusively Italian were not true. Study I published in 1974 details my findings. A chapter from my dissertation on the proposals for a permanent episcopal college in the Roman Curia was presented as a paper at the Sixteenth Century Studies Conference (1977), awarded a Carl Meyer Prize, and subsequently revised for the Remigius Bäumer *Festschrift* (1988); it appears here as Study V. While I was doing research on the dissertation, A. Lynn Martin, whom I met regularly at the Vatican Library's espresso machine, called my attention to what proved to be the draft of a lost speech of the imperial ambassador to the Council that he had accidentally discovered in the Chigi collection. I subsequently transcribed that document, researched its context, and presented my findings through the good offices of Myron P. Gilmore at the Alberto Pio conference (1978)–here Study III. Because my work on Lateran V had turned up repeated evidence of the papacy's concern for orthodoxy in the years prior to Luther's theses, a concern at variance with the standard portrayal of a doctrinally indifferent Leo X, I resolved to examine this issue in detail. My research (especially in 1979-80) revealed that the preoccupation of the papacy in the later years of Julius II's reign and at the beginning of Leo X's was the healing of the Pisan schism on terms that preserved the spiritual and temporal prerogatives of the papacy and extracted from schismatic clerics an admission that the denial of the pope's power over councils was heresy (Study II published in 1984).

Because work on Lateran V has been hampered by the lack of a critical edition of its *acta* and by the scarcity of printed sources, I have attempted over the years to transcribe and publish in the notes and appendices of my articles relevant documents that may be of assistance to future scholars working on this Council. I have, therefore, added to this reprinting some subsequent findings as two new appendices (XVI* and XVII*) to Study II and three (11*, 12*, and 13*) to Study IV. Another factor that has impeded research on Lateran V is the tendency of scholars to write this Council off as a failure because it did not prevent the Protestant Reformation. When studied free of this preoccupation, the Council can be seen as an important clearing-house for the concerns of leading churchmen. Indeed, contemporaries considered it a success, given the limitations imposed upon it by circumstances beyond its control. For some of my other studies on Lateran V, please consult the companion Variorum volume *The Catholic Reformation* (1993).

Over the years I have incurred numerous debts of gratitude to individuals and institutions for their support of my research on Lateran V. Principal among them are my former teachers: Heiko A. Oberman who introduced me to the topic and guided my initial research, Samuel J. Miller who helped me develop the topic into a master's thesis, William J. Bouwsma who encouraged my interest in this Council, the late Myron P. Gilmore who patiently directed my dissertation on the topic, even reading hand-written drafts, and Giles Constable who sacrificed part of his Christmas holidays in 1976 to give the final version a careful reading. Among my colleagues I am particularly grateful to John W. O'Malley, S.J., and Paul F. Grendler for having taken a personal interest in my work over the years, to Heinrich W. Pfeiffer, S.J., for having helped me to explore the artistic and liturgical aspects of the Council, and to Walter Brandmüller for his continued encouragement of further research and writing on this Council. To these distinguished and generous scholars I gratefully dedicate this volume. Among the institutions that have supported my studies and research over the years are the Society of Jesus, the Foundation for Reformation Research, Harvard University, the National Endowment for the Humanities, the American Council of Learned Societies, Villa I Tatti, the American Academy in Rome, the Richard Krautheimer Research Fund, the Catholic University of America, and the Societas Internationalis Historiae Conciliorum Investigandae. I am especially grateful to Paul F. Grendler for having encouraged me in various ways to publish this volume, to John Smedley for his editorial assistance, and to Joseph C. Linck for his help with typing and indexing.

NELSON H. MINNICH

The Catholic University of America
Washington, D.C.
4 July 1992

I

THE PARTICIPANTS AT THE FIFTH LATERAN COUNCIL

Summarium. — Duae accusationes frequentissimae de numero participantium necnon de nationibus repraesentatis in Concilio Lateranensi V examini subiciuntur. Ex criteriis internis et externis comprobatur elenchos participantium, qui in Actis Concilii inveniuntur, mendosos esse. Praelati praesentes eorumque sedes identificantur, inquantum fieri potuit. Numerantur 431 membra Concilii; plus quam tertia pars sedium in Concilio repraesentatarum extra Italiam sita fuisse ostenditur. Adduntur quattuor appendices: 1ᵃ exhibet nomina membrorum Concilii, additis datis biographicis, 2ᵃ sedes in Concilio repraesentatas, 3ᵃ religiosos in Concilio praesentes, 4ᵃ oratores dominorum civilium.

Ever since the time of the Fifth Lateran Council (1512-17), both the number and diversity of nationality of this general council's membership have been the object of disparaging statements by scholars.[1] In spite of (or perhaps better, because of) the absence of a careful study of the assembly's rolls, this council has been repeatedly labelled and libelled as poorly attended and of almost exclusively Italian membership.

A variety of writers who have treated this council in subsequent centuries have made mistaken or misleading statements. The Italian controversialist-theologian, Roberto Bellarmino (1542-1621), attempted to defend the ecumenicity of this council on legalistic grounds, conceding that very few bishops were present, not even a hundred. The church historian and proponent of moderate Gallicanism, Noël Alexandre (1639-1724), also pointed to deficiencies in the membership of this general council, affirming that the bishops in attendance were one-hundred and

---

[1] For a general bibliography on this council, consult that found in N. H. MINNICH, *Concepts of Reform Proposed at the Fifth Lateran Council*: Arch. Hist. Pont. 7 (1969) 163-64, n. 2. The long awaited study by Oliver de la Brosse scheduled for publication this year was, unfortunately, not available for consultation in preparing this article. Two useful works on the membership of medieval councils are Georgine TANGL, *Die Teilnehmer an den allgemeinen Konzilien des Mittelalters*, Weimar 1922, and Joseph RIEGEL, *Die Teilnehmerlisten des Konstanzer Konzils: ein Beitrag zur mittelalterlichen Statistik*, Freiburg/Br. 1916.

fourteen in number and these were almost all Italians.[2] The great collector of conciliar materials, Giovanni Domenico Mansi (1692-1769), was but a bit more generous in saying that the number of bishops hardly exceeded one-hundred and twenty[3]. While these statements may be true for particular sessions, they do not apply to the full membership of a council which sat for five years nor do they agree with the fourteen different rolls of prelates contained in the conciliar acts.[4]

Modern historians, unfortunately, have not gone much beyond the statements of their predecessors. In the last century Ferdinand Gregorovius (1821-91) apparently used the number and nationality of the council's members as the bases for the disparaging statement « this servile synod of a few Italian bishops ... audaciously called itself an Oecumenical Council. »[5] Karl Joseph Hefele (1809-93) erred on two counts in affirming that no Spanish prelate was present at the initial sessions apart from the ambassador of King Ferdinand, the Bishop of Vich.[6] The English historian Mandell Creighton (1843-1910) was also mistaken in holding that the kings of Europe did not trouble to send representatives to the council.[7] More recently the

---

[2] *Roberti cardinalis Bellarmini opera omnia*, ed. Xisto Riario Sforza, Naples 1857, II, 63, 66; Natalis ALEXANDRUS, *Historia ecclesiastica veteris noviąue testamenti ab orbe condito ad annum post Christum natum millesimum sexcentesimum*, Paris 1714, VIII, 607.

[3] Odoricus RAYNALDUS, *Annales ecclesiastici ab anno MCXCVIII ubi desinit cardinalis Baronius ad annum MDLXV*, revised and supplemented by Johannes Dominicus MANSI, Vol. 30, Lucca 1754, 607, ad annum 1512, n. 1. Hereafter references to this work will be cited as RAYNALDUS followed by the appropriate year and number subdivision.

[4] These fourteen rolls can be found in *Sacrorum conciliorum nova et amplissima collectio*, ed. Joannes Dominicus MANSI et post ipsius mortem Florentinus et Venetianus editores, Vol. 32 (1438-1549), reprinted Paris 1902, cols. 673e-80c, 707b-10e, 727d-31c, 743b-47b, 762d-66c, 785a-88c, 805e-09c, 858b-63a, 901a-05a, 936a-37e, 939b-42a, 977b-79b, 980a-83d. Hereafter this volume will be cited as M followed by the number of the column and its alphabetic subdivision.

[5] Ferdinand GREGOROVIUS, *History of the City of Rome in the Middle Ages*, trans. from the 4th German edition by Annie HAMILTON, London 1902, III, 241, 102.

[6] Charles-Joseph HEFELE, *Le Cardinal Ximenès et les affaires religieuses en Espagne a la fin du quinzième siècle et au commencement du seizième*, trans. from the German by Charles SAINTE-FOI et P.-A. DE BERMOND, Tournai 1856, 502. The ambassador of Fernando in Rome was the Baron de Llauri, Jeronimo Vich, not to be confused with his other ambassador, Jaime Conchilles, bishop of Catania, as did even Paride de Grassi in his *Diarium* (Joseph Ignatius von DÖLLINGER, *Beiträge zur politischen, kirchlichen und Cultur-Geschichte der sechs letzten Jahrhunderte*, Vienna 1882, III, 403). Excluding such Spanish prelates as Fernando de Castro of Scala, Pedro Florez of Castellamare, and Gaspar Torrella of Santa Giusta who held Italian sees, there were also then present from Spain Juan de Sepulveda of Tuy and Pascual de Ampudia of Burgos.

[7] Mandell CREIGHTON, *A History of the Papacy from the Great Schism to the Close of Rome*, New York 1897, IV, 234.

French scholar Pierre Imbart de la Tour (1860-1925) claimed that out of the six-hundred bishops of Christendom only one-hundred and ten, all of which, except three, Italian, and the generals of religious orders resident in Rome constituted the Council's membership. [8] Even the rightly renowned scholar on the council in the sixteenth century, Hubert Jedin has affirmed that the personnel of the Lateran Council was made up almost exclusively of Italian bishops. [9]

Perhaps the most forceful criticism of the number and nationality of Lateran's membership came at the time of the council and from the pen of Europe's leading humanist, Desiderius Erasmus of Rotterdam. Invited to accompany John Fisher, Bishop of Rochester, a member of the English legation to the council, Erasmus was forced to decline the offer since it came too late for him to make the necessary arrangements for such a trip. [10] Realizing the difficulties, especially for foreigners, involved in arriving at Rome in time for the council, Julius II (1503-13) on the advice of his relative cardinal Raffaello Riario postponed the initial session by two weeks. [11] Confusion over the opening date of the council delayed the departure and eventually altered the composition of the English delegation. [12] Piqued by the lost opportunity to revisit the home of humanism and piously offended by Julius' political and military exploits, Erasmus composed the derisive and at times maliciously libellous *Julius II. exclusus e coelis* which was presented on the stage at Paris in 1514. [13] In this play the pope is portrayed as boasting of having excluded from the council by trickery the representatives of transalpine Europe. Standing before the gates of heaven, Julius brags to St. Peter that he intentionally kept the number of bishops small and tried to prevent honest men

---

[8] Pierre IMBART DE LA TOUR, *Les origines de la réforme*, Vol. II: *L'Eglise catholique: La crise et la renaissance*, 2nd edition revised and augmented by Yvonne LANHERS, Melun 1946, 531.

[9] Hubert JEDIN, *Kleine Konziliengeschichte. Die zwanzig ökumenischen Konzilien im Rahmen der Kirchengeschichte*, Freiburg 1959, 78; and his *A History of the Council of Trent*, trans. Ernest GRAF, New York 1957, I, 128, 135.

[10] *Opus Epistolarum Desiderii Erasmi Roterodami*, ed. Percy S. ALLEN et al., Vol. I, Oxford 1906, Ep. 252 To Anthony Bergen (London, 6 February 1512), 498; *Letters and Papers, Foreign and Domestic, of the Reign of Henry VIII*, ed. J. S. BREWER, Vol. I, London 1862, nr. 2085 (4. II. 1512), 320; nr. 3108 (s. d.), 341.

[11] N. MINNICH, *Concepts of Reform*, 241-43; M691e-95a.

[12] *Letters and Papers*, nr. 3012 (16. II. 1512), 324; nr. 3109 (1. IV. 1512), 342; *Opus Epistolarum*, I, Ep. 255, To Andrew Ammonius (Cambridge, 19 February 1512), 502.

[13] *The Julius Exclusus of Erasmus*, trans. Paul PASCAL, introd. and notes by J. Kelley SOWARDS, Bloomington (Indiana) 1968.

from attending by advising the bishops and abbots to spare expenses and send only one or two from each province. Fearing that still too many would attend, he prorogued the council, telling them that they need not come and then proceeded to anticipate the date, opening the council with only his pawns present.[14] While such accusations against Julius made for a colorful stage character, they do not conform to fact. The pope never anticipated the date he had set, neither did he postpone it without just reasons such as the hazards to travel occasioned by hostilities in northern Italy, nor did he try to limit the number of prelates attending.[15]

Rome was aware from the start that men were ready to accuse the pope of trying to avoid a council and therefore labored to prove the contrary. Although Julius personally feared the council, as a schoolboy does his teacher's rod, so he confessed, and thus saw to it that he controlled its officials and machinery,[16] he spent much effort in trying to secure the presence of Europe at his council. Twice he postponed a session to allow a foreign delegation to arrive in time: the initial for Tamás Bakócz, Primate of Hungary, and for the Aragonese and English representatives; the third for Mathaeus Lang von Wellenburg, Bishop of Gurk and personal ambassador of Emperor Maximilian I. Julius' successor, Leo X (1513-21), postponed the seventh session for Jan Łaski, Primate of Poland, and the eighth for the French delegation.[17]. Grants of safe-conduct through the Papal States were given to all coming to the council and efforts were made to secure similar ones in other lands. Conciliar bulls and papal letters and legates to kings urged their personal attendance and that of their prelates at the council.[18]

---

[14] *Julius Exclusus*, 66, 69-70.

[15] *Julius Exclusus*, 104, n. 83, 128, n. 73.

[16] P. de GRASSI, *Diarium*, 418; Eugen GUGLIA, *Studien zur Geschichte des V. Lateranconcils. (1512-1517)*: Sitzungsberichte der phil.-hist. Classe der kaiserlichen Akademie der Wissenschaften 140 (1899) X, 34, hereafter this article is cited as GUGLIA; M 695a-97b; RAYNALDUS, 1512, nr. 34, q. 25.

[17] M 692d-93b, 716d-18a, 795c-96a, 818c-19c; N. MINNICH, *Concepts of Reform*, 241-43.

[18] M688c-89b, 872c-74b, 899a-900c; *Leonis X. Pontificis Maximi Regesta*, ed. Joseph HERGENROETHER, Freiburg 1884-91, nr. 4922, 4923, 6035, 6826, 6885, 14482, 15300, hereafter this work is cited as H followed by the number of the registry entry; *The Letters of James the Fourth 1505-1513*, ed. Robert Kerr HANNEY, Edinburgh 1953, nr. 477 (19. VIII. 1512), 264-65, nr. 478 (20. VIII. 1512), 265; *Corpo diplomatico Portuguez contendo os actos e relações politicas e diplomaticas de Portugal com as diversas potencias do mundo desde o seculo XVI até os nossos dias*, Vol. I: *Relações com a Curia Romana*, ed. Luis Augusto REBELLO DA SILVA,

Such measures were necessary given the political situation. Wars were then being waged through much of Europe, but especially in northern Italy. The French king threatened to take prisoner Spanish bishops on their way to the council. His enemy, the king of England, refused passage for the orators of Scotland, France's ally.[19] Many rulers required that their prelates first secure their permission before leaving the realm. Some princes refused such leaves, others determined the composition of their delegation. Threats of being held in contumacy and liable to excommunication and deprivation of ecclesiastical office were hurled at those who refused to come or could provide no acceptable excuse for their absence. Such threats were not ignored.[20] Prelates unable to attend in person were urged to send procurators and an apparently good number of bishops availed themselves of this option.

The extent of the powers of these procurators during the council is not always clear. Among the decisions made by Julius and the college of cardinals before the council even opened was that procurators like princes and their orators needed the permission of the pontiff before they could speak in the council.[21] Such a decision would seem to imply that they had only a consultative voice in spite of the fact that they represented prelates who by right had decisive voice in conciliar proceedings. The acts of the Lateran Council, however, show that at least a procurator bishop under Leo could vote in the name of those absent.[22]

Procurators' voting powers under Julius are difficult to discern. In his instructions to prelates justly prevented from attending the council, Julius ordered them to send suitable procurators with « legitimate mandates. » Their powers are not spelled out. The mandates recorded in the acts named as procurators both fellow bishops and others who seem to have

---

Lisbon 1862, 173, Vol. XI: *Relações com a Curia Romana: Supplemento aos tomos I a X*, ed. Jayme Constantino DE FREITAS MONIZ, Lisbon 1898, 59; José M. DOUSSINAGUE, *Fernando el Católico y el cisma de Pisa*, Madrid 1946, 505-07; M 711d; RAYNALDUS 1511, nr. 67.

[19] HEFELE-LECLERCQ, *Histoire des conciles d'après les documents originaux*, VIII-I, Paris 1917, 544; *Letters and Papers*, nr. 2085, 3109; *Corpo diplomatico Portuguez*, I, 153, 160; J. M. DOUSSINAGUE, *Fernando y el cisma*, 306-08, 520-23; *Letters of James*, nr. 478, p. 265, nr. 563, p. 315.

[20] M 688b, 715c, 733d; *Veterum scriptorum et monumentorum historicorum, dogmaticorum, moralium, amplissima collectio*, ed. Edmundus MARTÈNE and Ursinus DURAND, III, Paris 1724, cols. 1180-81.

[21] RAYNALDUS, 1512, nr. 33, q. 3.

[22] M 795bc; GUGLIA, 22 seems to hold that procurators had full power under both pontiffs.

been mostly clerics. These documents empowered them to be present at and take part in (*interessendo*) the council — the same term used for bishops at the council.[23] Other than the condemnation of the rival synod at Pisa, the agenda of Lateran under Julius scheduled no important votes. The mere presence at Lateran V of procurators without voting power, yet representing the hierarchy of Europe, was sufficient to defeat Pisa and posed few problems of control.

Leo, however, was at first eager for the active participation of prelates in the council. He even had them elect their own representatives to the conciliar commissions and ordered them under pain of excommunication to attend a general congregation. His instructions to prelates unable to attend the council commanded them in virtue of holy obedience and under pain of excommunication and perjury to send « suitable special procurators with full mandate for those things which are to be treated, acted upon, and deliberated » in the Lateran Council.[24] Leo was intent on having the revocation of the Pragmatic Sanction of Bourges and conciliar ratification of the Concordat of Bologna approved by a resounding vote and may, therefore, have wanted procurators to come empowered to cast decisive votes.

A major problem involved in determining the national representation at Lateran V is the use of terms like Italian, German, or Spanish. Since most scholars claim that the council's personnel was almost exclusively Italian, some attempt should be made at defining this term in particular. A recourse to political divisions is next to useless: the peninsula was divided into numerous units, the southern portion under Aragonese domination and parts of the north lying within the Holy Roman Empire. Sicily and Sardinia were also under Spanish hegemony while Genoa held Corsica. In the northwest the Duchy of Savoy included areas in present-day Italy, France, and Switzerland. The Venetian lands in the northeast and along the Illyrian coast with their mixture of Italian, native, and multi-national refugee populations can hardly all be subsumed under the heading of Italian. The geo-political categories used by the Roman Curia in the fifteenth century were no longer valid by the time of Lateran due to shifting national boundaries. Given these difficulties it may be wise to adopt the divisions used by the standard modern work on that period's hierarchy. Thus the

---

[23] M 688b, 692c, 715e-16c, 733d.
[24] M 794d-95b, 848de, 872e-73a.

term Italy would embrace the central, lower, and upper Italian peninsula, Sicily, Sardinia, Corsica, and adjacent minor islands.[25] An effort will be made to supplement the deficiencies of this listing by making allowances for the non-Italian portions of Savoy and the Imperial possessions in Istria and Venezia Giulia.

The term Italian even when applied only to the dioceses within the area thus circumscribed can be misleading. Just as Italians held sees outside their land, so too did foreigners in Italy. For example, during the Fifth Lateran the following non-Italian members of the council held bishoprics on the peninsula: the Greek scholar, Alexius Celadoni, was bishop of Molfetta; the Dutch astronomer, Paulus van Middelburg from Zealand, presided over Fossombrone; the Bosnian Franciscan, Juraj Dragišić (Giorgio Benigno Salviati), was transferred from Cagli to Nazareth-Canne; and a number of the bishops in southern Italy were of Spanish birth, the most famous of them being perhaps the diplomat Esteban Gabriel Merino, archbishop of Bari. Foreign cardinals, too, held Italian sees: thus the Spaniard Bernardino López de Carvajal administered the archbishopric of Rossano and the Swiss Matthäus Schinner was entrusted with Novara, while the Spaniard Francisco Remolines held seven different Italian sees.

Other countries also had their foreign prelates. The Austrian cardinal Matthäus Lang von Wellenburg was bishop of Cartagena in Spain, while in France the Spaniards Juan Villalva held the see of Elne and Antonio Flores Avignon. The Cretan scholar Markos Musuros became Latin archbishop of Malvasia in Greece. The see of Linköping in Sweden was apparently administered by the Spanish cardinal Jaime Serra. The Italian cardinal Innocenzo Cibò briefly attempted to administer the primatial see of Scotland, St. Andrews, until his Scottish successor Andrew Forman was transferred from the French archbishopric of Bourges. Although the Scot seems never to have attended the council, he labored to secure for it the adherence of both France and Scotland.[26] One of the ambassadors of

---

[25] J. I. von DÖLLINGER, *Beiträge*, II, Regensburg 1863; 1-296; Guilelmus van GULIK and Conradus EUBEL, *Hierarchia catholica medii et recentioris aevi, sive summorum pontificum, S. R. E. cardinalium ecclesiarum antistitum series*, Vol. III, rev. by Ludovicus SCHMITZ-KALLENBERG, reprinted Padua 1960, 348-51. Hereafter this volume is cited as E. Supporting references from Eubel regarding the bishops at Lateran V and the sees they held can be found at the end of this article in the lists of participants and dioeceses represented.

[26] *Letters of James*, nr. 388, pp. 213-15, nr. 415, p. 227, nr. 429, p. 236; *Letters and Papers*, nr. 3104, p. 341.

England to the Lateran was the Italian bishop of Worcester, Silvestro Gigli. Italy also supplied the representative from the New World, Alessandro Girolamo Geraldino from Amelia, the bishop of San Domingo in the Caribbean.

Given a Church hierarchy of such international composition, it is very difficult to determine the national origins of each bishop without doing extensive biographical research. One way of handling the problem is to concentrate on the location of the sees rather than on the birthplace of those who held them. Except for the clear case of the Spaniard Felipe de Urrea of Philadelphia,[27] most titular bishops appear to have been Italians.

A diocese could be represented at the council in a number of ways. Its own bishop or his coadjutor could be personally present. If the see were presently vacant and either held *in commendam* or administered by a prelate, that diocese would be represented by the cleric who thus controlled it. Should its bishop be unable to attend in person, he could delegate by mandate a procurator to act on his behalf in the council. A number of dioceses could be implicitly represented in the person of the orator(s) or procurator of the king in whose realm they lay, as was the case with the sees of Denmark and Norway whose procurator was probably the same as their king's, the curialist Zutfeldus Wardenburg from Mecklenburg,[28] or by the national primate or an archbishop (at times through their procurators) who headed the ecclesiastical region or province to which they pertained, especially when this was explicitly stated, as in the mandate sent by Jakob Ulfsson in the name of his archdiocese of Upsala and that of the province of Sweden.[29] While in no technical sense official delegates of their dioceses, the various officers of the Fifth Lateran such as the council procurator Thomas Regis of Rennes and the notaries Bernhard Schulz von Löwenborg of Leslau and Bernardino de Contreras from Burgos deserve mention when treating national representation.[30] To avoid excessive complications, no con-

---

[27] Carlos Ramon FORT, *Tratado LXXXIX: De los obispos Españoles titulares de iglesias in partibus infidelium ó auxiliares en las de España*, rev. and enlarged by Vicente DE LA FUENTE, Vol. 51 of *España Sagrada*, Madrid 1879, 140, 331.

[28] RAYNALDUS, 1512, nr. 83; *Regesta Diplomatica Historiae Danicae*, cura Societatis Regiae Scientiarum Danicae, Series 2, Vol. I-II: (1448-1536), Copenhaven 1889, nr. 10,059 (11. V. 1515), 1199.

[29] M 916c.

[30] E 86, H nr. 2323, 2324, 2375; H nr. 7652-53, Herman HOBERG, *Die Protokollbücher der Rotanotare von 1464 bis 1517*: Zeitschrift der Savigny Stiftung für Rechtsgeschichte, Kanonistische Abteilung 39 (1953), 200, esp. n. 11; *Codex diplo-*

* (See Addenda)

sideration will be given to the offices of national protector or of nuncio or of collector of revenues from various nations held by council members, although some kings may have felt they were represented by such ecclesiastics.[31]

Recording the names of those present whether in person or by procurator at the Fifth Lateran was entrusted to the council's protonotaries, notaries, and their subalternates, the scribes.[32] When cardinal Antonio del Monte three years after the council's closing set out with a commission from Pope Leo X to gather these records for the official publication of the acts of the council, he found that a number of the documents had already disappeared or were in need of emendation.[33] Lists of council members were not to be found either in the various speeches and bulls published individually during the council nor in the collection of Lateran's bulls printed at Milan in 1518.[34] Del Monte had to depend on the faulty written records. While a careful study of his version of the council's acts shows that he eliminated or modified records to project an image of harmony and consensus,[35] similar research sheds but a little light on his lists of council members.

By an examination of internal evidence, the council rolls published in the 1521 del Monte edition are found to be faulty. Names of bishops not listed among those present at a particular session later appear in the acts for that session — thus, while Lorenzo de Fieschi of Mondovì, Fernando de Castro of Scala, and Juan de Loayasa of Alghero are not listed as present at the fifth, tenth, and eleventh sessions respectively, they later appear in the acts of these sessions as procurators presenting mandates for absent prelates. Juan de Loayasa at that eleventh session claimed that he was procurator for more than one bishop, yet

---

maticus Brandenburgensis. Sammlung der Urkunden, Chroniken und sonstigen Quellenschriften für die Geschichte der Mark Brandenburg und ihrer Regenten, ed. Adolph Friedrich RIEDEL, Series III, *Namenverzeichniss*III, Berlin 1868, 196; H nr. 393, 7459-60.

[31] J. M. DOUSSINAGUE, *Fernando y el cisma*, 520-21.
[32] M 665b, 696e.
[33] M 650de, 652bd, 814d.
[34] *Bullae sacri concilii Lateranensis*, Milan: an unsigned work of Alexander Minutianus' press, printed for Johannes Jacobus et Fratres de Legnano, 15.ix.1518; British Museum Reading Room Shelfmark nr. 1609/891. Confer: Francis Swinton ISAAC, *An Index to the Early Printed Books in the British Museum*, Part II: 1501-1520, Section II. Italy, London 1938, nr. 13,584, p. 94. I am grateful to James J. BONO for having consulted this work for me. This rare edition of Lateran's decrees has thus far been ignored by writers on the council.
[35] GUGLIA, 9-12.

I

166

the name of only one was later given.[36] The famed champion of Italian liberty and father of the future cardinal president of the Council of Trent, Girolamo Morone, is reported to have defended as orator of Milan duke Massimiliano Sforza against the accusation made by Claude de Seyssel that he had prevented the French from coming to the council. Morone's name, however, is not listed among the orators at the council.[37] At the eleventh session, the orators of Simᶜān ibn Dāwūd ibn Ḥassān al-Ḥadatī, the centenarian patriarch of the Maronites in Syria (namely, Yūsuf al-Ḫūri, a priest, Ilyās ibn Zarzūr al-Ḥadatī, a deacon monk, and Ilyās ibn Ibrāhīm, a subdeacon monk), are mentioned in the acts as presenting to the pope and reading in Arabic the mandate of their patriarch. Their names, nonetheless, are to be found among neither the orators nor procurators listed as present.[38]

---

[36] M 774de, 916c, 975bd.
[37] M 869ab, 862d-63a.
[38] M 942ab, 939e-40b, 941e-42a, 975c-76b, 943b. The « cum Elias » of 943b should read « cum Moyse » according to Teseo Ambrogio and the authors who follow him. Ibrāhīm ḤARFŪŠ, *Alkunuz al Malfiah*: Al-Manārat, Revue mensuelle, Organ du Patriarch Maronite 4 (1933) 595, n. claims there were, as stated in the conciliar acts (M 943b: Acuri Joseph cum Elia, ac Elia monacho), two different procurators by the name of Ilyās: Ilyās ibn Ibrāhīm and Ilyās ibn Zarzūr al-Ḥadatī. His evidence is primarily a 1518 letter of the patriarch to Alberto Pio. Teseo Ambrogio, writing some twenty years after the council, may have confused the legation to Lateran V with that sent to Hadrian VI. Since this information became available to me when it was no longer feasible to replace Moyses (nr. 264 in the list of participants) with Elias (ibn Zarzūr) without a considerable juggling of numbers, Moyses remains in the list and Ilyās ibn Zarzūr al-Ḥadatī is mentioned in the same entry with Moyses. This Ilyās was in charge of the gardens of the monastery of Qannūbīn where the patriarch resided. . Acuri Joseph is difficult to identify. He may have come from Accura (Accurensis) in southern Lebanon. A papal bull lists a Jussiffus de Brachim as a member of the patriarch's family. The patriarch's nephew and son of a predecessor was Joseph filius Jacobi in whose honor, Mūsā ibn Saᶜādah al-ᶜAkkâri, the next patriarch, wrote a poem. Ilyās ibn Ibrāhīm was a student of the patriarch Simᶜān and carried his ceremonial patriarchal staff. While still in his late teens, Ilyās was sent by Simᶜān to Rome as a member of the Maronite legation in order to learn the Latin language. He spent two years in the city teaching Teseo Ambrogio Syrian and learning from him Latin. He helped Teseo translate the Maronite liturgy into Latin and made copies in Syrian of the Gospels and Psalms for cardinal Bernardino Lopez Carvajal and the humanist prince of Carpi, Alberto Pio. In 1521 this young monk is last mentioned as being in Rome. Pope Leo wanted to retain him at his court. Confer: Theseus AMBROSIUS, *Introductio in Chaldaicam linguam, Syriacam, atque Armenicam, et decem alias linguas*, Pavia 1539, 14r, Giorgio LEVI DELLA VIDA, *Ricerche sulla formazione del più antico fondo dei manoscritti orientali della Biblioteca Vaticana* (Studi e Testi, vol. 92), Città del Vaticano 1939, 107, 133-36; Michael LE QUIEN, *Oriens Christianus, in quatuor patriarchatus digestus, quo exhibentur ecclesiae, patriarchae, caeterique praesules totius orientis*, Vol. III, Paris 1740, cols. 64-66, 94-97; Tobias ANAISSI, *Bullarium Maronitarum*, Rome 1911, 41-42, 53, 55-56; William ROSCOE, *The Life and Pontificate of Leo the Tenth*,

External evidence reveals similar deficiencies in the acts. The Spanish reforming bishop of Burgos, the Dominican Juan Pascual de Rebenga (de la Fuentesanta),is reported to have attended the first and second sessions, but his name does not appear in the rolls.[39] Johann von Blankenfeld of Reval is never listed as orator for the Teutonic Knights yet appears as such in the 1518 collection of Lateran's decrees.[40] The humanist prince Gianfrancesco Pico della Mirandola claimed to have been present at the eighth session during the formal approbation of the decree on the soul's individuality and immortality. According to the rubrics of the council he could have been present then only if he had been officially incorporated into the council's membership. His name is missing, however, from the roll of temporal lords present at this session.[41] The papal master of ceremonies, Paride de Grassi of Pesaro, reported at almost every session that there were numerous procurators of bishops present and that they were incorporated into the council at the beginning of the session.[42] Del Monte listed procurators at only the second, fourth, fifth, sixth, tenth, and eleventh sessions and had them presenting their mandates after the voting at the close of each session.[43] It is known from Pietro Delfino's letters and not from the printed acts of Lateran that the procurator for this general of the Camaldolese at the winter session of 1512 was Pietro Bembo, fellow Venetian and humanist.[44] Given such internal and external evidence, there is little doubt that many more persons were present at the council than appear in the rolls of del Monte.

In addition to their incompleteness, the lists of council members provided by del Monte present a number of other

---

rev. by William HAZLITT, London 1846, I, 355; Celestino CAVEDONI, *Notizia letteraria di alcuni codici orientali e greci della Reale Biblioteca Estense che già furono di Alberto Pio, principe di Carpi*: Memorie di religione, di morale, di letteratura, Series 3, Vol. 17, Modena 1834, 2-8.

[39] S. BIEDNA, *Pascual de Fontecasto*: Biografia Eclesiástica Completa, Madrid 1863, XVI, 883.

[40] *Bullae sacri concilii*, K^r (leaf 41).

[41] Charles B. SCHMITT, *Gianfrancesco Pico della Mirandola and the Fifth Lateran Council*: Archiv für Reformationsgeschichte 61 (1970) 165, n. 17; e. g. RAYNALDUS, 1512, nr. 96, 100; M 831bd, 841e.

[42] E. g. RAYNALDUS, 1512, nr. 53, 95; 1513, nr. 24, 41, 90. De Grassi himself was present at the eighth session, listed among those who voted against a weak reform bull (M 847a), and at the twelfth session according to his diary (RAYNALDUS, 1517, nr. 1-17), but his name is not to be found in the official rolls of these sessions.

[43] M 715e-16c, 755bc, 774a-75c, 794ab, 915e-16d, 975c-76b.

[44] MARTÈNE-DURAND, *Veterum Scriptorum*, III, col. 1181.

* (See Addenda)

problems. According to the ruling of Julius and the college of cardinals, the council fathers, with the exception of the four privileged patriarchs and the papal assistants, were to sit according to the time of their promotion, as was the custom at Rome. The masters of ceremonies were charged with assigning places. That an effort was made to continue this practice under Leo is evident from a fight over precedence recorded in the acts.[45] There is, however, no firm arrangement in the names of bishops as they appear in the del Monte edition. If they actually did sit in order, the notaries at least failed to record that arrangement in its details. They may have sat in the order of their arrival at the council.[46]

Another problem with del Monte's rolls is the frequent misspelling of the names of episcopal sees — at times beyond recognition. Efforts at rectifying these mistakes have consumed the time and challenged the talents of subsequent editors of this council. Their labors allow one to trace up to a point sources used by the editors.

The basic text for all subsequent versions of the council's acts is that edited by Antonio del Monte and published at Rome in 1521 by Jacopo Mazzocchi. The monopoly for ten years granted this printer by Leo X [47] seems to have been unnecessary, for it was not until about thirty years later that the young layman Jean Quentel died trying to revise a 1538 collection of councils to include among other items the Fifth Lateran. The aged Franciscan Pierre Crabbe (c. 1471-1553/4) saw this revised edition to the press at Cologne in 1551, dying himself soon after.[48] This Cologne edition of the council preceeded by over fifty years the 1606 collection of Severinus Binius which Guglia cited as the first subsequent reprinting of Lateran V since del Monte. It is probably also the source of those

---

[45] RAYNALDUS, 1512, nr. 34, q. 17; M 697b, 977b.
[46] HEFELE-LECLERCQ, *Histoire des conciles*, VIII-I, 354-55, 364, 367.
[47] GUGLIA, 1 reports that the monopoly was granted for twenty-five years — the source for this statement is unknown to me. Confer: *Sacrum Lateranensis concilium novissimum sub Iulio .II. et Leone .X. celebratum*, ed. Antonio DEL MONTE, Romae: per Jacobum Mazochium, 1521, AAiv; hereafter cited as DEL MONTE; Fernanda ASCARELLI, *Annali tipografici di Giacomo Mazzocchi*, Vol. 24 of Biblioteca bibliografica italica diretta da Marino Parenti, Florence 1961, nr. 146, pp. 141-42.
[48] François SALMON, *Traité de étude des conciles, et de leur collections*, Paris 1724, 197-201; *Tertius Tomus Conciliorum omnium, tam generalium quam particularium, quae iam inde a synodo Basileensi usque ad concilium universale Tridentinum habita, nobis hac vice ad excudendum oblata fuerunt*, Cologne: ex officina Joannis Quentel, 1551. The Del Monte edition is reproduced on pp. 514-714. Hereafter this volume is cited as QUENTEL-CRABBE.

emendations in the Binius, Labbe, and Hardouin collections for which Guglia sought in vain.[49]

The Quentel-Crabbe edition of Lateran V is only ostensibly a reproduction of del Monte's, down to the detail of Mazzocchio's closing statement on where, when, and by whom the acts were published. The use of marginal notes and of a font of capital letters indicates, however, according to Crabbe's preface, that differing versions of the council's acts were consulted and their significant variants noted. The editor confessed that he was unable to check editions in the distant libraries of Rome or Venice or Bologna.[50] Given his critical apparatus and inability to visit Italian libraries where he would most likely have found the 1521 del Monte edition, it is questionable whether he had an original printed edition for consultation or only modified copies. A few examples of the Quentel-Crabbe departure from the original and of their marginalia on the list of participants include: at the second session Matheus Bethelen. of 1521 becomes Bitecteñ. or Bictecen.; Ieremias Crayneñ., Traneñ.; and Andreas Nulliteñ., Militeñ.; at the third Ioānes Anrainen., Arianeñ. and Paulus Luceorien., Lectorieñ.; at the eighth Benedictus Ouieñ., Chieñ. or Ogentinus and Iulianus Augustentiñ., Agrigentiñ.; and at the eleventh domino Montalicinen. becomes dno. Michaeli Monopolitano.[51] While some of these changes helped to identify the prelates, others were erroneous and have caused problems ever since.

As a result of the Quentel-Crabbe revisions in the text Jeremias of Trani has supplanted Geremia Contugii da Volterra of Krain (Krajina) even in Gams' *Series Episcoporum*. While avoiding this error, Ludwig von Pastor created a new one by identifying Craynensis in Albania with Carniola (Granea).[52] Johannes of Ariano has replaced Jean Lefranc of Orange and Paulus of

---

[49] GUGLIA, 2-3.
[50] QUENTEL-CRABBE, 714; the preface citation is in Vol. I, *a4r; Henri QUENTIN, *Jean-Dominique Mansi et les grandes collections conciliaires: étude d'histoire litteraire*, Paris 1900, 12-16.
[51] DEL MONTE, 25v-26r, 38r, 100v, 134v; QUENTEL-CRABBE, 546-47, 558, 616, 647.
[52] Pius Bonifacius GAMS, *Series episcoporum ecclesiae catholicae*, reprinted Graz 1957, 934; Ludwig von PASTOR, *Storia dei papi della fine del medio evo*, Italian version by Angelo MERCATI, IV-I, Rome 1960, 544; Eugen GUGLIA, *Craynensis-Tranensis?*: Mittheilungen des Instituts für Österreichische Geschichtsforschung 21 (1900) 537; Milan von ŠUFFLAY, *Die Kirchenzustände im vortürkischen Albanien. Die orthodoxe Durchbruchszone im katholischen Damme*: Illyrisch-Albanische Forschungen, ed. Ludwig von THALLOCZY, I, München 1916, 222; Daniel FARLATUS, *Illyrica Sacra*, VII, Venice 1817, 447-48; Vincenzo FORCELLA, *Iscrizioni delle chiese e d'altri edificii di Roma dal secolo XI fino ai giorni nostri*, Roma 1884, VII, 429, nr. 860; hereafter cited as FORCELLA.

Leictoure Paweł Algimunt, prince of Holszańy in Lithuania and bishop of Luck. Another Lithuanian Albert Radvilas of Vilnius was destined by their marginalia to become Albertus of Valva. For some strange reason the bishop of Montalcino, Girolamo Piccolomini, was replaced by Michele Claudi of Monopoli. A large number of these and other variant readings found in Quentel-Crabbe have been adopted by subsequent editors of conciliar collections. While Jean Hardouin avoided a few of these errors by referring to other codices and only rarely placed in the margins either variant readings or his own conjectures,[53] he seems to have followed in general the text or marginalia of the Cologne edition and its descendents. The version of Lateran V printed in the collection of councils published under the name of Giovanni Domenico Mansi and the editors who succeeded him is an exact reproduction of the edition of Nicola Coleti (1680-1765) based on the previous work of the Jesuits Philippe Labbe (1607-77), Gabriel Cossart (1615-74), and Jean Hardouin (1646-1729). Of the readily available collections, this versison of Lateran V, which is improperly called that of Mansi, is the most useful for studying the council's rolls since Coleti noted a number of the variations to be found in other collections.[54]

Recourse to the standard listings of the Catholic hierarchy for that period combined with research into the lives of these prelates, where doubts still remain, resolves most of the difficulties to be found in the rolls of council members. Consultation of the del Monte edition can on occasion clear up a problem immediately. Papal registers and the diary of de Grassi give additional clues on the presence in Rome of particular prelates. Histories of religious orders and their abbeys provide information on generals and abbots. Curial officials appear in a number of published lists.[55] A serious effort has been made to identify the family name of council members.

---

[53] Jean HARDOUIN, ed., *Acta conciliorum et epistolae, decretales, ac constitutiones summorum pontificum*, I, Paris 1715, Praefatio, xi-xij.

[54] *Sacrosancta concilia ad regiam editionem exacta quae olim quarta parte prodiit auctior studio Philip. Labbei et Gabr. Cossartii Soc. Jesu presbyterorum nunc vero integre insertis Stephani Baluzii et Joannis Harduini additamentis ... longe locupletior, et emandatior exhibetur curante Nicolao Coleti*, XIX, Venice 1732, title page; this volume is reprinted as Vol. 32 of Mansi's *Amplissima collectio*; one of the more important mistakes made by Coleti (M 765c) but avoided by Quentel-Crabbe and Hardouin was a confusion of the names and sees of two bishops at the fifth session (the Andreas Literen. and Philippus Adriacen. of DEL MONTE, 58ᵛ) so that they emerged as only one, namely, Andreas Adriacensis. The marginal additions of Adjacen. and Ajacen. seem to indicate that he realized there were difficulties with such an entry.

[55] For curial officials, confer: e. g. Walther von HOFMANN, *Forschungen zur*

I

In spite of such measures a number of conciliar prelates and their sees remain known only by the meager description supplied by del Monte. I have been unable to discover the family names or place derivations by which they were known for either Clemens of Kolossi, the uniate metropolitan of the Greeks on Rhodes, or for Matthaeus, the bishop of San Leone in southern Italy. A number of dioceses and thus also their ordinaries escape identification. *Bellicensis* with Vincentius at the third session and Georgius at the seventh may be the see of Balezo, *Balle(a)censis*, in Montenegro whose last known bishop was the Dominican Leonardo da Napoli (1459-88).[56] The sees of *Trabuniensis* with Joannes at the sixth, *Triburensis* without a Christian name at the congregation before the ninth session, and *Tribuniensis* also without a name but joined with the see of *Machariensis* at the eleventh may be one and the same diocese, namely Trebinje (*Tribuniensis*) in Herzegovina, but the sources list only a Georgius who died in 1513 and his successor Augustinus de Nabe who was appointed in early March of the following year. It is unlikely that a bishop Joannes held this see before the appointment of de Nabe. Attempts at identifying *Tra(i)bu(r)niensis* with other dioceses of a similar name having a bishop Joannes yield only conjecture.[57] Both the sees of *Mordaniensis* at the first and second sessions and *Archsensis* at the eighth list bishops with the name Michael. The first may be the diocese of Maronea in the province of Rhodes, the later the titular see of Arga in Armenia, but the sources examined indicate that neither see was occupied at that time.[58] Other possibilities are equally unlikely.[59] The Andreas

---

Geschichte der kurialen Behörden von Schisma bis zur Reformation of (*Bibliothek des kgl. Preuss. historischen Instituts in Rom*, Vols. 12 and 13) Rome 1914, hereafter cited as HOFMANN; Carolus CARTHARIUS, *Advocatorum sacri consistorii syllabum*, Rome 1656, hereafter cited as CARTHARIUS.

[56] M 730a, 808d; the Vincentius Bellicensis who appears in Mansi's roll for the fourth session (M 746b) is listed as Claudius Belicensis, Claude de Stavayer of Belley, in DEL MONTE 47ʳ; Fr. BULIĆ, *Balezo*: DHGE VI, col. 358; EUBEL, II, 101, 176; HARDOUIN, XI, 663 claimed Vincentius' see was Belley in Savoy (France).

[57] M 787e, 850b, 976a; DEL MONTE, 74ᵛ, neither 112ᵛ nor 190ʳ provide a Christian name for Tribu(r)nensis; E 318; HARDOUIN, XI, 887 claimed Joannes' see was Trebinje in Dalmatia (Herzegovina). Other candidates are: Joannes Perpignan Tinensis (E 313), Joannes Baptista de Misnis Tripoliensis, suff. Foroliviensis (E 319), Joannes Franciscus de Ruvere Taurinensis (E 309); Joannes Sartoris de Tremonia, O. F. M., Tefelicensis, suff. Paderbornensis (E 310, 346); Joannes Dominicus de Zaciis Terdonensis (E 310); Joannes Gosztonyi Jauriensis; etc.

[58] E 235, EUBEL, II, 93; HARDOUIN XI, 645 claimed Michael's see was Arca in Samnitibus or in Aprutia citeriori.

[59] « Mordaniensis »: Michael Marinoschi Moldauiensis (EUBEL II, 194), Mi-

Lausanensis who appears in the roll of the eighth session may be the retired bishop of Lausanne Aymone de Montefalcone or Andrea Franciotto of Lucca (*Lucensis*) or Andreas Mus of Oslo (*Asloensis*) or someone else — but biographical data is inadequate to eliminate some of the candidates.[60]

In spite of being listed with the names of dioceses clearly other than their own, some bishops are still identifiable. The orator of King Charles of Spain, Pedro de Urrea from Valencia, was called at the twelfth session *episcopus Caesaraugustanus*, but Zaragoza was an archbishopric and then held by Alfonso d'Aragona. De Urrea's diocese was Siracusa in Sicily.[61] The Martinus *Zarinensis* at the eighth session was most likely Martinus Lalexa, an episcopal assistant (*Albanensis*) to the Dominican bishop of Albania (*Arbanensis*), Giovanni Corona, who resided in Zara.[62] From other sources it is known that the Joannes Baptista *Brugnatensis* at the fifth session was Giovanni Battista Cibò of Mariana on Corsica[63]. Augustinus *Argiensis* listed in the roll of the tenth session is probably Agostino Fieschi, the bishop of Sagona also on Corsica, since the other candidates either are never listed otherwise, already listed for that session, or only later first appear at the council.[64]

Both the family name of an abbot-procurator and the exact location of his monastery are difficult to identify. Henrique Alvari de Coimbra, the famous Franciscan missionary to India who celebrated the first Mass in Brazil and labored to organize a crusade against the Moslems, is listed in the acts as bishop of Ceuta and primate of Africa . He was represented at the

---

chael Chesulius Boznensis (E 137); Sardanensis (E 292) apparently then vacant, or perhaps even Marcanensis if it were temporarily separated from Trebinje (E 318); the name of the religious appointed bishop of the then Spanish Oran (Oranensis in regno Marochitano — E 263) is not given in the sources consulted; HEFELE-LECLERCQ, 349-50, 354-55 ignores also this problem; even HARDOUIN XI, 791-92 left Mordaniensis unidentified. « Archsensis »: Michael Jorba Argolicensis, suffr. Brixinen. (E 340), Michael de Natera Alexiensis (E 103), Michael de Figueroa Pactensis (E 266), Michael Salonensis (E 289).

[60] E 220, 228, 120; Andreas de Novellis Albensis (E 100), Andreas Sirigo Sithiensis (E 301), Andreas Riccius Thelesinus (E 311); HARDOUIN XI, 762 claimed Andreas' see was Lausanne in Savoy (Switzerland).

[61] M 981a, E 144, 307. A letter from the officials of the Balìa of Siena dated 14 June 1517 addresses de Urrea also as episcopus Caragozensis (seu Caesaraugustanus) — confer: Biblioteca Angelica, Roma, Mss. nr. 1888, fol. 8r.

[62] E 100, 114; Giuseppe PRAGA, *Il vescovado albanese al principio del secolo XVI*: Rivista d'Albania, fasc. 2, July 1940, 143-44, 166-67.

[63] Giuseppe CAPPELLETTI, *Le chiese d'Italia* XIII, Venice 1857, 471; HARDOUIN IX, 1637c.

[64] M 904a; Augustinus de Ortis Satrianensis (E 293), Augustinus Spinola Aleriensis (E 102), Augustinus Justinianus Nebiensis (E 255), Augustinus de Grimaldis Grassensis (E 205).

fourth session by Rodericus Joannes *abbas Beatae Mariae de Tauoica, Tudensis diocesis*. Since the bishop of Ceuta as of 20 October 1512 became administrator of that section of the Tuy diocese lying within Portugal around the cities of Olivenca, Campo Maior, and Ouguella and was himself a Franciscan, his procurator may have been head of the Franciscan tertiary monastery and hermitage of Nossa Senhora da Ribeira de Távora established there in 1460.[65]

A number of ambassadors are not identified by name. At the third session on 3 December 1512 orators of Parma were listed as present, but no names were given. They may have been members of the legation which pledged allegiance to Julius II in mid-October — but once again their names are not mentioned. The Swiss Cantons had three representatives at the fourth session. A month earlier a delegation from the twelve cantons arrived in Rome, but most of its twenty members seem to have left by early December, including probably Johannes de Eylac from Luzern and Petrus Falcem from Fribourg.[66] Whether the village magistrate Daniel Babenberg and the municipal Gonfalonier Johannes Stölli were also among those who left early or decided to stay for the council is not clear.[67] The names of the other members of the delegation are not readily available. The Florentine orators at the eighth and their single representative at the ninth are both unnamed. Francesco Vettori, the friend of Machiavelli, was probably present both times since he remained in Rome until 1515 as the representative of Florence. Jacopo Salviati, however, left the City in early August and did not return to attend the eighth session. Giuliano Tornabuoni, a protonotary and the only ecclesiastic in

---

[65] Fortunato DE ALMEIDA, *História de igreja em Portugal*, Coimbra 1915, III-I, 7, 371, III-II, 981-82; F. Félix LOPES, *Henrique de Coímbra (Frei)*: Verbo: Enciclopedía Luso-Brasileira de cultura, IX, Lisbon 1969, cols. 1793-94; Prudencio DE SANDOVAL, *Antiguedad dela civdad y iglesia cathedral de Tuy y de los obispo*, Braga 1610, 201v, 202v; Pascual GALINDO ROMEO, *Tuy en la baja edad media siglos XII-XV*, Madrid c. 1950, Supplement to Vol. 22 of *España Sagrada*, ed. P. FLOREZ, Appendix II, 139-42.

[66] *I Diarii di Marino Sanuto*, ed. Federico STEFANI, Guglielmo BERCHET, Nicolò BAROZZI, Vol. XV (1512-13), Venice 1887, 252, 412, 418, 442. A manuscript copy of DE GRASSI's *Diarium* lists ten orators in the October 1512 legation from Parma: Paulus de Colla, Jacobus Baiardus, Antonius Bernerius, Salomon Tamatoldus, Joannes Franciscus Aloysii de Garimbertis, Julius de Tam de Mariis, Genesius de Balistreriis, Octavianus de Musachis, Joannes Christophorus de Cancellis, and Bartolomaeus de Gerardutiis. It does not, however, mention which, if any of these, represented Parma at the Council. Confer: Vat. lat. 12414, fols. 217r-226r.

[67] *Bullen und Breven aus italienischen Archiven, 1116-1623*, ed. Caspar WIRZ (Quellen zur schweizer Geschichte, vol. 21) Basel 1902, 280, 287-88.

the June 1513 embassy to Leo, may have stayed on in Rome as a member of Leo's court and represented Florence at the council later in the year.⁶⁸ At the ninth session there appears almost at the end of the list of « orators, senator, illustrious temporal lords » the mysterious entry *Orator patriarchae Hierosolymitani*.⁶⁹ Since the Latin patriarch Bernardino Lopez Carvajal was already listed among the council members, the Greek patriarch Dorotheos II was apparently hostile to Latin Christians, and the Armenian patriarch(s) went unmentioned in available contemporary Latin sources, the patriarch represented was probably of a seat other than Jerusalem. The nuncio Buṭrus Būlus sent by the Maronite patriarch in Syria arrived in Rome in time for this session, but it would be surprising that he be listed among the representatives of temporal powers and that his patriarch who was known to come from the region of Syria, even to the point of being called patriarch of Antioch, would be listed as Jerusalem. The mysterious orator could also be a representative of the fabled Prester John. The Portuguese orators at this session had recently informed Pope Leo of the desire of the Christian Emperor of Ethiopia, Lebna Dengel (David), and of his « patriarch », the abuna Mârqos, to send representatives to Rome to acknowledge him as head of all Christians. A member of the Ethiopian legation then in Lisbon may have accompanied these Portuguese to Rome, or Leo may have appointed one of the Ethiopians resident in the City to represent this Emperor and his abuna at the Council. On these details, however, the available sources are silent.⁷⁰ At the twelfth session the senator of Rome is listed as Johannes Baptista. He may be the Joannes Oricellarius (Rucellai) mentioned in a later document as having been senator about this time.⁷¹

Having briefly surveyed a few of the difficulties encountered in the membership rolls found in the conciliar acts, one can now turn to the catalogues of council participants and of the sees represented which are at the end of this study and draw from them a number of general conclusions.

---

⁶⁸ M 809b, 831c, 862e, 904d; Alessandro FERRAJOLI, *Il ruolo della corte di Leone X (1514-1516)*: Archivio della reale società romana di storia patria 36 (1913), 207-08. I am grateful to Melissa Bullard for the information on Salviati's stay at Rome.
⁶⁹ M 863a.
⁷⁰ Confer my forthcoming article in *Orientalia christiana periodica*.
⁷¹ Francesco Antonio VITALE, *Storia diplomatica de' senatori di Roma*, Roma 1791, II 498-500; Luigi POMPILE OLIVIERI, *Il Senato Romano nelle sette epoche di svariato governo da Romolo fino a noi colla serie cronologica-ragionata dei senatori dall'anno 1143 fino al 1870*, Roma 1886, I, 285-86.

The first list, that of the participants at Lateran V, reveals that four-hundred and thirty-one (431) named persons attended the council. By considering only the highest office which they held, since a number were promoted during the five years the council sat, there were from the Sacred Colleges of popes (2) Julius II and Leo X thirty-two (32) cardinals who held, besides numerous archiepiscopal and episcopal sees, also the Latin patriarchates of Jerusalem, Constantinople, and Aquileja. The Latin patriarchs (3) of Antioch, Alexandria, and the successor at Aquileja were also present and held an archiepiscopal and a number of episcopal sees. Thirty-seven (37) archbishops attended the council, of whom seven (Athens, Corinth — two, Krain, Nazareth, Patras, and Thebes) were only titular. Two-hundred and nine (209) bishops were also present. Of these, four were only titular (Bethlehem, Philadelphia, and Sebaste — two) and six others were from sees difficult to identify, possibly also titular. Heads of religious organizations were in attendance, too: ten (10) abbots, some of whom were heads of monastic congregations, one (1) praeceptor of a group of Roman hospitallers, and also four (4) generals and four (4) vicar-generals of religious orders. Non-episcopal procurators representing absent prelates were three (3) for the Maronite patriarch, two (2) for archbishops, seventeen (17) for bishops, and two (2) for abbots. Non-mitred orators of temporal rulers accounted for thirty-five (35) other participants. Four (4) senators and seven (7) conservators represented the city of Rome. Council officials (procurators, notaries, scribes, examiners of votes, guards for the assembly and the popes, etc.) numbered twenty-nine (29). Of the twelve recorded homilists at the council, four (4) did not clearly fall into any of the above categories. Twenty-six (26) temporal lords, nobles, and knights were also named.

Forty-six (46) prelates never attended the council personally but were represented there by procurators. These included two (2) patriarchs, seven (7) archbishops, thirty-five (35) bishops, and two (2) abbots. Of these, seventeen (17) held Italian dioceses while the others' sees ranged from Estonia to Morocco and from Lebanon (and Ethiopia?) to Haiti.

The future careers of the members of Lateran V deserve comment. Four prelates were later elected pope (Clement VII, Paul III, Julius III, and Paul IV). In the years after the council's close, at least twenty-seven (27) members were raised to the cardinalate and thirty-three (33) of its non-episcopal members eventually became bishops. Apparently only one of its members, the Polish orator Stanisław Ostrorog, joined the Protestant movement.

Men involved in the Pisan Council also attended Lateran V. Girolamo Morone who witnessed its edict of convocation and Guglielmo Capponi who represented the College of Cardinals in the negotiations to have it dissolved were both members of the Roman synod. The Spanish cardinal-president of Pisa, its Italian cardinal-legate in conquered papal territory, a French bishop at its sessions, and the Pisan Council's secretary, homilist, and leading propagandist were all admitted to membership in the Lateran Council after confessing their error.

The second list, that of ecclesiastical jurisdictions represented at Lateran V, shows that all the major political units of Latin Christendom outside Italy had someone representing at least one of their dioceses present at the council. These non-Italian sees constituted over one-third of the total number represented. The following list of these sees is organized according to the political units operative at the time of the council. When a diocese lies today in a different country, the name of that nation follows in parentheses that of the ecclesiastical unit. No consideration is here given to the seven sees which escape clear identification.

Sees outside of Italy represented in the Council

Anglia (5)
Bathonien. et Wellen.
Eboracen.
Leglinen. (Hibernia)
Tuamen. (Hibernia)
Wigornien.

Aviniona (2)
Avinionen. (Francia)
Cavallicen. (Francia)

Dania (2)
Lincopen. (Suecia)
Upsalen. (Suecia)

Francia (22)
Agathen.
Agenen.
Albien.
Aurasicen.
Dignen.

Ebredunen.
Elnen.
Grassen.
Malleacen.
Massilien.
Nanneten.
Narbonen.
S. Pontii Thomeriarum
(Redonen.)
Regen.
Tolonen.
Turonen.
Vauren.
Vencien.
Veneten.
Viennen.
Xanctonen.

Helvetia (1)
Sedunen.

Hispania (cum transmarinis) (19)
Aurien.
Burgen.
Carthaginen.
Compostellan.
Conceptionis (Rep. Dominicana et Haiti)
Conchen.
S. Dominici (Haiti et Rep. Dominicana)
Gadicen.
Gerunden.
Legionen.
Lucen.
Milevitan. (Malta)
(Oscen. et Jaccen.)
Placentin.
Salamantin.
Seguntin.
Tirasonen.
Tuden.
Urgellen.

Hungaria (5)
Agrien. (Jugoslavia)
Modrusien. (Jugoslavia)
Ottocien. (Jugoslavia)
Signien. (Jugoslavia)
Strigonien.

Janua transmarina (sine Corsica) (1)
Chien. (Graecia)

Polonia-Lithuania (5)
Gneznen.
Luceorien.
Warmien. (Polonia et USSR)
Vilnen. (USSR)
Vladislavien.

Portugallia (4)
Cepten. (Africa Hispanica)
Colimbrien.
Egitanien.
Portugalen.

Ragusa (3)
Ragusin. (Jugoslavia)
Stagnen. (et Curzulen.) (Jugoslavia)
Tribunien. (Jugoslavia)

Rhodi Milites S. Joannis Hierosolymitan. (1)
Colocen. (Graecia)

Sabaudia (extra Italiam) (5)
Bellicen. (Francia)
Gebennen. (Helvetia)
Lausanen. (Helvetia)
Maurianen. (Francia)
Nicien. (Francia)

Sacrum Imperium Romanorum (sine Aquilegia et Tergesto) (11)
Gurcen. (Austria)
Halberstaden. (Germania)
Havelbergen. (Germania)
Lubicen. (Germania)
Magdeburgen. (Germania)
Maguntin. (Germania)
(Merseburgen.) (Germania)
Misnen. (Germania)
Ratzeburgen. (Germania)
(Salzeburgen.) (Austria)
Trajecten. (Hollandia)

Scotia (1)
S. Andreae (Magna Britannia)

Theutonici Milites S. Mariae in Livonia (2)
Curonien. (USSR)
Revalien. (USSR)

Turcorum Imperium cum Aegypto (20)
Albanen. (Albania)
Alexandrin. - tit. (Aegyptus)
Antiochen. - tit. (Syria)
Argolicen. (Graecia)
Athenien. - tit. (Graecia)
Bethleemitan. - tit. (Jordanus)
Constantinopolitan. - tit. (Turcia)
Corinthien. - tit. (Graecia)
Coronen. - tit. (Graecia)
Crainen. - tit. (Albania)
Dyrrhachien. (Albania)
Hierosolymitan. - tit. (Jordanus et Israel)
Maronitarum (Lebanon)
Nazaren. - tit. (Israel)
Patracen. - tit. (Graecia)
Philadelphien. - tit. (Turcia)

Sappaten. (Albania)
Sebasten. - tit. (Turcia?)
Spigaten. - tit. (Turcia)
Theban. - tit. (Graecia)

Venetia transmarina (26)
Absaren. (Jugoslavia)
Agien. (Graecia)
Antibaren. (Jugoslavia)
Arben. (Jugoslavia)
Buduen. (Jugoslavia)
Calamonen. (Graecia)
Catharen. (Jugoslavia)
Chironen. (Graecia)
Curzolen. (et Stagnen.) (Jugoslavia)
Dulcinen. (Jugoslavia)

Famagustan. (Cyprus)
Hierapetren. (Graecia)
Jadren. (Jugoslavia)
Justinopolitan. (Jugoslavia)
Milopotamen. (Graecia)
Monobasien. (Graecia)
Nicosien. (Cyprus)
Nimocien. (Cyprus)
Nonen. (Jugoslavia)
Paphen. (Cyprus)
Parentin. (Jugoslavia)
Pharen. (Jugoslavia)
Polen. (Jugoslavia)
Sibenicen. (Jugoslavia)
Spalaten. (Jugoslavia)
Veglien. (Jugoslavia)

The following catalogues of council members and their dioceses are not exhaustive but limit themselves to recording the participants at the twelve sessions, the congregations before the last two, the membership in the various deputations, and the officials of the council. Lest a false impression be given that large numbers of prelates were absent at the opening session or other congregations because del Monte failed to provide the names of their participants or gave but a fraction of them,[72] only those fourteen sittings will be mentioned for which the 1521 edition attempted to provide a complete list. The papal cursors who appear throughout the acts but were not technically members of the council have not been included. The official homilists at the council, whether or not they were then prelates, merit mention in the list.

The first catalogue is arranged numerically in alphabetical order according to the family names as found in del Monte, Eubel, Gams, de Grassi, Garampi, and other Latin sources.[73] When only the Christian name or place derivation of a council member is given by the sources, as often happened with members of religious orders and minor officials, that person is listed solely by his baptismal name to keep the catalogue from be-

---

[72] E. g., M666b-67e, 794c-95b, 849b-50d, 938d-39a.

[73] GARAMPI refers to the 124 large volumes of handwritten schedules in the Archivio Segreto Vaticano prepared by Giuseppe Garampi (1725-1792) and his collaborators. These volumes are divided into eight categories, plus a chronological index. References to this collection are hereafter cited as ISG (*Index Schedularum Garampi*) followed by the volume and folio page number — e. g., ISG, 94, f. 9r.

coming too long by numerous cross-references.[74] In cases of doubt as to whether the name is of the family, or adopted by the individual, or merely of place derivation, it is treated as familial. Latin variations of the name, if any, and those in the vernacular which are somewhat different in spelling follow immediately in parentheses, the vernacular being separated when necessary from the Latin by a semi-colon. The specific position(s) held by each participant as listed in the acts and the particular roll(s) or text in Mansi where he is thus found come next. These lists of participants for each of the twelve sessions are identified by the arabic number of that session; the rolls provided for the congregations before the eleventh and twelfth are cited by the respective Roman numerals. A reference to a text in Mansi's edition of the council's acts is cited by « M » followed by the column number and appropriate letter of the alphabetic subdivision. Miscellaneous biographical information relevant mostly to the time during which he was present at the council, especially regarding other sees held by him, may then follow. What is included in brackets pertains to the period after his presence at the council.

The second listing is that of dioceses represented at the council. Their Latin names are arranged in alphabetic order according to the spelling given by Eubel. Significant variations from this form of the name which are found in the Mansi edition of the acts immediately follow in parentheses. Next come the vernacular name of the see, the geographic region in which it lies, the ecclesiastical jurisdiction to which it pertained (metropolitan, suffragan, or immediately subject to Rome), and whether or not it was titular. The arabic numeral(s) at the end of each entry refers to the person(s) thus identified in the first list who was connected with this diocese.

These two catalogues are prefaced by a list of abbreviations employed throughout them. In order that these lists can be more easily consulted by all scholars and because the sources for the technical terms found in them are in Latin, this classical language has been used in both catalogues.

---

[74] For an example of the difficulties involved in determining the family names of religious, confer the efforts of A. FERRAJOLI, *Il ruolo*, 191, n. 1 and 2 regarding the Franciscan Johannes de Prato, son of a Dominicus, probably of humble origins where four different surnames are suggested: Dagomari, Trombetti, Thomassiis, and Bonamici.

Abbreviationes

abbrev. = abbreviator
adm. = administrator
advoc. = advocatus
aep. = archiepiscopus
apost. = apostolicus
aud. = auditor
B. M. = Beata Maria
brev. = brevium
c. = circa
cam. = camera, camerarius
can. = canonicus, canonicatus
card. = cardinalis
cler. = clericus
comd. = commendatarius
comm. = commissio
conc. = concilium
cong. = congregatio
consist. = consistorialis
decret. = decretum
dep. = deputatio
diac. = diaconus
dioec. = dioecesis
doct. = doctor
dom. = dominus
domest. = domesticus
eccl. = ecclesia
el. = electus
ep. = episcopus
ex. = extra
fam. = familiarius
fisc. = fiscus, fiscalis
gen. = generalis
gub. = gubernator
immed. = immediatus
imp. = imperialis
infer. = inferior
ins. = insula
j. u. d. = juris utriusque doctor
lit. = litterae
m. = mortuus
mag. = magister
mand. = mandatum
metrop. = metropolitanus
n. = nota
nr. = numerus
nom. = nominatus a S. S.
not. = notarius
O. = Ordo:
    C. = de Monte Carmelo
    (S.) Cist. = Cisterciensis
    E. S. A. = Eremitarum S. Augustini
    F. M. = Fratrum Minorum
    H. S. Sp. = Hospitalariorum S. Spiritus
    P. = Fratrum Praedicatorum
    Praem. = Praemonstratensis
    S. A. = Canonicorum S. Augustini
    S. B. = S. Benedicti
    Burs. = Bursfeldensis
    Camald. = Camaldulensium
    Cassinien. = Cassiniensis
    Celes. = Coelestinorum
    C. V. U. = Cong. Vallis Umbrosae
    S. J. Hier. = S. Joannis Hierosolymitani de Rhodo
    S. M. = Servorum B. Mariae
    Theut. = S. Mariae Theutonicorum in Prussia
orat. = orator
patr. = patriarchus
pnot. = protonotarius
poenit. = poenitentiarius
praed. = praedicator
praep. = praeparativus
presb. = presbyter
proc. = dedit mandatum et/vel procurator
refm. = reformatio
reg. = rex
s. = sessio vel cong. gen.
    1 — 10. V. 1512
    2 — 17. V. 1512
    3 — 3. XII. 1512
    4 — 10. XII. 1512
    5 — 16. II. 1513
    6 — 27. IV. 1513
    7 — 17. VI. 1513
    8 — 19. XII. 1513
    9 — 5. V. 1514
    10 — 4. V. 1515
    11 — 19. XII. 1516
    12 — 16. III. 1517
    xi — 15. XII. 1516
    xii — 13. III. 1517
S. = Sanctus, sacer
script. = scriptor
secret. = secretarius
solic. = solicitor
S. S. = Sua Sanctitas
subalt. = subalternens
subj. = subjectus
subdiac. = subdiaconus
suffr. = suffraganeus
super. = superior
temp. = temporalis
tit. = titularis
vic. = vicarius
v. s. = vide supra (notam)
[ ] = biographical data enclosed in square brackets pertains to the period following the last session of the council at which this member was present

Participants personally present at the Fifth Lateran Council

1. Accoltis, Petrus de: card. presb. S. Eusebii s. 1-10, 12, xi, xii, comm. praep., dep. de fide - nom., proc. aep. Florentin. s. 5 (M 775a); ep. Anconitan. et Humanaten., Malleacen, adm. Gadicen. [m. 1532] (E 12, 107, 200, 234, HOFMANN, I, 309).
2. Acuri (al-Ḫūri, κῦρις, χορεπίσκοπος) Joseph (Yūsuf): proc. patr. Maronitarum s. 11 (M 943b, v. s. n. 38).
3. Albicis (Albizzi), Thomas de, O. P.: ep. Callien. s. 6 [m. c. 1535] (E 147).
4. Algimunt, Paulus: ep. Luceorien. s. 3-6; dux Alsanensis [ep.Vilnen., m. 1555] (E 229).
5. Alsay (Hulsay, Halsey), Thomas: ep. Leiglinen. s. 10, xi, poenit. nationis Anglicae Romae [m. 1521] (E 222).
6. Altavantis (Attavantis, Actavanti), Franciscus Dominicus de: conc. not. subalt. et scriba (M 696e); laicus, pater Petri Pauli (HOFMANN II, 119, 194).
7. Alvarottis, Alvarottus de: scrutator votorum (M 697a); abbrev. lit. apost. ex majori parco, can. Basil. S. Petri (H nr. 2464-65).
8. Alvensleben (Alvenschn, Alvestent), Busso de (Benso, Bussonus): orat. Joachim marchionis Brandeburgen. electoris imperii s. 8, 9; can. eccl. Magdeburgen., subdiac., j.u.d., [ep. Havelbergen., m. 1548] (E 208, H nr. 11, 521).
9. Amato, Aloysius Ludovicus de: ep. Liparen. s. 8, ep. S. Marci s. 10 [m. 1530] (E 226, 234).
Amerinus - v. Laureliis
10. Ampudia (de Fontecasto, Rebenga de la Fuentesanta), Paschal (Joannes) de, O. P.: ep. Burgen. s. 1, 2 [m. 1512] (v. s. n. 39, E 142).
11. Andreas: ep. Lausanen. s. 8 (v. s. n. 60)
12. Andreis, Vincentius de: ep. Ottocien. s. 7, 12, xii (E 299).
13. Antonini, Aegidius, O.E.S.A.: mag. gen. O. (Er.) S. A. s. 1-5, 7-9, xi, xii, dep. de pace - nom., praed. s. initiationis [card, ep. Viterbien, m. 1532] (E 16).
14. Apra, Ludovicus (Aloysius) de: ep. Interamnen. s. 1, 2, 6, 10 [m. 1520] (E 213).
15. Aragonia, Aloisius (Ludovicus) de: card. diac. S. Mariae in Cosmedin s. 1-12, dep. de refm. - nom., comm. praep.; frater naturalis reg. Siciliae, adm. Aversan., Caputaquen., ep. Legionen. [m. 1519] (E 6, HOFMANN I, 309).
16. Arbaudo, Lambertus: ep. Venusin. s. 1-4, 8, 9 (E 330).
17. Aretio, Angelus de, O.S.M.: mag. gen. O.S.M. s. 3, 4, 7, 8, 11, xi, dep. de pace - nom. [m. 1523].
18. Aretio, Petrus de: ep. Acernen. s. 11, 12, xi, xii (E 93).
19. Arianiti (Conunatus, Cominato, Comnene), Constantinus. custos gen. conc., capitaneus S. Lat. conc. (M 696d), dux Macedoniae et princeps Achaiae s. 2 [m. 1530].
20. Arsago, Hieronymus de: ep. Nicien. s. 3, 4, 9, 10 [m. 1542] (E 257).
21. Asonia (Sonica), Bartholomaeus de, O.P.: ep. Justinopolitan. s. 6, 7, 8, 10, dep. de fide - el., proc. ep. Clugien. s. 10 (M 916b); apost. referendarius, scriptor archivi Vat., auditor lit. contradict. [m. 1529] (E 216).
22. Avalzivo, Stanislaus de: proc. ep. Wladislavien. s. 5 (M 775bc); can. eccl. Wladislavien., decret. doct.

23. Averoldis, Altobellus de: ep. Polen. s. 1, 2, 11, 12, xii [m. 1531] (E 276).
24. Azeglio, Hercules de: ep. Augusten. et orat. ducis Sabaudiae s. 3, 4, 6, 7, dep. de refm. - nom. [m. c. 1515] (E 122).
25. Baduer (Badoer), Joannes (Zuan): orat. dominorum Venetorum s. 9.
26. Baglionibus, Hercules de: ep. Urbevetan. s. 8 [m. c. 1520] (E 323).
27. Bainbridge, Christophorus: card. presb. S. Praxedis s. 1-5, 7-9, dep. de refm. - nom.; aep. Eboracen., orat. reg. Angliae [m. 1514] (E 11, 190).
28. Bakòcz, Thomas: card. presb. S. Martini in montibus s. 1-7, dep. de pace - nom., comm. praep.; aep. Strigonien., reg. Hungariae cancellarius, patr. Constantinopolitan. [m. 1521] (E 7, 299, 304, HOFMANN I, 309).
29. Baldassinis (Bardasinis), Melchior de: advoc. conc. (M 697b), praed. s. 4 (M 750bc); consist. advoc. [m. 1525] (CARTHARIUS 101).
30. Ballistraro, Antonius, S. O. Cist.: abbas mon. S. Galgani ord. Cist., Vulteranen. dioec. s. 1, 2, 4, 5, 6; ?proc. gen. Cist. [aep. Amalfitan.] (E 105, H nr. 3190).
31. Baonia, Petrus de: orat. ducis Sabaudiae s. 10.
32. Begnius (de Begno, Kožičić), Simon: ep. Modrusien. s. 1-6, xi, xii, dep. de refm. - el., praed. s. 6 (M 798d) [m. 1536] (E 247).
33. Bembus, Petrus: secret. S. S., proc. prioris gen. ord. Camald. s. 3 vel 4 [card., m. 1547] (E 26, v. s. n. 44).
34. Benignus (Dragišić, Dobrotić, Dobrotech), Georgius (Juraj), O.F.M.. ep. Callien. s. 1, 2, aep. Nazaren. s. 3-12, xi, xii, dep. de fide - el., proc. ep. Tribunien. s. 11 (M 976a) [m. 1520] (E 147, 254).
35. Benzis (Benzon, Venzo), Hieronymus de: conservator Urbis s. 5, 6, 7 (cum sociis); mag., lit. apost. abbrev. (H nr. 17, 877).
36. Berrutus, Amadeus: ep. Augusten. et gub. Urbis s. 12, xii [m. 1525] (E 122).
37. Berthelay, Franciscus: ep. Milopotamen. s. 1, 2, 4, 9; residens in Rom. Curia, poenit. apost., can. Ebredunen. (E 244, H nr. 4452).
38. Bertuciis, Joannes Baptista de, O.S.B.: ep. Fanen. s. 9, per ep. Rapollan. s. 2, (M 716b); [m. 1518] (E 194).
39. Bibiena, Bernardus Dovizius de: card. diac. S. Mariae in Porticu s. 9-12; thesaurarius gen. [m. 1520] (E 14).
40. Blanchis, Julius de: aep. Corinthien. s. 4-9 (E 178).
41. Blankenfeld (Bencelvil), Joannes: orat. Joachim marchionis Brandeburgen. et Alberti Mag. O. Theut. 8, 9, 11, 12, etiam ep. Revalien. s. 11, 12, xi. xii; proc. Romae O. Theut., cler. dioec. Brandeburgen. [aep. Rigen., m. 1527] (E 285, M 836e, H nr. 11, 519).
42. Blasiolis, Jacobus de: ep. Signien. s. 1, 2, 6, 7 [m. 1513] (E 299).
Blasius - v. Mediolanense
43. Bobadilla, Franciscus de: ep. Salamantin. s. 12, xii [apost. secret., m. 1529] (E 289, HOFMANN II, 193).
44. Bonadies, Simon: ep. Ariminen. s. 1-7, 9, 11, 12, xi, xii [m. 1518] (E 118).
45. Boncianus, Joannes Baptista: ep. Casertan. s. 10-12, xi, xii; referend. S. S., pnot. [domest. praelatus, Datarius, m. 1532] (E 155).
46. Bondelmonte, Philippus de: orat. Florentinorum s. 7; Confalonerus [m. 1522].
47. Bongallus, Jacobus Antonius: ep. Sutrin. et Nepesin. s. 11, 12, xi; domest. praelatus (E 306).
48. Bonjoannes, (Joannes) Antonius Jacobus: ep. Camerinen. s. 3, 4 (E 149).
49. Bonjoannes, Joannes Baptista: ep. Vencien. s. 8-10, 12, xi, xii [m. c. 1522] (E 328).

50. Bonomus (Bonhomius), Petrus: ep. Tergestin. et orat. Imperatoris Maximiliani s. 9 [m. 1546] (E 310).
51. Borgasius, Paulus: ep. Nimocien. seu Limosien. s. 11, 12, xi, xii (E 259).
52. Boschettus, Laurentius: ep. Dulcinen. s. 10, 12, xii [aep. Antibaren.] (E 188).
53. Boveriis (Payeriis), Vincentius de: ep. Naulen. 1-5 (E 254).
54. Bovius, Jacobus: senator Urbis s. 9, 10; Bononiensis [m. 1522].
55. Briçonnet, Dionysius: ep. Tolonen. s. 8, 9; filius card. G. Briconnet, aderat conc. Pisan. [ep. Maclovien., m. 1535] (E 6, 315).
56. Britto (Guibé vel Challand), Robertus: card. presb. S. Anastasiae s. 1-7, dep. de fide - nom.; adm. Albien., Veneten. [m. 1513] (E 10).
57. Brognolis, Floremonte de (Floremondus; Fioramonte): abbas S. Gregorii de Urbe s. 1, 3-5, 7 [m. 1514] (ISG 113, fol. 9v, Hofmann II, 119).
58. Brognolis, Nicolaus de: abbas S. Gregorii de Urbe s. 8, 9, 12; nepos Floremontis (ISG 113, fol. 8v).
59. Bruni, Joannes Franciscus: ep. Nolan. s. 1, 2, 4, 5 [m. 1549] (E 260).
60. Brut (?de Silva), Michael: orat. reg. Portugalliae s. 10.
61. Buffalinis, Riccomanus de (Richardus, Racomanus): ep. Venafran. s. 9, 11 (E 328).
62. Buffalis, Baptista de: ep. Aquinaten. s. 3, 5, 7 [m. 1513] (E 114).
63. Byzantius, Tryphon: ep. Catharen. s. 9, 12, xii; de natione Hungariae [m. 1540] (E 160).
64. Cadapesario, Jacobus de: ep. Paphen. s. 1-7, 9, proc. ep. Montisviridis s. 5 (M 775b) (E 269).
65. Cadichio, Joannes Baptista de: ep. Valven. et Salmonen. s. 12, xi, per ep. Rapollan. s. 10 (M 916a) (E 326).
66. Caetani (Gaetani d'Aragona), Honoratus (Onorato III): dux Trajecti s. 12.
67. Cancellaris, Raynaldus (Rinaldo) de: ep. S. Angeli de Lombardia s. 7 (E 109).
68. Candia, Petrus de: proc. ep. Grassen. s. 11 (M 975c).
69. Caneti (Chaneti), Humbertus (Hubertus): proc. aep. Tarentin. s. 10 (M 916a).
70. Canigianus de Florentia, Joannes Maria, O.P., ?C.V.U.O.S.B.: gen. Vallis Umbrosae s. 11, 12, xi, cognatus fortasse nepos S.S. [ep. Hipponen., suffr. Pistorien., m.c. 1542] (E 211).
71. Canossa, Ludovicus de : ep. Tricaricen. s. 1-9; princeps Canossae [ep. Baiocen., m. 1532] (E 318).
72. Cantalicio, Valentinus: ep. Pennen. et Adrien. s. 10, 12, xi, xii [m. 1550] (E 271).
73. Capellaniis, Joannes de: ep. Bivinen. s. 9 [m. 1529] (E 135).
74. Capisuchi (Capozuchiis, Capizzuchi), Paulus de: conservator Urbis s. 2; cappellanus, aud. causarum S. Palatii Apost. [ep. Neocastren., m.c. 1539] (E 256).
75. Capiteferreo (Capodiferro), Bartholomaeus de: ep. Montisvirdis s. 3, 4, 10, 12, xi, xii (E 250).
76. Capponi, Guilelmus: ep. Cortonen. 1-4; commissarius s. Collegi ad conc. Pisan. [m. 1515] (E 179).
77. Capranica, Nicolaus: ep. Neocastren. 1, 2 [m. 1517] (E 255).
78. Capua, Fabritius de: aep. Hydruntin. s. 9 (E 212).
79. Carafa, Alfonsus: patr. Antiochen. s. 1-6, 8, 9, 12; ep. S. Agathae, Lucerin. [m. 1534] (E 97, 111, 229).

80. Carafa, Joannes Petrus: ep. Theatin. 6, 7, dep. de pace - nom. [aep. Brundusin., Paulus IV, m. 1559] (E 34, 311).
81. Carafa, Joannes Vincentinus: aep. Neapolitan. s. 1-10, 12, proc. ep. Isclan. s. 2 (M 715e) et Ruben. s. 5 (M 775a) [card., m. 1541] (E 20, 255).
82. Carbon, Stephanus: conservator Urbis s. 6.
83. Caretto, Carolus Dominicus de: card. presb. S. Caeciliae s. 6-8, dep. de pace - nom.; aep. Turonen., marchio Finarii [m. 1514] (E 11, 321).
84. Caretto, Fabricius de: Curator personae S.S. (M 696d, 697d), proc. O. S. J. Hier. s. 1, 2; frater card. Caroli, Admiratus [Magnus Mag. O. S. J. Hier., m. 1521] (M 850de).
85. Caretto, Galeottus de: orat. marchionis Montisferrati s. 8.
86. Caropipe, Blasius: ep. Thelesin. s. 11, 12 [m. 1524] (E 311).
87. Carosis, Justinus de: Advoc. fisc. conc. (M 697a); advoc. fisc. cam. apost. (HOFMANN II, 95, CARTHARIUS 78).
88. Carotus, Johannes (Valentinus): secret. conc. (de Grassi, *Diarium*, 418-19).
89. Carraciolis, Conradus de: ep. Ostunen. s. 1-6, 8 (E 265).
* 90. Carraciolis (Charatius), Marinus (Ascanius) de: orat. ducis Mediolanensis s. 6-8, 10; apost. pnot. [ep. Cathanien., card., m. 1538] (E 24, 159).
91. Carvajal, Bernardinus Lopez de: card. ep. Sabinae s. 8-12; patr. Hierosolymitan., adm. Rossanen., comd. Seguntin., praesidens conc. Pisan. [m. 1523] (E 4-5, 210, 286).
92. Carvara (Corvara), Galeatius: ep. Sarsinaten. s. 1, 2 (E 293).
93. Castellensis (Castellesi) de Corneto, Hadrianus: card. presb. S. Chrysogoni s. 6-12, dep. de pace - nom.; ep. Bathonien. et Wellen. [m. 1521] (E 8).
94. Castiglia, Arnaldus Ferdinandus: ep. Balneoregien. s. 1-5, 9 [m. 1521] (E 128).
95. Castillione, Joannes Jacobus de: aep. Baren. s. 1, 2 [m. 1513] (E 129).
96. Castro, Ferdinandus de: ep. Scalen. s. 2, 4, 10, proc. ep. Soran. s. 10 (M 916c) (E 294).
97. Cataneus, Thomas, O.P.: ep. Cervien. s. 1, 2 [m. 1515] (E 163).
98. Celadonius, Alexius: ep. Melfiten. s. 1-4, 6-11, xi, dep. de fide - nom., proc. ep. Melfien. s. 4 (M 755b) et Agrigentin. s. 11 (M 975d) et Bergomen. s. 11 (M 976a), praed. s. 3 (M 736d) [m. 1517] (E 241).
99. Cesis, Angelus de: Advoc. conc. (M 697a); advoc. consist., pater Pauli Emilii [m. 1528] (HOFMANN II, 118-19, CARTHARIUS 70).
100. Cesis, Paulus Emilius de: not. conc. (M 696e); pnot. apost., cler. Rom. [card., m. 1537] (E 17).
101. Cherio (Riva), Bernardinus de Prato de, O.F.M.: minist. gen. O.F.M. s. 8, 9, 11, 12, xi dep. de fide - nom. [aep. Athenien., ep. Cajacen. m. 1528] (E 122, 145).
* 102. Cibo, Franciscus: dom. temp. s. 7.
103. Cibo, Innocentius: card. diac. SS. Cosmae et Damiani s. 8-12; adm. S. Andreae, Taurinen, nepos S.S. [m. 1550] (E 14, 108, 309).
104. Cibo, Joannes Baptista: ep. Marianen. s. 1-10, 12 (E 235; v.s. n. 63).
105. Cibo, Julianus: ep. Agrigentin. s. 1-10, per ep. Melfiten. s. 11 (M 975d) (E 98).
106. Cibo (alias Borsiani), Lucas: ep. Fulginaten. s. 3, 4 [aep. Ephesin.] (E 199, 193).
+ Cina de Potentia, Joannes Franciscus, O.F.M.: nuntius S.S. cum proc. patr. Maronitarum s. 11 (M 943b) [ep. Scaren., Nazaren., m. 1527] (E 294, 254).

* (See Addenda)

107. Claudi (Tragurinus), Michael: ep. Monopolitan. s. 1, 2 (E 248).
108. Clemens: aep. Colocen. (Rhodien.) s. 11, 12 (E 285, H nr. 15, 659).
109. Columna, Joannes Franciscus de: dom. temp. s. 10.
110. Columna, Marcus Antonius de: dom. temp. s. 1, 7, 10 [m. 1522].
111. Columna, Mutius de: dom. temp. s. 10 [m. 1516].
112. Columna, Pompejus de: ep. Reatin. s. 6-10, dep de pace - nom. [card., m. 1532] (E 15-16, 283).
113. Columna, Prosper de: dux Caniae s. 10 [m. 1523].
114. Comitibus (alias dei Domicelli), Franciscus de: aep. Consanen. s. 1-8, 10 [card., m. 1521] (E 15, 175).
115. Comitibus, Stephanus de: dom. temp. s. 4; Mag. S. Hospitii Palatii Apost.
116. Contreras (Conteras), Bernardinus de: not. conc., scriba, not. subalt. (M 696e); mag. cler. Burgen., j.u.d. (M 935d, H nr. 393, 16, 283, 17, 942).
117. Contugi, Jeremias: aep. Crainen. s. 1-12, xi, xii, el. sed non membrum dep.; residens in Rom. Curia (E 180, v. s. n. 52).
118. Cophinis, Lucas de: ep. Guardien. s. 3-5 (E 206).
119. Cornarus (Cornelius, Corner), Andreas: ep. Absaren. s. 3-9; frater card. Marci [m. 1514 - sic E91, sed idem promotus = n. 120].
120. Cornarus (Corner), Andreas: aep. Spalaten. s. 10-12, xi, proc. ep. Calamonen. s. 10 (M 916d); ?idem ep. Absaren. [- sic!]
121. Cornarus (de Corneliis), Marcus: card. diac. S. Mariae in Porticu s. 3-8, S. Mariae in Via Lata s. 9-12, dep. de refm. - nom.; ep. Nimocien., Paduan., adm. Veronen. [patr. Constantinopolitan., m. 1524] (E 7, 259, 267, 177).
122. Corvaria, Joannes Antonius de: coadj. ep. Sarsinaten. s. 8 (E 293).
123. Corvinus, Maximus Brunus, O. S. J. Hier.: ep. Isernien. s. 9, 11, 12, xi, xii, praed. s. 12 (M 993c) [m. 1522] (E 214).
124. Costabilis, Beltrandus (Beltramo) de: ep. Adrien. s. 3-12, xi, xii, etiam orat. ducis Ferrariae s. 6-12, xi, xii [m. 1519] (E 95).
125. Crescentiis, Marius de: conservator Urbis s. 9, 10.
126. Cuccinis, Marianus de: proc. fisc. conc. (M 697b); proc. fisci cam. apost. gen [m. 1513] (HOFMANN II, 95).
127. Cunha (Aeugna, Cugna), Tristandus (Tristannus) de: orat. reg. Portugalliae s. 9.
128. Cupis, Joannes Dominicus de: aep. Tranen. s. xii [card., m. 1553] (E 15, 316).
129. Cuppis, Theseus de: ep. Racanaten. et Maceraten. s. 6, 8-11, xi, xii, ep. Maceraten. s. 12 [m. 1528] (E 281).
130. Curialis, Andreas: ep. Litteren. s. 3, 5-9 (E 226, v. s. n. 54).
131. Delphinus, Petrus: prior gen. O. S. B., Camald s. 8, 9, dep. de refm. - nom., per P. Bembum s. 3 vel 4 [m. 1525, venerabilis] (v. s. n. 44).
132. Despes (de Espes), Joannes: ep. Urgellen. s. 10, 11, xi, proc. aep. Conceptionis s. 11 (M 975e) [m. 1530] (E 324).
133. Dormes, Georgius: abbas S. Jacobi Pegauien. dioec. Merseburgen., O. S. B., Burs. s. 4 (ISG 94, fol. 9r).
134. Elias (Ilyās) filius Abrahae (ibn Ibrāhīm): proc. patr. Maronitarum s. 11 (M 943b); subdiac. monachus, discipulus patr. et baculum patr. tulit (mace-bearer) (v. s. n. 38).
+ Elias (Ilyās ibn Zarzūr al-Ḥadatī): proc. patr. Maronitarum s. 11 (M 943b); adm. hortorum monasterii de Qannūbīn, residentiae patr. (v. s. n. 38 et infra nr. 264).

* (See Addenda)

135. Eruli (Heruli), Franciscus: ep. Spoletan. s. 3-7, per ep. Stabien. s. 11 (M 975e), 12 (M 982e) [m. 1540] (E 303).
136. Este, Hippolytus de: card. diac. S. Luciae in Silice s. 9, 10; adm. Agrien., Capuan., Ferrarien., Mediolanen., Mutinen., frater ducis Ferrariae [m. 1520] (E 5, 252).
137. Falconibus, Marinus de: ep. Minerbinen. s. 8 [m. 1525] (E 245).
138. Fanzi, Vincentius: ep. Signin. s. 8-10, 12, xii, dep. de refm. - el., [m. c. 1528] (E 300).
139. Farnesius, Alexander: card. diac. S. Eustachii s. 1-12, xi, dep .de pace - nom.; comm. praep., ep. Parmen., S. Pontii Thomeriarum, adm. Beneventan., Montisflasconis et Cornetan. [Paulus III, m. 1549] (E 5, 23, 132, 248, 270, 277, HOFFMANN I, 309).
140. Farra (Faria), Joannes de: orat. reg. Portugalliae s. 9; miles O. Christi.
141. Favorinus (Phavorinus, Camerti), Varinus (Guarrinus, Guerrino): ep. Nucerin. s. 10, 11, xi, xii (E 261).
142. Ferrerius, Bonifatius: ep. Iporegien. s. 7, 11, 12, xi, per ep. Montisregalis s. 5 (M 774e) [card., m. 1543] (E 15, 214).
143. Ferrerus, Zacharias, O. S. B.: abbas S. Benedicti de Monte Subasio (Subasten.) s. 8, ep. Sebasten. s. 12, xi, xii; in conc. Pisan.: comm. praep., secret., scrutator votorum, praed., acta ejusdem protulit [ep. Guardien., m. 1524] (E 295, 206).
144. Filippi de Senis, Hilarius (Hylarion; Ilario), O. H. S. Sp.: praeceptor S. Spiritus in Saxia de Urbe s. 7,8 [m. 1514] (Ferrajoli 36, 1913, 530).
145. Flisco, Augustinus de: ep. Sagonen. s. 3-5, 9, 10 [m. 1528] (E 288, v. s. n. 64).
146. Flisco, Laurentius de: ep. Asculan. et vicecamerarius et gub. Urbis s. 1, 2, ep. Montisregalis et gub. Urbis s. 3, 4, 5, proc. ep. Iporigien. s. 5 (M 774d) et ep. Vercellen. s. 5 (M 774de) [m. 1519] (E 119, 250).
147. Flisco (Fieschi), Nicolaus de: card. presb. S. Priscae s. 1-12, dep. de pace - nom., proc. ep. Torcellan. s. 10 (M 916cd); aep. Ravennaten., adm. Agathen., Ebredunen., Tolonen. [m. 1524] (E 8, 97, 190, 283, 315).
148. Flisco, Petrus de: ep. Cervien. s. 10-12, xii [m. c. 1525] (E 163).
149. Flores, Antonius: aep. Avinionen. s. 1, 2 [m. 1512] (E 126).
150. Flores, Petrus: ep. Stabien. s. 1, 2, 5-12, xi, xii, dep. de refm. - el., proc. ep. Spoletan. s. 11 (M 975e) et 12 (M 982e) [m. 1540] (E 303).
151. Folch de Cardona, Petrus: ep. Urgellen. s. 6, 7 [aep. Tarraconen., m. 1530] (E 324, 308).
152. Forbin, Ludovicus: orat. reg. Franciae, dom. de Soleriis s. 8-10.
153. Foscarus, Franciscus: orat. dom. Venetorum s. 1, 2, 5-7.
154. Foschi, Thomas: ep. Comaclen. s. 9 [m. 1514] (E 173).
* 155. Foscus, Gabriel, O.E.S.A.: aep. Dyrhachien. s.1-12, xi, xii; adm. Castren., sacrista S. S. [m. 1533] (E 189, 157).
156. Franceschinis, Franciscus de, O. F. M.: ep. Hortan. s. 1-5 (E 211).
157. Francischis, Bonus de: orat. communitatis Lucensium s. 5.
158. Frangipanibus, Jacobus de: conservator Urbis s. 2 (M 697d).
159. Fregoso (Campofregoso), Federicus de: aep. Salernitan. s. 1-6, dep. de pace - el.; ep. Eugubin. [card., m. 1541] (E 26, 193, 289).
160. Gabloneta (Gabbioneta), Alexander: orat. marchionis Mantuae s. 7, 9, 12.
161. Gaeta, Josue de: ep. Asculan. s. 1, 2, 6-9 (E 120).
162. Gagliardi, Joannes Baptista: ep. Bivinen. s. 1-5 [m. 1513] (E 135).
163. Galeottis, Vincentius de: ep. Squillacen. s. 8 [adm. Caputaquen., m. 1522] (E 303, 152).

* (See Addenda)

164. Gargha (de Gargiis), Joannes Baptista, O. S. J. Hier.: praed. s. 8 (M 850d); eques, tutor Camilli de Chisiis.
165. Garsias, Dominicus, O. P.: ep. Sappaten. s. 9 [m. c. 1518] (E 292).
166. Garzonibus, Joannes Baptista de: ep. Absaren. s. 10 [m. 1516] (E 91) Geometius Lusitanus - vide Ulixibona
167. Georgius: ep. Bellicen. s. 7 (v. s. n. 56).
168. Georgius (Zorzi), Marinus: orat. dom. Venetorum s. 10.
169. Gerardinus, Alexander Hieronymus: ep. S. Dominici s. xi [m. 1525] (E 187).
170. Gerardus, Jacobus: ep. Aquinaten. s. 8, 9 [m. c. 1516] (E 114).
171. Gerteuvitz (Gertewitz), Jacobus: proc. ep. Misnen. s. 6 (M 794b); cler. dioec. Misnen., not. apost. et imp. auctoritate (HOBERG, 214).
172. Gilbert (Gylberd vel Giles), Guillemus, O.S.A.: abbas B. Mariae Briutonis (Britonis), dioec. Bathonien. s. 2-5 [ep. Maioren., m. 1533] (E 233).
173. Giliis (Gigles, de Ziliis), Silvester de: ep. Wigornien. s. 2, 3, 5, 7, 9, 10, etiam orat. reg. Angliae s. 7, 9, 10 [m. 1521] (E 334).
174. Ginutiis (Chinucci), Hieronymus de: scrutator votorum (M 697a) aud. apost. cam., can. Senis, ep. Asculan. s. 3-12, proc. ep. Calinen. s. 11 (M 975d) [ep. Wigornien., card., m. 1541] (E 23, 120, HOFMANN II, 91).
175. Gonzaga, Federicus: Marchio Mantuanus s. 2-5.
176. Gonzaga, Sigismundus: card. diac. S. Mariae Novae s. 5-7, dep. de pace - nom., adm. Mantuan., frater marchionis Mantuae [m. 1525] (E 11, 234).
177. Gorrevodo-Challant, Ludovicus de: ep. Maurianen. et orat. ducis Sabaudiae s. 10 [card., m. 1535] (E 21, 238).
178. Grassis, Achilles de: card. presb. S. Sixti s. 1-7, 10, 12, dep. de fide - nom., proc. abbatis gen. O. Praem. s. 2 (M 716c); ep. Bononien., Civitatis Castelli [m. 1523] (E 12, 168, 136).
179. Grassis, Belthasar (Balassar) de: ep. Civitatis Castelli s. 11, 12, xi, xii (E 168).
180. Grassis, Paris de: mag. ceremoniarum, assignator locorum (M 697b), proc. aep. Ravennaten. s. 5 (M 774c), ep. Pisaurien. s. 6-12, xi, xii (v. s. n. 42) [m. 1528] (E 274).
181. Gratianis, Raynaldus de, O.F.M.: aep. Ragusin. s. 3-7, dep. de fide - nom. non el. [m. 1529] (E 281).
182. Griffus, Petrus: ep. Forolivien. s. 3-5, 7, 9 [m. 1516] (E 198).
183. Grimaldis, Augustinus de, O.S.B., Cassinien.: ep. Grassen. s. 12, xii, per P. de Candia s. 11 (M 975c); abbas Lerinensis, filius Lamberti principis in Monaco [princeps in Monaco, m. 1532] (E 205).
184. Grimanis, Dominicus de: card. ep. Portuen. s. 1-12, xi, dep de fide - nom., proc. patr. Venetiarum s. 5 (M 774a) et ep. Cremonen. s. 5 (M 774b); patr. Aquilegien., adm. Urbinaten., Ceneten. [m. 1523] (E 5, 114, 162, 323).
185. Grimanis, Marinus de: ep. Ceneten. s. 3-10, patr. Aquilegien. s. 12 [card., m. 1546] (E 19, 162, 114).
186. Grimanis, Petrus de: curator personae S.S. (M 696d, 697d), miles O.S.J. Hier. et prior de Hungaria s. 1, 2.
187. Guascus, Alexander: ep. Alexandrin. s. 3-9, dep. de refm. - el. [m. 1517] (E 102).
188. Guastaferro, Franciscus: ep. Suessan. s. 1-6 [m. 1543] (E 305).
189. Guglielmucci, Petrus Priscus: ep. Lavellen. 12, xi, xii [m. 1539] (E 221).
190. Guidono, Franciscus de: orat. Magni Mag. Rhodi s. 8, 9.

191. Guillinis (Ghillinis), Guillinus (Ghillinus, Silvius) de: ep. Comaclen. s. 10 [m. 1549] (E 173).
192. Guiramandi, Franciscus: ep. Dignen. s. 11, 12, xii [m. 1536] (E 186).
193. Guzmanus (de Gormaz), Petrus: ep. Narnien. s. 2-9 [m. 1515] (E 253).
194. Hamon, Franciscus: ep. Nanneten. s. 8-10 [m. 1532] (E 252).
195. Herrera, Ferdinandus de: ep. Gaietan. s. 1-4 [m. 1518] (E 200).
196. Histello (Spello), Petrus Paulus Venantius de: ep. Aesin. s. 8-12, xi, proc. ep. Auximan. s. 10 (M 916d) (E 97).
197. Ingenvinkel (Ingenwinckel), Joannes (Jan): proc. ep. Trajecten. s. 11 (M 975e); not., script., secret. [Datarius, m. 1535] (H nr. 11, 630-31, 17, 837, 15, 646, Hofmann II, 104, 182, 240).
198. Inghirami, Thomas (Phedra): secret. conc. (M 696e); bibliothecae apost. praefectus (M 696e-97a) [m. 1516].
199. Inuciatis, Matthaeus de: ep. Bethleemitan. s. 2 (ISG 4, fol. 115^v).
200. Iusart (Insert, Iussurte, Juzarte), Franciscus: proc. ep. Portugalen. s. 2 (M 716a) et ep. Colimbrien. s. 6 (M 794b); cler. dioec. Ulixbonen., de nobile genere procreatus, mag., not., solic. lit. apost., famil. suus [collector in regno Portugalliae] (H nr. 2053, 3328).
201. Jaba (Juba, Giuppo della Rovere), Antonius (Antoniello): orat. Maximiliani imperatoris el. s. 8; nepos Sixti IV ex matre, frater Francisci de Ruvere ep. Vicentin.
202. Jacobatius (Jacovazzi, Giacobazzi) de Faceschiis, Dominicus: ep. Lucerin. s. 1-12, xii, dep. de refm. - nom. [card., m. 1528] (E 16, 229).
203. Joannes: ep. Trabunien. vel Triburen. s. 6 et M 850b (v. s. n. 57).
204. Joannes Baptista (? Oricellarius, Rucellai).senator Urbis s. 12 (v. s. n. 71).
205. Julius II (de Ruvere, Julianus): ep. Romae s. 1-4, per moderatorem card. Riario s. 5 [m. 20. II. 1513] (E 9).
206. Justinianus (Giustiniano), Augustinus, O.P.: ep. Nebien. s. 11, 12, xi, xii [m. 1536] (E 255).
207. Justinianus, Benedictus: ep. Chien. 1-12, xi, proc. ep. Faventin. s. 11 (M 975cd) [m. 1533] (E 165).
208. Laleza (Lalexa), Martinus: ep. Albanen. s. 8 (E 100, v. s. n. 62).
209. Lambertinus, Caesar: ep. Insulan. s. 9 (E 213).
210. Landuccus de Senis, Bernardinus, O. C.: vicarius gen. O. Carm. s. 1-5 (sed gen. B. Spagnoli non praesens nom. dep. de refm.) [m. 1523].
211. Landus, Petrus: orat. dom. Venetorum s. 8, 9.
212. Lang de Wellenburg, Matthaeus: ep. Gurcen. et locumtenens Maximiliani el. imperatoris s. 3 (M 731ab), card. diac. S. Angeli in foro piscium s. 8, 9; ep. Carthaginen., coadj. aep. Salzeburgen. [m. 1540] (E 13, 154, 207, 291).
213. Lapide (von Stein in Beiern, Stayn), Totus Lupus (Enttelvvolffo, Eitelwolf) de: orat. Joachim marchionis Brandeburgen. electoris imperii s. 8, 9 (Riedel III, 260).
214. Lasco (Łaski), Joannes de: aep. Gneznen. et orat. reg. Poloniae s. 7-10, dep. de pace - nom., proc. ep. Warmien. s. 10 (M 916a) [legatus natus, m. 1531] (E 204).
215. Laureliis, Laurentius (Aurelius Amerinus) de: not. et scriba (M 935c); not. cam. apost. (Raynaldus 1513 nr. 47).
216. Laurus (Loreo), Bernardus (Bernardinus): ep. Polycastren. s. 3-6 [m. 1516] (E 277).
217. Lefranc, Joannes: ep. Aurasicen. s. 1, 3, 9, 10, xi [m. 1524] (E 123, Hofmann II, 182).

218. Leo X (de Medicis, Joannes): ep. Romae s. 6-12 [m. 1521] (E 13).
219. Leonibus (Macarazzi), Tranquillus de: ep. Ferentin. s. 1, 2, 7-12, xi [m. 1548] (E 195).
220. Leonini, Angelus: aep. Turritan. s. 9 [m. 1517] (E 322).
221. Leonini, Camillus: ep. Tiburtin. s. xii [m. c. 1528] (E 313).
222. Leonissa, Jacobus Alpharidius (? Alaphridus) de: ep. Civitatis ducalis s. 2-6, 12, xii (E 169).
223. Lerma, Alphonsus de: not. conc. (M 696e); pnot. apost., script. brev. apost., prior eccl. Burgen. (H nr. 619, 2593).
224. Lippomanus, Nicolaus: not. conc. (M 696e), ep. Bergomen. s. 3-9, per ep. Melfiten. s. 11 (M 976a) (E 132, 271).
225. Loaysa, Joannes de: ep. Algaren. s. 11, 12, proc. ep. Tirasonen. s. 11 (M 975d) et alii (M 975bc) [ep. Mindonien., m. c. 1525] (E 104, H nr. 552).
226. Luca, Timotheus de, O.F.M.: (vicarius gen. Observ. Cismont.) « mag. gen. » O.F.M. s. 5 [m. 1513].
227. Lunellus (Bunel, Runel), Joannes Andreas: abbas S. Sebastiani S.O.Cist. extra Urbem s. 6-9, 11, 12; cler. Cenoman., nepos J. Bodier cui successit [ep. Sebasten.] (E 295, ISG 113, fol. 150ᵛ).
228. Maccafanis, Angelus de: ep. Lancianen. s. 11, 12, xi, xii [m. 1517] (E 218).
229. Maccafanis, Jacobus de: ep. Marsican. s. 1, 2, 7-10, 12, xi (E 236).
230. Madrignano, Archangelus (Michelangelus) de: ep. Avellinen. s. 12, xii [m. 1529] (E 126).
231. Maffeis, Marius (Marinus) de: ep. Aquinaten. s. 11, 12, xi [m. 1537] (E 114).
232. Maffeis, Vintius (Vincentius) de: ep. Cajacen. s. 6-9; ep. Coronen. [m. 1517] (E 145, 179).
233. Magdalenae (Maddaleni de' Capodiferro), Evangelista (Fausto): conservator Urbis s. 9, 10.
234. Magnani, Hieronymus, O.F.M.: ep. Buduen. s. 3-7, 10, 12, xi, xii, proc. ep. Larinen. s. 5 (M 774b) [ep. Vestan., m. 1527] (E 332).
235. Magnaninis (Magnacurius), Christophorus de: ep. Polygnianen. s. 5, 9, 11, 12, xi (E 277).
236. Malabaila, Vasinus: ep. Placentin. s. 9, 10 [ep Asten., m. 1525] (E 275, 121).
237. Malombra, Aloysius: ep. Arben. s. 9 [m. 1514] (E 115).
238. Marcellus, Christophorus: praed. s. 4 (M 755de); pnot. apost. [aep. Corcyren., m. 1528] (E 177).
239. Mari, Zacharias de: ep. Terracinen. s. 1, 2, 5, 7-10 [m. c. 1517] (E 310).
240. Martellis, Ugolinus de: ep. Licien. s. 1, 2, 6-9, 12, xi (E 224).
241. Mascardi, Basilius (Bertrandus): ep. Tudertin. s. 3-5, 12, xii [m. 1517] (E 321).
242. Matthaeus (? Michael de Amatis, m. 1518): ep. S. Leonis s. 11, 12 [m. ∗ 1518] (E 223).
243. Medicis, Julianus de: frater germanus S.S. s. 7; [Generalissimus Ecclesiae, m. 1516].
244. Medicis, Julius de, O. S. J. Hier.: aep. Florentin. s. 6, 7, dep. de pace - el., card. diac. S. Mariae in Domnica s. 8-12; consobrinus S.S., prior Capuae, aep. Narbonen. ep. Albien., adm. Vauren., vicecancellarius [Clemens VII, m. 1534] (E 14, 18, 101, 197, 327).
245. Medicis, Laurentius de: nepos S.S. secundum carnem, dux Urbinaten. s. 11 [m. 1519].
246. Mediolanense, Blasius (Basilius, Biagio) de, C.V.U.O S.B.: abbas et gen. Vallis Umbrosae s. 5, 8 [venerabilis] (H nr. 8152-53).

∗ (See Addenda)

247. Melis (Melle), Petrus Joannes de: ep. Montismarani s. 12 (E 249).
248. Merinis, Stephanus Gabriel de: aep. Baren. s. 7-12, xi, xii; ep. Legionen. [patr. Indiarum, card., m. 1535] (E 21, 129, 213, 221, H nr. 2420).
249. Merula, Bartholomaeus: ep. Agien. s. 3 (E 98).
250. Michael: ep. Archsen. s. 8 (v. s. n. 58, 59).
251. Michael: ep. Mordanien. s. 1, 2 (v. s. n. 58, 59).
252. Middelburg, Paulus de: ep. Forosempronien. s. 9-12, xi, xii [m. 1533] (E 198).
253. Miedzyleski (Miedzeleschh, Medizeldri), Laurentius: orat. Stanislai et Joannis ducum Mazoviae Russiaeque s. 7 (M 814bc); cath. Wilnen. praepositus, secret. reg., proc. spec. [ep. Camenecen., m. c. 1531] (E 148).
254. Minerbeti de Medicis, Franciscus: aep. Turritan. s. 10 (E 322).
255. Minius, Marcus: orat. dom. Venetorum s. 12.
256. Minuti, Andreas: aep. Monobasien. s. 1-10; ep. Hierapetren. [m. 1515] (E 209, 248).
257. Mocharus, Bernardus. proc. conc. (M 697b); Romanus.
258. Molon, Ludovicus: proc. ep. Ampurien. et Civitaten. s. 10 (M 916ab); cler. Caesaraugusten.
259. Montagna, Hieronymus de: aep. Antibaren. s. 1, 2, 5, 9, 12, xi [m. 1517] (E 110).
260. Monte (Ciocchi de Monte S. Savini), Antonius Maria de: card. presb. S. Vitalis s. 1-9, dep. de refm. - nom., card. presb. S. Praxedis s. 10-12, xi, xii, proc. ep. Caesenaten. s. 5 (M 774c) et aep. Upsalen. et prov. Sueciae s. 10 (M 916c); aep. Sipontin., ep. Novarien., adm. Papien., comm. praep. [m. 1533] (E 12, 260, 269, 300, HOFMANN I, 309).
261. Monte (S. Savini), Joannes Maria de: aep. Sipontin. s. 3-5, praed. s. 5 (M 775c) [card., Julius III, m. 1555] (E 31, 300).
262. Moriconibus, Justinianus de: ep. Amelien. s. 10 (E 106).
263. Moronus, Hieronymus: orat. M. Sfortiae ducis Mediolani s. 9 (M 869a); aderat publicationi ex parte principum edicti convocationis conc. Pisan., pater futuri card. J. Moroni [m. 1529].
264. Moyses (Mūsā): proc. patr. Maronitarum s. 11 (M 945b); diac. monachus — sic T. AMBROGIO. I. ḤARFŪŠ adfirmat Ilyās ibn Zarzūr al-Ḥadatī fuisse procuratorem (v. s. n. 38 et post nr. 134).
265. Musanus (Musurus, Mousouros), Marcus: aep. Monobasien. s. 11, 12, xi, xii; ep. Chironen., Hierapetren. [m. 1517] (E 166, 209, 248).
266. Nabe (Nallio), Augustinus de, O. P.: ep. Tribunien. s. 9, per proc. aep. Nazaren. s. 11 (M 976a) [m. c. 1528] (E 318).
267. Narnia, Simon de: ep. Andrien. s. 12, xii [m. 1517] (E 109).
268. Nichesolis, Galesius de: ep. Bellunen. s. 1-8, 11, 12, xii, proc. ep. Aesin. s. 5 (M 774d), per ep. Calinen. s. 10 (M 916d) [m. 1527] (E 131).
269. Nicolai de Viterbo, Baltassar: mag. ceremoniarum, assignator locorum (M 697b). Substitutus eiusdem absentis fuit Bernardus Gutteri Hispanus.
270. Niconitiis, Nicolaus de: ep. Curzolen. et Stagnen. s. 8, 9 [m. c. 1541] (E 183).
271. Nigusantius, Vincentius: ep. Arben. s. xi, xii [aderat conc. Trident.] (E 115).
272. Nini (de Amelia), Jacobus: ep. Potentin. s. 1-4, 6-12 (E 279).
273. Noendomman, Joannes: proc. ep. Lubicen. s. 11 (M 975c).
274. Novellis, Andreas de: ep. Alben. s. 3, 4 [m. 1513] (E 100).

275. Novellis, Hippolytus de: ep. Alben. s. 12, xii [m. 1530] (E 100).
276. Orfeus, Carolus: proc. ep. Brixien. s. 6 (M 794ab); praelatus domest., not. apost., frater Joannis Antonii [m. 1514] (Ferrajoli 36, 1913, 213-23).
277. Orfeus, Joannes Antonius: ep. Calinen. s. 1, 3, 4, 6-10, proc. ep. Bellunen. s. 10 (M 916d), per ep. Asculan. s. 11 (M 975d) [m. 1518] (E 147).
278. Oschillai de Portu (O'Fihely of Baltimore), Mauritius, O. F. M.: aep. Tuamen. s. 1, 2 [m. 1513] (E 320).
279. Ostrorog (de Osteroch), Stanislaus: orat. reg. Poloniae s. 7; palatinatus castellanus Calissiensis, consiliarius reg. [postea Lutheranus, m. 1568].
280. Pacheco, Didacus (Diogo): orat. reg. Portugalliae s. 9; doctor juris, auditor curiae reg.
? Paganottis (Pagagnotti), Benedictus de, O. P.: ep. Vasionen. s. ? [m. 1522] (E 327, Cavalieri 336).
281. Pallavicinis, Christophorus de: dom. temp. s. 4.
282. Pallavicinis, Joannes Baptista de: ep. Cavallicen. s. 1-6, 8-12, xi, xii, dep. de refm. - el., proc. ep. Alerien. s. 2 (M 716a) [card. m. 1524] E 15, 161).
283. Pallavicinis, Joannes Ludovicus de: dom. temp., marchio s. 8.
284. Pallavicinis, Octavianus de: dom. temp. s. 4.
285. Pallavicinis, Philippus de, O. F. M.: ep. Adiacen. s. 4, 5, 10 [m. 1518] (E 94, v. s. n. 54).
286. Pandolfinis, Jannocius (Jannotius, Joannocius, Genocius, Giannotti) de: ep. Trojan. s. 6, 8-12 [m. 1525] (E 319).
287. Pandonus, Silvius: ep. Boianen. s. 10 [m. 1519] (E 136).
288. Parente, Petrus de: ep. Algaren. s. 1-3 [m. 1514] (E 104).
289. Pasi, Jacobus: ep. Faventin. s. 3-10, dep. de pace - el., per ep. Chien. s. 11 (M 975cd) [m. 1528] (E 194).
290. Pels, Joannes: proc. abbatis S. Adalberti in Egmonda O. S. B. Burs. dioec. Trajecten. s. 11 (M 976a); ?can. S. Salvatoris Trajecten.
291. Perini, Petrus: proc. ep. Lausanen. s. 2 (M 716b); venerabilis vir dominus.
292. Peruschis, Marius de: proc. conc. (M 657e); proc. fisci cam. apost. gen. [m. 1528] (Hofmann II, 95).
293. Petruciis, Alphonsus de: card. diac. S. Theodori s. 1, 2, 4-10, dep. de fide - nom.; ep. Massanen. [m. 1517] (E 12, 237).
294. Petruciis, Angelus de: ep. Bretenorien. s. 9, 10 [m. 1515?] (E 139).
295. Petruciis, Lactantius de: ep. Suanen. s. 8-10 [m. 1527] (E 305).
296. Petruciis, Raphael de: ep. Grossetan. s. 2 [castellanus arcis S. Angeli de Urbe, card., m. 1522] (E15, 206).
297. Piccolominibus, Franciscus de: ep. Bisinianen. s. 1-9, dep. de pace - el.; nepos Pii III [m. c. 1530] (E 134).
298. Piccolominibus, Hieronymus jun. de: ep. Ilcinen. s. 1-9, dep. de fide - el. [m. 1535] (E 212, v. s. n. 51).
299. Picus de Mirandula, Joannes Franciscus: dom. temp. s. 8 [m. 1533] (v. s. n. 41).
300. Piis, Albertus de: orat. Maximiliani imperatoris el. s. 3-12; princeps de Carpo [m. 1531].
301. Piis, Latinus de: ep. Vestan. s. 1-9 [m. 1514] (E 332).
302. Piperariis (Peverari), Andreas de: secret. conc .(M 663c); not., cubic., secret. card. M. Cornari [ep. Absaren., m. 1527] (H nr. 17, 389, E 91).
303. Pisauro, Franciscus de: aep. Jadren. s. 1-5, 8, 9 [patr. Constantinopolitan.] (E 215, 177).

304. Planca, Paulus de: advoc. conc. (M 697a); advoc. consist., advoc. pauperum, abbrev. praesentiae majoris [m. 1523] (HOFMANN II, 185).
305. Platamone, Ludovicus de: ep. Sarnen. s. 12, xii [m. 1540] (E 293).
306. Plaude, Joannes Filibertus de: orat. ducis Sabaudiae, comes de Jaes s. 10.
307. Poetis, Virgilius de: orat. Bononien. s. 12.
308. Prato, Joannes Dominici de, O. F. M.: ep. Aquilan. s. 1-10, aep. Theban. s. 11, 12, xi, xii [m. 1517] (E 113, v. s. n. 74).
309. Pucius, Antonius: praed. s. 9 (M 887d); cler. cam. apost. [ep. Pistorien., card., m. 1544] (E 21).
310. Pucius, Laurentius: card. presb. SS. IV Coronatorum s. 8-12, xi, xii; ep. Pistorien., adm. Amalfitan., Melfien., Veneten. [m. 1531] (E 13, 105, 241, 275, 329); proc. reg. Daciae s. 12 (SANUDO, XXIV, 105).
311. Pugilla, Franciscus: orat. marchionis Montisferrati s. 8.
312. Rabus (Rallus), Manilius: scrutator votorum (M 697a), proc. ep. Argolicen. s. 5 (M 775ab); acolytus capellae papalis, cub., secret. vicecancellarii (HOFMANN II, 182), Graecus [aep. Monobasien. E 248].
313. Radzivil (Radvilas), Albertus: ep. Vilnen. s. 3-8 [m. 1519] (E 334, H nr. 11, 732).
314. Rangonibus, Hugo de: ep. Regien. s. 3, 4, 6-10 [m. 1540] (E 284).
315. Raymiardi, Petrus: proc. ep. Regien. s. 10 (M 916b).
316. Regis, Thomas: proc. conc. (M 697b); cler. dioec. Redonen., lit. aplic. script. et abbrev., cler. cam., famil. suus [ep. Dolen., m. 1524] (E 86, 186, H nr. 810).
317. Remolinis, Franciscus de: card. presb. S. Marcelli sed titulus SS. Joannis et Pauli conservatus s. 6-11, dep. de pace - nom., card. ep. Albanen. s. 12; aep. Surrentin., ep. Firman., adm. Gallipolitan., Lavellen., Panormitan., Sarnen. [m. 1518] (E 8, 196, 201, 221, 268, 293).
318. Remolinis, Gisbertus de: aep. Surrentin. s. 6, 9, 10; frater card. Francisci [m. 1525] (E 306).
319. Riarius, Caesar: patr. Alexandrin. s. 1-12; aep. Pisan. [m. c. 1541] (E 102, 274).
320. Riarius, Rafael (Sansonus): card. ep. Ostien. s. 1-12, dep. de refm. - nom., moderator conc. s. 5 (M 776d), comm. praep., proc. aep. Magdeburgen. et Maguntin. et adm. Halberstaden. ac marchionis Brandeburgen. s. 11 (M 975e); comd. Conchen., adm. Saonen., Milevitan., nepos Sixti IV, camerarius [m. 1521] (E 3, 174, 243, 291, HOFMANN I, 309).
321. Riarius, Thomas Joseph: ep. Saonen. s. 11, 12, xi [m. 1528] (E 291).
322. Riccius? Casulanus de Senis, Joannes Baptista: advoc. conc. (M 697a); advoc. consist. [m. 1529] (CARTHARIUS 94).
323. Rio, Balthasar del: praed. s. 7 (M 819d); scholasticus Mindonien., prot. apost., famil., secret. card. J. Serra [ep. Scalen., m. 1540] (E 294, H nr. 8213, M 658c).
324. Rocca (de Rocha), Raphael: ep. Caprien. s. 1, 2 (E 151).
325. Rodericus Joannes: proc. ep. Cepten. s. 4 (M 755b); abbas B. Mariae de Tauoica Tudensis dioec. (v. s. n. 65).
326. Rogeriis, Bernardus de: ep. Soran. s. 1-4, 6, 7, 11, 12, xi, xii, per ep. Scalen. s. 10 (M 916c) (E 302).
327. Rossi, Bernardus (Bertrandus): ep. Tarvisin. s. 1-12, xi, xii, dep. de pace - el., etiam gub. Urbis s. 7-9, proc. ep. Nonen. s. 10 (M 916b) [m. 1527] (E 309).
328. Rotariis, Carolus de: ep. Montisregalis s. 2 [m. 1512] (E 250).

329. Ruvere (Roboreus), Albertinus de: ep. Pisaurien. s. 1-4 (E 274).
330. Ruvere, Franciscus de: ep. Vicentin. s. 1-5, 7-9 (E 333).
331. Ruvere, Joannes Franciscus de: ep. Taurinen. s. 7, 8, 10, dep. de fide - el., proc. ep. Gebennen. s. 10 (M 915e-916a) [m. ex 1516] (E 309).
332. Ruvere, Leonardus Grossus de: card. presb. S. Susannae s. 2-12, dep. de refm. - nom.; ep. Agenen., comm. praep., poenit. major [m. 1520] (E 10, 98, HOFMANN I, 309).
333. Ruvere, Nicolaus de: dom. temp. s. 1, 3, 4; nepos S.S., capitaneus palatii (DE GRASSI, *Diarium*, 430).
334. Ruvere, Orlandus de Caretto de: aep. Nazaren. s. 1, 2, aep. Avinionen. s. 6-10; adm. Aurien., castellanus arcis S. Angeli de Urbe [m. 1527] (E 124, 126, 254).
335. Ruvere, Sixtus de Franciottis de: card. presb. S. Petri ad Vincula et vicecancellarius s. 4, dep. de fide - nom ; ep. Paduan., adm. Benevetan., Lucan., nepos S.S. [m. 1517] (E 11, 132, 228, 267)
336. Ruvere, Sixtus de: curator personae S.S. (M 696d, 697d), prior Urbis et miles O.S.J. Hier. s. 1, 2; ep. Salutiarum s. 8-10 [m. 1516] (Savio 123-125).
337. Sabellis, Jacobus de: dom. temp. s. 5.
338. Salicetus, Bartholomaeus. secret. conc. (M 697a); Bononiensis.
339. Salvaterra, Guillelmus de: proc. ep. Gerunden. s. 10 (M 916b); rev. pater dom. frater.
340. Salviatis, Jacobus de: orat. dom. Florentini s. 3, 4, 6, 7 (v. s. n. 68).
341. Salvinus, Joannes Franciscus: ep. Spigaten. s. 6, 9, ep. Vestan. s. 10 [m. 1516] (E 303, 332).
342. Sanna (Sanz), Andreas: proc. ep. Ussellen. s. 5 (M 774d); can. et [ep. Ussellan., aep. Arboren., m. c. 1556] (E 115, 324).
343. San Severino, Alexander de: coadj. ep. Urbevetan. s. 9, 10 (M 903e), aep. Viennen. s. 10 (M 902d), 11, 12 [m. 1527] (E 323, 333).
344. San Severino, Federicus de: card. diac. S. Angeli in foro piscium et orat. reg. Franciae (M 832ab) s. 8-10; aderat conc. Pisan., comd. Viennen., ?adm. Novarien. [m. 1516] (E 12, 260, 333).
345. Sansonibus, Hieronymus de: ep. Aretin. s. 1-5, 9, 12 [ep. Lauden., m. 1536] (E 116, 220).
346. Santucius, Gratianus, O.S.A.: ep. Alatrin. s. 12 (E 99).
347. Satmat, Laurentius de: dom. temp. s. 10.
348. Saulis, Bandinellus de: card. presb. S. Sabinae s. 1-10, dep. de fide - nom., card. presb. S. Mariae trans Tiberim sed cum titulo S. Sabinae s. 11, 12; ep. Hieracen. et Oppiden., adm. Albinganen. [m. 1518] (E 12, 101, 209).
349. Saulis, Philippus de: ep. Brugnaten. s. 11, 12, xi, xii [m. c. 1528] (E 141).
350. Scannafora, Bernardinus: ep. Castren. s. 1-5 (E 157).
351. Scaramellotti, Polydorus: abbas S. Eutychii dioec. Spoletan. s. 5 (PIRRI 36-38).
352. Schinner, Matthaeus: card. presb. S. Pudentianae s. 6, dep. de refm. - nom.; ep. Sedunen., adm. Novarien. [m. 1522] (E 12, 260, 295).
353. Scotius (Scotti), Joannes Antonius: ep. Anglonen. s. 1-5, 7-9, dep. de fide - el. [m. 1528] (E 109).
354. Scribonius, Dominicus: ep. Imolen. s. 3-7, 10, 12, xi, xii (E 213).
355. Sculteti (Schulz de Lowenburg), Bernardus: scriba et not. subalter. (M 696e); cler. dioec. Wladislavien., decanus Warmien., vicarius Magdeburgen., decret. doctor, not. Rotae, pnot. et script. apost. [m. 1518] (M 935c, v. s. n. 30).

* (See Addenda)

I

356. Secchia de Parma, Joannes Baptista, O. C.: vicarius gen. O. Carm. s. 12 [m. IV. 1517].
357. Senilis (Sanilio), Gibertus (Gisbertus): ep. Rapollan. s. 1-5, 7, 9-12, xi, xii, proc. ep. Fanen. s. 2 (M 716b) et ep. Valven. s. 10 (M 916a) [m. 1528] (E 282).
358. Senis, Matthaeus de: ep. Umbriaticen. s. 1-10; famil. card. N. de Flisco [m. 1517] (E 323).
359. Sepulveda, Joannes de: ep. Tuden. s. 1-5, 8, aep. Corinthien. s. xii (E 320, 178).
360. Serra, Jacobus (Jaime): card. ep. Albanen. s. 1-7, 9, dep. de fide - nom., adm. Burgen., Elnen., Lincopen. [m. 1517] (E 6-7, 142, 192, 225).
361. Serra de Munoz, Petrus: aep. Arboren. et S. Justae s. 4-8 [m. 1517] (E 115).
362. Sertorius, Joannes Matthaeus: aep. S. Severinae s. 7 [ep. Vulterran., m. 1545] (E 298, 337).
363. Setario, Joannes Franciscus: ep. Avellinen. et Frequentin. s. 6, 7 [m. 1516] (E 126).
364. Seysello, Claudius de: ep. Massilien. et orat. reg. Franciae s. 8, 9 [aep. Taurinen., m. 1520] (E 237, 309).
365. Sfortia, Galeatius: dom. temp. s. 8 [m. 1515].
366. Sfortia, Franciscus Maria: orat. Maximiliani imperatoris el. et dux Baren. s. 8, 9; frater ducis Mediolani.
 ? Sicilia (Siciliano) Thomas de, O. P.: ep. Minoren. s. ? sub Leone X [m. 1526] (E 246, CAVALIERI 341).
367. Silva, Michael (Viseus) de: orat. reg. Portugalliae s. 11, 12; vicarius Egitanien. [ep. Visen., card., m. 1556] (E 27, 190).
368. Simoneta, Jacobus: scrutator votorum (M 697a); aud. causarum sacri palatii [ep. Pisaurien., card., m. 1539] (E 23-24).
369. Sinibaldis, Antonius de: ep. Auximan. s. 4, per ep. Aesin. s. 10 (M 916d) (E 125).
370. Sinibaldis, Joannes Baptista de: ep. Auximan. s. 11, 12, xi [m. 1547] (E 125).
371. Sinibaldis, Maurus (Marcus, Marius) de: ep. Ogentin. s. 2, 6-10 [m. c. 1517] (E 262).
372. Soderinus, Franciscus: card. ep. Sabinen. s. 3-7, dep. de pace - nom., card. ep. Tiburtinen. s. 8-10; ep. Vicentin., adm. Narnien., Xanctonen., Anagnin. [m. 1524] (E 8, 107, 253, 333, 338).
373. Soderinus, Julianus: ep. Vulterran. s. 3-9; nepos card. Francisci [ep. Xanctonen., m. 1544] (E 337, 338).
374. Solino, Dominicus: ep. Aquen. s. 1, 2, 8 et orat. marchionis Montisferrati s. 8 [m. c. 1528] (E 113).
375. Soto, Petrus de: proc. aep. Compostellan. s. 11 (M 976a); cler. dioec. Compostellan., licen. in decret. [ep. Tripolien. et aux. Compostellan., m. c. 1533] (E 319, 341, H nr. 2236, 2371).
376. Spinola, Augustinus: ep. Perusin. s. 9-12 [card., m. 1537] (E 19, 271).
377. Spinola (Spinula), Franciscus: not. conc. (M. 696e).
378. Spiritibus, Christophorus de: ep. Caesenaten. s 8-12, xi, xii, per aep. Sipontin. s. 5 (M 774c) [aderat conc. Tridentin., patr. Hierosolymitan., m. 1556] (E 144, 210).
379. Squarcialupis (Starcelupis), Petrus de: senator Urbis s. 1-4; Florentinus.
380. Staphyleus, Joannes: ep. Sibenicen. s. 6-11, dep. de fide - nom., proc. ep. Pharen. s. 10 (M 916b); aud. Rotae [m. 1528] (E 299, H nr. 4925).

381. Staviaco (Stavayer), Claudius de, S. O. Cist.: ep. Bellicen. s. 4,6; abbas monasterii Altaecumbae, consiliarius ducis Sabaudiae [m. 1534] (E 130, v.s. n. 56).
382. Storciatus (de Scorciatis; Scorzati, Sonino), Julius (Julianus): senator Urbis s. 5,6; Neapolitanus.
383. Stroziis (Stroxis), Antonius de: orat. dom. Florentinorum s. 1,2.
384. Stroziis (Stroxis), Matthaeus de: orat. dom. Florentini s. 3,4.
385. Stunega (Zúñiga), Antonius de, O.S.J. Hier.: prior Castellae s. 9; prioratus litigatus [adjuvavit in suppressione rebellionis in Hispaniae contra Carolum V].
386. Sylva, Albertus de: ep. Sebasten. s. 6,7 (E 295).
387. Taleazis (Teglatius), Stephanus de: aep. Patracen. et ep. Torcellan. s. 1-3,6, aep. Patracen. s. 9-10, praed. s. 10 (M 916e) [m. 1515] (E 315).
388. Tapia, Joannes Rodericus de: proc. ep. Placentin. s. 4 (M 755c); venerabilis vir dom., portionarius ecclesiae Corduben.
389. Tassis, Aloysius (Alvisius) Ludovicus de: ep. Parentin. s. 3,4,10 [m. 1520] (E 270, 281).
390. Tedeschini-Piccolomini, Joannes Vincentius Nanni: aep. Senen. s. 1,2, 4,6-12, xii, dep. de refm. - el. [card., m. 1537] (E 15, 297).
391. Theobaldeschis, Robertus de: ep. Civitaten. s. 8 [m. c. 1517] (E 167). Timotheus - vide Luca
392. Tomacelli, Marinus (Martinus): ep. Cassanen. s. 10 (E 156).
393. Toreglias (Torrella), Gasparus: ep. S. Justae s. 2 (E 216).
394. Tornabonus, Julianus: ep. Salutiarum s. 11,12, xi,xii (E 290).
395. Tornafrancia, Joannes Evangelista: ep. Catacen. s. 10 [m. 1523] (E 158).
396. Treda, Joannes de: nomine ep. Gaietan. sive Liparen. proc. ep. Lucen. s. 11 (M 975d).
397. Trivultiis, Scaramutia de: ep. Cuman. s. 3-7,9,11, xi,xii, dep. de pace - el. [card., m. 1527] (E 15, 182).
398. Trombetta (Trumbeta), Antonius, O.F.M.: ep. Urbinaten. s. 2-9, aep. Athenien. s. 10, dep. de fide - el. (E 323).
399. Trulletti (Trulleri, Trocileti), Benedictus: scriba et not. subalt. (M 696e, 935c); Gallus.
400. Tuerdus (Stuerdus, Stewart, Stuart), (Joannes) Baltassar: secret. S.S. (M 711a); praelatus domest., collector Sabaudiae et Scotiae [m. c. 1519] (Ferrajoli 40, 1917, 262-67).
401. Turre, Natalis de: ep. Veglen. s. 10 (E 328).
402. Ubertis, Georgius de: ep. Castren. s. 12, xii (E 157).
403. Ugonibus, Matthias de: ep. Famagusten. s. 9 (E 194).
404. Ulixibona (Olisipo, Lusitanus; de Lisboa), Geometius (Gomesius, Gomes, Demetrius), O.F.M.: vicarius O.F.M. s. 1,2 [?aep. Nazaren.].
405. Urries (Urrea), Petrus de: ep. Syracusan et orat. reg. Hispaniae s. 12, xii (E 307, v.s. n. 61).
406. Urries (Urrea, Urias), Philippus de: ep. Philadelphien. s. xii; coadj. ep. Oscen (E 273, 264).
407. Ursinis, Aldobrandinus de: aep. Nicosien. s. 1-9, 11, 12; frater Ludovici comitis de Petiliano [m. 1527] (E 258).
408. Ursinis, Franciottus de: dom. temp., pater Octavii s. 4, 7 (cum filio), 12 [card., m. 1534] (E 17).
409. Ursinis, Franciscus de: dom. temp. s. 1.
410. Ursinis, Gabriel de: ep. Calven. s. 5,8,11 (E 147).
411. Ursinis, Julius de: dom. temp. s. 1-5; tamquam gentium praefectus ecclesiae (DE GRASSI, *Diarium*, 430).

412. Ursinis, Ludovicus de: comes Petiliani s. 6, 9, 10 [m. 1534].
413. Ursinis, Octavius de: dom. temp., filius Franciotti s. 7.
414. Ursinis, Robertus Latinus: aep. Rheginen. s. 3-6, 8-12, dep. de refm. - el. [resignavit aep. et duxit in matrimonium] (E 284).
+ Ursinis, alii illustres domini de: dom. temp. s. 3 (M 731c).
415. Valle, Andreas de: ep. Militen. s. 1-12, xi, xii, dep. de refm. - el [card., m. 1534] (E 15, 244).
416. Varano, Joannes Maria: dom. Camerini s. 7 [m. 1527] (H nr. 8219).
417. Vechis (de' Vecchi), Petrus Paulus de: conservator Urbis s. 2.
418. Vich, Hieronymus: orat. catholici regis et reginae Hispaniarum s. 1-12.
419. Vich, Joannes de, O.P.: ep. Acerrarum s. 5, 6, 9 [m. 1526] (E 93).
420. Victorius (Vettori), Franciscus: orat. dom. Florentinorum s. 6, 7, 10 [m. 1539].
421. Vigerius, Marcus, O.F.M.: card. ep. Praenestin. s. 1-10, dep. de refm. - nom.; comm. praep., ep. Senogallien., aep. Tranen. [m. 1516] (E 10, 298, 316, Hofmann I, 309).
422. Vigerius, Marcus de Ruvere: ep. Senogallien. s. 7-12, xi, xii; nepos card. et Marci Vigerius et L. G. de Ruvere [aderat conc. Tridentin., m. 1560] (E 298).
423. Villalva, Joannes de: ep. Elnen. s. 3-9 [ep. Calaguritan., m. c. 1523] (E 192, 145).
424. Vincentius: ep. Bellicen. s. 3 (v. s. n. 56).
425. Vio, Thomas (Gaetanus) de, O.P.: mag. gen. O.P. s. 1-5, 8, 9, 11, 12, xi, xii, dep. de fide - nom., praed. s. 2 (M 719d) [card., ep. Gaietan., m. 1534] (E 16, 200) ; proc. Georgii ducis Saxoniae (v. supra n. 28).
426. Visconti-Riario, Octavianus: ep. Viterbien. s. 1, 2, 4, 5, 8-10, 12, xii, per proc. aep. Spalaten. s. 6 (M 794b) [m. 1523] (E 335).
427. Viterbio, Ludovicus Gentilis de, O.P.: ep. Signin. s. 1, 3-5 [m. 1512 - sic Katterbach, 79, n. 1] (E 300).
428. Volsky (Volschi, Volski), Nicolaus: miles (Sepulchri Dominici Hierosolymitani) Polonus s. 10; laicus Poznanien. (H nr. 8784).
429. Wardenberg (Vardemberch, Vandemberch, Werdemberg, Noiodeburgensis, Guardemberg), Zutpheldus (Zutfeldus, Hodfelsus): proc. ep. Havelbergen. s. 10 (M 916a), 11 (M 976a), et ep. Ratzeburgen. s. 10 (M 916c) et ep. Curonien. s. 11 (M 975c); cler. dioec. Zwerinen., script. archivi Rom. Curiae, doctor decretorum, proc. Romae reg. Daniae (v. s. n. 28).
430. Zaciis (Zazi), Joannes Dominicus de: ep. Terdonen. s. 3-11, xi, xii, dep. de pace - el. [m. 1528] (E 310).
431. Zanni, Bernardus: aep. Spalaten. s. 1-9, dep. de fide - el., praed. s. 1 (M 700a), proc. ep. Viterbien. s. 6 (M 794b) [m. 1524] (E 302).
+ auditores causarum sacri palatii s. 4 (M 747b).
+ auditores Rotae s. 9 (M 863a).
+ clerici camerae s. 4 (M 747b), s. 9 (M 863a).
* + doctores (alii, quamplures) in diversis facultatibus, in utroque jure, diversarum professionum clerici et laici et magistri sacrarum literarum, in theologia s. 1 (M 680c), 4 (M 747b), 7 (M 805d), 8 (M 831d), 9 (M 863a), 12 (M 980a).
+ milites O.S.J. Hier. et domini et alii nobiles (quamplures) s. 5 (M 766c), 7 (M 805d), 10 (M 905a), 11 (M 942a), 12 (M 980a).
+ oratores dom. Florentini s. 8, 9 (v. s. n. 68).
+ oratores tres dom. Helvetiorum s. 4 (M 747a, v.s. n. 66, 67).

* (See Addenda)

THE FIFTH LATERAN COUNCIL 197

+ orator patriarchae Hierosolymitani s. 9 (v. s. n. 70).
+ oratores Parmensis s. 3 (M 731b, v. s. n. 66).
+ protonotarii apostolici (quamplures) s. 4 (M 747b).

Sees represented at the Fifth Lateran Council *

Absaren. (Absoren., Ansaren., Auxeren.), Ossero, Osor, in ins. Cherso, suffr. Jadren.: 119, 166.
Acernen. (Accernen., Acerraí.en.), Acerno, in Italia infer., suffr. Salernitan.: 18.
Acerrarum (Acceranus), Acerra, in Italia infer., suffr. Neapolitan.: 419.
Adiacen. (Adriacen., Ajacen.), Ajaccio, in ins. Corsica, suffr. Pisan.: 285.
Adrien., Adria in Italia super., suffr. Ravennaten.: 124.
Aesin. (Esin.), Jesi in Italia media, immed. subj.: 196, proc. 268.
S. Agathae, Sant'Agata dei Goti in Italia infer., suffr. Benevent.: 79.
Agathen., Agde in Gallia, suffr. Narbonen.: [147].
Agenen., Agen in Gallia, suffr. Burdegalen.: 332.
Agien. (Agrien.), Canea in ins. Creta, suffr. Creten.: 249.
Agrien., Eger vel Erlau in Hungaria, suffr. Strigonien.: [136].
Agrigentin. (Augustentin.), Girgenti in ins. Sicilia, suffr. Panormitan.: 105, proc. 98.
Alatrin. (Aletrin.), Alatri in Italia media, immed. subj.: 346.
Albanen., Albano suburban. Romae: 317, 360.
Albanen. (Zarnen.), Albania in Illyrico, tit.?: 208.
Alben. (Albae Pompeiae), Alba in Italia super., suffr. Mediolan.: 274, 275.
Albien., Alby in Gallia, suffr. Bituricen.: [56], 244.
Albinganen., Albenga in Italia super., suffr. Januen. [348].
Alerien., Aleria in ins. Corsica, suffr. Pisan.: proc. 282.
Alexandrin., Alexandria in Aegypto, patriarchatus, tit.: 319.
Alexandrin., Alessandria in Italia super., suffr. Mediolanen.: 187.
Algaren. (Othanen.), Aghero vel Ottana in ins. Sardinia, suffr. Turritan.: 225, 288.
Amalfitan., Amalfi in Italia infer., metrop.: [310].
Amelien. (Amerien., Amerinus), Amelia in Italia media, immed. subj.: 267.
Ampurien. et Civitaten. (Empurien.), Ampurias et Templo in ins. Sardinia, suffr. Turritan.: proc. 258.
Anagnin., Anagni in Italia media, immed. subj.: [372].
Anconitan. et Humanaten., Ancona et Umana in Italia media, immed. subj.: 1.
S. Andreae, St. Andrews in Scotia, metrop.: [103].
Andr(i)en., Andria in Italia infer., suff. Tranen.: 267.
S. Angeli et Bisacien., S. Angelo dei Lombardi et Bisaccia in Italia infer., suffr. Consanen.: 67.
Anglonen. et Tursien., Anglona et Tursi in Italia infer., suffr. Acheruntin.: 353.

---

* Symbols used in this appendix:
    [number] = see administered by the prelate thus numbered
    ⟨number⟩ = see held *in commendam* by the prelate thus numbered
    (see or number) = council member from this see was not the prelate
        in charge of the see

I

Antibaren., Antivari in Epiro, metrop.: 259.
Antiochen., Antiochia in Syria, patriarch., tit.: 79.
Aquen., Acqui in Italia super., suffr. Mediolanen.: 374.
Aquilan., Aquila in Italia infer., immed. subj.: 308.
Aquilegien., Aquileja in Istria (S. R. Imperium), patriarch.: 184, 185.
Aquinaten., Aquino in Italia infer., immed. subj.: 62, 170, 231.
Arben., Arbe vel Rab in Dalmatia, suffr. Jadren.: 237, 271.
Arboren., Oristano in ins. Sardinia, metrop.: 361.
Archsen., ? : 250.
Aretin., Arezzo in Italia media, immed. subj.: 345.
Argolicen., Argos in Graecia, suffr. Corinthien.: proc. 312.
Ariminen., Rimini in Italia media, immed. subj.: 44.
Asculan., Ascoli-Piceno in Italia media, immed. subj.: 146, 174.
Asculan., Ascoli-Puglie, in Italia infer., suffr. Beneventan.: 161.
Athenien., Athenae in Graecia, metrop., tit.: 398.
Augusten., Aosta in Italia super., suffr. Tarentasien.: 24, 37.
Aura(s)icen. (Anrainen., Arianen.), Orange in Gallia, suffr. Arelaten.: 217.
Aurien., Orense in Hispania, suffr. Bracharen.: [334].
Auximan., Osimo in Italia media, immed. subj.: 369, 370, proc. 196.
Avellinen. (Lavellen.) et Frequentin., Avellino et Frigento in Italia infer., suffr. Beneventan.: 230, 363.
Aversan., Aversa in Italia infer., immed. subj.: [15].
Avinionen., Avignon in Gallia, metrop.: 149, 334.
Balneoregien., Bagnorea in Italia med., immed. subj.: 94.
Baren., Bari in Italia infer., metrop.: 95, 248.
Bathonien. et Wellen., Bath et Wells in Anglia, suffr. Cantuarien.: 93, (172).
Bellicen., Belley in Gallia, suffr. Bisuntin.: 381.
Bellicen., ? : 167, 424.
Bellunen. (Viluen.), Belluno in Italia super., suffr. Aquilegien.: 268, proc. 277.
Beneventan., Benevento in Italia infer., metrop.: [139], [335].
Bergomen. (Pergamen.), Bergamo in Italia super., suffr. Mediolanen: 224, proc. 98.
Bethleemitan. (Bethelen.), Bethlehem in Palaestina, tit.: 199.
Bisinianen., Bisignano in Italia infer., immed. subj.: 297.
Bivinen. (Bovinen.), Bovino in Italia infer., suffr. Beneventan: 73, 162.
Boianen., Bojano in Italia infer., suffr. Benevent.: 287.
Bononien., Bologna in Italia super., suffr. Ravennaten.: 178.
Bretenorien. (Britonorien.), Bertinoro in Italia super., suffr. Ravennaten.: 294.
Brixien., Brescia in Italia super., suffr. Mediolanen.: proc. 276, (403).
Brugnaten. (Brumaten.), Brugnato in Italia super., suffr. Januen.: 349.
Buduen. (Bidrianen., Budinen., Biduanen., Bidrien.), Budua in Dalmatia, suffr. Ragusin.: 234.
Burgen., Burgos in Hispania, immed. subj.: 10, (116), (223), [360].
Caesenaten., Cesena in Italia media, immed. subj.: 378, proc. 260.
Cajacen. (Cayacen.), Cajazzo in Italia infer., suffr. Capuan.: 232.
Calamonen. (Calamoven., Rethymen.), Rethymo in ins. Creta, suffr. Creten.: proc. 120.
Calinen. (Calenen.), Carinola in Italia infer., suffr. Capuan.: 277, proc. 174.
Callien., Cagli in Italia media, immed. subj.: 3, 34.
Calven. (Gallinen.), Calvi in Italia infer., suffr. Capuan.: 410.
Camerinen., Camerino in Italia media, immed. subj.: 48.

Caprien. (Crapitanen., Capritan.), Capri in ins. cognom., suffr. Amalfitan.: 324.
Capuan., Capua in Italia infer., metrop.: [136].
Caputaquen., Capaccio in Italia infer., suffr. Salernitan.: [15].
Carthaginen., Cartagena in Hispania, immed. subj.: 212.
Casertan., Caserta in partibus Neapol., suffr. Capuan.: 45.
Cassanen., Cassano in Calabria, suffr. Reginen.: 392.
Castren., Castro vel Acquapendente in Patrimonio S. Petri, immed. subj.: [155], 402.
Castren., Castro in Apulia, suffr. Hydruntin.: 350.
Catacen. (Cajacen.), Catanzaro in Calabria, suffr. Reginen.: 395.
Catharen. (Cataren.), Cattaro in Dalmatia, suffr. Baren.: 63.
Cavallicen., Cavaillon in Gallia merid., suffr. Arelaten.: 282 .
Ceneten., Ceneda in Italia super., suffr. Aquilegen.: [184], 185.
Cepten. (Septen.), Ceuta in Africa septentr., primas, suffr. Bracharen.: proc. 325.
Cervien., Cervia in Italia super., suffr. Ravennaten.: 97, 148.
Chien. (Ouien), Chios in ins. Cyclad., suffr. Colocen.: 207.
Chironen., Herronesou vel Chiron in ins. Creta, suffr. Creten.: 265.
Civitaten., Città vel Civita in Italia infer., suffr. Beneventan.: 391.
Civitatis Castelli, Città di Castello in Italia med., immed. subi.: 178, 179.
Civitatis ducalis, Città ducale in Italia infer., immed. subj.: 222.
Clugien. (Clusien., Clodien.), Chioggia in partibus Venet., suffr. Venet.: proc. 21.
Colimbrien., Coimbra in Portugallia, suffr. Bracharen.: proc. 200.
Colocen. (Colossen.), Kolossi in ins. Rhodo, metrop.: 108.
Comaclen. (Comacen.), Comacchio in Italia super., suffr. Ravennat.: 154, 191.
Compostellan., Compostela in Hispania, metrop.: proc. 375.
Conceptionis, Concepcion de la Vega in ins. Hispanolae, metrop.: proc. 132.
Conchen., Cuenca in Hispania, suffr. Toletan.: ⟨320⟩.
Consan., Conza in partibus Neapolit., metrop.: 114.
Constantinopolitan., Constantinopolis vel Istanbul, patriarch. rit. lat., tit.: 28.
Corinthien. (Corinthus), Corinthus in Graecia, metrop., tit.: 40, 359.
Coronen., Coron in Graecia, suffr. Patracen., tit.: 232.
Cortonen., Cortona in Tuscia, immed. subj.: 76.
Crainen. (Craynen., Tranen.), Krain in Albania, metrop., tit.: 117.
Cremonen., Cremona in Italia super., suffr. Mediolan.: proc. 184
Cuman., Como in Italia super., suffr. Aquilegien.: 397.
Curonien. (Coronien.), Curland in Lettia, suffr. Rigen.: proc. 429.
Curzolen. (Corsulen., Curciolen.) et Stagnen., Stagno vel Stonj in Dalmatia, suffr. Duracen.: 270.
Dignen., Digne in Gallia merid.-orient., suffr. Ebredunen.: 192.
S. Dominici, San Domingo in ins. Hispaniolae, suffr. Conceptionis: 169.
Dulcinen., Dulcigno vel Olcini vel Olgun in Epiro, suffr. Antibaren.: 52.
Dyrrhachien., Durazzo in Epiro, metrop.: 155.
Eboracen., York in Anglia, metrop.: 27.
Ebredunen., Embrun in Gallia orient.-merid., metrop.: [147].
Egitanien., Idana cum sede in Guarda in Portugallia, suffr. Ulixbonen.: ⟨367⟩.
Elnen., Elne in Gallia orient.-merid., immed. subj., olim suffr. Narbonen.. [360], 423.

Eugubin., Gubbio in Umbria, immed. subj.: 159.
Famagustan., Famagosta in ins. Cypro, suffr. Nicosien.: 403.
Fanen. (Phanen.), Fano in Italia media, immed. subj.: 38, proc. 357.
Faventin., Faenza in Italia super., immed. subj.: 289, proc. 207.
Ferentin. (Firman.), Ferentino in Italia media, immed. subj.: 219.
Ferrarien., Ferrara in Italia super., immed. subj.: [136].
Firman., Fermo in Italia media, immed. subj.: 317.
Florentin., Firenze in Tuscia, metrop.: 244, proc. 1.
Forolivien., Forli in Italia super., immed. subj.: 182.
Forosempronien., Fossombrone in Italia media, immed. subj.: 252.
Fulginaten., Foligno in Italia media, immed. subj.: 106.
Gadicen., Cadiz in Hispania, suffr. Hispalen.: [1].
Ga(i)etan. (Cajetan), Gaëta in partibus Neapol., immed. subj.: 195.
Gallipolitan., Gallipoli in Italia infer., suffr. Hydruntin.: [317].
Gebennen., Genève vel Genf in Helvetia (Sabaudia), suffr. Viennen.: proc. 331.
Gerunden., Gerona in Hispania, suffr. Terraconen.: proc. 339.
Gneznen., Gniezno vel Gnesen in Polonia, metrop.: 214.
Grassen., Grasse in Gallia merid.-orient., suffr. Ebredunen.: 183, proc. 68.
Grossetan., Grosseto in Italia media, immed. subj.: 296.
Guardien., Guardialfiera in Italia infer., suffr. Beneventan.: 118.
Gurcen., Gurk in Corinthia, suffr. Salzeburgen.: 212.
Halberstaden., Halberstadt in Germania, suffr. Maguntin.: proc. 320.
Havelbergen., Havelberg in Germania, suffr. Magdeburgen.: proc. 429.
Hieracen., Gerace in Italia infer., suffr. Regin.: 348.
Hierapetren., Hierapetra vel Gera Petra in ins. Creta, suffr. Creten.: 256, 265.
Hierosolymitan., Jerusalem in Palestina, patriarch., tit.: 91, (v. s. n. 70).
Hortan. (Ortan.), Orte in Italia media, immed. subj.: 156.
Hydruntin. Otranto in Italia infer., metrop.: 78.
Ilcinen. (Insulen., Montalcinen.), Montalcino in Italia media, immed. subj.: 298.
Imolen., Imola in Italia super., suffr. Ravennat.: 354.
Insulan., Isola in Italia infer., suffr. S. Severinae: 209.
Interamnen., Terni in Italia media, immed. subj.: 14.
Ipor(eg)ien. (Hipporegien.), Ivrea in Italia super., suffr. Mediolan.: 142, proc. 146.
Isclan. (Neselitan.), Ischia in Italia infer., suffr. Neapolitan.: proc. 81.
Isernien., Isernia in Italia infer., suffr. Capuan.: 123.
Jadren. (Zaren.), Zadar vel Zara in Istria, metrop.: 303.
S. Justae, S. Giusta in Sardinia, suffr. Arboren.: 361, 393.
Justinopolitan., Capo d'Istria in Istria, suffr. Aquilegen.: 21.
Lancianen. (Lausanen.), Lanciano in Italia infer.: 228.
Larinen., Larino in Italia infer., suffr. Benevent.: proc. 234.
Lausanen., Lausanne in Helvetia, suffr. Bisuntin.: proc. 291.
Lausanen., ? : 11.
Lavellen., Lavello in Italia infer., suffr. Baren.: 189, [317].
Legionen., Leon in Hispania, immed. subj.: 15, 248.
Le(i)glinen. (Legelien., Lechlinen.), Leighlin in Hibernia, suffr. Dublinen.: 5.
S. Leonis, San Leone in Italia infer., suffr. S. Severinae: 242.
Licien., Lecce in Italia infer., suffr. Hydruntin.: 240.
Lincopen., Linköping in Suecia, suffr. Upsalen.: [360].

Liparen. (Iporien.), Lipari in ins. cognom., suffr. Messanen.: 9.
Litteren. (Literen., Adriacen.), Lettere in Italia infer., suffr. Amalfitan.: 130.
Lubicen. (Lubecen.), Lübeck in Germania, suffr. Bremen.: proc. 273.
Lucan., Lucca in Italia media, immed. subj.: [335].
Lucen. (Lucan.), Lugo in Hispania, suffr. Compostellan.: proc. 396.
Luceorien. (Lectoren.), Luck in Polonia, suffr. Leopolien.: 4.
Lucerin., Lucera in Italia infer. (Apulia), suffr. Beneventan.: 79.
Lucerin., Nocera dei Pagani in Italia infer., suffr. Salernitan.: 202.
Maceraten., Macerata in Italia media, immed. subj.: 129.
Magdeburgen., Magdeburg in Germania, metrop.: proc. 320.
Maguntin., Mainz in Germania, metrop.: proc. 320.
Malleacen., Maillezais in Gallia occid., suffr. Burdegalen.: 1.
Mantuan., Mantova in Italia super., suffr. Aquilegen.: [176].
S. Marci, San Marco in Italia infer., immed. subj.: 9.
Mar(i)anen. (Brugniaten.), Mariana in ins. Corsica, suffr. Januen.: 104.
Maronitarum in Syria, patriarchatus: proc. 2, 134, + post 134, (264), (+ post 106).
Marsican., Marsi in Italia infer., immed. subj.: 229.
Massanen., Massa marittima in Italia media, suffr. Pisan.: 293.
Massilien., Marseille in Gallia orient.-austr., suffr. Arelaten.: 364.
Maurianen., Saint-Jean de Maurienne in Sabaudia, suffr. Tarentasien.: 177.
Mediolanen., Milano in Italia super., metrop.: [136].
Melfien. (Malfien.), Melfi in Italia infer., immed. subj.: [310], proc. 98.
Melfiten., Molfetta in Italia infer., immed. subj.. 98.
(Merseburgen, Merseburg in Germania, suffr. Magdeburgen.: 133).
Milevitan., Malta in ins. cognom., suffr. Panormitan.: [320].
Militen., Mileto in Italia infer., immed. subj.: 415.
Milopotamen., Mylopotamos in ins. Creta, suffr. Creten.: 37.
Minerbinen. (Minernen.), Minervino in Italia infer., suffr. Baren.: 137.
Misnen., Meissen in Germania, suffr. Magdeburgen.: proc. 171.
Modrusien., Modrus vel Krbava in Croatia (Hungaria), suffr. Spalaten.: 32.
Monobasien. (Noboniasien., Nuboniasien.), Monembasia in Graecia, metrop.: 256, 265.
Monopolitan., Monopoli in Italia infer., immed. subj.: 107.
Montisflasconis et Cornetan., Monteflascone et Corneto in Italia media, immed. subj.: [139].
Montismarani, Montemarano in Italia infer., suffr. Beneventan.: 247.
Montisregalis, Mondovi in Italia super., suffr. Mediolan.: 146, 328.
Montisvirdis, Monteverde in Italia infer., suffr. Consan.: 75, proc. 64.
Mordanien., ? : 251.
Mutinen., Modena in Italia super., suffr. Ravennat.: [136].
Nanneten., Nantes in Gallia occid., suffr. Turonen.: 194.
Narbonen., Narbonne in Gallia merid. orient., metrop.: 244.
Narnien., Narni in Italia media, immed. subj.: 193, [372].
Naulen. (Nolen., Launen.), Noli in Italia super., suffr. Januen.: 53.
Nazaren., Nazareth in Palaestina, metrop., tit.: 34, 334.
Neapolitan., Napoli in Italia infer., metrop.: 81.
Nebien. (Nobien.), Nebbio in ins. Corsica, suffr. Januen.: 206.
Neocastren., Nicastro in Italia infer., suffr. Regin.: 77.
Nicien., Nice vel Nizza in Gallia merid.-orient., suffr. Ebredunen.: 20.
Nicosien., Nicosia vel Levkosia in ins. Cypro, metrop.: 407.
Nimocien. (Limosien.), Nemosia vel Limasol in ins. Cypro, suffr. Nicosien.: 51, 121.

Nolan., Nola in Italia infer., suffr. Neapolitan.: 59.
Nonen., Nona vel Nin in Dalmatia, suffr. Spalaten.: proc. 327.
Novarien., Novara in Italia super., suffr. Mediolan.: 260, [?344], [352].
Nucerin., Nocera in Italia media, immed. subj.: 141.
Ogentin. (Urgentin.), Ugentino in Italia infer., suffr. Hydruntin.: 371.
(Oscen. et Jaccen., Huesca et Jacca in Hispania, suffr. Caesaraugusten.: coadj. 406).
Ostien. et Velletren., Ostia et Velletri, suburb. Romae: 320.
Ostunen. (Astunen.), Ostuni in Italia infer., suffr. Brundusin.: 89.
Ottocien. (Osconen., Octotien.), Ottochaz vel Otocsácz in Croatia (Hungaria), suffr. Spalaten.: 12.
Paduan., Padova in Italia super., suffr. Aquilegien.: 121, 335.
Panormitan., Palermo in ins. Sicilia, metrop.: [317].
Paphen., Paphos vel Baffo in ins. Cypro, suffr. Nicosien.: 64.
Papien., Pavia in Italia super., immed. subj.: [260].
Parentin., Parenzo in Istria, suffr. Aquilegien.: 389.
Parmen., Parma in Italia super., suffr. Ravennat.: 139.
Patracen., Patras in Graecia, metrop., tit.: 387.
Pennen. (Parmen.) et Adrien., Penne et Atri in Italia media, immed. subj.: 72.
Perusin., Perugia in Italia media, immed. subj.: 376.
Pharen. (Faren.), Hvar vel Lesina in Dalmatia, suffr. Spalaten.: proc. 380.
Philadelphien., Philadelphia in Arabia vel Isauria, tit.: 406.
Pisan., Pisa in Italia media, metrop.: 319.
Pisaurien., Pesaro in Italia media, immed. subj.: 180, 329.
Pistorien., Pistoja in Italia media, immed. subj.: 310.
Placentin., Piacenza in Italia super., immed. subj.: 236.
Placentin., Plasencia in Hispania, suffr. Compostellan.: proc. 388.
Polen., Pola in Istria, suffr. Aquilegien.: 23.
Polycastren.. Polycastro in Italia infer., suffr. Salernitan.: 216.
Polygnianen. (Polinianen.), Polignano in Italia infer., suffr. Baren.: 235.
S. Pontii Thomeriarum, S. Pons de Tomières in Gallia merid.-orient., suffr. Narbonen.: 139.
Portuen. et S. Rufinae, Porto et S. Rufina, suburban. Romae: 184.
Portugalen., Porto vel Oporto in Portugallia, suffr. Bracharen.: proc. 200.
Potentin., Potenza in Italia infer., suffr. Acheruntin.: 272.
Praenestin., Palestrina, suburban. Romae: 421.
Racanaten. (Recanaten.) et Maceraten., Recanati et Macerata in Italia media, immed. subj.: 129.
Ragusin. (Relisin.), Ragusa et Dubrovnik in Dalmatia, metrop.: 181.
Rapollan., Rapolla in Italia infer., immed. subj.: 357.
Ratzeburgen. (Rhotheburgen.), Ratzeburg (O. Praem.) in Germania septentr., suffr. Bremen.: proc. 429.
Ravennaten., Ravenna in Italia media, metrop.: 147, proc. 180.
Reatin., Rieti in Italia media, immed. subj.: 112.
(Redonen., Rennes in Gallia septentr.-occid., suffr. Turonen.: 316).
Reg(i)en., Riez in Gallia merid.-orient., suffr. Aquen.: proc. 315.
Regien., Reggio-Emilia in Italia super., suffr. Ravennat.: 314.
R(h)eginen., Reggio-Calabria in Italia infer., metrop.: 414.
Revalien., Reval in Estlandia, suffr. Rigen.: 41.
Roman., Roma in Italia media, patriarch.: 205, 218, moder. 320.
Rossanen., Rossano in Italia infer., metrop.: [91].

Ruben., Ruvo in Italia infer., suffr. Baren.: proc. 81.
Sabinen., Sabina, suburban. Romae: 91, 372.
Sagonen., Sagona in ins. Corsica, suffr. Pisan.: 145.
Salamantin., Salamanca in Hispania, suffr. Compostellan.: 43.
Salernitan., Salerno in Italia infer., metrop.: 159.
Salutiarum, Saluzzo in Italia super., suffr. Taurinon.: 336, 394.
(Salzeburgen., Salzburg in Austria, metrop.: coadj. 212).
Saonen., Savona in Italia super., suffr. Januen.: [320], 321.
Sappaten. (Tabaten., Sabaten.), Sappae vel Nensiati in Albania, suffr. Antibaren.: 165.
Sarnen., Sarno in Italia infer., suffr. Salernitan.: 305, [317].
Sarsinaten., Sarsina in Italia super., suffr. Ravennat.: 92, 122.
Scalen., Scala in Italia infer., suffr. Amalfitan.: 96.
Sebasten., Sebaste in ?, tit.: 143, 386.
Sedunen., Sion vel Sitten in Helvetia, exemp. suffr. Tarentasien.: 352.
Seguntin., Siguenza in Hispania, suffr. Toletan.: ⟨91⟩.
Senen., Siena in Italia media, metrop.: 390.
Senogallien., Senigallia vel Sinigaglia in Italia media, immed. subj.: 421, 422.
S. Severinae, Santa Severina in Italia infer., metrop.: 362.
Sibenicen. (Sabinicen., Sebonicen.), Sebenico in Dalmatia, suffr. Spalaten.: 380.
Sign(i)en., Senj vel Zengg in Croatia (Hungaria), suffr. Spalaten: 42.
Signin. (Siginen., Signien.), Segni in Italia media, immed. subj.: 138, 427.
Sipontin., Manfredonia in Italia infer., metrop.: 260, 261.
Soran., Sora in Italia infer., immed. subj.: 326, proc. 96.
Spalaten., Spalato vel Spljet in Dalmatia, metrop.: 120, 431.
Spigaten. (Spigacen.), Pegae vel Spigant vel Bigha in Asia Minor, suffr. Constantinopolitan., tit.: 341.
Spoletan., Spoleto in Italia media, immed. subj.: 135, (351), proc. 150.
Squillacen. (Squilaten.), Squillace in Italia infer., suffr. Reginen.: 163.
Stabien. (Castelli maris, Castrimaris), Castellamare in Italia infer., suffr. Surrentin.: 150.
Strigonien., Esztergom vel Gran in Hungaria, metrop.: 28.
Suanen., So(v)ana in Italia media, immed. subj.: 295.
Suessan., Sessa Aurunca in Italia infer., suffr. Capuan.: 188.
Surrentin., Sorrento in Italia infer., metrop.: 317, 318.
Sutrin. et Nepesin., Sutri et Nepi in Italia media, immed. subj.: 47.
Syracusan. (Caesaraugusten.), Siracusa in ins. Sicilia, suffr. Montisregal.: 405.
Tarentin., Tarento in Italia infer., metrop.: proc. 69.
Tarvisin. (Trevisin.), Treviso in Italia super., suffr. Aquilegien.: 327.
Taurinen., Torino in Italia super., metrop. ab 1515: [103], 331.
Terdonen.. Tortona in Italia super., suffr. Mediolan.: 430.
Tergestin., Trieste in Istria (S. R. Imperio), suffr. Aquilegien.: 50.
Terracinen., Terracina in Italia media, immed. subj.: 239.
Theatin., Chieti in Italia infer., immed. subj.: 80.
Theban., Thebae in Graecia, metrop., tit.: 308.
Thelesin., Telese in Italia infer., suffr. Benevent.: 86.
Tiburtin., Tivoli, suburban. Romae et in Italia media, immed. subj.: 221, 372.
Tirasonen. (Tyrasonen.), Tarazona in Hispania, suffr. Caesaraugusten.: proc. 225.

* (See Addenda)

Tolonen., Toulon in Gallia merid.-orient., suffr. Arelaten.: 55, [147].
Torcellan., Torcello in Italia super., suffr. Venetiarum: 387, proc. 147.
Trabunien., ? : 203.
Trajecten., Utrecht in Hollandia, suffr. Colonien.: proc. 197, (290).
Tranen. (Traiocen.), Trani in Italia infer., metrop.: 128, 421.
Tribunien. et Marcanen., Trebinje et Mrkanj vel Macarsca in Hercegovina, suffr. Ragusin.: 266, proc. 34.
Triburen., ? : 203.
Tricaricen., Tricarico in Italia infer., suffr. Acheruntin.: 71.
Trojan., Troja in Italia infer., immed. subj.: 286.
Tuamen. (Tuanien.), Tuam in Hibernia, metrop.: 278.
Tuden., Tuy in Hispania, suffr. Compostellan.: 359, (325).
Tudertin., Todi in Italia media, immed. subj.: 241.
Turonen., Tours in Gallia, metrop.: 83.
Turritan., Sassari olim Torres in ins. Sardinia, metrop.: 220, 254.
Umbriaticen. (Vumbriacen., Uniblacen., Umbriatinen.), Umbriatico in Italia infer., suffr. S. Severinae: 358.
Upsalen., Upsala in Suecia, metrop. (et provincia Sueciae): proc. 260.
Urbevetan., Orvieto in Italia media, immed. sub.: 343.
Urbinaten., Urbino in Italia media, immed. subj.: 26, [184], 398.
Urgellen., Urgel in Hispania, suffr. Terraconen.: 132, 151.
Ussellen. (Usulen.) et Terralben., Ales et Terralba in Sardinia, suffr. Arboren.: proc. 342.
Valven. et Sulmonen., Valva et Sulmona in Italia infer., immed. subj.: 65, proc. 357.
Warmien. (Narnien.), Ermland in Prussia, suffr. Rigen.: proc. 214.
Vauren., Lavaur in Gallia merid., suffr. Tolosan.: 244.
Veglen. (Vigilien., Veglien.), Veglia in ins. cognominis, suffr. Jadren.: 401.
Venafran. (Venefran.), Venafro in Italia infer., suffr. Capuan.: 61.
Vencien. (Vintien., Veveren.), Vence in Gallia merid.-orient., suffr. Ebredunen.: 49.
Veneten., Vannes in Gallia, suffr. Turonen.: [56], [310].
Venetiarum, Venezia in Italia super., patriarch.: proc. 184.
Venusin., Venosa in Italia infer., suffr. Acheruntin.: 16.
Vercellen., Vercelli in Italia super., suffr. Mediolan.: proc. 146.
Veronen., Verona in Italia super., suffr. Aquilegien.: [121].
Vestan., Viesti in Italia infer., suffr. Sipontin.: 301, 341.
Vicentin., Vicenza in Italia super., suffr. Aquilegien.: 330, 372.
Viennen., Vienne in Gallia orient.-merid., metrop.: 343, ⟨344⟩.
Wigornien. (Vigornien.), Worcester in Anglia, suffr. Cantuarien.: 173.
Vilnen. (Valven., Viluen.), Vilnius vel Wilna in Lithuania, immed. subj.: 313.
Viterbien., Viterbo in Italia media, immed. subj.: 426, proc. 431.
Wladislavien. (Noladislanuen., ?Naulen. de Januen.), Wloclawek vel Leslau in Cujavia, suffr. Gneznen.: proc. 22, (355).
Vulterran., Volterra in Italia media, immed. subj.: 373, (30).
Xanctonen., Saintes in Gallia occid.-merid., suffr. Burdegalen.: [372].

Religious orders represented at the Council

O. C. (Ordo Fratrum B. Mariae Virginis de Monte Carmelo) vicarius: 210, 356.
O. E. S. A. (Ordo Eremitarum S. Augustini) magister generalis: 13; praelatus: 155; per procuratorem: 312.
O. F. M. (Ordo Fratrum Minorum) minister generalis: 101; vicarius: 226, 404; praelatus: 34, 156, 181, 234, 278, 285, 308, 398, 421; per procuratorem: 258, 325, 380, 234; [? praelatus: 321].
O. H. S. Sp. (Ordo Hospitalariorum S. Spiritus) praeceptor S. Spiritus de Urbe: 144, ?329.
O. P. (Ordo Fratrum Praedicatorum) magister generalis: 425; praelatus: 3, 10, 21, (70), 97, 165, 206, 266, ? post 280, ? post 366, 419, 427;
O. Praem. (Ordo Praemonstratensis) abbas et superior generalis: proc. 178; praelatus per procuratorem?: 429.
O. S. A. (Sacer et Apostolicus Ordo Canonicorum Regularium S. Augustini) abbas mon. B. Mariae Briutonis, dioec. Bathonien.: 172; praelatus: 346; per procuratorem: 184.
O. S. B. (Ordo S. Benedicti) abbas mon. S. Benedicti de Monte Subasio (Subasten.), dioec. Assisinaten. et postea praelatus: 143;
O. S. B., Burs. (Ordo S. Benedicti, Congregatio Bursfeldensis) abbas mon. S. Adalberti in Egmonda, dioec. Trajecten.: proc. 290; abbas mon. S. Jacobi Pegauien., dioec. Merseburgen.: 133.
O. S. B., Camald. (Ordo S. Benedicti, Congregatio Monachorum Eremitarum Camaldulensium) prior generalis: 131; per procuratorem: 33.
O. S. B., Cassinien. (Ordo S. Benedicti, Congregatio Cassiniensis) abbas S. Gregorii de Urbe, dioec. Roman.: 57, 58; praelatus: 38, 183.
O. S. B., Celes. (Ordo S. Benedicti, Congregatio Coelestinorum) abbas mon. S. Eutychii in Valcastoriana (Norcia), dioec. Spoletan.: 351.
O. S. B., C. V. U. (Ordo S. Benedicti, Congregatio Vallis Umbrosae) abbas et generalis: 70, 246.
O. S. Hier. (Ordo S. Hieronymi) praelatus per procuratorem: 339.
O. S. J. Hier. (Ordo S. Joannis Hierosolymitani de Rhodo) proc./orat.: 84, 190; prior. de Capua - 244; de Castella - 385; de Hungaria - 186; de Urbe - 336; praed.: 164; praelatus: 123, 244, ?335.
O. S. M. (Ordo Servorum B. Mariae) magister generalis: 17.
O. Theu. (Ordo S. Mariae Theutonicorum in Prussia) orat. et praelatus: 41.
S. O. Cist. (Sacer Ordo Cisterciensis) abbas S. Galgani, dioec. Vulterran.: 30; abbas S. Sebastiani ad Catacumbas extra Urbem (Pontiniacen.), dioec. Roman.: 227; praelatus: 381; per procuratorem: 184.

Ambassadors of temporal rulers

Angliae (England) regis: 27, 173.
Bononiensis (Bologna): 307.
Brandeburgensis (Brandenburg) marchionis sacri imperii electoris: 8, 41, 213, 320.
Ferrariensis (Ferrara) ducis: 124.
Florentini (Firenze) domini/dominorum: 46, (243), (245), 340, 383, 384, 420, (v. s. n. 68).

* (See Addenda)

Franciae (France) regis: 152, 344, 364.
Helvetiorum (Schweizer Kantone) dominorum: (v. s. n. 66, 67).
Hierosolymitani (Jerusalem) patriarchae: (v. s. n. 70).
Hispaniarum (España) regis et reginae: 405, 418.
Imperatoris electi sacri imperii Romanorum (das Reich der deutschen Nation): 50, 201, 212, 300, 366.
Lucensium (Lucca) communitatis: 157.
Mantuae (Mantova) marchionis: 160, (175).
Mazoviae (cum regno Polonia in 1526 unitae — Mazowsze) ducum: 253.
Mediolanensis (Milano) ducis: 90, 263.
Montis ferrati (Monferrato) marchionis: 85, 311, 374.
Parmensis (Parma) domini: (v. s. n. 66).
Poloniae (Polska i Litwa) regis: 214, 279.
Portugalliae (Portugal) regis: 60, 127, 140, 280, 367.
Rhodorum (Rhodos) militum S. Joannis Hierosolymitani ordinis: 84, 190.
Romae (Roma) Urbis: conservatores - 35, 74, 82, 125, 158, 233, 417; senatores - 54, 204, 379, 382.
Sabaudiae (Savoia, Savoie) ducis: 24, 31, 177, 306.
Theutonicorum in Prussia (Preussen) S. Mariae militum ordinis: 41.
Venetorum (Venezia) domini: 25, 153, 168, 211, 255.

ADDENDA AND CORRIGENDA

p.164, n.28, add to end of note: Pucci is reported to have served as the procurator of the king of Denmark at session 12, see SANUDO, XXIV, 105; the Dominicans Tomasso de Vio and Nicholas von Schönberg were appointed in 1513 procurators of Ducal Saxony, see Th. KOLDE, 'Zum V. Lateranconcil,' in *Zeitschrift für Kirchengeschichte* 3 (1879), 599-609, here 601-07.

p.167, n.39, add to end of note: For de Rebenga's absence, see Joaquin Luis ORTEGA MARTÍN, 'Un reformador pretridentino: Don Pascual de Ampudia, obispo de Burgos (1496-1512),' in *Anthologica Annua* 19 (Rome 1972), 408-412.

p. 184, n.90: 'de: orat.' should read 'de: secret. conc. (Vat. Lat. 12269 fol.536^v), orat.'.

p. 184, n.102, add to end of note: filius Innocentii VIII, pater Innocentii et J. Baptistae.

p.185, n.108: 'Clemens:' should read 'Clemens, mon. S. Catherinae Sinaitici:'.

p.185, n.108: '(E 285, H nr. 15,659).' should read '(E 285 et Z. TSIRPANLIS, in *Thesaurismata* 21 [1991], 64-68).'

p.186, n.155: 'Dyrhachien' should read 'Dyrrhachien'; add at end of entry: [forse nomen gentile erat Mascioli].

p.189, n.242, read: Matthaeus de Senis: ep. S. Leonis s. 11, 12 (forse idem ep. Umbriaticen., nr. 358) [m. 1517] (E 223, FORCELLA VII 536 nr. 1092).

p.193, add between n.352 and n.353: 352A. Schönberg, Nicolaus de, O.P.: proc. Georgi; ducis Saxoniae (v. supra n. 28).

p.196 + doctores, add at end: sed non facultates ut corpora moralia 6 (M784e).

p.203, line 29, add extra entry: Spiren., Speyer in Germania, suff. Maguntin.: per proc. s. 12 (SANUDO, XXIV, 105).

p.205, line 1, add extra entry: (O.C....): Monasterii S. Catherinae Sinaitici, praelatus: 108.

p.205, line 12, add at end: per proc. 132.

p.205, line 19, add at end: Silvestrina 141.

p.205, line 44, add extra entry: Daciae (Danmark) regis: mandatum s. 4 et per proc. 310 in s. 12 (SANUDO, XV, 390, XXIV, 105).

II

The Healing of the Pisan Schism (1511—13)*

The tragedy of the Pisan schism, which afflicted the Church on the eve of the Reformation, lasted for three years (1511—13), despite two major attempts to prevent its occurence and protracted negotiations under Julius to end it once begun. The election of Leo X in 1513 finally opened the way to a restoration of Church unity. While scholars have studied in detail the theological and canonical arguments for and against the Pisan Council propounded by various propagandists, relatively little attention has been given either to the intricacies of the diplomatic efforts to heal the schism or to the papacy's concern to defend its theological and feudal prerogatives throughout these negotiations.[1]

---

* Research on this study was made possible by generous financial support from the American Council of Learned Societies, Villa I Tatti (Florence), the American Academy in Rome, and the Richard Krautheimer Research Fund. A Research Grant-In-Aid from the Catholic University of America helped defray the cost of typing.

[1] For the standard treatments in passing of the healing of the Pisan schism, see: F. GUICCIARDINI, Storia d'Italia, ed. C. PANIGADA, Bari 1929, Vol. III for Books IX—XII—hereafter this work is cited as GUICCIARDINI, Book, chapter, ed. PANIGADA, Volume, page; relevant sections of P. DE GRASSI's diary are printed in Le due spedizione militari di Giulio II tratte dal Diario di Paride Grassi bolognese, ed. L. FRATI, in: Documenti e studj pubblicati per cura della Reale Deputazione di Storia Patria per le Provincie di Romagna, I Bologna 1886; passim in: O. RAINALDI, Annales ecclesiastici post Baronium ab anno 1198 ad annum 1565, ed. and rev. G. D. MANSI and A. THEINER, Paris 1877—80, vols. 30—31, ad annos 1511—13; and in: Beiträge zur politischen, kirchlichen und Culturgeschichte der sechs letzten Jahrhunderte, ed. J. J. I. VON DÖLLINGER, III Wien 1882, 363—433, esp. 390—429; L. VON PASTOR, The History of the Popes from the Close of the Middle Ages, trans. F. I. ANTROBUS et alii, vols. 6—8 St. Louis ²⁻⁴1923; M. CREIGHTON, A History of the Papacy from the Great Schism to the Sack of Rome, V London 1897; F. FERRATA, L'opera diplomatica pontificia nel trienno 1510—1513 e l'opposizione del Concilio lateranense a quello scismatico di Pisa (1511—12), Grotte di Castro 1910; J. HERGENROETHER, Histoire des conciles d'après les documents originaux, trans. and rev. H. LECLERCQ, VIII/1 Paris 1917; and O. DE LA BROSSE, Latran V, in: Latran V et Trente: Part I by O. DE LA BROSSE, J. LECLER, H. HOLSTEIN, and CH. LEFEBVRE (= Histoire des conciles oecuméniques X) ed. G. DUMEIGE, Paris 1975.

For some of the modern studies on the canonical and theological arguments for and against the Pisan Council, see: H. JEDIN, Giovanni Gozzadini: ein Konziliarist am Hofe Julius' II, in: RQ 47 (1939) 193—267 reprinted in his Kirche des Glaubens — Kirche der Geschichte: ausgewählte Aufsätze und Vorträge, 2 vols., Freiburg 1966, 17—74 and his Nochmals der Konziliarist Gozzadini, in: RQ 61 (1966) 88—93; J. KLOTZNER, Kardinal Dominikus Jacobazzi und sein Konzilswerk: ein Beitrag zur Geschichte der konziliaren Idee (= Analecta Gregoriana 65) Rome 1948; O. DE LA BROSSE, Le Pape et le Concile: La comparaison de leurs pouvoirs à la veille de la Réforme (= Unam Sanctam 58) Paris 1965; F. A. OAKLEY, Almain and Major: Conciliar Theory on the Eve of the Reformation, in: AHR 70 (1965) 673—90 and his Conciliarism in the Sixteenth Century: Jacques Almain Again, in:

The origins of the schism are to be found in a complex of factors, canonico-theological and personal; but political considerations were chiefly responsible for bringing the schism into existence and inhibiting a quick resolution.

As head of the Papal States, Julius II (1503—13) sought two principal goals: to regain control over his territory and to secure its independence from outside incursions by expelling foreign armies from the Italian peninsula. Aided by the fortuitous illness of Cesare Borgia and his own diplomatic skills, Julius was able soon after his election to eliminate the incipient territorial dynasty of the Borgias established under Alexander VI in the northeastern portion of his state. To recover the cities which Venice had occupied during the temporary weakness of the papacy, Julius organized the League of Cambrai which brought the combined might of the Empire, France, and Spain against the republic of the lagoons. When the Venetian army was destroyed at Agnadello in 1509, Julius feared that with no Italian states strong enough to resist them, the foreign monarchs might proceed to carve up Italy among themselves and so control the pope that he would be reduced to the status of their personal chaplain. He, therefore, withdrew from the League and made a separate peace with Venice, much to the resentment of his French and German allies who had been counting on his assistance to achieve their own war aims of dispossessing Venice of its territory on the Italian mainland.[2]

ARG 68 (1977) 111—32; R. BÄUMER, Nachwirkungen des konziliaren Gedankens in der Theologie und Kanonistik des frühen 16. Jahrhunderts (= RST 100) Münster 1971; W. ULLMANN, Julius II and the Schismatic Cardinals, in: Schism, Heresy and Religious Protest, ed. D. BAKER (= SCH[L] 9) Cambridge 1972, 177—93; F. TODESCAN, Fermenti gallicani e dottrine anti-conciliariste al Lateranense V: un capitolo della teologia politica del secolo XVI, in: Cristianesimo, secolarizzazione e diritto moderno, eds. L. LOMBARDI VALLAURI and G. DILCHER (= Per la storia del pensiero guridico moderno 11/12) Milano 1981, 567—609.

[2] On Julius, see in addition to the above-mentioned works, A. J. DUMESNIL, Histoire de Jules II: Sa vie et son pontificat, Paris 1873; M. BROSCH, Papst Julius II und die Gründung des Kirchenstaates, Gotha 1878; E. RODOCANACHI, Histoire de Rome: Le Pontificat de Jules II, Paris 1928; F. SENECA, Venezia e Giulio II, Padova 1962; F. GILBERT, The Pope, His Banker and Venice, Cambridge, Mass. 1980; and L. PARTRIDGE and R. STARN, A Renaissance Likeness: Art and Culture in Raphael's ‚Julius II', Berkeley 1980.

For the Venetian perspective on these events, see M. SANUTO, I Diarii di Marino Sanuto, ed. R. FULIN et alii, Venice 1879—1903, 58 vols., esp. vols. 11—24; H. KRETSCHMAYR, Geschichte von Venedig, II Gotha 1920; and, in addition to his earlier cited work, F. GILBERT's Venice in the Crisis of the League of Cambrai, in: History: Choice and Commitment, Cambridge, Mass. 1977, 269—91.

For the Imperial role, see: H. ULMANN, Kaiser Maximilian I.: Auf urkundlicher Grundlage dargestellt, 2 vols., Stuttgart 1884—91; A. SCHULTE, Kaiser Maximilian I. als Kandidat für den päpstlichen Stuhl 1511, Leipzig 1906; and the magisterial work of H. WIESFLECKER, Kaiser Maximilian I. Das Reich, Österreich und Europa an der Wende zur Neuzeit, Vols. 1 ff., Wien 1971 ff.

The major role played by the Aragonese in these politico-military maneuvers is described in two works by J. M. DOUSSINAGUE, La politica internacional de Fernando el Católico, Madrid 1944, and Fernando el Católico y el cisma de Pisa, Madrid 1946; and by L. DE MANGLANO Y CUCALÓ DE MONTULL (= Barón de TERRATEIG), Politica en Italia del Rey Católico 1507—1516, 2 Vols. (= Biblioteca [Reyes Católicos]: Estudios XII/1—2) Madrid 1963.

The French perspective on the Pisan Council is studied by: P. IMBART DE LA TOUR, Les origines de la Réforme, 4 vols., II: L'Eglise catholique, la crise et la renaissance, rev. 1909 ed. with bibliography

The Healing of the Pisan Schism (1511—13)   61

This reversal of allegiances was not as risky as it may at first seem or later have become. Julius was not alone in supporting Venice, but continued to retain Fernando of Aragon as his powerful ally. The pope rewarded such loyalty by formally investing the Aragonese king with the throne of Naples, a papal fief, in autumn of 1510. Prior to this grant, the rival claimant to Naples,

---

augumented by Y. LANHERS, Melun ²1944; and A. RENAUDET, Préréforme et humanisme à Paris pendant les premières guerres d'Italie (1494—1517) rev. 1916 ed., Paris ²1953, esp. 524—56.

The principal French sources for this period are: Lettres du Roy Louis XII: Avec plusieurs autres lettres, mémoires et instructions écrites 1504 jusque et compris 1514, ed. J. GODEFROY, 4 Vols., Brussels 1712; Négociations diplomatiques entre la France et l'Autriche durant les trentes premières années du XVIe siècle, ed. A. J. G. LE GLAY, 2 Vols., Paris 1845; and the appendices in A. CAVIGLIA, Claudio di Seyssel (1450—1520): La vita nella storia de' suoi tempi (= Miscellanea di Storia Italiana 54) Torino 1928.

For still other perspectives on these events, see: CH. W. FERGUSON, Naked to Mine Enemies: The Life of Cardinal Wolsey, Boston 1958; J. J. SCARISBRICK, Henry VIII, Berkeley 1968; V. FRANKNÓI, Ungarn und die Liga von Cambrai, 1509—11: Nach unbenutzten Quellen, Budapest 1883, and his Erdödi Bakócz Tamás Élete, Budapest 1889; L. FINKEL, Sprawy Wschodu przed Soborem Lateraneńskim R. 1512, Lwów: Nakładem Autora, 1900, 1—25, esp. 14—17; A. THEINER, Vetera monumenta historica Hungariam sacram illustrantia, II: 1352—1526, Rome 1860; P. TOMICKI, Acta Tomiciana, collected by ST. GÓRSKI, eds. W. KETRZYŃSKI and Z. CELLCHOWSKI, 8 vols., II and III, Poznen 1852—53; P. B. T. BILANIUK, The Fifth Lateran Council and the Eastern Churches, Toronto 1975, 134—54; Regesta historico-diplomatica ordinis S. Mariae Theutonicorum 1198—1525, Pars II: Regesta privilegiorum ordinis S. Maria Theutonicorum: Regesten der Pergament-Urkunden aus der Zeit des Deutschen Ordens, and I: Regesten zum Ordensbriefarchiv, Vol. 3: 1511—1525, ed. E. JOACHIM and W. HUBATSCH, Göttingen 1948, 1973; Correspondance de l'Empereur Maximilien Ier et de Marguerite d'Autriche, sa fille, gouvernante des Pays-Bas, de 1507 à 1519, ed. A. J. G. LE GLAY, 2 Vols., Paris 1839; L. DE LA BRIÈRE and R. DE MAULDE, Rapport de M. Mond sur une communication de MM. de la Brière et René de Maulde: Lettres de Ferry Carondelet à Marguerite d'Autriche, in: Bulletin historique et philologique du Comité des travaux historiques et scientifiques, Année 1895, Paris 1896, 97—134; C. F. WEGNER, Aarsberetninger fra det Kongelige Geheimearchiv, indeholdene Bidrag til Dansk Historie af Utrykte Kilder, I Copenhagen 1852—55; Regesta Diplomatica Historiae Danicae. Index chronologicus diplomatum et literarum historiam Danicam inde ab antiquissimis temporibus usque ad annum 1660 illustrantium quae in libris hactenus editis vulgata sunt, Cura Societatis Regiae Scientiarum Danicae, Ser. 2, Tom. I/2 (1448—1536), Havniae 1889; The Letters of James the Fourth 1505—1513, calendared by R. K. HANNAY, eds. R. L. MACKIE and A. SPILMAN (= Publications of the Scottish History Society, 3 Ser., Vol. 45), Edinburgh 1953; F. DE ALMEIDA, História de Igreja em Portugal III/2, Coimbra 1915; Corpo diplomatico Portuguez contendo os actos e relações politicas e diplomaticas de Portugal com as diversas potencias do mundo des de o seculo XVI até ao nossos dias, I: Relações com a Curia Romana, ed. L. A. REBELLO DA SILVA, Lisboa 1862; Quadro elementar das relações politicas e diplomaticas de Portugal com as diversas potencias do mundo desde o principio da monarchia Portugueza até aos nossos dias, IX: Curia Romana (1137—1533), ed. V. DE SANTAREM and L. A. REBELLO DA SILVA, Lisboa 1864; R. RIDOLFI, The Life of Niccolò Machiavelli, trans. C. GRAYSON, Chicago 1954/63; R. D. JONES, Francesco Vettori: Florentine Citizen and Medici Servant, London 1972; M. M. BULLARD, Filippo Strozzi and the Medici: Favor and Finance in Sixteenth-century Florence and Rome, Cambridge 1980; A. RENAUDET, Le concile gallican de Pise-Milan: Documents florentins (1510—1512), Paris 1922; G. MORONE, Lettere latine di Girolamo Morone pubblicati sugli autografi, ed. D. PROMIS and G. MÜLLER, and Documenti che concernono la vita pubblica di Girolamo Morone, ed. G. MÜLLER (= Miscellanea di storia italiana edita per cura della regia Deputazione di storia patria 1, 2) Torino 1863—65; P. PRODI, Relazioni diplomatiche fra il ducato di Milano e Roma sotto il duca Massimiliano Sforza (1512—1515) in: Aevum 30 (1956) 437—494, and the lengthy studies of A. BÜCHI, Korrespondenzen und Akten zur Geschichte des Kardinals Matthäus Schiner, 2 Vols., Basel 1920—25 and Kardinal Matthäus Schiner als Staatsmann und Kirchenfürst, 2 Vols., Zürich-Fribourg 1923—37.

Louis XII of France hoped to win Julius back to his side with the proposal of conferring on the papal nephew, Francesco Maria della Rovere, the territories of Piombino and Siena, neither of which, however, were then under French control.[3] Julius was not to be dissuaded from his efforts to rescue the imperiled Venetians and expel from Italy his former northern allies, especially the French.

This diplomatic about-face created many problems for Julius. While he succeeded in recovering from the Venetians the cities they had earlier illegally occupied, he earned the hostility of Louis XII of France who accused him of treachery and of ingratitude since French armies had restored to papal control such important cities as Imola, Forlì, Bologna, Ravenna, Faenza, and Rimini. When Julius' vassal, Alfonso d'Este, the duke of Ferrara who had distinguished himself alongside his French allies in the fight against Venice, resisted Julius' call to make peace with Venice, the pope on 9 August and 14 October 1510 deposed him from his ducal office and placed him and his helpers under major ecclesiastical censures.[4]

This example of resorting to spiritual weapons in what was essentially a political struggle was not lost on Louis XII. In the hope of punishing Julius and of distracting him from his military and political ventures by attacks in the area of his spiritual powers, Louis had the clergy of France meeting in a synod at Tours in September of 1510 reassert the liberties of the Gallican Church from papal control, declare in advance the nullity of any ecclesiastical measures Julius might impose on Louis for coming to the aid of such allies as the d'Este duke, and demand that the pope convoke a council.[5] The French were supported in their call for a council by emperor Maximilian, especially after the new alliance with France negotiated by his ambassador Matthaeus Lang von Wellenburg, bishop of Gurk, and signed at Blois on 17 November 1510.[6]

Julius II was particularly vulnerable to a call for a church council. Among the election capitularies he had signed as cardinal in the conclave of 1503 and had reconfirmed under oath after his election as pope was the pledge to convoke within two years a general council. The last two councils of the previous

---

[3] On the continued powerful backing of the Aragonese and the rival French offers, see TERRATEIG I 204—19, II 153—54 (for the oath of Fernando at the Neapolitan investiture); on Julius' calculation of eventual imperial assistance, see GILBERT, The Pope, His Banker, 91—92.

[4] On Louis' feelings of having been unappreciated and betrayed, see the draft of the French ambassador's letter of credence, Bibliothèque Nationale-Paris, Fond Ancien Français 3087, fols. 101r—02v reprinted in Appendix II; the bull against Alfonso d'Este dated 9 August 1510 *Romani Pontificis autoritas* can be found in ASV, Reg. Vat. 984, fols. 137v—46r (sections 139r—40v are printed in RAINALDI, 1510, nr. 15) and the bull anathematizing the French forces sent to assist Alfonso *Decet Romanum Pontificem* dated 14 October 1510 is registered in ASV, Reg. Vat. 984, fols. 162r—64v (this bull is summarized in RAINALDI, 1510, nr. 16). These events are treated in HERGENROETHER - LECLERCQ VIII/1, 269—75.

[5] The French response in the area of spiritual jurisdiction is summarized in HERGENROETHER - LECLERCQ VIII/1, 275—80.

[6] On the French-Imperial alliance, see TERRATEIG II 143—44; HERGENROETHER - LECLERCQ VIII/1, 294—95; and GUICCIARDINI IX, i, iv, ed. PANIGADA II 5, 19.

II

The Healing of the Pisan Schism (1511—13)

century, both Konstanz in 1417 and Basel in 1431, had ordered the periodic celebration of such solemn assemblies. Belief that a council was superior to the pope and the fitting instrument for a reform of the Church found fervent supporters not only in the conciliarist stronghold of the University of Paris and elsewhere throughout Europe, but even at the papal court. Fearful of what kinds of reforms a council might legislate for the Roman curia, Julius ignored his pledge and church legislation mandating its convocation. In the opinion of leading canonists, not only Christian princes, but especially members of the college of cardinals, had the right, even the obligation to convoke a council when the Church was in danger of suffering great harm from papal failure to call one. Julius' position became all the more precarious in October of 1510 when five cardinals (two Spanish, two French, and one Italian) fled out of a personal fear of the pope to the protection of the French armies and allies and threatened to add their names and authority to that of Maximilian and Louis in convoking a council.[7] Given Julius' opposition to a council, especially one outside his control, schism seemed imminent.

In an effort to avoid Church disunity and to strengthen their position by scrupulously following legal forms, the principal proponents of a council sought the pope's approbation of a conciliar convocation. Maximilian on 16 January 1511 and Louis XII on 15 February 1511 commissioned procurators to request of the pope that he call a council. Julius rejected their petition and thereby gave

---

[7] Julius' election capitularies are printed in RAINALDI, 1503, nr. 3—9, esp. 6, and in Acta primi concilii Pisani celebrati ad tollendum schisma anno Domini M.CCCC.IX. et concilii Senensis M.CCCC.XXIII. ex codice MS. Item constitutiones sanctae in diversis sessionibus sacri generalis concilii Pisani ex bibliotheca regia, Paris 1612, 15—20 (for Julius' election capitularies), the second part of this book separately paginated and entitled Apologie sacri Pisani concilii moderni contains such supportive material as the Consilium CLI of Filippo Decio (pp. 69—107), an oration on the same theme (pp. 108—29), various letters, etc. In his bull *Sacrosanctae Romanae ecclesiae* of 18 July 1511 which convoked the Lateran Council, Julius attempted to refute these arguments justifying the calling of the Pisan Council — see Sacrosanctum Lateranense Concilium Novissimum sub Iulio II. et Leone X. Celebratum, ed. A. DEL MONTE, reprinted in MANSI 32, 649—999 — hereafter this volume is cited as MANSI — the relevant sections of this bull are found at MANSI 32, 681 A—86 C.

On contemporary support for the conciliarist position, see: O. DE LA BROSSE, Le Pape et le Concile: La comparaison de leur pouvoirs à la vielle de la Réforme, Paris 1965; M. GILMORE, The Lawyers and the Church in the Italian Renaissance, in his Humanists and Jurists: Six Studies in the Renaissance, Cambridge, Mass. 1963, 61—86, esp. 72—78; F. OAKLEY, Almain and Major: Conciliar Theory on the Eve of the Reformation, in: American Historical Review 70 (1964—65) 673—90, and his Conciliarism in the Sixteenth Century: Jacques Almain Again, in: ARG 68 (1977) 111—32. On conciliarist thought at the papal court, see H. JEDIN, Giovanni Gozzadini, ein Konziliarist am Hofe Julius' II. (1939), reprinted in his Kirche des Glaubens — Kirche der Geschichte: Ausgewählte Aufsätze und Vorträge, I Freiburg 1966, 17—74; and F. TODESCAN, Fermenti gallicani e dottrine anti-conciliariste al Lateranense V. Un capitolo della teologia politica del secolo XVI, in: Cristianesimo, secolarizzazione e diritto moderno, ed. L. LOMBARDI VALLAURI and G. DILCHER, Milano 1981, 567—609.

On the flight of the cardinals to French protection due to a fear for their lives aroused by the recent deaths of non-Italian cardinals such as Georges d'Amboise and Melchiorre de Copis which they attributed to the pope's evil plots, see: GUICCIARDINI IX ix, x, ed. PANIGADA III 42, 48—49; HERGENROETHER - LECLERCQ VIII/1, 280—81, and TERRATEIG I 200—04, II esp. 144, 146—48.

grounds for accusing him of intransigence.[8] Still in hope of avoiding an impending schism, an attempt was made to resolve the outstanding political issues preventing peace.

In the Spring of 1511 a major effort was made at Mantova by the former members of the League of Cambrai to resolve their differences. To prevent any divisions in the ranks of those still resolved on the defeat of Venice, the Empire, France, Burgundy, and possibly also Hungary had taken the precautionary measure earlier at Blois on 17 November 1510 of pledging to make no agreements with their former ally, the treacherous Julius II, unless first having obtained the consent of all. The sketch for a Spring offensive against Venice was drawn up and Louis promised to pay Maximilian 100,000 ducats to bring his army into northern Italy. These plans for the final conquest of the Venetian mainland were temporarily blocked by Fernando of Aragon. Working through Jaime de Conchillos, bishop of Catania and Aragonese ambassador to the Imperial court, the Spanish king persuaded Maximilian to seek his goals in Italy first through peace negotiations rather than resorting initially to arms, and to appoint as his special representative at these discussions the trusted imperial councillor, Lang. Also pressured by Fernando into joining this peace parley, Louis XII dispatched as his ambassador Étienne Poncher, bishop of Paris, grand chancellor of the duchy of Milan and member of the quadrumvirate which directed French affairs after the death of cardinal d'Amboise. Louis enlisted by letter the good offices of Andrew Forman, bishop of Moray and ambassador to the papal court of his Scottish ally, James IV. In the hope of agreeing upon a common bargaining position before entering into negotiations with Julius, many of the ambassadors met first at Mantova. Lang came accompanied by Conchillos and Giovanni Gonzaga. Poncher intentionally dallied to arrive last and be received by his colleagues with great honors. Also present were Alessandro Gabbionetta, the archdeacon of Mantova and confidant of Julius II, and Jeronimo de Vich, the baron de Llauri and Aragonese representative at the papal court. The ambassadors of Florence and Ferrara joined them.[9]

---

[8] HERGENROETHER - LECLERCQ VIII/1, 295; W. ULLMANN, Julius II and the Schismatic Cardinals, in: Schism, Hersey, and Religious Protest (= Studies in Church History 9) Cambridge 1972, 177—93, esp. 181—87; for the edicts of Maximilian and Louis, see Acta primi concilii Pisani 22—25, a notarized but mutilated copy of the cardinals' edict of convocation is preserved in Wien, Haus-, Hof- und Staatsarchiv, Maximiliana, box 24, folder III, fol. 98.

[9] TERRATEIG I 210—13, 227—28, II, 148—49; DOUSSINAGUE, Politica internacional, 395—416, 431; while not a formal signatory to the Blois accords, Hungary tentatively agreed to them during the negotiations at Konstanz in October of 1510, but subsequently failed to ratify this agreement — see FRAKNÓI, Ungarn und die Liga, 67—71, 75—77, 82, 94—96; M.-C. GARAND, La carrière religieuse et politique d'Étienne Poncher évêque de Paris (1503—1519), in: Huitième centenaire de Nôtre-Dame de Paris (Congrès des 30 Mai—3 Juin 1964): Recueil de travaux sur l'histoire de la cathédrale et de l'eglise de Paris, Paris 1967, 291—343, esp. 311, 318; GUICCIARDINI IX xii, xv, xvii, ed. PANIGADA III 59—62, 78—83, 89; PASTOR VI 345; GODEFROY, Lettres de Louis II 111; for the report on Lang's expectations of a peace accord and Poncher's delay at Cremona due to "illness," see the letter of Andrea del Burgo to Marguerite of Austria, Bourges, 13 March 1511, in: LE GLAY, Négociations I 387—89.

The Healing of the Pisan Schism (1511—13)

The principal spokesmen began their rendezvous on 17 March 1511. On instructions from Julius, Gabbioneta urged Lang to consult first personally with the pope. Vich warned Poncher that probably because of the pope's earlier anathema against the supporters of Alfonso d'Este, Julius refused to receive the French bishop in his role as ambassador of king Louis, Alfonso's principal ally, but that the pontiff urged him to come to him in a private capacity. Poncher rejected such a procedure and on the advice of Vich named Lang to negotiate in his stead. To strenghten the Imperial ambassador's commitment to the French cause, Poncher eventually turned over to Lang an initial 10,000 ducats toward the full 100,000 promised the emperor. French interests were also to be protected by Forman.[10] Despite these efforts at coordination, the goals and strategies of some of the participants were at variance.

The vacillating emperor Maximilian was by then primarily concerned with regaining Imperial territories in northern Italy lost over the years to Venice and with guaranteeing his peaceful possession of those recently recovered. While personally offended by Julius' refusal to honor his obligations under the terms of the League of Cambrai, the emperor was not intent on exacting a revenge. In keeping with his chivalric ideals, Maximilian wanted to keep his commitments to his recent ally and former rival, Louis of France, but as the paternal grandfather of the half-orphaned heir apparent to the Spanish throne, duke Charles of Burgundy, the emperor was ultimately more concerned with coordinating his policies with those of Fernando, Charles' maternal grandfather.[11]

As the Imperial ambassador, Lang entered the negotiations with a set of instructions. Maximilian wanted the pope to desert Venice and rejoin the League of Cambrai. Should Julius refuse to do this, Lang was to urge him to work out a universal peace for Christendom or at least an acceptable peace between Venice and the Empire and a resolution of the Ferrarese dispute. Failing this, Lang was to follow through on the articles signed at Blois, proceed with the convocation of a church council, and carry out other actions detailed in his instructions.[12]

King Louis of France wanted to secure his possession of the duchy of Milan and of those neighboring territories on the Venetian mainland which he had gained under the terms of the League of Cambrai. He preferred to accomplish this by peaceful means and a reconciliation with Julius. But when the pope pressed his attacks against the territories of the rebellious papal vassal, Alfonso

---

[10] TERRATEIG I 228; GARAND 318, n. 147; GUICCIARDINI IX xv, ed. PANIGADA III 83—84; DOUSSINAGUE, Politica internacional 433.
[11] ULMANN, Kaiser Maximilian II 419—25; A. SCHULTE, Kaiser Maximilian I als Kandidat 57—58; TERRATEIG I 209; PASTOR VI 294, 299—300.
[12] Letter of Lang to Maximilian, from Riva on Lago di Garda, 16 May 1511, HHStA Wien, Maximiliana 24, III 81r; GUICCIARDINI IX xvi, ed. PANIGADA III 88; and DOUSSINAGUE, Politica internacional, 433—34, citing a letter of the English ambassador to Maximilian, Robert Wingfield, to Henry VIII, dated 24 May 1511.

d'Este, whom Louis had taken under his royal protection, the king ordered the commander of his army in Italy, Charles d'Amboise, lord of Chaumont and Grand Master of France, to defend Ferrara and force the pope's retreat by counterattacks on territories controlled by the pope. Despite some initial military successes, French advances were stymied when on Vich's urgings Julius turned over to the Imperial representative, Viet von Furst, some of the intended targets of d'Amboise's attacks. The Grand Master's death two weeks later left the command of the French army in the hands of the skillful and experienced Gianiacopo de Trivulzio. But before he could demonstrate his abilities, Louis became involved in the peace negotiations of Mantova and therefore ordered a suspension of all military actions against the Papal States.[13]

The king's concerns were not only over the uses of his army in Italy, but also over the reliability of his political alliances. The peace agreements he had negotiated with Fernando were fraught with dangers. The Aragonese king was not to be trusted: by trickery and arms he had ousted Louis earlier from Naples. For the present this Spanish monarch was assembling an army and navy for the announced intention of an expedition against the North African Moors, but such military might could be easily redirected against his neighbor Louis and in support of Julius. Although invited to sign the articles of Blois with his former allies in the League of Cambrai, Fernando had resisted and pledged his full support to Julius.[14]

The French alliance with the Empire was also subject to stress. Having earlier reneged on a marriage alliance between his daughter Claude and duke Charles, the grandson of Maximilian, which would have settled by way of dowry the outstanding territorial disputes in Italy and Burgundy, Louis now sought by protestations of fraternal affection for Maximilian to encourage Imperial adherence to treaty obligations favoring France. The Valois king also worked to have Julius fulfil his obligations toward Maximilian under the terms of the treaty of Cambrai, thus proving to the emperor the value of friendship with France. What Louis most feared was a separate peace between the Empire and Venice which could leave France alone in Italy against the combined forces of Venice, the papacy, and Aragon. If peace agreements were to be made for northern Italy, all the contending parties should be included.[15]

The Italian resources at Louis' service were equally unreliable. French domination of Genoa was continually threatened by revolts. At the very time Louis had halted hostilities so that the peace negotiations could go forward, Julius

---

[13] PASTOR VI 333; TERRATEIG I 215—16, 222; GUICCIARDINI IX v—vi, x—xv, ed. PANIGADA III 22—29, 43—47, 53—81.

[14] DOUSSINAGUE, Politica internacional 396—402; TERRATEIG I 216, 222—26; GUICCIARDINI IX xv, ed. PANIGADA III 79—81.

[15] GARAND 311—13; GODEFROY, Lettres de Louis III 81; TERRATEIG I 211—12, II 176; GUICCIARDINI IX xv, ed. PANIGADA III 80.

sent the bishop of Ventimiglia, Alessandro Campofregoso, on a secret mission to stir up a revolt among his fellow Ligurians. French possession of Milan was also subject not only to internal unrest, but also to external threats from the pope's Swiss allies and from a possible assertion of Hapsburg claims on the duchy. Louis' ally Alfonso d'Este was hard pressed trying to keep papal and Venetian forces from his Ferrarese duchy. Although pledging their loyalty to the French, the Florentines were reluctant to field any troops in their ally's defense, especially against Julius. On his return from France, Niccolo Machiavelli convinced the Florentine government that there would be a war between Louis and Julius and that the Florentines would likely become involved. He, therefore, received a commission from the government to ready the fortresses and raise troops, activities which absorbed his attention at the time of the peace negotiations at Mantova and Bologna. Feeling itself particularly vulnerable to threats against its merchants and bankers in the Papal States, Florence wanted at all costs to avoid conflict with the pope, if such could be done without alienating the French.[16] Given such shaky alliances, Louis had reason for being indecisive.

Understandably, Louis was desirous of peace with the pope. Already in autumn of 1510 he had enlisted Fernando's assistance in the hope of securing peace, and had sent to Rome as his ambassador, Alberto Pio, prince of Carpi, an imperial fiefdom near Modena. Pio was to offer Julius generous terms. On the difficult issue of Alfonso d'Este, the disobedient papal vassal enjoying French protection, Julius was to be given wide discretion in settling the issue of duties and of Ferrarese salt manufacture at Comacchio in contravention of the papal monopoly. Through the mediation of Francesco Alidosi, a favorite of Julius and the cardinal-bishop of Pavia then under French control, Louis sought to win peace with the papacy by the offer of troops for a Turkish crusade, by the suggestion that Piombino and Siena be conferred on the pope's nephew Francesco Maria della Rovere, and by the promise of French pressure on Alfonso d'Este so that the Ferrarese duke would surrender to the pope Cento and Pieve and other territories in the Romagna and agree to the payment of the traditional annual tribute of 4,000 ducats earlier abrogated by Alexander VI on the occasion of the marriage of his daughter Lucrezia to Alfonso. Although France was, thus, willing to sacrifice some of Alfonso's personal gains, it would not agree to his deposition from the ducal office or to his loss of its traditional rights.[17]

---

[16] PASTOR VI 321—29; GUICCIARDINI IX i, vii, xv—xvi, ed. PANIGADA III 2—4, 29—33, 80, 88; EUBEL III 334; R. RIDOLFI, The Life of Niccolo Machiavelli, trans. C. GRAYSON, Chicago 1954 Italian, 1963 English, 114—22; RENAUDET 626—27.

[17] GUICCIARDINI IX i—ii, v, xviii, ed. PANIGADA III 4, 6, 25, 100; TERRATEIG I 212, 216, 218, II 155; PASTOR VI 333; on Alexander VI's favors to his son-in-law Alfonso, see the 1522 response of Alberto Pio to the letter of Alfonso d'Este addressed to Charles V in September or October of 1521 lamenting the hostile attitudes of both Julius II and of Leo X toward their Ferrarese vassal, in: Due Documenti per la Storia di Alberto Pio, Conte di Carpi, ed. G. SEMPER, in: Memorie storiche e documenti sulla città e sull' antico principato di Carpi, IV, Carpi 1888, 253—326, at 295 — hereafter these documents are cited as SEMPER.

Unfortunately for Louis, the men he initially chose as mediators proved ineffectual. Fernando outwardly worked for peace, but secretly instructed Vich to pursue other goals. Pio also proved himself a doubledealer. Reports reached the French court first of his unauthorized activities and then of his outright treachery. Pio's recall was ordered in February of 1511. Not even the good offices of Alidosi could mollify the pope's stiff resolve on Ferrara. Julius derided Louis' proposals as mere triffles and demanded the complete surrender of the duchy before peace negotiations with France could progress. Any future services Alidosi could have rendered Louis were terminated by this cardinal's murder in May of that year. Following the initial failures of Fernando, Pio, and Alidosi to secure the peace, Louis turned to his trusted diplomat and royal councillor, Poncher. He was dispatched to Italy to do all within his power to bring about a settlement without abandoning the essential interests of France's allies, especially Maximilian, or of those taken under its protection, notably Alfonso.[18]

France loomed as Aragon's chief rival on the Italian peninsula. Although technically allied and at peace with Louis, Fernando feared that France could come to dominate Italy. Already in control of Genoa and Milan, Louis could easily gain sway over the northern part by a defeat of Venice. Assured of Florentine support or neutrality, the French king could then establish himself in central Italy by a military victory over Julius' armies and by a check on his spiritual authority through the calling of a church council. From his base in southern Italy, Fernando felt threatened by Louis' perduring legal claim to the throne of Naples and by his ability to assert that claim militarily. A papal investiture had recently strengthened Fernando's hold on Naples, but brought with it obligations to defend the interests of Julius.[19]

A strong papacy was ultimately Fernando's best bulwark against the French. He thus refused to join in the Blois reaffirmation of the war aims of the League of Cambrai directed against Venice and its recent ally Julius. He pledged his troops, instead, to the papal cause. To bolster the pope's temporal authority in the Papal States, he gave Julius a free hand in dealing with his rebellious vassal Alfonso, while counseling him to moderate his punishments. When Fernando's efforts to reconcile the rebellious cardinals and pope failed, he fully backed Julius' excommunication, deposition from office, and removal from benefices

---

[18] GUICCIARDINI IX v, xviii, ed. PANIGADA III 24, 100; TERRATEIG I 216, 218—19; GODEFROY, Lettres de Louis II 100, 218, 220. By July of 1511 Louis had formally judged Pio guilty of treason and dismissed him from his service but did not proceed to punish him because he was a vassal of Maximilian — see the letters of Andrea del Burgo to Maximilian, from Romans, 1 July 1511, Maximiliana 25 I 3a[r] and from Blois, 23 September 1511, Maximiliana 25 III 87r; GARAND 317—18; EUBEL III 10—11, n. 2.

[19] On the agreements between Fernando and Louis, see PASTOR VI 291; GUICCIARDINI VI xvi, VII, viii, xiii, VIII, ii, ed. PANIGADA II 163—65, 210—11, 243—44, 257—58; DOUSSINAGUE, Politica internacional 372—412, 510, and especially the more relevant documents on 551—53, 576—77, 581—83, 616—19, 620—35; and TERRATEIG I 212, 226—27.

of these wayward churchmen. Fernando also resisted the pressures from his fellow monarchs to join in the call for a church council which would have undermined Julius' position.[20]

To check Gallic power in Italy, Fernando sought to destroy the French-Imperial alliance which secured it. On the supposition that Maximilian's personal dislike of France would determine imperial policy once the emperor no longer needed French assistance to achieve his war aims against Venice, Fernando worked to bring about peace between Venice and the Empire. Julius was asked to do his part by restoring captured Imperial territories to the emperor, by avoiding armed conflict with Imperial forces, and by winning over the emperor's special emissary Lang through a show of public honors and a proffer of promotion to the cardinalate and to a rich see in return for negotiating a peace. Julius was also to pressure Venice into making generous concessions.[21]

In a letter to his ambassador Vich on the eve of Mantuan parley, Fernando detailed his policy toward France. His principal desire was for the universal peace of Christendom and continued friendship with Louis. To this end, Fernando intended to keep his agreements with France, provided Louis did not interfer with his defense of Aragonese and papal interests. Should ambition lead Louis to attack Julius and the Papal States, the armed might of Spain would come to the pope's defense. For Fernando, the peace of Italy depended on a negotiated settlement between the Empire and Venice. Unless this were achieved, no agreement was to be made between Julius and Louis over the fate of Ferrara. The ruler of that duchy, in the opinion of Fernando, should remain Alfonso d'Este and his heirs.[22]

If Maximilian and Louis were often indecisive and irresolute, slow to seize an opportunity, and inclined toward peace, Julius was clear about his goals and determined to achieve them. He dedicated his efforts to a restoration of the rights and privileges of the papacy.

Julius was very sensitive about protecting the spiritual powers of the papacy. He seems, however, to have felt himself personally bound by the limitations on his powers stipulated in the capitularies he swore at the time of his election to the papacy. He worked to terminate Venetian autonomy in the appointment of bishops. He resisted the petitions of Fernando of Aragon to have the royal right of patronage enjoyed over lands won from infidels and pagans extended over the whole Spanish church and insisted on the papal prerogative of naming the successor to a benefice which became vacant when its encumbant died "in the Roman curia". The most serious challenge to his papal power of appointment came soon after the death of Georges d'Amboise, cardinal-legate for

---

[20] DOUSSINAGUE, Politica internacional 395—412, 510; TERRATEIG I 200—03, 208, 212, 217.
[21] GUICCIARDINI IX xiv, xv, ed. PANIGADA III 74—76, 80, 83; TERRATEIG I 213, 215—16, 218—19, 222.
[22] DOUSSINAGUE, Politica internacional 416—20, 655—58; TERRATEIG I 218, 225—27.

France, when the Synod of Tour in September of 1510 advised Louis to withdraw France from obedience to Julius and to let the Gallican Church be governed according to the Pragmatic Sanction of Bourges. What perhaps most upset Julius about the decisions of Tours was the call for a general council. He had been outraged the year earlier by the Venetian call for such a council and saw this French call as a potentially more serious threat to his spiritual authority in that it was backed by the emperor and a number of rebellious cardinals. For Julius, so egregious was their offense against papal authority that he eventually not only excommunicated and deposed these cardinals, but stated on his deathbed that although as a private Christian he gladly forgave them, as pope he insisted that justice be served in their regard and that they be refused admission to the conclave or even the city, lest Rome be polluted. To restore the spiritual reputation of the papacy, he issued at Bologna in 1510 an earlier constitution forbidding simony in the election of a pope and had the decree reaffirmed by the Lateran Council on the eve of his death.[23]

The reassertion of the pope's temporal rights as head of the Papal States, as noted earlier, consumed much of Julius' time and energy. His first priority on assuming office was to break the power of Cesare Borgia and gain control of his dukedom in Romagna. Within a year the duke went into exile and many of his strongholds were in papal hands. The next target of Julian attention was Venice. This republic had taken advantage of papal weakness in the previous century to gain control of Ravenna and Cervia. During the confusion accompanying the Italian wars and death of Alexander VI, Venice occupied much of Romagna on the pretext of removing Cesare Borgia. The duke's exile to Spain and the pope's unanswered demand for a restoration of his territories unmasked Venice's true intent. So determined was Julius on the restoration of these territories that he forged an alliance with foreign powers to defeat the republic and divide up its holdings on the mainland. The victory of the League of Cambrai at Agnadello in 1509 prompted Venice to surrender to the pope his traditional territories and sue for peace with Rome. The war against Venice also had the unexpected result

---

[23] For indications that Julius felt himself bound to some extent by his oath, see his arguments against the Pisan convocation which did not deny the validity of his obligation to call a council, but listed reasons why he could not fulfill this up until then — MANSI 681B—85E, esp. 682C, E, 684A. Julius feared the power of a council to discipline him — see DE GRASSI, Diarium, ed. DÖLLINGER III 418.

On Julius' insistence on the papal right of appointment, see PASTOR VI 257—58, 264, 291, 301, 319—20, 327; P. PRODI, Organization and Structure of the Venetian Church, in: Renaissance Venice, ed. J. R. HALE, London 1973, 409—30; TARSICIO DE AZCONA, La elección y reforma del episcopado español en tiempo de los Reyes Catolicos, Madrid 1960, 174—93 and his Juan de Castilla, rector de Salamanca: Su doctrina sobre el derecho de los Reyes de España a la presentación de obispos (= Vol. IX, Text 2 of Bibliotheca Salmanticensis) Salamanca 1975, 47—114; and HERGENROETHER - LECLERCQ VIII/1 276—77.

On the challenges from a council and rebellious cardinals, see: ULLMANN, Julius and the Schismatic Cardinals 180—88, and RAINALDI, 1513, nr. 8. On the bull against simony, see PASTOR VI 440 and MANSI 768A—72B.

of drawing Alfonso d'Este into the orbit of the French. In contravention of the terms of the treaties of Cambrai and Biagrassa, Louis took under his protection a papal vassal, Alfonso. When the duke repeatedly refused to obey the pope's orders to cease hostilities against Venice because of the recently negotiated peace, Julius was incensed. He initiated legal proceedings against this rebellious vassal and declared him deprived of his lands, titles, and offices. Julius blamed such insubordination in part on Louis who had offered him his protection. Papal rule was also extended to other parts of his territory, so that local tyrants either acknowledged his authority or were driven into exile.[24]

The pope was concerned with asserting not only his feudal authority over all the vassals and cities in the Papal States, but also with protecting his economic interests and prerogatives. Venice was forced to allow ships flying the papal banner free passage through the Adriatic Sea. The monopoly throughout Christendom on the sale of alum granted by Paul II in 1465 to those managing the Tolfa mines in the Papal States was enforced by Julius. Through prohibitions against the import of Turkish alum, letters of protest against violations, and negotiations over a reasonable price, he succeeded in controling the trade as far away as England and the Low Countries and enriched the papal coffers. The monopoly the pope enjoyed in the Papal States on the manufacture of salt at Cervia was also safeguarded by Julius. Because Comacchio lay supposedly outside the Papal States in Imperial territory, Alfonso d'Este claimed that his saltworks there did not fall under the prohibition. Julius, however, regarded them as an infringement on his monopoly and demanded that salt production there be terminated.[25] Thus, on a whole range of issues touching papal prerogatives, Julius insisted on his rights.

For the Julius of 1511, the greatest threat to papal power came from France. Its troops dominated northern Italy, its king gave unlawful protection to a rebellious papal vassal, and its prelates at Tours supported the call for a general council. From the peculiar perspective of Julius, the remedy for these dangers lay not in fulfilling treaty obligations nor accepting the generous terms offered by Louis for resolving the Ferrara dispute, but in driving the French from Italy. Instead of expelling all foreigners from the peninsula, this solution led to Hapsburg hegemony in the person of Charles, the common heir of Maximilian of Austria and Fernando of Aragon. To prepare the way for the French expulsion, Julius followed the advice of Fernando and sought to weaken the French-Imperial alliance by getting Maximilian to make a separate peace with Venice. The cooperation of Lang was considered essential to this plan.[26]

---

[24] M. BROSCH, Geschichte des Kirchenstaates, I: Das 16. und 17. Jahrhundert, Gotha 1880, 23—31; PASTOR VI 216, 232—89; DOUSSINAGUE, Politica internacional, 509; GUICCIARDINI IX ii, ed. PANIGADA III 7.
[25] GILBERT, The Pope, His Banker, and Venice, 76—90; PASTOR VI 317, 328.
[26] GUICCIARDINI IX i—ii, xv—xvi, ed. PANIGADA III 1—2, 7—8, 80; TERRATEIG II 144, 157; BROSCH, Julius II und die Gründung, chps. 5—6.

The key man in these negotiations was Lang. On Vich's advice, Poncher had empowered him to represent both French and Imperial interests. Vich also conveyed to Julius Fernando's suggestions that the prospect of promotion to the cardinalate and translation to a rich episcopal see be dangled before Lang as the reward for concluding peace between the Empire and Venice. In anticipation of Lang's cooperation, Julius on 10 March 1511 while still with his army at Ravenna included among the names of those promoted to the Sacred College as replacements for the rebellious cardinals, that of a ninth cleric which he kept *in pectore*, but was known to be that of this Austrian bishop. To receive the Imperial emissary in a fitting setting, Julius moved his court to Bologna. On the night prior to Lang's ceremonial entrance into that city, Julius granted him a secret audience lasting some four hours and on the following day again allowed him every possible honor. Over the protests of his master of ceremonies, Julius allowed Germanic processional practices to be followed and Lang to wear the simple garb of a traveling layman. At the public consistory held the next day for the presentation of his letters of credence, Lang was granted the place of honor usually given to persons of great importance — the last seat in the benches of the cardinal deacons. His elevation to the cardinalate had not yet been announced. In their speeches before the consistory both Lang and Conchillos urged the pope to embrace peace in Italy so that Christian weapons could be redirected against the Turks. In response Julius complained of Louis XII who prevented him from making peace and disciplining his vassals.[27]

Lang was not to enjoy for long these private and public direct discussions with Julius. To work out the details of a settlement, the pope appointed as his negotiators the three cardinal priors: Raffaele Riario, Pedro Isuales, and Giovanni de'Medici. Although initially amenable to discussing these matters with the cardinals, Lang eventually sent three representatives of his own to the negotiations. For over two weeks the discussions dragged on.[28]

The issues most susceptible to a compromise solution were the terms for a peace settlement between Venice and the Empire. True to his instructions, Lang began by insisting that Julius abandon Venice or force it to make concessions in accord with the goals of the League of Cambrai. Thus, it was to surrender to the emperor those areas he had not yet recovered: Padova, Treviso, and the region around Cividale. As compensation to the emperor for the revenues he lost when Venice seized his cities earlier and for the expenses of the war he was thus forced to wage to recover them, Venice was to pay some 70,000

---

[27] On Lang's promotion to the cardinalate at Ravenna, see: PASTOR VI 344; the letter of Andrea del Burgo to Marguerite of Austria, Bourges, 13 March 1511, in LE GLAY, Négociations I 388; and GUICCIARDINI IX xvi, ed. PANIGADA III 85, but EUBEL III 13 gives 19 November 1512 as the date of his promotion.

The ceremonies surrounding Lang's entrance into Bologna are described in GUICCIARDINI IX xvi, ed. PANIGADA III 86 and by de Grassi in DÖLLINGER III 402—04, and RAINALDI, 1511, nr. 52.

[28] GUICCIARDINI IX xvi, ed. PANIGADA III 86—87; RAINALDI, 1511, nr. 57.

ducats. Should Venice resist restoring to the emperor his due, the pope was to back the emperor in his efforts to recuperate his losses.[29]

After weeks of negotiations the pope was able to work out the following compromise which he hoped would be mutually acceptable to Venice and the Empire. Venice was to acknowledge the emperor's complete control over Verona and Vicenza. Maximilian was to allow the Venetians to retain in peace the cities of Padova and Treviso, provided they recognized his imperial sovereignty over these cities and paid him for them a substantial annual tribute. Although this solution was ultimately rejected by the Venetian Senate, Julius succeeded in getting Lang to agree to these terms. In this effort, the pope was assisted by his allies Conchillos and Vich.[30]

Other factors, however, came into play. The Empire would make no separate peace, but observe the Blois accords. On the question of Ferrara, Julius insisted on conquering this rebellious vassal himself and not being bound by a settlement worked out with others. The pope was similarly bellicose toward France. He demanded that Louis beg pardon for supporting Alfonso and that he end his aggressive policy in Italy. Julius even tried to get Lang's agreement to a united papal-imperial campaign to drive Louis from the peninsula. Despite the progress made on the terms of an Imperial-Venetian peace, the widening gap on the other issues led to a collapse of the discussions. On April 25th Lang paid his parting respects to Julius and left Bologna.[31]

Finally realizing the seriousness of the situation, Julius made desperate last minute efforts to rescue these negotiations. As soon as Lang left the city, the pope sent word after him to return. But Lang continued on his way to Modena where he rejoined Poncher. Together they headed for Parma. On the fourth day after the breakdown of the negotiations, a special emissary of the pope, Forman, finally caught up with the two ambassadors in the hope of persuading them to reopen the discussions. Doubting the sincerity of Julius and fearing the dangers born of further delay, Lang was reluctant to return to Bologna. Poncher was also entreated to hasten there to speak with the pope in a private capacity and not as the official ambassador of Louis. The bishop of Paris also suspected the pope's real intentions and expected little results from such discussions. When Lang despaired of a new parley and left Parma for the Tyrol, Poncher was even more hesitant to deal separately with Julius. He figured that Lang wanted to negotiate the peace terms himself and feared that Julius would try to split the Franco-Imperial alliance. Nonetheless, Poncher was willing to take risks for

---

[29] GUICCIARDINI IX xvi, ed. PANIGADA III 86—87; RAINALDI, 1511, nr. 57; DÖLLINGER III 404.
[30] *Ibid.*
[31] GUICCIARDINI IX xvi, ed. PANIGADA III 87—89; L. MACFARLANE, Forman (Andrew), in: DHGE 17 (1971), 1071; TERRATEIG I 229—30; GILBERT, The Pope, His Banker, and Venice, 128 n. 41, 144 n. 97. According to BORSCH, Julius II, 221, Julius on April 16th (in the middle of the negotiations) issued a bull excommunicating Alfonso, the French marshall Trivulzio, and those holding Milan and the Lombard state — indirectly Louis XII was condemned too.

peace. He wrote to Louis explaining the situation and asking for instructions. The royal response was to question the pope's sincerity. In the meantime, Forman had returned to Bologna and wrote Poncher to say that Julius again urged him to come, claiming that he wanted peace with Louis, that he understood the concerns and positions of the two ambassadors, that he had proposals of his own to make, and that all the issues in dispute could be worked out on his arrival. Poncher could now negotiate for Lang, just as the Austrian had earlier represented him. As tempting as these proposals were, Poncher decided not to go. The reason was Lang's veto on negotiations conducted in his absence.[32]

Responsibility for this collapse of these negotiations has been variously assessed. The papal master of ceremonies blamed Lang for having been so seduced and corrupted by Louis XII that he disregarded the pope's spiritual office in dealing with Julius and arrogantly broke off negotiations when the papal proposals were not to his liking. Echoes of de Grassi's accusations are to be found in subsequent apologists for the papacy. But historians from the time of Guicciardini on have pointed to Julius' hatred of the French and insistence on punishing Alfonso as the real causes of the collapse. The pope was intent on protecting the independence of the Holy See and on asserting its authority over its own vassals. But while the pope's personal animosity toward Louis and Alfonso may have been involved, Lang's adherence to his instructions proved the determining factor. Instead of appearing arrogant, disrespectful, and unyielding, Lang properly conducted himself as the emperor's special emissary, first councillor, and vicar for Italian affairs, and thus deserving of exceptional honors. As an intelligent diplomat, he was conscious of the usefulness of the trappings of power, and as a cleric engaged in essentially secular matters he opted not to be attired in episcopal robes. Despite the temptations of a rich benefice, cardinal's hat, and possible legation to Germany, Lang remained faithful to his mission. He carried out the emperor's instructions and did not betray the trust Poncher had placed in him. Responsibility for the French ambassador's absence from the Bolognese parley was not due to the "deceptions" of Lang, as claimed by de Grassi, but to the pope's duplicity which led to a loss of his credibility in the eyes of Louis and Lang, to papal insistence on merely private discussions with the French king's official emissary, and to the strategem of Vich who worked to separate Lang from Poncher in the hope that individually they could be the more easily cajoled by Julius.[33]

---

[32] GUICCIARDINI IX xvi, xvii, ed. PANIGADA III 88—89; GODEFROY, Lettres de Louis, II 206—09, 216—21, 223, 227; GARAND 318—19.

[33] For de Grassi's attacks on Lang (motivated in part because this Austrian bishop openly contravened some of the ceremonial practices of the papal court), see: DÖLLINGER III 402—03 and RAINALDI, 1511, nr. 52, 56—57. For the claim that Lang's deception, arrogance, and harshness caused the collapse, see: HERGENROETHER - LECLERCQ VIII/1, 274; Lang's arrogance is emphasized in PASTOR VI 344—46. What may have seemed to a contemporary Italian or to later papal historians as arrogant conduct, may merely have been Lang's insistence that fitting honor be shown the personal representative of the

The Healing of the Pisan Schism (1511—13)

With the final collapse of these negotiations, the stage was set for the convocation of a council. In accordance with his instructions from Maximilian, having failed to obtain either the pope's adherence to the treaty of Cambrai or an acceptable peace with Venice and resolution of the Ferrara dispute, Lang moved to comply with the emperor's wishes that the terms of the articles of Blois be observed and a council called. On his departure from Bologna, Lang consulted with his fellow imperial councillors and with Poncher. They agreed that Julius would never himself call a council due to his great abhorrence of one and that the number of cardinals then in Milan favoring a council was inadequate for their convoking it. Responsibility for the convocation, therefore, fell on the emperor and king of France as heads of the temporal aspects of the Christian religion. After consulting with Poncher, Lang dispatched to Milan for further discussions with this French ambassador and the dissident cardinals there three of the six procurators empowered by Maximilian to convoke a council in his name. The press of business elsewhere or the lack of skill in such matters prevented the other three procurators from joining them. While the cardinals and lay representatives concurred on the need to convoke a council, a dispute arose over the adequacy of the mandate of those sent by the Empire. Lest the delay caused by awaiting the arrival of new mandates result in yet greater harm

---

emperor, that leader specially charged with resolving the political quarrels of Christendom. On the procedures and ceremonies of diplomacy at that time, see: M. A. R. DE MAULDE-LA-CLAVIÈRE, Histoire de Louis XII. Deuxieme partie: La Diplomatie à l'epoque de Machiavel, 3 vols., Paris 1893, esp. II 171—96 (for the ambassador's entrance ceremonies) and notably 175 (for the observation that the pope's insistence that Poncher come only as a private individual effectively prevented him from coming at all).

That the principal blame for the collapse was due to Julius' insistence on punishing Alfonso and Louis, despite the generous concessions offered, is suggested by GUICCIARDINI IX xvi, ed. PANIGADA, III 87—89. TERRATEIG I 218, 228—30; DOUSSINAGUE, Politica internacional, 440—41; and GILBERT The Pope, His Banker and Venice, 128 n. 41, 144 n. 97 also support this assessment. Poncher felt the Ferrarese dispute could be resolved — see GODEFROY, Lettres de Louis, II 218.

For a general study of Lang, see: H. ULMANN, Lang, Matthaeus, in: ADB 20, Leipzig 1884, 610—13; for an example of Lang's caution and scrupulous observance of the terms of his mandate, see the letter of Alberto Pio to Maximilian, from Rome, 6 January 1514 in: Maximiliana 30 III 18r; for Lang's contention that it was more useful to wear secular garb when dealing with political questions, see his remarkable letter to Maximilian, from Rome, 24 November 1513, Maximiliana 30 II 89v; for Francesco Vettori's fascinating description of Lang's customary negotiating style — *lui e huomo molto secreto, et col parlare pocho et non exprimere in tutto i concepti suoi, fa credere che porti grande cose et grande comessioni, le quale qualche volta non riescono, et di questo si vede lexemplo ... a bologna anchora non fece conclusione alchuna* — see his letter to the Dieci di Balìa, from Rome, 18 November 1513, in AS Firenze, Dieci di Balìa, Carteggi, Responsive, Nr. 118, fol. 298r.

Whatever the allurements of ecclesiastical promotion and revenues dangled before him by Fernando and Julius, they were not enough to get Lang to betray his trust at Bologna — see P. KRENDL, Spanische Gesandtenberichte über Maximilian I., den Hof und das Reich, in: MIÖG 87 (1979) 101—20, esp. 105—06, 109, 116—19. For the extravagant praise of Lang's loyalty by Louis, see the letter of Andrea del Burgo to Maximilian, from Grenoble, 15 June [sic] 1511, Maximiliana, 25 I fol. 55r—v. According to a report of Francesco Chieregato, Lang sacrificed the red hat, legation to Germany, patriarchate of Aquileja, and other benefices worth 10,000 ducats proffered by Julius — see SANUTO, Diarii XII 77.

being done to Christendom and especially to the Empire by Julius, the procurators decided to act. On May 16th they issued their edict convoking a council to meet in Pisa later that year. Two days later, they received a letter from Maximilian effectively confirming their action. Subsequent documents from the emperor were more explicit in approving their actions. On the day after the arrival of the emperor's letter, the cardinals gathered at Milan also issued their edict of convocation.[34] One of the most serious challenges to the pope's position as head of the Church had thus been made by the two principal lay leaders of Christendom and by members of the pope's own Sacred College.

The indomitable Julius refused to yield to his opponents. When Bologna fell on 23 May 1511 to the French army under Trivulzio and the Bentivogli were reinstated there, the college of cardinals urged the pope to enter into peace negotiations with the French. Julius agreed in the hope of using these negotiations to win time enough to recoup his forces and organize an anti-French league. His lack of earnestness was evident in the appointment of one of the mediators and in the restricted mandate given the other. For the delicate and difficult task of initiating these negotiations, Julius appointed his son-in-law, Gian Giordano Orsini, a client of Louis XII, inexperienced in diplomacy, and someone he himself did not trust. Not until July did Orsini return from his recent sojourn in France with proposals for a papal-French settlement. The other negotiator Julius employed was a skilled diplomat. He sent the Breton cardinal Robert Guibé to Trivulzio to obtains a truce. When the general ascertained that the cardinal's instructions allowed him to make only vague protestations of the pope's desire for peace, were devoid of specifics regarding the conditions for that peace, and did not respond to the French proposals, Trivulzio refused to negotiate. On commands from Louis who earnestly hoped for peace, public celebrations of the French victory at Bologna were forbidden and Trivulzio was ordered to withdraw his troops from the Papal States to the duchy of Milan, leaving Annibale Bentivoglio in command of Bologna.[35]

---

[34] That Lang on departing Piacenza had left orders for the imperial procurators to convoke a council was reported on 7 May 1511 to the Florentine government by Roberto Acciajuoli from Saint-Cher near Vienne, see RENAUDET 27—28; for the letters of Lang to Maximilian, from Riva on Lago di Garda, 16 May 1511, and from Trient, 18 May 1511, and the edict of the cardinals, Milano, 19 May 1511, see in Maximiliana, 24 III fols. 81r—v, 96r, 98. The letter of the procurators to Lang, from Milano, 20 May 1511, is printed in J. OBERSTEINER, Eine Gurker Urkunde zum Konzil von Pisa aus dem Jahre 1511: Ein Beitrag zur Stellung des Gurker Bischofs Matthäus Lang von Wellenburg zum genannten Konzil, in: Festschrift zur Vollendung des 60. Lebensjahres des Hofrates Universitätsprofessor Dr. Gotbert Moro, ed. H. BRAUMÜLLER, (= Beigabe zum 152. Jahrgang der Carinthia I/1962), Klagenfurt 1962, 105—111, esp. 109—11. For the emperor's approval of the procurators' actions, see his letter to them from Mühldorf, 5 June 1511 and his edict of 15 June from Mühldorf and of 16 June from Weylheim in Bavaria, the Mühldorf material is printed in Acta primi concilii, 49—51 and a copy in German of the Weylheim edict is preserved in the ÖNB Wien cod. 12589, fol. 168r—174r.

[35] DOUSSINAGUE, Fernando y el cisma 176 and his Politica internacional 450; BORSCH, Julius II, 221—26, 354—55 nn. 60—61.

Because Trivulzio would not negotiate with Guibé, Julius commissioned the Scottish ambassador Forman and the apostolic nuncio in France Angelo Leonini to approach directly the French court about mutually acceptable conditions for peace. The pope's temporarily weak military and political positions led him to propose through his agents moderate terms. Alfonso d'Este as duke of Ferrara was to pay the traditional annual tax of 4,000 ducats and not the reduced tax of 100 granted to the detriment of the Holy See by Alexander VI on the occasion of Alfonso's marriage to his daughter Lucrezia. The duke was to surrender Lugo and other places disputed with Rome and was to accept a joint-lordship with the Holy See over his duchy of Ferrara which would allow the papacy to intervene and eventually supplant him in the administration of Ferrara. He was also to pay an indemnity for the cost of war Rome waged against him as a rebellious vassal. The protection which Louis had given the members of the Bentivogli family in Bologna was to be withdrawn so that the papal forces could move against them without having to fight their French allies too. In the spiritual order Julius would impose an interdict on Bologna as a rebellious city and move against the Pisan council.[36]

---

[36] Doussinague, Fernando y el cisma 176—77; Renaudet 39—42, 45—46; Guicciardini X ii—iii, ed. Panigada III 110—11, 117.

When Julius proposed a joint-lordship over Ferrara, he was merely claiming for the papacy what had earlier been granted to Venice. By a series of treaties from the twelfth century on, Ferrara was forced to grant Venice an increasing role in the commerce and government of the duchy. Under the guise of a resident *vice-dominus* who ostensibly protected the republic's trading rights, Venice gained a series of legalized monopolies, immunities, and jurisdictional rights. In 1308 Fresco d'Este even ceded his claims on Ferrara to Venice and in 1481 Girolamo Riario offered to the Venetians, apparently in the name of his uncle Sixtus IV, the duchy of Ferrara if they could conquer it. The Venetians failed, but retained their traditional rights there. Sixtus' other nephew Julius II in 1509 insisted that the Venetian official in Ferrara exchange the title *vice-dominus* for that of consul which was less suggestive of lordship. On 15 February 1510 Venice finally agreed. Julius thus effectively transformed Venetian rights into privileges bestowed by Ferrara's overlord. By now claiming for himself the right of *vice-dominium*, Julius seems to have wanted to assert the solely papal prerogative to intervene in Ferrarese affairs. On this topic, see: Moroni, Dizionario XXIV 121 ff., XCII 69, 135, 287, 289, 293; W. L. Gundersheimer, Ferrara: The Style of a Renaissance Despotism, Princeton 1973, 32—34, 45; Pastor IV 350—86; and Guicciardini VIII xiii, xvi, ed. Panigada III 318—19, 334.

Julius II saw Forman as a likely intermediary with France because the Scottish king was an ally of Louis XII. The pope had Forman write James IV to urge Louis to make peace with him — see the letter of Julius to James IV, from Bologna, 7 April 1511, in ASV, Arch. Miscel., Acta Consist. 3, fols. 34v—35v. The imperial ambassador to France reported that Forman was claiming at the French court that Julius truly inclined to a peace acceptable to the Empire. Del Burgo then spoke with Jean de Gannay, the grand chancellor, and they agreed that Forman was a good person but deceived by the pope, *concludens cancellarius, quod, si papa inclinaret ad concordiam, illa esset vera via bene faciendi ; sed si stat obstinatus, ut ipse cancellarius credit eum facturum, verum remedium esset quod exercitus dirigeretur potius contra terras ecclesias* ... rather than wasting time, men, and money attacking Padova and Trevisio — see letter of Andrea del Burgo to Maximilian, from Grenoble, 23—24 June 1511, Maximiliana 24 III fol. 66r—v. The Aragonese king, Fernando, was kept informed and approved the proposals Julius sent to Forman in France — see letter of Fernando to Vich, Hontiveros, 16 July 1511 in Terrateig II 171. Leonini brought the papal terms to Louis while the king was at Valence — see the letter of Andrea del Burgo to Marguerite of Austria, Lyon, 26 August 1511 in: Le Glay, Négociations I 431—32.

While most eager for peace with the pope, Louis was also concerned to safeguard the interests of his allies. He thus wanted the emperor to be secure in his territories and rights, the duke of Ferrara to retain all his state, the cardinal of Auch and the son of the marchese of Mantova to be set free, the Pisan cardinals to be totally absolved, and some other small items to be resolved. On the question of Bologna, Louis was willing to have it returned to papal control. He seems to have felt that his obligations to the Bentivogli were fulfilled when he restored them to power in May. Forman arrived in Rome in mid-July with word of the king's latest proposals.[37]

Negotiations dragged on through the heat of the summer. While Julius agreed to a new investiture of Alfonso with Ferrara, the duke was to pay the traditional tribute, accept a visdominio of the Church, and surrender Comacchio, Lugo and other territories Alfonso held in Romagna. Julius indicated a willingness to release the French cardinal François Guilhem de Clermont-Lodève, if a security of 40,000 ducats was deposited against his leaving Rome and if he promised to do all possible to see that the bishops Massimo Corvino and Niccolo Capranica taken prisoner by the French at Bologna were set free. On June 29th, the first anniversary of his imprisonment, the cardinal of Auch was finally released. Federico II Gonzaga, however, remained a hostage in Rome in accordance with the terms of the agreement which had secured his father's release from Venetian captivity the year earlier. The position of the Bentivogli in Bologna was precarious. For fear of a papal expedition to recover the city, the Bentivogli were proposing to surrender the city to the pope's forces, provided they were able to retain their private property there. Out of respect for Louis, Julius agreed to pardon all the rebellious cardinals, except for Carvajal and Borgia, the Spanish prelates whom Fernando wanted to see punished. At a consistory of July 28th Julius yielded to the unanimous wish of the Sacred College and promised to pardon and restore to his benefices and dignities any cardinal who within sixty-five days begged his pardon. A special letter in the name of the Sacred College was entrusted to Alessandro Guasco, bishop of Alessandria, to be delivered to these cardinals. The College pledged that Julius would abide by the offer and if the cardinals insisted on some other form of security, the College would do what was asked. Guasco was to beg them to lay aside any personal animosity toward Julius for the sake of church unity. On August 5th a report of these concessions by the pope was brought to the French court by Leonini. The papal proposals were considered unclear and inadequate in some areas.[38]

---

[37] Borsch, Julius II, 227; Renaudet, 43—46, 63, 69, 71—72; Terrateig I 231—33; letter of Andrea to Marguerite, Négociations I 431; G. R. Marek, The Bed and the Throne: The Life of Isabella d'Este, New York 1976, 173—77, 180—81.

[38] Doussinague, Fernando y el cisma, 177; Renaudet, 48, 57, 61—62, 71, 81—82, 87, 92 n. 109, 101; for the pope's monitorium of 28 July 1511 which included the sixty-five day grace period for obtaining pardon and restoration, see ASV., Reg. Vat. 967, fols. 314r—19r, reprinted in Rainaldi, 1511, nrs. 24—29; on Fernando's desire that Carvajal and Borgia be deprived, see Terrateig II 166;

II

The Healing of the Pisan Schism (1511—13)

The king's reply focused on the restitution of the cardinals who had fled to his protection for what he judged were honest reasons. He insisted that they be restored to their offices and dignities and be allowed to reside where they wished. In return, he proposed to eliminate the council convoked at Milan and promised to enter into a mutual defense pact with the pope. Should Julius refuse to restore them, Louis pledged all his earthly goods to the cause of their restoration and the council.[39]

The desire for an accommodation with France was still strong in the Sacred College. In mid-August the cardinals still urged Julius to agree to a settlement. Bologna was to be left to the pope, and the Bentivogli were to go into exile, but continue to enjoy their private goods in the city. Alfonso d'Este, having requested papal pardon, would remain duke of Ferrara, pay an annual tribute of 4,000 ducats, avoid a papal visdominio in Ferrara, discontinue salt production, and restore Cento and Pieve to the papacy. No mention was made of reimbursing Julius for the expenses of his Ferrarese war. The rebellious cardinals were to be pardoned and allowed to live where they wished. The pope was to adhere to the terms of the League of Cambrai.[40]

Julius responded to a number of these proposals. He did not want to be obliged to join in the attacks on Venetian-controlled Padova and he insisted that Lugo, Bagnacavallo, and Cotignola be surrendered by Alfonso and restored to the Papal States. He agreed that the Bentivogli once in exile could retain their goods and that the rebellious cardinals be pardoned in accord with the king's wishes. These negotiating positions Julius sent to Leonini in France, together with a new and provocative proposal. Let Louis abandon his allies to make a separate peace with the pope.[41]

When Louis learned of these most recent proposals on August 24th, he grew angry. He resented the suggestion that he betray the emperor and his other allies and engage in deception. He declared that he would never come to an agreement with the pope, unless he first obtained the consent of the emperor and security of his allies. Unless the pope also agreed to a settlement of the emperor's interests, Louis refused to negotiate any further.[42]

DE GRASSI, Diarium, ed. DÖLLINGER III 410; GUICCIARDINI IX ix X iii, ed. PANIGADA III 37, 117; PASTOR VI 367—69.

On Guasco's missions, see RENAUDET 82, 88, 109, 114, 120; for the letter of the Sacred College to the rebel cardinals, Rome, 7 August 1511, see ASV, Arch. Miscel., Acta Consist. 3, fol. 36r—v and RAINALDI, 1511, nrs. 17—18, for the response of these cardinals, from Borgo San Donnino, 11 September 1511, see Acta primi concilii, 67—74, and RAINALDI, 1511, nrs. 20—21. For an overview of these negotiations, see HERGENROETHER - LECLERCQ VIII/1, 304—05; RAINALDI, 1511, nrs. 16—22; and GUICCIARDINI X, ii, ed. PANIGADA III 110; for Raffaelle Riario's advice given in consistory to go slow in condemning these cardinals, see BAV, Chigi I.III.89, fols. 57r—71r.

[39] RENAUDET 93—94, 101, 111—12.
[40] Ibid. 114—15; letter of Fernando to Vich, s.l., 17 September 1511, in TERRATEIG II 176.
[41] RENAUDET 115, 140, 158.
[42] Ibid. 140, 158—59. Acciajuoli claimed the interview between Louis and Leonini was held on August 24th (p. 140), Tosinghi reported that Leonini wrote on August 25th to say he had not as yet

Instead of having sought a reasonable solution to the difficulties between the papacy and the northern monarch, Julius intentionally dragged out the negotiations. When they were near success, he sabotaged them by introducing conditions he knew Louis would reject. The king's patience wore thin. He advised Leonini that if he had no other business to conduct at the French court, he could return to Avignon. The papal nuncio elected to stay on and reported to Rome on the king's response.[43]

On 25 September 1511 Rome provided Leonini and Forman with new mandates and negotiating instructions. Julius demanded the restitution of Bologna and Alfonso d'Este's petition for pardon and payment of the annual tribute. Provided these were done, neither the pope nor his allies would attempt anything against Milanese territory. The schismatic cardinals, already under the threat of a monitorium, were to make their submission to the pope. He promised to grant them pardon. Once absolved, they would be free to return to their native lands. Cardinal Clermont-Lodève, however, was obliged to remain in Rome, unless the pope specifically allowed him to leave. On September 26th Forman was supposed to depart for France with his new set of instructions. Little hope of success was held out for his mission.[44]

Louis' response to such proposals was unfavorable. He became increasingly convinced that the negotiations had not been carried out in good faith, but that Julius was all the while arranging a new anti-French league which would include himself, Venice, Spain, England and the Swiss Cantons. When Louis learned that it might also include his former ally, the Empire, he rejected the urgings of the Spanish and English representatives at the French court and refused to surrender Bologna or to abandon his plans for a council. Julius had been offered many opportunities to make peace, but he had preferred war.[45] Ironically his new alliance was called the "Holy League".

The tremendous expenditure of energies on the part of the aging pontiff to organize this league took its toll on his health and in August his condition grew grave. The news that Julius might be at death's door sent the Spanish cardinals

---

spoken with the king and hoped to reach an agreement (p. 159). See also the report of Andrea del Burgo to Marguerite of Austria, Lyon, 26 August 1511, in LE GLAY, Négociations I 431—32.

[43] RENAUDET 159, 170.

[44] GODEFROY, Lettres de Louis, III 40—50, and RENAUDET 278 n. 196.

[45] DOUSSINAGUE, Fernando y el cisma 178; RENAUDET 133, 141, 158, 420; letter of Andrea del Burgo to Marguerite of Austria, Blois, 24 September 1511 in: LE GLAY, Negóciations I 438; on Louis's insistence on maintaining his protection of Bologna and Ferrara, see SANUTO XIII 158; on the pope's efforts to form a new military league while seeming to negotiate peace, see GUICCIARDINI X, iii—v, ed. PANIGADA III 117—27; for the strong support of Fernando who won over England to the pope's side and for the Aragonese promises of troops to help him reconquer Bologna, and for the delay of two months before this new league was finalized in October, caused by Julius' doubts about Venetian military strength and his own grave illness in August, see TERRATEIG I 234—42 and GILBERT, The Pope, His Banker, and Venice, 55—62, 92—93; on Louis's suspicions of an agreement between Julius and Maximilian and the French king's reactions, see TERRATEIG II 176.

The Healing of the Pisan Schism (1511—13)

Carvajal and Borja on their way from French-controlled territory in northern Italy to a possible conclave in Rome. When they learned of his recovery, they sent messengers to Julius requesting a safe-conduct so that they could defect from the French. The pope promised they would not be molested, provided they returned to the unity of the Church by renouncing their adherence to a council he had already anathematized. When Louis learned of their intentions, he urged them not to fear the pope, but trust in the king's assistance. The cardinals were in a quandry and hoped to keep a foot in both camps by not completely deserting Louis nor wholly adhering to Julius. This position was not acceptable to the pope. When the period of his monitorium expired, Julius held a public consistory on 24 October 1511 and deprived them and two other Pisan cardinals of their offices.[46]

The Pisan Council was equally unsuccessful in its efforts to reach an understanding with the pope. A week after Julius' deprivation of the cardinals, the council formally opened in Pisa. Still hoping for a compromise, it commissioned on November 12th four procurators among whom were Jean de Reby, abbot of Cluny and vicar of the Clunic congregation, and Ambrogio Zancha, a Neapolitan who was Louis' procurator to the council. The conciliar fathers charged them to invite Julius to attend personally and, if the location at Pisa was not acceptable, to choose a neutral site for its sessions. Julius refused to grant these emissaries a safe-conduct and threatened them with imprisonment should they attempt to come to Rome. When he scorned the council's summons to come and to justify his numerous hostile actions against them, the conciliar fathers

---

[46] RENAUDET 115, 119, 133—34, 141—42, 150—54, 162—63 (pope's illness and recovery), 152, 162 (cardinals depart for Rome). On the cardinals' efforts to be reconciled with Rome, see DE GRASSI, Diarium, ed. DÖLLINGER III 413—14; the letter of Andrea del Burgo to Maximilian, Ste. Marie de Cléry, 26—27 October 1511, in: Maximiliana 25, IV, fols. 124v—25r; the reports in RENAUDET 408, 412—15, 431; and RAINALDI 1511, nr. 34.

On the Pisan Council supporters' last minute efforts to be reconciled with Julius by sending two emissaries to Rome, Gian Battista de Teodorici a Roman medical doctor and Francesco de Treio a cleric from Piacenza, to negotiate a settlement, see Acta primi concilii, 75, RENAUDET 207 n. 69, and RAINALDI 1511, nr. 22.

On Julius' formal punishment of Briçonnet, Borgia, Carvajal, and de Prie, see ASV, Arch. Miscel., Acta Consist. 3, fols. 36v—37r and RENAUDET 415; in two studies the name of Sanseverino is incorrectly substituted for that of de Prie, e.g. RAINALDI 1511, nrs. 32—36 and EUBEL III 4 n. 1b. The judgment against Sanseverino was not finally pronounced until 30 January 1512 — see RENAUDET 608. In ASV, Arch. Miscel., Acta Consist. 3, fol. 37r—v, the name of Borgia (card. Cusentin) is given in place of Sanseverino as the person declared an excommunicate and schismatic on 30 January 1512.

Once the formal deprivations of October had been pronounced, Julius rejected the petitions of the Aragonese and imperial representatives, Vich and Ferry Carondelet, that the deposed cardinals be spared their benefices and goods. The pope claimed he could not revoke his earlier actions, because these cardinals had spurned numerous paternal appeals to return to the Church, and not to have deprived them would have scandalized the whole Church, especially now that they have celebrated the Pisan Council — see letter of Ferry Carondelet to Maximilian, Rome, 16 December 1511, in Maximiliana, 26 II fol. 42r and L. DE LA BRIÈRE, Dépêches de Ferry Carondelet, procureur en cour de Rome (1510—13), Bulletin historique et philologique du Comité des travaux historiques et scientifiques, Paris 1895, 118—19 for his letter to Marguerite of Austria from Rome, 18 December 1511.

ignored the more drastic measures urged on them by Louis such as deposing Julius and electing a successor, but instead chose to suspend him from the exercise of his office. They did not want to deepen the divisions already in the Church. Such moderation was not matched by Julius. On 13 February 1512 the pope in consistory declared as heretics and schismatics and deprived of their ecclesiastical offices other prominent members of the Pisan Council: two sons of cardinal Guillaume Briçonnet, Guillaume, bishop of Lodève, and Denys, bishop of Toulon; Zaccaria Ferreri, abbot of Subasio; and the jurists Filippo Decio and Girolamo Bottigella.[47]

At the same time Julius was hurling his censures at the Pisan partisans, the pope continued negotiations aimed at a settlement of political differences. Leonini and Forman functioned as his negotiators at the French court. Emperor Maximilian was also proposed as a possible mediator between Julius and Louis, but the latter had reservations. Although French military forces were still strong enough to raise the papal and Spanish siege of Bologna, Louis was unsure of his Austrian ally. The emperor's ambassadors kept assuring Louis of their master's sworn bonds of friendship, yet reports reached the French court that negotiations for a separate truce between the Empire and Venice were well advanced.[48]

In addition, the emperor's support of the Pisan Council was so ambiguous as to disqualify him as a trusted mediator in the eyes of the French. Maximilian had commissioned procurators to convoke the council and had confirmed their actions. But no German representatives ever participated in its sessions. Nor

---

[47] Acta primi concilii 109—14, 175—82, 185—86, 192—206; RENAUDET 519—20 n. 135; letter of Jean Hannart to Marguerite of Austria, Milan, 21 December 1511, in: LE GLAY, Négociations I 464 n. 1; on the papal penalties against supporters of the council, see the two papal monitoria of 3 December 1511 addressed to the prelates at the Pisan Council and to Ferreri, Decio, and Bottigella in MANSI 35, 164A—71B and reported in RENAUDET 561—62, 564; for the 13 February 1511 deprivation of the Briçonnets, Ferreri, Decio and Bottigella, see ASV, Arch. Miscel., Acta Consist. 3, fol. 37v, RENAUDET 616—17 n. 74, SANUTO XIII 331, and PASTOR VI 396. For the bull *Exigit contumacium* of 18 February 1513 threatening the king and queen of Navarre with excommunication and deprivation for assisting Louis and the Pisan cardinals, see ASV, Reg. Vat. 1190, fols. 173r—78r, printed in V. PRADERA, Fernando el Católico y los falsarios de la Historia, Madrid ²1925, 417—23.

[48] On Forman's continuing mission, see L. MACFARLANE, Forman (Andrew), in: DHGE 17 (1971) 1071; on Leonini's presence at the French court as a possible negotiator, see RENAUDET 317, 453, 676; for a report on a diplomatic exchange between Louis and Julius using the services of these two bishops, see, SANUTO XIII 286 and the letter of Agostino Somenzo to Maximilian, Mantova, 9 January 1512, in Maximiliana, 26, III 21r; on Maximilian as a possible mediator, see the letters of Paolo da Lodi to N. N., Blois, 3 February 1512 in Maximiliana 26 IV fols. 8r and 19r; on the successful French resistance at Bologna and report of an as yet unratified imperial-Venetian truce, see the letter of Paolo da Lodi (?) to Andrea dal Burgo, Blois, 5 February 1512, Ibid. fol. 14v; for evidence that these negotiations had been going on for sometime now, see the reports in: GODEFROY, Lettres de Louis III 120, the letters of Jean le Veau to Marguerite of Austria, Blois, 3, 16, and 29 December 1511, in LE GLAY, Négociations I 459, 468, 479, the reports of Giovanni Colla to Maximilian, Rome, 22, 25, and 30 December 1511, in Maximiliana, 26, II, fols. 72v, 80r—81v, 84r—85r and the later report in SANUTO XIV 24. On 9 April 1512 a truce was in fact concluded for eight months between the Empire and Venice, see HERGENROETHER - LECLERCQ VIII/1, 337.

The Healing of the Pisan Schism (1511—13)

did its transfer from Pisa to Milan, so much nearer to Hapsburg lands, produce the promised delegates. Unable to gain for this council the backing of his own German episcopate, Maximilian tried to enlist the support of the neighboring kings of Poland and Hungary, but again was unsuccessful. If no German prelate was willing to attend the council, Maximilian at least would be personally represented by delegates. He appointed Girolamo Nogarola, a Veronese count, and Pigello Portinari, his Florentine secretary and a member of a prominent Florentine banking house. The delegates' departure from Trent was initially delayed until questions of finance were settled. The agreement of Carvajal and his fellow conciliar cardinals to pay the expense of the imperial delegation still did not secure its arrival in Milan. Maximilian hesitated to give such formal backing to the council, while negotiating his own Venetian peace with papal assistance.[49]

Louis tried desperately to dissuade Maximilian from making a separate peace with Venice using the pope as mediator. He argued that Julius was not to be trusted, for if he really wanted Maximilian to regain Padova, Treviso and Giulia-Veneto earlier seized by Venice, he would support the emperor with money and his ally Fernando would send troops so that the Venetians would be quickly defeated. Instead, the pope acts to protect them. If Maximilian was still intent on these negotiations, Louis declared that he too would send an ambassador to join Lang in these discussions at Rome. The French king recalled all that he had done for the emperor and how he trusted in the Austrian's fidelity to his promises.[50]

Lest any truce be contrary to French interests, Louis enumerated his concerns. Alfonso d'Este was to retain the duchy of Ferrara as was earlier agreed upon by the pope. Louis was ready to discontinue the Pisan Council and merge

---

[49] On Maximilian's wavering stance toward the Pisan Council, see: HERGENROETHER - LECLERCQ VIII/1, 292—97, 324, 330; MINNICH, The 'Protestatio' of Alberto Pio (1513), in: Società, politica e cultura a Carpi ai tempi di Alberto III Pio: Atti del Convegno Internazionale (Carpi, 19—21 maggio 1978), ed. R. AVESANI et al. (= Medioevo e umanesimo 46) Padova 1981, 268—76; and FRAKNÓI, Ungarn und die Liga 85—86, 91—96.

In RENAUDET, some of Maximilian's attitudes toward the Pisan Council can be traced: he supported it (417, 537, 541), hesitant toward it (521), possibility of participating in person (494, 624), his efforts to get German bishops to attend (541, 585—86, 610—11), talk of sending Lang, Georg von Neideck of Trent, Nogarola, and Faella (416—17, 420, 444, 451, 623), his ambassador to France Andrea del Burgo came to Milan but quickly left (563) or came without a mandate (628).

For the appointment of Pigello Portinari and Girolamo Nogarola as imperial procurators to the Council, but failure of the Emperor to send them, see the letters of Pigello Portinari to Jakob de Bannissis, Trient, 2 January 1512 and of Girolamo Nogarola to Maximilian, Trient, 8 January 1512, in: Maximiliana 36 [sic] III, fol. 2r and 26 III fol. 14r respectively. On Portinari, see: R. DE ROOVER, The Rise and Decline of the Medici Bank 1397—1494, New York 1963, passim and genealogical chart on 387, and R. D. JONES, Francesco Vettori: Florentine Citizen and Medici Servant, London 1972, 19—20, 23.

[50] For Louis' arguments, see the letter of Andrea del Burgo to Maximilian, Blois, 14 March 1512, in Maximiliana, 26, IV, fols. 66v—67r; for Louis' appeal to gratitude and intention to send an ambassador to Rome, see the letter of Paolo da Lodi to N. N., Blois, 3 February 1512, Ibid. fols. 7v—8r.

it with the upcoming Lateran Council in a way that would be very acceptable to Julius. The Pisan cardinals were to be restored and some reform of the Church undertaken. On these points, Louis felt that he, Maximilian, Julius, Fernando, and others could readily agree. However, one significant difficulty remained.[51]

Louis insisted that the Bentivogli retain power in Bologna. Their replacement by direct papal rule was seen as placing "a sword into the furiously angry hand" of Julius, as a threat to French interests in Italy, especially in the Duchy of Milan, as harmful to the emperor and helpful to the Venetians. The French king insisted that he did not want Bologna for himself, for it belonged to the Church. Instead, let Bologna return to its earlier status under a joint Bentivogli lordship and papal legation as was the case under Julius' predecessors and as was confirmed initially by him with bulls and privileges. If Maximilian were to secure the principle of a return to the former condition as the determining factor in these negotiations, he would thereby also recover his territories lost to Venice.[52]

The French king was anxious to protect his interests. He not only explained his concerns to the imperial representative, but decided to send a special embassy to Maximilian consisting of the count of Guise and Claude de Seyssel. While protesting his enduring trust in Maximilian and his preference for the emperor, rather than anyone else, as the mediator of a peace with Julius, Louis sought to bind the Emperor's hands. He wanted Maximilian to promise in secret letters patent to be guided in these negotiations by French concerns, especially those regarding Bologna — a provision which the imperial representative at the French court suspected of being a ploy for assuring the failure of these negotiations. Meanwhile, Louis was quietly sending out his own peace feelers through the Hungarian cardinal then in Rome, Tamás Erdödi Bakócz.[53]

---

[51] Letter of Andrea to Maximilian, Ibid. fol. 67r—v.

[52] Ibid. fol. 67v: *obtineatur hunc punctum quod papa habeat Bononiam tanquam gladium in manu furiosi.*

[53] For the conversation with Andrea, desire for letters patent, and intent to send an ambassador to Maximilian, see Ibid. fols. 66v—67v; for the plan to send the *Dominus de la Guiza* who knew no Latin together with the skilled Latinist and diplomat, Claude de Seyssel, to Maximilian to work out the terms of a peace, see the letters of Andrea dal Burgo to Maximilian, Blois, 27 March and 2 April 1512 in Maximiliana, 26, V, fol. 46r and 27, I, fols. 9v—10r respectively. The lord of Guise was probably Pierre de Rohan-Guéménée (d. 22. IV. 1513) who had served on a previous embassy to Maximilian and was now emerging from the shadow of an earlier judgment against him for treason. The county of Guise was one of his numerous territories. On Rohan, see M. A. R. DE MAULDE-LA CLAVIÈRE, Procédures politiques du regne de Louis XII in: Collection de documents inédits sur l'histoire de France. Première Série: Histoire, Paris 1885, lxxxii n. 2, ci, cxxv n. 3, cxxvii, 697, 1173 n. (5). Claude of Lorraine, count of Aumale, did not become duke of Guise until 1527 — see L. BATIFFOL, The Century of the Renaissance, trans. E. F. BUCKLEY, New York 1925, 131. On Bakócz as peacemaker, see the letter of Andrea dal Burgo to Maximilian, Blois, 2 April 1512, in Maximiliana, 27, I, fol. 12r.

Andrea dal Burgo's suspicion that Louis' insistence on a Bentivogli Bologna was a ploy to sabotage the negotiations was not without grounds. In earlier negotiations the French king had agreed to their exile but retention of private property. And in the negotiations following the fall of Ravenna, he quickly returned to this earlier position. Paolo da Lodi, however, felt Louis' stand on a Bentivogli

If Louis was not aggressively seeking a peace settlement in the first months of 1512, neither was Julius. Having formed the "Holy League" against France, the pope sought to activate its military provisions. The combined papal Spanish forces engaged in attacks on Ferrarese and Bolognese territories, but were unable to dislodge the d'Este duke or the Bentivogli. The Venetians were no more successful, losing Brescia soon after regaining it. Julius hoped for better results on other fronts. The Swiss were to attack the French in Milan, Fernando to demolish Louis' Navarrese allies, and Henry VIII to attack France itself. As an incentive to the English king, Julius issued on 15 March 1512 a brief bestowing on Henry and his heirs the title "Most Christian king of France" together with the enjoyment of the rights of that kingdom. This transfer from Louis "the son of iniquity and of ingratitude and the nourisher of heretical depravity" to Henry on whom "not unworthily the crown of justice was placed by God" was to be effected if God granted Henry victory over Louis. Until that day, this papal brief was not to be published.[54] How seriously Julius was pursuing a peaceful solution to the conflict is surely open to question.

Early April seemed to mark a turning point in these negotiations. On 9 April 1512 Julius finally succeeded in arranging a truce between the Empire and Venice to last until January of 1513, thus weakening the emperor's dependence on his French alliance. Two days later Gaston de Foix at the head of a French army and assisted by the devastating artillery of Alfonso d'Este routed the combined papal-Spanish forces outside Ravenna. Ten thousand died, many were wounded, and the list of the prisoners included Giovanni de'Medici, the cardinal legate to the now defeated army. Unfortunately for the French, they lost in the battle their commander de Foix — but this loss was not known at first by the panicky papal forces. Fearful of a French march on Rome, the

---

lordship was sincere — see his letter to Andrea dal Burgo, Blois, 6 February 1512, in Maximiliana, 26 IV fol. 18r; that Louis' intent was not peace but sowing discord among the pope's allies by proposing vague and unacceptable terms yet yielding to Julius on the questions of Bologna and the council is asserted by TERRATEIG I 285 and 304.

On Bakócz's initial peace negotiations, see the letter of Andrea dal Burgo to Maximilian, Blois, 2 April 1512, in Maximiliana, 27, I, fol. 12r and V. FRAKNÓI, Erdödi Bakócz Tamás Élete, Budapest 1889, 122—25. He arrived in Rome on 27 January 1512 — see SANUTO XIII 445. By early February he discussed with Julius the terms of an imperial-Venetian peace — see Ibid., 470 and urged him to come to a settlement with France by giving up his attempts to regain Bologna which he will never achieve — see Ibid., 490. By early March he was joined by Guibé in the effort to fashion a general peace so that Christians would be united in their defense against the Turks — see Ibid. XIV 24.

[54] On Julius' military efforts and hopes, see BORSCH, Julius II 237—44; GUICCIARDINI X, viii—xi, ed. PANIGADA III, 146—75; TERRATEIG I, 284—86; PASTOR VI, 396—99.

On the transferral of the French title and rights to the English king, see: the brief of Julius to Henry, Rome, 15 March 1512 in ASV, A. A., Arm. I—XVIII, nr. 4063; the report of Matteo Strozzi to the Dieci di Balìa, Rome, 10 December 1512, BAV, Vat. Lat. 6232, fol. 61v; and the study of A. FERRAJOLI, Un breve inedito per la investitura del regno di Francia ad Enrico VIII d'Inghilterra, in: Archivio della Reale Società Romana di Storia Patria, 19 (1896) 425—31 and GUICCIARDINI XI, viii, ed. PANIGADA III 256.

cardinals importuned the pope to make peace. His situation at that moment left him few other options. For his part Louis wanted to avail himself of his temporary military advantage to make a favorable settlement. He therefore secretly dispatched to Rome as his peace-maker the brother of the Ligurian cardinal-archbishop of Tour, Fabrizio del Caretto, lord of Finale in Liguria, a high-ranking member of the Knights of St. John of Jerusalem and Rhodes, and a skillful diplomat. On his arrival in Italy he was given as his papal counter-parts in the negotiations two cardinals: Tamás Bakócz, archbishop of Gran, primate of Hungary and friend of France and Venice, and Robert Guibé, papal administrator of the diocese of Albi, loyal Breton supporter of the papacy to the point of losing all his French revenues, and widely recognized promoter of peace. These negotiators reached agreement on almost all of the major issues.[55]

The most difficult issue was Bologna. While Louis was willing to see it restored to the Papal States, *pleno jure*, he preferred a return to former arrangements which would have kept the government of the city in the hands of his allies, the Bentivogli. Papal opposition to this family must have been such that some thought the Bentivogli would not only be expelled from the city but also have their property confiscated. The terms agreed upon by the negotiators were that the Bentivogli would recover their private goods in Bologna, but be required to live in exile at least one-hundred miles distance from the city.[56]

An easier settlement was worked out for Louis' other lay ally the d'Estes. The French king wanted Alfonso absolved of ecclesiastical censures and restored to his ducal title, rights, and privileges. For his part, the pope insisted on an acknowledgement of his suzerainty, a fulfillment of feudal obligations, and a restoration of territories. The negotiators agreed to the absolution and reintegration of Alfonso to his former position, but he was to accept over Ferrara a joint-dominion with the Holy See and restore to it all the lands he had received from it earlier in Romagna up to the Po River, especially the border towns of Lugo and Bagnacavallo to the west of Ravenna. The castelli of Cento and Pieve to the north of Bologna given to Alfonso by Alexander VI as part of his wife's dowry were to be detached from his duchy of Ferrara and restored to the bish-

---

[55] On the imperial-Venetian truce, see HERGENROETHER - LECLERCQ VIII/1, 337, on the emperor's need to discuss this truce first with his councillors and the princes, and on the complaints of the French ambassador that the emperor was still obligated by the treaties of Cambrai and Blois and could not treat anything else with the Venetians apart from the French, see the letters of Maximilian to Andrea dal Burgo, Trier, 4 May 1512, in Maximiliana 27 II fols. 11r—12r, 19r; for the emperor's claim that the truce had been concluded without his consent, see GUICCIARDINI X, xv, ed. PANIGADA III, 199; for the battle of Ravenna and its consequences, see: HERGENROETHER - LECLERCQ VIII/1, 537—39; PASTOR VI, 399—404, GUICCIARDINI X, xii—xv, ed. PANIGADA III 175—202, and RAINALDI, 1512, nrs. 22—23; for a list of prisoners taken, see the Nota de li capitani morti e presi nel conflicto facto fra Francesi et Spagnoli, in Maximiliana, 26, III, fol. 66r; on the negotiators, see RAINALDI, 1512, nrs. 23—24, RENAUDET 664—65 n. 140, TERRATEIG I 304, FRAKNÓI, Bakócz, 125—28; and GUICCIARDINI X, xiv, ed. PANIGADA III 197; for Louis' initial proposals, see Ibid.

[56] RAINALDI, 1512, nr. 23, RENAUDET 665, 674; and SANUTO XIV 189.

The Healing of the Pisan Schism (1511—13)

opric of Bologna. The feudal military tribute and the former annual tax of 4,000 ducats were also to be paid in due time. Because the papacy claimed an exclusive right in its territory to manufacture salt in the marshes of Cervia, he was to desist from its production in the lagoons of Comacchio, even though he had claimed that his salt-bearing areas were in imperial territory and hence not subject to the papal ban.[57]

On the question of the schismatic cardinals agreement was reached with some difficulty. Louis wanted the cardinals readmitted to the pope's favor and restored completely to their former positions so that they would not be inferior to all the other cardinals in their grade and honor. Julius recoiled at this proposal. Such a restoration without some fitting expiation would give a terrible example to posterity of unpunished rebellion against papal authority involving an assertion of the superiority of councils and the convocation of one contrary to the wishes of the pope. Since Julius was reluctant to agree formally to such a restoration, he promised, instead, to be bound by the decision of the college of cardinals in this regard. Many members of the college worked out with Julius a procedure whereby the repentant schismatics would not be simply restored, but recreated cardinals. This second promotion could be interpreted as confirming the justice of their earlier deprivation.[58]

Louis' role in the demise of the Pisan Council was to be significant. In order to annul this assembly and its acts, the king was to divorce himself completely from its proceedings, to forbid any of his subjects who were prelates to adhere to it or support it by their presence and writings, and to declare null and void whatever it had enacted. Those who formerly participated in this council were to give their allegiance to the Lateran Council in Rome and seek to achieve through it the good of the Church. Their restoration to their former church dignities was initially requested by the king, but apparently was not included in the compromise proposal.[59]

The last issue to be agreed upon by the negotiators was one specifically demanded by some of the cardinals in Rome. They wanted Louis to give them the possession of those benefices in France conferred on them by the pope.[60]

The release of cardinal Giovanni dei Medici, the cardinal legate captured at Ravenna, was also demanded by Rome but apparently not made a formal article of this agreement. Julius threatened Louis with excommunication and deprivation of his kingdom if he did not release him. At the request of the college of cardinals he delayed implementing this monitorium until Louis re-

---

[57] Ibid.; on the restoration of Cento and le Pieve to the bishopric of Bologna, see SANUTO XIV 404 and GUICCIARDINI IX, vi, ed. PANIGADA III 27.
[58] RAINALDI, 1512, nrs. 23—24; RENAUDET 665, 673 n. 151; SANUTO XIV 189.
[59] RAINALDI, 1512, nr. 23; RENAUDET 665, 673—74; GODEFROY, Lettres de Louis, IV 249; GUICCIARDINI X, xiv, ed. PANIGADA III 197.
[60] RENAUDET 674.

sponded to a letter the college wrote him in its own name requesting the same. Cardinal dei Medici's subsequent escape rendered meaningless this demand.[61]

For a while hopes ran high that this set of negotiations might finally bring peace. On April 20th Julius signed a draft of the agreed upon articles and promised the cardinals to ratify them formally if they were confirmed by Louis. On the following day this document and a letter of the pope were sent on their way to France, being entrusted to a delegation composed of the secretaries of cardinals Guibé and Bakócz (the Hungarian's was a Venetian named Francesco Marsupina), and a M. de Clermont who had been kept as hostage in Rome since the release from the Castel Sant'Angelo of his brother François, the cardinal-archbishop of Auch. Once in France the dispatches were handed over to Angelo Leonini, the apostolic nuncio at the royal court, and to cardinal Carlo Caretto who had been sent from Genoa to France to help negotiate the peace. Although commissioned to secure the king's approval, they were not empowered to conclude the agreement.[62]

Louis signed most of the articles sent to him, but others he found difficult to accept, especially those seen as an affront to his honor. Having given his royal protection to Alfonso, the Bentivogli, and the Pisan cardinals, he sought to minimize the penalties they might have to pay for having taken his side. He thus asked that Alfonso be restored to the duchy of Ferrara with all his censures and penalties removed. The duke's supporters were to have their goods returned. On the question of Bologna, Louis suggested that it be placed in the hands of Bakócz who would decide its fate. The French king also proposed that the Pisan cardinals have their case heard by the council instead of the college of cardinals or that these deprived prelates be simply restored to their dignities and benefices and allowed to reside wherever they wished. And finally, Louis stated his willingness to aid the Papal States in all its military needs, but he expected the pope to be similarly obligated toward France. He did not want such a mutual defense pact, however, to include Fernando of Aragon. These minor emendations in the articles signed by Julius were within the range of

---

[61] RENAUDET 673—74 n. 151; SANUTO XIV 294, 317. That Julius threatened Louis with excommunication and deprivation of his kingdom implies that the French king was not as yet excommunicated for his support of Alfonso d'Este, for his occupation of papal territory in contravention of *In Coena Domini*, or for his backing of the Pisan Council, and that the pope's brief transferring the French crown to Henry VIII had not been promulgated. DE GRASSI claims that Julius did excommunicate Louis at a consistory in June of 1512, but no record of such a decree seems to exist — see RAINALDI, 1512, nr. 62 and MANSI's footnote 1 to that section and also GUICCIARDINI X, xv, ed. PANIGADA III 202. For the 17 April 1511 version of *In Coena Domini* which inserts an explicit mention of the excommunication of Alfonso d'Este and of any one who helps him no matter what his status or condition, even pontifical or regal, see Reg. Vat. 956, fol. 164r—v. The bulls *Pastor ille caelestis* of 21 July 1512 and *Exigit contumacium* of 18 February 1513 denounced Louis for offering help, counsel, and support to Alfonso d'Este and the schismatic cardinals — see PRADERA 411, 413, 417.

[62] GUICCIARDINI X, xiv, ed. PANIGADA III 197; RAINALDI, 1512, nr. 24; RENAUDET 664—65 n. 140, 673, 676—77; SANUTO XIII 286; TERRATEIG I 304; and the letter of Jean le Veau to Marguerite of Austria, Blois, 3 December 1511, in: LE GLAY, Négociations I 459—60.

The Healing of the Pisan Schism (1511—13)

earlier agreements. The status of Bologna, however, was left less clear, but was not meant to become an obstacle to a settlement — indeed, Louis was ready to make the changes necessary for peace. In the hope of facilitating agreement in what seemed the approaching final stage of the negotiations, Louis tried to enlist the assistance of the Florentine government, and he empowered Geoffrey Carles, the president of the Parlement of Grenoble whom he dispatched to Florence to be nearer Rome, to conclude a final agreement in his name. Louis also sent a Genoese knight named Giannotto, the secretary of Leonini, to Rome to ask the pope to grant Leonini and Caretto authority to finalize the peace in France should Julius not want to call Carles from Florence.[63]

External factors of political alliances and of military might, rather than the specific provisions of an agreement, determined the fate of the negotiations. The mutual fears of Louis and Julius had led them to adopt conciliatory positions. The costly French victory at Ravenna not only left Louis' forces in Italy greatly debilitated, but seemed to invite France's neighbors to attack its ally Navarre and its weakened frontier defenses in Flanders and along the Pyrennes. For his part Julius feared that with the destruction of the papal and Spanish armies at Ravenna, the path lay wide open for an assault on Rome. If nothing else, peace negotiations would hopefully put a halt to French advances. Despite the earnest effort of the Spanish ambassadors at the papal court to sabotage the negotiations lest France be left the dominate power in Italy, Julius went forward with the peace-making process.[64]

In late April peace had seemed near at hand. But then Giulio dei Medici, a knight of St. John and emissary of his cousin, cardinal Giovanni who was still a prisoner of the French in Milan, arrived in Rome to report that the schismatic cardinals might be willing to abandon their Pisan Council and adhere to the pope and participate in his council at the Lateran, provided he pardoned them and the princes of Christendom who gave them protection. Indeed, many were

---

[63] For Louis' proposed emendations, see: TERRATEIG I 304—05; the letter of Antonio Strozzi to the Signori (The Standard-bearer of Justice and Priors of Liberty), Rome, 2 June 1512 in: A S Firenze, Signori, Carteggi, Serie: Responsive originale, Filza cartacea 33 (Lettere esterne alla Signoria de 1511 e 1512), fols. 164r—65r, in his transcription of this letter on pp. 679—80, RENAUDET failed to include the *capituli* recorded on fol. 165r, and see also the letter of Carondolet to Marguerite, Rome, 19 May 1512, in DE LA BRIÈRE, Dépêches 123; on Louis' willingness to further compromise, see Ibid. fol. 164r and GUICCIARDINI X, xv, ed. PANIGADA III 200; on the negotiators, see ASV, Arch. Miscel, Acta consist. 3, fol. 37v (a payment of 24 golden ducats on 19 May 1512 to *Johannoto Januen. Caballario* sent to Rome by Leonini *super certis articulis*) and ASV, Fondo Camerale, Introitus et exitus, nr. 551, fol. 117r (a payment of 136.5 large golden florins to Johannes Curtius de Tybure *pro totidie expositis in diversis cursoribus missis per R. D. Angelum Archiepiscopum Turritanum Gubernatorem Avinionensis* under a mandate of 25 July 1512); RENAUDET 679—80; P. HAMON, Carles (Geoffroy), in: Dictionnaire de biographie française 7 (Paris 1956) 1154—55 and the older studies by LE GLAY, Négociations I, vi and by A. PIOLLET, Audience solennelle de rentrée de la cour d'appel de Grenoble du 3 novembre 1882... Étude historique sur Geoffroy Carles, Grenoble 1882.

[64] GUICCIARDINI X, xiv—xvi, XI, i, vi, ed. PANIGADA III 193—210, 244—49; SANDRET 449; RENAUDET 663, 665.

the Frenchmen who on begging pardon for their fault and promising never agan to harm the Church had received absolution from their prisoner, the cardinal. At the Lateran Council in Rome sentiment also favored peace. When cardinals Accolti, de Grassi, Vigerio, and del Monte consulted with the episcopal members of the Lateran Council on May 15th, two days prior to its second sessions, they learned that the bishops favored granting the schismatic cardinals ample time and a safe-conduct for their return to Rome. The consulting cardinals assured the bishops that Julius was of the same mind. The decree *Cum inchoatam* presented for the bishops' approval at the next sessions was not, however, conciliatory in tone or content. It reaffirmed three earlier letters of the pope nullifying the Pisan Council and imposing numerous ecclesiastical censures and penalties on its adherents. No period of grace nor safe-conduct was granted to the schismatics. While over one-hundred conciliar fathers approved this decree, one openly opposed it. The Greek bishop of Molfetta in southern Italy, Alexius Celadoni, insisted that the schismatic cardinals and prelates be first granted the opportunity to be heard before being condemned. Julius dismissed his protest as just another example of the typical Greek refusal to agree with Latins.[65] But then Julius had come to doubt the wisdom of moderation.

Julius became less and less interested in peace. Giulio dei Medici had not only brought him news of the demoralization of the schismatics, but also of the precarious military situation of the French. Their withdrawal from Romagna and then from Milan had left the position of their Bentivogli allies in Bologna untenable. Word also came from Fabrizio Colonna, a former prisoner of Alfonso d'Este, that the duke was eager to make his peace with the pope. The Spanish and Swiss were rallying their forces to expel the French completely from Italy.[66] From a political and military perspective it was not longer in Julius' interest to compromise.

The pope now worked to defeat the peace treaty. When the Florentines, responding to the request of Louis, offered their peace-making services, Julius politely thanked them for their offer but claimed he should await first the re-

[65] For Giulio de' Medici's report, see SANUTO XIV 188, 297, 317 and GUICCIARDINI X, xv, ed. PANIGADA III 202—03. On the Lateran Council, see: DE GRASSI, Diarium Concilii, ed. DYKMANS 848 : 4 q. 6 (consultation of bishops), 848 : 22 (condemnation of Pisan Council), 27—28 (vote of Celadoni and Julius' reaction); MANSI 714A—15D (reading of the bull *Cum inchoatam* and the claim it was approved unanimously); SANUTO XIV 233 (report that bishops favored assisting the return of the deprived cardinals).

[66] PASTOR VI 402—03; W. ROSCOE, The Life and Pontificate of Leo the Tenth, London ²1806, II 168—83; GUICCIARDINI X, xvi, ed. PANIGADA III 203—10; SANUTO XIV 188; RENAUDET 677, 679; TERRATEIG II 214 for the arrival of 20,000 Spanish reinforcements in Naples, of which Julius learned only after having signed the draft peace treaty, see A. CHITI, Scipione Forteguerri (il Carteromaco): Studio biografico con una raccolta di epigrammi, sonetti e lettere di lui o a lui dirette, Firenze 1902, 37 and the report in the letter of Ferry Carondelet to Marguerite d'Autriche, Rome, 19 May 1512, in: DE LA BRIÈRÈ, Dépêches de Carondelet 124. For an account of the reasons for and course of the French retreat, see the letter of Girolamo Morone to Stephen Poncher, Mortara, 21 June 1512, in: Lettere latine di Morone ed. PROMIS and MÜLLER 178—87.

The Healing of the Pisan Schism (1511—13)

sponse Louis would give to the papal delegation. The pope also instructed the Florentines not to allow Carles to come to Rome. Having pledged his willingness to abide by the articles he had signed, Julius had to find some way to be freed from the commitment. Louis unwittingly cooperated by asking for an alteration in the article on Bologna, although he insisted that he would be willing to compromise on this point. Julius claimed that in order to finalize the treaty he needed the consent of the college of cardinals. Meanwhile he worked with the Spanish cardinal Serra and the English Bainbridge to oppose its approval. Because the college, therefore, did not give its unanimous consent, Julius could claim absolution from his pledge to make peace.[67]

By a series of papal documents that summer Julius II dealt an even more serious blow to any prospects of peace with France. At the specific urgings of Fernando of Aragon and in accord with the pope's pledge to assist his allies in the Holy League with both temporal and spiritual weapons, Julius issued on July 21st a monitorium, *Et si hii qui christiani*. This document threatened with excommunication within three days of its publication all who took up arms under any pretext to assist, defend or protect heretics and schismatics. In the bull *Pastor ille caelestis* of the same date Julius identified one of these helpers of the schismatics as none other than the ally of Alfonso d'Este, Louis XII of France who had taken schismatic cardinals under his protection. Whether or not Julius proceeded formally to excommunicate Louis is unclear. In his diary the papal master of ceremonies, Paride de Grassi, reported that in June the pope had promulgated in consistory a sentence of excommunication. But de Grassi would seem to be in error, since the monitorium was not issued until a month later. The text of the decree of excommunication, if it ever existed, has yet to be found. The bull *Ad reprimendum nepharios conatus perversorum* of August 13th, reaffirmed at the third session of the Lateran Council on December 3rd, while placing France under interdict because of the actions of Louis and of French civil and ecclesiastical officials favoring the Pisan Council, does not seem to excommunicate the king. The brief of Julius to the bishop of Liège dated September 7th, however, ordered this prelate to stop favoring Louis on the grounds that the king was a schismatic and separated from the communion of the faithful. The brief does not go on to explain whether the king's status was due to a formal excommunication or the automatic result of having failed to heed the monitorium. The ambiguity of Louis' status was a problem Julius' successor Leo X would later seek to resolve.[68]

---

[67] RENAUDET 665—66, 679—80; ROSCOE II 171—72; GUICCIARDINI X, xv, ed. PANIGADA III 201—20.

[68] On Fernando's urgings and the papal pledge, see TERRATEIG I 343, II 214; for the text of *Etsi hii qui christiani*, Ibid. II 221—23; on *Pastor ille caelestis*, see Ibid. I 343, 345—47 and PRADERA, Fernando el Catolico 145, 431; on the inability of scholars to locate the decree of excommunication, see the comment of Mansi in RAINALDI, 1512, nr. 63, n. 1; on *Ad reprimendum*, see MANSI 32, 734 B—D and TERRATEIG I 347; on the brief to the bishop of Liège, see Ibid.; and on Leo's effort to resolve this ambiguity, see his constitution *Aeternae vitae claviger*, below, in Appendix V.

Julius' firm stand against Louis, involving a rejection of his peace offers and at least a threat of excommunication, proved to be the politically astute course for one intent on breaking French power in Italy. In order to protect France itself from invasion by the Aragonese and English, Louis was forced to recall his forces from Italy. This left his Italian allies vulnerable to attack by the Holy League. On June 13th Bentivogli control of Bologna ended when the city under Gonfaloniere Fantuzzi refused to mount a defense against the advancing army of the pope's nephew, Francesco Maria della Rovere. The Bentivogli were thus forced into exile, pursued by the threat of an interdict on any place which received them. Their property in Bologna was subject to confiscation and their adherents there were initially kept under Church censures and forced to pay heavy fines. Broken, the Bentivogli took refuge with their fellow outlaw in-laws in Ferrara or in Venetian territory.[69]

The rebellion of Alfonso d'Este seemed also near an end. Without the protection of the French military, the Ferrarese duke availed himself of the intercessions of Fabrizio Colonna, Jeronimo Vich, and his brother-in-law Gianfrancesco Gonzaga who paved the way for a reconciliation with the pope. Granted a safeconduct by both Julius and the Aragonese ambassador and accompanied by Fabrizio Colonna who had been taken prisoner at Ravenna but freed by Alfonso, the d'Este duke came to Rome on July 4th to beg pardon. Several days later in a public consistory of cardinals, with trembling voice and tears, he confessed his sins and errors, threw himself on the pope's mercy, and promised to accept whatever penalty was deemed fitting, even if it meant the loss of his duchy and personal property. The pope, having reminded Alfonso of his various crimes, finally granted him absolution. To celebrate the return of the prodigal son, a banquet followed.[70]

The ultimate fate of the d'Este duke was still to be determined. Julius was reluctant to reinvest Alfonso with Ferrara which had finally come under papal control. He also eyed the d'Este duchy of Modena and the city of Reggio and tried to occupy them with papal troops while Alfonso awaited in Rome a decision on his future status. The duke grew increasingly suspicious of the pope's intentions. Instead of being granted an audience to voice his concerns, Julius instructed him to plead his case before a commission composed of cardinals Vigerio, Flisco, L. G. della Rovere, del Monte, d'Aragona, and a sixth unnamed. Alfonso was informed that because he had not freed his two brothers,

---

[69] P. LITTA, Famiglie celebri italiani, Bentivoglio di Bologna, tavola V, Annibale; GUICCIARDINI X, xvi, ed. PANIGADA III 210; PASTOR VI 415 n.; G. DE CARO, Bentivoglio, Ermes, in: DBI 8 (Roma 1966) 618—19, esp. 619.

[70] LITTA, Famiglie celebri, d'Este, tavola XIII, Alfonso; PASTOR VI 419; RAINALDI, 1512, nr. 71—75; DE GRASSI, Diarium Julii, ed. DÖLLINGER III 420—21; GUICCIARDINI XI, i, ed. PANIGADA III 211—12; the date of July 16th for the public consistory and absolution is given in ASV, Arch. Miscel., Acta Consist. 3, fol. 38r, that [of July 9th by R. QUAZZA, Alfonso I d'Este, in: DBI 2 (Rome 1960) 332—37, at 335.

The Healing of the Pisan Schism (1511—13)

Giulio and Ferrante, from prison as earlier promised, his safe-conduct was nullified and he himself could be justly put into chains. Alfonso protested that they had attempted to kill him and had been condemned to incarceration as a lesser penalty. But if the pope insisted on their release, he would grant it. The cardinals also notified him of a plan not to restore him to Ferrara, but to compensate him instead with the county of Asti which enjoyed an annual income of 20,000 ducats and had recently been captured from French partisans (Massimiliano Sforza was its puppet count) by an army of the Holy League. To this proposal Alfonso objected, claiming he did not merit deprivation of Ferrara, especially since he had already been publicly absolved of his former crimes. If the pope wanted him to give up anything else, he was ready.[71]

The harsh penalties contemplated by Julius destroyed the reconciliation. When the cardinals relayed to the pope in private consistory the protests of the d'Este duke, Julius threatened to throw him in prison. Alerted to the danger, Alfonso had recourse to Fabrizio Colonna who was indebted to him for his own release after Ravenna. This Roman nobleman went to the pope to plead Alfonso's cause. When he realized that Julius was indifferent to his pleadings, Fabrizio in the early morning hours of July 19th, before Julius could act on his plans, intimidated the guards at the Lateran gate, secured Alfonso's escape from the city, and accompanied him as far as the Colonna stronghold of Marino on Lago Albano. Hidden in the suite of Prospero Colonna, Alfonso was brought to Florence and from there made his way back to Ferrara accompanied by Ludovico Ariosto. The duke quickly reassumed control of the city and its defense.[72] Made wiser by this experience, Alfonso was not inclined to seek reconciliation on terms Julius would dictate. The pope had been offered a prime opportunity to resolve one of the major outstanding differences, but had tried, instead, to exploit Alfonso's temporary weakness, only to find that he had lost in the process the prospects for peace.

The French retreat from Italy also had a detrimental effect on their council. When their troops evacuated Milan, the conciliar fathers accompanied them. These prelates stopped briefly at Asti to celebrate on June 12th the ninth session, but then continued on their way over the Alps to the safety of French soil. On July 6th the last remnants of the council gathered at Lyon to hold its tenth and final session. Never having attracted support outside the system of

---

[71] RAINALDI, 1512, nr. 76; de GRASSI, Diarium Julii, ed. DÖLLINGER III 421—22; GUICCIARDINI, XI, i, ed. PANIGADA III 212—13; on the plot of his second brother Ferrante and half brother Giulio, see QUAZZA 333—34.

[72] Ibid.; according to de Grassi (in RAINALDI, 1512, nr. 76 and in DÖLLINGER III 422—23) and according to GUICCIARDINI (XI, i, ed. PANIGADA III 213), Alfonso, once left at Marino, was blocked from returning to Ferrara by land and thus fled into Neapolitan territory and from there took a boat headed for Dalmatia. He was finally installed safely into his duchy by Prospero Colonna. But according to a letter of Ludovico Ariosto who claims to have accompanied Alfonso in his flight, the duke made his way in disguise through Umbria and Florentine territory back to Ferrara — see L. ARIOSTO, Opere Minori, ed. C. SEGRE, Ricciardi 1954, 760—61 and QUAZZA, Alfonso I d'Este, 335.

French alliances and now confined to the orbit of France itself, the council lost any claim to ecumenicity. Even France's allies moved to support openly the rival Lateran Council. At a public consistory on August 6th three ambassadors of Hans von Oldenburg, king of Denmark, Norway, and Sweden and ally of France, announced his formal adherence to the Lateran Council and reported the intention of James IV, king of Scotland, to do the same. The French council at Lyon was without hope of foreign support. In his sermon in the cathedral of Lyon marking the council's first anniversary on November 1st, Zaccaria Ferreri lamented that of all the princes of Christendom only Louis XII had consistently adhered to and defended this council. But still unwilling to admit defeat, the council's secretary appealed to prophecies in Isaiah, the Book of Revelations, and the writings of Joachim of Flora to predict that the kings of the earth would in the end adhere to this council. Support for it, however, even in France was on the wane. Despite the levying of special taxes for the council and the appointment of four bishops to receive these subsidies, conciliar revenues proved inadequate. The proposal of cardinals Carvajal and Briçonnet to increase income by charging a fee for their expediting of benefices was, however, sharply rejected by Louis.[73] Thus, even the council's last regal mainstay no longer accorded it his untiring support.

If the French military reversals had opened up opportunities for resolving some of the outstanding issues, they also created a new obstacle to peace, the fate of the duchy of Milan. Louis XII had prided himself in having made good for the last twelve years French claims to Lombardy. In the aftermath of his army's retreat, the troops of the Holy League occupied it. The papacy, Venice, Aragon, and the Swiss Confederation each sought to hold on to the cities its troops had seized. In addition, the emperor worked to have his grandson, Charles Hapsburg, invested with this imperial fief. To prevent open warfare among the members of the Holy League over a division of the Milanese spoils, a conference was held at Mantova in mid-August. In addition to deciding to replace the pro-French Soderini government in Florence with a pro-papal Medici regime, the conference found a figure-head ruler for Milan acceptable to both the pope and the emperor. It agreed to install as duke Massimiliano Sforza the nineteen-year-old heir to the throne who had grown up as an exile in Burgundy

---

[73] Promotiones et progressus sacrosancti pisani concilii moderni indicti et incohati anno domini M.D.XI. (s.d., s.l.) notarized by Zaccaria Ferreri and Nicolaus Chalmot (in BAV, R. G. Concilii II 55 / Membr. II. 23), 42v—43v (Asti session), 43v (Lyon session), 44r—v (Sermon of Ferreri); on the Danish adherence, see DE GRASSI, Diarium Concilii, ed. DYKMANS 877: 1—7; for the financing of the council, see MANSI 35, 162D—63E and the letter of the Florentine ambassadors to the Committee of Ten Men, Roma, 31 December 1512 in BAV, Vat. Lat. 6232, fol. 72r; for the report on 9 January 1513 of Guillaume de La Marque, the procurator-general of the Grand Council of Mechelen, sent to the councils of Flanders, Lille, and Douai protesting against the conferral of benefices by the cardinals of the French council and against the provisions made by the University of Paris in accordance with the Pragmatic Sanction of Bourges, see Archives Générales du Royaume de Belgique (Brussel), Grand Conseil de Malines, nr. 143, fols. 299—303.

and Germany under the emperor's watchful eye. Prior to this decision, Louis had allowed himself an illusion. He hoped that the pope would indeed conclude a peace and help him regain Milan. He thought of sending Claude de Seyssel to work out such a settlement and even looked to the emperor for help in negotiating this peace. Any interest Maximilian may have showed in these negotiations was primarily directed at protecting his own interests. Already in April he was moving away from his French alliance. With the help of Julius he negotiated a truce with the Venetians, and even worse had recalled the German contingent in the French army at the very moment this army was most debilitated due to the terrible losses at Ravenna. By June Maximilian was ready to order the imperial vassals Florence, Siena, Lucca, Modena, and Mantova to withdraw all support for the Pisan Council and adhere to the Lateran. He was also prepared to send Lang to Rome to approve the truce with Venice, thus leaving Louis alone to confront the armies of the Republic. Far from helping the French, the emperor capitalized on their temporary weakness, negotiated favorable terms with their opponents, and sought to dominate the Milanese duchy through a Sforza puppet installed by Louis' enemies.[74] The French king was finding himself more and more isolated.

Louis lost not only Milan but also his sole significant, even if vacillating, ally, Maximilian. Suspecting that the French were no longer in a position to help him achieve his goal in Italy of regaining territories occupied by Venice, the emperor turned increasingly toward the pope for this assistance. Encouraged at Mantova to explore the possibilities of such a new alliance, Maximilian dispatched Lang to Rome. Because Julius was still anxious to have the emperor formally withdraw his support for the French council and adhere to the Lateran, Lang was welcomed into the city on November 4th with honors usually reserved for a king. As a price for the emperor's adherence, Julius agreed to support him in his struggle with the Venetians and to allow him admission to the Holy League on terms which did not require him to fight his former ally France. With great pomp this treaty was formally announced on November 25th and at the third session of the Lateran Council on December 3rd Lang officially announced the emperor's adherence. A major victory was thus registered in the papal effort to isolate Louis and his council at Lyon.[75]

---

[74] GUICCIARDINI X, xvi, XI, i—ii, ed. PANIGADA III 203—22; for an account of the French retreat from Milan, see the letter of Girolamo Morone to Étienne Poncher, Mortara, 21 June 1512 in: Lettere latine di Morone, ed. PROMIS and MÜLLER 178—87; on the Mantuan conference, Florence, and Massimiliano Sforza, see also JONES, Francesco Vettori 50—54, PASTOR VI 420—22, and P. PRODI, Relazioni diplomatiche fra il ducato di Milano e Roma sotto il duca Massimiliano Sforza (1512—1515), in: Aevum 30 (1956) 437—94, at 440—43; on Louis' illusions, see Paolo da Lodi to Maximilian, Blois, 11 July 1512 in Maximiliana 27, IV, fols. 94v—95v and his letter to Marguerite of Austria, Blois, 10 July 1512 in LE GLAY, Négociations II 511—12; on Maximilian's readiness to approve the truce, see TERRATEIG II 219.

[75] On Lang's thinking prior to his visit to Rome, see his letter to Maximilian, Modena, 11 October 1512, in Maximiliana, 28, II, fols. 50r—53v; on his visit to Rome, see the letters to

Louis strove desperately to break out of his isolation. Both he and cardinal Philip von Luxemburg wrote friendly letters to the pope at the same time Lang was negotiating the new alliance. Julius dismissed these French efforts at peace because Louis would not renounce his claims to Milan. At the third session of the Lateran Council the pope placed all of France (less Brittany) under interdict and continued his hostile attitude toward the Valois king. The queen of France, Anne of Brittany, sent in January an agent to Rome who joined with cardinal Guibé in futile efforts to work out a peace. In the hope of weakening the papal league, Louis sent to the Swiss in the opening months of 1513 a delegation headed by Claude de Seyssel and Louis de la Trémouille. In order to address the Swiss diet at Lucerne, the French were required to pay 70,000 francs and surrender the fortresses of Lugano and Locarno in Ticino. Despite a long and eloquent discourse begging an alliance of friendship and proffering a pension, the French offer was rejected in favor of a treaty with Massimiliano Sforza. The defeat of the French proposal was attributed in part to the concerted effort of the pope and emperor to prevent such an alliance. Given the vacillations and duplicity of Maximilian, Louis turned to his former enemy Venice in the hope of forging a new alliance. But before these two victims of Julian treachery could formally conclude a mutual defence treaty, the pope died on 21 February 1513.[76]

Negotiations under Leo X

With the death of Julius there were new opportunities to make peace. On learning of Julius' approaching death, Louis wrote to the cardinals in general and to select number of them in particular such as Guibé to affirm his great desire for the unity and peace of the Church and to urge them to seek the good of the Church and to work for a healing of any schism or divisions. Louis named Guibé as his official spokesman. As soon as the warrior pope died, the cardinals for their part sent a letter to the French king urging him to end the schism,

---

Marguerite of Austria from Lang, Rome, 23 November 1512, in LE GLAY, Négociations II 513—14, from Jehan Hannart, Rome, 23 November 1512, Ibid. 515—16, and from Ferry Carondelet, Rome, 14 and perhaps 20 November 1512, in de LA BRIÈRE, 128—32; on the treaty and third session, see DE GRASSI, Diarium Julii, ed. DÖLLINGER III 424—26, RAINALDI, 1512, nrs. 89—102, MANSI 32, 731D—35B, PASTOR VI 422—28, and C. O'REILLY, 'Maximus Caesar et Pontifex Maximus': Giles of Viterbo Proclaims the Alliance Between Emperor Maximilian I and Pope Julius II, in: Augustiniana 22 (1972) 80—117.

[76] GUICCIARDINI XI, vii, ed. PANIGADA III 251—52; for the French peace offensive in Rome, see the reports of Jacopo Salviati and Matteo Strozzi to the Decem Baliae, Rome, 27 November 1512, 31 December 1512, and 28 January 1513 in Vat. Lat. 6232, fols 34r—v, 72r, and 79r; on Julius' continuing hostility toward Louis, see his letter to Maximilian, Rome, 11 January 1513 in Maximiliana, 28, V, fols. 8r—v and 10r—v; on the French negotiations with the Swiss, see the letters of Johann Storch to Maximilian, Zurich, 16 February 1513 and of Maximilian to Mathias Schiner, Landau, 21 February 1513, in Maximiliana, 28, V, fols. 132r and 165r—v; on the French-Venetian negotiations, see the letter of Salviati and Strozzi to the Decem Baliae, Rome, 28 January 1513, in Vat. Lat. 6232, fol. 79r and the fuller account in GUICCIARDINI XI, vii, ix, ed. PANIGADA III, 252—54; 262—65.

II

The Healing of the Pisan Schism (1511—13)

dissolve the Pisan Council then in Lyon, and act as a good son of the Church. Included among the election capitularies they agreed upon was one obliging the new pontiff to work for a healing of the schism and a restoration of peace to Christendom.[77]

The election of Giovanni dei Medici as pope Leo X on 11 March 1513 was seen as a hopeful sign for peace. Even though his family had been expelled from Florence with French assistance some twenty years earlier and he himself had been taken prisoner by the French at the battle of Ravenna, Leo was known as a mild mannered man, temperamentally quite different from his predecessor. On the day of his coronation, March 19th, Leo officially confirmed and subscribed to the election capitularies. He was well aware that he had been elected to bring peace to Christendom and welcomed opportunities to demonstrate that this was the primary goal of his pontificate. He openly protested this desire to the imperial ambassador Alberto Pio who on reporting the conversation to Maximilian observed that far from being the ferocious lion his name Leo suggested, the new pope was more easily compared to the gentle lamb. The hope among leading Romans that Leo would be a peace-maker was manifested in various artistic representations and inscriptions which decorated the route of his triumphal procession on April 11th when he took possession of the Lateran Basilica.[78]

Alfonso d'Este of Ferrara

These ceremonies were the occasion for one of Leo's first symbolic gestures toward resolving the legacy of discord left by Julius. Cardinal Luigi d'Aragona helped prepare the way for this by arranging with Leo on the day of his election for a three-month suspension of the interdict against the cardinal's first cousin, Alfonso d'Este. Bernardo Dovizi da Bibbiena, who had been released from his captivity in Ferrara so that he could accompany his patron Giovanni dei Medici to the conclave, also interceded with the new pope to allow the duke to come to Rome to offer his obeisance. Quickly availing himself of this opportunity, the duke hurried to Rome with an embassy of some sixteen gentlemen, including members of his own family and of the Bentivogli and Ludovico Ariosto,

---

[77] Letter of Louis to College of Cardinals, from Blois, 5 March 1513, in Sanuto XVI 34—35; letter of Louis XII to an unnamed cardinal, from Blois, ca. February 1513, in: Documents relatifs au Regne de Louis XII et sa politique en Italie, ed. L. G. PELISSIER (= Notes Italienne d'Histoire de France 35) Montpellier 1912, 306—07; for the letter of the college to Louis, see ASV, Arch. Miscel., Acta consistorialia 3, fols. 40v—41r and the letter of Jean le Veau to Marguerite of Austria, Milan, 5 March 1513, in: GODEFROY, Lettres de Louis IV 61—62; for Leo's election peace capitulary, see ASV, Miscel. Arm. I, nr. 43, fol. 16v and in SANUTO XVI 84—115, esp. 109.

[78] Leonis X. Pontificis Maximi Regesta, ed. J. HERGENROETHER, Freiburg i. Br. 1884, I 2—3; ROSCOE V 203, 211, App. 70; PASTOR VII 27 43; letter of Francesco Vettori to the Dieci di Balia, Rome, 6 September 1513, in: ASF, Carte Responsive, nr. 117, fol. 154r; Letter of Alberto Pio to Maximilian, Rome, March 1513, in: GODEFROY, Lettres de Louis IV, 77, 79.

to pay homage. He arrived on April 4th, took up residence in the home of his cousin, and soon obtained a papal audience. The desires of both Leo and Alfonso to find a peaceful resolution of the conflict produced results. On April 10th Leo absolved him for the present in so far as necessary from the bonds of excommunication, granted him a safe-conduct, and invited him to participate in the festivities surrounding his taking possession of the Lateran. The following day, before setting out for the Lateran, Leo in a ceremony in the Sistine Chapel reinstated Alfonso d'Este as Gonfaloniere of the Church, with the proviso that this act did not prejudice the rights of the Church over this vassal. Robed in a ducal mantle of office, Alfonso helped Leo mount his horse and then joined in the procession which escorted the new bishop of Rome to his cathedral church.[79]

To resolve the outstanding issues involving Alfonso, Leo announced in consistory the establishment of a commission of seven cardinals. Accounts agree on the names of six: Riario, Farnese, Soderini, Bakòcz, Flisco, and Castellesi. But the seventh is variously identified as d'Aragona, Gonzaga, or Vigerio. Of these cardinals, Flisco, Vigerio, and d'Aragona had sat on a similar commission a year earlier. The Leonine commission met during the month of April and tried to work out what should constitute the privileges of the d'Este family. By April 22nd the cardinals had agreed that the annual tribute for Ferrara be set at 25,000 ducats, the production of salt at Comacchio cease, the fate of Cento and la Pieve be decided by a special commission of cardinals, and the question of d'Este control over that portion of the duchy of Modena the duke presently occupied be left to the emperor on whom this fief depended. No consensus was reached on the status of the city of Reggio. For the next four months Alfonso, as papal vassal in Ferrara, was to be allowed to enjoy his offices and prerogatives. A final settlement could be worked out when his brother, cardinal Ippolito, came to Rome. While these proposed terms for reconciliation could not be considered generous from the duke's perspective, they did at least signal the end of open conflict.[80]

The pope promptly acted to formalize some of the progress made toward a resolution of the Ferrara conflict. In a letter dated April 22nd, Leo granted to Alfonso, to members of his household, and to his domestic servants an absolution from all bonds of excommunication, interdict, and other penalties incurred from violation of the monitoria of his predecessor, Julius II. No stipulations as to conditions and time restrictions were attached to this absolution. In a sepa-

---

[79] On Luigi d'Aragona's and Bernardo Dovizi's efforts on behalf of Alfonso, see SANUTO XVI 58, 148, 152, 678 and SEMPER 280—81; for the embassy, see QUAZZA 335 and SANUTO XVI 58, 148, 152; on the grant to Alfonso of a temporary absolution, see ASV, Arm. XLIV, vol. 5, fol. 6r; for the ceremony of reinstatement, see SANUTO XVI 682; on Alfonso in the procession, see RAINALDI, 1513, nr. 20 and PASTOR VII 36, 38.

[80] On the commission of cardinals, see SANUTO XVI 148, 153, 678; on its workings and recommendations, see Ibid. 179, 188, 678.

rate document, Leo suspended, this time for four months, the interdict Julius had imposed on all the territory subject to Alfonso. During this period of suspension, Alfonso could be called duke of Ferrara and enjoy all of the traditional rights and privileges attached to this title. On the evening of April 22nd Alfonso dined with Leo, and on the following day departed for Ferrara.[81]

Despite this progress, difficulties remained. Alfonso, having been formally deprived of his Ferrarese duchy by Julius, had not as yet been reinstated by Leo. This Medici pope was suspected of eyeing a number of d'Este territories, perhaps even Ferrara, which could be united into a new principality for his brother Giuliano. Leo pressured Alfonso to release from prison members of the pro-papal Fantuzzi family of Bologna and to supply the Spanish viceroy with cannons for the defense of Verona. A full reconciliation was yet to be worked out.[82]

Over the summer further steps were taken toward a resolution. At the end of July cardinal Ippolito d'Este arrived in Rome. In the hope of facilitating a reconciliation of his brother with the pope, Ippolito as regent during the duke's absence in Rome had ordered the destruction of the salt mines in Comacchio. What success the cardinal enjoyed over the summer in negotiating a full solution is not known, but in mid-August a papal brief renewed for six months an earlier suspension of the Julian interdict. The duke also regained the Garfagnana portion of his Modenese duchy when in accordance with Leo's wishes, the representative of Lucca which had seized this mountainous territory during the war came to Rome to restore it.[83]

Not until the following year was a fuller resolution of the issues concluded. On 12 April 1514 Leo granted to cardinal Ippolito and members of his household full absolution from any penalties they may have incurred for having helped Alfonso during his struggle with Julius. After detailed negotiations with this cardinal, Leo issued on June 14th a much revised secret brief which absolved Alfonso of his penalties and censures and restored him to his former honors and grade. He was reinstated as duke of Ferrara and as ruler of Cento and la Pieve, and the annual tribute for these was fixed at the reduced levels set by his father-in-law, Alexander VI. Leo also took him and his successors and state under

---

[81] For the papal absolutions, see ASV, Arm. XLIV, vol. 5, fols. 8r (Alfonso, household, and domestics), 33r—v (suspension of interdict for four months), 35r (absolution of Lucrezia, his wife); on the dinner and departure, see SANUTO XVI 188.

[82] On Leo's ambitions for Giuliano at the d'Estes' expense, see SANUTO XVII 21, 342, and QUAZZA, 335; on his later plans to give Ferrara to his nephew Lorenzo, see AS Florence, Mediceo Avanti Principato 113, nr. 94 — letter of cardinal Giulio dei Medici to Lorenzo dei Medici, Rome, 3 March 1516; on his request of favors from Alfonso, see HERGENROETHER, Regesta I 177, 195, nrs. 3030, 3333.

[83] On the cardinal's visit to Rome, see SANUTO XVI 419, 533, 548; on the restoration of Garfagnana, Ibid., 566; on the destruction of the salt works, see GILBERT, The Pope, His Banker 90; for the extension of the suspension, see SANUTO XVI 663.

papal protection and promised to include him in a future alliance and to restore to him within five month Reggio-Emilia. On June 15th the cardinal agreed to cede to the Apostolic Camera the duke's rights to manufacture salt in Comacchio, an imperial fief. Tensions mounted when on 17 June 1514 Leo made a bid to acquire Modena outright from the emperor by the payment of 40,000 golden ducats. Given his imperial and papal overlords' seeming disregard of some of his family's traditional rights, Alfonso once again looked to France for a protector. The duke's trust in the new king there, Francis I, seemed at first well placed for the young king pressured Leo to return Reggio and Modena to Alfonso. But d'Este interests soon became a casualty of big power politics. If Leo had succeeded in resolving the outstanding differences between Alfonso and his predecessor, he also left to his successor a new but similar set of problems regarding the relations between Rome and Ferrara.[84]

The Bentivogli of Bologna

For Alfonso's relatives and fellow banned papal vassals, the Bentivogli of Bologna, the election of Leo X had also raised hopes of reconciliation with the papacy and of a restoration of their property and lordship. The new pope, whose father had been an ally and friend of this Bolognese family, granted Alfonso permission to include in the embassy of homage from Ferrara his brothers-in-law, Annibale II, head of the Bentivogli in exile, Antongaleazzo the cleric, and Ermes the soldier. In Rome they were courteously received by the Medici pope. Leo, however, while reported to favor a return of their family property and revenues, was not inclined to restore their ancestral lordship nor to allow them to reside in Bologna or its neighboring territory. To a special commission of seven cardinals, which included the Venetians Grimani and Cornaro, the pope entrusted the case of the Bentivogli. The terms of a settlement were quickly worked out.[85]

On 25 May 1513 Leo published his decisions in a document which basically restipulated the terms of settlement tentatively agreed upon a year earlier by

---

[84] On the absolution offered Ippolyto see ASV, Arm. XL, vol. 2, fol. 105r; on the exchange of salt manufacturing rights for Reggio, see QUAZZA 335; on the other settlements of 1514, see MORONE, Dizionario 24, 123; on Leo's bid for Modena and French opposition to it, see QUAZZA 335—36 and the letter of Lang to Maximilian, Rome, 10 April 1514, in: Maximiliana, 31, II, fol. 34r; for the papal-Ferrarese negotiations and the papal brief, see: ASF, Manoscritti Torrigiani, Filza III, Inserta XIV Leone X e Ferrara, nrs. 1—10; L. A. MURATORI, Delle antichità Estensi ed Italiane tratto, 2 vols., Modena 1717—40, II 317—18; and Appendices XII—XV of this article; and if Leo sought to regain Ferrara, it was primarily for the good of the Church (so claimed Pio) and not for the advantage of his own family; also, whether Comacchio was an imperial fief or pertained to the Church and the Ravennati was disputed — see SEMPER 260, 279, 281—85, 290, 298, 305, and 307.

[85] G. DE CARO, Bentivoglio, Annibale, 595—600, esp. 598—99, Bentivoglio, Antongaleazzo, 600—02, esp. 602, Bentivoglio, Ercole, 612—14, esp. 613, and Bentivoglio, Ermes, 618—19, esp. 619, in: DBI 8 (Rome 1966); SANUTO XVI 58, 148, 152, 179.

The Healing of the Pisan Schism (1511—13)

Julius II and Louis XII. The Bentivogli brothers were absolved of all their crimes and sins against the Church, freed from ecclesiastical censures and penalties, and granted the restoration of that personal property their parents possessed before 10 October 1506, the date of the bull by which Julius II had declared their father Giovanni II (1443—1508) and them rebels of the Church. The adherents of their faction were absolved of ecclesiastical censures, restored to their secular goods, and allowed to return to Bologna. The prospect was held out to the Bentivogli that they too might some day return to their homes, provided they proved themselves worthy of trust.[86]

Leo took steps to implement the property provisions of this settlement. To facilitate a restoration of the family's private goods, he commissioned on June 13th Andrea Griffi to see that the brothers recovered all their properties, once the legitimate claims of their creditors had been settled from their liquid assets. On June 9th, Leo ordered the magistrates of Bologna to give speedy justice to the Bentivogli by eliminating all legal subterfuges and appeals. A month later a papal brief threatened with a ban all those who still retained the property of the Bentivogli and that of other political exiles. When those who had taken possession of these goods in virtue of the papal bull of 1506 excommunicating the rebellious Bentivogli appealed their cases directly to the Roman curia and Rota, a solution was found in compensating them for what was returned to the Bentivogli. The restored property included not only mobile goods and war spoils, but also agricultural lands and even the lucrative office of collector of taxes on the Bolognese Jewish community. This process of restoration took over a year to implement.[87]

Leo was not ready, however, to welcome the Bentivogli back into Bologna. From Julius II he inherited a ruling Council of Forty composed of many republicans hostile to a restoration of a Bentivogli lordship. On the election of Leo, this government sent to Rome to pay homage an embassy of six leading citizens, some of whom were known opponents to a return of the old signoria.

---

[86] HERGENROETHER, Regesta I 165, nr. 2833 gives only a summary of this brief and dates it 25 May 1513, SANUTO XVI 337—39 publishes its text and cites a date of 21 May 1513, see also Ibid. 385; on the 1510 bull of excommunication, see DE CARO, Bentivoglio, Giovanni, 598.

[87] On Gritti's commission, see ASV, Arm. XXXIX, vol. 30, fols. 41v—42v and HERGENROETHER, Regesta I 184, nr. 3155, for the letter to the magistrates to eliminate subterfuges, see Ibid. 210, nr. 3559; for the papal letter putting under a ban all those still retaining the Bentivogli goods, see SANUTO XVI, 608; on reimbursing those who made restitution, see the letter of Leo to Achille de Grassi, Rome, 11 May 1514 in ASV, Arm. XXXIX, vol. 30, fols. 310v—11v, on the restoration of the office of tax collector, see the letter of Leo to Andrea Griffi, Rome, 5 November 1513, Ibid, fol. 78r—v; on the restoration of spoils and fields, see the letter of Leo to Achille de Grassi, Rome, 24 May 1514, Ibid. fols. 309v—310r; for the restoration of goods to Lorenzo Battista Malvetti, see the letter of Leo dated 25 June 1513 in HERGENROETHER, Regesta I 165, nr. 2834; for an instance of cardinal de Grassi presiding over a transfer of land and its revenues earned since 1506 involving Giovanni Bentivoglio and dated 12 January 1515, see Archivio di Stato-Roma, Archivio del Collegio dei Notari Capitolini, vol. 1914 (Inghirami), fol. 265r—v.

Leo apparently consulted with them on the composition of a new government for Bologna. On June 22nd he announced his decision to constitute a new Council of Forty and appoint to it men known for their loyalty, virtue, and family status. After waiting a month to learn if they were willing to serve on it, the pope published a document on July 29 which formally replaced the Julian council with a senate of thirty-nine councillors. Among these senators were members of the Malvizzi family (bitter opponents of the Bentivogli), the Fantuzzi (who had urged them to go into exile), and Agamenon, a brother of cardinal Achille de Grassi. The only Bentivogli named, Ercole, was a cousin of the ruling family known for his steady loyalty to the papacy. The unusual number of thirty-nine senators gave rise to speculation that Annibale might eventually be named the fortieth senator. Given Leo's insistence that at least for the time being the Bentivogli brothers were not to reside in Bologna, they retired to Ferrara on leaving Rome.[88]

Opposing factions sought to disrupt this settlement. Even before the formal naming of the new senators, Leo had to defend his political reorganization of Bologna. On learning of the stealthful return of Bentivogli partisans contrary to the conditions and precautions he had established, the pope wrote to the city magistracy and council on July 25th ordering them to have these persons punished and expelled, lest for the sake of a few men the peace of the whole city be disrupted. His fears were justified. By mid-August suspicion on the part of some Bolognesi that Leo might throw his support behind the Bentivogli led to civil unrest.[89]

To end these disturbances, Leo took a number of measures. He ordered some of the leading citizens opposed to the Bentivogli to come to Rome to discuss the situation. Excuses for not coming were either rejected, accepted for the period only of the illness, or allowed provided other close members of their family came. Having heard from the Bentivogli's enemies, Leo summoned Anni-

---

[88] For the embassy to offer homage composed of Bonifatio Fantuzzi, Ercole Bentivoglio, Alessandro Pepoli, Alberto Albergati, Ovidio Bargelini, and Matteo Malvezzi, see Archivio di Stato-Firenze, Signori — Carteggi: Responsive originali, filza cartacea nr. 35, fol. 19 which is a letter of the elder consuls and the standard-bearer of justice of Bologna to the priors of liberty and standard-bearer of justice of Florence, Bologna, 14 March 1513; on the continued presence in Rome on June 24th of six Bolognese orators, see DE GRASSI, Diarium Leonis, BAV, Vat. Lat. 12275, fol. 47r; on Leo's consultation of Bolognese representatives and tentative appointment of a new Council of Forty, see his letter to the Gonfaloniere and elders of Bologna, Rome, 22 June 1513 in ASV, Arm. LXIV, vol. 5, fols. 9r and 32r and in HERGENROETHER, Regesta I 193, nr. 3313; on his replacement of the Julian Council of Forty with thirty-nine named senators, see the bull of 29 July 1513 in ASV, Reg. Vat. 999, fols. 293r—94r; on Ercole, see DE CARO, Bentivogli, Ercole, 613; on Agamenon see LITTA, Famiglie celebri, Grassi di Bologna, tav. II; on the possible appointment of Annibale to be the fortieth senator, see DE CARO, Bentivoglio, Annibale, 599 and LITTA, Famiglie celebri, Bentivoglio di Bologna, tav. V; on the Bentivogli's retirement to Ferrara, see SANUTO XVI 385.

[89] HERGENROETHER, Regesta I 266, nr. 3793 and its text published in Pietro BEMBO, Epistolarum Leonis Decimi Pont. Max. nomine scriptarum libri XVI, Lyon 1538, Bk 4, ep. 6, pp. 82—84; on the unrest in Bologna, see G. FANTUZZI, Notizie degli scrittori bolognesi, Bologna 1781—94, III 235.

bale and his son Costantino on August 28th to come immediately to Rome to clear themselves of various charges. In hope of quickly quelling the civil unrest, Leo dispatched with ample faculties and a letter of commendation dated August 19th the native-born cardinal-bishop of Bologna, Achille de Grassi. His efforts to stop attacks on the life and property of the Bentivogli partisans were in vain.[90]

The hope which Leo had held out to the Bentivogli that they might some day return to power had been a factor in the disorders. The peace of Bologna required a clear decision. The opposition of eminent citizens of Bologna to a resurrection of the Bentivogli signoria, the relative weakness yet subversive intrigues of this family and its partisans, the danger of continued civil disorders, the failure of the Bentivogli's former French allies to insist on their restoration, and the prospect of placing this important city under tighter controls from Rome — all led Leo in the end to deny the exiled lords' request to return to their native city.[91] The Bentivogli had ceased to be an obstacle to the achievement of a comprehensive peace.

The Pisan Cardinals

The death of Julius II had also provided new opportunities for reconciling the schismatic cardinals with Rome. From Lyon Sanseverino wrote to the college of cardinals asking that they await his arrival so that he could participate in the conclave. Carvajal also wrote insisting that he had been deprived of his office without just reason and wished to be judged according to the legal merits of his case. From Marseille they both took passage by ship, but arrived at Livorno too late for the conclave. The Florentine authorities at this port took them under guard to Pisa and then Florence. In response to his brother Giuliano's request for instructions, the newly elected Leo ordered that these prelates be detained in Tuscany. The pope also wrote directly to the two cardinals and sent the youthful bishop of Orvieto, Ercole Baglioni, as his personal emissary to assure them of his intention to deal leniently with them. They were told to lay aside their robes as cardinals and to remain in Florence until Leo had prepared the way for their return to Rome.[92] Thus, at the same time that the pope was working out a resolution of the conflict with Alfonso d'Este and the Bentivogli, he also sought a way for reconciling the schismatic cardinals.

---

[90] On Leo's handling of excuses, see his letters of 15 August 1513 from Rome to Ercole Marescotti (send sons instead), Lorenzo Malvetti (rejects excuse), and Angelo Cospi (come when recovered from illness) in BEMBO, Epistolarum libri XVI, Bk 4, epp. 11—13, pp. 87—88; for his summons of Annibale and Costanzo, see Ibid, ep. 14, p. 88; on Achille's mission, see FANTUZZI, Notizie III 235—36 and SANUTO XVI 663.
[91] LITTA, Famiglie celebri, Bentivoglio di Bologna, tav. V; DE CARO, Bentivoglio, Annibale, 599 and Bentivoglio, Ercole, 613.
[92] SANUTO XVI 38, 58, 72—73, 76, 153, 158; ROSCOE II 312—13.

Opinion in Rome was divided on the question of their restoration. Within a couple of days of his election, the case of the deprived cardinals had been brought up in the consistory. Guibé and Caretto of the pro-French party suggested that they be pardoned, if they requested it, and that the college write to king Louis. Bainbridge later opposed this, insisting that the process of reconciliation begin with the humiliation of him who had so harmed the Church, namely, Louis XII. The English cardinal reportedly found much support among his colleagues for this stance. His principal allies in opposing a restitution of the schismatic cardinals were the Swiss Schiner, the Catalan Remolines, the eminent canonists del Monte and de Grassi, and the vice-chancellor Sisto di Franciotti della Rovere. Fernando II of Aragon and Henry VIII of England instructed their ambassadors in Rome to join in the opposition. In support of the deprived cardinals were emperor Maximilian I and Louis XII whose ambassadors Pio and Forbin respectively interceded with Leo on their behalf. Open support also came from the Roman nobles, Giovanni Giordano Orsini and Fabrizio Colonna. In order to reach a decision on the matter, Leo met repeatedly with the cardinals in consistory.[93]

The dean of the college of cardinals, Raffaele Riario, urged a reconciliation. In his speech before the consistory he recalled how from the beginning he had personally urged the Pisan cardinals to desist from their actions and the pope to avoid taking harsh measures against them. Neither listened to the dean. Now that Julius, who harboured a deep dislike for and indignation against these cardinals, was dead and they openly sought pardon, Leo should show them mercy and forgiveness as did Christ Peter. Riario thought two factors important in the reconciliation. First, the dignity and authority of the Holy See and of the college of cardinals must be safeguarded. This required that the schismatic cardinals acknowledge their grave errors, renounce the French council and its adherents, beg pardon for their sins and errors, promise emendment, submit themselves in all things to the judgment and will of the pope, and observe the legal and customary procedures prescribed for such a reconciliation. Riario's second concern was that the pope show clemency and generosity toward the penitents. Because of their sins and errors they have already suffered condemnations and the inconveniences and labors of wanderings in exile. The more kindly their treatment now, the more grateful and loyal should be their devotion to the Holy See. While Riario favored a full return of their "pristine dignity and prior places," he questioned a restoration of their titular churches lest undesirable consequences follow. The authority by which the Holy See had legitimately and canonically deprived them of these churches should not be

---

[93] SANUTO XVI, 72—74, 179, 308; D. S. CHAMBERS, Cardinal Bainbridge in the Court of Rome 1509 to 1514, Oxford 1965, 45—47; for the congregation of cardinals meeting on 21 April 1513, see the letter of the Florentine ambassador to the Decem Baliae, Rome, 21 April 1513, in Vat. Lat. 6232, fol. 111v.

open to question. And those innocent cardinals on whom the churches were then conferred should not now be disgraced by having them taken away.[94]

After numerous discussions of the factors involved in a reconciliation of the penitent cardinals, the college in May entrusted the pope with finding a fitting resolution of the case. Leo favored a restoration of the deprived cardinals provided they accepted their deposition from office and sought a return to their former honors not by claims of justice but by the mercy of the pope. In early June the consistory agreed in effect to their absolution and committed the details of the reconciliation to three cardinals, one from each of the three orders, the cardinal deacons being represented by the Venetian Marco Cornaro.[95]

The terms by which their restoration would be effected were not easily accepted by Carvajal and Sanseverino. They had insisted that Julius had deprived them of their office without justification, a claim that could have found scholarly support in the writings of eminent contemporary canonists, notably in those of Leo's former teacher, Filippo Decio.[96] The cardinals were not, therefore, inclined to accept the papal view of their actions as erroneous and schismatic, nor were they ready to throw themselves on the mercy of the pope. Since Leo would not allow them to come to Rome unless they acknowledged their deprivation, the proud Sanseverino resorted to a dramatic gesture to register his reluctance to accept this condition. On the very day the cardinals were meeting in consistory to discuss his case, a train of carriages and some twenty mules draped with the insignia of this cardinal entered the City. Leo was extremely annoyed. He sent word to Sanseverino in Florence that unless he changed his position as to how he was to make his entry into Rome, nothing further could be done to help him. When the Pisan cardinals finally capitulated, they were granted a papal safe-conduct for the trip from Florence.[97]

Prior to their restoration to the cardinalate, Carvajal and Sanseverino were to acknowledge that they had been legitimately deprived of their offices. The cardinals hostile to their restoration wanted them to put aside their cardinal's robes and dressed as simple priests go on foot through the street of Rome. Their route was to begin at the Lateran Basilica, where their petition for pardon was to be read to the council they had openly opposed, and terminate at the Vatican, where their humiliation would end in absolution.[98]

---

[94] R. RIARIO, De restitutione, in Consistorialia, Tom. II, nr. 3, BAV, Chigi I. III. 89, fols. 72r—76r, for his ealier comments on the deprivation see fols. 57r—71r; to alleviate the problem of restoring titles, Leo thought of restoring the cardinal bishoprics of Tivoli and Veletri, see SANUTO XVI 308.
[95] SANUTO XVI 58, 308, 369.
[96] SANUTO XVI 38, 307; ULLMANN 177—93, esp. 180—88; GILMORE 74—78; P. DECIUS, Consilium CLI and Sermo de eadem materia, in: Acta primi concilii Pisani, in the section Apologie sacri Pisani concilii moderni 69—129; G. B. PICOTTI, La giovinezza di Leone X, Milano 1927, 245—46.
[97] SANUTO XVI 58, 157—58, 179, 307—08, 415; G. FRAGNITO, Carvajal, Bernardino Lopez de, in: DBI 21 (Roma 1978) 28—34, esp. 31—32; and DE GRASSI, Diarium concilii, ed. DYKMANS, nr. 989 : 7.
[98] SANUTO XVI 400.

With some minor modifications this plan was followed. On June 17th, prior to their arrival in Rome, a signed confession of their errors was read at the seventh session of the Lateran Council. In their letters patent, Carvajal and Sanseverino revoked and condemned the Pisan Council and praised and approved the Lateran which they recognized as the only legitimate and true council. For their former actions as schismatics they begged pardon. By the format of their signatures, which consisted merely of their names without their cardinalitial titles, they implicitly acknowledged their deprivation from office. With the consent of the Sacred Consistory the humiliation of their penitential walk through Rome was lessened. While they could not wear the robes of a cardinal, they were now allowed to make their entrance into the City at night, a time also chosen by the penitent Venetian ambassadors three years earlier, and the humble fashion of the cardinals' entrance being in sharp contrast to the lavish procession of Sanseverino's suite a month earlier. Under the cover of darkness on June 26th, dressed as simple priests, they made their way to the Vatican palace where they spent the night. In the morning, when on Leo's orders the master of ceremonies, de Grassi, went to see them, the penitents insisted that they be allowed to appear before the consistory robed as cardinals, not be required to walk through the halls of the Vatican palace dressed as priests, nor be called heretics and schismatics at the restoration ceremonies. Only upon learning of the harsher terms urged by their opponents did the two reluctantly agree to abide by the terms laid down by Leo. The Pope had warned that if they did not conform, they would not receive pardon and restoration. As minor concessions they were allowed to wear at the secret consistory the simple attire of archpriests and university graduates and not be called heretics in their formula of confession.[99]

The two former leaders of the Pisan Council reluctantly endured the humiliating ceremonies of confession, absolution, and reconciliation. So many persons jammed the stairs, corridors, and halls of the Vatican to view the once proud cardinals now robed as priests that there was danger that the recently frescoed Stanze of Raphael might suffer damage. When the penitents arrived at the consistory hall, de Grassi ordered them both to exchange their red birettas for ones of violet or black which they were to carry in their hands, and also to remove the hoods which covered their shoulders and necks. Then robed in simple mantles with none of the honors accorded prelates, they entered the consistorial chamber, genuflecting thrice as they made their way to the papal throne. Despite Leo's request that the full college of cardinals be present for this ceremony, three of the twenty-four members then in Rome failed to attend: Sisto di Franciotti della Rovere for reasons of chronic illness, and the Englishman

---

[99] MANSI 32, 814D; DE GRASSI, Diarium concilii, ed. DYKMANS, nrs. 985 : 12, 989: 1—3,6; SANUTO XVI 429—30; PASTOR VI 316, VII 55—56 n., 448—49.

Christopher Bainbridge and the Swiss Matthäus Schiner to register their opposition to the reconciliation.[100]

Leo initially dealt sternly with the penitents. Kneeling before the pope, Carvajal recited the text of his petition which had been earlier approved. Due to his sins, he protested his unworthiness to lift his eyes and look into Leo's face. Prostrate, he begged mercy for his innumerable sins. In response Leo assured him that the Church customarily grants mercy to all requesting it, but also imposes a fitting penance on penitents lest they ever glory in their offenses. The pope then enumerated their crimes and asked if they had not indeed done them. Once they confessed their guilt, Leo pointed out their ingratitude. How did the Roman Church which had bestowed so many favors on them come to deserve to be vilified by them and turned into a brothel? The pope demanded an answer and pressed them to suggest what their sentence should be. They were stunned into silence and on the verge of crying when he handed them a sheet, telling them first to read it quietly and decide if they were willing to swear to observe it, for only then would they be granted pardon.[101]

According to the formula given them to read, Carvajal and Sanseverino freely confessed their fault and begged pardon. They openly acknowledged that their deprivation from office by Julius II was a fitting, lawful, and just sentence against them for having adhered to the schismatic Pisan Council. Repeating their abjuration of this council read ten days earlier at the seventh session of the Lateran Council, they once again abjured and anathematized the schismatic assembly, declaring its acts null, vain, without significance, and the work of audacious, unauthorized persons. God's grace having rescued them from the cloud and errors of schism, they begged pardon for their faults from the pope and college of cardinals, swore never again to destroy the unity of the Church or disregard the obedience owed to the pope, acknowledged the legitimacy of the Lateran Council, and promised to fulfil whatever penance the pope might impose on them for their errors.[102] Throughout this formula their faults were described as errors, rather than as crimes or sins.

Despite the moderate tone of this confession, Carvajal had difficulty reading it aloud. His voice could not be clearly heard. Leo interrupted him to insist that he speak loudly enough for all the cardinals to hear. Carvajal excused his poor diction on the grounds that he was hoarse. In rejecting this explanation, the pope opined that the real reason his voice faltered was because his heart was not in his words. He reminded the Spaniard that he still had his safe-conduct and could freely return to Florence if he found the formula too burdensome and did not wish to abide by it. He was either to read it and swear to obey it or else leave. Such speech problems were not shared by his colleague Sanse-

---

[100] DE GRASSI, Diarium concilii, ed. DYKMANS, 989: 1—6, 11.
[101] Ibid. 989: 6.
[102] Ibid. 990.

verino, who recited the formula in a voice for all to hear. In the presence of the pope and cardinals and with Lorenzo de Laureliis, a notary of the apostolic camera, as witness, they both signed the sheet, and with their hands touching the Gospels, they swore to observe what was contained in the formula.[103]

Satisfied as to their full confession of guilt, humble petition for pardon, and promise of amendment, Leo proceeded to their absolution and restoration. His mitre removed, he read the sentence he had worked out in consultation with the two penitents. On the full authority of his office Leo absolved them from every bond of excommunication, censure, and penalty, and freed them from the irregularities, disqualifications, sentences of deprivation, and other liabilities contained in the tenor or precise wording of the letters of condemnation issued by his predecessor. Thus freed, the penitents were formally restored by the pope to the unity of the Church, to participation in its sacraments, and to the fellowship of the faithful. Leo also restored to them their reputations, honors, and dignities. These offices included the cardinalate, any ecclesiastical benefice formerly held and not already bestowed on another by the Holy See, and their benefices in France. As a penance Leo imposed a one-day fast each month for the rest of their lives. Should they be unable to fast, they could substitute on that day of penance a visit to two churches.[104]

Carvajal and Sanseverino were then promoted anew to the cardinalate. Their mantles were removed, and on their heads Leo placed the red birettas. De Grassi and de Laureliis clothed then in the rochet and presented them with the violet cloth skull caps. Leo gave to each not new but used hats with the wide brim of a cardinal. Rising from their knees, they recited the oath customarily taken by new cardinals and each kissed the pope on his feet, hands, and mouth. Leo then declared them to be his brothers because now they did his will, and he rejoiced in the Lord for the sheep who had been lost but were found. After Leo's speech the restored cardinals greeted each member of the sacred college with a kiss. Returning to the pope, they asked him to assign them their places in the college. Leo ordered Carvajal to reassume his position as prior of the order of cardinal-bishops, that is, second in rank behind Riario, the dean of the college. To Sanseverino the pope restored his position as dean of the cardinal-deacons. To underline their full restoration to the cardinalate, Leo asked their opinions on an appointment pending before the consistory.[105]

A number of special activities marked this reconciliation. Following the consistory that noon, Leo dined with the two prodigals to celebrate their return. As evening approached a huge escort of fifty bishops and some four-hundred horsemen accompanied the new cardinals to their residences in the City with great pomp, as if celebrating a triumph. Both on that day and on the one fol-

---

[103] Ibid. 989: 6, 990.
[104] Ibid. 989: 7, 10; 991.
[105] Ibid. 989: 7—10.

lowing the consistory, Leo wrote to the rulers of Europe informing them of the reconciliation and justifying it on the grounds that Christ never refused forgiveness to anyone who sought it. As his vicar, the pope must follow his example and teachings.[106] Leo also worked to restore to the cardinals their former titles and benefices.

Within four months Carvajal regained his titular church in Rome and suburban see of Sabina. Antonio del Monte, who had been assigned his church of Santa Croce in Gerusalemme on 24 October 1511 following Carvajal's excommunication as a schismatic, resigned it on 10 September 1513 so that it could be restored to its former occupant. A month later on October 7th, Carvajal regained the title of cardinal bishop of Sabina when Francesco Soderini exchanged it for that of the resurrected suburban see of Tivoli.[107]

Carvajal's numerous rich benefices were not easy to restore, since many had already been given to others. By granting in July of 1513 to Fedrigo de Portugal various reservations in compensation for not giving effect to his translation to Siguenza, a see which he had received after Carvajal's deprivation, Leo was able to restore this bishopric to the Spanish cardinal. Actual possession of Siguenza, however, was dependent on the good will of king Fernando. In hope of securing it, Carvajal tried to pressure the emperor into interceding for him. He also asked Maximilian to urge Leo to grant him benefices *(honori)* commensurate with the burden *(oneri)* of his recovered dignity and to restore to him a pension on the monastery of St. Blaise in the archdiocese of Salzburg. While amenable to interceding with the pope on Carvajal's behalf and to any agreement the Spanish cardinal could work out on his own with those currently in control of that monastery's revenues, Maximilian seems to have been reluctant to intervene in Spanish affairs in order to overcome Fernando's opposition to a restitution there of the cardinal's former churches and benefices. When Leo on the death of Fernando tried to restore these to Carvajal, Maximilian protested

---

[106] Ibid. 989 : 12; SANUTO XVI 429—32; PASTOR VII 448—50; ROSCOE V 241—53; HERGENROETHER, Regesta Leonis I 198 nrs. 3373—77 (27 June 1513) for the letters to the kings of France, Scotland, Portugal and England and to the Regent of Burgundy, and I 200 nr. 3410 (28 June 1513) for the letter to emperor Maximilian I printed in RAINALDI, 1513, nr. 50; for the letter to the doge of Venice (27 June 1513), see SANUTO XVI 479—81; for Leo's letter to Louis XII of 27 June 1513, see ASV, Arm. LXIV, tom. 5, fols. 11r—12v, for the pope's absolution formula see fol. 13r; emperor Maximilian praised Leo's handling of the reconciliation and urged him to continue his kindnesses toward the penitents — see the letter of Maximilian to Leo, Lille, 12 September 1513, in: Maximiliana 29, IV, fol. 61r—v; for the Milanese agent's effort to get his duke and the Swiss to rejoice in the reconciliation of Carvajal and Sanseverino who were so humbled that they begged pardon, see the letter of Marino Caracciolo to Massimiliano Sforza, Roma, 11 November 1513, in: Maximiliana 30 II, fol. 33v.

[107] For Carvajal's regaining of Santa Croce in Gerusalemme, see HERGENROETHER, Regesta Leonis I 270 nr. 4431 and the copy of Leo's letter to Carvajal, Rome, 10 September 1513 in ASV, Arm. XXXIX, vol. 30, fols. 64v—65r; for Antonio del Monte's possession of this church after Carvajal's excommunication, see EUBEL III 62b n. 4; for Soderini's obtaining his see of Sabina, see RAINALDI, 1511, nr. 36; for his resigning it to Carvajal and receiving in compensation the restored see of Tivoli, see HERGENROETHER, Regesta Leonis I 300 nr. 4883 and SANUTO XVI 308.

both against the pope's failure to consult with the new king Charles and because of the problem such an action created in Spain. The new king of France, Francis I, was also brought into the Carvajal affair. He instructed his ambassadors in Rome, Guillaume and Denys Briçonnet, to urge Leo and his nephew Lorenzo de' Medici to see that this Spanish cardinal was restored to his former benefices and secured actual possession of them. Where benefices could not be recovered, Leo apparently sought to provide him with new ones.[108]

Perhaps the clearest indication of Carvajal's restoration occured on 16 March 1517. He, who had played such a prominent role in the convocation of the Pisan Council whose president he became, now celebrated the Mass opening the twelfth session of the Lateran Council which voted to dissolve the council now that it had achieved its goals, among which was the healing of the Pisan Schism.[109]

Sanseverino also encountered difficulties in regaining his titles and benefices. His former title of cardinal deacon of S. Teodoro was assigned to Alfonso Petrucci when Sanseverino was deprived of his office. The title he used during the Pisan Schism was that of cardinal deacon of Sant' Angelo in Pescheria, a title conferred on him a year before the convocation of the Pisan synod. When Julius raised Matthias Lang, bishop of Gurk and representative of the emperor, to the cardinalate, he took the title of cardinal deacon of Sant' Angelo. Neither Petrucci nor Lang resigned their titles on Sanseverino's restoration. When he also insisted on using that of Sant' Angelo, an anamoly occurred with both Sanseverino and Lang being listed with the same title both in papal chancery documents and in the official acts of the Lateran Council. In an attempt to

---

[108] On Fernando's readiness to confer on others the benefices held in Spanish lands by the schismatic cardinals Carvajal and Borja, see TERRATEIG II 162—63, 166, 171, 178—79; on Leo's preventing Fedrigo's translation to Siguenza from taking effect and compensating him with a reservation over certain benefices in Palencia, Astorga, and Salamanca, see EUBEL III Segutin, n. 3; on his restoration to Rossano, see Ibid. III 286; on Leo's repeated efforts to give effect to this restoration, see ASV, Reg. Lat. 1193, fols. 84r—89v, 1194, fols. 127r—134r, 1197, fols. 84r—89r where Leo even threatened Fedrigo de Portugal and Juan Rodrigo Fonseca with interdict for unlawfully retaining these sees; Leo also repeatedly issued letters affirming the restoration of Carvajal to the cardinalate, titles, dignities, and benefices he held before his deprivation, e.g. Reg. Lat. 1193, fols. 44r—49v, 1194, fols. 68r—73v, 81r—86r, 1198, fols. 85r—89v; for a detailed listing of his former benefices, see Reg. Lat. 1193, fols. 62v—63r and EUBEL III 296 Segutin. n. 2; for some of the numerous benefices Carvajal acquired after his restoration, see Ibid. 4a—5b, n. 9 and ASV, Arm. XXXIX, vol. 36, fols. 96v—97r and vol. 31, fols. 136r—v; on the effort to enlist the help of Maximilian, see the correspondence: Carvajal to Maximilian, from Rome, 15 July 1513, in: Maximiliana 29, III, fol. 47r; Maximilian to Pio, from Lille, 12 September 1513, in Maximiliana 29, IV, fols. 50v—51v; Maximilian to Carvajal, from Lille, 12 September 1513, in: Maximiliana 29, IV, fol. 62v; Maximilian to Pio, s.l., s.d. (1516?), in Maximiliana 42, II, fol. 407r; on the effort to enlist French assistance, see the letters of Leo to Louis XII, from Rome, 28 May 1514, in ASV, Arm. XXXIX, vol. 30, fol. 322r—v and of Guillaume and Denys Briçonnet to Lorenzo de' Medici from Rome, 20 February 1517 in AS Firenze, Le Carte Strozziane, Prima Serie, Filza 8, fol. 174r; the efforts to restore Carvajal are also treated in PASTOR VI 367, HERGENROETHER - LECLERCQ VIII/1, 409, and DOUSSINAGUE, Fernando y el Cisma 177.

[109] MANSI 32, 983D; DE GRASSI, Diarium concilii, ed. DYKMANS 1231 : 2.

resolve the conflict, Lang turned to the emperor and pope for a decision. The death of Sanseverino on 7 August 1516 left Lang in secure possession of the title and church. The bishopics of Maillezais and Novara which he held in administration until they were assigned on his deprivation to cardinals Accolti and Schiner respectively were not officially restored to him after his absolution. The archbishopric of Vienne in France, however, he seems to have retained until he resigned it to his nephew Alessandro in 1515. The regress which Sanseverino had to the bishopric of Terouanne was over-ruled by Leo out of respect for the emperor's wishes. To compensate for the benefices he had permanently lost, the cardinal received from Leo a significant number of revenues and benefices in France and Italy.[110]

The reconciliation and partial restoration of Carvajal and Sanseverino prepared the way for the return of the other schismatic cardinals. Reports reached Rome that they would make their peace in September; but, as became evident later, the public humiliation exacted from the two penitents could prove an obstacle to their coming in person to Rome.[111] Alerted to the possibility of a similar affront to the honor and dignity of his office, Louis XII would give clear instructions to his ambassador to refuse any reconciliation on such terms.

Louis XII of France

Central to a resolution of the Pisan Schism was a reconciliation with Louis XII of France who was the principal author and sustainer of the rival Pisan

---

[110] On Sanseverino's title of S. Teodoro and its bestowal on Petrucci, see EUBEL II 21, III 4b nn. 1—3, 76 and MANSI 32, 691A; for his transfer to the titular church of S. Angelo, see EUBEL III 72; for Sanseverino's continued use of this title at the Pisan Council, see SANDRET 436; for the use of both titles in one document, see MANSI 32, 832A, 833D, 834D; in the rolls of the eighth and ninth sessions both Sanseverino and Lang used the title of S. Angelo, see MANSI 32, 827E—28A, 858D—E, in the bull affirming the legitimacy of Giulio dei Medici's birth, Sanseverino signed his name with the title Sti. Angeli, see ASV, Reg. Vat. 1198, fol. 34v; in papal documents both Sanseverino and Lang bore the title S. Angeli, e.g. HERGENROETHER, Regesta Leonis I 105 nr. 1870, 177 nr. 3026, 333 nr. 5349 and those mentioned in EUBEL III 4b n. 3; on Lang's efforts to resolve the confusion, see the letter of Lang to Maximilian, from Viterbo, 16 November 1513, in Maximiliana 30, II, fol. 64r. On 8 August 1516, the day following Sanseverino's death, Leo ordered that Lang or his procurators be given actual possession of the church of S. Angelo and its properties — see ASV, Reg. Vat. 1207, fol. 118r—v. For Leo's efforts to restore Sanseverino to his revenues in Spain, see his three letters of 13 June 1514 to Fernando, the archbishop-elect of Zaragoza, and the nuncio in Spain in ASV, Arm. XXXIX, vol. 30, fols., 407v—09r; for his more general letters affirming Sanseverino's restoration to his former benefices, honors and titles, see Reg. Vat. 1205 fols. 152r—55v and 1206, fols. 589r—93v, and Arm. XXXIX, vol. 36, fols. 73v—75v. Whether Sanseverino retained Maillezais is unclear, see EUBEL II 184, III 234; DE GRASSI, Diarium concilii, ed. DYKMANS 989 : 7; and E. BOURLOTON, La nomination des évêques au XVe siècle: Fédéric de Saint-Séverin, évêque de Maillezais 1481—1511, in: Revue de Bas-Poitou 18 (1905) 108—24, esp. 123—24. On Novara and Vienne, see EUBEL II 268, III 260, 333. For Terouanne and Sanseverino's regress on this bishopric, see the letter of Pio to Maximilian, from Rome, 8 November 1513, in Maximiliana 30 II, fol. 24v, EUBEL II 197, and C. G. CRUICKSHANK, The English Occupation of Tournai 1513—1519, Oxford 1971, 193, 267—68. For some of Sanseverino's subsequent benefices under Leo, see EUBEL III 4b n. 3.

[111] SANUTO XVI 432.

Council. His grievances toward Julius II were numerous and deep and his efforts at reaching a reasonable settlement of the conflict had been sabotaged or manipulated to strengthen the pope's position. The election of Giovanni dei Medici as Julius' successor raised the hope that a reconciliation between Rome and France could at last be achieved.

The new pope's policy toward France was dictated by a number of considerations. Of primary importance was ending the Pisan schism. A return to Roman jurisdiction was affirmed as a pre-condition for any political or military agreements with the French. To facilitate this Leo made overtures of friendship, took initially a public stance of neutrality in the conflicts between France and its enemies, and in hope of hastening the reconciliation hinted repeatedly through the Florentine ambassador in France at numerous favors he wished to bestow on the French king if only he were not a schismatic. When national pride prevented an abandonment of the Pisan schism, the pope hoped that a series of humiliating military defeats would temper French arrogance and prompt them to make peace with the papacy.[112]

To protect the rights and independence of the Papal States, especially by asserting control over its vassals, the former French allies, the d'Estes in Ferrara and Bentivogli in Bologna, and to block Louis' ambition to dominate the peninsula with power bases in Genoa, Milan, and Naples, Leo resolved to exclude the French from Italy.[113] To this end he was willing to supply money and troops to the opponents of France.

As head of Christendom, Leo longed to organize a crusade to stem the advancing armies of the Turks and ultimately win back from Moslem control the

---

[112] Pastor VII 43; F. Nitti, Leone X e la sua politica, Firenze 1892, 11—13; letters of the Dieci di Balìa to Roberto Acciaiuoli, from Florence, 10 and 24 September 1513, in Archivio di Stato Firenze (= ASF), Dieci di Balìa, Carteggi Missive Legazioni Commissarie (= Dieci, Mis.), nr. 40, fols. 142v, 161v, Francesco Vettori to the Dieci di Balìa, from Rome, 6 September 1513, in ASF, Dieci di Balìa, Carteggi, Responsive (= Dieci, Resp.), nr. 117, fol. 154r; the emperor also recognized the need to heal the schism as a pre-condition to peace and a united crusade effort, see his mandate to Lang, from Koblenz, 13 August 1513, in Maximiliana 29, III, fol. 36r; his ambassador Lang advised Leo that the French needed to be humbled before they would abandon their schism, see the letter of Lang to Maximilian, from Viterbo, 16 November 1514, in Maximiliana, 30, II, fol. 66r—v.

Another way of viewing Leo's handling of Louis XII is to compare it to the strategy typically used in hunting boars and deers, Leo's favorite sport. To capture the game, the hunter would determine first where he would like the animal to try to make its exit from the woods and then station himself and his nets there. Beaters would encircle the area where the game was. Cutting off all other exits, they drove it toward the pre-determined one where the hunter quietly and patiently awaited it. In the conduct of his French policy, Leo systematically encircled that country with foes who pressed Louis in from the Pyrennes, Artois, Hainaut, and Burgundy, using Spanish, English, Imperial, and Swiss forces. Navarre, Scotland, and Venice, Louis' principal allies, each suffered crushing defeats. The only avenue of escape open to Louis was to make his peace with Leo, a route the pope patiently and repeatedly urged Louis to take. On Leo's enthusiasm for the hunt, see Pastor VIII 157—63.

[113] Pastor VII 61—62; letters of Pio to Maximilian, from Rome, 6 July and 8 November 1513, in Maximiliana 29, III, fol. 17r and 30, II, fol. 23v; letter of Lang to Maximilian, from Viterbo, 16 November 1513, in Maximiliana 30, II, fol. 66r.

holy places in Palestine. The current struggle among leading Christian princes for lands in Italy dimmed prospects for a united crusade effort and put Christendom in the real danger of leaving its frontiers inadequately defended.[114] Peace and French cooperation in the crusade were seen as essential.

As protector of Medici interests, Leo hoped to secure from a well-disposed French king or from one defeated in battle and in need of friends, favors for members and supporters of this Florentine family and a possible renewal of the traditional Gallic-Tuscan alliance which would guarantee Medici control of Florence and free Leo from his great dependence on the Spanish.[115]

Leo tried to show himself receptive to French overtures. In mid-March the imperial ambassador considered Leo certainly not a friend of France but then not its bitter enemy and wondered whether the pope's attitude might not change. By the end of that month Leo let it be known that he was ready to examine anything Louis wished to propose in hope of resolving the differences between France and the papacy. The Treaty of Blois concluded on March 23rd between France and Venice signaled Louis' intention to return to power in Italy. He planned to invade in May and quickly retake Milan. Leo first learned of this alliance from France's enemies. When the French and Venetians eventually offered him membership in their league, he politely declined the invitation. In the hope of wooing him, the French dangled before him the possibility of states and royal marriages for members of the Medici family. Counter-offers of marriage and military alliances were soon proffered by France's opponents, notably Maximilian.[116]

In response to such proposals from both sides Leo protested a policy of neutrality. He claimed that as pope he must be a common father to all. He wanted to avoid doing anything publicly which might offend the French. When Mario de Perusco, the procurator of the Lateran Council, called for a sentence of contumacy against the French clergy for failing to appear at the sixth session on April 17th, Leo made no response, thus preventing a judgment. In May he assured the Venetian ambassador of his neutrality in the struggle over Milan and of his opposition to the Spanish and imperial requests for money to fight the League of Blois. He also denied having ever supplied such funds. But in

---

[114] K. M. SETTON, Leo and the Turkish Peril, in: Proceedings of the American Philosophical Society 113 (1969) 367—424; letter of Pio to Maximilian, from Rome, 6 July 1513, in: Maximiliana 29, III, fol. 20r; and the letter of Vettori to the Otto di Pratica, from Rome, 28 July 1514, in ASF, Otto di Pratica, Carteggi, Serie Responsive 1471—1533, Registro Carteceo (= Otto, Resp.), nr. 11, fol. 73r—v.
[115] PASTOR VII 87—93, 106, 112—13; NITTI 18.
[116] Letter of Pio to Maximilian, from Rome, 16 March 1513, in GODEFROY, Lettres de Louis, IV 79; NITTI 14 n. 1; SANUTO XVI 385; Vettori to Dieci di Balia, from Rome, 6 September 1513, in: ASF, Dieci, Resp. nr. 117, fol. 154r; letter of Paolo Somenzo to Marino Caracciolo, from Rome, 11 July 1513, in: Maximiliana 29, III, fol. 29v; letter of Antonio Giuppo della Rovere to Leo, from the imperial camp at Tournai, 20 September 1513, in: Maximiliana 29, IV, fols. 86r—87r; letter of Pio to Maximilian, from Rome, 8 November 1513, in: Maximiliana 30, II, fols. 23v—24r; letter of Maximilian to Lang, from Wels, 25 February 1514, in: Maximiliana 30, III, fol. 231r.

secret he did send France's enemies subsidies to purchase Swiss military intervention. In an effort to preserve his facade of neutrality he refused to join in the public festivities celebrating the defeat of the French army in early June. Indeed, he openly exhorted the victors to peace and mercy.[117] If in public the pope had striven to project the image of impartial peace-maker, he had also privately sought to defeat French political ambitions in Italy.

To help bring about a defeat of the French Leo gave his support to its enemies. On repeated occasions he indicated his opposition to a return of the French into Italy. He affirmed his support, after some initial hesitation, for a continuance of the Sforza regime in Milan, backed Ottaviano Fregoso as doge of Genoa and confirmed Fernando of Aragon as king over the papal fief of Naples.[118]

Leo also backed military measures against the French. Another so-called "Holy League" formed by England and the Empire on April 5th to oppose the French and Venetian alliance contained a clause welcoming the pope and Spain to membership. Leo at first refused formal partnership in the league, claiming some of its articles were unbefitting the dignity of the Holy See and his role as common father of all Christians. He, nonetheless, backed the league's effort to block the French invasion of Italy and provided it with secret funds to hire Swiss mercenaries. To the Venetian ambassador he subsequently denied having any such involvement. The defeat of the French at Novara on June 6th did not end Leo's collaboration with the Holy League. He wanted the war effort pushed hard to force France to make peace. An invasion of France was discussed and Henry VIII urged Leo to launch an attack over the Alps. The pope wanted to dash once and for all French hopes of returning to the peninsula, for he saw that a conjunction of the French and Venetian forces would inflict great harm on Italy.[119]

To eliminate this danger, Leo sought to break the French-Venetian alliance by forcing Venice to make a separate peace or truce with its major enemy the Empire. The emperor was well disposed to such a peace and empowered his representative Lang to negotiate an honorable settlement so that Maximilian could devote his attention to the war with France. The terms were discussed in detail at Rome and involved a return of captured cities and payment of indem-

---

[117] PASTOR VII 51—53; letter of Louis de Forbin to Louis XII, from Rome, 8 July 1513, in: Bibliothèque Nationale, Paris (= BNP), Dupuy 261, fol. 121r; MANSI 32, 657E, 792AB, 816B; SANUTO XVI 179.

[118] PASTOR VII 48—52; SANUTO XVI 179, 188, 481—82; letter of Pio to Maximilian, from Rome, 6 July 1513, in: Maximiliana 29, III, fols. 17r and 20r; letter of Forbin to Louis, from Rome, 8 July 1513, in BNP, Dupuy 261, fol. 121r; NN to Louis, from Rome, 29 June 1513, in Dupuy 262, fol. 60r; letter of Guibé to Louis, from Rome, 6 July 1513, in Dupuy 262, fol. 17r.

[119] PASTOR VII 50; SANUTO XVI 172; the Papal States formally joined the league on 18 April 1513 according to NITTI 15; letter of Pio to Maximilian, from Rome, 6 July 1513, in: Maximiliana 29, III, fols. 17r—20r.

nities and tribute. To overcome Venetian reluctance to make a settlement the Holy League continued to apply military pressure. Despite the pope's displays of displeasure when asked to support the league with funding and troops, he promised and sent to Maximilian both money and his own lancers, infantry, and cavalry in support of the league's war effort against Venice. Leo did not, however, want Venice pushed too hard for fear that it would in desperation invite the Turks into Italy to fight its opponents. The pope also resisted attempts to make him end his official neutrality. To bring the pope into formal alliance with members of the league, the emperor empowered his ambassadors to alter the articles which Leo found offensive or to propose a new league with much the same membership. Maximilian's readiness to accommodate the pope did not succeed in bringing Leo to join formally this defensive league. The pope's intention was to exclude Louis from Italy but not to alienate him by siding publicly with his enemies.[120]

The French king grew increasingly willing to come to terms with the new pope. He initially hoped to win papal favor or neutrality in the struggle for control of northern Italy. To this end he sent two representatives, one the official ambassador to the Roman court, the other a former friend of the pope.

The new French orator was Louis de Forbin, lord of Solliès, Luc, and Peyruis, former first president of the Parlement of Provence, and royal councillor who had earlier concluded French participation in the League of Cambrai. He traveled to Italy in the company of the schismatic cardinals Carvajal and Sanseverino and when they were detained in Tuscany, he proceeded on to Rome where he arrived in time for Leo's coronation. On the following day he joined the pro-French cardinals Guibé and Flisco in the loggia above the gardens of the papal palace where they urged Leo to favor the French and permit the schismatic cardinals then in Florence to come to Rome. While Leo eventually brought the two Pisan cardinals to the papal court for reconciliation, this did not further French interests but weakened still more the Gallican Pisan schism. Forbin's efforts in early June to win the pope to the French camp were singularly unsuccessful. By late June and through July of 1513 Forbin was failling repeatedly in his attempts just to see the pope. His petty protest over Leo's acceptance of a gift from king Fernando followed by a puerile altercation with the Spanish ambassador earned him the laughter of all present at the papal

---

[120] Letters of Pio to Maximilian, from Rome, 29 June, 6 July, and 30 July 1513, in Maximiliana 29, II, fol. 179v, III, fols. 17r—18r, 20r, and 85r; letter of Jacques Hanock to Marguerite d'Autriche, from Rome, 6 July 1513, in: GODEFROY, Lettres de Louis, IV 173—74; memorial of Lang to Maximilian, from Rome, 13 November 1513, in: Ibid, IV 206; mandate of Maximilian for Lang, from Adenarde, 5 August 1513, in: Maximiliana 29, III, fol. 91r—v; letter of Jacopo de Bannissi to Pio, s.l., 17 July 1513, in: Maximiliana 29, II, fols. 50r—51r; letter of Maximilian to Pio, from Lille, 12 September 1513, in: Maximiliana 29, IV, fols. 47r—50v; letter of Maximilian to Lang, from Wels, 25 February 1514, in: Maximiliana 30, III, fol. 230v; SANUTO XVI 481—82; letter Maximilian to Marguerite, from Frankfurt, 5 July 1513, in LE GLAY, Correspondance II 173.

ceremony on June 29th.[121] If French interests were to be advanced at the papal court, new faces and strategies were needed.

Louis' hopes of winning over Leo through an unofficial emissary were equally disappointed. Soon after the papal election, Louis chose as carrier of a personal letter to Leo, Janus Lascaris, the exiled Greek scholar whose friendship with the new pope dated from his days spent in the Florence of Lorenzo the Magnificent and who had since entered the service of the French. He was sent by the Council of Pisa the year before to win support from the German emperor, princes, and prelates and also functioned as French ambassador to the marchese of Monferrato. Louis now empowered him to negotiate in Rome on his behalf. His arrival there was welcomed by Leo who extended him an invitation at the end of March in the hope of learning from him Louis' true intentions. Although Lascaris is reported to have exercised his good offices with Leo on Louis behalf, no papal-French alliance or truce emerged, and the Greek soon passed over into the service of the pope who commissioned him and his disciple Marcus Musurus to promote Greek studies by a school and press in Rome.[122] The French king was, thus, still without an effective representative in Rome. The failure of his policy must also be blamed on his determination to retake Milan and on his continued backing of the Pisan schism, both of which Leo adamantly opposed.

The cause of the Pisan Council suffered much since the election of Leo. The death of Julius II, whom Louis felt to be his personal enemy, followed by the election of the mild-mannered Medici pope eliminated the principal reason for the king's support of this anti-Julian council. His wife, Anne of Brittany, had long opposed the schism and entreated him repeatedly to terminate it, especially after the death of their child which she saw as God's punishment for the schism. Support for the Pisan Council now at Lyon was definitely on the wane. Even its ardent backers at the Sorbonne had already in January of 1513 discussed warning the king and bishop of Paris not to place too much confidence in it. The theological faculty delayed giving a response to Cajetan's attack on the assembly. When Louis consulted in the spring of 1513 the new rector of the Sorbonne, Girolamo Aleander, on the authority of the Pisan Council, this Italian theologian who had earlier declined representing the university at its sessions now worked to get the king to dissolve it. Defections to the Roman camp by the council's Spanish president Carvajal and its Italian legate Sanseverino were followed by rumors that other schismatic cardinals would soon

---

[121] R. D'AMAT, Forbin, Louis de, in: DBF 14 (Paris 1976) 409; SANUTO XVI 158—59, 173, 179, 216, 385; letter of Hanock to Marguerite, from Rome, 25 August 1513, in: Archives départmentales du Nord, Lille (= ADNL), coté B 18859, nr. 30846; HERGENROETHER, Regesta Leonis I 201.

[122] SANUTO XVI 157, 173, 178—79, 188; ROSCOE II 336—40, 358, V 266—67, App. 90; HERGENROETHER, Regesta Leonis I 111, nr. 1963; Apologie sacri Pisani Concilii moderni 163; PASTOR VII 148; D. J. GEANAKOPLOS, Byzantium and the Renaissance: Greek Scholars in Venice, Studies in the Dissemination of Greek Learning from Byzantium to Western Europe, Cambridge, Mass. 1962, 147.

also make their peace with the papacy.¹²³ By June the Pisan Council had no chance of success, but was only an obstacle to French efforts to mend the damage at Novara by coming to terms with the papacy. To explore ways of ending this schism, both France and Rome thought of exchanging new emissaries of peace.

The choice of a papal envoy was complicated by many factors. On 17 June 1513 the seventh session of the Lateran Council decreed the sending of legates or nuncios to all Christian princes in the hope of establishing a universal peace in Christendom and of uniting them in a crusade. This was not the only pretext under which the papal envoy could be sent. The papal territories of Avignon and Venassin in southern France were governed by a legate or his delegate often sent from Rome. Leo and the cardinals decided to use the Avignonese legation as the cover for renewing negotiations on a termination of the schism. On July 8th the commission of the papal governor of Avignon, Angelo Leonini, was rescinded. Robert Guibé was then appointed vicar general for both spiritual and temporal affairs in Avignon, Venassin, and the neighboring ecclesiastical provinces south of the Rhone and along the Mediterranean coast and also constituted papal legate with full faculties. This French cardinal was the logical man for the legation not only due to his proven loyalty to the Holy See which had cost him dearly in lost revenues from schismatic France and due to his acceptability to Louis who had earlier appointed him as his spokesman, but also because of his reputation as a peace maker. When apparently for health reasons he he did not go to France but sent in his stead his nephew François Hamon, bishop of Nantes, Louis sought to have a more prestigious prelate and partisan of the French sent to him in virtue of the Lateran Council's peace mandate. He suggested cardinal d'Este. Leo opposed such an appointment and also rejected the candidacy of Sanseverino proposed by Forbin. Instead, he named in mid-August Luigi Canosa as the council's peace nuncio, but his departure was delayed.¹²⁴

The French king was prompter in naming his deputy. Reports reaching Rome claimed he would send the bishop of Paris, Etienne Poncher, in the hope that Leo would promote him to the cardinalate. Louis, however, chose as his new

---

[123] GUICCIARDINI XI, xiii, ed. PANIGADA III 282; J. PAQUIER, L'humanisme et la réforme: Jerome Aléandre da sa naissance à la fin de son séjour a Brindes (1480—1529) avec son portrait, ses armes, un fac-simile de son écriture et un catalogue de ses oeuvres, Paris 1909, 60—63; letter of G. Aleandro to Paul III (1534) in A. MAI, Spicilegium Romanum, Rome 1839—44, II 240: Aleandri cardinalis epistolae nr. 6; SANUTO XVI 432; RENAUDET, Préréforme 544—55.

[124] MANSI 32, 817A—D, 818DE; SANUTO XVI 600, 652; EUBEL III 10b n. 3; HERGENROETHER, Regesta Leonis I 209 nr. 3549; letter of Pio to Lang from Rome, 30 July 1513, in: Maximiliana 29 III, fol. 85v; report probably of Forbin, from Rome, s.d., in BNP, Ancien Fond Français 2933, fol. 135r; letter of Forbin to NN (Louis?), from Rome, 8 July 1513, in Dupuy 261, fol. 121r; DE GRASSI, Diarium Leonis, BAV, Vat. Lat. 12275, fol. 99r; letter of Vettori to the Dieci di Balia, from Rome, 8 November 1513, in ASF, Dieci, Resp. nr. 118, fol. 267r; S. FANTONI CASTRUCCI, Istoria della città d'Avignone e del contado Venesino, stati della Sede Apostolica nella Gallia, Venezia 1678, I 353.

ambassador the bishop of Marseille, Claude de Seyssel, an experienced diplomat, noted humanist, and personal friend of the pope. What may have recommended Seyssel most for this post, however, was his reputation as an intrepid defender of the king's reputation. Indeed, so lavish was his praise of Louis that his enemies accused him of flattery, a charge he answered at length with his *Apologie* of 1510. Given the humiliating confessions and absolution ceremony required of Carvajal and Sanseverino, Louis was in need of this skilful champion of his good name. The royal instructions given Seyssel prohibited him from agreeing to anything which might offend the king's honor and required the king's prior approval before any agreement was concluded.[125] He was also provided with a forceful defense of the king's actions in having backed the Pisan Council.

The letter which Seyssel brought exculpated Louis, attacked Julius, and suggested ways in which Leo could resolve the conflict.[126] The king's previous policies were characterized as a justified self-defense against a cruel, unjust, and ungrateful Julius II. The pope, who acted like a wild and powerful wolf, abused church authority and attacked the French king even though Louis had done more for the Church than any other Christian prince by restoring to it lands and cities in Romagna. To defend himself Louis had recourse to every effective means without, however, intending in any way to support an evil sect or schism, for his wish was always to remain a loyal and devoted son of the Roman Church and of its canonically elected pontiffs. When the new pope Leo indicated his opposition to the Pisan Council, Louis ordered the conciliar fathers, then in Lyon awaiting word of the pontiff's intentions, to disband without further use of this council's authority. A fitting way to eradicate the Julian legacy of iniquity would be for Leo X to follow the example of Clement V. On his own, without the then French king Philip the Fair having requested any absolution or abolition of papal decrees, Clement declared in his "extravagante" *Meruit* that all the measures his predecessor Boniface VIII had taken against Philip and France were null and without effect.

Leo would do well also to ignore the advice of Louis' enemies, to have regard for the many injuries the king has already suffered at the hand of Julius and his allies, to be concerned about the grave weakness of the French military forces, and to consider the ambitions of certain princes who prepare for war so

---

[125] SANUTO XVI 322, 385; A. CAVIGLIA, Claudio di Seyssel (1450—1520): La vita nella storia de' suoi tempi (= Miscellanea di Storia Italiana 54) Torino 1928, 274, 276 n. 8; C. DE SEYSSEL, Apologie des Louenges de Lovys XII, Roy de France, pour respondre aux detracteurs — composée l'an 1510, in Histoire de Lovys XII. Roy de France . . ., ed. TH. GODEFROY, Paris 1615, 157—176, esp. 159, 165, 173—76; letter of Jean le Veau to Marguerite, from Rome, 24 August 1513, in GODEFROY, Lettres de Louis, IV 200—01.

[126] A copy of this letter is to be found in BNP, Fond Ancien Français 3087, fols., 101r—102v. This document is transcribed in Appendix II. I am grateful to Profs. Ellen S. Ginsberg and Joseph P. Williman and to Dr. Gino Corti for their kind and expert assistance in helping me read some difficult passages in this text.

as to bring under their dominion the greater part of Christendom. The pope should, therefore, make peace among Christian princes by seeing that lands seized unjustly are restored and should also organize a crusade against the infidels.

In response to such measures by the pope, Louis promised to remain a loyal son of the Church and to render to the papacy all possible services.

This position paper brought to Rome by Seyssel is remarkable in many ways. According to its logic the king, far from making an open and humiliating confession of guilt in having caused the Pisan schism, is depicted as the victim of ingratitude who defends himself with any effective means at his disposal. Questions concerning the validity of the conciliar thesis or the legitimacy of the Pisan Council are never confronted. Instead of the king shifting blame for the schism onto the Pisan cardinals, his advisors, or the emperor, Louis insists that recourse to a council was justified and that blame belongs properly to Julius whom he compares to ferocious animals. The new pope is to correct the misdeeds by nullifying the decrees against the king. Thus the papacy, rather than France, is to suffer a humiliation — a clever defense by counter-attacking. While Seyssel's letter offers a persuasive analysis and plausible resolution of the conflict, it seriously distorts the facts in at least one of its claims.

King Louis did not disperse the Pisan prelates on learning of Leo's opposition to the Council at Lyon. Royal agents blocked the attempt to flee Lyon for the court of Rome made by the council's secretary and former prime animator, Zaccaria Ferreri, the Italian abbot of Subasio. The bishop of Luçon, Pierre de Sacierges, refused to allow Ferreri to leave Lyon. When he attempted by stealth to flee the city taking passage on a boat down the Rhone, he, his household, and possessions were captured at Viviers near Avignon. Despite the vain efforts to free him undertaken by the local bishop, Claude de Tournon, Ferreri spent three days in prison before being returned to Lyon. Unswayed by the threats and pressures applied, he kept his resolve to reach Rome and beg pardon. While still in Lyon he penned a poem describing his dream about the election of Leo to the papacy and confessing the error of the Pisan Council. He dated the poem the 18th of March. To the printed edition of this poem he appended a petition he sent to Louis from Lyon on August 23rd. In this letter he urged the king to withdraw royal support for the council and insisted that he and the other members of the council had been led into error by ignorance rather than ill will. He also complained of being held in Lyon against his will and in violation of ecclesiastical liberties. Let Louis, therefore, allow him to go to Rome.[127]

---

[127] Z. FERRERI, Lugudunense somnium de divi Leonis decimi pontificis maximi ad summum apostolatus apicem divina delectione ... et est Sylva centesima decima quae Leonina titulatur, Lyon 1513, B_{ii}^v, C_{ii}^r, C_{iii}^v, C_v^v—C_{vi}^r; B. MORSOLIN, L'Abbate di Monte Subasio e il Concilio di Pisa (1511—1512): Episodio di storia ecclesiastica, in: Atti del R. Istituto Veneto di scienze, lettere, ed arti, Tomo IV, Serie VII (1892—93), 1689—1735, esp. 1723.

Thus, instead of making the council fathers leave Lyon, as claimed in Seyssel's letter, Ferreri's experience suggests that the king was still backing the council and conspiring to detain its members lest they make their individual peace with Rome.

The arrival of the French ambassador sent to negotiate for the king and the Gallican Church the terms for healing the Pisan schism was of concern to many in Rome. Because he came only as an orator and not to present his king's obeisance, Leo did not allow cardinals or members of the papal household to escort Seyssel into the city when he appeared at the gate near St. Peter's on Sunday July 23rd. The pope decided that he should be greeted instead by members of the households of the four pro-French cardinals: Guibé, Sanseverino, Caretto, and Flisco. His lodgings were in the palace of Domenico Massimo, the wealthiest private citizen of Rome, who often offered hospitality to ambassadors.[128]

Within a week of his arrival, Seyssel had presented his credentials at two public ceremonies. The imperial ambassador, Pio, was worried, for he knew Seyssel to be a very skillful diplomat and considered him truly sinister *(nigemosus)*. What Pio most feared was what dampening effect Seyssel might have on Leo's supposed anti-French ardor should the pope ever have private discussions with him. Leo was careful to keep men like Pio in the dark. The Venetian ambassador reported the pope's public admonition to Seyssel on the occasion of the presentation of his credentials which was both an interpretation of Louis' current misfortunes as a punishment for having harmed the Church and a prediction that the king would pay yet more for his misdeeds. While Leo's public pronouncements were threats to the French, his stance in a top-secret three-hour long meeting with Seyssel was decidedly conciliatory and agreement was quickly reached on a termination of the Pisan Schism with other matters being left unresolved.[129]

The progress of the papal-French negotiations are difficult to trace. Seyssel's reports have not been found but information from other sources permits a partial reconstruction. The rapid agreement reached in the initial meetings was apparently followed by a series of snags. The principal problems were two. Leo insisted that Louis not only end the schism but that he formally acknowledge having wrongly, unreasonably, indirectly and without cause brought about the

---

[128]Diarium sub Julio II ab anno 1509 die 3 Martii usque ad 1540 die 6 Octobris — Gallice, BAV, Barb. Lat. 3552, fol. 19r; L. MADELIN, Le Journal d'un habitant français de Rome au XVIe siècle (1509—1540), Étude sur le Manuscript XLIII — 98 de la Bibliothèque Barberini, in: Mélanges d'Archéologie et d'histoire — École Française de Rome 22 (1902) 251—300, esp. 276 — according to this diary, five pro-French cardinals sent their staffs to greet Seyssel, but only four names are given by SANUTO XVI 548; LITTA, Famiglie celebre, Massimo di Roma, Milano 1839, tavola III.

[129] Letter of Pio to Lang, from Rome, 30 July 1513, in: Maximiliana 29, III, fol. 85v; SANUTO XVI 587; letter of Jacopo Salviati and F. Vettori to the Dieci di Balìa, in: ASF, Dieci, Resp. nr. 117, fols. 2v—3r.

II

The Healing of the Pisan Schism (1511—13)

convocation and assembly of the Pisan Council. To repair this injury to the Holy See, he was, in addition to his confession, to dispatch the larger part of the principal prelates who attended that council. In Rome they were bitterly to repent their role in the Pisan schism and humbly to beg pardon and mercy from the pope and Holy See. For his part, Louis not only resisted any agreement which might impugn his royal honor, but he even sought an alliance with Leo which would support French ambitions in Italy, something Leo hitherto abhorred.[130]

Various measures were taken by both the French ambassador and the pope to overcome these difficulties. Seyssel spent long hours enlisting the assistance of Leo's brother, Giuliano dei Medici, with renewed pledges of the king's affection for him and similarly soliciting the sympathy of various cardinals with promises of royal favor. He had recourse also to his fellow ambassadors. Such a campaign for gathering support was necessitated by Leo's reluctance to deal directly with him any further on a question involving the honor of the Holy See. In mid-August the issues of the Pisan Council and the Pragmatic Sanction of Bourges were discussed in a congregation, perhaps the same twenty-member deputation of the Lateran Council established two months earlier for handling these topics. Seyssel is reported to have participated in its discussions. In an apparent move to facilitate these negotiations, Leo established by August 20th a smaller commission and by August 25th fixed as its members four cardinals and the French orators, of whom one was probably also a cardinal.[131]

The composition of this commission is not clear. The cardinals Leo initially appointed were supposedly neutral regarding French affairs: Accolti, Farnese, and Soderini. When the latter could not come to Rome in time, his place was taken by Vigerio and another cardinal, variously reported as del Monte or L. G. della Rovere. The French orators were apparently Sanseverino, Seyssel, and Forbin. Seyssel was considered the principal negotiator for the French.[132]

Given the fragmentary and seemingly contradictory evidence, the course of the commission's work is difficult to trace. The overlapping reports of contentment with progress and amazement at delays, of deadlines fixed for royal consent while discussions were still in progress, may find resolution if one posits two-track negotiations dealing with both the political and ecclesiastical

---

[130] CAVIGLIA 275 n. 6; letter of Acciaiuoli to the Dieci di Balìa, from Paris (?), 10 August 1513, in: ASF, Dieci, Resp. nr. 117, fol. 40r; letter of Jean le Veau to Marguerite, from Milan, 24 August 1513, in GODEFROY, Lettres de Louis, IV 199—201.

[131] SANUTO XVI 616, 652; letter of Giuliano dei Medici to Louis, from Rome, 30 August 1513, in BNP, Fond Ancien Français 2964, fol. 14r; letter of Hanock to Marguerite, from Rome, 25 August 1513, in ADNL, coté B 18859, nr. 30846, fol. 1r.

[132] Letter of Vettori to the Dieci di Balìa, from Rome, 20 and 25 August 1513, in ASF, Dieci, Resp. nr. 117, fols., 68r, 90v where del Monte is named a substitute; letter of Hanock to Marguerite, from Rome, 25 August 1513, ADNL, Coté B 18859, nr. 30846, fol. 1r gives the replacement as *Agen.*, i.e., L. G. della Rovere; letter of Jean le Veau to Marguerite, from Milan, 24 July 1513, in: GODEFROY, Lettres de Louis, IV 200.

issues and the need to expand Seyssel's mandate which was initially limited to renouncing the Pisan Council in a way which would preserve the king's honor and required specific royal consent before any agreement could be concluded. What is clear from the various ambassadors' reports is that Leo followed the negotiations very closely with daily inquiries into their progress and expressions of concern for their success.[133]

The political issues separating France and the Papal States were slowly negotiated. After the defeat of Novara, the French were under increasing pressure to make peace with the Holy League. In late August they suffered another reversal with the capture of Terouanne by the English. In September the military might of France's closest ally was virtually destroyed on the fields of Flodden with the slaughter of the Scottish king and of many of his highest civil and ecclesiastical lords. Louis' woes would not end there, for in mid-September his own city of Dijon was spared a siege and sacking by Swiss troops only on the promise of paying an immense sum of money, and in October his Venetian allies were defeated at Olma near Vicenza, and the Ghelder contingent abandoned the French army fearing lest they be the only Germans fighting against the Holy League. In hope of avoiding disaster, Louis sought an honorable peace. While Leo was willing to listen to French proposals, he reportedly refused to conclude an agreement without the consent of his allies. Given France's precarious position and papal efforts at reconciliation, Leo marveled in early September when Louis initially resisted cajolement by papal threats of military actions and ecclesiastical censures should the king not respond positively within twenty days to a tentative treaty. While this treaty protected the Papal States and Medici interests in Florence, it was favorable to France and was apparently used as bait. Through the Florentine ambassador in Paris, word was sent that Leo would like to help defend the king and bestow on him numerous favors as tokens of the great affection he bore him, but that his hands were tied as long as Louis remained a schismatic. If there was an element of duplicity in Leo's tactics, it did not lie in the priority of a resolution of spiritual issues or in the possibility of a treaty of friendship with France, but rather in his purported need to consult first with his allies. Had the League not won at Olma, Leo was prepared to side with the French in the hope of driving his Spanish and German former allies out of Italy.[134]

---

[133] Letter of Jean le Veau to Marguerite, Ibid. 200—01; letter of Vettori to the Dieci di Balìa, from Rome, 20 August 1513, in: ASF, Dieci, Resp. nr. 117, fol. 90v.

[134] SANUTO XVII 31, 73—74, 102, 205; letter of Giovanni Battista Spinelli to Maximilian from Brescia, 12 October 1513, in: Maximiliana 30, I, fols. 57v—58r; letter of Vettori to the Dieci di Balìa, from Rome, 5 September 1513, in: ASF, Dieci, Resp. nr. 117, fol. 160r; letters of the Dieci di Balìa to Vettori and Acciaiuoli, from Florence, 10 and 24 September 1513, in: ASF, Dieci, Mis. nr. 40, fols. 142v, 145v—46r, 161v; draft of a treaty between Louis and the Holy League dated September 1513 and signed by Jacopo Sachi the chancellor Pavia, in: ASF, Mediceo avanti il Principato (= MAP), Filza 147, nr. 34, fol. 117r; letter of Lang to Maximilian, from Viterbo, 16 November 1513, in: Maximiliana 30, II, fols. 66v, 68r.

The Healing of the Pisan Schism (1511—13)

The negotiations to resolve the differences in spiritual matters between France and the papacy can be traced in some detail. The mandate which Seyssel brought to Rome empowered him to renounce the Pisan Council. In a secret meeting with Leo soon after Seyssel's arrival it was agreed that the schismatic council would be dissolved and its members pardoned. Because his mandate did not extend to other issues which Louis wanted to decide personally, messengers had to travel back and forward between the two courts. The twelve days it normally took to convey a message in one direction meant that a month could pass before a response was received. Leo's twenty-day deadline proved impractical and only accentuated his impatience for a speedy resolution.[135] From the fragmentary records surviving it would seem that on three occasions an exchange of messages was required before an agreement was concluded.

The first messenger was apparently dispatched from Rome by the French orators toward the end of August. Leo demanded a response from Louis within twenty days or he threatened to proceed against him and his Venetian ally with military might and ecclesiastical censures. When Leo learned in early September that the French would not meet his deadline, he marveled at their delay. By September 17th, however, he had his response. The contents of this message are not known, but seem to have involved the degree of humiliation the French were willing to accept in renouncing their council.[136]

Much more is known about the second exchange of messages. The commission of papal and French representatives made rapid progress at Leo's urgings. Earlier difficulties had centered on the French reluctance to nullify the numerous benefices and dispensations granted by the Pisan Council. The papal negotiators objected to approving them because they had been conferred by schismatics. Given Julius' explicit invalidation of these conciliar grants, their approval now would result in confusion. The commission found a resolution to this problem and others. Its tentative solution to eleven outstanding issues was presented to the pope for his approval. By September 6th agreement was reached in Rome and the proposed terms of reconciliation were sent to France to secure royal assent.[137]

---

[135] Letter of Jean le Veau to Marguerite, from Milan, 24 August 1513, in: GODEFROY, Lettres de Louis, IV 199—201; for examples of the twelve-day trip: Seyssel's agent left Amiens on September 22rd (see the letter of Acciaiuoli to the Dieci di Balìa, from Amiens, 21 September 1513, in: ASF, Dieci, Resp. nr. 117, fol. 247v) and arrived in Rome on October 4th (see the letter of Vettori to the Dieci di Balìa, from Rome, 6 October 1513, in: ASF, Dieci, Resp. nr. 118, fol. 44v and MAP, Filza 105, nr. 37); Seyssel in Rome received a letter of October 3rd from Amiens on October 15th (see SANUTO XVII 227), and of October 28th on November 10th (see SANUTO XVII 318).

[136] Letter of Jean le Beau to Marguerite, from Milan, 24 August 1513, in: GODEFROY, Lettres de Louis, IV 200—01; letters of Vettori to the Dieci di Balìa, from Rome, 6 September and 17 October 1513, in: ASF, Dieci, Resp. nr. 117, fols., 154r, 215r.

[137] Letters of Vettori to the Dieci di Balìa, from Rome, 20, 25 and 29 August and 5 September 1513, in: ASF, Dieci, Resp. nr. 117, fols. 68r, 90v, 104r, 160r.

The proposals of the commission and Leo's response reveal some insistence on principle, concessions to the powerful, and gentleness with penitents.[138] To protect the dignity of the Holy See, Leo refused to ratify outright the decisions of the Pisan Council, to guarantee automatic mercy and reintegration to those not seeking it, or to denounce the decrees of his predecessor Julius II. In some respects following the example of Clement V as had been urged in the royal instruction of Seyssel, Leo agreed that once Louis had dissolved and disbanded the Pisan Council and had adhered to the Lateran, he would send to the king a legate with a bull declaring that Louis was not included in any of the censures or penalties decreed by Julius or the Lateran Council; but if in some way he was subject to those decrees, this was not to prejudice his majesty either in the past or future. This provision may have reference to the Julian proposal to transfer the French crown from Louis de Valois to Henry Tudor of England. Leo's treatment of Louis, therefore, not only preserved papal dignity, but it exculpated the French king while denying to his English enemy the promised reward and stimulus to military exploits. Those who followed Louis' lead in the schism were similarly freed from the full penalty of their deed.

Absolutions were to be granted, as was earlier agreed, to the participants of the Pisan Council. Out of consideration for their past and future services to both the French king and Roman Church, the deprived and penitent cardinals Briçonnet and de Prie were to be dealt with gently, and if the restored cardinals Carvajal and Sanseverino agreed, they were to be spared the solemn humiliating ceremony of absolution and restoration. A general absolution from censures and interdict in the forum of conscience would be granted to all adherents of the Pisan Council once there arrived in Rome orators or procurators sent to renounce that council and adhere to the Lateran.

The delegation from the Pisan Council was the subject of almost half of the articles. Because wartime conditions required the presence of prelates in France, the commission proposed to the pope that only four prelates, a doctor, and other major officials from the Pisan Council come to Rome. Leo, however, insisted that six prelates together with four masters in sacred theology or canon law, all from among the more prestigious participants at Pisa, come to confess their error and beg pardon. They were to bring with them mandates from the other participants repudiating this schismatic assembly. They were free either to attempt to defend their conduct at Pisa on legal grounds with Leo promising to grant them a hearing in accordance with legal procedures or to beg mercy with a papal pledge to treat them with as much kindness as possible. In their quest for full rehabilitation and reintegration, most of the former members of the Pisan Council were expected to beg mercy rather than make a legal defense. On account of the wars, the pope agreed to grant these prelates ample

---

[138] See appendix IV for my transcription of a copy of these eleven articles which is preserved in the ADNL as Coté B Entrée 1462 nr. 18060, fols. 1r—2r.

time for the trip and to provide them with safe-conducts so they could come and return without molestation.

Given Leo's refusal to ratify the decisions of the Pisan Council, a way had to be found to legitimize the current situation resulting from the council. Instead of a blanket validation even of those transactions done in good faith and by impartial procedures, Leo required personal recourse either to his curia or legate to secure the desired legitimization. Once the legal decisions of the Pisan Council had been declared null by rescript, the pope was willing to affirm that cases resolved by the council should remain in their current state, thus avoiding the expense and labor of new litigation. Those who obtained from this council provision to such major benefices as cathedral churches and monasteries were not to be deprived of them or denied their revenues but would be given papal provision provided the king favored this provision and it was requested within three months of the council's dissolution. Minor benefices which normally depend on local ordinaries but were conferred by the council could be re-conferred by the ordinary once the holder renounced the Pisan Council and its provision. The pope agreed to be most liberal in allowing the retention of revenues improperly acquired and in granting the necessary dispensations.

Almost a month passed before final agreement was reached on these terms for reconciliation. Seyssel sent his agent to the king to secure his approval. He arrived at the royal court then at Amiens on September 15th and left for Rome a week later. While Louis generally agreed to the negotiated terms, he was sensitive to anything which might seem to dishonor the French crown and decided to argue his case. The point with which he took issue is not identified in the report, but may have concerned the wording of the mandate by which he renounced the Pisan Council. The Venetian orator at the French court reported that the king would send four orators to renounce the Pisan Council (two less than agreed at Rome) and would entrust to Leo the resolution of the war. To secure the king's speedy approval of the terms, the Florentine ambassador to France, Roberto Acciaiuoli, under instructions from his government encouraged ratification, claiming that a resolution of the spiritual issues would allow Leo to deal favorably with France in other areas. Indeed, rumors spread that Leo was already completely on Louis' side in the war. So delicate was Acciaiuoli's role in securing royal assent to the negotiated articles that his superiors in Florence refused to allow a new ambassador to take his place, as requested by Acciaiuoli, for fear the French might interpret his arrival as an investigation into the progress of the negotiations. On his return to Rome on October 4th, Seyssel's agent brought a commission which empowered the French orators to agree to Leo's decisions on all the articles affecting spiritual matters.[139]

---

[139] Letters of Acciaiuoli to the Dieci di Balìa, from Amiens, 18 and 21 September 1513, in: ASF, Dieci, Resp. nr. 117, fols. 224v, 247v; letters of Vettori to the Dieci di Balìa from Rome, 15 September and 6 October 1513, Ibid. nr: 117, fol. 211r and nr. 118, fol. 44v (= MAP, Filza 105,

Having secured royal assent, the papal-French commission in Rome worked out the details of the reconciliation. It met on October 5 and 6th and fixed the wording of the mandate whereby Louis would renounce the Pisan Council and adhere to the Lateran. Had Louis complained about any possible offense to the French crown in an earlier draft of the mandate, he could only praise the skill and prudence of his representatives who negotiated a final text that almost completely exculpated Louis.[140] Its wording and tone were far different from the humiliating confession demanded of Carvajal and Sanseverino, and reflected some of the arguments advanced in Seyssel's letter of July.

Blame for the former papal-French conflict is placed in Rome. There the enemies and rivals of Louis by their wily and false insinuations so misled Julius II that he abandoned his paternal affection for this oldest and most loyal son of the Church and became, instead, an open and bitter enemy of the French king.[141]

Louis' comportment in this situation is described in a way which exonerates him of any guilt. The wrathful brunt of papal attacks the French king bore patiently in hope of an eventual reconciliation with the pope. Contrary to his own thinking on the matter, an assembly of many important and learned ecclesiastics, even cardinals, met in Pisa claiming with clever and persuasive arguments to be legitimately convened as a general council. The need to defend his cause against the provocations of Julius, the imperial backing given to this assembly, and the counsel of the numerous learned men and prelates consulted led Louis to adhere to this "supposed council," to permit those prelates, so interested, to attend it, to welcome the transferred council into his domains, and to allow its decrees and provisions to ecclesiastical benefices to have effect there. By these measures Louis never intended to charge the Apostolic See with any possible fault nor to inflict a schism on the Roman Church. Once the new pontiff Leo had condemned the Pisan Council and continued that at the Lateran, Louis realized that only the Roman assembly was legitimate.[142]

Only the most honorable considerations now led Louis to reject the Pisan Council for the Lateran. The death of Julius removed all reason for hatred and suspicion of the pope. The new pontiff Leo who commands respect not only by the authority of his office but also by the innocence of his life sent letters of paternal exhortation admonishing Louis to withdraw from the Pisan Council which he declared illegitimate and to adhere to the Lateran as the only ecumen-

---

nr. 37); letters of the Dieci di Balìa to Acciaiuoli, from Florence, 24 September and 11 October 1513, in: ASF, Dieci, Mis. nr. 40, fols. 161v and 171r; letter of the Dieci di Balìa to Vettori, from Florence, 4 October 1513, Ibid. fol. 169v; letter of Antonio Giuppo della Rovere to Leo, from the imperial camp, 20 September 1513, in: Maximiliana 29, IV, fol. 86v; SANUTO XVII 180.

[140] Letter of Vettori to the Dieci di Balìa, from Rome, 6 October 1513, in: ASF, Dieci, Resp. nr. 118, fol. 44v; MANSI 32, 835C.

[141] MANSI 32, 832C.

[142] MANSI 32, 832C—33B.

ical assembly. Inspired solely by a zeal for religion, judging this pope's opinions to be holier and graver than those of any other mortal, especially on questions of scandal and schism, desiring not only to follow his predecessors in their devotion to the Holy See but even to surpass them in so far as possible, longing for a universal peace among Christians under the guidance of Leo so that the arms of the faithful could be soon redirected against the enemies of the orthodox faith, and considering that some of the cardinals and the emperor who had convoked the Pisan assembly had already renounced it and joined the Lateran Council, the French king hereby appointed three procurators to do the same in his name. The only suggestion that Louis may in the least have shared in the blame for the Pisan schism was the statement that his representatives withdrew from the supposed Pisan Council with "fitting reverence and humility."[143] Such a wilful distortion of the historical record would not go unnoticed or unchallenged when brought before the members of the Lateran Council.

The negotiated text of the French mandate, having thus absolved the king of any guilt as agreed upon in the first of the eleven articles, went on to restate some of the other agreements recently concluded. The royal procurators promised that Louis would withdraw all favor or assistance to the Pisan Council and expel as schismatics within two months from his domains, even by means of military force if necessary, any person no matter what his status who stubbornly adhered to that council. A pledge was also given that six prelates and four doctors or university graduates chosen from among the more prestigious members of the Pisan assembly would be sent in its name and with a mandate to represent all who participated in that council. These ten men were to appear in person before the pope by January 1st. In their own name and in that of the other participants in the Pisan Council they were to abjure that council, beg humbly from Leo pardon and absolution according to a format approved by the pope, and incorporate themselves into the Lateran Council, acknowledging it to be the only true and undisputed council. Should these delegates fail to do the above, Louis warned that the papal sentences and censures against them would be put into effect. As soon as conveniently possible other prelates and notables with proper mandates from the whole Gallican Church were also to come to Rome to assist at the Lateran Council in the same way as did other nations.[144]

On October 6th at a formal ceremony in the papal antechamber at the Vatican the French procurators, Sanseverino, Seyssel, and Forbin, signed a copy of this mandate. Present on this occasion were Leo X and cardinals Accolti, Farnese, del Monte, Pucci, and dei Medici. The first three of these cardinals had apparently been appointed to the papal-French commission due to their supposed impartiality regarding France. Accolti, however, was already administrator of

[143] MANSI 32, 833A—E.
[144] MANSI 32, 833E—34D.

the French see of Maillezais, while del Monte administered that of Pavia in often French-controlled Milanese territory. The absence from this ceremony of the other commission member, cardinal Vigerio, may be explained by a bout of rheumatism. Pucci and dei Medici were among Leo's closest advisers and had only just recently been named to the cardinalate.[145]

On October 9th the papal constitution *Aeternae vitae claviger* was issued in what seems a direct response to the requests in Seyssel's July credential letter repeated in the first article of the papal-French commission's report. Claiming inaccurately that he was acting *motu proprio* and not at the urging of others, Leo followed, without acknowledging it, the precedent set by Clement V's *Meruit* which nullified the penalties imposed by his predecessor Boniface VIII.[146]

This Leonine constitution completely absolved the French king. Ecclesiastical penalties could have been imposed on Louis XII for having backed either the schismatic Pisan Council or the rebellious vassal Alfonso d'Este. Julius issued separate letters on April 16 and July 18 of 1511 imposing penalties of excommunication, interdict, and censure on them and their supporters. The Lateran Council reaffirmed the latter while other papal decrees were also issued penalizing the same.[147] Given Louis' ardent support for both the Pisan Council and duke Alfonso, he logically incurred the papal penalties imposed for this. Some, however, seem to have claimed he did not fall under the sanction.

Leo gave an official pronouncement which freed Louis from any of these penalties. He based this action on the powers a pope has to lift or interpret the sentences of his predecessors, especially in consideration of the many benefits conferred on the Church by a present ruler and his predecessors. This papal power was also to be activated when there was the question of resolving doubts weighing on the conscience of the faithful and when an elimination of scandals and schism or an encouragement of union, peace, and tranquility among Christians and of a crusade against the infidel were dependent on such a pronouncement. Leo, therefore, declared that Louis and his successors were not in the least subject to any penalties contained in former papal letters, even those confirmed by the Lateran Council, nor were the king and his successors to be prejudiced by them in either the spiritual or temporal realm. Even if Louis was expressly and specifically named in these papal documents, Leo absolved him to the extent necessary of all penalties applicable to the reputation and titles of

---

[145] Mansi 32, 834D—35A; Eubel III 234, 267; Chambers 52; Pastor VII 67, 86, VIII 87, 90.

[146] See appendix V for a transcription of the original of this constitution preserved at the Archives Nationales de Paris as L 329 nr. 1 and dated 9 October 1513.

[147] For the bull of 18 July 1511 convoking the Lateran Council and condemning the Pisan adherents, see Mansi 32, 681B—91A, esp. 686B and 690B; for the papal condemnation of the supporters of Alfonso d'Este issued 14 October 1510, see ASV, Reg. Vat. 984, fols. 162r—64v, esp. 163r—v; for the *In Coena Domini* of 16 April 1511 which excommunicated Alfonso explicitly and Louis indirectly, see Reg. Vat. 956, fols. 162v—66r, esp. 164r—v; for the condemnations of 21 July 1512 and of 18 February 1513, see Pradera 411—23.

this king and fully restored and reintegrated him. No judge or delegate was to interpret these former papal decrees in a way contrary to Leo's constitution. The decrees of former pontiffs such as *Inter Caetera* of John XXII were also ruled as not applicable to Louis.

The French mandate approved on October 6th and the constitution issued three days later exemplify to what limited extent Leo would go to end the Pisan schism. He successfully defended the papal position that the Pisan Council was invalidly convoked by those lacking the requisite authority and that hence this "pretended" council was schismatic. Instead of vilifying the memory of his predecessor Julius as the cruel tyrant and wild animal defamed in Seyssel's letter, Leo had him depicted as the unwitting victim of malevolent advisors. Louis was provided with a similar excuse. Supposedly misled by high churchmen, learned consultants, and imperial precedent, the French king had backed the Pisan assembly without, however, intending to inflict any harm on the Roman see. To placate Gallic pride Leo had agreed to this gross falsification of the historical record regarding the prominent role of Louis at Pisa. He also nullified the penalties Julius had imposed on the king for his schismatic and illegal acts. If Leo preserved the principle of papal authority, he was also willing to undo its logical application and to shift blame for failure to obey it.

Explicit reference to a formula for confessing guilt and promising amendment demanded of minor supporters or collaborators of the Pisan assembly first appeared apparently in a papal letter of provision dated 3 May 1513, but the formula itself, in the text of a papal provision dated October 15th.[148] Due to its being contemporaneous with the work of the commission on reconciliation, to its generalized way of abjuring the Pisan Council, and to its possible relationship to two of the commission's eleven articles, this formula, like the

---

[148] At the beginning of Leo's reign, those who had received a benefice from the Pisan Council and now sought to regularize that provision with the Roman Curia were required to abjure in the hands of their ordinaries the Pisan Council and its schismatic adherents according to a formula of abjuration (*iuxta formam*) sent them, but not included apparently in the register's copy of the pope's letter to them. Whether this formula of abjuration was general or specifically tailored to the context of the Pisan schism is not clear. For a copy of the letter containing the reference to this *formam*, see the papal letter to Johannes de Roca of the diocese of Montauban, from Rome, dated 3 May 1513, in: Reg. Vat. 1035, fols. 52r—53v, esp. 53r. The letter of Leo to Bartholomaeus de Oleriis of the diocese of Marseille, from Rome, dated 6 October 1513, in: ASV, Reg. Vat. 1004, fols. 264v—66v, esp. 265r mentions an abjuration made in the hands of cardinal L. G. della Rovere, but does not indicate if this abjuration was according to a special formula. The typical papal letter in these cases of abjuration and regularization began with the words: *Sedes apostolica pia mater recurrentibus ad eam post excessum cum humilitate filiis libenter se propitiam exhibet et benignam ad eos quoque dexterum suae liberalitatis extendit quos ad id propria virtutum merita multipliciter recommendant exhibita siquidem nobis nuper pro parte tua petitio continebat quod* ... with minor variants, see ASV, Reg. Vat. 1004, fol. 264v, 1035, fol. 52r.

See appendix VI for a transcription of the earliest formula of abjuration I have been able to find. It is contained in the letter of Leo to Johannes Dronni of the diocese of Arles, from Ostia, dated 15 October 1513, in: ASV, Reg. Vat. 1005, fols. 153r—54v. This version has been checked against that found in Leo's letter to Johannes Cailhon of the diocese of Limoges, from S. Severa (on the coast near Tolfa), dated 27 January 1514, in: ASV, Reg. Vat. 1010, fols. 267r—68r.

constitution *Aeternae vitae claviger* may also have been the fruit of these negotiations. While a few of its phrases echo the formula of abjuration used by Carvajal and Sanseverino, the more general confession of guilt does not belabor the nullity of the Pisan Council nor include a promise to perform penance. It does specify, however, the crime as being not just a schism but also heresy, and devotes almost half of its text to solemn pledges to obey and defend the pope. The precise nature of this heresy is not given, but from the context it would seem to be a denial of the pope's power over councils, an error which led to schism. The relationship between heresy and schism was further emphasized by the assertion that the backers of the Pisan Council were true schismatics and to be punished just as *(tamquam)* heretics — a prescription of canon law commonly accepted at the time.[149] Not only was the penitent required by the formula to swear never to harm the papacy, plot against it, or divulge its counsels, nor to aid those so doing, but he had also to promise to the best of his ability to reverence, obey, defend, and protect the papacy, and to oppose actively anyone, no matter what his status, attempting to harm the pope. This formula would thus suggest an attempt by the papacy to raise the question of its authority over a council to the status of Church doctrine and to bind to itself by solemn oath future defenders of its prerogatives — a strong antidote against any recurrence of a similar schism.

No sooner had the commission finalized its work and the constitution *Aeternae vitae claviger* been issued than a third messenger was dispatched to Louis. If the carrier who brought the terms of reconciliation was an agent of Seyssel, the bearer of the formal agreement and much desired constitution was the loyal servant and member of Sanseverino's household, Sebastiano da Pistoia. The cunning attempts by Sanseverino to be regarded as the sole spokesman and effective member of the French delegation, so evident in later correspondence, may be already foreshadowed in this appointment of a messenger. That Louis was aware of and utilized these differences within his delegation is suggested by his sending of a special message to Seyssel which he wanted to arrive in Rome before Sebastiano's return there. This struggle between Sanseverino and Seyssel does not seem to have influenced seriously the negotiations on resolving the Pisan schism, but did cause much confusion later in matters of military

---

[149] For a study of the meaning of the term "heresy" at this time, see A. LANG, Der Bedeutungswandel der Begriffe "fides" und "haeresis" und die dogmatische Wertung der Konzilsentscheidungen von Vienne und Trient, in: MThZ 4 (1953) 133—46; for a punishment of schismatics as heretics by Boniface VIII in 1303 *(indicavit schismaticos et tanquam haereticos puniendos)*, see Extravag. Commun., lib. V, tit. 4, c. 1. (FRIEDBERG II 1293); for the opinion of an eminent theologian just prior to the Pisan Schism who carefully distinguished heresy from schism, see A. TROMBETTA, Opus in metaphysicam Aristotelis Padue in Thomistas discussum: Cum questionibus perutilissimis antiquioribus adiectis in optimam seriem redactis et formalitates eiusdem cum additionibus et dilucidatione diligenti exculte, Venice 1502, fols. 106v—107r; for the views of Leo's former teacher and eminent canonist, Filippo DECIO, on absolution for heresy and on the legal status of the Pisan Council, see consilia 137 and 151 respectively in his Consilia sive responsa, 2 vols., Frankfurt 1588, and PICOTTI 245—46.

The Healing of the Pisan Schism (1511—13)

strategy and political alliances. A royal confirmation of the agreement signed in Rome on the 6th was given on the 26th at Corbie to which Louis had fled to avoid a plague and to consult with his captains fighting the nearby English. By the 8th of November, Sebastiano was back in Rome reporting on the success of his mission.[150]

Plans to ratify these agreements in mid-November at a solemn session of the Lateran Council had to be altered. At the seventh session on June 17th the date for the next session was set for November 16th and this date was apparently maintained by the French-papal commission in early October as the day on which the agreement would be published in the council. In preparation for this session, Leo held toward the end of October frequent meetings of the various conciliar deputations. Plans were altered, however, in early November soon after Sebastiano's return. Together with Louis' confirmation of the accords, he apparently brought an accompanying letter dated also October 26th. While earlier reports gave the impression that efforts were already underway to send to Rome the French prelates promised, the king's letter requested a delay due to war conditions and the inability thus far of the French clergy to assemble and choose their delegation. If the eighth session could not be postponed, Louis requested that its agenda at least not treat in the absence of a French delegation the Pragmatic Sanction of Bourges. Keenly desirous of an abrogation of this Sanction, especially when agreed to by the Gallican Church, Leo prorogued this session for a month. It is interesting to note that both the eleven articles of accord and the French mandate made no mention of such an abrogation. The Lateran Council had repeatedly demanded that the French hierarchy appear before it to explain why the Sanction should not be abolished. When reporting to Florentine authorities the contents of the French mandate, Vettori claimed that it contained a pledge to send prelates in the name of the Gallican Church who would debate the Pragmatic Sanction and agree to what the Lateran Council decided regarding it.[151] Perhaps some verbal understanding was reached on this issue during the negotiations. The importance of resolving this conflict between the Roman and Gallican Churches soon became apparent.

The death on November 8th of the French cardinal resident in Rome, Robert de Guibé, famed for his peace-making efforts, became the occasion for a bitter

---

[150] On 10 October 1513 Sebastiano was provided with a letter of recommendation to the doge of Genoa whom Leo requested to aid this messenger on his way to Louis, see HERGENROETHER, Regesta Leonis I 303, nr. 4919. For the message of Louis to Seyssel, see the letter of Acciaiuoli to the Dieci di Balìa, from Amiens, 20 October 1513, in: ASF, Dieci, Resp. nr. 118, fol. 138r—v and SANUTO XVII 318; MANSI 32, 835AB; letter of Pio to Maximilian, from Rome, 8 November 1513, in: Maximiliana 30, II, fol. 23r—v.

[151] MANSI 32, 750D—54E, 791E—92B, 815C—16C, 817DE, 818C—19C; letters of Vettori to the Dieci di Balìa, from Rome, 6, 24, 29 October, 24 November, and 20 December 1513, in: ASF, Dieci, Resp. nr. 118, fols. 44v, 162v, 200r, 317r, 421r; letter of Acciaiuoli to the Dieci di Balìa, from Amiens, 23 October 1513, in: Ibid. fol. 139r; letter of the Dieci di Balìa to Acciaiuoli, from Florence, 13 November 1513, in: ASF, Dieci, Mis. nr. 40, fol. 185v.

conflict. This cardinal had been appointed perpetual administrator of the rich diocese of Albi in 1510, but due to his loyalty to Julius II was denied by Louis real possession of it and its revenues. The man who came into pacific possession of this bishopric and held it for the two years prior to Guibé's death was Charles Robertet, brother of the royal treasurer and principal adviser of the king, Florimond Robertet. Because Leo did not recognize Charles' claims and wanted to retain Roman control of so rich a church which had become vacant in the Roman curia by the death of Guibé, the pope decided to confer it immediately on another curial cardinal. Although his cousin Giulio dei Medici was already archbishop of Florence, Leo granted him a dispensation so that he could continue to hold that church while being named also bishop of Albi. The bull of provision was dated November 21st. When the Florentine ambassador at the French court, Roberto Acciaiuoli learned of this, he feared for the worst since each claimant to the see of Albi was supported by a very powerful and close family member. Leo was in danger of losing the good will of Florimond Robertet, considered essential for the success of matters handled at court. Acciaiuoli worried that the agreement for ending the Pisan schism might even be in danger. From Rome, Vettori reported the arrival of a letter from Florimond on his brother's behalf. Leo refused to yield, insisting that Guibé had been properly appointed to Albi by Julius and that with this cardinal's death, the pope had to maintain the papacy's right to confer benefices becoming vacant in the Curia. Who would question that the pope's cousin Giulio was most worthy of this see? Did Florimond think his own desires should take precedence? Surely Louis would grant Giulio real possession of Albi once things quieted down. The flurry over this provision was not grounds for going back on agreements already reached, especially about the Pisan Council.[152]

Leo underestimated the difficulty of making effective this provision. Unwilling apparently to remove from the see of Albi the brother of one of his principal ministers, Louis sought in late spring of 1514 to placate the pope by giving his cousin instead the recently vacated bishopric of Lavaur. Robertet backed this appointment in hope of securing thereby for his brother papal provision to Albi. From Paris, Pandolfino urged cardinal Giulio to be generous to Robertet by resigning Albi to his brother. Such liberality would put the minister into his debt and besides Giulio had never been able to get real possession of the church. Robertet's hopes for Albi were blocked not only in Rome but also in Paris. Just as cardinal Sanseverino sought to oust from his position of leadership in the French delegation to the papal court Claude de Seyssel whom Robertet backed, so also did the cardinal's brother, Galeazzo Sanseverino, the Grand-Shieldbearer of France, seek to replace Robertet as a principal adviser

---

[152] Letters of Vettori to the Dieci di Balìa, from Rome, 10 November and 10 December 1513, in: ASF, Dieci, Resp. nr. 118, fols. 267r, 391r, letter of Acciaiuoli to the Dieci di Balìa, from Blois, 26 November 1513, in: Ibid. fol. 332r—v.

of the king. The issue of Albi became one of their battlefields. As the death of the peace-maker Guibé had ironically occasioned the conflict over Albi, so too would the demise of a clerical and a lay leader of the divisive Pisan Council opened a way to its resolution. On 14 December 1514 the restored cardinal Guillaume Briçonnet died leaving vacant the wealthy Church of Narbonne. On New Year's Day 1515 the ineffectual Louis XII was replaced by François I who eagerly desired the pope's favor. A month later the new king conferred Narbonne on Giulio dei Medici who had failed thus far to get possession of either Albi or Lavaur. With this handsome compensation, Giulio willingly resigned his claim to Albi and on 14 March 1515 Charles Robertet finally secured papal provision to the see.[153]

Leo's initial attempt to appoint his cousin to the see of Albi had not been well received by the French clergy and only increased its already negative feelings toward the papacy. To implement the agreement he ratified on October 26th, Louis commissioned the Parlement of Paris a month later to organize and send the delegation of former Pisan prelates and doctors on its way to Rome. Out of respect for the king, Parlement confirmed the mandate Louis and his royal council had approved. The parlementary provisions for implementing this agreement differed only slightly from the royal intent. Had it not been for the favorable attitude toward the papacy which the king and his council manifested, this Parlement with its prelates would have used the occasion for insults. They seem to have been particularly concerned about having to obtain a new provision from Rome for benefices already conferred by the Pisan Council. News of Giulio dei Medici's provision to the see of Albi pleased no one. While plans went ahead in early December for dispatching the promised delegation of penitent prelates, a proposal to send soon after them an embassy to pay Leo homage lost the enthusiastic support it had enjoyed at court prior to the arrival of word of the Albi provision. The project was left suspended in Parlement.[154] Events had proved Leo right, for the Albi affair did not alter the agreement already reached in healing the schism.

A major factor influencing the course of the negotiations to resolve the ecclesiastical issue of the schism was the prospect of a diplomatic and even military alliance between France and the papacy. After successive military defeats of the French and of their Scottish and Venetian allies, Louis was in desparate

---

[153] Letters of Francesco Pandolfini from Paris to: Giuliano dei Medici, 7 June 1514, Lorenzo dei Medici, 8 June 1514, Giulio dei Medici, 8 June and 17 July 1514, Leo, 9 June and 10 July 1514, Giulio and Giuliano, 2 and 4 February 1515, Otto di Pratica, 11 February 1515, in: ASF, Signori, Dieci di Balia, Otto di Pratica, Legazione e Commissarie — Missive e Responsive (= Sig., Dieci, Otto, Leg. e Com.) Registro nr. 55, fols. 44r—45r, 47v, 48v—49r, 74r—75r, 80r, 192v, 195r, 209r; HERGENROETHER, Regesta Leonis I 339, II 48, 50, nrs. 5430—35 (21 November 1513), 14,543—50 (14 March 1515), 14,587 (16 March 1515); EUBEL III 10, 101, 253, 327; for Poncher's failed effort to secure the archdiocese of Narbonne, see GARAND 323.

[154] Letters of Acciaiuoli to the Dieci di Balìa, from Blois, 26 November and 4 December 1513, in: ASF, Dieci, Resp. nr. 118, fols. 332r, 361r.

need of new support and of an end to his isolation. For a variety of reasons Leo was also willing to give serious consideration to a possible French alliance. By having his agent, the Florentine ambassador in France, dangle before the king the bait of numerous unspecified favors which the pope wished to bestow on him once he resolved the question of the schism, Leo not only used hopes of an alliance as a tool to hasten the spiritual reconciliation, but encouraged the king to look to him as a potential friend and defender of his interests. From such a relationship Leo could gain a new protector of papal and Medici interests and a counterbalance to an increasing domination of Italy by the Germans and Spanish.[155]

Attempts were made to negotiate a papal-French alliance. In September Louis tested Leo's intentions by agreeing in principle to an end of the schism and entrusting to him negotiations to end the state of war with Leo's allies. A draft treaty was drawn up and signed by Jacobus Sachus, chancellor of Pavia. By it Louis pledged to protect the Papal States and Medici control of Florence and he also renounced his claim to Milan and Asti. Such a shift in papal policy could not be kept completely secret and rumors reached the imperial camp that Leo was now completely on the side of the French. These rumors were promptly denied by Antonio Giuppo della Rovere, who in practice functioned at times as the pope's double agent. On the same day that the king formally ratified the mandates renouncing the Pisan schism and constituting as his representatives at the Lateran Council Sanseverino, Seyssel, and Forbin, Louis also appointed these three ambassadors as his procurators for resolving the dispute over Milan between France and its opponents: the Empire, Spain, England, the Swiss, and the Sforzas. The defeat of France's ally Venice at Olma, which gave an initial set back to these negotiations, was quickly turned to Louis' advantage through the skill of Seyssel who played on Leo's fears of imperial-Spanish dominance of the Italian peninsula. Instead of France proving an effective counterbalance, its weakness became apparent in its loss of Tournai and in the confidence of its captors shown in the impending departures from the city of Henry Tudor for England and of Maximilian Hapsburg for Germany. Rumor had it that Louis was nonetheless planning an invasion of Italy to recover his territories there lost. As yet lacking a clear understanding and friendship with the French, Leo was reluctant to welcome their return. He hoped, however, to use them to expel from the peninsula the Germans and Spanish and to provide his brother Giuliano with the thus vacated throne of Naples. Much to the displeasure of the Spanish who accused the pope of gross ingratitude, lengthy negotiations

---

[155] Letter of Acciaiuoli to the Dieci di Balìa, from Amiens, 21 September 1513, in: ASF, Dieci, Resp. nr. 117, fol. 147v; letters of the Dieci di Balìa to Acciaiuoli, from Florence, 24 September and 11 October 1513, in: ASF, Dieci di Balìa, Legazione e Commissarie, Istruzione e Lettere Missive (= Dieci, Leg. e Com., Ist. e Let. Mis.), nr. 40, fols. 161v, 171r; letter of Lang to Maximilian, from Viterbo, 16 November 1513, in: Maximiliana 30, II, fols. 66v, 68r.

The Healing of the Pisan Schism (1511—13)

were carried out between Leo and the three French orators in hope of forming a league including the Papal States, France, Venice, and the Swiss. These discussions continued up to the eve of the eighth session, thus giving Louis added reason to follow through with the promised renunciation of Pisa and adherence to Lateran.[156]

Another incentive for France to make peace was the danger of increased vulnerability and isolation should its ally Venice come to terms with the Empire and Aragon. Already in early July Maximilian had empowered Lang to negotiate an honorable peace with the Venetian Republic so that he could the better fight France. To apply psychological and economic pressures, Lang as the emperor's representative in Italy issued in late October an edict ordering the Venetians to retreat from lands they had seized and forbidding any trade with them. Willing to conclude a favorable peace, Venice did not deal directly with the Empire but entrusted to Leo much authority to settle their affairs with the Empire and Aragon. The Republic knew that its enemies hoped to despoil it of its territory on the mainland. Fernando even entertained the secret design of conquering the Republic, changing its government, and placing on its ducal throne his much beloved grandson and namesake left otherwise empty-handed by his elder brother's vast inheritance. The Venetians had reason to confide in Leo, for he was deeply opposed to any Hapsburg domination of Italy and was concerned lest there be truth in the rumors that Venice was ready to call in the Turks if its position in Italy was too threatened. On his arrival in Rome Lang spent long hours in discussions with Leo and with his fellow orator Pio and the representatives of his Spanish ally, Vich and Remolines. In hope of winning over the pope to approving a treaty despoiling Venice of all its mainland possessions less Padova and Treviso, Lang proposed that Leo's brother Giuliano be given imperial investiture of Lucca, Pisa, and Siena. While these negotiations gave concern to the French, neither Leo nor the Venetians were ready to see the Republic seriously weakened. For its part Venice insisted it would not desert its French ally.[157]

---

[156] Sanuto XVII 180, 217, 318, 373; Capituli per lo apunctamento et pace facta, signed by Jacobus Sachus comitatis Papiae cancellarius, September 1513, in: ASF, MAP, filza 147, nr. 34, fol. 117r — I am grateful to Professor Melissa Meriam Bullard for having confirmed this reference for me; letter of Antonio Giuppo della Rovere to Leo, from the imperial camp at Tournai, 20 September 1513, in: Maximiliana 29, IV, fol. 86v; letter of Pio to Maximilian, from Rome, 8 November 1513, in: Maximiliana 30, II, fol. 23r—v; C. Guasti, ed., I Manoscritti Torrigiani donati al Reale Archivio di Stato di Firenze: Descrizione e Saggio, Florence 1878, 459; Cruickshank 1—31.

[157] Letter of Maximilian to Marguerite, from Frankfurt, 5 July 1513, in: Le Glay, Correspondance II 173; edict of Lang against the Venetians, from Mirandola, 23 October 1513, in: ASF, Dieci, Resp. nr. 118, fols. 151r—52r, 157r—58v; letter of Vettori to the Dieci di Balìa, from Rome, 18 November 1513, in: Ibid., fol. 298r—v; Sanuto XVII 341—42, 353; letter of Lang to Maximilian, from Viterbo, 16 November 1513, in: Maximiliana 30, II, fol. 68r—v; Instructio secretissima a Leone X data Reverendissimo Gurcensi pro pace inter principes, from Rome, 29 April 1514, in: ASV, AA. Arm. I—XVIII, nr. 2621, fol. 1v; letter of Pio to Maximilian, from Rome, 6 July 1513, in: Maximiliana 29, III, fol. 20r.

In the context of these diplomatic, military, and ecclesiastical negotiations, the pope and college of cardinals decided to hold the eighth session of the Lateran Council at which the representatives of the French king were to renounce formally in his name the now defunct Pisan Council. In order that the promised delegation of French bishops could also arrive to abrogate at this time the Pragmatic Sanction of Bourges, this session had already been delayed for one month. But the unlikelihood of their attendance became clear when the Florentine ambassador reported on December 4th that the full delegation of bishops had yet to assemble at Blois and depart for Rome. If the absence of the French prelates eliminated from the conciliar agenda a discussion of the Pragmatic Sanction, other items were almost ready for approval. At a congregation of cardinals on December 12th, the schedule for the eighth session was established. To allow adequate time for the preparation of the conciliar decrees, the pope on the following day postponed this session from the 16th to the 19th of December.[158]

On the eve of the session a crisis arose when the precise wording of the French mandate became known to the imperial ambassador, Alberto Pio. He took offense at the way in which the emperor Maximilian was made to bear principal responsibility for the Pisan Schism. At the marathon meeting of the cardinals on December 12th, Lang seems to have worked out with Leo a compromise solution to this problem. The French mandate was to be left unaltered, but its recitation at the eighth session would be so garbled as to eliminate the offending passages. To prove his conscientiousness as the emperor's ambassador, Pio penned for inclusion in the official records of the council a detailed refutation of the impugned reputation of Maximilian.[159]

On 19 December 1513 at the eighth session the French mandate was read, formally renouncing the Pisan Council and adhering to the Lateran Council. Immediately following the Mass, sermon, chanting of a Gospel text, and obeisances of the almost 150 conciliar fathers in attendance, Claude de Seyssel and Louis Forbin presented the first of two mandates of Louis XII to the pope. They excused Louis' former adherence to the Pisan Council on the ground that the king had been mislead by many prelates into thinking it was legitimate. On learning from Leo that only the Lateran Council was canonical, Louis disbanded the Pisan assembly, adhered to the Lateran, and asked that he be pardoned his mistake. The ambassadors then pointed out that the king's position was more

---

[158] For the prorogations of the eighth session, see MANSI 32, 818B—19C and the letter of Vettori to the Dieci di Balìa, from Rome, 14 December 1513, in: ASF, Dieci, Resp. nr. 118, fol. 409v; on the delayed departure of the French delegation, see the letter of Acciaiuoli to the Dieci di Balìa, from Blois, 4 December 1513, Ibid. fol 361r; on the congregation of cardinals, see SANUTO XVII 398.

[159] On the reported contents of the French madate, see the letter of Vettori to the Dieci di Balìa, from Rome, 20 December 1513, in: ASF, Dieci, Resp. nr. 118, fol. 421r; on Pio's countermeasures, see MINNICH, 'Protestatio' of Pio 261—82.

fully described in the first mandate. Leo responded to the ambassadors' speech by praising the king's intention and accepting his excuse. The pope next accepted the second mandate constituting Sanseverino, Seyssel, and Forbin as representatives of Louis. Leo handed these two documents to Tommaso Inghirami, the council's secretary, to read them aloud from the pulpit. The first mandate contained the verbatim text which had been so carefully negotiated and signed in October. The second, also dated October 26th, named his three ambassadors to the council and asked that the council not take action on the question of the Pragmatic Sanction until the full French delegation had arrived.[160] Whether Inghirami actually garbled his recitation of the first mandate, as instructed, is not known.

Reaction to these mandates was mixed. While Pio apparently quietly submitted to the conciliar officials his written protestations against the implicit attack on the emperor contained in the first mandate, an ambassador of the duke of Milan interrupted the conciliar proceedings to register his objections. In both mandates, Louis had included among his titles that of duke of Milan. Following Inghirami's reading of these documents, one of the members of the Milanese delegation, either Francesco Sforza or Marino Caraccioli, approached the papal throne to register his protest to this usage. A few days earlier the pope had formally accepted the obeisance of the Milanese delegation given in the name of Massimiliano Sforza as duke of Milan. He had also supported the Sforza claim to this title when the French had objected. When Seyssel once again protested, this time against the Milanese intervention at the eighth session, Leo sided with the Sforza duke and silenced the French. Most of the conciliar fathers, and especially Leo X, found in the French mandates ground not for a minor objection but for great joy. Asked by de Grassi if he wanted the *Te Deum* sung at the conclusion of the session, the pope responded affirmatively, insisting that the restoration of Church unity effected by the French mandates was a matter of great importance.[161]

The ease with which this reconciliation had thus been formalized displeased the emperor who, on learning of the conciliar ceremonies, warned that such indulgence could have detrimental consequences. The French had already con-

---

[160] DE GRASSI, Diarium Concilii, ed. DYKMANS 1039: 8—12; MANSI 32, 831E—36B.

[161] On Pio, see MINNICH, 'Protestatio' of Pio, 280, 289; on Louis' use of the ducal title, see MANSI 32, 832A and 835C; on the protest of Marino Caraccioli, see MANSI 32, 836B, DE GRASSI, Diarium Concilii, ed. DYKMANS 1039: 12, and the letter of Jacques Hannock to Marguerite d'Autriche, from Rome, 21 December 1513, in: ADNL, Coté B 18861, nr. 31067, fols. 1v—2r, on fol. 2r he gives the date of December 16th for the obeisance ceremony, but in ASV, Arch. Consist., Acta Miscel. 3, fol. 54v the date of Wednesday December 14th is given and there also Seyssel is identified as the protesting French orator, see also PRODI 463 for the date of December 14th; for part of the text of the Milanese protest, see MORONE, Lettere latine, ed. PROMIS and MÜLLER, App. 133, pp. 326—27; on the pope's satisfaction with the mandates, see the letters of the Dieci di Balìa to Vettori and Acciaiuoli, from Florence, 24 and 25 December 1513, in: ASF, Dieci, Leg. e Com., Ist. e Let. Mis., nr. 41, fols. 6v—7r, and DE GRASSI, Diarium Concilii, ed. DYKMANS 1039 : 15.

tumaciously neglected with impunity a deadline given them. The leniency, nonetheless shown them, would not stiffen their resolve never to return to their former sinful condition. In addition, a bad example of contempt for papal authority was thereby given to others. In answer to Maximilian's objections, Lang reported that the French had only been admitted to membership in the council, but had not been absolved. The bishop of Gurk promised not to neglect his duty in this regard, but to seek to impede this absolution as opportunities arose.[162]

The reading of the French mandates at the Lateran Council, while very significant, did not of itself heal the Pisan Schism. The process of reconciliation still hinged in good part on the French fulfilment of the terms set out in the eleven articles and two mandates.

Partial French fulfillment of the terms for reconciliation

The papacy had kept its pledge to free the French king from any concern over the penalties he may have incurred due to his role in the Pisan Schism. The constitution *Aeternae vitae claviger* of 9 October 1513, which contained sweeping declarations and absolutions to that effect, had been sent to the king.[163]

The restoration of the remaining two Pisan cardinals who had been deprived of their offices and excommunicated was accomplished within little more than four months of the formal ceremonies at the Lateran Council. Guillaume Briçonnet and René de Prie were not required to come in person to Rome or suffer the humiliations previously inflicted on Carvajal and Sanseverino. In a public consistory on 7 April 1514 cardinal Briçonnet's son, Denys, read his father's signed statement retracting his former errors. The pope then restored him to the cardinalitial dignity, to the metropolitan church of Narbonne, and

---

[162] For the letter of Maximilian to Lang, from Wels, 25 February 1514 and of Lang to Maximilian, from Rome, 22 March 1514, see Maximiliana, 30, III, fol. 228r and 31 I, fol. 104v.

[163] How this constitution was delivered to Louis is not clear. According to the first article, this papal document was to be sent by a *legatus a latere*. The most likely candidate for this post would have been Robert de Guibé, but he died on 8 November 1513, see Vettori to the Dieci de Balìa, from Rome, 10 November 1513, in: ASF, Dieci, Resp., nr. 118, fol. 267r. Forbin would have preferred Sanseverino or d'Este as legate, see below, Appendix III. Perhaps one of the messengers in the negotiations, such as Sebastiano da Pistoia or Amadeo de Marseille, conveyed the document to the king. Leo may have thought of entrusting this task to Ludovico Canossa whom he planned to send as his nuncio to France, providing him with instructions dated September 14th and special faculties on October 11th, but his departure was delayed until May of the following year — see Pastor VII 63 n., 98 and the letter of Baltassare Turini to Lorenzo dei Medici, from Rome, 22 May 1514, in: ASF, MAP, filza 107, nr. 27, fol. 27v. Not until 28 July 1514 did Leo appoint a cardinal as his *legatus de latere* to France, namely François Guilhem de Clermont-Lodève (de Castelnau) — see R. d'Amat, Clermont-Lodève (François Guilhem de), in Dictionnaire de biographie française VIII (Paris 1959), cols. 1507—08, at 1507. The cardinal's faculties were apparently restricted to the ecclesiastical provinces of Avignon, Vienne, and Embrun. Clermont was already in France — see the letter of Marino Caraccioli to Massimiliano Sforza, from Rome, 2 August 1514, in: Maximiliana 32 II, fol. 88r—v.

to his other former churches, monasteries, privileges, indults, and concessions. On April 24th de Prie was similarly restored to his pristine status.[164]

The other three Pisan cardinals did not apparently undergo the same type of reconciliation, or any at all. Francisco de Borja, who was represented at the opening ceremonies of the Pisan Council by a procurator, died three days later. So that he could later be interred with cardinalitial honors in Rome, Leo on 31 October 1513, granted him a posthumous absolution. Philippe de Luxembourg, who was also represented at Pisa by a procurator, was not deprived of his offices nor excommunicated. Indeed, Leo sent him apparently in October of 1513 a special invitation to attend the Lateran Council where his wisdom, experience, authority, and good example were needed. Amanieu d'Albert who attended in person the Pisan Council, was also not formally punished for his actions. His loss of the administration of the church of Pamplona in 1512 was probably due to the conquest of this diocese by Fernando of Aragon and the cardinal's family ties to the defeated royal family of Navarre. In December of 1513 Leo granted him a monastery *in commendam* in the diocese of Poitiers and six months later confirmed his administration of Pamiers.[165]

What Leo intensely desired and Louis pledged to produce was a delegation of six bishops and four theologians or canonists drawn from among the more important former participants at the Pisan Council. In their own name and in that of the other Pisan adherents they were to abjure that council, beg pardon from the pope, and incorporate themselves into the Lateran Council where they would enter into negotiations for an abrogation of the Pragmatic Sanction of Bourges. Such a delegation left Blois for Rome in early December of 1513. Among its members were five bishops: Jean de Poupet, O.S.B., of Châlons sur Saône, Jean le Veneur de Tillières of Lisieux, François de Halwin of Amiens, Antoine d'Estaing of Angoulême, and Symphorien Boullioud of Glandeves.

---

[164] On the restorations of Briçonnet and de Prie, see EUBEL III 6b n. 2, 11; HERGENROETHER' Regesta Leonis, I 498 nr. 7854 (= ASV, Reg. Vat. 1198, fols. 192r—95r — a copy of the cardinal's statement is not included in this document), 728 nr. 11795, and the letter (without author, date, or origins given) to the Dieci di Balìa, in ASF, Dieci, Resp. nr. 118, fol. 480r; for an overview of the role of de Prie at the Pisan Council, see G. OURY, Autour du Concile de Pise de 1511: le Cardinal René de Prie, maître de la chapelle de Louis XII, in: Bulletin Trimestriel de la Société Archeologique de Touraine 38 (1977) 469—84, esp. 476—82.

[165] For the presence by procurators of cardinals de Borja and de Luxembourg at the opening ceremonies, see Acta Primi Concilii Pisani 79—80; for the presence of d'Albret, see Ibid. 79; on Borja's death and burial, see EUBEL III 7 and HERGENROETHER, Regesta Leonis I 319 nr. 5171; for the letter of Leo to de Luxembourg, see ASV, Arm. XLIV, vol. 5. fol. 48v; for the confirmation by Leo on 7 May 1513 of a pension conceded by Julius on 9 July 1511 to cardinal de Luxembourg, see HERGENROETHER, Regesta Leonis I 146 nrs. 2482—83; for the claim that d'Albret submitted to the pope and obtained his pardon, see HERGENROETHER - LECLERCQ VIII/1, 445; for HERGENROETHER's admission that he was unable to find any record of d'Albret's reconciliation with Rome, see his Regesta Leonis I 375 n. 1; for the absence of de Luxembourg's and of d'Albret's names from among those specifically condemned by Julius in late 1511 and early 1512, see above nn. 46 and 47; for d'Albret's confirmation as administrator of Pamiers, see EUBEL III, 111; for his *commenda* in Poitier, see HERGENROETHER, Regesta Leonis I 375, nr. 5916.

The first four of these bishops had been present at the opening ceremonies of the Pisan Council. Of these prelates only one could claim to have held a position of leadership at that council. At its second session, Antoine d'Estaing was named one of the four judges charged both with examining questions of faith, schism, and church reform and with proposing solutions for adoption by the council. Boullioud may have attended the final session of the council held in Lyon. The two theologians accompanying the bishops were Jean Le Lamiens and Antoine Seurre, who was a canon of Meaux, master of arts, doctor of theology from the University of Paris, and preacher at the eighth session held in Milan. The two canonists were Guillaume de Nory, a doctor of both laws and archdeacon of Lisieux, and Jean du Fresne, also a doctor of canon and civil laws, archdeacon of Toulouse, procurator of the University of Toulouse, and one of the four deputies appointed at the third session to negotiate with the pope and college of cardinals a mutually agreeable site for holding the council. Thus in each category of bishop, theologian, and canonist, at least one cleric was among the more distinguished members of the council.[166]

If the French delegation failed to arrive in Rome in time for the eighth session, five former members of the Pisan Council had been present to hear the reading of the French mandates. Cardinals Carvajal, the former president of the Pisan Council, and Sanseverino, its legate in captured papal territories, were both in attendance at the Lateran. So too were Denys Briçonnet, son of the deprived cardinal and bishop of Toulon who had first attended the schismatic council in Pisa, and Giambattista Bongiovanni, bishop of Vence who joined the assembly in Milan. Perhaps the most famous of the Pisan adherents at the eighth session was the abbot of Subasio and former secretary, promotor, homilist, and propagandist of the schismatic assembly, Zaccaria Ferreri. To the following ninth session of the Lateran Council came as ambassador of the Sforza duke Girolamo Morone who had witnessed the convocation of the Pisan Council three years earlier in Milan. Also present was Vasino Malabaila, bishop of Piacenza, who had earlier backed the Pisan Council. If these seven men had succeeded in making their way to the Lateran Council, the members of the French delegation repeatedly claimed that insurmountable obstacles blocked their route.[167]

---

[166] For the promised composition and functions of the French delegation, see MANSI 32, 834A—C, 835E—36A; for the members of this delegation and their former roles at the Pisan Council, see Ibid. 864E—65A and Acta primi concilii Pisani 80, 96—97, 109—110, 189; on Bullioud, see H. FISQUET, La France pontificale (Gallia Christiana): Histoire chronologique et biographique des archevêques et évêques de tous les dioceses de France, VI: Métropole de Reims: Soissons et Laon, Paris s.d., 76—77 and R. D'AMAT, Bullioud, Symphorien, in: DBF 7 (Paris 1956) 663; and on Antoine d'Estaing's prominent role at the Pisan Council, see C. BELMON, Un évêque français à l'Assemblée de Tours et au Concile de Pise: François d'Estaing, in: Revue des études historiques, Année 89 (1923) 295—312, esp. 304—10.

[167] For the presence of these prelates at the eighth and ninth sessions, see MANSI 32, 827C, E, 829A, 830A, E and 860D; for Morone at the ninth session, see Ibid. 869A; for their presence and roles

The initial deadline of 1 January 1514 came and went without the French prelates presenting themselves before the pope, as had been promised earlier in Louis' mandate. To excuse their absence, the bishops wrote to Rome explaining their difficulties. Neither Massimiliano Sforza of Milan under the control of Swiss and imperial advisers nor Ottaviano Campofregoso of Genoa who looked to the Aragonese for guidance and was engaged in fighting off the Adorni faction had been willing to grant a safe-conduct through their territories. As a result the French delegation was forced to find shelter from the Alpine winter in the Augustinian priory of SS. Pietro e Paolo e San Lorenzo at Ulzio on the Dora Riparia River, half way between Briançon in Dauphiné and Susa in Savoy. In this desolate place of penance and solitude, they awaited word to proceed to Rome.[168]

So that their willingness to fulfil their mission would be apparent to all, the French prelates made before a public tribunal on 11 January 1514 a formal statement in their own names and in those of all the other Pisan fathers, especially of those for whom they had explicit procurations, namely: Gaspar de Tournon, bishop of Valence and Die who had attended the schismatic assembly in Milan; Claude de Longwy bishop-elect of Mâcon who had been present at the opening of the council in Pisa; Guiscard de Beysard (Lessart), titular bishop of Hierapolis and auxiliary bishop of the archdiocese of Lyon, who had celebrated the Mass of the Holy Spirit opening the tenth session of the council in Lyon; and Jean Arzelier, a doctor of both canon and civil laws living in Lyon. A procuration of this type had, of course, been allowed by the seventh of the eleven articles of the papal-French accord. Before two apostolic notaries and masters, Jean de Alverina of the diocese of Limoges and Pierre Quesvel, a priest of the diocese of Lisieux, the members of the French delegation publicly renounced the Pisan Council which had been already dissolved, adhered to the Lateran Council, and asked to be absolved of any penalties they had incurred for having supported the schismatic assembly.[169]

In late February they received word from the pope. By his letter of 17 February 1514, Leo praised their efforts to reach Rome and informed them that he had written to Massimiliano Sforza and Ottaviano Campofregoso asking that they provide the French delegation with a safe-conduct and with whatever else

---

at the Pisan Council, see Acta primi concilii Pisani 48 (Morone as witness), 91 (Carvajal as president), 139—47 (Sanseverino as legate); 80, 82, 91, 122—30, etc. (Ferreri as secretary, homilist, etc.) and Promotiones et progressus, 42v—44v (Ferreri as celebrant, homilist, and notary).

[168] For the deadline of 1 January 1514, see MANSI 32, 834B; for the inability to obtain safe-conducts from Milan and Genoa, see below, Appendix VII; on Swiss and imperial domination of Milan, see PRODI, 469; on the unrest in Genoa and Aragonese control, see MANSI 32, 865AB and GUICCIARDINI XI, xiv, xvi, ed. PANIGADA III 286—87, 298. The French delegation arrived at Ulzio by mid-January, see MANSI 32, 864DE, 865A—C, 866BC, 867A, 868B—E. On the priory at Ulzio (until 1937 called Oulx), see L. H. COTTINEAU, Répertoire topo-bibliographique des abbayes et prieurés, 2 vols., Mâcon 1935—37, II 2159—60.

[169] MANSI 32, 865E—67D.

was needed for their protection. He urged the bishops to put aside fear and proceed on their way. However, at about the same time they received this papal exhortation, they were also counseled by the governor of Asti to delay until they had actually received the requisite safe-conduct. For twenty days they waited only to learn that the duke of Milan denied the pope's request for a safe-conduct brought to him by a papal mazziere.[170]

The French delegation on March 19th wrote to the pope explaining why they could not come. They thanked the pope for his efforts to obtain for them a safe-conduct and explained how Massimiliano had refused it. To assure Leo of their readiness to fulfil their mission, they forwarded to him a notarized document detailing how before a specially constituted tribunal they had renounced the Pisan schism, adhered to the Lateran Council, and "humbly and devoutly" sought a papal absolution. This document was dated March 17th. They noted that four months had passed since they had set out on this journey and that they had for the last sixty days been forced to reside in this place of solitude and penance. With Easter approaching, they felt a pastoral obligation to return to their dioceses to provide for the liturgical needs of their flocks and they asked the pope's permission to do just that.[171]

At the ninth session of the Lateran Council on May 5th the conciliar procurator Mario de Perusco accused the French bishops of contumacy for failing to attend the Council and he asked for a declaration against them. In their defense Seyssel explained how they had come as far as the Alps but had not been able to obtain the safe-conduct needed to complete their journey to Rome. In proof of his claims he produced the notarized statement of the special tribunal, a letter of the Savoyard ducal council noting the advice of the governor of Asti not to proceed without a safe-conduct, and the letter of the delegation to Leo explaining their predicament. On the basis of these, Seyssel asked that they be formally excused. The Milanese ambassador, Girolamo Morone, claimed that Massimiliano Sforza had not denied the safe-conduct to the French bishops, but had only delayed giving it to them so that he could first legitimately deliberate and consult on the matter. Besides, there were roads to Rome other than those which passed through Milanese territories. Leo admitted the excuse of the French and postponed until the next session the deadline for their arrival. And so that all those invited could come to the council, Leo had Seyssel read a decree which, among other things, required civil authorities to grant to these persons safe-conducts, and threatened penalties on anyone who tried to impede them.[172]

---

[170] For Leo's letter, see Appendix VII; for the warning not to proceed, see MANSI 32, 867D—68A; on Sforza's refusal, see Ibid. 868C.

[171] MANSI 32, 868A—69A; for the notarized document, see 864D—67D.

[172] MANSI 32, 864B—69C, 873A—74B; for Morone's defense of Massimiliano, see MORONE, Lettere latine, ed. PROMIS and MÜLLER 332—36 and the letter of Vettori to the Dieci di Balìa, from Rome, 6 May 1514, in: ASF, Dieci, Resp., nr. 118, fol. 649r.

The Healing of the Pisan Schism (1511—13)

In November of 1514 and March of 1515 Leo made a major effort to secure the presence of a French delegation at the upcoming tenth session. On November 26th he prorogued that session from 1 December 1514 to 23 March 1515, and on the day before that session was to meet he again moved its date to May 4th. Ample time was thus allotted for the arrival of the French. Free passage for them was also solicited from the three states controling the routes into Italy along the borders of France and of her Savoyard ally.[173]

Leo concentrated his attention on securing the cooperation of the doge of Genoa, Ottaviano Campofregoso. On 8 March 1515, the pope reminded the doge that two important goals of the Lateran Council remained to be achieved: a thorough extinction of the Pisan Schism and an abrogation of the Pragmatic Sanction of Bourges. Without the presence of the French bishops at the council neither goal could be fittingly accomplished. Although cited to come to Rome, these bishops had excused themselves on the ground of a fear arising from the safe-conducts having been denied them. Leo therefore urged the doge to grant the French an ample and free safe-conduct through his territory and thereby eliminate any pretext they might claim for not coming.[174]

In his response to the pope's request, Campofregoso on March 22nd issued a "secure, full, valid, and general safe-conduct" to the prelates of France or of any other nation invited by the pope to attend the Lateran Council. This safe-conduct applied to their full retinues, was valid on both land and sea subject to Genoese jurisdiction, and remained in force no matter what controversies or battles raged between Genoa and another country. The authenticity of the signatures of the doge and of his chancellor and of the ducal seal affixed to this document was attested to in Rome on April 26th by Eduardo Doria and Tommaso Pecunia, merchants of Genoa. On that same day cardinal Antonio del Monte, acting on instructions from the pope, personally entrusted this document to the conciliar scribes and notaries Bernhard Schulz von Lowenburg and Bernardino de Contreras of Burgos to note its authenticity and have it forwarded to the French ambassadors. Five days later on April 28th the master of the papal couriers Edouard Du Vivier attested to the fact that the couriers Jean Duvet and Giovanni Bernardi had that day handed over the Genoese safe-conduct to the French ambassadors in Rome, Louis de Forbin and Nostromars.[175]

On 10 March 1515 Leo wrote three letters in an effort to obtain a safe-conduct for the French bishops from the Swiss who dominated Milanese foreign policy. The pope noted that a thorough extinction of the Pisan Schism and an abrogation of the Pragmatic Sanction, both ends of the Lateran Council,

---

[173] Mansi 32, 898A—99A. The official reason given for postponing the session was that the preparatory commissions had not as yet completed their work.
[174] For this letter, see below Appendix VIII.
[175] Mansi 32, 899A—900C.

were yet to be accomplished, although much progress had already been made on the first goal. Leo and the council still wanted the French to come to Rome, seek pardon for their error, and abjure it with new oaths of loyalty to the Roman Church and pope. An abrogation of the Pragmatic Sanction in a way more in keeping with human nature and fitting precautions also required the presence of the French bishops. They had already been cited to come but had been prevented from completing their journey due to a denial of safe-conducts by the Swiss, among others, as had been reported to the pope. Leo observed that this denial provided the French with a welcome and pleasing excuse for not coming. If only the Swiss would recognize this and the danger that they could fall under the penalties imposed by the pope and council on anyone impeding access to the council, they would not only provide the French with a safe-conduct but assist them on their way. Leo asked that the Swiss send him immediately a full safe-conduct for the French delegation for passage through their territories and through those over which their influence extended. A similar letter bearing the same date was also sent to the client of the Swiss, Massimiliano Sforza of Milan. Copies of the letter to the Swiss were sent that same day to cardinal Matthias Schiner and to the papal nuncio in Switzerland, Ennio Filonardi. They were urged to use their influence with the Swiss to obtain the safe-conduct for the French.[176]

Despite these efforts of Leo, a French delegation failed to appear at the tenth session on 4 May 1515. To put added pressure on the French, the pope had Pedro Flores read a degree which exposed the fallaciousness of the excuse they had proffered and ordered them to come. Leo recalled how he had obtained from the Genoese government a safe-conduct through its territories for the French prelates wanting to come to the council in Rome and how he had seen that this document was handed over to the French representatives. For the last time he once again postponed taking legal action against them for contumacy and set 1 October 1515 as the final date for their arrival in Rome. If this deadline was not met, he threatened to proceed against them and to a determination of the question of the Pragmatic Sanction at the next session of the council, which he scheduled to meet on 14 December 1515.[177]

After the reading of this decree, the French ambassador Louis Forbin offered an excuse for the absent French bishops. He noted that usually no one who has been cited is obliged to endure the risks of a sea voyage or dangers from robbers, enemies, or long journeys. The French prelates had been justly impeded by the continuing conflicts in the areas of the Dauphiné, Liguria, and Lombardia. They had asked the pope to hold them excused and had promised

---

[176] For the letters to the Swiss, Schiner, Filonardi, and Sforza, see ASV. Arm. XLIV, vol. 5, fols. 203v—204r and 206r—07r; on Filonardi as papal nuncio to Switzerland see PASTOR VII 93 n., 110, 158 n.; for a transcription of the letter to Sforza, see below Appendix IX.
[177] MANSI 32, 913D—14D.

II

The Healing of the Pisan Schism (1511—13)   145

that if a safe passage were open to them they would come to the council to explain their position on the Pragmatic Sanction. In conclusion Forbin requested that the conciliar notaries draw up instruments both of the excuse he had offered on the French bishops' behalf and of the decree just read, so that he could forward these to officials of the French Church. Not until July 8th, however, did he receive from Schulz and Contreras on orders from Leo and del Monte an authentic instrument of his protest at this tenth session.[178]

Leo did not let Forbin's excuse for a moment go unchallenged. He pointed out to the ambassador that the bishops could easily have traveled safely from Provence into Genoese territory where they enjoyed a safe-conduct attested to in a document which the pope had ordered to be handed over to them. If they needed a better and surer safe-conduct, he would see that it was provided them. The decree just read, however, should stand in force.[179] Surely, in accord with the eighth of the eleven articles agreed upon in October of 1513, the pope had granted the French bishops more than ample time for their journey to Rome.

It is interesting to note that unlike the pope's letters of March 1515, the discussions at the Lateran in May of that year did not mention a thorough extinction of the Pisan Schism but focused on an abrogation of the Pragmatic Sanction as the reason for the desired presence of French prelates at the council. By the time of the eleventh session in 1516 there was no longer a need for the former Pisan adherents to come to Rome. Although a French delegation never appeared in Rome prior to the October 1st deadline, the new king of France, Francis I, obtained from Leo X at Bologna on 13 December 1515 a papal letter absolving the French clergy of any penalties they may have incurred for having adhered to the Pisan Council. To spare them the labors and expenses of coming to Rome as promised but never accomplished, due to wars and territorial changes, Leo absolved them of this obligation to appear personally or through procurators for abjuring the Pisan Council.[180]

According to the fourth of the eleven articles of October 1513, until the French delegation had arrived in Rome, no general absolution was to be granted to the former Pisan adherents. While most who were prelates waited for the general absolution, a few made their separate peace with the pope.

Within days of Leo's election, Antonio Trivulzio, who as bishop of Asti had attended the council at Milan, was urged by the new pope to assume the government of the church of Piacenza to which Julius had transferred him five years earlier only to reinstate him in 1509 as bishop of Asti. A month after Leo's exhortation, Vasino Malabaila who contended Trivulzio's claim to the church of Piacenza but had been deposed from this see by Julius for having

---

[178] Mansi 32, 914D—15D, 934B—35E.
[179] Mansi 32, 915D.
[180] For a transcription of this papal letter of 13 December 1515, see below Appendix X.

supported the Pisan Council, was restored as bishop of Piacenza, now that he had made satisfactory penance for his earlier schismatic action. Trivulzio thus remained bishop only of Asti. At what point he had renounced the Pisan Schism is not clear.[181]

The reconciliation of Zaccaria Ferreri with Rome was accomplished within nine months of Leo's election. The death of Julius, the hasty departure of Carvajal and Sanseverino from Lyon in the hope of attending the conclave in Rome, and the news of the election of Giovanni dei Medici occasioned a change of heart in the Italian abbot. No longer lamenting in apocalyptic terms the near demise of the Pisan Council as he had at its anniversary celebration, Ferreri described in verse form what he had seen in a "dream" and proclaimed his rejection of the Pisan Schism, acceptance of the Lateran Council, and plea for permission to go to the Rome of Leo X to confess his error. To this *Lugudunense somnium* or *Sylva centesima decima* he gave the title *Leonina* and dated the poem 18 March 1513. In his letter to Louis XII of August 23rd, Ferreri insisted that his support for the Pisan Council was an error born of ignorance, and since he was not ashamed to repudiate it, he requested permission to seek pardon in Rome. His earlier attempt to make this pilgrimage of penance had ended in his capture, imprisonment, and subjection to pressures by adherents of the Pisan Council. Royal consent for the journey, however, seems to have been delayed until the king had finalized his agreement with Leo, for only in December did Ferreri make his formal peace with Rome.[182]

---

[181] HERGENROETHER, Regesta Leonis I 100, 127 nrs. 1777, 2202, II 198, nr. 17695; EUBEL III 121, 275.

[182] FERRERI, Lugudunense somnium, $A_{viii}{}^v$—$C_{iii}{}^v$, some of the more appropriate verses are:

... *Uno foedere iunctae*
Relligionis agunt coetum, generaleque patrum
Concilium: qua sunt laterana palatia sancto
Praeside pontifice et totoque petentibus illuc
Orbe sacerdotum turmis Roma undique plena est.

O fortunatam tanto sub praeside Romam:
Quo duce schismaticus passim delebitur error:
Et Romanus apex solutus rehabebit honores.
Quo duce relligio toto reparabitur orbe:
Atque per eoas procul amplificabitur oras.

(Obsecro) quam primum fuge de squallentibus umbris
Conciliablaeae gentis. Iam ad corda reuersus
Errores agnosce graues: gemituque patenti
Dilue tot maculas. Claemens tibi nanque sacerdos
Indulgebit.

(Si qua tibi pietas) ors mihi pande recessus:
Pande modum: uel si nunc fas est degere Romae
(Si Roma haec) nusquam patiare relinquere Romam
Me rogo.

For Ferreri's letter to Louis, see Ibid. $C_v{}^v$—$_{vi}{}^r$ and the account in MORSOLIN 1723.

II

The Healing of the Pisan Schism (1511—13)

The papal letter of absolution issued on 11 December 1513 clearly detailed Ferreri's offenses and granted his request for pardon. Listed among his crimes for which Julius had justly punished him were urging the convocation of the Pisan Council, counseling and defending its indiction, editing an apology and other treatises on its behalf, arguing its cause in public sermons and disputations, attending its meetings, casting a definitive vote in them, dictating, organizing, signing, and publishing its acts, serving as a notary, *referendarius*, registar, and in other ways preparer of conciliar documents, celebrating the liturgy at conciliar ceremonies, being a recipient of benefices conferred by this council, imposing and receiving revenues from conciliar tithes on the benefices of France, and treating with contempt the decisions of the pope and Lateran Council. But because Ferreri had repented of these deeds and had abjured them both in published writing and in accord with juridical form, and had professed his desire to reject the Pisan Council and adhere to the Roman Church, Leo absolved him of all penalties and restored him to his former status.[183]

In mid-April of 1514, at about the same time that cardinals Briçonnet and de Prie were reconciled with Rome, two archbishops in France obtained absolution for their support of the Pisan Schism. François de Rohan, archbishop of Lyon and bishop of Angers, who attended the council from its early days in Pisa, celebrated Mass at its sixth session in Milan, together with seven other prelates officially cited Julius II for contumacy just prior to his suspension at the eighth session also held in Milan, and welcomed the assembly into his primatial see, was pardoned on April 15th. Giovanni Ferreri, the archbishop of Arles, who seems to have attended the council only at Lyon and then out of fear, was granted his letter of absolution eight days later. Both men were required to read a formula of abjuration provided by Rome and have a public instrument of this act drawn up by notaries and scribes.[184]

By this formula the archbishops abjured the Pisan Council and pledged their loyalty to the Lateran Council and Roman pontiff. God's light and grace having saved them from the cloud and snare of schism, they anathematized the Pisan Council and held as null, vain, insignificant, unauthorized, and presumptuous whatever was done or decreed by it. The sentences and penalties imposed by Julius on the Pisan Council and its adherents were recognized as correct and legitimate. The Lateran Council, called for just and legitimate reasons, they acknowledged as the only true council. Under the pain of suspension from the exercise of their priestly office, the loss of their churches, and the bond of anathema, they promised never to return to any form of schism. And they

---

[183] Except for its concluding formula, this papal document is printed in RAINALDI 1513, nrs. 51—52. For Ferreri's *Apologia* on behalf of the Pisan Council, see J. KLOTZNER, Kardinal Dominikus Jacobazzi und sein Konzilswerk: Ein Beitrag zur Geschichte der konziliaren Idee (= Analecta Gregoriana 45) Rome 1948, 227—36 and BÄUMER 253.

[184] On de Rohan at the Pisan Council, see Acta primi concilii Pisani 80, 148, 192—93, and Promotiones et progressus 43v; on Ferreri, see EUBEL III 116, and RAINALDI, 1514, nr. 8.

swore on the Gospels to remain always in the unity of the Catholic Church and in true obedience to the pope, Christ's vicar. The formula which Ferreri used went on to promise to perform whatever penance Leo has imposed on him for his errors and to come personally to Rome and appear before the pope, once the current impediments have ceased. Ferreri also acknowledged that he would once again fall under the pains of the former censures and penalties should he fail to fulfil what was imposed on him.[185]

Whether any other prelates made their separate peace with Rome or argued their case on its legal merits is unclear.[186] Former adherents of the Pisan Council whose names appear in the papal registers and who enjoyed the ecclesiastical rank of bishop or below did not apparently seek absolution from the papacy unless such a pardon were preliminary to the validation of a provision previously made by the Pisan Council. In these cases Leo seems to have granted pardon with the kindness and mildness promised in the sixth of the eleven articles of the papal-French accords.

A good number of provisions had been made by the Pisan Council. As its relations with Julius worsened, the council increasingly provided for its adherents the functions normally exercised by Rome. At the second session in Pisa the council forbad anyone to take litigation to Rome but ordered, instead, that cases be heard and decided by four bishops it appointed. At the eighth session in Milan on 21 April 1512 the council suspended Julius II from both the spiritual and temporal administration of his papal office. Those who would earlier have sought from the pope ecclesiastical appointments and favors now had to look to the council for these. By letters patent dated June 16th and registered by the parlement of Paris on June 25th, Louis XII approved this conciliar decree suspending Julius. While it remained in effect, French subjects were forbidden to seek from the pope any legal judgment or provision. The parlement of Paris was to judge its cases according to the bulls and provisions issued by the Pisan Council. Anyone seeking or carrying a papal bull was to be subject to arrest and punishment as a violator of a royal edict and ordinance. With such strong royal backing, the Pisan cardinals as presiding officers of the council issued in its name numerous letters of collation, presentation, reservation, provision and other favors regarding the dignities and benefices in the kingdom of France and in lands claimed by it, such as Flanders.[187]

---

[185] The formula used by Ferreri is printed in RAINALDI 1514 nr. 9; for de Rohan's formula which drops the section: *omnem poenitentiam . . . si contrauenero, ac*, inserting *quod* before *dum et quoties*, see ASV, Arm. XXXIX, vol. 36, fol. 29r.

[186] At times the incentive for a separate reconciliation was weak, as when, for example, according to GUICCIARDINI XI, xiii, ed. PANIGADA III 282, Leo by conciliar decree restored to the French bishops and other prelates (against whom as schismatics Julius had rigorously proceeded with official warnings) the faculty of purging themselves of contumacy during all of the coming November. This seems to be a reference to the decree *Meditatio cordis nostri* of the seventh session which postponed the deadline of the citation until the next session scheduled for November 1513 — see MANSI 32, 816C.

[187] For the termination of Roman litigation, see SANUTO XIII 331; for the suspension of Julius, see

Resistance to these provisions came from both civil and religious authorities. The government of Flanders under the guidance of Marguerite d'Autriche issued at Ghent, Lille, Douai, and Mechelen prohibitions against the provisions made by the Pisan Council. Any Flemish subject seeking such promotions was to be punished. The Lateran Council at its fourth session on 10 December 1512 declared null any provision made by the Pisan Council and ordered anyone who had received such a provision to resign it within two months and restore its revenues or else suffer the loss of other ecclesiastical benefices to which they have a just title.[188]

Given this decree by the Lateran Council and the need to protect the dignity of the Holy See, Leo refused to grant a blanket validation of these actions of the Pisan Council. In the ninth article of the papal-French accord, he did agree to confer again on those, on whose behalf Louis wrote, the churches and monasteries and other benefices they had earlier received from the Pisan Council. Lesser benefices at the disposition of local ordinaries, but conferred by the Pisan Council, could be granted anew by those ordinaries to those who renounced both the Pisan Council and the provisions they had received from it.[189]

At least two French bishop appointed irregularly at the time of the Pisan Schism had their nominations confirmed by Rome. On 5 October 1513 Martin de S. André, an eighteen year old subdeacon from Carcassonne who had been entrusted with the administration of that church by the Pisan Council on the death of its bishop Pierre Oliz in September of 1512, was absolved of an irregularity and censures now that he had abjured the Pisan Council and indicated a willingness to do penance. Two days later he was named administrator of that diocese and on October 9th given permission to be consecrated its bishop once he reached his twenty-seventh year. King Louis backed his appointment.[190]

A more complicated situation existed for Tournai. Both Louis XII and Maximilian I claimed sovereignty over the cathedral city and its immediate environs. In early June of 1513 the bishop of Tournai, Charles de Hautbois, a schismatic adherent of the Pisan Council, died soon after resigning his see to Louis Guillard, the twenty-one year old son of the vice-president of the parlement of Paris. On June 19th in a series of bulls issued at Rome, Guillard was appointed administrator and bishop-elect of this see. On August 24th he was formally admitted into possession of the see. When the city of Tournai sur-

---

Acta primi concilii Pisani 193—206; for Louis' letter, see Recueil général des anciennes lois française depuis l'an 420 jusqu'a la Révolution de 1789, ed. F. ISAMBERT et alii, 29 vols., Paris 1821—33, IX 631—32, nr. 107; for attempts to make provisions in Flanders, see the report of Guillaume de Marque dated 9 January 1513 in Archives Générales du Royaume de Belgique (Brussel), Grand Conseil Malines 143, fols. 299—303.

[188] Report of de Marque, fol. 301—03; MANSI 754A—C.
[189] See below Appendix IV.
[190] On Martin de S. André, see EUBEL III 152 and HERGENROETHER, Regesta Leonis I 297 nr. 4846, 300 nrs. 4871—82, 303 nr. 4918.

rendered to the troops of Henry VIII on 23 September 1513, the question of removing this French bishop came to the fore. Maximilian had already written to Pio in Rome on September 9th in an effort to replace Guillard with cardinal Castellesi. He based his case on the grounds that Guillard was underage, a supporter of the Pisan Council, and appointed according to the terms of the Pragmatic Sanction in territory under Hapsburg sovereignty. In addition, the former bishop de Hautbois, whose resignation had opened the way to Guillard's appointment, had also adhered to the Pisan Council. As a consequence of the papal-French accord in October, the arguments based on the Pisan Schism lost their force. Leo agreed to revoke Guillard's appointment only if it could be proven that he was twelve-years old instead of twenty-two. In his bid to be appointed bishop of Tournai, Thomas Wolsey did not apparently argue on the ground of an irregularity stemming from the Pisan Schism. While Wolsey did for awhile secure the status of administrator of the see, he eventually resigned his claim on Tournai to Guillard in lieu of an annual pension from the French king.[191]

Although not required by the papal-French accord to have recourse to Rome, a number of recipients of benefices and favors from the Pisan Council did seek to have these reconferred by the pope instead of by the local ordinary. The few dozen cases which are recorded in the papal registers do not fit into any single pattern. Many involved the resignation of a benefice into the hands of the presidents of the Pisan Council and its subsequent conferral by them. Some concerned secular clergy receiving monastic benefices or regulars a secular church. For others it was the case of receiving a benefice in a diocese other than one's own. Some cases dealt with a simple provision. Efforts were also made to confirm a dispensed pluralism, to let stand the absolution of an irregularity, or to pardon the confirmation of a papal collation by the council, since Louis had forbade access to Rome. Not only was the subject matter diverse, but the dioceses from which the supplicants came were numerous, some with bishops who had attended the Pisan Council, others without.[192]

The papal letters reconferring benefices earlier granted by the Pisan Council did follow a general format. They began with the words *Sedes apostolica pia mater*

---

[191] On Guillard's June appointment, see EUBEL III 316; for Maximilian's efforts to remove him, see the letter of Maximilian to Pio, from Lille, 12 September 1513, in: Maximiliana 29 IV, fols. 48v and 52r, and the letters of Pio to Maximilian, from Rome, 8 November 1513 and 3 January 1514, in: Maximiliana 30 II fol. 24v and 31 I, fol. 11r; on Wolsey's efforts to obtain Tournai, see CRUICKSHANK 143 —87 and the letter of Francesco Pandolfini to Giulio dei Medici, from Poissy, 27 July 1514, in: ASF, Sig., Dieci, Otto, Leg. e Com., nr. 55, fol. 88r.

[192] In HERGENROETHER, Regesta Leonis I, are examples of: resignations (140 nr. 2401, 253 nr. 4191, 408 nr. 6420, 409 nr. 6423, 409 nr 6426, 448 nr. 7065), regular-secular benefices (408 nr. 6420, 409 nr. 6430, 448 nr. 7065, 498 nr. 7849, 508 nr. 8027), another diocesis (227 nrs. 3801—03, 273 nr. 4478, 298—99 nr. 4854), simple provision (512 nr. 8098, 534 nr. 8524), absolved irregularity (227 nrs. 3801—03, 345 nr. 5517) dispensed pluralism (409 nr. 6430), and confirmed collation (279 nr. 4565).

and explained how the Church customarily showed mercy and liberality to her children humbly returning to her bosom after their excesses. The merits of the supplicant recommended him to her kindness. His crime was then described as having received a particular benefice from the hands of the presidents of the Pisan Council which had been condemned by Julius II and the Lateran Council. Because of this action, the supplicant incurred a number of ecclesiastical penalties. In accord with the statutes of the Lateran Council, the benefice was declared vacant and its conferral devolved upon the Holy See. Before it could be reconferred, however, the supplicant was to resign it into the hands of an official or officials named by the pope, and to abjure the Pisan Council. In each case specific officials were appointed to receive this abjuration. They could be the local ordinary, officials from another diocese, or even an abbot. In Rome the cardinal penitentiary, Leonardo Grosso della Rovere, received the abjuration. It was to be made in the hands of the officials named, according to a prescribed formula, sworn to on the Gospels and followed by a fitting penance imposed by a confessor of the supplicant's own choosing. If he failed to perform this penance, the papal letter was to have no effect.[193]

If the need for such papal bulls had been eliminated for the most part by the papal-French accord of October 1513, the papal bull of December 1515 granting to all former adherents of the Pisan Council sweeping absolutions, restorations to former titles and status, and a validation of the orders and benefices conferred by council members and their supporters removed yet further any reason for recourse to Rome. That bull also provided faculties for a priest of the supplicant's choosing to grant either in the forum of conscience or outside it absolution and restoration and to impose a fitting penance. By this provision of the bull, former adherents of the Pisan Council no longer needed to seek such pardons from the pope or his legate, as stipulated in the tenth article of the papal-French accord. When Leo formally announced in accord with the eleventh article that litigation decided by the Pisan Council should remain as decided is not clear.[194]

While the eleven articles spelled out in some detail how the major issues involved in the Pisan Schism were to be resolved, the king's second mandate of 26 October 1513 which promised to send to Rome a delegation of French clergy for discussing the Pragmatic Sanction gave hope of a permanent removal

---

[193] This composite reconstruction is based on the following sections from papal letters: Reg. Vat. 1004 fols. 264v—66v; 1010 fols. 264v—68r; 1026 fol. 77r—v; 1035 fols. 52r—53v; 1093, fol. 166r; 1206 fol. 102r—v; and Arm. XXXIX, vol. 30, fols. 153r—55r. The formula of abjuration is transcribed in Appendix VI. Its efforts to secure from the penitent declarations of loyalty to the papacy were discussed earlier. This formula is not apparently included among the ninety studied in TH. FRENZ, Armarium XXXIX Vol. 11 im Vatikanischen Archiv. Ein Formelbuch für Breven aus der Zeit Julius' II, in: Römische Kurie. Kirchliche Finanzen. Vatikanisches Archiv. Studien zu Ehren von Hermann Hoberg, ed. Erwin GATZ, 2 vols. (= Miscellanea Historiae Pontificiae 45—46) Roma 1979, I 197—213.
[194] See below Appendix X.

of one of the principal irritants in papal-French relations. Even since its enactment in 1438, the Pragmatic Sanction of Bourges had been opposed by the papacy because it seemed to justify an autonomous French church. Popes repeatedly denounced it and worked for its revocation. The Lateran Council was enlisted in this campaign. It distinguished the important diplomatic aspects of the issue of the schism from the doctrinal questions of the Pragmatic Sanction and thus placed the first under the care of the deputation on peace and made the abrogation of the Sanction the concern of the deputation on the faith. Leo initially thought that a thorough resolution of both depended on the cooperation of the French episcopate. The failure of its representatives to come to Rome despite the guarantees of a Genoese safe-conduct was due in large part to the reluctance of the French clergy to see abrogated this charter of Gallican liberties. Just as the terms for ending the Pisan Schism were negotiated independently of the French episcopate, so too would an abrogation of the Pragmatic Sanction.[175]

Negotiations between the king of France and pope eventually succeeded in abrogating this Sanction. Louis XII who had difficulties at times in securing under the terms of this French adaptation of the conciliar legislation of Konstanz and Basel the appointment of prelates to his pleasing suggested to a Medici representative at the beginning of October 1514 that the Pragmatic Sanction be replaced with a concordat, as had been done in the time of Louis XI. Little progress, however, could have been made on this proposal, for within three months of the letter reporting it Louis XII had died. His successor Francis I was eager to come to an arrangement with Leo X. The French military victory at Marignano on 14 September 1515 set the stage for a wide-ranging accord. Leo wanted to reach an agreement not only safeguarding the temporal rights of the Holy See over its vassals, salt monopoly, and tribute for cities held by France, but also acknowledging the pope's right to make church appointments in France. Although an agreement was reached in mid-October on the question of temporal rights, a full resolution of the spiritual rights had to await the meeting in Bologna in December between Leo X and Francis I. As a result of their private negotiations not only was the Pragmatic Sanction to be abrogated in France, but the outlines of a concordat were agreed upon. Its details were worked out by 18 August 1516. At the eleventh session of the Lateran Council on 19 December 1516 both the abrogation and concordat were given conciliar approbation. Under great pressure from Francis I the Parlement

---

[195] On the Pragmatic Sanction of Bourges, see the recent study of John A. F. THOMSON, Popes and Princes, 1417—1517: Politics and Polity in the Late Medieval Church, London 1980, esp. 148—51 and 159—64; on the conciliar deputations, see MANSI 32, 796B, 797B, and 989D; on Leo's joining of a thorough extinction of the schism and an abrogation of the sanction see below App. VIII and IX; for the refusal of Guillaume and Denys Briçonnet to attend the eleventh session of the Lateran Council which abrogated the Pragmatic Sanction because they knew the French clergy opposed it, see SANUTO XXIV 105 and RAINALDI, 1516, nr. 21.

of Paris finally registered on 22 May 1517 both the concordat and the royal letters patent of May 17th abolishing the Pragmatic Sanction. Thus in addition to a resolution of the Pisan Schism Leo had secured an elimination of the legal pretext for an autonomous French church and had bound the French king to the papacy by a generous concordat.[196]

The principles which had guided Leo X throughout these negotiations for healing the Pisan Schism had been early on enunciated by cardinal Riario: a preservation of the authority and dignity of the Holy See and a pardon and restoration of the penitents. A recognition of papal authority underlay the acknowledgement of the justice of the penalties imposed on the former schismatics, a confession of their errors, a plea for pardon, and a pledge of loyalty to the papacy in the future. The purpose behind the generous pardon and restoration was not only a following of the Gospel teachings in the story of the prodigal son and pardon of Peter but also a hope that such generosity would bind the penitent to the papacy with the strong bonds of gratitude.

The wisdom of this policy was open to question. Henry VIII warned that papal leniency with schismatics only encouraged others to use the threat of schism in their conflicts with the papacy![197] Maximilian had complained that the French were granted absolution even though they contumaciously failed to come to Rome as agreed upon in the papal-French accord. Some of the cardinals had also counseled against excessive indulgence being shown the former schismatics. Yet despite such warnings, Leo pursued a policy of leniency.

In the negotiation of the papal-French accord of October 1513 and in its subsequent implementation Leo showed great flexibility and toleration. He placated the French king's pride by issuing the constitution *Aeternae vitae claviger* which completely absolved Louis XII of any ecclesiastical penalties imposed by Julius II or the Lateran Council. Leo also accepted the French mandate which distorted the historical record in an effort to exonerate the king. The pope allowed Briçonnet and de Prie to avoid the humiliations suffered by their former colleagues, Carvajal and Sanseverino. Despite all his threats, Leo never penalized the French delegation for its repeated failures to come to Rome. He issued letters reconferring and revalidating the appointments and grants of the Pisan Council. And in the end he issued a bull absolving all the Pisan adherents. Such leniency did not pose great problems to Leo, for he had carefully seen that the central issue of papal authority was resolved to his satisfaction.

---

[196] For the king's proposal of a concordat, see the letter of Francesco Pandolfini to Giulio dei Medici, ex Bevilla, 2 October 1514, in: ASF, Sig., Dieci, Otto, Leg. e Com. — Mis. e Resp., nr. 55, fol. 147r; on the negotiations with Francis I, see PASTOR VII 123—46; for a proposed treaty which reflects the outlines of what Leo hoped would be included in a concordat but never succeeded for the most part in obtaining, see BAV, Vat. Lat. 12,208, fols. 93r—95r; on the abrogation of the Pragmatic Sanction and approval of the concordat by the Lateran Council, see MANSI 32, 947E—970D, by the king and Parlement of Paris, see ISAMBERT XI 75—97, 114—18, nrs. 36 and 51.
[197] On the warning of Henry VIII, see CREIGHTON V 218 n. 1.

Leo's primary concern was the same as that of his predecessors ever since the days of the councils of Konstanz and Basel. And to a remarkable degree he succeeded in asserting papal authority over a council or national church and even had the Lateran Council confirm his victories. But one of his more subtle successes was in emphasizing the doctrinal issue raised by schism. From each of the former adherents of the Pisan Schism who sought reconciliation with Rome, whether king or cleric, Leo extracted a confession not so much of disobedience as of error. The nature of this error was not spelled out with precision, but seems to have been a denial of papal authority over councils. In the formula of abjuration demanded of clerics, belief in the schismatic Pisan Council was even denounced as heresy.

The time and energies expended by Julius II and Leo X to meet the challenge of the Pisan Council suggest that the papacy on the eve of the Reformation was still pre-occupied with the conciliarist issue of the previous century. While papal diplomacy could succeed in resolving many of the minor difficulties involving Gallic pride, papal sovereignty over Bologna and Ferrara, and new political and military alliances, a permanent resolution of the conciliarist threat would only be found when the issue of papal power over councils was raised from the realm of canon law to that of theology. By his efforts to identify as heresy belief in the Pisan Council, Leo furthered that process. And by his skillful negotiations with Louis XII and Francis, he eventually eliminated royal support in France for this "error".

APPENDICES*

I.

Consistorial Speech of Raffaele Riario on the Restoration of Carvajal and Sanseverino Rome, April — June 1513

Bibliotheca Apostolica Vaticana, Mss. Chigiani I. III. 89: Consistorialia Raph. Riarii, Tom. II: De Restitutione, fols. 72r—76v.

Cum sepius fuerit dictum de hoc negotio in hoc sacro loco, non est opus iterum replicare quantum et mihi et (ut puto) ceteris Reuerendissimis Dominis displicuerit, et molestum fuerit uidere res istorum Reuerendissimorum Dominorum absentium[1] ruere et deferri ad hos terminos ad quos (ut uidemus) deuenerunt. Quod licet fuerit omnibus molestum ac graue, tamen non uisum est posse aliter fieri, partim ob eorum contumaciam, partim ob materiam per se ipsam non solum abhorrentem ab honestate et ratione, verum etiam ualde scandalosam et periculosam huic Sancte Sedi et uniuerse Sancte Romane Ecclesie.

Post autem has nostras molestias et angores supererat tantummodo optandum et precandum ab omnipotenti Deo quemadmodum alias dictum est, quod posset reperiri aliquis bonus et condecens modus, per quem dignitas et authoritas huius Sancte Sedis et totius sacri collegii seruaretur, et ipsi tanquam errantes filii ad gremium parentis redirent ac reducerentur. Et hoc fere totum, aut saltem magna ex parte, in eo positum uidebatur, ut ipsi desisterent a tam deuio itinere, et deinde peterent ueniam et reditum cum bona et conuenienti humilitate et cum ea maiori ostensione et significatione penitentie qua fieri posset. Quamobrem, quum nunc, ut proposuit Sanctitas Uestra[2], suppliciter et humiliter petant ueniam, quumque etiam subsint alie rationes quas eadem allegauit, sum in uoto cum his dumtaxat circumstantiis de quibus alias dictum est, ut concedatur reditus et recipiantur ad ueniam et ad gratiam quod erit condecens et conueniens pietati

---

* My transcriptions of the following documents have retained peculiar spellings where they occurred, avoided contractions and abbreviations, and modernized to some extent the use of capital letters and punctuation. In the Latin documents I have consistently used *e* for the diphthongs *ae* and *oe*, *i* for *j*, and *u* for *v*. In the two French pieces I have not inserted the diacritical marks used in modern French but not found in these documents; I have, however, made use of the apostrophe indicating the contraction of two words, even though this mark is not to be found in the documents.

I am very grateful to Professors Daniel J. Sheerin and F. A. C. Mantello of the Catholic University of America for their help in resolving some difficulties in the Latin manuscripts. Professors Ellen S. Ginsberg and Joseph P. Williman and Ms. Maria Rebbert of the same university and Dr. Gino Corti of Villa I Tatti, the Harvard University Center for Italian Renaissance Studies, in Florence were particularly helpful with the French texts. Father Luigi La Favia, also of the Catholic University, and Professor Agostino Borromeo of the University of Rome kindly helped me with the Italian text. Responsibility for any misreadings of the documents is solely mine.

[1] The absent cardinals were Bernardino Lopez de Carvajal and Federigo Sanseverino.

[2] Leo X (1513—21).

et clementie Sanctitatis Uestre, et ipsi Reuerendissimi Domini in posterum sentient se esse tanto magis obnoxios et obligatiores Sanctitate Uestre et huic sacro collegio, quanto intellexerint clementius et benignius secum actum esse.

In actionibus humanis frequenter solent aliqua occurrere, que prima sua facie et intuitu apparent implicita et difficilia et multoties minus equa et minus honesta, sed postea in decursu rationis, ubi omnia fuerint bene considerata, illa eadem reperiuntur facilia et ad conuenientiam iuris et equitatis commode et salubriter rediguntur et deducuntur. In quorum numero uidetur potissimum esse hoc ipsum negotium, quod habetur nunc pre manibus, de restitutione priuatorum, de quo breuissime dicam quod sentio, repetitis prius pauculis que occurrunt.

Ego ab initio, quo uidi illos suscipere eam uiam per quam sunt progressi et uidi etiam Summum Dominum Nostrum[3] predecessorem Sanctitatis Uestre procedere et deuenire ad grauissimum odium et indignationem contra eos, cepi mecum ipse rem detestari et sicuti docebat pro debito et officio meo grauiter et moleste ferre, considerans (ueluti postea accidit) rem hanc non posse sortiri alium finem quam difficilem et scandalosum huic Sancte Sedi et omnibus nobis et illis ipsis periculosum et plenum laborum et erumnarum. Ad quod ne per negligentiam meam (quantum ad me spectabat) uel per illorum culpam deueniretur, Deus est testis, quod omnia egi publice et priuatim, que sciui et potui, supplicando rogando et suadendo ut et illi ab incepto desisterent et Summus Dominus Noster ad mitiora remedia se conuerteret. Fecerunt hoc idem pro eorum bonitate multi ex aliis Reuerendissimis Dominis. Sed siue preces nostre non fuerint digne exaudiri siue Deus ex aliqua bona causa ita permiserit, res deuenit ad hunc exitum, quem modo uidemus, nec sine mestitia et molestia omnium nostrorum nec sine nota et iactura illorum.

Nunc autem quod Sanctitas Uestra proposuerit de restitutione potest sibi persuadere, quod quemadmodum non sine magna molestia omnium nostrorum deuentum est ad ipsam priuationem, ita etiam est futurum gratissimum, si possit reperiri aliqua bona et condecens uia ad id faciendum. Qua in re duo potissimum mihi uidentur esse consideranda: primum scilicet, ut sit talis modus per quem seruetur dignitas et authoritas huius Sancte Sedis, Sanctitatis Uestre, et totius sacri collegii; deinde ut, quantum fieri possit, consulatur eorum commodo et honori et indemnitati.

Quo ad primum, quando ipsi suppliciter petant ueniam cum recognitione erroris et professione uere emendationis, seruando alias debitas circunstantias que in huiusmodi actibus siue de iure siue de approbata consuetudine requiruntur, existimarem ualde bene et commode satisfactum esse authoritati et dignitati Sanctitatis Uestre et Sancte Sedis Apostolice.

Quo ad interesse illorum, Sanctitas Uestra faciat erga ipsos officium dignissimum bonitate pietate et clementia sua, et ipsi ex tanta hac beneficentia et

---

[3] Julius II (1503—13).

pietate tanto obligatiores se esse intelligent Sanctitati Uestre et Sancte Sedi Apostolice, quanto intelligent se esse donatos uenia maioris errati. Nec est dubitandum pro eorum bonitate, quin in posterum tanto studiosiores sint futuri compensandi peccata et errata preterita, quanto Sanctitas Uestra benigniorem se exhibuerit ad gratiam et ad ueniam. Nam licet errata sint grauissima (neque enim potest aliter dici), presertim ob exemplum quod inde subsequi potest, tamen quicunque uoluerit respicere ad personam et decentiam Sanctitatis Uestre uel etiam ad personam illorum, fatebitur in hoc casu, non minus debere esse locum clementie et uenie quam nimie seueritati et rigori, attento quod ad omnes principes, sed potissimum ad Romanos Pontifices, nihil magis uidemus decere et pertinere quam clementiam et pietatem. Cuius nulla unquam tanta obliuio esse debebit, ut quicunque Pontifex in hac Sancta Sede sederit non multo magis meminerit exemplum illius cuius uices et cuius locum gerit in terris, qui non solum indulsit Petro post trinam negationem sed ouilis curas sibi committens sublimauit ad apicem summi Apostolatus[4], et ab eodem etiam, cum discipuli Samaritanos celesti igne uellent consumere, sunt prohibiti et Samaritani sunt ad penitentiam misericorditer expectati.[5] Quantum etiam ad personam illorum, si quis uoluerit considerare damna incommoda et labores et itineris seu potius exilii molestias et perigrinationes que sunt perpessi, reperient non tulisse impune quicquid peccauerunt, immo talia passos esse ut et ipsi quoad uixerunt possint recordari et ceteri omnes eorum exemplo moniti nisi fuerint plusquam insani perpetuo possint et debeant ab huiusmodi abstinere et precauere. Quamobrem et cetera.

Beatissime Pater, credo Sanctitatem Uestram habere pro certo et indubitato quod nihil mihi et (ut arbitror) ceteris Reuerendissimis Dominis potuisset accidere molestius et grauius quam primo uidere causas depositionis seu priuationis istorum Reuerendissimorum Dominorum, deinde uidere finem et actum ipsius priuationis. Quum nullum membrum siue paruum siue magnum a reliquo corpore abscindi et separari possit sine dolore et afflictione totius corporis, et quemadmodum totum hoc, ut Sanctitas Uestra potest cogitare, fuit molestissimum, ita etiam potest iudicare futurum esse gratissimum, quod hec ipsa uulnera et he cicatrices reducantur a Sanctitate Uestra per aliquam bonam uiam ad sanitatem et incolumitatem.

Cause huius priuationis sunt omnibus note et (ut dixerim) ad oculos patentes et euidentes, propterea de qualitatibus rei ego non curabo aliter commemorare et recensere. Unum est quod non potest [*word missing*] nisi quod fuerint graues et urgentes. Et licet in huiusmodi casibus uideri possit non minoris momenti futurum esse exemplum quod exinde nasci et sumi potest, quam sit causa et materia rei; tamen multoties uidemus quod gratia et benignitas principum solet supplere et preuenire culpis et deffectibus alienis, quum ex huiuscemodi gratia

---

[4] John 13 : 38; 18 : 17, 25, 27; 21: 16—17.
[5] Luke 9: 53—55; John 4: 39—42.

II

errantes studeant preteritam culpam redimere et in melius compensare et indulgentes Saluatoris nostri exemplo prebeant largiorem causam et materiam redeundi ad optimam frugem. Ipse enim Saluator noster non modo post primum lapsum sustinuit Petrum, sed etiam post trinam negationem Principem Apostolorum instituit. Et ille tanto fidelior est factus et tanto magis postea in fide et gratia profecit, quanto apertius cognouit se fidem perdidisse, ex quo maiorem gratiam (ut ait Ambrosius)[6] ex uenia meruit reperire quam ex culpa et peccato amiserit. Quamobrem [dash].

Causa hec (ut manifestissime apparet) est grauissima et maximi ponderis et in qua multa et uaria possent dici. Ego tamen quam breuissime potero me absoluam, relinquens ordinatiorem apparatum doctrine et sapientie Dominorum Reuerendissimorum.

Beatissime Pater, ab initio, quo isti Reuerendissimi Domini uocati a predecessore Sanctitatis Uestre recusarunt uelle uenire et ceperunt tacito quodam modo se subtrahere ab illius obedientia, fuit mihi et omibus [sic!] aliis ualde molestum et graue. Et profecto est data omnis conueniens opera et adhibita omnis possibilis diligentia, ut illis liceret sine contumacia et indignatione Sanctitatis Sue abesse, tamen nunquam potuit adhiberi tale remedium quod huic tanto malo sufficeret. Et sic postea illi deuenerunt ad indictionem illius conciliabuli[7] et Sanctitas Sua ad illorum priuationem, ex quibus secuta sunt omnia ista mala que uidimus, et poteramus suspicari ac timere quod secutura essent multo maiora et grauiora, nisi pietas diuina apposuisset manum suam.

Nunc autem quod Sanctitas Uestra proponat de compositione huius materie potest sibi persuadere quod quemadmodum omnia ista que precesserunt, fuerunt nobis molestissima, ita futurum sit gratissimum quod possit reperiri aliquis bonus et condecens modus per quem isti reducantur ad obedientiam Sanctitatis Uestre et ad gremium Sancte Romane Ecclesie. Et ad hoc efficiendum duo potissimum mihi occurrunt consideranda: in primis, scilicet, ut habeatur condigna et condecens ratio dignitatis et honoris huius Sancte Sedis; deinde ut quantum commodius fieri possit consulatur et prouideatur rebus illorum.

Quo ad primum, uidetur mihi condecens et conueniens, immo necessarium, ut illi ante omnia recognoscant et fateantur errores eorum, renuncient conciliabulo et omnibus inde secutis, et demum suppliciter petant ueniam a Sanctitate Uestra, submittendo se in omnibus et per omnia iudicio et arbitrio Beatitudinis Uestre. Quod si fecerint, uidetur mihi abunde cautum et prouisum esse honori Sanctitatis Uestre et authoritati huius Sancte Sedis.

Quantum ad res illorum, quandocunque ipsi fuerunt restituti ad dignitatem pristinam et ad priora loca in quibus erant, meo iudicio, non poterunt dicere neque existimare quod non sit actum cum eis humaniter et benigne. Quin immo, si uoluerint recto examine pensitare rem suam, nunquam poterunt agere tot

---

[6] I have been unable to locate this citation from St. Ambrose.
[7] Pisan Council (1511—12).

gratias diuine clementie neque etiam tantum obsequi Sanctitati Uestre, ut adequent et impleant minimam partem debiti et meritorum Sanctitatis Uestre.

De titulis[8] autem non loquor, quia non potest de illis agi ut non grauissime ledatur existimatio huius Sancte Sedis, tum propter dehonestamentum illorum qui possident, tum etiam quod in illorum restitutione uideremur aperte fateri ea que fuerunt per nos gesta fuisse minus legitime et canonice facta, immo uideremur approbare et authorizare gesta per eos. Et propterea quando altera partium sit grauanda, equius est, ut sors cadat super eos qui peccauerunt quam super innocentiam huius Sancte Sedis.

Neque propter hoc uolo inferre quod gratia de qua modo agitur non sit ualde magna et non sit supra errores et merita illorum, sed quod hec Sancta Sedes semper consueuit potius inclinare ad partes clementie et benignitatis quam rigoris et seueritatis.

II.
A Justification of Louis XII's Actions Against Julius II
S. 1., July 1513?

Bibliothèque Nationale de Paris, Fonds Ancien Français 3087, fols. 101r—102v.

Le Roy tres chrestien veult vivre et mourir bon et devot filz de l'eglise de pape Leone Xme, a present gouvernant l'eglise comme vicaire de nostre Seigneur et Redempteur Jhesus Crist et successeur du glorieux apostre Monsieur St. Pierre, et ne veult adherer ne consentyr a mauvaises sectes ne scismes en maniere que ce soyt.

Et au regart du Concille de Pise, parce qu'il a sceu qu'il desplaisoyt a nostre sainct pere, il a fait deppartyr les prelatz et autres gens qui estoient a Lyon[9], qui y estoient demourez depuis le trespas de feu pape Julle[10] en attendant savoir l'intencion de nostre sainct pere Leon, laquelle entendue les a fait separer et retourner en leurs maisons sans plus user d'autorite dudit Concille.

Maiz au regard du temps dudit feu pape Julle, parce qu'il s'est monstre sy grant ennemy dicelluy roy tres chrestien et de la nacion gallicane, et useur d'une tres grande ingratitude, crudelite, injustice et non faissant office de pasteur, mais plus tost de tyrain et ennemy, en maniere qu'il semble audit roy tres chrestien que du temps dicelluy pape Julle se pouvoyt deffendre par toutes voyes tant de droyt que de fau contre luy et mesmement celles qui estoient trouvees bonnes par grans lectrez savans et experimentez. Et s'il y a eu erreur d'un couste et d'autrui, ce n'a este pour vouloyr desobeyr au sainct siege appostolique, ny a

---

[8] The title of Carvajal was "Sanctae Crucis in Jerusalem" — EUBEL III 62b n. 4, of Sanseverino "Sancti Angeli in foro piscium" — Ibid. 72.
[9] The Pisan Council transferred from Asti to Lyon by a decree of the ninth session held at Asti on 12 June 1512. It solemnly entered Lyon on 27 June 1512 and celebrated the tenth session there on 6 July 1512 and an anniversary Mass in the cathedral on 1 November 1512 — see Promotiones et progressus, fols. 42v—44r.
[10] Julius II (1503—13).

l'eglise, ne au saincts papes qui sont entrez canoniquement au siege appostolique, maiz pour resister aux malices, iniquitez, crudelitez dudit pape Julle, qui abusoyt tant de l'autorite de l'eglise que on le pouvoyt fuyir *tanquam a facie Saulis*[11], et que tiran et loup puissant; et ainsi par son trepas entend ledit roy tres chrestien toutes erreurs d'un coste et d'autre estre abolies, et pourvoyt nostre sainct pere le pape faire a present comme avant fist le pape Clement V[ieme][12] apres le trespas de Boniface VIII[ieme][13], lequel Clement fist une estravagante qui se commence *Meruit*[14], par laquelle il abolist et voulut que tout ce que avoyt fait ledit Boniface contre le Roy de France lors regnant n'avoir aucun effet, ce qu'il fist sans ce que ledit roy nomme Phillipe[15] demandast absolution ne aucune abolicion, *sed proprio motu*.

Et ainsi plus prie ledit roy tres chrestien a nostre sainct pere qu'il ne veuille adherer ne suyvre les oppinions de ceulx qui sont et ont tousiours este ses ennemys, ne de les dits adherans, ne pareillement de ceulx qui ont conforte ledit feu pape Julle en telles crudelitez et inniquitez, et aussy qu'il luy plaist avoir regard aux injustices, iniures, dommaiges et pertes a luy faictes par ledit feu pape Julle et ses adherans, ennemys dicelluy roy tres chrestien, qui userent dudit pape Julle comme de leur ministre et justicier d'iniquite contre ledit roy tres chrestien, sans que ledit pape Julle est *[sic]* regard aux services par luy faiz a l'eglise Romaine, par le moyen duquel ont este renduz et restituez audit sainct siege appostolique les terres et services de Ymole, Fourly, Boulongne, Ravenne, Fayence, Ariminy et autres terres de la Romaigne.[16] Et non ont autant fait tous les autres princes chrestiens ensemble pour ladite eglise Romaine.

Et aussy prie ledit roy tres chrestien a nostre sainct pere avoir regard a la paix universalle de la chrestiente, affin que tous les princes chrestiens puyssent employer leurs forces et armes contre les infidelles, a l'exaltacion de nostre saincte foy, prosperite et unyon de l'eglise. Et que en faissant ladite paix universalle chascun desdits princes soyt remis et reintegre en ses vrayes et justes possessions et services, et les invaseurs en soient expellez, parce que autrement ne se peut faire paix en ladite chrestiente, *quia pax et justicia osculate sunt*.[17]

Et aussy vueille avoir regard nostre sainct pere aux grandes ambicions d'aucuns desdits princes qui ja se veulent avoir toute la chrestiente en leur main.

Et soyt aussy adverty nostre sainct pere que ledit roy tres chrestien ne luy demande or, argent, ne autre chose pour faire guerre contre les chrestiens,

---

[11] 1 Samuel 21: 10, another suggested reading would be: *tant que a faire sanlier.*
[12] Clement V (1305—14).
[13] Boniface VIII (1294—1303).
[14] For the text of *Meruit*, see FRIEDBERG II 1300.
[15] Philip IV (the Fair) of France (1285—1314).
[16] For Louis XII's help in restoring to the Holy See control over Imola, Forlì, Bologna, Ravenna, Faenza, Rimini, and other places in Romagna, see GUICCIARDINI VII, iii, VIII, i, v—vi, xvi, ed. PANIGADA II 174—82, 248—55, 274—82, 333.
[17] Psalm 85: 10.

comme font les autres princes qui la veullent faire et font a ses despens; et vueille considerer que la guerre a longue queue, et quant elle est escamote d'un coste, elle s'alume de l'autre, et que l'Ytallye est plus subgecte a mutacion que autre region de chrestiente.

Et y a plusieurs autres choses lesquelles de sa grande prudence saura mieulx considerer et qu'il ne vueille extimer: ledit roy tres chrestien est sy bas, comme ses ennemys le luy vouldroient donner a entendre.

En luy faissant assavoir que touiours le trouvera son tres bon, devot et obeissant filz, delibere de luy faire tous les services qu'il pourra, comme plus amplement luy dira monsieur de Marseille[18] son ambassadeur.

III.
Anonymus letter (perhaps of Louis de Forbin to Etienne Poncher)[19] Rome (?), August or September 1513 (?)[20]

Bibliothèque Nationale de Paris, Fonds Ancien Français 2933, fol. 135r.

Par les lettres que Monsieur de Marseille[21] et moy esspedions au Roy[22], entendrez tout ce que icelluy de Marseille a peu gaigner de pape.[23] Et ny a eu remede par ce bout. Quoy voyant et considerant le dangier provehant, Majeste sue retyre a Monsieur de Saint Sevrin.[24] Lui recordant le besoing que avoyt le

---

[18] Claude de Seyssel, bishop of Marseille (1511—17) — see EUBEL III 237—38.

[19] Louis de Forbin was the resident ambassador in Rome prior to Seyssel's arrival and had failed to negotiate the reconciliation between Leo and Louis. In the struggle for influence in the French delegation, he sided with Sanseverino over Seyssel. Ever since the death of Jean de Gannay in June of 1512, Étienne Poncher had functioned as chancellor of France without, however, being formally granted that title. See D'AMAT 409 and GARAND 320—21.

[20] The date of August or September 1513 is suggested by the status of the negotiations at that time which coincided with the conditions enumerated in this letter: Seyssel has arrived and begun to negotiate, no conclusion has yet been reached, Louis XII has yet to disband the Pisan Council and adhere to the Lateran, Sanseverino has dispatched his own messenger, and there is talk of sending a special legate to Louis (see below, Appendix IV article 1 and above footnote 163).

[21] Claude de Seyssel was bishop of Marseille (1511—1517) — see EUBEL III 237—38.

[22] Louis XII (1498—1515).

[23] Leo X (1513—21).

[24] Cardinal Federigo Sanseverino (1463—1516) was the second of six sons of Roberto Sanseverino, himself the son of Lisa Attendolo, a natural daughter of Muzio Attendolo (surnamed Sforza due to the vigor of his character), the father of Francesco Sforza, duke of Milan (d. 1466). Roberto's title was Count of Cajazzo. Federico's mother was either Isabella d'Urbino or Giovanna de Correggio. The Sanseverino family was married into the major royal and nobles families of Europe and ranked among the highest nobility of Naples. Roberto served not only Ferrante I of Naples, but also Innocent VIII, Ludovico Sforza, and Venice. Federigo's brother Galeazzo married Bianca, a natural daughter of Ludovico Sforza, served Ludovico for a while, and then passed over to the service of Charles VIII of France. Louis XII in 1505 named him Grand Esquire of France, a title he retained until his death at the battle of Pavia in 1525. See: PH. DE COMMINES, The Memoirs, ed. Andrew R. SCOBLE, 2 vols., London 1892, I 52, II 101—03, 108; BOURLOTON 111—13; L. CARDELLA, Memoire storiche de' cardinali della Santa Romana Chiesa, Rome 1793, III 243—44; A. DE SAINT-MARIE, Histoire générale et chronologique de la maison royale de France, Paris 1726—33, VIII 502; T. DE MOREMBERT, Frédéric de San Severino, in: DHGE 18 (Paris 1977) 1172—73.

Roy et le temps ou il devoyt employer son credit qu'il avoit du pape, duquel souvent favory estirpt du Roy, Monsieur de Sainct Sevrin, y alla de celluy pas, et conclud avec le pape la seurete du Roy des maintenant. Sy le Roy dissipe le concille pisan, envoyant chacun en sa maison adherant au concille Lateran, et de ce envoye a diligent procuracion expresse et bien ample a qui luy playra, et non seullement a asseure le fait d'icy, maiz celluy par dela incontinent auriuee icelle confederacion grosse intelligeure, amortissant le feu par dela et plusieurs autres choses que le Roy entendra par Monsieur le Grant Escuy[25], auquel Monsieur de Sainct Sevrin envoyt homme expres.[26] Maiz cecy esvente mectroyt en dangier les affaires du Roy, le stat [—] vie de tous ceulx qui y tiennent le main par deca. Or m[——] je vous prie, vueillez comprendre par ce que a fait Monsieur de Marseille et remis et vecrez sy les matieres ont este si faciles de mon temps.[27] Qui nay sceu avoir aucune nomme puissance pour riens traicter avec le pape present. Et qui ay eu du quartier de la plusieur des faveurs sans aucun port pleust a dieu eu eusst, je eu la montre du ciedu et du pouoir, non pour moy, maiz pour avoir peu exequter le groz vouloyr que j'ay de faire au Roy quelque bon service. Et vous asseur, Monsieur, quelque part que je soys, le Roy me trouveora loyal, tres obeissant, et tout plein de bon et groz coeur. Et ne seray a perpetuite autre que vostre tres humble serviteur ycy a ma maison et ailleurs. Sy le pape doyt envoyer devers le Roy legat[28] meilleur seron pervenyr et que le Roy requist Monsieur de Sainct Sevrin. Et surtout ne soyt nomme le cardinal de Ferrare[29], car le Roy y seroit trompe pour tout vray.

IV.

Response of Leo X to the Eleven Proposals of the Papal-French Commission on How to End the Pisan Schism
Rome, September 1513

Archives départmentales du Nord-Lille: Coté B, entrée 1462, nr. 18,060, fol. 1r—2r, identified on fol. 2v as: Conciles de Pise et de Latran: Copie des articles propostes au pape par la France et repondus par le pape pour labolition du Concile de Pise en faveur du Concile de Latran.

Imprimis, quia Sua Sanctitas declarauit, quod dummodo Christianissimus Rex dissolui faciat conuentum Pisanum et discedere eos qui sub illius nomine Lugduni

---

[25] The Grand Esquire of France was the brother of Federigo, Galeazzo (d. 1525).

[26] Federigo's messenger was often Sebastiano da Pistoia.

[27] In his treatise on the Gospel of St. Luke, penned within months of these events, Claude de Seyssel complained of those who out of jealousy plot against and seek to find fault in the words and deeds of upright and talented men — see his Tractatus de triplici statu viatoris, s.l. 1518, fol. 122F.

[28] The proposal to send a legate to Louis XII with a bull declaring that the king had not been censured by Julius was contained in the first of the eleven articles worked out by the papal-French commission. See below Appendix IV.

[29] The cardinal of Ferrara was Ippolyto d'Este (d. 1520).

resident, et adhereat Consilio Lateranensi, contentus erit facere omnia que desiderabuntur, ex quibus sit cautum dignitati sue et honori ac etiam utilitati.

[1] P: Petitur quod Sua Sanctitas in euentum predictorum declaret prefatum regem non fuisse comprehensum in aliquibus censuris priuationibus aut aliis decretis bone memorie domini Julii et prefati Consilii Lateranensis, in eiudem regis odium et preiudicium promulgatis. Et casu quo pretendi posset illum quouis modo comprehensum esse, illud omnino non preiudicasse nec preiudicare posse in futurum sue maiestati, sed haberi perinde ac si numquam factum esset in ampla et serenissima forma.

R: Sanctissimus dominus noster est contentus absque prouisione facere que petuntur, cum primum Christianissimus Rex fecerit contenta in articulo, et mittet legatum de latere, qui portabit sue maiestati bullam predicta[m] continentem in sufficienti forma.

[2] P: Item circa dominos Maclouiensem[30] et Baiocensem[31] Cardinales per dictum quondam Julium priuatos, quod Sua Sanctitas, attentis et consideratis multis tum meritis eorum tum authoritate erga prefatum regem, necnon seruiciis que inde faciunt et facere possunt in regno, et etiam Sanctissimo domino nostro et uniuersali ecclesie, dignetur Sua Sanctitas uti cum eis benignitate, etiam plusquam ceteris priuatis, et eos restituere sine ulla graui solempnitate.

R: Sanctissimus dominus noster retinet ista in pectore suo, sed si dicti cardinales uenerint ad Sanctitatem Suam tractabit eos humaniter; et mitius etiam aget cum eis, quam cum aliis cardinalibus priuatis[32] egerit, accedente eorum consensu.

[3] P: Tertio, quantum ad prelatos et alios qui interfuerunt conuentui Pisano, quia Sanctitas prefata intendit et uult omnino quod ueniant in sufficienti numero ad confitendum errorem et petendum absolutionem, habeat respectum Sua Sanctitas ad bella et alia grauia negocia et onera, que nunc sunt in Gallia, pro defensione regni. Ob que, non solum est opus presentia prelatorum, sed etiam auxilio eorum et subditorum suorum, et sic esse contenta paruo numero quattuor prelatorum et dominorum doctorum aut principalium officiatorum dicte congregationis.

R: Sanctissimus dominus noster contentabitur, quod ueniant sex prelati et

---

[30] Cardinal Guillaume Briçonnet, bishop of Saint-Malo (1493—1514), was deprived of his offices on 24 October 1511 — see Eubel II 183; III, 4b n. 1, 6, 227 Lodoven. n. 2. He retracted his errors in a public consistory on 7 April 1514 through his son Denys as his procurator — see Hergenroether I 498, nr. 7854.

[31] Cardinal René de Prie, bishop of Bayeux (1498—1516), was deprived on 24 October 1511 and restored on 24 April 1514 — see Eubel III 11, 127.

[32] Cardinals Carvajal and Sanseverino.

quattuor magistri in sacra theologia aut in iure canonico de his, qui interfuerunt dicte congregationi, ex honorabilioribus.

[4] P: Item quod interim fiat una absolutio generalis quoad omnes qui in dicto conuentu interuenerunt et illi adheserunt.

R: Fiet statim post illorum oratorum seu procuratorum aduentum, et exinde dicto casu adueniente, absoluantur a censuris et interdicto in foro conscientie.

[5] P: Item, et concedatur amplus saluus conductus pro iis qui uenient, ut re facta uel infecta absque ulla molestia tute redire possint; etiam pro ueniendo obtinenptur securitas ab omnibus, etiam ita ut secure uenire possint.

R: Placet Sanctissimo domino nostro, et faciet quod poterunt ire et redire secure.

[6] P: Item et quod ipsi prelati et alii, qui uenient nomine dicte congregationis, possint eligere uiam iuris et gracie uel unum sine preiudicio alterius; et casu quo eligant uiam gracie, ut creditur, dignetur Sua Sanctitas audire patienter eorum excusationes, et illis intellectis absoluere et rehabilitare ac reintegrare tam eos quam alios quorum uoce loquentur, scilicet qui dicte congregationi interuenerunt, in ampla forma et cum omni mansuetudine, non seruato rigore iuris et sine scandalo.

R: Sanctitas Sua erit parata audire quoscumque petentes iusticiam, seruatis terminis iuris; petentibus autem graciam, concedet et utetur humanitate et mansuetudine, quantum cum Deo poterit, seruata dignitate Apostolice Sedis.

[7] P: Item, et ne sit necesse conuocare denuo omnes qui interuenerunt dicte congregationi, sufficiat quod illi qui uenient habeant mandatum ab his qui nunc reputant [sic] dictam congregationem Lugduni.

R: Concedet Sua Sanctitas.

[8] P: Item, et quantum ad ecclesiam Gallicanam, quod tempus conueniens detur ad comparendum in Consilio Lateranensi, habita ratione guerrarum.

R: Est contenta Sua Sanctitas quod detur tempus conueniens, prout petit.

[9] P: Item, quantum ad gesta in dicto conuentu Pisano, postquam Sua Sanctitas non uult illa ratificare, dignetur eadem Sanctitas saltem quoad collationes et prouisiones taliter prouidere[33], seruata dignitate Sedis Apostolice, quod illi qui eas obtinuerunt non priuentur, sed petita noua prouisione a Sede Apostolica quoad ecclesias cathedrales et monasteria, non possint molestari etiam pro fructibus perceptis et fiat sine compositione. Quantum autem ad alia beneficia que pertinent ad prouisionem inferiorum prelatorum, quod illi qui obtinu-

---

[33] For the nullification of these provisions by the Lateran Council, see MANSI 32, 754AB.

erunt a dicta congregatione possint illa petere ab ordinariis uel Sede Apostolica aut etiam legato eius, prout uoluerunt, nec aliis conferentur sub obtentu quod acceperint a dicta congregatione prouisiones.
R: Sanctitas Sua est contenta de nouo concedere ecclesias monasteria et alia beneficia per dictam congregationem collata his pro quibus scribet Christianissimus Rex, etiam si habuerint prouisiones a dicta congregatione, dummodo petant infra trimestre a die dissolutionis dicte congregationis. Et de his que pertinent ad collationem ordinariorum, concedat quod ipsi ordinarii possint dispensare super restabilitate et de nouo conferre, dummodo abrenuncient dicte congregationi et prouisioni habite ab ea. Et utetur liberalitate maxima quoad fructus indebite perceptos, quantum ad prelatos tantum cum aliis dispensabit liberaliter.

[10] P: Item, circa ea que concernunt graciam aut conscienciam, dignetur etiam eadem Sanctitas habere rationem, quod saltem ea que sunt sortita effectum ualidentur, et de aliis fiat aliqua generalis prouisio, prout uidebatur Sue Sanctitati, que satisfaciat his qui fuerunt in bona fide.
R: Sanctissimus dominus noster recurrentibus ad Suam Sanctitatem exhibebit se in omnibus gratiosum, et legatus de latere quem mittet habebit facultatem de multis, ad quem poterunt recurrere.

[11] P: Item, circa ea que respiciunt forum contentiosum, dignetur Sua Sanctitas ea conualidare, saltem inter omnes regnicolas et eos qui dicte congregationi adheserunt.
R: Sanctissimus dominus noster, ad euitandas lites et ut partium parcatur laboribus et expensis, erit contentus omnibus gestis, uirtute rescriptorum dicte congregationis declaratis nullis, tamquam factis a non habentibus potestatem, decernere quod ea, que iam gesta sunt, maneant in statu in quo sunt.

V.

Constitution of Leo X *Aeternae Vitae Claviger* Declaring Louis XII of France Free of Ecclesiastical Censures
Rome, 9 October 1513

Archives Nationales de Paris, L 329, nr. 1.

Leo, episcopus, seruus seruorum Dei, ad perpetuam rei memoriam.

Eterne uite clauiger, Romanus Pontifex, hereditarie pacis testamentique Saluatoris nostri perpetuus custos et iudex, portas salutis perpetue etiam a predecessoribus suis iuste clausas, quandoque etiam non requisitus, pro redemptione gregis sibi crediti more uigilia *[sic]* pastoris aperit sententiasque excommunicationis et censuras omnes etiam predecessorum, ut prefertur uel tollit uel interpetratur *[sic]* aut declarat, ne Christi fidelium mentes in hiis que periculum animarum concernunt in anbiguo aut cum conscientie scrupulo aliquo remaneant, temporum conditione id exigente, presertim pro restituenda uniuersali ecclesie extirpatis radicitus scismatibus unione, proque Christi fidelium uniuersali pace, que, prohic *[sic]* dolor, tandiu exulauit, et tranquillitate consequenda, sanctaque expeditione in orthodoxe fidei hostes concordibus omnium Christianorum principum animis quantocius facienda, recuperandaque sancta Hierusalem, pacis uisione, aliaque facie, prout in Domino salubriter conspicit, expedire.

Dudum, siquidem felicis recordationis Julius papa II predecessor noster, ut conuentum siue Conciliabulum Pisanum pernitiosumque scisma quod inde oriebatur tanquam communem pestem in ipso ortu extingueret, prefatum Conciliabulum nullum et a non habentibus potestatem nulliterque illegitime immo uero temere congregatum declarauit, ac quatinus de facto processit, et ad habundantem cautelam reuocauit, necnon contra ibi conuenientes, illudque congregantes, aut prosequentes seu adherentes, fauctores, illique consilium auxilium uel fauorem quomodolibet dantes, excommunicationis interdicti ac alias censuras et penas multiplices fulminauit, ac unicum uerum legitimum et ex legitimis causis congregandum sacrosanctum Lateranense Concilium indixit, aliaque fecit, prout in litteris sub dato quintodecimo Kalendas Augusti pontificatus sui anno octauo[34], quorum tenores ac clausulas perinde ac si de uerbo ad uerbum insererentur pro insertis et expressis haberi uolumus, plenius continetur, ac per diuersas eius litteras, tam ex prefata causa quam ex pluribus aliis, etiam tam antequam post sententias excommunicationis et interdicti aliasque censuras et penas, tam contra receptatores fauctoresque adherentes ac auxilium consilium uel fauorem, ut prefertur quomodolibet dantes, quam etiam contra receptatores uel fautores Alphonsi Extensis ciuitatem Ferrariensem ut asserebat tunc ocupantem[35] *[sic]*, quam etiam contra ocupantes aut quomodolibet terras ecclesie hostiliter inuadentes, ac alias quomodolibet contra prefatam ecclesiam militantes exercitusque hostilis huiusmodi duces capitaneos stipendiarios eorumque fauctores omnes et singulos eisque auxilium consilium uel fauorem quomodolibet dantes, presertim per suas quas in „Cena Domini" contra eundem Alphonsum[36] aliosque prefatos legi et publicari fecit, diuersis respectibus et causis diuersimode ac multipliciter tulit et promulgauit, prout in multis ac diversis eius litteris desuper confectis, quarum omnium et singularum tenores causas ac clausulas formasque, etiam cum irritantibus decretis, perinde ac si de uerbo ad uerbum insererentur et exprimerentur, simili modo uere et non ficte pro expressis ac de uerbo ad uerbum insertis haberi uolumus, plenius continetur, que quidem sententie censure

---

[34] The bull *Sacrosanctae Romanae ecclesiae* of 18 July 1511 is published in MANSI 32, 681B—91A, see esp. 686B and 690B.

[35] The decrees against Alfonso d'Este and his supporters are *Romani Pontificis auctoritas* of 9 August 1510 and *Decet Romanum Pontificem* of 14 October 1510, in: ASV, Reg. Vat. 984, fols. 137v—46r, esp. 142r and fols. 162r—64v, esp. 163r—64r, respectively.

[36] For the bull *Coena Domini* of 16 April 1511 condemning Alfonso by name see ASV, Reg. Vat. 956, fols. 162v—66r, esp. 164r—v.

et pene seu earum alique fuerunt forsan per prefatum Lateranense Concilium solemniter confirmate[37] propter quarum et in eis contentarum clausularum et formarum pregnantiam uerborumque generalitatem et eruberantiam dubitari contingit, hesitarique posset, tempore procedente, an carissimus in Christo filius noster Ludouicus Francorum Rex Christianissimus in illis ac penis et censuris in eis contentis quomodolibet comprendatur.

Nam igitur ad huiusmodi ambiguitatem tollendam, necnon scandalis que inde uerisimiliter prouenire possent obuiandum, unionique universalis ecclesie ac paci et tranquillitati Christi fidelium consulendum, expeditionemque prefatam in hostes fidei acerlerandum, premissa paterno considerantes affectu, at[t]endentesque quod tam ipse Rex quam predecessores sui ob religionis zelum multaque beneficia in Sedem Apostolicam sanctamque Romanam ecclesiam aliquando collata, laudabiliaque opera et seruitia eidem aliquando impensa, de Sede Apostolica ac sancta Romana ecclesia predicta bene meriti fuerunt, dictum Regem a quibusuis aliis excommunicationibus censuris et penis a iure uel ab homine quauis occasione uel causa latis, si quibus quomodolibet innodatus existit, ad effectum presentium duntaxat consequendum, harum serie absoluentes et absolutum fore censentes.

Motu proprio, non ad alicuius super hoc nobis oblate petitionis instantiam, sed ex nostra certa scientia ac libera et spontanea uoluntate et clementia presentium uigore declaramus sententias censuras penasque predictas in prefatis litteris contentas, litterasque ipsas omnes et singulas etiam ut prefertur per predictum Lateranense Concilium confirmatas, omniaque alia et singula in eis contenta, personam prefati Ludouici Francorum Regis Christianissimi ab earum omnium et singularum datis minime comprehendisse nec comprehendere, aut ad eius uel successorum suorum personas extendi quomodolibet potuisse uel posse, aut illi uel illis tam in temporalibus quam in spiritualibus quomodolibet preiudicare, etiam si in eis uel earum aliqua prefatus Ludouicus Rex Christianissimus quomodolibet expresse et spetialiter nominaretur; et quatinus opus sit et ad omnem habundantiorem cautelam, eundem Ludouicum Regem a prefatis sententiis censuris et penis ac aliis omnibus et singulis in prefatis litteris contentis, motu scientia et uoluntate similibus absoluimus, in omnibus et per omnia, quo ad omnes effectus tam temporales quam spirituales; eundemque Ludouicum Regem, quatinus opus fit, aduersus omnes sententias censuras et penas prefatas omniaque alia et singula inde secuta et ad famam honores dignitates titulos etiam regales regnumque ac ducatus principatus marchionatus comitatus dominia

---

[37] Probably a reference: to the 17 May 1512 bull *Cum inchoatam* of the second session which confirmed three previous decrees against the Pisan Council — see MANSI 32, 714A—15D, esp. 714C; to the 3 December 1512 bull *Ad illius* of the third session condemning the supporters of the Pisan Council — see MANSI 32, 733E—35A, esp. 734A—C; and to the 10 December 1512 bull *Saluti gregis* which among other things cited French officials, even those of regal status, for failing to appear before the Lateran Council to answer charges against them for violating the liberty of the Church — see MANSI 32, 753A—754E, esp. 753D—54A.

iurisdictiones ac feuda etiam ecclesiasticas successionesque quaslibet ac alios quoslibet actus legitimos et ad eum prorsus statum in quo ante premissas sententias censuras penas ac litteras quomodolibet existebat, perinde ac si sententie censure et pene littereque predicte, quas omnes et singulas ab earum datis pro nullis et infectis haberi uolumus, nullatenus emanassent, restituimus et plenarie reintegramus, sicque per quoscumque iudices ecclesiasticos uel laycos tam ordinarios quam delegatos quacunque auctoritate fungentes iudicari interpetrari *[sic]* ac declarari uolumus, sublata eis et eorum cuilibet quauis aliter iudicandi imterpetrandi *[sic]* ac declarandi facultate decernentes, nichilominus irritum et inane totum id et quicquid contra premissa uel eorum aliquod a quoquam quauis auctoritate scienter uel ignoranter contigerit atemptari; non obstantibus premissis ac constitutionibus et ordinationibus apostolicis, illa presertim Johannis xxii predecessoris nostri que incipit „Inter Cetera" contra ocupantes aut inuadentes terras ecclesie edita[38], necnon quibusuis litteris similibus uel dissimilibus a nobis seu predecessoribus nostris quomodolibet emanatis, sub quibusuis formis et clausulis etiam similibus motu proprio et ex certa scientia ac de apostolice potestatis plentitudine, quibus etiam si pro illarum sufficienti derogatione de ipsis earumque totis tenoribus ac clausulis, spetialis specifica expressa indiuidua ac de uerbo ad uerbum non autem per clausulas generales ad importantes mentio seu queuis alia expressio habenda aut alia exquisita forma seruanda esset illarum omnium tenores formas ac clausulas pro sufficienter expressis et insertis habentes illis preterquam quo ad premissa inter alias in suo robore permansuris spetialiter et expresse motu ac scientia similibus derogamus, ceterisque contrariis quibuscunque.

Nulli ergo omnino hominum liceat hanc paginam nostre absolutionis declarationis restitutionis reintegrationis uoluntatis decreti et derogationis infringere uel ei ausu temerario contraire. Si quis autem hoc atemptare presumpserit, indignationem omnipotentis Dei ac beatorum Petri et Pauli Apostolorum eius se nouerit incursurum.

Datum Rome apud Sanctum Petrum, anno incarnationis dominice millesimoquingentesimo tertio decimo, septimo Idus Octobris, pontificatus nostri anno primo.

B. de Accoltis[39]

---

[38] For the decree *Inter caetera* of John XXII against those occupying and invading the lands of the Church, see perhaps the decree *Inter caetera* of 1 April 1321, in: Bullarum diplomatum et privilegiorum sanctorum Romanum pontificum Taurinensis editio, ed. F. GAUDE et alii, Torino 1860, IV 297—98, app. 29; a more likely candidate would be *Ad hoc dignoscitur* of 23 December 1321, Ibid. 299—300, app. 32.

[39] The signature would appear to be B. de Accoltis, but Benedictus Michaelis de Accoltis was only 19 years old and named to the office of *abbreviator praesentiae majoris* in 1513, a post he resigned in 1521 upon being promoted to bishop of Cadiz. Under Clement VII, he served as domestic secretary. His uncle cardinal Pietro de Accoltis functioned under Leo X as *referendarius et signator litterarum gratiarum* — see W. v. HOFMANN, Forschungen zur Geschichte der kurialen Behörden vom Schisma bis zur Reformation, II (= Bibliothek des königlich-preußischen historischen Instituts in Rom 13), Rome 1914, 124, 133, 191, 196.

VI.
Formula for Renouncing the Pisan Council Used by Those Who Had Received a Provision by Its Authority
Rome, 15 October 1513

Archivio Segreto Vaticano, Reg. Vat. 1005, fols. 153r—54v*.

Tenor autem forme iuramenti abiurationis sequitur, et est talis: Ego, Ludouicus Dronnii, rector parrochialis ecclesie Sancti Sulpicii de Gidiaco Aurelianensis diocesis, comperto diuisionis et scismatis[40] ac heresis laqueo, quo tenebar credendo faciendo et adherendo Conciliabulo Pisano et credentibus fauentibus receptatoribus adherentibus defensoribus complicibus et sequacibus eiusdem, prestando auxilium consilium uel fauorem, et propterea nunc diutina mecum[41] deliberatione propria et spontanea uoluntate ad fidem catholicam et unitatem Sedis Apostolice diuina gratia incensus, fateor publice me tenuisse et de presenti[42] tenere fidem catholicam et credere et tenere ut docet sancta mater ecclesia, cui preest sanctissimus dominus Leo diuina prouidentia papa X., et quod idem dominus Leo fuit et est uerus Romanus pontifex et uerus uicarius Jhesu Christi Petrique successor, canonice electus intronisatus et coronatus in Romanum Pontificem per cardinales, ad quos, uacante sede per obitum sancte memorie Iulii pape ii, electio intronizatio et coronatio pertinebat; quodque scismatici manifesti et inuasores et destructores totius Christianitatis, a luminibus[43] sancte matris ecclesie separati et a Christifidelibus persequendi sunt, donec ad cor reuersi, suos recognoscant errores, et ad gremium reuertantur ecclesie antedicte; et quod tam illi qui conciliabulum indixerunt, quam omnes alii illis adherentes credentes receptatores defensores complices et sequaces eorum fuerunt et sunt, uere scismatici apostatici excommunicati anathematisati ac diuisi et separati a communione fidelium et ab unitate sancte ecclesie et tamque heretici puniendi, meque talem fuisse, et esse iuste et sancte de scismate[44] credentia fautoria[45] adhesione sequela et erroribus predictis condempnatum, et incidisse in penas et sententias, tam a iure quam ab homine in talia perpetrantes inflictas et promulgatas, et in processibus prefati Iulii pape contra Conciliabulum Pisanum et illi adherentes factis contentas et declaratas.

Et ne simulate reuersus extimer, sub honoris mei casu et anathematis obligatione et sub pena que relapsis a iure imponi deberet anathematizo et abiuro

---

* This version, which appears first in the following notes, is, where appropriate, compared to that which appears in Reg. Vat. 1010, fols. 267v—68r.

[40] scismatis *corr. ab* scismaticis: scismatius.
[41] mecum: mera.
[42] de presenti (?) *abbrev.* de pūti: deputari (?).
[43] luminibus: luminbus [liminibus?].
[44] scismate: scismatne.
[45] credentia fautoria: credentis fautoris.

II

omnem heresim et scisma extolentem[46] se adversus et contra sanctam Romanam ecclesiam et prefatum dominum nostrum[47] Leonem papam X., et euominatum damnatum scisma credentiam[48] adhesionem prefati Conciliabuli Pisani, et me ad eamdem heresim et scisma de quibus Redemptoris nostri gratia ereptum[49] sum numquam reuersurum, sed semper me in fide et unitate[50] sancte ecclesie catholice, cui preest prelibatus noster dominus[51] Leo papa X., mansurum.

Ac sponte promitto, uere et non ficte sed uoluntarie et sincere, iuro ad sancta Dei euangelia et corporaliter per me tacta, quod stabo et parebo mandatis ecclesie et dicti domini Leonis pape super huiusmodi excessibus rebellionibus fautoriis et ceteris penis et sententiis, quas ob premissa et ea tangentia[52] incurri; et quod dicto domino nostro pape[53] et eius successoribus canonice intrantibus obediens et fidelis de cetero ero, et eis reuerentiam debitam exhibebo. Non ero in consilio uel tractatu, ut uitam perdant aut membrum, uel capiantur mala captione. Consilium, quod michi credituri sunt per nuncium uel litteras, ad ipsorum damnum[54] uel preiudicium scienter nemini pandam uel communicabo. Et si sciuero fieri uel tractari aliquid, quod in ipsorum damnum[54] uel preiudicium uergeret, illud pro posse impediam, ne fiat. Et si id per me impedire non potero, hoc eis aut alii seu aliis, per quem uel per quos id credam ad noticiam ipsorum peruenire personaliter uel per litteras aut per nuncios significare curabo.

Papatum Romanum, et regalia Sancti Petri ac iura, et iurisdictiones prefate Romane ecclesie, et dicti domini nostri pape maiestatem et honorem ac statum illesos manutenebo. Totis uiribus et defendam et iuuabo ad illesos recuperandum, et recuperatos manutendendum contra omnes homines et specialiter quoscumque credentes adherentes fautores receptatores[55] defensores complices et sequaces huiusmodi Conciliabuli Pisani, cuiuscumque preeminentia ordinis religionis conditionis uel status existant, etiam si pontificali regali seu regniali aut quauis alia prefulgeant dignitate, etiam si fuerint sancte Romane ecclesie cardinales.

Et contra quoscumque per dictam[56] ecclesiam denotatos uel imposterum denotandos[57], quamdiu extra gratiam et communionem dicte ecclesie permane-

---

[46] extolen.: extollentem.
[47] dominum nostrum: dominum nostrum dominum.
[48] credentiam: credentia in.
[49] ereptum: ereptus.
[50] unitate: uoluntate.
[51] prelibatus noster dominus: prefatus dominus noster dominus.
[52] tangentia: tagentia.
[53] pape: papa.
[54] damnu: dampnum.
[55] receptatores: receptores.
[56] dictam: dictum.
[57] denotatos uel imposterum denotandos: denotatos uel imposterum denotatos uel imposterum denotandos.

bunt, nec cum prefatis scismaticis et rebellibus et ipsorum fautoribus et sequacibus, per prefatum Iulium denotatis deinceps ero. Nec eis seu quibuscumque aliis contra dictam ecclesiam et dominum nostrum papam dabo auxilium consilium uel fauorem, per me uel alium seu alios directe uel indirecte, publice uel occulte. Nec ab aliis, quantum in me fuerit, si id impedire potero, prestari seu dari permittam. Nec cum dictis scismaticis et rebellibus aut quibuscumque aliis in rebellione prefate ecclesie existentibus contra ipsam ecclesiam colligationem uel conspirationem faciam siue ligam, sed eos et eorum quemlibet iuxta tenorem processuum predictorum, pro posse meo, persequar et inuadam, donec conuertantur et reuertantur ad gremium ecclesie memorate, sic me Deus adiuuet et hec sancta Dei euangelia.

Nulli [possibly two words cancelled[58]] nostre absolutionis dispensationis abolitionis collationis prouisionis mandati uoluntatis et decieti[59] infringere et cetera. Signis eorum.

VII.
Letter of Leo X to the French Delegation Impeded from Coming to the Council
Rome, 17 February 1514

Archivio Segreto Vaticano, Arm. XLIV, vol. 5, fol. 58r*.

Uenerabilibus fratribus Joanni Cabilonensi[60], Joanni Lexouiensi[61], de Englosinensi[62], Symphoriano Gladecitensi[63], et ceteris.[64]

Uenerabiles fratres. Legimus litteras uestras, quibus uos paratos esse ad ueniendum ad sacrum Lateranense Consilium, maiestatis et Sedis Apostolice mandatis obediendum significastis, sed cum minime tutum iter uobis ostendatur, in ipsa uia restitisse, in quo nos uestram obedientiam in Domino commendamus.

Quo uero secure proficisci ad nos possitis, dedimus operam cum dilectis filiis nobilibus uiris Maximiliano Mediolani[65] et Octauiano duce Genue[66] ut

---

[58] words cancelled: ergo omnino huiusmodi liceat hanc paginam.
[59] absolutionis dispensationis abolitionis collationis prouisionis mandati uoluntatis et decreti: absolutionis abolitionis dispensationis collationis prouisionis decreti mandati et uoluntatis.
* HERGENROETHER, Regesta Leonis I 436 nr. 6885.
[60] Jean de Poupet, O.S.B., bishop of Chalôns sur Saône (1503—31) — see EUBEL III 148.
[61] Jean de Tillieres (le Veneur), bishop of Lisieux (1505—39) — see EUBEL III 22, 224.
[62] Antoine d'Estaing, bishop of Angoulême (1506—23) — see EUBEL III 192.
[63] Symphorien Bullioud, bishop of Glandèves (1508—21) — see EUBEL III 203.
[64] The other members of this delegation were apparently François de Halwin (bishop of Amiens), the theologians Jean Le Lamiens and Antoine Seurre, and the canonists Jean du Fresne and Guillaume de Nory — see MANSI 32, 864E—65A.
[65] Massimiliano Sforza, duke of Milan (1512—15) — see CAPPELLI 331.
[66] Ottaviano Campofregoso, doge of Genoa (1513—15 November), governor under French domination (1515—22) — see CAPPELLI 317.

uobis de saluoconductu, et si opus fuerit, etiam de scutis et aliis ad iter tute agendum necessariis rebus prouideant, quemadmodum plenius ad uos perscribet uenerabilis frater Claudius episcopus Massiliensis regis Christianissimi apud nos orator[67], cuius litteris adhibebitis fidem.

Uos, itaque, fratres, hortamur in Domino, ut deposito metu ad nos et predictum consilium proprio quoque tempore uos conferatis. Datum Rome, die xvii Februarii 1514, anno primo.

VIII.
Letter of Leo X to Ottaviano Campofregoso, Doge of Genoa
Rome, 8 March 1515

Archivio Segreto Vaticano, Arm. XLIV, vol. 5, fol. 203r.

Dilecte fili. Quanto intersit Romane ecclesie et totius Reipublice Christiane sacrum Lateranense Concilium, quod a felicis recordationis Iulio ii predecessore nostro in Spiritu Sancto legitime indictum, et per nos continuatum est, ad optatum finem perduci, facile tibi pro tua prudentia notum esse confidimus.

Cum uero due uel grauissimi momenti res in eo sint pertractande, una perniciosi scismatis penitus extinguendi, altera pragmatice abusionis[68] que in paitibus Gallie tot iam annis uiguit tollende et eiiciende.

Neutrum satis commode et secundum institutum sacri Concilii ordinem sine Gallicorum prelatorum presentia perfici potuit. Itaque nos et alios prelatos Gallice nationis citari iussimus ad comparendum, et quoniam adhuc iusto, ut ipsi attestati sunt, metu propter negatos saluosconductus non uenerunt, denuo eos euocamus, cum autem eorum aduentus nobis et sacro concilio admodum optatus et pene necessarius sit. Sitque nostre et eiusdem concilii dignitatis afficere ut ad id uenientes tutum ubique iter et liberum habeant.

Nobilitatem tuam hortamur in Domino et paterno affectu requirimus, ut nostro et uniuersalis ecclesie que tota in concilio ipso representata est intuitu predictis prelatis sine armis accedentibus, si per tuos fines iter facere instituerint, amplum et liberum saluumconductum conficere, eumque ad nos quam primum mittere studeas[69], ut erepta illis omni tergiuersandi causa, que Dei et fidei honori conducunt maturius efficere ualeamus. Erit hoc nobis gratissimum. Datum Rome, 8 Martii 1515, anno secundo.

---

[67] Claude de Seyssel, bishop of Marseille (1511—17) — see EUBEL III 237—38. For a reference to this letter of Leo and to Seyssel's informing the French delegation of Leo's efforts to obtain safe-conducts, see MANSI 32, 865CD, 868B.

[68] The Pragmatic Sanction of Bourges (1438).

[69] For a copy of the doge's safe-conduct, see MANSI 32, 899D—900A.

IX.
Letter of Leo X to Massimiliano Sforza, Duke of Milan
Rome, 10 March 1515

Archivo Segreto Vaticano, Arm. XLIV, vol. 5, fols. 206r—07r[70].

Dilecte fili, et cetera. Sacrum Lateranense Concilium, quod a felicis recordationis Iulio secundo predecessore nostro in Spiritu Sancto legitime indictum, et per nos eodem cooperante Spiritu continuatum, multa proposuit ad ordinem et instaurationem Christiane relligionis pertinentia, que aut lapsa fuerant aut iam collabebantur, in melius reformanda.

Duo inter alia tractanda et peragenda suscepit. Unum est [u]terror scismatis que ex partibus Gallie contra fidei unitatem et sancte Romane ecclesie autoritatem intentatus fuerat, infringeretur. Alterum, ut pragmatica abusio, que in eadem natione Gallicana tot iam annis uiguit, tanquam huic Sancte Sedi apostolice et summo uniuersalis ecclesie pontifici aduersaria atque infesta abrogaretur penitus atque eiiceretur.

Quorum primum, quod fidei Catholice incolumitatem concernit, et si per Dei misericordiam et Sancti Spiritus illuminationem illis ouibus, que uagate ac errantes fuerant, ad uerum pastorem iam conuersis, magna ex parte sublatum est. Tamen ut radicitus extirpari possit, uisum nostre et ipsius concilii circumspecte grauitati est, ipsi[s]met qui aberrauerunt presentibus et pristinum errorem cum humili petitione uenie abiurantibus, nouis eos sacramentis sancte Romane ecclesie et Christi uicario Beati Petri successori obligari.

In secundo uero quod ad pragmaticam attinet, quamquam illam, ut notorie nullam et a non habentibus autoritatem editam ac libertatis ecclesie contrariam, liceat nobis et eidem sacro concilio iure optimo, non expectata alia citatione, abrogare et amouere, tum ut humanius cum illis ageretur et ad abundantiorem cautelam uisum fuit citata ad contradicendum, siquid allegare uellet, parte procedere, ut ipsi quoque conuicti errorem suum faterentur. Quo circa, ut omnia seruatis iuris et iustitie terminis perficerentur, prelati Gallice nationis ab ipso primum predecessore nostro, deinde a nobis, sacro approbante concilio, citati fuerunt cum amplo et libero saluoconductu, ut qui accederent ad concilium tutum ubique iter et liberum haberent, grauissimis censuris in quoscunque impedientes promulgatis, sicut in litteris predecessoris nostri et nostris super hoc editis plenius continetur.[71]

Cum uero superioribus mensibus quemadmodum nobis litteris et nunciis ac etiam instrumentis autenticis fuit intimatum, prelati Gallici iam iter arripuis-

---

[70] This letter is the same as that sent to the Swiss recorded on fols. 206r—07r, with certain alterations indicated on fol. 207r and required by the usage of the second person singular (for Massimiliano) in place of the plural (for the Swiss).

[71] For the previous citations of the French prelates by the Lateran Council, see MANSI, 32, 750B—54E, 772E—73D, 783B—E, 791E—93E, 815C—18A, 818C—D.

sent, seseque ad nos et ad concilium ipsum conferre intenderent, quo melius id facere pergerent iusto, ut ipsi attestati sunt, metu propter negatum illis a tua Nobilitate saluumconductum sunt retardati[72], quod quidem illis fortasse gratum et optatum, utpote inuitis uenientibus, nobis uero et sacro concilio perquam incommodum accidit.

Sumus autem certi, Nobilitatem tuam, si credidisset in huiusmodi prelatorum transitu impediendo illorum, quos non amat, commodis et uoluntati consulere, sacri autem Lateranensis Concilii cui fauet autoritatem ledere, nunquam suam uim illorum aduentui oppositurum fuisse, sed daturam potius operam, ut illi inuiolati et tuti ad nos peruenirent.

Nunc postquam non sine nostro et sacrosancti concilii incommodo factum est, ut illorum aduentus impediretur, sine quibus due maxime et grauissime res, scismatis uidelicet et pragmatice, perfici secundum supradictos respectus et absolui non possunt, deuotionem tuam pro nostra erga te paterna charitate primum commonefaciendam teque requirendum duximus, ut animaduertere diligenter velis, ne iis quibus nocere intendis rem gratam illis causam more obiiciendo, nobis uero et sacro concilio incommodam facias, cauereque studeas, ne illos censurarum grauissimarum laqueos, qui impedientibus proficiscentes ad concilium per binas iam litteras apostolicas eodem sacro approbante concilio[73] intenti sunt, implicemini. Quod esset penitus alienum uirtute et probitate tua et ea, quam debes sancte Romane ecclesie, a qua maximis tuis in rebus semper adiutus fuisti gratitudine. Deinde, hortamur te in Domino et paterno affectu requirimus, ut eisdem prelatis ad concilium proficiscentibus, eorum comitatibus, tam equestribus quam pedestribus, necnon honeribus sarcinis impedimentis, dum sine armis, sed ornatu et comitatu ecclesiastico ueniant, amplum et liberum saluumconductum per loca et regiones tuas conficeres, non solum tuas, sed eorum etiam apud quos tua auctoritas uiget, conficiendum curare, eumque ad nos quamprimum mittere studeas, ut nos, Deo et Spiritu Sancto concedente, que ad summum decus Christiane fidei et sancte Romane ecclesie pertinet sine ulteriore dilatione et prorogatione temporum agere et perficere ualeamus. Quod erit tue solite relligioni consentaneum, nobis uero et huic sacro concilio commodum atque gratum.

Datum Rome, x Martii 1515, anno 2.

---

[72] For Massimiliano's denial of a safe-conduct and the justification of his action by his ambassador at the ninth session of the Lateran Council, see MANSI 868BC and 869AB; the text of Morone's response is printed as App. 136 in: MORONE, Lettere latine, ed. PROMIS and MÜLLER 332—36.

[73] The two letters of Leo X approved by the Lateran Council imposing penalties on anyone impeding those coming to the Council are referred to in MANSI, 32, 793CD, 816B. The earlier safe-conduct of Julius is in MANSI 32, 688D—89C.

X.

Letter of Leo X Absolving the French Clergy for Adhering to the Pisan Council
Bologna, 13 December 1515

Archivio Segreto Vaticano, Reg. Vat. 1204, fols. 122r—24r.

Leo, episcopus, seruus seruorum Dei, ad futuram rei memoriam.

Clementissimi regis in excelsis imperantis uices licet immeriti gerentes in terris, ad ea uigilantie nostre curas libenter impendimus, per que singulorum utriusque sexus Christi fidelium animarum salus procuratur, ac intensum pie matris ecclesie gremium singulis post lapsum liberaliter exhibemus,[74] et piis fidelium presertim Catholicorum Regum[75] id a nobis exposcentium desideriis, fauorem apostolicum libenter impartimur.

Sane dilectus filius noster Franciscus Francorum rex Christianissimus nobis nuper exposuit, quidem alias postquam felicis recordationis Iulius papa ii predecessor noster excommunicationis suspensionis et interdicti aliasque sententias censuras et penas ecclesiasticas, in et contra omnes et singulas tam ecclesiasticas quam utriusque sexus personas, qui Conciliabulo Pisano adhererent et interessent, ac illi necnon personis eidem adherentibus auxilium consilium uel fauorem prestarent, inflixerat et promulgauerat, necnon ciuitates loca et terras, ubi dictum Conciliabulum illique adherentes fautores et sequaces stare morari fieri et sedere permitteretur, ecclesiastico interdicto subiicerat, nonnulli archiepiscopi episcopi abbates priores decani archidiaconi et alii, in dignitate ecclesiastica constituti, et beneficiali et parrochialium ecclesiarum rectores et alie utriusque sexus persone, tam ecclesiastice quam seculares, etiam nobiles duces barones principes comites milites, tam de suo regno Francie quam aliis prouintiis et dominiis sibi pertinentibus, adheserunt et interfuerunt, ac eidem Conciliabulo et adherentibus huiusmodi auxilium consilium et fauorem fecerunt prestiterunt et dederunt, excommunicationis suspensionis et interdicti aliasque ecclesiasticas sententias censuras et penas, tam per eundem Iulium predecessorem quam alias contra tales a iure uel ab homine latas incurrendo.

Quare dictus Franciscus Rex [dum in ciuitate nostra Bononensi filialem obedientiam et reuerentiam personaliter nobis prestitit][76] suorum subditorum animarum salutem cupiens, nobis humiliter supplicauit, ut eosdem, qui sic aut alias quomodolibet, post damnationem Conciliabuli huiusmodi et ex tunc imposterum usque hodie Conciliabulo huiusmodi interessendo deliquerunt, ac

---

[74] This echoes the general formula introducing an absolution document — see above n. 193.

[75] Fernando V, king of all Spain (1512—16), his second wife Germaine de Foix, queen of Aragon (1506—16), and his daughter Juana, queen of Castile (1506—16).

[76] This phrase has been cancelled out and the cancellation signed by "Cardinalis" [Sanctorum Quattuor Coronatorum = Lorenzo Pucci]. Leo X and François I met at Bologna from 11—15 December 1515 — see PASTOR VII 135—40.

II

censuris et penis huiusmodi uel alias ligati seu irretiti existunt, ab excessibus sententiis censuris et penis predictis absoluere, interdictum relaxare, et super irregularitate quam ecclesiastice persone, etiam episcopali archiepiscopali aut alia ecclesiastica uel mundana dignitate fingentes, censuris eisdem ligate, Missas et alia diuina officia etiam non absque clauium contemptu celebrando, seu interdictum uiolando, aut alias quomodolibet premissorum occasione contraxerint, dispensare, omnemque inhabilitatis et infamie maculam siue notam ex premissis prouenientem abolere, aliasque eis et eorum statui in premissis optime prouidere, de benignitate apostolica dignaremur.

Nos igitur, qui illius uices gerimus in terris, cuius proprium est misereri semper et parcere huiusmodi supplicantibus, inclinati omnes et singulos archiepiscopos episcopos abbates priores decanos archidiaconos et alios, dignitates personatus administrationes et officia canonicatus et prebendas ac alia beneficia ecclesiastica tam in cathedralibus quam metropolitanis, uel collegiatis et aliis ecclesiis, quam extra eas obtinentes, parrochialium ecclesiarum rectores et generaliter omnes et singulas utriusque sexus personas tam ecclesiasticas quam seculares, cuiuscunque dignitatis status gradus ordinis uel conditionis, etiam si nobiles duces comites milites et alii principes fuerunt, quorum ac archiepiscoporum episcoporum abbatum priorum decanorum archidiaconorum et beneficatorum aliarumque personarum singularum predictarum, necnon eorum archiepiscopalium episcopalium monasteriorum prioratuum dignitatum canonicatuum et prebendarum aliorumque beneficiorum ecclesiasticorum nomina cognomina titulos et qualitates presentibus pro expressis habemus, qui Conciliabulo huiusmodi quomodocunque adheserunt et interfuerunt, ac tam eidem Conciliabulo quam illi adherentibus et fautoribus auxilium consilium et fauorem publice uel occulte directe uel indirecte dederunt et prebuerunt, a quibusuis excommunicationis suspensionis et interdicti aliisque ecclesiasticis sententiis et penis, tam per eundem Iulium quam alios Romanos pontifices predecessores nostros, ac alias iure uel ab homine contra tales latis et promulgatis de apostolice potestatis plenitudine tenore presentium absoluimus, et absolutos fore nuntiamus.

Ac cum eisdem archiepiscopis episcopis abbatibus prioribus decanis archidiaconis, et dignitates personatus administrationes uel officia et alia beneficia et officia ecclesiastica cum cura et sine cura obtinentibus, canonicis et aliis personis ecclesiasticis, tam secularibus quam religiosis super irregularitate quam ipsui, tam propter premissa quam alias Missas et alia diuina officia etiam tempore interdicti celebrando, et alias se diuinis immiscendo et administrando, in eisdem incurrerunt; et quilibet eorum incurrit; quidque ipsi archiepiscopi episcopi abbates et alii prelati in regimini et administratione ecclesiarum et monasticorum suorum, et tam ipsi quam alie persone predicte, et singuli ex eis in susceptis per eos et eorum quemlibet ordinibus etiam in altaris ministerio ministrare, ac archiepiscopatus episcopatus monasteria prioratus prepositures prepositatus dignitates personatus administrationes officia canonicatus et prebendas ceteraque beneficia ecclesiastica, cum cura et sine cura, secularia et regularia, que in titulum commendam et administrationem aut alias obtinent, in titulum et commendam simul et respectiue ut prius retinere, libere et licite ualeant, dispensamus.

Necnon tam ipsas ecclesiasticas quam alias utriusque sexus personas predictas, etiam si nobiles duces comites milites et alii principes fuerint, ad pristinos et eos status gradus nobilitates formas dignitates et honores, in quibus ante adhesionem et fautionem huiusmodi erant, et quilibet eorum erat, plenarie restituimus et reintegramus. Omnemque inhabilitatis et infamie maculam siue notam per eos et eorum quemlibet premissorum occasione contractam penitus et omnino abolemus. Necnon interdictum et interminationem ac intronizationem per eundem Iulium predecessorem tam in ciuitatibus terris et locis quam singulis personis, predictarum apposita et facta penitus et omnino tollimus et relaxamus.

Et insuper, cum alias clare memorie Ludouicus Francorum Rex, dicti Francisci Regis predecessor, cupiens scismatis huiusmodi uiam amputare, dictum Conciliabulum per eius procuratorem legittimum[77] in Concilio Lateranensi publice abiurauerit et illi renuntiauerit, ac archiepiscopos episcopos abbates prelatos et alias personas ecclesiasticas sui regni seu aliquas ex eis, tam suo quam reliquorum nominibus, pro similibus abiuratione et renuntiatione faciendis, ac absolutionibus et rehabilitationibus necessariis impetrandis, destinare et mittere sub eius regia fide promiserit; tamen, cum dictus Franciscus Rex, qui dicto Ludouico, Rege eo postmodum de medio sublato, in dicto regno et dominiis successet, etiam nobis nuper exposuit, licet alias nonnulli ex prelatis dicti regni pro premissis faciendis et adimplendis iter arripuerint, seu arripere conati fuerint, tamen propter guerrarum turbines et dominiorum mutationes usque ad apostolicam sedem accedere ausi non fuerint; nos indempnitatibus archiepiscoporum episcoporum abbatum et aliarum personarum predictorum consulere, eorumque expensis et laboribus parcere uolentes eos et eorum singulos ab obseruatione promissionis huiusmodi absoluimus.

Et illis et eorum cuilibet quidem ad Romanam Curiam ac Concilium Lateranense, alias pro abiuratione et renuntiatione premissis faciendis accedere, per se uel procuratorem eorum minime teneantur, de similis potestatis plentitudine indulgemus.

Et si qui delinquentium et censuris predictis irretitorum, pro eo quidem absolutio predicta eis personaliter per se ipsos illam petentibus impensa non est, seu alias de ipsius absolutionis uiribus hesitantes, cuperent pro conscientiarum suarum ampliori puritate ab excessibus censuris et penis predictis alias absolui, ac cum eisdem super dicta irregularitate dispensari, eis concedimus ut presbyter secularis uel cuiusuis ordinis etiam mendicantium regularis, quem quilibet eorum per se duxerit eligendum, possit absolutionem restitutionem ac omnia et singula alia premissa per nos sic, ut presertim in genere facta et concessa ac decreta erga

---

[77] legittimum [sic]; at the eighth session of the Lateran Council, Claude de Seyssel presented the mandate of Louis XII renouncing the Pisan Council — see Mansi 32, 831E—36B.

II

178

eligentem, tum et in eius fauorem tam in foro conscientie, quam etiam in foro fori, auctoritate nostra, in spetie et nominatim eidem facere et decernere, eisque concedere iniunctis inde sibi pro modo culpe penitentia salutari et aliis que eidem sic electo uidebuntur iniungenda.

Non obstantibus premissis ac aliis constitutionibus et ordinationibus apostolicis, necnon predictorum archiepiscoporum episcoporum abbatum ecclesiarum et monasteriorum ac aliarum ecclesiarum in quibus dignitates personatus et administrationes et officia canonicatus et prebende ac alia beneficia secularia et regularia huiusmodi existunt, iuramento confirmatione apostolica uel quauis firmitate alia roboratis statutis et consuetudinibus priuilegiisque et indultis ac litteris apostolicis illis concessis, quecunque quotcunque et qualiacunque fuit, quibus hac uice dumtaxat specialiter et expresse derogamus, ceterisque contrariis quibuscunque.

Nulli ergo et cetera nostre absolutionis nuntiationis dispensationis restitutionis reintegrationis abolitionis amotionis relaxationis indulti concessionis et derogationis infringere, et cetera.

Si quis, et cetera.

Datum Bononie, anno incarnationis Dominice, millesimo quingentesimo quintodecimo, Idibus Decembris, pontificatus nostri anno tertio.[78]

Ioannes Cheminart.[79]

Laurentius Cardinalis Sanctorum Quattuor.[80]

XI.

Excerpt from the Letter of Francesco Pandolfini to Cardinal Giulio de Medici
Beville-le-Comte, 2 October 1514, hora ii noctis

Archivo di Stato, Florence: Signori, Dieci di Balìa, Otto di Practica, Legazioni e Commissarie — Missive e Responsive, Registro No. 55, fols. 147r.

Noi[81] parlamo oggi al Cristianissimo[82] del placet per li beneficii che furono della bona memoria del Reverendissimo di Phinale[83], secondo che per la ultima

---

[78] This concluding section replaced that cancelled out by Lorenzo Pucci which reads: *Rome apud Sanctum Petrum, anno incarnationis Dominice, millesimo quingentesimo sextodecimo, sextodecimo Kalendas Octobris, pontificatus nostri anno quarto.*

[79] Jean Cheminart was a *scriptor litterarum apostolicarum* and an official at the church of S. Louis in Rome — see Archivio di Stato, Roma, Archivio del Collegio dei Notari Capitolini, vol. 1914, Inghirami, fol. 237r.

[80] Lorenzo Pucci continued to function as a *corrector litterarum apostolicarum* on occasions even after his promotion to the cardinalate — see HOFMANN II 78; for his curial career, Ibid. II 97—98.

[81] Francesco Pandolfini and perhaps also Ludovico di Canossa.

[82] Louis XII.

[83] Cardinal Carlo Domenico de Caretto was marchese of Finale in Liguria, archbishop of Tours

The Healing of the Pisan Schism (1511—13) 179

di costi ne fu commesso per parte di Nostro Signore. Sua Maiesta ci ha mostro essere del tutto resoluta (e cosi crediamo) che e benefici predicti pervenghino nelle mani di coloro ad chi sono suti resignati, ma soprattienne il placet, sperando cum questo mezo redurre le cose di Cominge[84] et di Redun[85] piu facilmente al disegno suo; dicendoci che, per essere vacati di qua, era cum diminutione della auctorita sua, et cosi carico apresso de sue patlamenti quali gridavano; confortandolo ad mantenere le iurisdictioni sue; subiungendoci conoscere che faceva cosa iniusta ritenendo il placet sopradicto. Ma lo faceva, perche anche la Santita del papa piu facilmente revocassi quello che fuora del consueto haveva fatto circa le due sopradicte chiese; monstrando farlo piu per satisfactione de populi et de parlamenti che per contento suo particulare; dicendo essere resoluto mantenere sempre la auctorita et iurisdictione del papa nelle cose beneficiali; ma che dal laltro [sic] canto era necessario et ragionevole che sua Santita non volessi romperli, ma conservali le constitutioni di questo regno et affirmandoci che per torre via simili disordini, quali conosce che possono nascere ogni giorno, saria contento di venire ad uno concordato cum la Santita del papa come fu fatto al tempo de Re Luigi.[86] Promisseci sua Maiesta in ultimo che si facessino tutte quelle provisioni che fussino possibili, perche non nascessi alcuno disturbo ne beneficii sopradicti et che non ne fussi di qua fatta electione alchuna et cosi domani habbiamo ad essere per tale officio cum Parigi[87] et Robertet.[88] Et speriamo che da obtenere il placet, in fuora si hara ogni altra provisione intorno ad cio necessaria. Circa ad chi noi non mancheremo dogni nostra diligentia.

---

which he resigned by July of 1514, bishop of Cahors which he resigned in favor of his brother Luigi on 12 August 1514, and holder of a number of lesser benefices and pensions in France and Italy. He died *in curia Romana* on 15 August 1514 — see EUBEL III 11, 160, 321.

[84] Cominges, contested between Galhardus de Hospitali elected by the chapter in 1502 and Amanieu d'Albret appointed by Alexander VI in 1499. On death of de Hospitali, Leo tried twice, on 21 August and 7 November 1514 to confirm the earlier provision of d'Albret — see EUBEL III, 177.

[85] Redon, the Benedictine monastery of St. Sauveur in the diocese of Vannes in Brittany, over which Anne duchess of Brittany and queen of France exercised a right of nomination — see THOMSON 164—65. When its abbot Pierre de Brigniac died, Leo on 2 June 1514 gave the monastery *in commenda* to Luigi de Rossi, a cleric of Lyon, blood-relative of the pope, and apostolic notary. Rossi had difficulty securing actual possession of the monastery due to the opposition of the king's confessor. On 20 September 1514 Leo wrote to Louis XII asking his help in eliminating all delays — see HERGENROETHER, Regesta Leonis I 587, 597, 729, nrs. 9302—03, 9458, 11814.

[86] Louis XI (1461—83) who in 1461 and again in 1472 abrogated the Pragmatic Sanction of Bourges; in 1461 the French Church returned to the status quo of 1438, in 1472 a new concordat was negotiated — see THOMSON 160—61.

[87] Étienne Poncher, bishop of Paris (1503—19) and acting chancellor of France (1512—15) — see EUBEL III, 270 and GARAND 320—23.

[88] Florimond Robertet, grand treasurer of France since 1508, died 1527 — see RENAUDET 7 n. 14.

XII.

Proposed Terms of an Accord Between Leo X and Alfonso d'Este Read to the Duke by Francesco Armellini[89], Together with the Duke's Responses to Certain of These Proposals

s.l., s.d.
Archivio di Stato, Florence: Manoscritti Torrigiani, Filza III, Inserta XIV Leone X e Ferrara, Nr. 1: Capitula cum Duce Ferrarensi

Primo. Dominus Dux seruiet Summo Domino Nostro et Sancte Romane Ecclesie contra quoscumque, nemine excepto, totis uiribus cum persona et statu, sed cum persona equitare non teneatur nisi cum conuenienti stipendio, et Summus Dominus Noster accipiat Ducem filios et statum sub protectione sua, et aliquis alius principes *[sic]* neque dominatus cum consensu ipsius Ducis protectionem non capiet.[90]

Secundo. Regienses et Mutinenses quicumque in ipsis ciuitatibus et eorum territoriis habitantes non puniantur aliquo modo exquoque defecerint a Duce et redierint sub Sancta Romana Ecclesia inmediate.[91]

Tertio. Summus Dominus Noster sit iudex inter ipsum Ducem et Dominum Albertum de Carpi super quibuscumque eorum diferentiis super Carpi, qui declarationi Sanctitatis Sue parere debeant etiam sub penis et censuris.[92]

Quarto. Subditi ecclesie liberati fuerunt et sic Dux dicit quod Summo Domino Nostro soluat censum centum ducatorum annorum preteritorum et etiam quotanus satisfecit ducatorum mille pro Domino Petro Grifo quos amiserat dum ex Ueneteiis Romam redibat.[93]

Quinto. Dominus Dux soluet annuatim censum centum ducatorum et quod possit publicare breue et litteras restitutionis ad sui beneplacitum que dicit in manibus et sub potestate sua habere.[94]

Sesto. Dictus Dominus Dux soluet annuatim calicem ualoris x ducatorum in festo apostolorum Camere apostolice pro censu Regii et eius territorii, et istud

---

[89] In 1514 Armellini was a cleric of the Camera; for his curial career, see HOFMANN II 87—88.

[90] In his biref, *Cum mente nobiscum*, of 14 June 1514, Leo took Alfonso, his sons, successors, and state under his protection — see MURATORI II 317.

[91] For the effects in Reggio of the papal penalties imposed on Alfonso, see G. PANCIROLI, Storia della città di Reggio, 2 vols., Modena 1846—48, II 99—100.

[92] For the conflict between Alfonso d'Este and Alberto Pio, see P. GUAITOLI, Memorie sulla vita d'Alberto III° Pio, in: Memorie storiche e documenti sulla città e sull'antico principato di Carpi, I, Carpi 1877, 133—313 passim, and MINNICH, Protestatio 276—78.

[93] On Pietro Griffi, former collector of papal taxes for England and currently bishop of Forlì and administrator in the Papal States, see M. MONACO, Il ,De officio collectoris in regno Angliae' di Pietro Griffi da Pisa (1469—1516), (= Uomini e dottrine 19) Rome 1973, 17—79, esp. 69—74, and D. HAY, Pietro Griffo, an Italian in England: 1506—1512, in: Italian Studies 2 (1938—39) 118—28, esp. 125—26. On his return to Rome, he stopped in Ferrara in August of 1512 — see SANUTO XIV 561.

[94] Leo restored the level of tribute for Ferrara set by Alexander VI, see MURATORI II 317.

The Healing of the Pisan Schism (1511—13)

donec legitime declaratum fuerit hoc fieri posse sine preiuditio ipsius Ducis si legitime esset alteri pro censu huiusmodi obligatus.[95]

vii°. Se domanda la lunga del Po per laparte de Briselli et la custodia di la Rocha di Montechii in Regiana de le quale cose Santa Maria in Portico e lonepote ne hanno lanno circa a ducati 750.[96]

Responde il Duca che la Santita Domini Nostri disse non se uolere impacciare in quanto tamen e contento. Sua Santita per fare cosa grata adicto Cardinale di Santa Maria in Portico et durante uita ipsius Cardinalis darli ducati doicento lanno, e cosi dice che Sua Signoria Reuerendissima disse al Cardinale di Ferrare[97] che non fructaua piu de dicti ducati doicento doro lanno. [N.B. Capitolo vii° has been crossed out]

viii°. Quanto al datio de ogni sale se facesse passare sub nomine Summi Domini Nostri uel Camere apostolice per tutto lo stato de esso duca e che altro sale non possa passare.

El duca domanda per la conuentione fatta ducati doimilia cinque cento octanta et doiterzi de uno altro ducati doro largi lanno e lo tempo sia cominciato a di xi de luglio 1514 che a quello tempo lui chiuse il passo quanto a la oblegatione de leuare el sale et piglare lanno sacha sesmilia quatro cento di sale de libre 360 il sacco al peso Bolognese, e contento che cominci in kalendas de dicembre 1514, et cosi cautera idoneamente in Ferrare de pagare de anno in anno iusta le capitoli, che se po fare stima che sera, a di primo de dicembre 1516, che allora sera debitore de doi anni ho circa et montera circa a ducati [blank] netti del suo datio et tanto piu quanto rehauesse Reggio e Modena et li altri lochi, et che, poi sera restituito Reggio et altri lochi, habbi a piglare lanno sacca quatordecemilia sei cento. Come se contene in lo contracto e cosi habbi piglare sacca 3850 lanno simili de piu ultra la dicta somma uolendo il dicto duca come il contracto dice et li sali habbi adarse in li lochi dice il contracto e che il sale se le desse di Ceruia de Cesenatico ho di altri lochi uoleno siano de libre doimilia cinque cento uinte di sale, che sonno sacca sei, per e libre quatro centouinte per sacco al peso Bolognese et non hauere adare piu donatiui ne Callo ne altra tarra respecto ala qualita di essi et cosi intende ogni libre doimilia cinque cento uinte di sale al peso Bolognese, ducati cinque e unoquarto doro pagare.[98]

---

[95] Leo promised to restore Reggio-Emilia to Alfonso within five months of the ratification of the accords, see MURATORI II 317. Leo could also delay the return another five months — see Appendix XIII.

[96] Brescello is a town on the Po River eleven miles NW of Parma, Montecchio is nine miles W of Reggio — see L. E. SELTZER, ed., The Columbia Lippincott Gazetteer of the World, New York 1952, 267, 1234; the cardinal-deacon of S. Maria in Portico was Bernardo Dovizi da Bibbiena (d. 1520) — see EUBEL III 14, 75.

[97] Ippolyto d'Este, see EUBEL III 5.

[98] For the conflict over the manufacture and sale of salt by Alfonso and for a copy of the detailed accords worked out on 15 June 1514 between Leo X and Ippolyto d'Este in the name of his ducal brother, see L. A. MURATORI, Piena esposizione de i diritti imperiali ed Estensi sopra la città di

II

viiii°. Domandase che habbi il Duca a mantenere la locatione de datii di Reggio facta a Leonardo Iustiniani[99] per anni cinque da finire a di 27 di maggio 1518.

Responde il duca uolere donare ducati mille cinque cento doro e che le datii remanghino al dicto duca.

x°. Domandase che paghi ali Datieri dicti il sale che setrouera conducto per Reggio il di de la restitutione.

Il duca responde che pagera ad ragione de ducati cinque et uno quarto doro ogni libre doimilia cinque cento uinte al peso Bolognese e le spese de la conductura et tale prezo se contene in la somma che deue piglare annuatim.

xi°. Domandase che obserue tucte le altre donatione et concessione facte da la Santita di Nostro Signore de piu intrate et altre cose tanto a Briselli quanto in li altri lochi.

Il duca dice non uole essere tenuto obseruare, perche dice che la Santita Domini Nostri ha dicto che intende che le cose dicte durino secondo quanto la Santita di Nostro Signore et sede apostolica tenera li lochi doue sonno le cose predicte.

xii°. Domandase che il duca obserua la locatione facta de datii di Briselli.

Dice il duca che per essere li datieri da Briselli li contentera et cosi la Camera non patera pena pro obseruatione contractus.

xiii°. Domandase la restitutione de ducati cinquantatre milia doro se dice hauere pagati per rahauere Modena da lo imperatore quali uolemo contanti quando se dara la possessione de Modena.[100]

Responde il duca che la Santita di Nostro Signore disse uolea una somma notabile de quello hauia pagato. Donarlo ad esso duca et de lo resto ne uolia una parte contanti et de li altri farne tempo de anno in anno et deputarlo ala fabrica de Santo Petro siche il duca supplica la Santita di Nostro Signore che chiarifia la quantita et i tempi, hauendo consideratione a le promesse sopradicte et seruita de esso duca.

xiiii°. Domandase che habbi a restituire Modena a lo imperatore in fine de Cenerii uel alio tempore prout continetur in istrumento quale se hauera amostrare ad esso duca.

A questo il duca dici: Uenga lo istrumento e faro in modo che la Santita di Nostro Signore et sede apostolica seranno conseruate sensa danno et illese, e cosi se obligera.

Comacchio ... Modena 1722, 294—317, esp. 312—15 (an account of these accords), 395—401 (App. XXII which transcribes this agreement). The original accords signed by Giulio dei Medici and Ippolyto d'Este are preserved in ASF, Manoscritti Torrigiani, Filza III, Inserta XIV, nr. 4.

[99] Probably Leonardo qu. Lorenzo qu. Bernardo Giustiniani, a wealthy Venetian patrician, knight, and holder of high offices: e.g., procurator, senator, governor of the *intrade*, etc. — see SANUTO XX 577, XXI 180—81, XXII 408.

[100] Julius and Leo held Modena as collateral for a loan of 40,000 ducats made to emperor Maximilian — see GUICCIARDINI X viii, XII vii, xviii, ed. PANIGADA III 255, 329, 378.

xv°. Domandese la restitutione de ducati cinque milia doro prestatoli sub nomine di Andrea Gentile[101] tempore felicis recordationis Julii.

Responde il duca grauandose perho che pure quando Nostro Signore li uorra obedi dara ex tunc che Messer Andrea gli casse el contralto.

xvi°. Domandase che il duca habbi sempre acomodare a la Santita di Nostro Signore et sede apostolica cento homini darme pagati, e la Santita di Nostro Signore et sede apostolica li possa operare doue et contra chi li parera, aliquali solum la prefata Santita habbi adare loro le stantie ho tasse, che se daranno ali soldati di santa chiesa.

Responde il duca che dandoli la Santita di Nostro Signore soldo per quatro cento homini darme se contento non hauere pagamento piu che per tre cento cinquanta, et quando lui caualcasse uole uno quarto ho uno quinto de le fantarie farle lui et condure le artiglarie soi aspese di Nostro Signore et similiter lifanti.

xvii°. Domandase la restitutione de li denari pagati al Conte Guido per Robera.[102]

Il duca dice grauandose perho che pagera quello se e pagato et lo resto pagera et exequira la promessa facta. [in the margin in another hand: sono ducati 1500 doro inoro]

xviii°. Domandase la restitutione de le artiglarie e monitione che seranno in Modena, Reggio, e loro teritorii.

Il duca dice che tucta quella, che non haiara le arme sue, ho che non fosse stata sua, la restituera, ho se porti uia a posta de Nostro Signore.

xviiii°. Restituendose il Polesine de Rouico cioe quello fo tolto al tempo de duca Hercole che e dallo Addice prima in qua incluso lo fiume de lo Addice.[103]

Il duca e contento dare achi uorra la Santita di Nostro Signore in esso tante possessione che fructeranno lanno ducati quatromilia doro e la iurisdetione del sale. Remanga sotto li capitoli delo altro stato del duca a cosi per lo fiume dello Addice, ne per altro loco de quillo territorio possi passare altro sale che quello uorra la Santita di Nostro Signore et sede apostolica, et cosi la Santita di Nostro Signore sia supplicata fare ogni diligentia dicto Polesine se restituisca, auisandola che la cosa del sale importera assai, perche non possono altro che sua Santita usare, il fiume de lo Addice non porra andare altro sale che il suo, per loco nessuno de la Lombardia.

---

[101] Andrea Gentile was a Genoese merchant who did business at the Roman curia — see MONACO 192.

[102] Count Guido Rangoni received 2,000 ducats for the fortress of Rubiera, according to GUICCIARDINI XII xiii, ed. PANIGADA III 353; see also MURATORI II 314 and PANCIROLI II 109—10.

[103] Polesine is the low-lying marshy delta region typical of the area where the Po and neighboring rivers empty into the Adriatic Sea. The Adige River flows S and E from the Alps, meeting the sea just south of Chióggia. Rovigo lies between the Adige and Tártaro Rivers, half-way between Padova and Ferrara. Alfonso hoped to gain this region by joining in the war of the League of Cambrai, see SENECA 113, 138.

xx°. Domandase che habbi alassare continouare il passo de nauicello a Modena a Messer Johannes Matteo Ghiberti.[104]

Il duca e contento darli lanno solum ducati octanta de prouisione e questo respecto al Reuerendissimo Cardinale de Medici et durante uita ipsius Johannis Mattei.

xxi°. Super quibus omnibus expedicantur lectere apostolice et istrumenta rebus tamen confectis cum conuenientibus clausolis prout uidebitur Summus Dominus Noster cum obligatione censurarum et aliarum rerum in forma experimendo in oblegationibus nomina omnium ciuitatum et locorum ea recognoscendo a sede apostolica et a Summo Domino Nostro et annuatim in futurum pro ipsis locis censum centum ducatorum soluendo in festo apostolorum Camere apostolice ut moris est et non ultra, cum quietatione de preterito.

xxii°. Domanda el Signore Enea de Pii da Carpi[105] ducati doicento doro lanno de intrata intanti benefitii ho pensione ho altre cose e questo per recompensa di tanti benefitii che renuntio al quondam Messer Andrea da Modena ad istantia de la Santita di Nostro Signore.

xxiii°. Lecte tucte le cose sopradicte dopo molte persuasione de Messer Francesco Armellini, respuse il duca, quando io ueda, non me siano date parole, e che uoi facciate lo efecto de la restitutione, uorro che la Santita di Nostro Signore ho Reuerendissimo legato per suo nome dica: io uoglio cosi; et alora sero bon figlio de obedientia tanto impagare quanto inseruire et hauere respecto ale cose sopradicte di Santa Maria in Portico et saro da bon et fidel seruitore de la Santita di Nostro Signore de la santa chiesa.

---

[104] At this time Gian Matteo Ghiberti was apparently ending his studies at Padova and beginning his career at Rome as secretary of cardinal Giulio dei Medici and as holder of various curial posts and benefices — see A. PROSPERI, Tra evangelismo e controriforma: G. M. Giberti (1495—1543), (= Uomini e dottrine 16) Rome 1969, 9—11.

[105] Enea Pio was the youngest brother of Giberto III who co-ruled Carpi with his cousin Alberto from 1494 until 1499 when he finally sold his share to Ercole d'Este. Giberto and his brothers were then forced to move away from Carpi and live in Bologna. Enea tried to gain possession of a commendatory parish benefice in Carpi on the death of his brother Galeotto on 6 August 1513 — see A. L. TROMBETTI BUDRIESI, Sui rapporti tra i Pio e gli Estensi: lo scambio Carpi-Sassuolo, in: Società, Politica e Cultura a Carpi, II 395—425, here 396—402; A. PRANDI, Il patrimonio fondiario dei Pio nello ‚Stato' di Carpi, Ibid., II 469—502, here 485 n. 38; and G. ZARRI, La proprietà ecclesiastica a Carpi fra Quattrocento e Cinquecento, Ibid., II 503—59, here 535 n. 86.

XIII.
An Agreement with Leo X Signed by Hippolyto d'Este in His Own Name and That of Duke Alfonso d'Este

Rome, 15 June 1514
Archivio di Stato — Firenze: Manoscritti Torrigiani, Filza III, Inserta XIV Leone X e Ferrara, Nr. 7

Ego Hipolitus Sancte Lucie in Silice diaconus cardinalis Estensis, nomine proprio promitto quod Dominus Dux frater meus ratificabit omnia que in presenti cedula continetur. Et tamquam procurator dicti Domini Ducis promitto etiam per presentem cedulam quod prefatum Dominus Dux fideliter ex totis uiribus serviet summo Domino Nostro Leoni x⁰ et sancte Romane ecclesie contra quoscumque nemine excepto cum persona et statu, ita tamen quod non teneatur equitare in castris nisi cum stipendio conuenienti.

Item, cum summus Dominus Noster acceperit prefatum Dominum Ducem et eius filios et statum in protectionem suam polliceor quod dictus Dominus Dux non dabit se neque statum neque filios in protectionem alieni alii principi uel potentatui, neque admittet si quis illam sponte capere uellet nisi de mandato et consensu sue sanctatis, sed firmiter permanebit cum summo Domino Nostro.

Item, promitto nominibus quibus supra, quod ipse Dominus Dux in personis et in bonis parcet in totum Regiensibus, qui ab ipso defecerunt ad partes ecclesiasticas, et similiter quibuscumque aliis comunitatibus et priuatis personis in territoriis Regii et Romandiole constitutis qui cum illis consensissent, aut quouis modo ecclesiastice partes iuuassent alias declarandis si de aliquibus fuerit dubium infra terminium unius anni proxime futuri per Summum Dominum Nostrum, que omnia extendi possint in ampliori forma [words cancelled: Summo Domino Nostro grata].

Item, cum Christianissimus Francorum Rex in presentiarum sit extra Italiam et dominium Mediolanense in quem alias prefatus Dominus Dux compromisit differentias suas oppidi Carpi uertentes cum Domino Alberto de Piis et idcirco ad ipsas sedandas minime uacare possit, cumque Summus Dominus Noster ex innata sua benignitate, ut differentiis finem imponat, manum sue sanctitis aponere dignetur, promitto nominibus quibus supra quod prefatus Dominus Dux remittet omnes differentias suas quas habet cum dicto Domino Alberto prefate sue beatitudini, et quod ratificabit omnia que per eam laudata iudicata uel sententiata fuerint, suplicantes tamen illi ut dignetur bene et mature omnia considerare et habere rationem magni pretii quo par[s] ipsius oppidi super quo est controuersia acquisita fuit a genitore nostro.[106]

---

[106] On the complicated financial transaction by which Ercole d'Este purchased half of Carpi, see TROMBETTI BUDRIESI 401—18.

II

Item, promitto quod prefatus Dominus Dux liberabit omnes captiuos dominii ecclesiastici exceptis Ferrariensibus et dicto Duci attinentibus.

Item, promitto nominibus quibus supra quod prefatus Dominus Dux intuitu Summi Domini Nostri restituet uel satisfaciet Domino Nicholao Estensi[107] bona que iuste et legittime possidebat et que tempore belli propter eius fugam et alias causas fuerunt confiscata, dummodo appareat et constet sufficienter prefatum Dominum Nicholaum defecisse intuitu et causa felicis recordationis Iulii secundi et sancte sedis apostolice, et ea bona amisisse ob seruitia collata in summum Pontificem et sedem apostolicam.

Item, quod prefatus Dominus Dux soluet et restituet Summo Domino Nostro ducatos mille auri de Camera pro pecuniis et bonis ablatis Domino Petro Gripho cum Uenetiis Romam redibat, infra tres menses proxime futuros.

Item, quod prefatus Dominus Dux soluet Summo Domino Nostro infra dictum terminum trium mensium censum [...] centum ducatorum decursum a die priuationis.

Item, cum Summus Dominus Noster pro tranquillitate et securitate mentis Domini Ducis fratris mei et mee concesserit et mihi tradiderit unum breue absolutorium et restitutorium cum quibusdam aliis gratiis et promissionibus manu sua subscriptum et anulo piscatoris signatum, promitto nomine proprio illud aut eius sententiam nemini preterquam Domino Duci prefato et Domino Gherardo Saraceno propalare et notum facere, et nomine Ducis predicti quod etiam similiter nemini reuelabit aut notum faciet nisi dicto Domino Gherardo aut in euentum contrauentionis sue Sanctitis contentis in illo breui cum additione contenta in subsequenti capitulo. Et hoc sub pena excomunicationis ipso facto incurrenda, tam pro me quam pro prefato Domino Duce et Domino Gherardo a qua non possimus absolui nisi a Summo Domino Nostro aut eius successoribus causa expressa prout ma[n]dauit Sanctitas sua. [Signed:] Ego Hippolytus cardinalis Estensis manu propria

Item, si quis casus euenerit quo Summus Dominus Noster protrahere et differre uelit restitutionem ciuitatis Regii ultra spatium quinque mensium per alios quatuor aut quinque menses proxime et immediate sequentes, promitto nominibus quibus supra quod prefatus Dominus Dux dictum tempus tacite expectabit, neque antea publicabit breue absolutionis et restitutionis predicte. Ita tamen quod post primos quinque menses omnes redditus et introitus dicte ciuitatis Regii aliorumque locorum detractis ordinariis expensis pertineant ad Dominum Ducem sicut a prefata Beatitudine promissum fuit.[108]

Item, promitto nominibus quibus supra quod dictus Dominus Dux secuta restitutione Regii et aliorum locorum in territorio dicte ciuitatis ad ipsum spectantium obligabit se et suos heredes et successores ita quod teneatur soluere

---

[107] Perhaps the Niccolo da Este *(fo dil Signor Sigismondo)* who participated in the solemn procession to the Lateran Basilica when Leo took possession of this church — see SANUTO XVI 680.

[108] On the partial fulfilment of this clause, see MURATORI II 318—19.

Summo Domino Nostro et sedi apostolice singulis annis recognitionem unius calicis non excedentem ualorem decem ducatorum quo usque legittime declaratum fuerit dictam recognitionem non posse solui sine preiuditio iurium ipsius Ducis uel successorum suorum.

Item, promitto quod dictus Dominus Dux expediet litteras apostolicas sub plumbo iuxta formam predicti breuis.

Item, promitto quod ipse Dominus Dux contentabitur et obligabit se quod omnia suprascripta possint extendi in ampliori forma sub censuris et penis honestis et conuenientibus que uidebuntur Summo Domino Nostro declarandis per suam Sanctitatem infra terminium unius anni proxime futuri non alterando sensum suprascriptum in preiudicium ipsius Ducis uel rerum suarum.[109]

Et ego Hippolytus Sancte Lucie in Silice sancte Romane ecclesie diaconus cardinalis Estensis nomine meo proprio et procuratorio Domini Ducis ut supra dictum est promitto quod ipse Dominus Dux omnia et singula suprascripta confirmabit et ratificabit in forma ualida uel manu propria infra dies xx. et in fide premissorum presentem cedulam manu aliena scriptam propria manu subscripsi et solito paruo sigillo meo signaui. Rome, die xv° iunii 1514.

XIV.
Rejected Draft[110] of a Brief Absolving Alfonso d'Este and Restoring Him to His Former Positions and Privileges, Rome, June 1514

Archivio di Stato — Firenze: Manoscritti Torrigiani, Filza III, Inserta XIV Leone X e Ferrara, Nr. 2. Brief of Leo X Absolving Alfonso and Restoring Him to His Formal Dignities. Minuta 2

Cum mente nobiscum recolimus, animoque diligenter attendimus quot et quanta scandalorum genera ecclesie Dei ex eo tempore parata sint, quo per felicis recordationis Julium ii predecessorem nostrum contra dilectum filium nobilem uirum Alfonsum Estensem Ferrarie ducem, ad priuationem usque ducatus et uicaricatus et eiusdem ciuitatis nostre Ferrarie processum est, ingenti

---

[109] On 23 May 1515 Leo issued a brief taking Alfonso and his state under papal protection — see MURATORI II 319—20.

[110] In the form of a bull *(Ad futuram rei memoriam)*, this version of the decree of absolution and restoration was written on parchment, but left undated and unsigned. It still exists as ASF, Pergamene, Provenienza Torrigiani, 1514 Giugno 14. The draft version identified as Minuta 1 (old marking 9) is similar to Minuta 2 (old marking 10), but drops references to Reggio. Minuta 3 is similar to that version published in MURATORI II 317—18, but with minor stylistic variants and with the insertion of the here highlighted words: in the sentence restoring Cento and la Pieve „ac si dicta priuatio *in hoc casu* facta non foret", and in that promising to restore Reggio „ipsam ciuitatem Regii cum omnibus oppidis, fortilitiis, et pertinentiis suis *sub honestis tamen aliquibus conditionibus* restituemus." According to Cesare GUASTI, I manoscritti Torrigiani donati al R. Archivio di Stato di Firenze: Descrizione e saggio, Firenze 1878, 411, Minuta 1 was annotated by cardinal Lorenzo Pucci.

quidem dolore afficimur. Non solum enim temporale respicimus bellum ex quo tanta humani sanguinis profusio emanauit totque locorum et ciuitatum excidia prouenerunt, sed ipsum maxime spirituale bellum consideramus, quo detestabile atque mortiferum in ecclesia Dei fabricatum est scisma eoque fabricato uniuersa fere Cristiana fides pessumdata est. Unde cum pro abolenda nephandissimi scismatis peste, omnem quam potuimus operam, consilium, et auctoritatem adhibuerimus, idemque pro uniuersa Cristianorum principum reconciliatione atque concordia adhibere curemus, rati pro totius Italie pace ad quam componendam prono inhiamus affectu, non mediocriter esse facturos si ipsum Alfonsum Ferrarie Ducem et persone nostre supra modum affectum de hac sanctissima sede in prima Bononie expugnatione optime quidem meritum, singulari liberalitatis nostre beneficio complecteremur, ipsum uidelicet ea dignitate honerando atque decorando, qua ante eiusmodi priuationem honestatus decoratusque existebat.[111]

Ea propter prefatum Alfonsum Ducem ex certa nostra scientia et de apostolice potestatis plenitudine et omnes et quoscumque alios qui illi post literas monitorii penalis contra ipsum Alfonsum ducem et illi adherentes decreti adheserunt, eiusque familiares a quibusuis sententiis, censuris et penis ecclesiasticis ob non paritionem predictam, et quarumcumque literarum monitorialium ab eodem Iulio predecessore contra ipsum Alfonsum Ducem et illi coherentes emanatarum per ipsum Alfonsum et illi adherentes forsan incursis auctoritate apostolica absoluimus, et absolutos fore pronunciamus. Predictam priuationem et omnia contenta in quibuscumque supradictis literis et alia quecumque inde subsecuta, que omnia pro sufficienter expressis haberi uolumus, ex uberiori nostra gracia annullamus et nulla pronunciamus. Ipsumque Alfonsum ducem et illos qui illi adheserunt in pristinum et eum statum in quo antequam dicte litere ab eodem Iulio predecessore emanassent, erant, restituimus, reponimus, et reintegramus; omnemque inhabilitatis et infamie maculam siue notam per ipsum Alfonsum et alios qui ei adesserunt *[sic]* premissorum occasione contractam abolemus. Necnon et reductionem census qui pro predicta ciuitate nostra Ferraria et aliis locis per predecessores dicti Alfonsi sancte Romane ecclesie soluebatur, per Alexandrum ui predecessorem nostrum factam similiter et alienationem Centi et Plebis Oppidorum per eundem in parentem dicti Alfonsi celebratam et transactionem super inde secutam que omnia etiam pro expressis, ut iaceat, habere uolumus. Eisdem scientia et potestate confirmamus et approbamus.

Nosque dictum Alfonsum et filios in fidem et protectionem nostram accipimus et aduersus eos omnes, qui sibi et statui, ac rebus suis periculum atque iniuriam inferre contenderint, cuiuscumque sint dignitatis et status,

---

[111] This document is similar to *Aeternae Vitae Claviger* in that a former enemy of Julius II is praised for his services to the Church and Julius is implicitly blamed for the conflict which followed — see Appendix V.

omni nostra et huius sancte sedis auctoritate et potestate tueri in fidem pontificis pollicemur.

Insuper approbantes dacia et gabellas que et quas predecessores dicti Alfonsi, et presertim eius genitor in dicta ciuitate nostra Ferraria eiusque ducatu exigere consueuerant consentaneum iuri fore decernimus ut Alfonsus ipse eiusque sucessores eadem dacia et gabellas pro rebus que per territorium eiusdem ciuitatis nostre, aliaque loca sue ditioni supposita Uenecias proficiscuntur, queue ex Ueneciis ad alia loca ducuntur, exigere possint et ualeant, que et quas pro rebus que alibi et ex aliis locis proficiscuntur ipse et eius predecessores percipere consueuerant ad quod maxime mouemur, cum predicta ciuitas nostra ipsiusque Dux et populus per prefatum Iulium predecessorem liberati fuerunt a pactis et obligationibus, quibus regimini Ueneciarum ipsique ciuitati tenebantur, et quorum occasione duntaxat pro dictis rebus minus quam pro aliis soluebatur.[112]

Preterea, ex ea die quo nos diuina potius operante clementia quam nostris id exigentibus meritis ad sumum apostolatus apicem euecti sumus, nihil sane, ut eorum omnium Cristi fidelium pastorem patremque decet, flagrantiori animo ardentiorique studio intendimus atque curauimus quam tum uniuersa Cristianorum regna tum ipsam presertim Italie regionem, tot tantisque diuturnis bellis et seditionibus agitatam uexatam afflictatam ac fere consumptam in amenissimum pacis quietis ac tranquillitatis statum reducere atque firmare; unde cum non sine immenso animi nostro merore depopulationes predas rapinas homicidia incendia ex superiori bello, quod in humanis agente felicis recordationis Iulio ii predecessore contra dilectum filium nostrum Alfonsum predictum gestum est, emanata recolimus, ipsumque Alfonsum, ciuitate Regii ad Romani pontificis potestatem redacta, priuatum fuisse, paterna clementia aduertentes Estensis familie nomen celebre in Italia exititisse optate que Italie paci summopere conducturos, si ipsum Alfonsum de Romana olim ecclesia ante initum bellum optime meritum aliqua liberalitate nostra prosequeremur, cogitauimus, proposuimus, decreuimus atque firmiter uolumus eidem Alfonso Ferrarie duci predictam ciuitatem Regii cum omnibus iuribus et pertinentiis suis restituere. At cum certis rationabilibus causis hoc in presentia prestare non ualeamus, utque tum prefatus Alfonsus intelligat breui omnino nos id prestaturos, idcirco dilecto filio Hippolyto cardinali eius fratri et nomine ipsius accipienti in fide pontificis promitimus quod intra quinque mensium spacium a data presentium incoandorum eidem Alfonso libere et sine aliqua pecuniarum aut alterius rei solutione ipsam ciuitatem Regii cum omnibus castris et fortilitiis tam in planitie quam in montibus positis et ab ea ciuitate dependentibus realiter restituemus, similiter et quecumque alia loca si que possidemus ex his que alias per ipsum possessa fuerint. Quam tamen ciuitatem et alia loca predicta, si dicto termino pendente pacem fieri aut' nos nouam confederationem inire

---

[112] See above n. 36 of text.

contingerit, in quibus predictum Alfonsum semper includere promitimus, altero horum casuum adueniente illico et sine mora prefato Alfonso restituere promitimus.

Et hanc scripturam manu nostra propria subscriptam, manuque dilectorum filiorum cardinalium infrascriptorum signatam illammet uim robur et efficatiam habere uolumus, ac si esset bulla apostolica in publico concistorio de consensu omnium cardinalium emanata. Et predicta omnia promitimus, facimus, et disponimus, motu proprio, ex nostra certa scientia, ac de plentitudine potestatis, non obstantibus quibuscumque in contrarium facientibus, etiam si essent talia de quibus specialissima habenda foret mentio.

Datum Rome apud Sanctum Petrum sub annullo piscatoris.

XV.
Letter of Johannes Franciscus Calcaneus[113] to Cardinal Laurentius Pucci, Ferrara, 13 July 1515

Archivio di Stato — Firenze, Manoscritti Torrigiani, Filza III, Inserta XIV, Nr. 9

Reuerendissime Domine, Domine mi obseruandissime. Non ho prima scripto quanto habia dicto et instato per obedire al Nostro Signore come promisse per la cedula de mia mane, non essendo uenuto il Reuerendissimo et illustrissimo signore cardinale ad Ferrara prima che dominica de sira[114], et stracho forte si per il mare come per li excessiui caldi, et la tarditate e processa perche uolendose imbarcare in quelo de Pesare e stato constrecto al lassare cessare li uenti li erani in contrario.

Da poi la uenuta sua, ho facto instantia cum lo illustrissimo signore mio che prometa et confessa secundo me obligai fare, et prima quanto sia per quela additione apposita in lo breue de la protectione, oue se dice, prout etiam nobilitas sua etiam consentit per te ad omnia promissa obligare possimus et ualeamus.[115]

Epso signore mio dice che non uolendo la Santita de Nostro Signore che sua excellentia possa hauere dependentia da ueruno altro che da sua beatitudine, come se contene in li capituli, la instantia si e facta che sua signoria se intenda

---

[113] Perhaps the secretary to cardinal Ippolyto d'Este, Calchagnin, who was sent to France with a credence letter from him in April of 1513 — see SANUTO XVI 168.

[114] The previous Sunday was July 8th.

[115] Apparently a reference to the brief of 23 May 1515 — see MURATORI II 319—20. The secrecy surrounding Alfonso's earlier absolution was such that it does not seem to have shown up in the Venetian reports of that time, but was still awaited. Giambattista Spinelli, the Aragonese ambassador to Venice, reported as news from Rome and Bologna in May of 1515 that Leo had lifted the penalties against Alfonso and reinvested him with Ferrara — see SANUTO XX 53, 101, 174, 198, 364, etc. and the letter of Spinelli to Maximilian, Verona, 10 May 1515, in: Maximiliana 33, IV, 25r.

comprehessa et nominata in le lighe etc. e fundata in ogne ragione et equitate, perche altramente restaria solo, non petendo da se tractare ueruna cosa. Che quando mose ragiona de obligare sua Excellentia ad altri, che li pareria fosse conueniente che intendesse specifice quelo ad che hauesse ad essere obligato, hauendoli sua Santita ad ponere la uita et il stato et cio che ha in questo mondo. Et se beni sua Excellentia me dice firmamente credere che per essere sua Santita prudentissima non seria per obligarlo se non ad cose proficue, pur hauendoli ad ponere sua Santita tanto quanto ha, et ancho per essere quelo deuotissimo seruitore a sua Santita che li e, desidereria de intendere ad quanto se hauesse ad obligare, che se non come persona che li hauesse interresse al meno come suisceratissimo seruitore de sua Santita.

Poteria recordare qualche cosa che seria proficua non solo a se, ma ancho in seruitio de sua beatitudine.

Me ha ancho subiuncto sua excellentia circa ad questa parte, che il predecto reuerendissimo suo fratello prima li haueua scripto che sua Santita doueua de propria mane sottoscriuere epso breue, et che ge lhaueua replicato quelo giorno se parti da Roma, hauerne parlato cum Nostro Signore et cosi stabelito, et che perho suplica sua Santita se uolia dignare farlo reformare et sottoscriuere de sua mane propria.

Circa laltra parte per la quale io haueua ad curare, cioe chel signore Duca mio confessasse che ogne cosa li fusse stata promessa, li era stata obseruata, excepto che il darli actualmente la possessione de Regio, et che quando li fusse data, che seria quando se li daria le bulle che prometeua, non allegare che non fusse stato satisfacto ad quanto li fu promesso.

Sua Santita me ha resposto che, se bene il differrire, si e facto in dare executione al quanto li era stato promesso. Et datili la fede piu uolte, lha ruinato et ne lhonore et ne lo utile, pur per la reuerentia che porta a Nostro Signore, quando sua Santita se degni de presente farli dare liberamente la possessione et intrate de la cose, come se contene in la cedula.

Non intendendo perho uolere parlare, ne fare contra al quanto ha promesso il Reuerendissimo Signore Cardinale per Modena, che sua excellentia sera per fare decta confessione, ma quando sua Santita uoglii differrire in darli dicta possessione, et che cosi continua in renouare danno et uergogna, che lei non e per fare decta confessione.

Et piu me ha decto che ad parlare de bono et deuoto seruitore de sua Santita come e, non e per restare beno satisfacto, non li essendo obseruato quanto li e stato promesso.

Et perho me ha decto che supplica sua beatitudine che se degna di farli questa gracia, de non uolere dare piu dillatione ad dicta obseruatione, come tene per fermo che sua Santita clementissima sera per fare, supplicandoli che uolia considerare, quanto e il danno at carico ha sua excellentia per non hauere Regio, et la pocha utilitate ne ha sua Santita, la quale omnino e patrona de cio

II

che ha et hauera sua Signoria, et uolendo io significare questo a Nostro Signore ad cio sua Santita cognosca et intenda quanto ho facto.

Mi e parse pregare uostra Reuerendissima Signoria, conscia del tuto che se uoglia dignare, acceptare questo officio, del che apresso a le altre infinite obligatione ho a uostra Signoria Reuerendissima, ge ne sentiro obligo grandissimo.

Et perche in li capituli de li quali se ragiona, li e uno capitulo chel Signore Cardinale promeso, che se staria a quanto declarasse la Santita predicta circa le differrentie se hauanno per il Signor Duca cum Signor Alberto di Pii supra Carpo, sua Excellentia me ha dicto che, hauendo lei obseruato quanto promesso epso Signor Cardinale li pareria conueniente che sua beatitudine ordenasse che ambe le parte se remetessene in sua Santita, et che lei hauesse quela potestate et auctoritate che era data per il contracto ala Majeste del re Christianissimo et che lei hauesse ad determinare secundo che in decto capituli se contene.

Signore mio Reuerendissimo se beno sono subdito del Signor duca, non e perho ancho, come e il debito, non sia seruo de Nostro Signore et de uostra Signoria, per il che ardisco de dire che uedendo io la bona mente e fidele et integra dispositione del predecto Signor Duca mio uerso sua Santita et Casa Sua non saperia se non recordare preghare et supplicare che sua beatitudine uolesse contentare sua excellentia, perche li e seruo de core, et promptissimo in ogne seruitio de sua Santita a di li sui.

Le bulle et il breue sono apressa a me. Cosi le tenero secundo promesso a sua Santita sino per quela non me sera data licentia, che le dia al Signor Duca. Et in bona gracia de uostra Signoria Reuerendissima, me raccomando et offerro.

Ferrarie xiii Julii 1515

Humilis seruitor Joannes
Franciscus Calcanus

The Healing of the Pisan Schism (1511-13)

XVI.*

Excerpts from a Draft Letter of Alberto Pio to Matthäus Lang[116]
Rome, 26 August 1513

Philadelphia, University of Pennsylvania, Charles Patterson Van Pelt Library, Rare Book Collection, Henry Charles Lea Library, Ms. 414 (letters of Alberto Pio), section 4 (correspondence with the imperial court), letter 12, fol. b^{r-v}, letter 52, fols. a^r-b^v.

Quoad confoederationem ineundam, vidi quae scribit Dominatio Vestra Reverendissima. Mihi valde perplacuit illi satisfacere vt illa ineatur; quam si probasset diebus praeteritis, aut forte iam initia esset vel non longe essemus a re perficienda.

Conveni Sanctissimum Dominum Nostrum[117] una cum Cardinali Surrentino[118], oratore Anglico[119], et oratore Ducis Mediolani[j][120]; eaque de re agere nos pacatos esse Sanctitati Suae exposuimus quae respondit, ut una cum Thesaurario[121] agere de articulis incipere poteramus. Verum non inest ei ille ardor nec se tam cupidum esse [*word illegible*] ut illa perficerentur nunc, vti

---

[116]The transcription of the letters in appendices XVI* and XVII* has retained the original orthography, but has silently expanded abbreviations, represented the e-cedilla as ae, and has to some extent normalized according to modern taste and convenience the paragraphing, punctuation, and capitalization. Where the sense of the passage requires alterations, words and letters added have been placed between parentheses, while those to be omitted were enclosed in brackets. Because the documents here transcribed are rough drafts of letters with corrections, deletions, and additions but without a final revision, it is at times difficult to determine the referents to pronouns and whose ideas or words are being reported in the sections where indirect discourse is not consistently followed. I am most grateful to Professor Frank A.C. Mantello for carefully checking my transcription and for suggesting valuable emendations. Responsibility for any misreadings, however, remains solely mine.

The information contained in this letter of 26 August 1513 confirms what is known from other sources (see above pp. 120-23), but adds fascinating details about how Leo X and the ambassadors in Rome of the members of the Holy League reacted initially to the French peace overtures. From Pio's report on various meetings and conversations, it is clear that Leo X found himself in a very difficult position, trying to reconcile his secular role as a key member of a politico-military alliance with his spiritual role as head of the Church. He uncharacteristically openly bristled at Remolines' apparent suggestion that he was not acting as a loyal ally, and he insisted that his duty as pope to restore church unity took precedence over his other concerns. Perhaps in part to minimize such unpleasant encounters with the anxious ambassadors of his allies, Leo preferred to conduct negotiations through intermediaries -- e.g., Dovizi and the cardinalatial commission of which del Monte (and not L.G. della Rovere - see above p. 121) was a member.

[117]Pope Leo X (1513-21).
[118]Francisco Remolines (d. 1518) (E 8).
[119]Silvestro Gigli (d. 1521) (E 334).
[120]Marino Carracioli (d. 1538) (E 24).
[121]Bernardo Dovizi da Bibbiena (d. 1520) (E 14).

II

194*

diebus praeteritis cum illo de ea disputatum fuit ostendebat. Id autem unde contingat non intelligo. Suspicor autem animum Beatitudinis suae et si non immutari valde tamen remitti posse ob multiplices et varias continuasque Gallorum pratichas quae certe durum lapidem moverent. Ipse autem, ut multotiens scripsi et Dominatio Vestra Reverendissima scit, facillimu(s) et mitissimu(s) ingenii est.

Cum Thesaurario autem nihil agere potuimus, eius morbo impediti; verum in eam rem vnusquisque nostrorum meditari incepit, unde paratam habebimus materiam cum Thesaurarius convaluerit, quapropter citius negocium peragemus. Si autem (diu)tius ipse laborauerit, agam cum pontifice vt Domino Iuliano[122] vel alteri hoc munus iniunga(m).

De omnibus articulis antea factis transigatur. Nec ego praeteribo quicquam eorum in hac re de quibus Dominatio Vestra Reverendissima me commissione(m) facit, eamque certiorem reddam [fol. b$^{r/v}$] etiam si procuratorium iam recepissit.

Cum oratores Galli[123], praecipue autem episcopus Marsiliensis[124], continue instent apud summum pontificem, idemque procurent apud omnes reverendissimos cardinales sibi respondere ad ea quae proposuerunt in consistorio: regem videlicet suum, tanquam Christianissimum[125], nunquam cupiuisse ecclesiam diuidere, irreligioso aut impio animo nihil egisse, nec vnquam molestare sedem apostolicam sibi statuisse, quam summe semper veneratus fuerat et venerabatur, et pleraque alia quae dixerat in suo qvanqvam ad defensionem actorum regis pertinentia; ultimo loco dixit regem sibi facultatem prestitisse et procuratorium habere consentiendi in sacrum concilium Lateranense; se paratum esse id perficere, dummodo honor et dignitas regis illesa conseruaretur. Cum rex vllo pacto se nec suos erga sanctam sedem apostolicam deliquisse arbitraretur, cui responsum fuit brevissimum per Sanctissimum Dominum Nostrum se vna cum reverendissimorum cardinalium collegio intellexisse quae proposuerat, sibi placere regem habere erga sedem apostolicam eam pietatem et reverentiam quam deberet, se cogitaturum vna cum reverendissimis cardinalibus et deinde responsurum.

Isto igitur instante de responso, vt dixi, Sanctissimus, antequam quicquam respondere vellet, nos oratores ad se vocari iussit, quibus humanissimis verbis dixit se nihil decernere in ea re velle nobis inconsultis; quid autem ipse excogitasset nobis conmunicare velle, vt si ipsius consilium probaremus, illud perficeretur; sin minus, consilium mutaretur eius aut consilium tale erat. [12b^v/52a^r] Sibi videri respondendum esse istis oratoribus quod, cum hoc negocium magni ponderis esset, diligenter tractandum esse et maturius peragendum. Ideo designasse quattuor reverendissimos cardinales, videlicet Senagaliensem[126], Sancte Vitalis[127], Anconitanum[128], et Farnesium[129], qui

---

[122]Giuliano dei Medici (d. 1516), brother of Leo X
[123]Federigo de Sanseverino, Louis Forbin, and Claude de Seyssel
[124]Claude de Seyssel (d. 1520) (E 237)
[125]Louis XII (1498-1515)
[126]Marco Vigerio (d. 1516) (E 10)
[127]Antonio Maria Ciochi del Monte (d. 1533) (E 12)

The Healing of the Pisan Schism (1511-13) 195*

eos audire deberent et singula discutere secumque pertractare, ac inde cuncta referre Beatitudini suae et sacro Collegio.

In primis autem hoc eis indicere se et sacrum collegium statuisse, vt nichil ageretur nisi rex cogeret praelatos qui conciliabulo interfuerant supplices Romam venire ad petendam veniam, vel eos obstinatos ex regno suo pelleret, sibique tempus viginti dierum aut triginta constituere; quo elapso, si rex non pareret, illis predicere se aduersus regem nominatim excommunicationem promulgaturum et schismaticum declaraturum et regno priuaturum, foedusque integrum cum vniversis principibus Christianis ad eum tanquam schismaticum exterminandum initurum.

His dictis, perquisiuimus nos a Sanctitate sua si casu rex pareret quidnam Beatitudo sua factura esset; respondit nichil erga regem, quoniam de persona sua nihil nunc agebatur; illam aliam esse controuersiam; se tantum de ecclesia Gallicana vnienda; eamque, si veniret et errasse et peccasse fateretur, imposita ei exemplari penitentia, cum magna grauitate et dignitate sedis apostolice reciperet, quam vltro venientem et penitentiam salutarem non renuentem reijcere et non recipere non poterat, cum ecclesia redeunti gremium non claudet. Immo quod et si Boemi[130] venire vellent, eos reijere non posse. Tunc ego dixi Sanctitatem suam posse committere tantum causam cardinalibus vt Gallos audirent. Nil autem nunc. [fol. a$^{r/v}$] Hoc probarunt caeteri oratores omnes; hancque existimationem magnum inferre incommodum principibus nostris posse et ipsam petere, nullam legem imponere, sed hoc aliquantulum differre, ne Galli conditiones impositas acceptarent, ne si se iritarent apud Elvetios, Anglicos et caeteros populos absolutos esse et in gratiam sedis apostolice esse receptos, quod et regi quandam conditionem sequere multum prodesse posset cum non distingueretur praelatos tantum et ecclesiam tantum esse recipiendam sed etiam Regem ad amicitiam suae sanctitatis et sedis apostolice esse restitutum, sine cuius iussu existimaretur ecclesiam Gallicanam nunquam fore redeundam.

Respondit Beatitudo sua se non posse diutius hoc differe cum jam quintum mensem id distulissit. Oratores autem Galli instent sibi responsum dari, respondere non posse, se nolle reditum ecclesiae Gallicanae, petereque vt consensus ipsius in sacrum concilium Lateranense accipiatur absolute et ecclesiam peccasse minime fateri, ipsum excogitasse hanc viam avt eos penitus excludendi, si leges impositas recusaverint, aut cum honore sancte sedis apostolice in futurorum exemplo eos recipiendi, si paruerint vt videlicet delictum suum humiliter fateantur et penitentiam supplices peteant.

Tunc nil aliud replicare nobis visum est. Diximus autem nos ire recogitaturos et invicem, disceptaturos, redituri ad Sanctitatem suam, bisque convenimus in domo domini oratoris Vich[131], qui adhuc valetudinarius est, remque longa

---

[128]Pietro de Accolti (d. 1532) (E 12)
[129]Alessandro Farnese (d. 1549) (E 5)
[130]Hussites
[131]Geronimo Vich, orator of Spain

verborum serie disputauimus. Deinde ad Sanctissimum Dominum Nostrum rediuimus.

Reverendissimus Cardinalis Surrentinus pro omnibus allocutus est, plurimaque verba fecit de arduitate et grauitate negocii, et in primis nos non posse ob magnitudinem rei quicquem dicere aut consultare [fols. a^v/b^r] in ea re, inconsultis principibus nostris. Ideo rogauit Sanctitatem suam vt adhuc differe vellet.

Quod responsum ingrate tulit Sanctitas sua, vel ob modum loquendi parca verba ip(s)ius cardinalis aut quia, vt aliis meis scripsi, iam de Hispanis ob eorum importunitatem et morositatem stomachatus esse vix uidetur, aut quia consilium nostrum omnino descripabat ab eo quod apud se statuisset; quid fuerit nescio, sed aliquantulum collorem ostendit, ipsique cardinali respondit se egre ferre, non eo animo nec ea sinceritate secum agi qua ipsa nobiscum agebat, se omni pulsa passione solum honeste et commode omnium principum confederatorum rationem (habentem) [Ms.: habens] non minus quam honoris et dignitatis sedis apostolicae consilia sua communicasse. (Sus)picor autem in hac responsione nostra nos de eo diffidere et nullam rationem haber(e) honoris sui et sancte sedis apostolice. Se etiam cognoscere nos omnes aut aliquos sic respondere vt ipsum revertitum et in maximis necessitatibus positum et anxium semper habeamus, vt ei dominari pro arbitrio possimus; verum longe falli si existimamus eum quicquam potius necessitate aut timore fecisse; facturum vi esse quam voluntate; se foedum firmasse cum principibus confederatis in initio sui pontificatus voluntate, nullo eum cogente; Eluetios pecunijs, breuibus, nuncio suo sollicitasse adversus Gallos; Regi Anglie scripsisse ne animum [non] remitteret; studuisseque potius illi spiritus subgerere quam remittere. Multa, preteria alia perfecisse ad commodum principum confederatorum, nulli rei parcens. Nos autem loqui tali modo quo ostendimus de eo diffidere et quasi suspicari [fol. b$^{r/v}$] ipsum animum inclinasse ad conueniendum cum Gallis, a qua re nunquam magis alienus fuit; verum cum Summus Pont(ifex) sit et omnium Pastor, non posse illam portam [non] reserare quam Dominus voluit esse apertam; verum nobis velle morem gerere et potius satisfacere ob id quod promiserat quam proprie dignitati et officio; cardinalibus iniuncturum tantum vti nos audiant, nihil aliud iniungant; verum ob id nos non existimare debere ovicollo maius vinculum aut cathenam imponere (ipsum) [Ms.: ipse] voluntate sibi imposuisse. Haec fere (pro)pria verba dixit.

Tunc cardinalis Surrentinus placidis verbis lenire animum ipsius studuit; post ipsum quoque et Anglicus qui jam verba dixit; post ipsum ego quoque aliqua dixi an forte non aliena. Idem fecit et orator ducis Mediolani et vltimo loco diximus nos in vno loco co(m)muni venturos tutos et adinvicem disputaturos.

Postea die Sanctissimus consistorium habuit in quo designavit illos quattuor cardinales quibus iniunxit vt oratores Gallos tantum audirent et deinde referrent....

II

The Healing of the Pisan Schism (1511-13) 197*

XVII.*

Excerpts from a Draft Letter of Alberto Pio to Matthäus Lang[132]
Rome, 28 October 1513

Ibid, Ms. 414 (letters of Alberto Pio), section 4 (correspondence with the imperial court), letter 14, fol. b^{r-v}.

Quod ad Eluetios et absolutionem Gallorum attinet, qui ab episcopo Constantiensi[133] a vinculo exco(m)municationis absoluti fuerunt, respondit mihi Sanctissimus[134] se scripsisse episcopo Verulano[135], qui apud Reuerendissimum Sedunense[136] est, vt ad Eluetios orator reuertatur; mittit praeterea vnum alium secretarium suum, nomine Dominum Gorum[137], ad eos, vt, intellecto statu omnium rerum, statim ad Sancitatem Suam reuertatur; episcopus autem ibi persistat. Dixit praeterea episcopum Constantiensem nec suo iussu nec permissione absolutionem impartitum fuisse vllis Gallis; verum esse quod, instantibus ipsis Eluetijs, ei per breve authoritatem prebuisse absoluendi illos Eluetios qui cum Gallis tractassent aut eorum partibus favissent; et, vti petebam, annuit ut ipsi episcopo Constantiensi scriberetur se ab absolutione Gallorum omnino abstinere; quod breve, in presentia his alligatum, mitto ad Dominationem Vestram Reuerendissimam. Oratorque qui ad ipso(s) iturus est eis declarabit Gallos minime adhuc absolutos esse nec rediisse in gratia cum sede apostolica aut Sanctitate Sua, minimeque licere eis secum communicare aut quicquam agere; et eos hortabitur vt arces Duci Mediolani[138] restituant, si Galli illas eis tribuent, plurimumque commendabit res Ducis Mediolanis....[fol. b $^{r/v}$].... Falsum est Pontificem scripsisse breve ad episcopum Constanciensem in quo tamen nulla fiebat mencio de Gallis ut supra dixi. Jure enim iurando mihi dixit ipsum Marsiliensem[139] nec vnum verbum de ea re sibi vnquam fecisse.

---

[132]These excerpts from Pio's report document an apparent papal strategy not to grant absolution to individual French adherents of the Pisan Council, but to wait for the formal abjuration of that council by the French king and bishops as agreed to in article 4 (see above p. 164) by the papal and French representatives at Rome on October 6th. On October 28th Louis XII formally agreed to the terms, but word of his assent did not reach Rome until about November 8th (see above pp. 124, 131). Leo's order to Filonardi, sent at Pio's request, not to absolve the French may also have been a way of temporarily placating his imperial ally, Maximilian I, who opposed the absolution.

[133]Adrian de Gouffier, bishop of Coutances (1510-19) (E 176)
[134]Pope Leo X (1513-21)
[135]Ennio Filonardi, bishop of Veroli (1503-38) (E 331)
[136]Cardinal Matthaeus Schiner, bishop of Sitten (d. 1522) (E 12)
[137]Goro Gheri of Pistoia, a principal Medici agent.
[138]Massimiliano Sforza, duke of Milan (1512-15)
[139]Claude de Seyssel, bishop of Marseille (1511-17) (E 237)

III

THE « PROTESTATIO » OF ALBERTO PIO (1513) *

On December 19th, 1513, one hundred and twenty-two conciliar fathers assembled in the *conciliabulum* of the Lateran Basilica to hear the secretary of the Council, Tommaso Inghirami, read on behalf of the orator of France, Claude de Seyssel, a mandate of King Louis XII which ended the Pisan Schism and brought France into adherence with the Fifth Lateran Council.[1] Only with difficulty could this mandate be heard. On instructions from Pope Leo X (1513-21), the lector intentionally garbled his recitation to disguise the derogatory statements against both Emperor Maximilian I (1493-1519) and Pope Julius II (1503-13) contained in this mandate. No sooner had Inghirami finished than Marino Caracciolo, the orator of Duke Massimiliano Sforza, rose to protest the asserted claim of the French King to the title of Duke of Milan. While the acts of the Council duly record the mandate of Seyssel and report that Caracciolo contested the title, they are completely silent about any protest the imperial ambassador Alberto Pio may have

---

* I would like to thank Professor Austin Lynn Martin of the University of Adelaide, South Australia, for having called to my attention the scribal draft of Pio's speech preserved in the Vatican Library. Much of the archival research on which this study is based was made possible by a summer stipend from the National Endowment for the Humanities.

1. The official acts of this council were published by A. DEL MONTE, ed., *Sacrosanctum Lateranense Concilium Novissimum sub Julio II et Leone X Celebratum*, Romae 1521, reprinted in *Sacrorum Conciliorum nova et amplissima collectio*, ed. G. MANSI *et al.*, reprinted Paris 1902, Vol. 32, cols. 649-999, hereafter this collection of the acts is cited as MANSI; the pertinent material related to the eighth session can be found in MANSI 827B-836C. The account of this session given by the papal master of ceremonies, Paride de Grassi, makes no mention of Pio's intervention but does report the other events here mentioned – see *Diarium*, Codex Vaticanus Latinus 12275, ff. 91r-93r in the Bibliotheca Apostolica Vaticana; some relevant parts of this diary are also reprinted in O. RAINALDI, *Annales Ecclesiastici post Baronium ab anno 1198 ad annum 1565*, ed. and rev. G.D. MANSI and A. THEINER, Paris 1877, Vol. 31, ad annum 1513, nr. 85-97, hereafter cited as RAINALDI, and in *Il Diario di Leone X di Paride de Grassi*, ed. P. DELICATI and M. ARMELLINI, Roma 1884, 10-12.

lodged against the impugned reputation of the Emperor. Almost all the historians of the Council are similarly silent about what role, if any, Pio may have played at this session.[2] While documents from the time of the Council exist which seem to disagree about Pio's precise role, they clearly indicate that he was not indifferent to this French affront to the imperial honor.

The mandate of Louis XII approved a document previously negotiated by his delegation to the Council which absolved the King of responsibility for the Pisan schism and blamed others. The rivals and enemies of Louis XII at the papal court were accused of turning Julius II against the King by their false and devious insinuations. With patience and in hope of reconciliation did Louis sustain the unjustified provocations and attacks of a wrathful pontiff. Contrary to the expectations of Louis, a large number of ecclesiastics, even cardinals, and other learned and illustrious men, assembled a council at Pisa, claiming with numerous artful reasons that it had legitimate power. Imperial consent and authority were also bestowed on this assembly. Responding to the advice of many prelates and learned men of the French Church and nation, Louis adhered to the Pisan Council and allowed his prelates to attend, the council to transfer to his territory, and its decrees to have effect there. In so doing, he intended in no way that the Church suffer harm or schism. The death of Julius II, the paternal exhortation of Leo X, the adherence to the Lateran Council by such former conveners of the Pisan Council as the cardinals and Emperor-elect, the realization that Pisa was in error and only the Lateran

---

2. Among the historians who ignore Pio's role at the eighth session are: K. HEFELE and J. HERGENROETHER, *Histoire des conciles, d'après les documents originaux*, rev. and trans. H. LECLERQ, Vol. VIII, Part 1, Paris 1917, 416-18 hereafter this volume is cited as HEFELE-LECLERQ; L. VON PASTOR, *Storia dei papi dalla fine del medio evo*, trans. A. MERCATI, Vol. IV, Roma 1960, 46-47, hereafter cited as PASTOR-MERCATI; M. CREIGHTON, *A History of the Papacy from the Great Schism to the Sack of Rome*, London 1897, Vol. V, 217-19; and O. DE LA BROSSE et al., *Latran V et Trente*, Vol. 10 of *Histoire des Conciles oecuméniques*, ed. G. DUMEIGE, Paris 1975, 65. Attention to Pio's activities was drawn by E. GUGLIA, *Studien zur Geschichte des V. Lateranconcils. (1512-1517.)*, «Sitzungsberichte der philosophisch – historischen Classe der kaiserlichen Akademie der Wissenschaften – Wien», 140 (1899), X, 20-21.

was legitimate, the desire for universal peace among Christians who could then unite in a crusade against the Turks, and especially his own zeal for religion have all led Louis to renounce the Pisan assembly, threaten its remaining supporters with expulsion from his realm, adhere to the Lateran Council, and promise to send his prelates to Rome. While the King is thus absolved of guilt, he agreed that his procurators had renounced Pisa and adhered to the Lateran with a fitting reverence and humility and that the participants at the Pisan assembly should seek pardon and absolution.[3]

This contrived account of Louis' involvement in the Pisan Schism was recognized by its listeners as a clever but indefensible fabrication.[4] Although there is evidence that personal animosity existed between Julius II and Louis XII,[5] the portrayal of the King as the guileless victim of eminent but erroneous advisers does not match the facts. Louis took the initiative in meeting the papal challenge of spiritual weapons by convoking the synod of Tours and seeking the support of the French clergy for his counter-offensive.[6] Instead of their pressuring him to call an anti-Julian council at Pisa, the synod meeting in September of 1510 urged that deputies be first sent to admonish Julius and only if he refused correction should a reform council be contemplated. It was Louis in conjunction with Matthias Lang, the roving imperial ambassador, who resolved at Blois a month and a half later to call such a council, and its location at Pisa, instead of Lyon as favored by Louis or Konstanz preferred by Maximilian, was due to the insistence of the Italian cardinals whom they won over to their plan.[7] Many

3. MANSI, 832A-835B.
4. PASTOR-MERCATI, IV-I, 47, n. 1.
5. F. GUICCIARDINI, *Storia d'Italia*, ed. C. PANIGADA, Bari 1967, reprint of 1929 edition, III, 1-2, 22-27, 41.
6. L. SANDRET, *Le concile de Pise (1511)*, « Revue des questions historiques », 34 (1883), 427-28; HEFELE-LECLERCQ, 275-79.
7. SANDRET, *Concile de Pise*, 431; HEFELE-LECLERCQ, 279-82; H. ULMANN, *Kaiser Maximilian I: Auf urkundlicher Grundlage dargestellt*, II, Stuttgart 1891, 419-20, hereafter this work is cited as ULMANN. Other sites suggested for the Council before its convocation included Vercelli and Modena, v. Letter of Lang to Maximilian, *ex Ripa*, 16.V.1511, in Wien, Haus-, Hof- und Staatsarchiv, *Maximiliana*, box 24, folder III, folio 81v.

of the eminent jurists who wrote in favor of the council did so not to urge the King to support the council but rather to satisfy the King's request and even command that they write in its defense.[8] While it is true that Maximilian on 16 January 1511 was the first ruler to commission procurators to request of the pope the convocation of a general council, Maximilian did not act independetly but in close collaboration with Louis and hence is not to be blamed for misleading a naive and confused French monarch. Indeed, it was Louis who first actually called for the council somewhat precipitately on 25 February 1511 and Maximilian who first waited until his efforts at making peace with Julius has failed in mid-May before joining in the convocation.[9] Louis was not surprised by the assembly of a council at Pisa, but had worked long and hard to bring it about and secure its success.[10] Not included among the reasons given for the King's abandonment of Pisa in favor of Lateran are the failure of his military and diplomatic efforts against the pope's allies in northern Italy, the stunning victories of the Holy League at Novara, Guinegate, Flodden, and Vicenza, the practical demise of the French synod at Lyon, and the urgent need for France to break out of its increasing iso-

8. HEFELE-LECLERCQ, 314-18; F. OAKLEY, *Almain and Major: Conciliar Theory on the Eve of the Reformation*, « American Historical Review », 70 (1964-65), 673-90: M. GILMORE, *The Lawyers and the Church in the Italian Renaissance*, in *Humanists and Jurists: Six Studies in the Renaissance*, Cambridge, Mass. 1963, 72-78; and O. DE LA BROSSE, *Le Pape et le Concile: La Comparaison de leur pouvoirs à la veille de la Réforme*, Paris 1965. As a result of having written in support of the council Filippo Decio found his goods confiscated by the papal forces and wrote to Louis for assistance, v. Bibliothèque Nationale, *Dupuy*, 85, f. 30r.

9. *Acta primi concilii Pisani celebrati ad tollendum schisma anno Domini 1409 et concilii Senensis 1423 ex codice manuscripto constitutiones sanctae in diversis sessionibus scari generalis concilii Pisani ex bibliotheca regia*, Paris 1612, 22-23; ULMANN, 433-34; HEFELE-LECLERCQ, 295; PASTOR-MERCATI, III, 781, n. 2; Letters of Lang to Maximilian 16.V.1511, *ex Ripa*, and 18.V.1511, Trient, *Maximiliana*, 24, III, ff. 81r, 92r, 96r.

10. A. RENAUDET, *Le concile Gallican de Pise-Milan: Documents florentins (1510-1512)*, Paris 1922, i-iii, 578-84, 655; Letters of Andrea de Burgo to Maximilian: 15.VI.1511, Grationoboli; 25.VII, 3.VIII, and 10.VIII, Valence; 18.X, *in Boiansi*; 26.X, in Santa Maria Cleriaci; v. *Maximiliana*, 25, I, ff. 55r-v, II, 101r-v 40v, IV, 86v-87r, 124r-v; for Louis' efforts to provide adequate funding for the Pisan Council, see Bibliothèque Nationale, *Fund Ancien Francais*, no. 5501, f. 52v.

lation. If the French mandate read at the eighth session was so full of half-truths, misrepresentations, and even blatant inaccuracies, why then did it receive papal approbation?

The pre-conditions which Leo initially placed on a reconciliation with the supporters of Pisa were their confession of guilt and humble request for absolution. Such were the terms on which the excommunicated Federigo Sanseverino and Bernardino Carvajal were padroned and restored to the cardinalate.[11] Leo sought the same from Louis [12] but was willing to modify his demands for the sake of Church unity. Among his election capitularies was a pledge to work for peace among Christian princes and for an end to the Pisan schism. To facilitate the achievement of these goals he declared that he would do nothing to antagonize the French. By the treaty of Mechelen on 5 April 1513, however, Leo entered into an anti-French alliance with the Emperor, Aragon, and England. He secretly provided the Swiss with a large financial subsidy which supported their renewed offensive against the French and resulted in the remarkable victory of Riotta near Novara on June sixth. Still hoping for reconciliation, Leo urged his allies to deal mercifully with the French.[13] He sent the nephew of Cardinal Ro-

---

11. MANSI 814D-15B; PASTOR-MERCATI, IV-I, 36-39.

12. Letter of Jean le Veau to Margaret of Austria, Milan, 24.VIII.1513 in *Lettres du Roy Louis XII. Avec plusieurs autres lettres, mémoires et instructions ecrites 1504 jusques et compris 1514*, ed. J. GODEFROY, Brussels 1712, IV, 199-200: « a quoy [Claude de Seyssel] nostredit sainct Pere ne veult aucunement entendre ains de prime face a respondu audit Ambassadeur qu'il veult premierement et avant toutte euvre que l'honneur du saint Siege Appostolique soit repare par ledit Roy de France non seulement en ostant le Cisme et Concile de France, mais qu'il congnoisse par lettres authentiques que à tort, sans cause, indirectement, et contre raison le dit Roy de France a fait convocquer et assembler ledit Concile... ».

13. W. ROSCOE, *The Life and Pontificate of Leo the Tenth*, 2nd ed., rev., London 1806, II, 261-300, V, 230-45; the treaty of Mechelen is printed in J. DU MONT, *Corps universel diplomatique du droit des gens...*, Amsterdam 1726, IV-I, 173-74; a memorial on this anti-French alliance is in Paris, Bibliothèque Nationale, *Fond Ancien Francais*, no. 2930, ff. 154v-58r; in a letter from Rome on 8 July 1513 the French orator Louis Forbin reported that Leo wanted to be neutral and a common father to all, but also did not want the French back in Italy and would send Robert de Guibé to France as legate on a mission of peace, v. Bibliothèque Nationale, *Dupuy*, no. 261, f. 121 r; GUICCIARDINI, *Storia d'Italia*, III, 282-83; R. DEVONSHIRE JONES, *Francesco Vettori*:

bert de Guibé, François Hamon, the Bishop of Nantes, to France as his delegate to prepare the way for reconciliation.[14] When in July of 1513 the ambassador of King Louis XII, Claude de Seyssel, Bishop of Marseilles, arrived in Rome to work out the terms for ending the Pisan schism, Leo X insisted on the non-interference of the French in Church affairs, tried to woo France away from Venice, and feigned an initial reserve and coolness toward Seyssel's overtures. The French orator was ordered to explain his King's position to a special commission of four neutral cardinals.[15] Leo X insisted that Louis confess his error in having supported Pisa. Seyssel, however, was not empowered to accept this humiliating condition.[16]

In hopes of working out a mutually acceptable statement whereby Louis would renounce Pisa and adhere to the Lateran Council, Leo appointed another commission. Representing the papal side were cardinals Antonio del Monte, Pietro Accolti, Lorenzo Pucci, and Giulio de Medici; on the French side were Federigo Sanseverino, Louis Forbin, and Claude de Seyssel.[17] The composition of this commission strongly favored France. In addition to these Tuscan cardinals were their frequent Gallic sympathies, this group had as its secretary Pietro Bembo from Venice, the ally of France. Antonio del Monte who favored the Holy League, but Medicean interests more, was probably the chief critic of the French proposals.[18] Seyssel was credited with bringing these negotiations to a conclusion acceptable to Louis. He was helped in this not only by the francophile majority on the commission and by Leo's earnest desire to restore Church unity, but also by Louis' greater tractability in the wake of the defeats suffered by his soldiers at Guinegate in August and by his allies at Flodden in September and at Olma (Vicenza) in October and after his enemies formed

Florentine Citizen and Medici Servant, London 1972, 91-92; D.S. CHAMBERS, *Cardinal Bainbridge in the Court of Rome, 1509-1514*, Oxford 1965, 45.

14. DE GRASSI, *Diarium*, Vat. Lat. 12275 ff. 59r, 99r; PASTOR-MERCATI, IV-I, 43.

15. A. CAVIGLIA, *Claudio di Seyssel (1450-1520): La vita nella storia de' suoi tempi*, Vol. 54 of *Miscellanea di Storia Italiana*, Torino 1928, 275-78.

16. *Lettres du Roy*, IV, 200-01.

17. MANSI, 832AB, 834D-35A; CAVIGLIA, *Seyssel*, 278.

18. CHAMBERS, *Bainbridge*, 44, 47, 109-110; CAVIGLIA, *Seyssel*, 595.

a new alliance against him in mid-October.[19] Fearing Spanish hegemony over Italy and frustrated in his attempts to provide his brother Giuliano with an imperial title to territories neighboring Florence, Leo inclined more and more toward a pro-French policy which would guarantee Medicean control of Florence and provide support for the candidacy of Giuliano to the throne of Naples.[20] Leo, therefore, approved the document agreed upon in early October by the papal-French commission, even though its text basically absolved Louis of blame for the Pisan council and contained the numerous other inaccuracies already indicated. On 26 October 1513 Louis XII while at the monastery of Corbie in Picardy formally ratified this document.[21]

Months later Maximilian wrote of his displeasure at the ease with which France was reconciled to Rome. He complained that while Leo could not refuse to accept Louis and his kingdom back into unity with the Church, this absolution and reunion should not have been done with such great ease and indulgence since others would be thereby encouraged to disobey the Holy See without fear of serious penalty. The papacy was also in danger of being held now in even greater contempt, because France was reconciled even though it remained contumacious by not fulfilling all the terms of the absolution.[22]

In answer to the Emperor's complaints, Lang wrote from Rome that the French had not been absolved, but only admitted to membership in the Lateran council, which both the pope and all the cardinals favored. An absolution for the French depended upon fulfilment of their obligations.[23]

---

19. CAVIGLIA, *Seyssel*, 27; ULMANN, *Maximilian*, II, 482-83; PASTOR-MERCATI, IV-I, 39-43.

20. M. SANUTO, *I Diarii*, ed. F. STEFANI, G. BERCHET, N. BAROZZI, XVII, Venezia 1886, 21-22, 342, 373; ULMANN, *Maximilian*, II, 460; Letter of Marino Carraciolo to Massimiliano Sforza, Roma, 11.XI.1513, *Maximiliana*, 30, III, ff. 33v-34br; Letter of Lang to Maximilian, Viterbo, 16.XI.1513, *Maximiliana*, 30, III, f. 66v.

21. MANSI, 834E-35B; CAVIGLIA, *Seyssel*, 280.

22. Letter of Maximilian to Lang, Wels, 25.II.1514, *Maximiliana*, 30, III, f. 228r.

23. Letter of Lang to Maximilian, Roma, 22.III.1514, *Maximiliana*, 31, I, f. 104v.

What the likely reaction of Maximilian was to the attack on his reputation contained in the French conciliar mandate can be readily inferred from his response to a similar accusation coming from the leader of the schismatic cardinals at Pisa, Bernardino Lopez de Carvajal. In a letter of 15 July 1513 this Spanish prelate claimed that he had joined the dissident council on the authority of Maximilian and therefore the Emperor was responsible for Carvajal's loss of his benefices and was obliged before God and men to provide him with compensation.[24] Maximilian claimed he was amazed at this assertion and proceeded to defend his reputation.

Maximilian's response is found in two letters, one to Leo and the other to Carvajal, both from *in Insolis* and dated September twelfth. Although he wrote to the pope on Carvajal's behalf, the Emperor denied responsibility for his plight and chided him for not having earlier trusted him and followed his kind suggestions whereby he probably could have avoided his current predicament.[25] Should Carvajal persist in these calumnies, Maximilian sent a detailed refutation for Pio's use at Rome.

The Emperor denied that Carvajal acted with his counsel. Without imperial advice or knowledge, this cardinal withdrew from the court of Julius II. That he fled to the French camp and joined in their opposition to the pope was a well known fact of which Maximilian was neither ignorant nor forgetful. While it was true that the Emperor consented to the convocation of a council and issued a mandate for this purpose, his directives in this regard were not followed. He had wanted that the pope and cardinals in Rome be legitimately first asked by the imperial procurators, Louis XII, their secular allies, and the dissident cardinals to convoke a general council for the needs of the whole Christian republic. Only if these Roman prelates refused, was the convocation to be issued by imperial authority and the council's assembly to be fixed for a fitting

---

24. Letter of Carvajal to Maximilian, Roma, 15.VII.1513, *Maximiliana*, 29, III, f. 47r.
25. Letters of Maximilian to Leo and Carvajal, *in Insulis*, 12.IX.1513, *Maximiliana*, 29, IV, ff. 61r-v, 62r-v.

time and place. Maximilian complained that his instructions were not followed: neither the pope nor certain cardinals were properly asked, the council was not summoned principally on their authority, its location was inconvenient, and its opening scheduled for an impossible date. Never before was such a procedure used, except for the council of Pisa which met a century earlier and merited a similiar condemnation. When it became clear that the intention of the Pisan cardinals was not the welfare of Christendom but the oppression of Julius with the weapons and favor of those on whose power they depended, the Emperor withdrew his support. What course that council then took, its goals, and its plans were well known and thus Carvajal had no grounds for blaming his error on the Emperor.[26] Maximilian was not willing to take sole or principal blame for the Pisan Council.

Knowing the Emperor's sensitivity to charges that he was the chief architect of the schismatic assembly and being forewarned about the contents of the French conciliar mandate, Alberto Pio prepared a response.[27] That such a rebuttal had been penned by Pio has been known by scholars over the centuries. The where-abouts of this document, however, had not been identified nor were its contents ever studied in detail.[28] An examination of this formal protest by Pio reveals a

26. Letter of Maximilian to Pio, in Insulis, 12.IX.1513, Maximiliana, 29, IV, ff. 50v-51v.
27. GUGLIA, Studien zur Geschichte, 20.
28. A letter of Jacopo Bannissi to Margaret of Austria from Innsbruck dated 17 January 1514 mentioned Pio's rebuttal and stated that a copy of it was appended. In 1712 Jean Godefroy published this letter but not the rebuttal in his Lettres du Roy Louis XII, IV, 236. The original of this letter is to be found at the Archives départmentales du Nord (Lille), Cote B, Entrée 18863, no. 31164. The rebuttal no longer accompanies the letter. I am grateful to the Director M. ROBINET, for allowing me to consult this archive, even though it was officially closed for a summer vacation. The relevant part of Pio's letter to the Emperor, explaining briefly the context and content of his protest which he sent along, was published in 1899 by GUGLIA, Studien zur Geschichte, 20. The whole letter is kept in the Maximiliana, 31, I, ff. 9r-12v. The rebuttal is not to be found with the letter. The only version of Pio's protest which I know to still exist is the Protestatio contra oratores Regis Franciae per oratores Caesareae Majestatis facta in Concilio di Laterano sotto Leone X⁰, in Raccolta di Diverse Scritture Minute, Mss. Chigiani, L. III. 60, Entry no. 84, ff. 158r-59r preserved in the Bibliotheca Apostolica Vaticana. This document is apparently a scribal

repetition of some of the arguments used by the Emperor to vindicate himself from the accusations of Carvajal, but also some other lines of defense and counterattack which probably originated with his Italian ambassador.

Pio sought to exonerate the Emperor. He insisted that as representative of Maximilian he could not let pass in silence Louis' unjust and undeserved calumnies against the German ruler. Inghirami's attempt to garble these accusations was unsuccessful and demanded a rebuttal. Whereas the Emperor in answer to Carvajal had openly admitted to backing the edict of convocation but sought to lessen his degree of culpability by claiming that his instructions were not followed, Pio's defense of the German was confused and even contradictory. He counterattacked by asserting that Maximilian, unlike Louis, did not seek to blame others for his mistaken initial support for convoking the council. He then adamantly denied that the Pisa Council was called by the cardinals with imperial approval and authority and that once convoked Maximilian had consented to it. And yet he also admitted that the German ruler had agreed to the convocation of a council and had empowered procurators to convoke it. Echoing the Emperor's earlier arguments, Pio protested that Maximilian had insisted that this was to be done only in accordance with the proper procedures and time-honored custom and that Julius II was to be advised and invited to attend. While the Emperor granted at Louis' request a procuratorship for convoking a council, he resisted the French King's enticing promises and never consented to the anti-papal measures taken by those who convened and promoted the Pisan Council. Imperial opposition to this Council was such that no German prelate attended its sessions. The reason for this shift in imperial policy was Julius' decision to call

draft, corrected by the hand of Pio (identified by Myron Gilmore), and revised yet again by a third hand. These changes in the original draft were apparently guided by considerations of stylistic elegance and did not significantly alter its content. While the *protestatio* is written in the first person plural and identified as having been composed by the imperial ambassadors (i.e., M. Lang, F.M. Sforza, A. Pio, A. Giuppo della Rovere, and P. Bonomi), Pio claimed in his cover letter to Maximilian that he was its author (*responsionem meam*), v. GUGLIA, *Studien zur Geschichte*, 20.

his own council to meet at the Lateran. When this assembled Maximilian soon admitted his error in having initially supported Pisa and adhered to the Lateran Council.

In attempting to vindicate Maximilian's reputation, Pio has like his French opponents distorted the historical record. The Emperor had an important role in the calling of a council. He was in full agreement with the plan worked out at Blois by Lang and Louis. In accord with traditional canonical procedures he empowered in January of 1511 an imperial delegation to urge the pope to convoke a council. It was unsuccessful. His ambassador Lang had a personal meeting with Julius in Bologna in which he tried to get the pope to agree to terms of peace. When Julius insisted on exacting revenge on Ferrara and France, Lang dispatched to Milan three procurators: Girolamo de Nogarola and Ludovico Faella, both of Verona, and Antonio Capodivacca. There on May 16th they joined with the French procurators, and at the urgings of the dissident cardinals convoked a council. Questions were, however, raised regarding the exact extent of their procuratorial powers. Étienne Poncher, the Bishop of Paris and representative of Louis, pointed out numerous deficiences in the imperial mandate and urged that Maximilian immediately issue a new one modeled on the French. The bishop went so far as to claim that with their present commission the imperial procurators could not convoke a council. The cardinals at Milan also questioned the delegates' powers, but were more concerned about any detrimental effect a delay in the convocation might cause. For their part, the imperial procurators insisted that their commission was adequate. Nonetheless, they cushioned their edict of convocation with such phrases as *quantum jure melius possumus et debemus* and *quantum in nobis est*. Similar wording also appears in the cardinals' edict of convocation three days later. The papal master of ceremonies in Rome, Paride de Grassi, begrudgingly complimented the cardinals on their skillful wording which could allow them later to disclaim responsibility on grounds that they lacked the proper authority to convoke a council. Although Maximilian did not send a new mandate to his procurators in time for the convocation, he did write to them on June 5th expressing pleasure in what they had done and asking them to thank in his name the cardinals for their cooperation and to promise them his firm support and continued help throughout the council's sitting. Writing from Muldorf on June 15th the Emperor formally approved all the actions of his procurators in Milan.[29] Unless Pio were to claim that the faulty mandate and the *quantum* phrases absolved the Emperor of responsibility for calling the council, his assertion that the Emperor never gave his approval and consent to the convocation is clearly indefensible. While Lang at the third session of the Lateran Council made the same claim as Pio, the Emperor in his mandate formally admitted that he had empowered procurators to convoke the Pisan Council and therefore now revoked their powers. In a letter to King Fernando of Aragon dated 1 September 1511, Maximilian seemed to assume sole responsibility for the conciliar convocation. He did not even mention the part played by Louis and reduced the role of the dissident cardinals to one of consenting to the imperial edict of convocation.[30] His ambassadors to the Lateran Council were apparently more jealous of his reputation than was he.

Pio was close to the truth when he claimed that Maximilian, in spite of enticing promises, never consented to the military and anti-papal activities of the Pisan supporters. Legal and financial factors seem to have dampened imperial enthusiasm for the council. In the opinion of leading canonists the Emperor's action in convoking the council was initially neither illegal nor schismatic. On 25 July 1511, however, the situation changed when Julius published a bull of the previous week convoking his own council to meet in Rome. Continued support for Pisa was thereby rendered illegal and Maximilian began to distance himself from it. During the year when the council met at Pisa, then Milan, Asti, and Lyon, Maximilian never

29. GUICCIARDINI, *Storia d'Italia*, III, 86-89, 101; ULMANN, *Maximilian*, II, 433-34; *Acta primi concilii Pisani*, 20-23 49-51; Letter of Lang to Maximilian, ex Ripa, 16.v.1511, *Maximiliana*, 24, III, f. 811r-v; Princes' and Cardinals' Edicts of Convocation, Bibliothèque Nationale, *Dupuy*, 85, ff. 28-29; P. DE GRASSI, *Diarium Julii*, Vat. Lat., 12414, f. 115v.

30. MANSI, 732BC, 733B; Letter of Maximilian to Fernando, Trient, 1.IX.1511, *Maximiliana*, 25, III, f. 10r.

formally withdrew his indeterminate support for the council – a fact noted in the sixth session at Milan. Financial considerations seem to have seriously limited the support he may otherwise have given. His daughter Margaret of Austria advised him that the treasury had not a penny to spare on the council. In order to fulfill his pledge to protect the council Maximilian had recourse to Louis and requested 150,000 ducats as a subsidy for his troops. The French King offered 50,000 ducats in November of 1511 if the Emperor would invade Italy and march on Rome. Maximilian hesitated on the grounds that he needed Spanish support for such an expedition. In the end whether for reasons of finance, military strategy, diplomacy, or canonical prohibition, the Emperor never engaged his troops in a defense of the Pisan Council.[31] His failure to rescind his initial indeterminate approval of the council, his pledge of protection, and his subsequent negotiations with Louis, however, all diminish his title to innocent by-stander, as suggested by Pio.

The claim that no German prelate was willing to participate at Pisa was advanced by Pio as evidence of the Empire's loyalty to the papacy. The absence of German names from the rolls of the council would seem to corroborate this assertion. That German participation was expected at Pisa is suggested by the appointment at the first session of a notary for the German nation and by the decision of the fourth session to divide membership on the conciliar deputations evenly among the four nations (Spanish, French, Italian, and German), if any of their representatives were present.[32]

The failure of Germans to attend the Pisan Council was in spite of rather than because of Maximilian's efforts. His initial delegation of six procurators commissioned to join with the

---

31. W. ULMANN, *Julius II and the Schismatic Cardinals*, in *Schism, Heresy and Religious Protest*, ed. D. BAKER, Vol. 9 of *Studies in Church History*, Cambridge 1972, 181-84, 187; GUICCIARDINI, *Storia d'Italia*, III, 116-17; MANSI, 681B-91D; *Acta primi concilli Pisani*, 172; *Lettres du Roy Louis XII*, III, 90; A. SCHULTE, *Kaiser Maximilian I als Kandidat für den päpstlichen Stuhl 1511*, Leipzig 1906, 63-64.

32. *Acta primi concilii Pisani*, 80, 91-92, 159.

French in convoking the council included at least two Germans: count Veit von Fürst and a high official in the Tyrolean chancery. Other more pressing responsibilities, however, prevented them from assisting at the convocation ceremonies. The Emperor's daughter Margaret and the abbot Trithem both warned him that Germany would not follow him to Pisa. His vain attempts to persuade individual prelates to attend confirmed their predictions. Even a lesser German cleric like the canon of Trient, Nikolaus von Neuhaus, was reluctant to serve as an imperial emissary in matters touching the council. In hopes of attracting Germans to the council by making access more convenient, Maximilian urged that the council be transferred to Verona or Trient, promising that he would attend in person if held there. When this proposal was rejected by Louis and the cardinals who reminded him of his promise to send procurators and prelates, Maximilian wrote that he was sending Pietro de Motta, a professor of sacred theology, as his representative to Pisa and, in hopes of securing the support of the whole German nation for the council, that he intended to consult with his bishops at the up-coming diet at Augsburg. To impede possible supporters of the rival Lateran Council he forbad passage through his territories to any prelate heading for Rome. He also wrote to Poland, Hungary, and Florence, urging in vain that representatives be sent to Pisa. When few bishops appeared at Augsburg in January of 1512 and these concluded that the Council of Pisa-Milan was schismatic, Maximilian hoped for a reconsideration of the question at the next diet which eventually met in April of 1512 at Trier and then moved to Köln. King Louis and the Pisan cardinals were not happy with these delays since their council was weakened by the absence of the Germans. Pressured by the active supporters of Pisa, Maximilian in early January of 1512 prepared a delegation headed by count Girolamo de Nogarola to be sent to the council which had by then relocated in Milan. This embassy apparently never left German territory; neither did the Emperor's Italian agent, Andrea de Burgo, who arrived in Milan the next month, come with an imperial mandate accrediting him to the Council; nor did

THE « PROTESTATIO » OF ALBERTO PIO 275

the spring diet at Trier elect ways of supporting this council.[33]

Faced with the German prelates' indifference or opposition to Pisa, without money or troops to advance the cause of the council, no longer hopeful of using the council to bring about his own election to the papal throne,[34] skeptical of the military strength of his French allies in Italy, especially after the Phyrric victory of Ravenna, and wooed by Spanish and papal diplomats, Maximilian lost interest in the council and moved away from the League of Cambrai. He allowed the Swiss to transit the Tyrol for their descent on the French forces in Lombardy. He also withdrew the *Landsknechte* contingent from the French army and thus forced his former ally to retreat from Italy. With the troops went the council, first to Asti and then to Lyon. There on 1 November 1512 at the Mass of All Saints celebrating the first and only anniversary of the council, Abbot Zaccaria Ferreri, the council's secretary, lamented that only the French King had shown himself a firm supporter of the council.[35] Even though the Emperor had not as yet formally repudiated Pisa, he had failed to keep his promise of sending German representatives. Exhortations to individual prelates, requests that they take up the cause of Pisa at the diet, attempts

33. Letter of Lang to Maximilian, *ex Ripa*, 16.V.1511, *Maximiliana*, 24, III, f. 81r; Instructions for imperial ambassadors to Hungary, *Maximiliana*, 25, I, f. 111r-v; Christoph von Schrofenstein to Maximilian, nach 24.VIII.1511, *Maximiliana*, 25, II, f. 115r; Nikolaus von Neuhaus to Maximilian, Trient, 26.IX.1511, *Maximiliana*, 25, III, f. 93r; Girolamo de Nogarola to Maximilian, Trient, 8.I.1512, *Maximiliana*, 26, III, f. 14r; ULMANN, *Maximilian*, II, 435-37; GUICCIARDINI, *Storia d'Italia*, III, 116-17, 144; *Lettres du Roy Louis XII*, III, 33; SCHULTE, *Maximilian als Kandidat*, 59-60, 64; P. VILLARI, *Niccolò Machiavelli e i suoi tempi*, 2nd ed. rev., II, Milan 1895, 556; HEFELE-LECLERCQ, 296-330; RENAUDET, *Concile Gallican*, 610-11, 628.

34. PASTOR-MERCATI, III, 1117-20, App. 132; H. WIESFLECKER, *Kaiser Maximilian I. und die Kirche*, in *Kirche und Staat in Idee und Geschichte des Abendlandes. Festschrift von Ferdinand Maass*, ed. W. BAUM, Wien 1973, 157-59, and his specialized study, *Neue Beitrage zur Frage des Kaiser-Papst Planes Maximilians I im Jahre 1511*, « Mitteilungen des Instituts für Österreichische Geschichtsforschung », 71 (1963), 311-32.

35. R.G.D. LAFFAN, *The Empire Under Maximilian I*, in *The Renaissance 1493-1520*, ed. D. HAY, Vol. 1 of *The New Cambridge Modern History*, New York 1961, 215; *Promotiones et progressus sacrosancti pisani concilii moderni indicti et incohati anno domini MDXI*, n.p., n.d. f. 44r preserved in the Bibliotheca Apostolica Vaticana.

to transfer the council to a more convenient location, and the commissioning of conciliar delegates all failed to produce a single German at Pisa. This was not due to a supposed loyalty to the papacy, as suggested by Pio, but to the ineffective efforts and calculated vacillations of the German Emperor.

Various reasons can be offered to explain why Pio engaged in such distortions of the historical record in his attempt to defend Maximilian's reputation. Ignorance of the facts is unlikely, for this Italian prince was during this period at such centers of information as the French, imperial, and papal courts, and even acted as the agent of the contending parties. That he protests too much about the Emperor's innocence could suggest an indirect attempt to excuse his own earlier role as servant of the schismatic French.[36] A recognition of the injustice of the French mandate in portraying the Emperor as the principal author of the schism, Pio's knowledge of the Emperor's sensitivity to a similiar charge made previously by Carvajal, and a sense of responsibility as imperial ambassador to defend Maximilian's reputation all help to explain why he penned his protest, but not why he resorted to such obvious exaggerations. They resemble arguments framed from desperation.

Alberto Pio, as prince of Carpi, was in a very difficult position. For years now he had struggled to preserve his hereditary title to Carpi and to assert his claims to that half of
* his territory which had during his minority come into the *de facto* possession of his uncle Marco whose son Giberto later obtained an imperial title to this portion which he subsequently sold to Carpi's powerful expansionist neighbor, Ercole d'Este of Ferrara. By appealing directly to the Emperor who was the feudal overlord of Carpi, Pio was able to gain title to the whole county in 1509.[37] His diplomatic and military service

---

36. P. GUAITOLI, *Memorie sulla vita d'Alberto III. Pio*, in *Memorie storiche e documenti sulla città e sull'antico principato di Carpi*, I, Carpi 1877, 163-209; R. BRANDOLINI, *Dialogus Leo nuncupatus*, ed. F. FOGLIAZZI, Venezia 1753, 82, 97-98; H. SEMPER, *Alberto Pio III als Herrscher und Staatsmann. Seine äusseren Schicksale*, in *Carpi: Ein Fürstensitz der Renaissance*, ed. H. SEMPER, F.O. SCHULZE, and W. BARTH, Dresden 1882, 3-9.

37. GUAITOLI, *Memorie sulla vita*, 133-55, 168.

* (See Addenda)

in the cause of France won him another important protector of his claims.

In the winter of 1510-11 this situation changed. During these months Julius II came northward to direct the military operations against his rebellious vassal and son of Ercole, Alfonso of Ferrara, who was supported by the French. The pope took personal command of the siege of Mirandola, promising to restore this fortress to its rightful lord, Gianfrancesco Pico, a cousin of Pio. Although Julius managed to capture this castle, he was unable to press his attack on Alfonso and by late spring Mirandola was back in French hands. Whether in hopes of restoring this town once again to his cousin with whom he had spoken at length during the Franco-papal negotiations over Bologna, or to protect his own nearby territory from future papal attacks, or to make a separate peace with his indomitiable former patron, Julius II, now that both France and the Empire had failed in their negotiations with this pope and were threatening a council, or also just to rescue his faltering finances which prevented him from meeting his obligations toward Alfonso and which eventually forced him to sell off some of his estates, Pio entered into secret negotiations.[38] For a reportedly large sum of money, he promised to betray into the pope's hands the neighboring territory of his cousin, Mirandola. The French learned of the plan and took their own ambassador, Pio, as prisoner. Louis XII involved himself personally in the case. Many important and respected persons, even captains in the imperial and Venetian armies, came forward to give oral testimony and written depositions against Pio. Because he was technically the subject of the Emperor, Louis took no formal action against him and had him released. He openly resolved, however, never again to admit him into his service and declared that justice was done when d'Este despoiled Pio of half of his possessions. In the near future at least the prince of Carpi could anticipate the combined hostility of France, Ferrara, and their Venetian ally.[39] Given the fluctuating fortunes of papal and

---

38. GUAITOLI, *Memorie sulla vita*, 172-82, 187-91, 195; GUICCIARDINI, *Storia di Italia*, III, 62-89.

39. Letters of Andrea de Burgo to Maximilian, from Valence, 1.VII.1511,

Aragonese arms, Pio's only remaining mainstay was the other major military power in the area and his own feudal overlord, the Holy Roman Empire.

Pio travelled to Germany where he sought the assistance of Maximilian. The Emperor welcomed this Italian prince who was known to be acceptable to Julius II and whose diplomatic skills he now utilized by sending Pio on missions to Venice and Rome. Within months of entering the imperial service, this count of Carpi was able to obtain from the Emperor's tribunal a decision requiring Duke Alfonso of Ferrara to restore to Pio that half of Carpi claimed by the d'Estes and to compensate the count for any damages suffered or expenses incurred. Maximilian went on to reward his Italian ambassador's services with words of praise, grants of money, protection for Carpi, investiture with additional titles and lands, and increased responsibilities at Rome. After years of struggle, Pio seemed to have gained at last the power and influence he needed to secure full possession of and a period of peace for the county of Carpi.[40] In the month just prior to his writing the *Protestatio*, however, this imperial ambassador came to fear that his position at court was in danger.

The arrival at Rome of Antonino Giuppo della Rovere caused Alberto Pio much consternation. This cousin of the former pontiff and brother of the bishop of Vicenza came with ample credentials as a special legate of the Emperor.[41] Pio was

---

Maximiliana, 25, I, f. 3ar, from Blois, 23.IX.1511, *Maximiliana*, 25, III, f. 87r, from *in Boiansi*, 18.X.1511, *Maximiliana*, 25, IV, f. 87v; Letter of Maximilian to Lang, Innspruck, ?.I.1514, *Maximiliana*, 30, III, f. 133r. In the light of this evidence it becomes increasingly difficult to continue the defense of Pio's reputation attempted by former historians: A. MORSELLI, *Notizie e documenti sulla vita di Alberto Pio*, in *Memorie storiche e documenti sulla città e sull'antico principato di Carpi*, XI, Carpi 1931, 56, 60, 62; GUAITOLI, *Memorie sulla vita*, 182-83, 190; by contemporaries such as Guicciardini, Pio was considered insincere and self-serving, v. *Storia d'Italia*, II, 333, III, 24, 65.

40. GUAITOLI, *Memorie sulla vita*, 197-204; Letter of Veit von Fürst to Lang, Modena, 9.V.1511, *Maximiliana*, 24, III, f. 46v; Letter of Maximilian to Pio, *in Insolis*, 12.IX.1513, *Maximiliana*, 29, IV, f. 47r; Letter of Maximilian to Margaret of Austria, Kaufbeuren, 6.V.1513, *Correspondance de l'Empereur Maximilien Ier et de Marguerite d'Autriche sa fille, gouvernante des Pays-Bas de 1507 a 1519*, ed. A. LE GLAY, Paris 1839, II, 139.

41. Letters of Maximilian to Lang, Giuliano de' Medici, D. Giacobazzi, B.

astonished and perplexed. How could the Emperor entrust affairs of state to a man known for his levity, mendacity, bungling, and sympathy for the Emperor's bitter enemy, Venice? Pio refused to be his colleague. He complained openly to Lang who quietly sought to find some honorable way to return Giuppo to Germany. In the letter to the Emperor which accompanied a copy of his *Protestatio*, Pio stated his displeasure at Giuppo's appointment and explained why it so upset him. The new ambassador was not his equal in birth or ability. Was the Emperor suggesting that Pio was negligent in his duties or not capable of handling great and difficult tasks? [42]

Pio was anxious to prove his worth. He sent a long report detailing his handling of imperial business. Together with Lang he labored day and night to negotiate a truce or peace treaty with Venice. They both wrote to the Emperor that they had never before worked so long and hard on such difficult material and each singled out the other for words of special praise. The French were denounced for having engaged in astute machinations to block these negotiations, but in the end Pio could claim to have won Leo over to the imperial peace plan.[43]

When seen in this context the distortions, exaggerations, and counter-attacks of the *Protestatio* are more easily understood. To some extent they were the predictable by-products of desperation. Pio's position as imperial ambassador which secured the safety of Carpi seemed threatened by Giuppo's arrival. The French who had earlier uncovered his own treachery now acted with shrewdness and cunning to defeat the peace negotiations by which Pio hoped to prove his worth as an ambassador. It is not surprising then that the *Protestatio* written at this time should contain attacks on the French. Its

Carvajal, A. Castellesi, T. Bakocz, M. Schiner, and P. Accolti, from Namur, 5.X.1513, *Maximiliana*, 30, I, ff. 24r-26v.

42. Letters of Lang to Maximilian, Viterbo, 16.XI.1513, and Roma, 1.XII.1513, *Maximiliana*, 30, II, ff. 64r, 118r-v; Letter of Pio to Maximilian, Roma, 3.I.1514, *Maximiliana*, 31, I, ff. 9r-10r.

43. Letters of Pio to Maximilian, Roma, 3.I, 6.I, 3.III.1514, *Maximiliana*, 30, III, ff. 10r-v, 17r-18v, 31, I, ff. 9r-12v; Letter of Lang to Maximilian, Roma, 28.II.1514, *Maximiliana*, 30, III, 242r.

distortions of historical fact and obvious exaggerations regarding Maximilian's innocence were but over-anxious attempts to defend the Emperor's reputation and thereby prove Pio an industrious and effective ambassador worthy of continued imperial support.

Whether Pio's carefully elaborated if misleading response in the form of a speech addressed to the conciliar fathers was ever delivered by him at the council is a question open to speculation. The imperial councillor and secretary at Innsbruck, Jacobus de Bannissis, seems to have thought that Pio presented his protest orally at the eighth session. In a cover letter accompanying a copy of the speech sent to Maximilian, Pio stated to the contrary that it was not necessary for him to make an oral presentation at the council because those statements in the French mandate hostile to the Emperor were at Leo's request effectively suppressed by Inghirami's garbled recitation. Nevertheless, in the text of his *Protestatio* Pio insists that this confused delivery did not adequately eliminate the derogatory comments made against the Emperor.[44] If this was true and not just a literary convention to justify keeping a record of Pio's written response, his silence at the eighth session becomes difficult to explain. Other ambassadors, notably Claude de Seyssel and Girolamo Morone, did not hesitate to interrupt papal ceremonies to contest any statement critical of their respective lords. In his letter to Margaret of Austria detailing the proceedings of this eighth session, Pio's colleague in Rome, Jacques Annocque, noted the protest of the Milanese orators but made no mention of Pio's response. A similar failure by Paride de Grassi, the conciliar master of ceremonies, to record in his carefully kept diary such an intervention by Pio would also strongly argue against it having ever happened.[45]

A variety of factors may have led Pio to keep silent. It is

---

44. *Lettres du Roy Louis XII*, IV, 236: « Comes Carpiensis protestatus est in Concilio contra eandem taxationem... »; GUGLIA, *Studien zur Geschichte*, 20; PIO, *Protestatio*, f. 158r.

45. DE GRASSI, *Diarium*, ff. 89r, 91v-93v, 118r, 122v; MANSI, 869AB; SANUTO, *Diarii*, XVII, 399; Letter of Jacques Annocque to Margaret of Austria, Roma, 21.XII.1513, Archives départmentales du Nord (Lille), Cote B, Entrée 18861, no. 31067, ff. 1v-2r.

unlikely that any protest he could have lodged just prior to the eighth session would have altered the text of the French mandate which had been negotiated with difficulty and finally approved at the end of October. The clever diplomatic solution whereby the text of Louis' mandate was left as approved by King and pontiff but not distinctly read aloud in its entirety was negotiated at the marathon meeting of the sacred consistory on December twelfth which reviewed the materials to be treated in that session of the council. Lang was credited by Pio with playing a central role in these negotiations.[46] This decision of the consistory relieved Pio of the need to make an immediate protest that could only have embarrassed the pope and cardinals who had agreed to the distortions and misrepresentations contained therein. Ever since Leo's election Pio was busily engaged in securing active papal support for the war-effort against Venice and France. Alone or more often in the company of the Spanish ambassador Geronimo Vich and others, he entered into lengthy discussions with the pope in hopes of forging a new alliance directed primarily against Venice. By December the French, too, were bargaining with Leo for a rival league involving France, Venice, the Swiss, and Papal States. As a further complication Maximilian was treating with Louis for a marriage alliance between the Houses of Valois and Hapsburg which would have given the Austrians an uncontested dominance in Italy.[47] He was also proposing a nuptial contract between the pope's brother Giuliano de' Medici and a member of the imperial family. It was primarily for this purpose that Giuppo had been sent to Rome.[48] A public protest over distortions of historical fact could have hindered these already involved negotiations affecting future relations with the papacy and France. Prudence may have counseled

---

46. Letter of Pio to Maximilian, Roma, 3.I.1514, *Maximiliana*, 31, I, f. 10v; Letter of Vetori Lippomani, Roma, 18.XII.1513; SANUTO, *I Diarii*, XVII, 398. *

47. SANUTO, *Diarii*, XVI, 72, 148, 153, 172-73, 179, 216, 295, 481-82, XVII, 31, 47-48, 205, 353, 373; *Lettres du Roy Louis XII*, IV, 215, 230.

48. ULMANN, *Maximilian*, II, 485-87; Letter of Antonino Giuppo della Rovere to Leo X, from the imperial camp, 20-21.IX.1513, *Maximiliana*, 29, IV, ff. 86r, 86v-87r; Letter of Pio to Maximilian, Roma, 8.XI.1513, *Maximiliana*, 30, II, ff. 23v-24r.

* (See Addenda)

that a defense of the Emperor's reputation be done discreetly. Because the French mandate was submitted in its entirety for inclusion in the official acts of the Lateran Council, Pio formally requested the conciliar notaries and protonotaries to insert immediately after it his own rejoinder. The acts of the council published at Leo's command in 1521 contain the text of the French document; they do not, however, make even a passing reference to Pio's response.[49]

The failure to include Pio's *Protestatio* in the official acts of the Fifth Lateran Council admits various explanations. If it was deliberately suppressed, it may have been at the urgings of either Leo, who at the time of publication was feigning affection for France while concluding an offensive alliance with Charles V, or Pio, who was by then more sympathetic to the French than Germans.[50] The cardinal charged with editing the council's acts was Antonio del Monte, a former member of the papal commission which had approved the mendacious French mandate. The suppression of Pio's protest would not only have relieved him of possible embarrassment, but would also have been in keeping with his editorial policy of minimizing or eliminating from the record instances of discord.[51] The cardinal may also have argued that since Pio never delivered his speech on the floor of the council, it did not properly belong in the acts. But then this criterion was not evenly applied to other documents. A simpler explanation may be found in del Monte's lament that many of the documents he sought to include in the acts had already disappeared by the time he set about gathering them for publication.[52] Could one of those documents have been the much revised scribal draft of Pio's speech which until recently has gone unnoticed among the numerous manuscripts in the Vatican library?

This speech is presently bound in a collection of mostly

---

49. GUGLIA, *Studien zur Geschichte*, 20; PIO, *Protestatio*, f. 159r; MANSI, 832A-36B.
50. PASTOR-MERCATI, IV-II, 307; GUAITOLI, *Memorie sulla vita*, 229-34; F. NITTI, *Leone X e la sua politica: secondo documenti e carteggi inediti*, Firenze 1892, 405-38.
51. GUGLIA, *Studien zur Geschichte*, 9-13.
52. MANSI, 652D, 814D.

late sixteenth-century documents which are identified merely as *Raccolta di diverse scritture minute* and catalogued as *Manoscritti Chigiani*, L.III.60.[53] It is numbered entry 84 and foliated 158r-59v. On the back of this last folio appears the title *Protestatio contra oratores Regis Franciae per oratores Caesareae Majestatis facta in concilio di Laterano sotto Leone X*. The Latin and Italian parts of this title are written in different hands and colored inks: the vernacular apparently added by a later curator or owner in order to identify the particular council, while the Latin is in a hand similar to that with which the text of the speech was written. In the index of this codex, on folio 6r, entry 84 is listed as *Minuta dell'invettiva e protesta fatta nel concilio di Laterano sotto Leone X da gli oratori di Cesare contra il Re di Francia dove si parla del conciliabolo di Pisa*. This speech is written on paper measuring 29 by 21 centimeters. Folios 158r and 158v both contain 32 lines of text while 159r has only 9 lines. Additions and corrections appear interlinearly and in both right and left hand margins. Those few at the top or bottom of a folio are corrections of the neighboring line.

Three different principal hands seem to have contributed to the final text. A clear, humanistic script, in an almost printed form, provides the basic text and can probably be assigned to one of Pio's scribes. I have used this text as the basis of the transcription which follows, noting in the apparatus the various emendations. What has been identified as Pio's autograph by Myron P. Gilmore appears in a cursive and printed form in this document. The cursive with its distinctive *e*, *d*, and double *s* is written with a brown colored ink which varies from light to dark and is noted in the apparatus as hand *A*. A printed script which contains some of Pio's characteristic lettering appears in the notes as hand *B*. The final script, almost printed, to which is assigned the letter *C*, is apparently different from

---

53. In the Vatican Library's manuscript inventory of the *Fondo Chigi*, this codex is described as containing letters and various other writings from princes and prelates and orators of the sixteenth and seventeenth centuries and as having come from the library of the *principe* Chigi — *Mss. Chigiani Inventario*, Vol. III, fols. 814v-815r.

that of the scribe and Pio, corrects both of them and is not itself revised, and adds to the text elements of stylistic elegance. Hand C may belong to one of Pio's humanist friends who helped him polish the final text.

My transcription of these hands has not reproduced their differing orthographies but has standardized the spelling, avoided contractions and abbreviations, and modernized to some extent the use of capital letters and punctuation. In the apparatus, I have recorded first a normalized version of the words as they appear in the scribal text and have separated them with a colon from the emendations which follow.

Before concluding this section, I would like to acknowledge the gracious assistance I have received on this project. In addition to those mentioned earlier in my notes, I am grateful to the following for their expert help in resolving some of the more difficult problems posed by the text: Professor Augusto Campana of the Università di Roma; Rev. Joseph Cos, O.P., of the Leonine Commission; Msgr. José Ruysschaert, vice-prefect of the Bibliotheca Apostolica Vaticana; Professor Daniel J. Sheerin of the University of North Carolina; Dr. Virginia Brown of the Institute of Medieval Studies in Toronto; and Dr. Agostino Borromeo of the Università di Roma. I am also grateful to Frs. John O'Malley, S.J., of the University of Detroit and Robert Trisco of the Catholic University of America for their careful reading of the text and helpful suggestions for revision. Professor Myron P. Gilmore of Harvard University has encouraged this project from its beginnings. For her patient typings of the manuscript I am grateful to Mrs. Jane Steimel.

ADDENDA AND CORRIGENDA

p.276, line 25-6: 'his territory which had during his minority come into the *de facto* possession of his uncle Marco whose son Giberto later' should read 'the territory which belonged to his cousin and guardian Marco and then passed to his son Giberto who in 1490'.

p.281, n.46: 'of Vetori Lippomani' should read 'of Francesco Vetori to Pietro Lippomani'.

Mss. Chigiani L. III. 60 *Raccolta di Diverse Scritture Minute.*
Entry # 84, ff. 158r-159r.

Nostrarum quidem partium esse existimamus, pater [1] beatissime vosque caeteri amplissimi patres,[2] cum hic apud sanctitatem vestram et hanc sacratissimam sedem sacrae caesareae majestatis [3] oratorem agamus, defendere quaecumque aut agantur [4] aut dicantur contra [5] honorem commoda aut [6] dignitatem ipsius majestatis. Quamobrem neutrique silentio dissimulandum fuit, quod hic in conspectu [7] vestrae beatitudinis et hujus sacratissimi consessus recitari audivimus procuratorium serenissimi Franciae regis, in quo inter caetera nonnulla dicta sunt, quae et taxare et calumniari caesaream majestatem, involutis quibusdam verbis [8] satis tamen expressis, videntur.[9] Quod profecto indigne nimis et injuste factum est, quando caesarea majestas, cum huic sacrosancto concilio adhaesit, etsi arguendi et calumniandi ipsum serenissimum Franciae regem et plurimos alios non falso magna [10] materia et facultas [11] ei offerretur,[12] neminem tamen lacescere [13] voluit,[14] ut est summae modestiae [15] praeter caeteras heroicas virtutes princeps. Silentioque potius [16] plurima [17] vera, et

1. pater: por (pastor?) *A.*
2. patres: antistites *A.*
3. sacrae caesareae majestatis: *cancell. et in marg.* caesareae majestatis semper augustae *A.*
4. agantur: fiant *B.*
5. contra: praeter *A.*
6. aut: *cancell. et novem ordinem verborum ind.* b - commoda, a - dignitatem *A.*
7. conspectu: con- *rep. sed cancell.*
8. quibusdam verbis: *inter verba inser.* prima specie *B.*
9. expressis videntur: *inter verba inser. in marg.* si quis diligentius attendat *A.*
10. magna: multiplex *C.*
11. et facultas: *inter verba inser.* magna *C.*
12. etsi arguendi ... ei offerretur: *cancell. sed postea rest. et in marg. scrips. sed etiam cancell.* quamvis suppeteret amplissimus obloquendi campus cum de aliis plurimis tum de ipso serenissimo Franciae rege *A.*
13. lacescere: *corr.* lacessere *A.*
14. voluit: sustinuit *A.*
15. summae modestiae: *inter verba inser.* ac divinae *A.*
16. silentioque potius: *inter verba inser. sed cancell.* involvit (?) *A.*
17. plurima: permulta quae erraverunt perlate (?) *A.*

III

quae[18] ab re sua non[19] fuissent, praeterire maluit[20] quam verbis[21] quemque provocare. Cujus rei locupletissimus testis est universus hic sacratissimus consessus. Nunc autem recitatum est ipsum serenissimum Francorum regem huic sacrosancto concilio adhaerere decrevisse, cum perspexerit et caesaream majestatem illi adhaesisse, cum qua una[22] et concilium (ut verbis ipsius utar) praetensum Pisanum, quod tamen verius nedum[23] conciliabulum sed[24] satanae synagoga appellari potuisset.[25] Quod si adductus[26] ipse eius exemplo[27] hoc perfecit,[28] profecto plurimum gaudebit caesarea majestas,[29] quod non solum ipse pio officio et principi Christianissimo convenienti[30] satisfecerit, verum et principes illos aut[31] reges, qui a recta via aberraverant, qui ab unitate ecclesiae[32] recesserant, suo exemplo[33] resipiscere fecerit, et ad piissimum sanctissimae matris gremium redire coegerit. Verum majestas sua[34] numquam fatebitur (cum id omnimo a veritate alienum sit) ut[35] conciliabulum illud Pisanum, ejus voto[36] et auctoritate, a cardinalibus fuisse indictum, nec[37] postquam indictum fuerat, in illud[38] consensisse.[39] Non fuit tamen opinione aliena majestas sua, a rege Franciae sollicitatus,[40] quin ex usu esset

18. quae: *cancell.*
19. ab re sua non: caesareis (?) si *et in marg. inser. sed cancell.* rebus caesareis plurimum praeferrendis (?) *A.*
20. praeterire maluit: *cancell.*
21. quam verbis: *subscrips. et inser. inter verba sed A, et alia verba postea cancell. et obsc.* ut dixi tacere malim (?) *A.*
22. cum qua una: *cancell.* cum *et inter alia verba inser.* cum approbavit (?) *A.*
23. nedum: quam (?) *A.*
24. sed: *cancell.*
25. potuisset. Quod: *inter verba inser. sed postea cancell.* probavit (?) *C* (?)
26. adductus: secutus *A.*
27. exemplum: exemplo *A.*
28. perfecit: profecit *A* (?)
29. majestas: augustissimus *A.*
30. Christianissimo convenienti: *inter verba inser. in marg.* qualis ipse est *A, et 'convenienti' mut. in* consentaneo *A.*
31. aut: et *A.*
32. ecclesiae recesserant: *inter verba inser.* Romanae *B.*
33. suo exemplo: sua pietate et authoritate *C.*
34. sua: caesarea *A.*
35. ut: *ras. aut in atramento pallido.*
36. eius voto: ex ejus nutu *C* (?)
37. nec: et *C* (?)
38. illud: ipsum *A.*
39. in illud consensisse: *cancell. et in marg. inser. sed postea cancell.* illi acquievisse (?) *A.*
40. a rege Franciae sollicitatus: rege Franciae urgiter sollicitante *A.*

reipublicae Christianae, ut concilium oeconomicum [!] celebraretur. Quapropter judicavit opportunum[41] ut et illud indiceretur, sed ut rite et more[42] maiorum id fieret[43] semper censuit, monito et requisito summo[44] pontifici nostro Julio felicis recordationis sanctitatis vestrae praedecessore. Quod re ipsa ostendit, quoniam, eo indicto[45] et incepto, mox illi adhaesit, et omnia acta conciliabuli Pisani quantum in se[46] erat damnavit et improbavit, irritavitque[47] et revocavit, quaecumque etiam circa indictionem conciliabuli,[48] ut regi[49] Franciae morem gereret, concesserat.[50] Quod si eius exemplo rex Franciae movebatur, id tunc[51] facere debuisset anno iam transacto, cum reverendissimus ac illustrissimus dominus cardinalis Gurcensis eius locumtenens generalis et ad hoc procurator specialis, in[52] hoc sanctissimo loco, verbis suae majestatis sacrosancto huic concilio adhaesit. Sic omnes arbitrarentur quaecumque ab eo[53] antea facta fuissent[54] errore ductum fecisse. Caeterum omnibus notum est: quis de indicendo conciliabulo primus verba fecerit; ad quem cardinales confugerint; cujus nutu et auspiciis congregatum fuerit conciliabulum; quales praelati[55] in eo interfuerint, Germanine an Galli; quis illud foverit; cujus armis Bononia fuerit occupata; quis tyrannos et rebelles ecclesiae in fidem et tutelam suam receperit.[56] Cladem Ravennatem omitto, ne vestrae beatitudinis invidiam[57] in aliquem commovere velle videar. Si recenserem[58] quaenam pro ecclesia sancta Dei, cujus

41. opportunum: *cancell. et in marg. inser.* optimum factum *A*.
42. sed ut rite et more: rite tamen et more *A*.
43. fieret: fieri debere *B*.
44. requisito summo: *inter verba inser.* in primis *C* (?)
45. eo indicto: *inter verba inser.* per ipsum *B*.
46. se: ipso *A*.
47. irritavitque: cancellavitque *A*.
48. quaecumque ... conciliabuli: quodcumque procuratorium ad indicendum concilium *C*.
49. ut regi: *inter verba inser.* serenissimo *A*.
50. concesserat: inconcessisset *A*.
51. tunc: *cancell.*
52. specialis in: *inter verba inser.* qui et dignitatis hujus sanctae sedis acerrimus defensor fuerat *C*.
53. ab eo: *cancell.*
54. facta fuissent: fecisset eum *A*.
55. quales prelati: *inter verba inser.* aut qui tandem *A*.
56. quis tyrannos ... receperit: *cancell. sed rest., et in marg. scrips.* sed postea *cancell.* multa hic praetereo *A*.
57. invidiam: *cancell. sed rest.*
58. recenserem: recensere velim *A*.

III

tunc summum fastigium ascendere meruisti, cum tot et tanta [59] perpessus sis, ut illam et hanc sanctam sedem a crudelissimis hostibus et saevissimis perduelionibus defenderes.[60] Haec omnia omitto, ne in calumniam alicujus [61] ea dicere existimer, cum neminem verbis lacessere mihi sit animus,[62] sed tantum ea dicere, quae ad defendendum caesareae majestatis honorem pertinent. Haec inquam non minus impie quam imprudenter facta non ab exercitu caesareae majestatis, non a Germanis facta sunt, nec unus quidem ex natione Germanica repertus est, qui particeps conciliabuli esse voluerit, tanta est illius gentis erga hanc sanctam sedem observantia. Quantum autem caesar sollicitatus fuerit, quam magnae ei fuerint factae pollicitationes ut in hoc nephandissimo [63] bello conspiraret, optimi testes esse possunt nonnulli reverendissimi cardinales qui hic praesentes [64] adsunt. Numquam tamen a pietatis officio et a devotione [65] hujus sanctae sedis dimoveri potuit. Res ipsa testatur. Vos inquam appello amplissimi patres, te summum pastorem et (?) Christi vicarium.[66] Res ipsa loquitur. In quanto nam [67] discrimine versabatur res ecclesiastica,[68] si impiis consiliis et coeptis aliorum caesar [69] consentire [70] voluisset. Verum non modo assentiri noluit, sed ut optimus advocatus et fidissimus ecclesiae protector [71] toto animo, summis viribus, omnibus modis ecclesiam opprimere conantibus se objecit.[72] Cujus virtute, ductu, imperio (absit invidia verbo), vestra etiam sapientia et divina opitulante clementia, res ecclesiastica [73] e magno naufragio et tempestate in portum salutis reducta est; et hostes iam supplices undique ad implorandam veniam ad pedes vestrae beatitudinis pro-

---

59. tanta perpessus: *inter verba inser.* constantissimo animo *C*.
60. a crudelissimis ... defenderes: ab hostibus saevissimis et impiis defenderes *C*.
61. in calumniam alicujus: in calumniandi studio *A*.
62. animus: in animo *A*.
63. nephandissimo: plus quam crudeli (?) *A*.
64. praesentes: coram *B*.
65. devotione huius: *inter verba inser. in marg.* et caritate *B*.
66. te summum ... vicarium: te summum pontificem et Christi vicem *A*: te summe pontifex qui Christi vice in terris geris *C*.
67. nam: *cancell. et in marg. inser.* adhuc *A*.
68. versabatur res ecclesiastica: versare fides orthodoxa *B*.
69. aliorum caesar: *inter verba inser.* Christiano nomine indignis *A*.
70. consentire: accedere *A*.
71. protector toto: *inter verba inser. in marg.* et vindex *A et sup. lin.* opportuno tempore *A*.
72. obiecit: *cancell. et in marg.* opposuit *A*.
73. res ecclesiastica: navicula Petri *C*.

strati accedunt. Quapropter, et laudandus esse videtur serenissimus rex Franciae, qui si errore aut alio quovis modo ductus in hanc sanctam sedem deliquerit, pie tamen resipiscit, et spreto conciliabulo, erroribus [74] et pessimis consiliis, in hoc verum et sacrosanctum, rite, et more majorum indictum concilium consentit et colla huic sanctae sedi et beatitudini vestrae submittit. Praeterea, hoc sibi persuadeat beatitudo vestra, tantam esse devotionem et summam observantiam majestatis caesareae erga hanc sanctam sedem et beatitudinem vestram ut semper ea praestaturus sit, quae ab optimo advocato et a pientissimo et reverendissimo filio beatitudinis vestrae et hujus sanctae sedis praestari debent. Hicque coram sanctitate vestra et hoc sacratissimo[75] consessu[76] nos oratores majestatis suae profitemur et protestamur majestatem suam numquam consensisse in his, quae adversus hanc sanctam sedem per indicentes conciliabulum et foventes illud facta sunt. Rogamusque singulos [77] prothonotarios ac [78] notarios hic praesentes,[79] praecipue autem illos quibus demandata est cura notandi acta concilii, ut hujusce nostrae defensionis, responsionis, ac protestationis, unum vel plura conficiant instrumenta.

74. conciliabulo erroribus: *inter verba inser.* subterhabitisque B.
75. sacratissimo: sacratissimorum A.: *sed postea cancell.* sacr.
76. consessu: coetu C *et in marg. add.* amplissimorum patrum A.
77. Rogamusque singulos: *inter verba inser.* universos et A.
78. ac: et B.
79. hic praesentes: quinam adsunt A: *cancell.* 'adsunt' *et in marg. add.* intersunt nostro sermoni A.

IV

CONCEPTS OF REFORM PROPOSED AT THE FIFTH LATERAN COUNCIL [1]

Summarium. — Ex ideis quae quinto Concilio Lateranensi de reformanda Ecclesia proponebantur, elucet quae fuerit mens hierarchiae italicae et hispanicae in pervigilia « Reformationis ». 25 schemata individualia vel collectiva crisi subiciuntur et inter se comparantur. Imprimis quaeritur, quomodo auctores reformationem requisitam intellexerint, quas origines malorum viderint, quales causas ad reformationem proposuerint. Ex hoc studio fontium apparet permultos tunc temporis de reformanda Ecclesia sincero animo sollicitos fuisse. Eis persuasum erat Ecclesiam divinas punitiones subituram esse, videlicet aggressionem islamicam, schisma haeresimque, nisi reformatio perficeretur.

Historians today recognize that reform within Renaissance Catholicism was not merely a reaction to the challenge of Luther but was also the natural outgrowth of a call to reform found throughout Western Christendom after the healing of the Great Western Schism. Frequently cited as examples of pre-Reformation attempts at renewal are the *Devotio Moderna*, Observantism, the efforts of such humanists as Colet and Erasmus and of such prelates as Ximenes and Nicholas of Cusa. Given slight attention is the work of the Fifth Lateran Council (1512-1517) [2].

---

[1] I would like to express my gratitude to Heiko Oberman of Tübingen University for having directed me in the initial stages of this research, to Samuel Miller of Boston College for having guided this work to completion, and to John O'Malley, S. J., of the University of Detroit for having helped me prepare this article for publication. Whatever deficiencies are found herein, however, are to be attributed solely to my own limitations.

[2] The del Monte edition of the official acts of the Council is published in *Sacrorum conciliorum nova et amplissima collectio*, edited by John Dominic Mansi and certain Florentine and Venetian editors, Paris 1902, Vol. 32 (1438-1549), col. 649-1002. Hereafter this will be cited as « M ». A number of the Council's decrees have been published in *Bullarum Diplomatum et Privilegiorum Sanctorum Romanorum Pontificum*, Taurinensis editio, Turin 1860, Vol. 5 (1431-1521), pp. 534-684, hereafter cited as « *Bull. Rom.* » Other printed primary materials can be found in *Opuscula Varia ad Conc. Latera.* (Romae, n. d.) in the Vatican Library. Most of the pertinent sections of the diary of the papal Master of Ceremonies, Paris de Grassis, are printed in *Beiträge zur politischen kirchlichen und Cultur-Geschichte der Sechs Letzten Jahrhunderte*, ed. J. I. VON DÖL-

Lateran V treated at length the problem of reform. Convoked to undermine the politico-ecclesiastical reform Synod of Pisa, the Council was formally assigned the task of renewal by Julius II:

> For we hope, the Lord helping, in this sacred Lateran synod to weed out completely the thorns and brambles from the field of the Lord; to lead morals back to a better state of virtue, and finally to decree an expedition against the enemies of the faith who are at variance among themselves ... [3]

Although the Council's decrees failed to effect significant reform, the sixteen speeches delivered in the Lateran halls, several written proposals, and a few fragments of consistorial speeches provide us with a unique picture of reform sentiment in the highest echelons of the Church during the five years immediately preceeding the Wittenberg theses.

A number of interesting discoveries and questions emerge from a careful examination of these documents. These proposals would seem to indicate a widely accepted sentiment in favor of reform. What is perhaps more surprising is the ease with which their authors could paint the blackest picture of the conditions in Christendom while producing little if any empirical evidence

---

LINGER, Vienna 1882, Vol. 3, 413-431. Many useful documents can be found in Caesar Baronius, Odocius Raynaldus, and Jacobus Laderchii, *Annales Ecclesiastici*, ed. THEINER, Paris 1877, Vols. 30 and 31. Hereafter this will be cited as « Raynaldus » with the year and number reference given.

Although a number of new books on the Council are presently in preparation, the best secondary materials thus far published are sections of larger works or articles. The best of these remains the sections in HEFELE-LECLERCQ, *Histoire des Conciles d'après les documents originaux* VIII-I, Paris 1917, 297-572. Also useful are Vols. 5-13, but especially 7 and 8, of L. PASTOR, *The History of the Popes from the Close of the Middle Ages*, St. Louis 1891 ff.; Vols. 4 and 5 of MANDELL CREIGHTON, *A History of the Papacy from the Great Schism to the Close of Rome*, New York 1897; R. AUBENAS and R. RICARD, *L'Eglise et la Renaissance (1449-1517)*, Paris 1951, 163-189, which is Vol. 15 of Fliche-Martin, *Histoire de l'Eglise;* and Vol. 1 of H. JEDIN, *A History of the Council of Trent*, New York 1957, 127-138. A good brief article on the Council is that by F. VERNET, *Latran (Ve Concile Oecuménique du)*: DThC VIII-II, 2667-2686. For a summary of some of the official speeches and decrees, confer: F. DITTRICH, *Beiträge zur Geschichte der katholischen Reformation im ersten Drittel des 16. Jahrhunderts. Das V. Lateran-Concil und Leo X*: Hist. Jahrbuch 5 (1884) 319-398. A treatment of the inner workings of the Council is offered by E. GUGLIA, *Studien zur Geschichte des V. Laterankonzils (1512-1517)*: Sitzungsberichte der Philosophisch-Historischen Classe der Kaiserlichen Akademie der Wissenschaften 140 (1899), X, 1-34, while 152 (1905-06), III, 1-50 provides a history of the reform bull's origins and fortunes during and after the Council. Two specialized but helpful recent works are: FELIX GILBERT, *Cristianesimo, Umanesimo e la Bolla ' Apostolici Regiminis ' del 1513*: Rivista Storica Italiana 79 (1967) 976-990; and JOHN W. O'MALLEY, *Giles of Viterbo on Church and Reform: A Study in Renaissance Thought* (Leiden, 1968).

[3] M 667D; Raynaldus, 1512, N⁰ 42; and Appendix 1 of this article.

IV

as proof of their assertions. The parade of stock phrases, the general failure to prescribe detailed remedies, the frequency of what seems to be obvious exaggerations, and the argument by rhetoric force the twentieth-century reader to question the actual extent of the evils. While not doubting the presence of moral weakness in the Church or the sincerity of the speakers, one wonders if the Council Fathers were not victims of « reform hysteria ». Confronted by no scientific data, whether historical or sociological, was it not all too easy to believe and declaim that the Church was without charity, deathly sick, extinct?

As interesting as this question is, the direct intent of the following analysis will be to identify the various concepts of reform proposed at the Fifth Lateran Council. Attention will be given to the various ecclesiologies and eschatologies which underlaid these proposals and to their differing views on the essential nature of reform, its agencies, means, motivation, and goal. Special effort has been made to identify any texts which mention doctrinal abberations.

In their personal addresses to the Council the two popes, Julius II (1503-1513) who convoked Lateran V and Leo X (1513-1521) who guided it to its conclusion, asserted the necessity of reform.

In his brief address read at the opening session, Julius outlined his conceptions of the Council and of the tasks it faced [4]. His references to the Council as his best means of effecting reform and his assigning the Fathers the sole practical function of offering advice would seem to indicate that he espoused a theory of papal supremacy over the Council. This assertion of papal supremacy, however, may have been prompted by practical rather than theoretical considerations. He was reported to have feared at first a rebuke from the conciliar Fathers for having delayed in fulfilling his election pledges to reform the Church [5]. To prevent this he carefully controlled the personnel and machinery of the Council, thus giving a certain reality to the theory of supremacy [6].

In his speech Julius both praised the Council and exhorted its members. The most important affairs of the day he entrusted to the Council « from which all good things come ». Its scope

---

[4] The extant text of this speech is contained in Appendix 1 of this article.

[5] The papal Master of Ceremonies reported a comment by Julius to the effect that he feared going to the Council as a boy going to school fears the teacher's rod; confer: de Grassis, *Diarium*, 418, 423-424.

[6] Raynaldus, 1513, N° 27, 1512, N° 42; M 696D-697B; GUGLIA, *Studien* 140 (1899), x, 33-34.

was to range from the restoration of peace and convocation of a crusade to the healing of schism and the reform of morals. He pleaded with the conciliar Fathers to join with him in prayer and consultation. And let all realize, he warned, that the world is watching their efforts and judging whether they have neglected any possible areas of reform.

The work of the Council he envisioned as including the calling back of the lost sheep and the ending of the recent heresy (the Pisan schism). He fully acknowledged the neglected condition of the « Lord's field » and closed his speech with the traditional rhetoric of reform:

> Not only has ecclesiastical discipline turned far from its proper course, but every institution of human life has collapsed and a great upheaval of morals has occurred in every age group and social class. This being the case, we are able to hope that we will return, through this holy synod legitimately gathered in the Holy Spirit, to the norm, and from harmful ways to the rule. Evil customs will be eradicated, good ones planted, the seedlings of virtue will prevail, and the field of the Lord, having been cleansed of thorns and weeds, will produce richer fruit in proportion to the care and greater diligence spent in its cultivation.

Reform then for Julius consists in a return to a norm or rule, a restoration of discipline and of morals. He spoke only in the most general terms: particular problems were never identified nor were any solutions proposed. This refusal to descend into particulars may have been dictated by his desire to leave such things for the consideration of the conciliar Fathers or may also have been necessitated either by his ignorance of the details involved in the work of reform or by his concern not to create false expectations by committing himself to a reform program which he had no intentions of executing.

At the first session Julius personally spoke a few words to the Council Fathers. Taking as his theme « You have come together, Fathers », the pope exhorted them to reflect on and seek eagerly those things which pertain to the peace and welfare of the Church, a termination of the schism, peace among Christian princes, a crusade against the infidels, and a reformation of the Church. That he went into any detailed elaboration of the Council's reform agenda at this time is unlikely and his words not recorded in the official acts [7]. His interest in the cause of reform does not seem to have extended beyond establishing a formal reform commission to examine complaints and

---

[7] Raynaldus, 1512, N° 38; M 680D.

having the Council reaffirm his 1505 prohibition against simony in papal elections and his apostolic letters published March 30, 1512 against certain malpractices in the Curia. Julius' prime concern was defeating the Pisan Synod and strengthening papal authority. Concern for reform was subordinate to, if not a means to, this end — in spite of his fine-sounding words to the opening session [8].

The reform thought of Julius' successor, Leo X, is difficult to ascertain, the evidence piecemeal. At the sixth session the new pope had a bull read which proclaimed his intense pastoral concern for the proper cultivation of the Lord's field and his eagerness to use the general Council as a means to this end. He then personally addressed the Council Fathers, assuring them that as Julius had convoked this Council so that « the state of the Church might be reformed for the better » so too would he now continue the Council to bring about « a reformation of the City and world, and peace and quiet in the Christian Republic ». This brief, very general, and inadequate statement of Leo's thought at the time is all that is recorded [9]. Other conciliar documents indirectly provide similiar glimpses into the mind of the pope on reform [10]. The fragmentary remarks of Riario, however, reveal a bit more. Leo is pictured as not content with the reform of the curial officials carried out by Julius and determined that his reform of the Church would begin first with the Curia. To secure this end Leo had the Council Fathers elect representatives for membership in the reform commission, personally attended the meetings of its particular congregations, and saw to it that delays and difficulties were minimized [11]. When hostilities between the bishops and the cardinals allied with the mendicants threatened to stymie the Council's work of reform, Leo acted as conciliator [12].

A brief address to the Council Fathers seems to have immediately followed the speech read in the name of Julius at the opening of the Council [13]. Contained in it are some of the first conciliar statements on reform. A great disintegration and collapse is said to have occurred primarily in the « ecclesiastical

---

[8] *Bull. Rom.*, Leo X, V, N° 2, p. 571; M 768A-772B, 753A-B, 772E; JEDIN, *Council of Trent* I, 127; HEFELE-LECLERCQ VIII-I, 340, n. 2.

[9] Raynaldus, 1513, N° 24; DE GRASSIS, *Diarium* 418; M 783A, 788D.

[10] Confer: M 815C-817A, 794D, 845D-846E, 874D-875A, 907D-E; *Bull. Rom.*, Leo X, V, N° 2, 4, pp. 571-572.

[11] Confer below, footnote 10 of Appendix N° 9.

[12] Raynaldus, 1513. N° 97.

[13] The extant text of this speech is contained in Appendix N° 2 of this article.

order ». Heresies infect the Church, while internal evils and vices close at hand beset us. Let this evil be taken from our midst, our hearts be converted to Christ, and our good works shine before men. Let us do truth in charity and thus build up the Church which is united by love in Christ its head (Eph. 4: 15-16). The Council is described as the most efficacious remedy for the correction of morals and the restoration of good and ancient institutions. This Council, the great ornament of our times, is to lend its authority and assistance to the pope to whom Christ has committed the care of all souls and the offices of judging, teaching, and ruling all the faithful. The speaker, thus, thought that reform was needed; he was very vague in identifying the evils or their particular remedies (reform rhetoric?) and saw the Council as an agent of reform, but subordinate to the pope who has care of the Church. Noteworthy in the speech is the emphasis on Christ and a frequent use of biblical expressions.

The single major extant source of those reform concepts proposed for the consideration of the Fifth Lateran Council are the conciliar speeches given at the opening of each session. Thirteen in number, they offer a good cross section of the views of the various conciliar Fathers. Among the speakers were to be found a future pope, a future martyr, the leading theologian of the day, the reforming general of a large religious order, a tutor to kings, a secretary to a curial cardinal, a member of the Curia, a Knight of Rhodes, a prince-humanist, and a battle-tested bishop from Dalmatia. Common to most of the speakers was birth in Italy, a humanistic [14] background, and conviction that the Church was in need of some reform.

The first and most famous speech was given at the solemn opening of the Council (May 3, 1512) by Giles Antonini of Viterbo (1469-1532) [15] whose eloquent pleas for reform brought tears

---

[14] Although scholars disagree on the precise meaning of the term « humanism » and its variants, they do acknowledge that Renaissance humanism had something to do with the study of classical literature and civilization. Only this very general meaning is intended by the use of the term in this paper. For an excellent précis of the scholarly debates over the term, confer: William J. BOUWSMA, *The Interpretation of Renaissance Humanism*, 2d. ed., N° 18 of the AHA Pamphlet Series published by the Service Center for Teachers of History (Washington 1966).

[15] Entering the Augustinian Eremites in 1488, Giles later studied at Padua whose Aristotelian philosophers he later opposed and at Florence where he became an enthusiastic disciple of Ficino's Platonism. A skilled philologist, man of letters, noted cabalist, Scripture scholar, popular preacher, and leading reformer, he became chief administrator of the Augustinians (1506-1518) and later served as papal ambassador, bishop of Viterbo, and cardinal. Among his

to the eyes of the conciliar Fathers, as de Grassis and Sadoleto report.[16]

From the outset of his speech Giles cast his theology of reform into an historico-metaphysical framework. Reminding his listeners that for the last twenty years he had preached throughout Italy an imminent eschatological purification to be followed by a final renovation, Giles exclaimed that his prophecy was giving way to fulfillment: « my eyes have seen the salvific and sacred beginning of the expected restoration. »[17] The golden age was now returning to the Church.

Giles's theory of reform, which seems to have incorporated Hesiodic, patristic, Joachimite, and cabalistic schemes, took the first age of the Church, from Christ to the time of Constantine, as the exemplar of perfection and predicted that the Church of the tenth or last age would resemble its reputed holiness by being also poor, pure, ascetical, and spiritual. Using the metaphysical principle of decreasing strength the further the distance from the exemplar source, Giles envisioned the present ninth age as one of greatest decay.[18] Reform then which ushers in the last or golden age will be achieved not by innovations in divinely ordained doctrines and institutions, such as were attempted by Arius, Sabellius, and Photinus,[19] but by a conscious effort to recall a « fallen religion to its pristine purity, ancient light, original splendor, and to its sources, » and to « restore charity, once washed of every committed sin, to its ancient splendor and cleanness. »[20] In its most concise expression, Giles's principle of reform was: « It is a divine command that

---

important writings were: « Sententiae ad mentem Platonem », « Historia xx saeculorum, » *Scechina,* and his speech before the Fifth Lateran. Confer: J. O'MALLEY, *Giles of Viterbo,* esp. 4-8, 40-66, 74-88, 168-170; also his *Historical Thought and the Reform Crisis of the Early Sixteenth Century:* Theological Studies 28 (1967) 531-548; FRANCIS X. MARTIN, *Giles of Viterbo and the Monastery of Lecceto: the Making of a Reformer:* Augustiniana 12 (1962) 225-253; and his *The Registers of Giles of Viterbo:* ibid. 142-160, see also E. GARIN, *Italian Humanism: Philosophy and Civic Life in the Renaissance,* Oxford 1965, 88-94, 113; H. HURTER, *Nomenclator Literarius* II, 1215-1216, N° 572; J. W. O'MALLEY, *Giles of Viterbo: A Reformer's Thought on Renaissance Rome:* Renaissance Quarterly 22 (1967) 1-77.

[16] M 668D; *Vat. lat.* 12269, fol. 525ᵛ; see quote in O'MALLEY, *Giles of Viterbo* 14, n. 3.
[17] M 669B-C.
[18] O'MALLEY, *Giles of Viterbo* 104-117, 139-142.
[19] M 671A-B.
[20] M 669C, 676A-C: « ablui potius ab omnibus conceptis maculis, et in antiquum splendorem munditiamque restitui. »

* (See Addenda)

men be changed by sacred things, not the sacred things by men. »[21]

Giles drew an intimate connection between the holding of councils and the vitality of the Church. All reality he divided into three categories: the divine which is unchanging, the sempiternal celestial bodies which return from their wanderings and are restored, and those transitory things which are destined to die. These latter, such as the human body, are either continually restored, as with food, or else suffer swift destruction. Into this category Giles seems to place the Church. Unless she is continually renovated by a return to the past under the care of synods, she is unable to function properly.[22] « Indeed, without synods we are unable to be saved. »[23] So essential are councils, that « as often as synods have ceased to be held, that often do we see the divine bride deserted by the Spouse. »[24] During this time of abandonment, the Church suffers a litany of evils and only when, responding to the admonitions of the Spirit, the Fathers again hasten to a synod, are these evils corrected and does the bride revive. Now that the winter of the Song of Songs has passed, the bride rises up and beholds the Groom Who had said, « In a short time you will no longer see me, and then a short time later you will see me again. »[25] Although Christ withdraws from the Church, he does so only temporarily, and the waves of wickedness which beat against the bark of Peter while Christ sleeps do not actually submerge it. The institutional Church is clearly meant in this context due to accompanying references to her authority and majesty. In another rhetorical passage, Giles refers to the Church as having died (*extinctae ecclesiae*) and then calls upon Julius to restore it to life by the synod. While the essential holiness of the Church seems to be called into question by Giles, he did not opt for a spiritual and interior church in the face of a temporarily sinful institution.[26]

As is evident from the preceding statements, councils hold a central position in Giles's reform thought. Nothing is more efficacious; indeed, they have saved the Church in the past. For

---

[21] O'MALLEY, *Giles of Viterbo* 139-141; M 669C: « homines per sacra immutari fas est, non sacra per homines ... »

[22] M 669E-670A; O'MALLEY, *Giles of Viterbo* 142.

[23] M 670C: « Atqui sine synodis stare non potest fides: absque synodis igitur salvi esse non possumus. »

[24] M 670A: « quoties a synodis habendis cessatum est, toties vidimus divinam sponsam a sponso derelictam ... »

[25] M 670B-D; Song of Songs 2:11; St. John 16:16.

[26] M 670B, 674A; F. X. MARTIN, *The Problem of Giles: A historiographical survey*: Augustiniana 10 (1960) 58.

Giles the Council is « the fear of the wicked, the hope of the honorable, the banishment of errors, the source and restoration of virtue, by which the deceit of demons is overcome, illicit inclinations are removed, reason retakes its lost citadel, and justice returning from heaven is restored to the earth »[27] — in short, it is the « single medicine for all evils. »[28] That in spite of such praeconia Giles did not espouse some form of the conciliar thesis must be proven from his other writings — but even in these he does not directly confront the issue.[29]

Joining forces with St. Jerome this time, Giles identified one of the major sources of the evils which afflict the Church — « the times of Constantine, which insofar as they added much splendor and ornament to the sacred things, so also did they enervate strictness in morals and life... »[30]. Ecclesiastical wealth, then, in his theology of reform is a cause of corruption. With St. Jerome he seems to imply that the practice of monastic virtues will bring about the reform of the Church.

While the golden light of the last age was dawning on the horizon, Giles looked about and saw everywhere evils which in their extent and intensity clearly indicated that the Church had not as yet left the ninth age. Never before was life softer, ambition more petulant, cupidity more inflamed, license more impudent, boldness in speaking, disputing, and writing against piety more frequent or carried on with greater security. Never did the people have a greater neglect and even contempt for sacred things, the sacraments, the keys of authority, and precepts of the saints. Never before was the Christian religion and faith more openly held up to the derision of the rabble. In such times truth is set upon by the fury of heretics. The boldness of wicked men rages against the laws, authority and majesty of the Church. Schism, war, force, plunder, slaughter, adultery, incest — every evil infects both sacred and profane alike[31].

Giles's analysis of the situation is certainly exaggerated at times by humanistic rhetorical flourishes. His chief emphasis is in the area of morals. References to heresy and derisions of

---

[27] M 673A.
[28] M 675E.
[29] O'MALLEY, *Giles of Viterbo* 121, 174-175.
[30] M 670A. On Jerome's view of Constantine, confer: GERHART LADNER, *The Idea of Reform: Its Impact on Christian Thought and Action in the Age of the Fathers*, Cambridge (Mass.) 1959, 152, n. 57. According to Giles, it was the misuse of this wealth and subsequent greed, selfishness, and gradual loss of former fervor which caused the decline of the Church from the second to ninth ages; confer: O'MALLEY, *Giles of Viterbo* 104-117.
[31] M 675B-C, 670B.

the faith are directed possibly against the Turks but more than likely against the Averroist and Alexandrine schools of Aristotelianism. Philosophy is made the villain at Nicea. And in his other writings he singles out philosophy as the cause of innumerable heresies and calamities which afflict the Church [32].

Any attempt to tag certain attitudes cited here and in other speeches as being « pagan » because of their reputed irreverence and criticism of certain aspects of religion is a bit precipitous. The evidence at our disposal indicates that the vast majority of the critics of organized religion, such as Erasmus and More, were quite Christian in their outlook. Even the accounts of contemporary writers must be approached with great caution since such labeling was a favorite device of sixteenth-century polemics [33]. Thus certain outspoken humanists and Aristotelian philosophers who aroused the wrath of some of the conciliar orators were readily denounced as impious, irreverent, disrespectful, and irreligious. It is also important to realize that many things written by the ancient pagans do not contradict Christian truths and that the teachings of Christianity can be expressed in literary terms and figures borrowed from pagan philosophy and mythology without thereby adopting the doctrinal errors of classical paganism. It is quite possible that certain Renaissance critics of humanism failed to make these essential distinctions.

According to Giles the principal human agents of this Church reform are the pope and the conciliar Fathers. God has chosen Julius as His vicar on earth, begged and requested him to call a Council, and even miraculously restored his health that he might restore life to a dead Church by a most holy synod. Giles closely associated the conciliar Fathers with the pope and addressed now the pope, now the Fathers with a plea for ecclesiastical reformation. To Julius, however, he seemed to assign the task of bringing peace, while to the Fathers the actual reform of the Church [34].

The major motives which should impel these Churchmen to undertake this reform are three in kind: the warning voices of God heard in the recent events of history, the threat of a Moslem takeover as a punishment, and the supplications of the whole Christian people [35].

---

[32] M 671A; O'MALLEY, *Giles of Viterbo* 33, 44-46, 188-189.
[33] P. KRISTELLER, *Renaissance Thought: Classical, Scholastic, and Humanistic Strains*, New York 1961, 70-91.
[34] M 673D-674B, 675D-676C.
[35] M 675B-E, 674D, 675A, 676A-C.

Giles is very weak in practical suggestions on what specific remedies the Fathers should adopt. In one section he tells Julius not to trust in armies and weapons. « Our arms, however, are piety, religion, probity, supplications, prayers, the breastplate of faith, the armor of light, to use the words of the apostle »[36]. Prayers for help are to be directed in particular to Sts. Peter and Paul. In speaking of the Fathers of the ancient councils, he digressed briefly to assert the importance of having holy men appointed to the episcopacy. Beyond this, Giles indulged in the generalities of rooting out vice and planting virtue[37]. Thus, when it came down to the practical order on how to effect reform, Giles was weak and covered up with generalities his lack of a constructive, detailed program of renewal such as we shall see in Giustiniani and Quirini.

On May 10, 1512, one week after the official opening of the Council, Bernard II Zanni († 1514)[38], Archbishop (1503-1514) of Spalato (modern-day Split), addressed the Fathers assembled in their first session. By birth, training, intelligence, first-hand knowledge of some of the conditions of the Church in Rome and Dalmatia, and experience as a reform-minded prelate, Bernard was the obvious choice of Julius for speaker on this solemn occasion.

Because he had been a forceful and effective advocate of reform in his own diocese, Bernard's speech before the reform Council is a disappointment. The first half of it he spends on irrelevant introductory comments, on a discussion of the nature of faith, and on the role of the pope. The last quarter is given to a pitiful picture of Turkish atrocities in Dalmatia and to a plea for help. It is only in the third part that he identifies the two things which most disturb the Church as being, surprisingly enough, the ambition of princes and, what is most dangerous, heresy and infidelity[39].

---

[36] M 674B; Eph. 6:13-17; a criticism of Julius' military interest and programs seems here implied.

[37] M 675E, 671E-672B, 669C.

[38] Born of Venetian nobility and related to popes, Bernard was trained in the classics, philosophy, and theology and earned the title of Doctor of Arts and Master of Theology. His work in the Curia and skill as an orator brought him to the attention of Alexander VI who marked him for the metropolitanate of Dalmatia. As Archbishop he protected the poor, actively opposed the Turks, and saw to the reform of his clergy and laity alike by his visitations, programs of instruction, disciplinary decrees, and convocation of a reform synod in 1511. At the Fifth Lateran he figured significantly in the reform deliberations. Confer: DANIELE FARLATUS, *Illyrici Sacri*, Venice 1765, III, 422-431; HEFELE-LECLERCQ, *Histoire des Conciles d'après les documents originaux* VIII-I, 458; M 702B-706C, 797C, 847A, 850D; HURTER 1278, n. 1.

[39] M 700A-707A, 703A-B.

Those most guilty of ambition, luxury, and a desire for dominion are princes. Violence, fires, slaughter and the corruption of virgins he blames on them. These evils would be corrected if the Council, under the pope's presidency, were to decree: « that all princes who are content with their own boundaries should advance no further. Let them retain whatever camps, towns, cities and regions they presently possess since a continued possession of them over a long time gives them title, provided no one has reclaimed them in the meantime »[40].

The second and greatest cause of disturbance in the Church, he claimed, was the combined evil of heresy and infidelity. With the help of St. Paul and the Latin Fathers, Bernard presents an erudite examination of the cause and effect of heresy. Echoing the words of Pope Leo, he traces its origins to subjectivity. Not trusting the wiser and more learned, heretics fall into foolishness since whenever

> they are confronted in their search for truth with something obscure, they have recourse not to the voices of the prophets, the apostolic epistles, the evangelical authorities, but to themselves, and thus they become teachers of error because they were not disciples of truth.[41]

Taking Jerome as his next authority, Bernard asserts that heresy « leads many to choose a way of life which they think is better, putting aside the catholic and apostolic discipline, sowing diverse errors, and introducing schism »[42]. Heresy then leads to schism and he has clearly in mind, although never directly mentioned or named, the schismatic Pisan Council which was called to bring about better discipline. Having listed emperors and kings whom popes have excommunicated for opposing divine and ecclesiastical *instituta*, he urges that schismatics (Louis of France, Emperor Maximilian, Pisan Cardinals?) be severely punished: excommunication for having left the communion of the faithful and deprivation of every papal privilege for having refused to submit themselves to the vicar of Christ, the head of the body of the Church[43].

Reformation then involves ending wars and schism. The pope is the primary agent of this reform. He is the « ruler of the whole world », « vicar of Christ », head of the body of the Church, in possession of a free and fullest jurisdiction given him

---

[40] M 703B.
[41] M 703E-704A.
[42] M 703D.
[43] M 704B-705A.

by Christ, the good shepherd, the only one who can provide for the flock of Christ the pasturage of

unity in believing, belief in loving, love in embracing, embracing in fulfilling, fulfillment in observing the Catholic, apostolic, divine, and most holy *instituta* by which strife will be removed, wars ended, acts of sedition, betrayals, perjuries, sacrileges, murders, acts of usury, luxury, adultery, and the old detested crimes of the human race will be rooted out and destroyed.[44]

If any reform is to come to the Church, then it must come somehow from papal and conciliar concern for observance of the *instituta*.

The *instituta* to which Zanni frequently referred but never explicitly identified seem to be divine and ecclesiastical ordinances, regulations, canons, and the customs of our ancestors. Their origins are to be found in the sacred scriptures, in the teachings of the doctors, and in the official pronouncements of the Church. By adherence to them (e. g. belief in the twelve articles of the Apostles' Creed and observance of the Ten Commandments) the baptized attain salvation. Hence reform must include a restoration of these *instituta* which have fallen into disuse and are neglected[45].

This speech is disappointing. Offered the opportunity of a lifetime for sharing with others his ideas on Church reform based on his experiences as curialist and archbishop, Bernard squandered it. His proposal embraced little more than urging a papal effort at restoring the *instituta* which would reform morals and thereby undo the Pisan schismatics. The pressing question of the means and methods for achieving this restoration was left practically untouched.

On May 17, 1512, one week after Bernard's speech, the leading theologian of the day and **Master General** of the Dominicans addressed the second session of the Ecumenical Council — Thomas de Vio (Cajetan) (1468-1534). His intelligence, reforming zeal, devotion to the papacy, and part played in the decision to convoke the Fifth Lateran made him the logical choice for this honor[46].

---

[44] M 700B, 702C-D, 702E.
[45] M 703E-704A, 701C, 704C-705B, 702D.
[46] At sixteen years of age Cajetan gave up the privileges of nobility to enter an Observant convent of the Dominicans. He devoted himself to the study of Aquinas and proceeded to teach philosophy and theology at Padua and Pavia and at Rome where he also discoursed on theology before Alexander VI and Julius II. Within his order he was procurator (1500-1507), vicar general (1507), and Master General (1508-1518). As General he promoted reform by updating the Constitutions, curtailing dispensations, and enforcing substantial

Standing now before this assembly Cajetan took as his theme the New Jerusalem of the Apocalypse which he identified with the Roman Church. Each quality attributed by St. John to this heavenly Jerusalem — that it was a city, holy, peaceful, new, and descended from heaven — Thomas de Vio in turn proved was not applicable to the schismatic Pisan Synod but only to the Roman Church assembled now in Council [47].

Two images are employed by him in describing the Church. It is the *civitas*, the perfect republic, in possession of all its parts, containing first of all the *sacra* or sacraments, then the apostles, evangelists, prophets, pastors, teachers, martyrs, and finally gifts of the Spirit, faith, prophecies, miracles, the power of the keys, and even the revelation of angels and illuminations [48]. As the one mystical body of Christ it unifies its members into an intimate society whereby they become members of each other and mutually foster each other by communication. The head of this body is the Vicar of Christ, the Pope [49].

The holiness of the Church Cajetan first submitted to a speculative examination. Only God, by nature pure act, is wholly free from stain and of Himself clean and holy. By an application of the philosophical principle that only similar things can be joined together, Cajetan asserts:

> it is doubted by no one, I think, that the ecclesiastical *civitas*, which is most closely joined to God, exists pure, clean, holy, and immaculate. Freed of all error by the very first Truth by which it is strengthened and on which it is founded, [the Church] perseveres in a pure mind and in the perpetual love by which it remains in Christ and Christ in it until the consummation of time. It is removed from all filth of

---

observance by the sending of visitors. He wrote the major refutation of the Pisan Synod and urged the convocation of the rival Lateran Council. At the Council he opposed certain views of the Aristotelians and defended the privileges of mendicants. Raised to the cardinalate in 1517, he became one of the leading figures in the Lutheran controversy. Confer: P. MANDONNET, *Cajetan (Thomas da Vio)*: DThC II, 1313-1329; G. M. LOHR, *De Caietano Reformatore Ordinis Praedicatorum*: Angelicum 11 (1934) 593-602; P. MORTIER, *Histoire des Maitres Généraux de l'Ordre des Frères Prêcheurs*, Paris 1911, V, 141-230; J. F. GRONER, *Kardinal Cajetan: Eine Gestalt aus der Reformationszeit*, Fribourg 1951, 43-52, 69; A. RENAUDET, *Préréforme et Humanisme à Paris pendant les premières guerres d'Italie 1494-1517*, rev. ed., Paris 1953, 545-547; HEFELE-LECLERCQ, *Histoire des Conciles* VIII-I, 300, n. 1; M 797D, 843D; A. COSSIO, *Il Cardinale Gaetano e la riforma*, Cividale 1902; I. MANCINI, *Cardinale Caietanus et Montes Pietatis*, Jerusalem 1954; HURTER 1201-1209, N° 566, 1387; G. HENNIG, *Cajetan und Luther: Ein historischer Beitrag zur Begegnung von Thomismus und Reformation*, Stuttgart 1966, 34-35.

[47] M 720A-726B.
[48] M 720D-721A.
[49] M 721B-C, 726B, 725C.

vice and contagion and is so perfected and strong in virtue and goodness that ... no other creature is able to separate it from the love of Christ.[50]

If these same attributes are applied to the image of Spouse of Christ which he uses elsewhere [51], Cajetan would seem to stand in direct opposition to Giles of Viterbo in his predication of the Church's holiness.

In the last quarter of his speech [52], however, Cajetan put aside speculative theology and tried to come to grips with the corrupted condition of the Church. While the *civitas* or mystical body may be holy with a sanctity granted from above, its members here on earth can err and sink to a low level of morals — and this they have done. The Fathers, therefore, are confronted with a serious situation and should not feel, just because a legitimate Council is in session, that automatically something holy and useful has been brought about. Vigilance, diligence, and care must be exercised immediately. Many things are expected and demanded of this Council.

Refusing to pass over in silence the evils confronting the Church, Cajetan bemoaned the boasts of some that the chief pastor has been stricken and placed under interdict by the Pisan Synod and that the sheep are now dispersed. The Council Fathers must seek an end to this schism, he asserted, and should also concern themselves with reconciling heretics, converting infidels, and reforming the Church. The present low level of morality and widespread corruption demand that Church law and its sanctions be strengthened. In this way will the well-deserving be appointed to ecclesiastical dignities, while those lacking in virtue will be either punished or at least denied access to honors and rewards. Let the Council come to quick agreement on a course of action on this question of reform. With consultation and care let it carry out its announced intention of Church reformation, and in so doing remove any reason for continued contradiction or opposition to this Council.

The agents of this reform are the pope and conciliar Fathers. The pope who is entrusted with the government and defense of the Christian faith is the only one who can convoke a council and whose responsibility it is that the Council achieve its ends. With his spiritual sword he is to vanquish errors, heresies, and

---

[50] M 721E-722B.
[51] M 724E.
[52] For the text of this section of the speech which is missing from the Del Monte edition of the official acts, confer Appendix N° 3 at the end of this article.

dissensions. His temporal sword does not seem to be of much use to him in this work of reform since he shares it with the other princes of this world (as ruler of the Papal States). By imitating the divine mercy and forgiving his enemies, he will restore unity to the Church and bring them to submission into the Council. Having called famous men from many nations to this Council, let them fulfill the hope of Christianity and provide whatever is good, auspicious and fortunate for this synod. Then will everyone join with this Roman Council and be devoted « to the discipline of the Christian religion, to the majesty of apostolic authority, to the common welfare of the faithful people, to the restoration of fallen things, to the defense henceforth of the whole Church ... » [53].

It is incumbent on the Fathers of the Council to cooperate and by their consultations and observations provide for the sheepfold, for the authority of the pastor, and for the salvation of all the churches. In this way they will be imitating the Fathers of the ancient councils. Just as Chalcedon defeated Dioscorus and his rival council at Ephesus, and Constantinople condemned Photius « the sower of all discords », so too will Lateran now undo Pisa and give no one the reason or opportunity for desiring or even thinking of causing new discords in the Church [54].

Little did Cajetan suspect that one greater than Photius was now at Wittenberg, and would within five years stir up such discords over the Church Lateran failed to reform that eventually the unity of Western Christianity would be shattered. Within six years from this speech, Cajetan, then Cardinal legate, would reason with this new Photius and attempt unsuccessfully to bring him back to the traditional teaching of the Church. In fact the rest of Cajetan's life was to be devoted to healing the new discords and to reforming the Church which Lateran neglected.

If judged by this speech alone, however, Cajetan would with some difficulty be ranked among those leading, ardent advocates who had a detailed program of conciliar reform. The bulk of his talk contained speculative theological considerations on the validity of the Lateran Council and the illegality of the Pisan. Besides his attacks on the Pisan schismatics, he urged, but only in passing, the conversion of infidels (presumably the Turks or the natives of the newly discovered lands) and the calling back of heretics (whom he never identified; perhaps the followers of Pomponazzi or Hus). The only concrete suggestion he made

---

[53] M 726C-727B.
[54] Confer the concluding comments of Appendix N° 3.

for bringing « those things which far and wide we discern as depraved and deformed » into conformity with the perfect virtue of the New Jerusalem was the application of two approaches he had found helpful in his reform of the Dominicans — the strengthening of laws and their sanctions and the promotion of only worthy candidates to ecclesiastical dignities. Granted the need of such measures, how far did they go in providing a comprehensive program of reform and how realistic were these recommendations given the administrative personnel in the Church at that time?

The third session of the Council, which opened on December 3, 1512, was addressed by Alexius Celadoni (1451-1517), bishop of Molfetta on the southern Adriatic coast of Italy [55]. In spite of his unabashed independence, his vast learning and prestige as tutor of kings commended him for this honor. Forced to abridge his three-hour long speech [56], Alexius chose to delete, unfortunately for our purposes, those sections which treated reform and devoted his time instead to a discourse on the definition, origins, causes, number and goals of the past councils. In this passage, however, Alexius describes in general terms applicable to the Fifth Lateran the causes and functions of a council.

A council occurs when bishops confronted with heresy and grave matters come together in a fitting place chosen by the pontiff and approved by them where they can think over and discuss among themselves what things need correction and how they can conserve religion, restore and strengthen public honesty, good morals and the salvation of souls. In these grave affairs and uncertainties they consult with the supreme head, the pope as common master and teacher of all. As a result of their consultations they determine upon remedies which they promulgate throughout the world in their decisions and decrees. The pope is to see that the council achieves these ends [57].

---

[55] Born in Sparta during a brief period of political and economic revival, Alexius was raised a Roman Catholic. After the Moslem conquest of his homeland in 1460, he went into voluntary exile. He became at Rome one of the most outstanding students of Bessarion and later at Naples the tutor of the two sons of Ferdinand I. Bishop of Gallipoli on the eastern shores of the Gulf of Taranto from 1494-1508, he was transferred to Molfetta where he promoted piety and patronized the arts. At the Fifth Lateran he figured prominently in the deliberations and debates on various reform measures. Confer: FRANCESCO LOMBARDI di Bari, *Notitie Istoriche della Città, e vescovi di Molfetta*, Naples 1703, 111-116; M. JUGIÉ, *Alexis Celadoni*: DHGE II, 395; PARIS DE GRASSIS, *Diarium* 419; M 797D-E, 847A, 849C-D, 850D, 913D, 975A.
[56] M 742B.
[57] M 738B-D, 739B.

For this reason councils are seen as punishing wickedness and strengthening goodness, as stirring up efforts, stamping out heresy, clarifying the faith by their chapters and articles, and as providing canons for virtuous conduct. So important are councils that their decrees carry no less authority than the gospels themselves and when they are despised or omitted morals decline — a point on which Alexius and Giles agreed wholeheartedly [58].

Those evils which infest the Church and which demand the attention of the Council Alexius mentions in passing at the end of this speech. Heresy is not a great threat to the Church, rather it is the wrath of God which should most concern the Council. The list of evils which anger him are seemingly endless: the great corruption of morals, pernicious ambition, intolerable luxury, venality in all things, abominable kinds of license, accursed entertainments and their accompanying blasphemies on the holiest days, evil advice, deceit, mutual fraud, and a covetousness of others' property from which arise discords, wars, and the slaughter of Christians by Christians. Remedies for these evils may have been suggested in the major portion deleted from the speech but in the first part which is preserved, this Greek prelate looks to conciliar decrees and canons of some kind as the solution to evils. Let the Western Church beware, for repentance can come too late [59].

It is difficult to evaluate Alexius' ideas on reform since his speech was significantly abridged. The few references he made to conditions needing reform or the remedies to be adopted were too vague to be of any real value. Of particular interest, though, was his closing observation on the prelates of his day:

> I wasted away in my soul out of indignation ... ascribing it to the perversity of men and the times that, when for so long and with such insistence men called for and desired a council now it is begun, they delay even though called and ordered. [60]

Why this absence of prelates? Was it because the prelates were insincere in their pleas for reform? Was it due to the perversity of men whereby they are unwilling to spend the necessary effort to effect reform? Or is it possible that many prelates, while sharing in a firm conviction found in all levels of society that ecclesiastical reform was mandatory since the millenium

---

[58] M 738D-739A.
[59] M 741D, 742A, 740D-E.
[60] M 742C.

was near at hand, nevertheless, sensed the real religious fervor of the times, judged that the condition of the Church was not as black as preachers had painted, and gave up hope anyway that a Roman Council would seriously espouse the cause of reform?

One week later the fourth session was addressed on its opening day by Christopher Marcellus († 1527), elected Archbishop of Corcyra or Corfu [61]. He owed this honor to the kindness of Julius who could overlook the fact that he was not yet a bishop, nor one of the conciliar Fathers. As might have been expected, Marcellus' speech was directed almost exclusively to Julius who was for the last time presiding over the Council.

Reform of Christian society depends upon the example and skill of the pope who has supreme power on earth. If he is himself a virtuous man, others will imitate him. His art of governing must be directed toward establishing love between himself and his subjects for this is « the fountain and spring of all virtue » and the cause of cooperation, dedication and sacrifice. God desires to bring about through Julius a peaceful restoration of the Church and an end to the schism. The Church, mother of all, looks only to Julius her loving spouse to rescue her from the contempt of her children, to cleanse her of filth, to restore to her beauty and brilliance. All men beg and expect Julius to restore the Church since he is pastor, doctor, ruler, and in words echoing Sacred Scripture and Gregory II, « the other God on Earth » [62].

Frequent ecumenical councils composed of Fathers from almost the whole world are to assist the pope in his work of

---

[61] Born into a patrician family of Venice, Marcellus devoted himself to the study of classics, philosophy, and theology, becoming eventually a canon and doctor of Padua. Under Julius II he was made apostolic protonotary and designated Archbishop-elect of Corcyra; under Leo X he was installed as archbishop but never seems to have resided in his see. With a seeming proclivity for controversy he published « Universalis de anima traditionis opus libri VI » (1508) against the « pagan » Aristotelians, battled Paris de Grassis over his publication of the *Caeremoniale Romanum* (1516), and was one of Luther's earliest antagonists in Italy, publishing in 1521 a defense of papal supremacy over a council and a refutation of Luther's positions on penance, satisfaction, purgatory, and indulgences. He was captured and martyred in the sack of Rome. Among his other writings are: « Dialogus de animae sanitate, » « De fato, » « Questiones IV philosophicae, » and some commentaries on the Epistles and Psalms. Confer: E. VANSTEENBERGHE, *Marcel, Christophe*: DThC IX-1, 1993; L. ELLIES DU-PIN, *Histoire de l'Eglise et des auteurs ecclesiastiques du seizième siècle*, Paris 1701, 444-446: A. J. SCHULTE, *Caeremonial*: Catholic Encyclopedia, New York 1908, III, 538; PASTOR VIII, 252; X, 342-343; IX, 410; HURTER, 1274, N° 596.

[62] M 759A, 756D, 757A-C, 759C-D, 761B-C, 762B, 761D; PASTOR VI, 430, n.

reform. It is their function to strengthen the holy laws, change institutions, erase errors and heresies, solve difficulties, test truth, eliminate dissensions, restore concord and teach the faith. Their laws silence kings, remove vice and reform the Church [63].

The evils which face the Church are not listed endlessly, instead Marcellus points to their causes. In a revealing passage this curial official asserted that engaging in sin has so become the present pattern of life that, with few exceptions, everyone obstructs each virtue and violates every law, even the smallest. Convenience, not conscience, rules the heart and guides the mind. As a result everything now deviates from the proper path of justice and the Church itself has been abandoned and wastes away [64]. Within its fold are ravening wolves in sheep's clothing who mock mortal men by their deceptions of piety and religion while they are really ruled by impiety, servitude, greed, ambition, anger and spite [65]. This is, indeed, the sad commentary of a curialist on the Church of his direct experience.

The pre-condition for reform is the establishment of peace since from it proceeds virtue and religion. Once war is checked it is the pope's task « to reform, correct, and make illustrious the Church depraved by morals ». This reform is not to be carried out with weapons but by laws. « Without laws everything is in flux, everything wavers and is held in a state of disturbance ». Not only must the traditional laws be enforced, but new ones must be established for the changed times. To encourage observance rewards, favors, liberality, benefices, and offices should be given to the deserving, while to the non-observant belong many punishments, corrections, exile, and even amputation from the body [66]. Thus in Marcellus' thinking, laws that are obeyed are the key to reform.

Various images are used to describe the goal of this reformation. In the words of the Gospel, the sheepfold of Christ will be cared for and fed. From St. Paul comes the image of Christ's family in which He will dwell and in which there will be one

---

[63] M 758E-759B.

[64] M 760D-E: « In tanta namque peccandi licentia constituti sumus, ut, paucis quibusdam exceptis, nullus sit, qui virtutibus non officiat omnibus, qui leges neque minimas quidem observat. Omnia improbitas et intemperantia complet et occupat, omnia a recto aequitatis, et justitiae tramite deviant, in obliquum tendunt; neque ullus est, qui ad seipsum, ad cor suum mentemque respiciat. Quisque commoditatem suam privatamque utilitatem praetendit. Ipsa vero respublica, ipsa ecclesia derelinquitur, et derelicta conqueritur, et lanquet, et plorat. »

[65] M 761A.

[66] M 760A, 760D, 761C, 758D-E.

mind, one soul and one will. Also from St. Paul, with echoes of the Song of Songs, comes the image of the bride who will be restored to her former likeness, grace and beauty. The golden age is also seen on the horizon when the earth will grow fertile under the sprinkling of dew by Julius. In the closing words of his speech, taken in part from the Psalms, Marcellus predicts the restoration of the Pope's inheritance « which so often the boar leaving the forests spreads out to devour »[67].

Eight years later Marcellus' prophecy was still not fulfilled but his closing words introduced a bull of excommunication — « Arise, O God, and judge Your own cause .... The boar out of the woods has laid it waste, and a singular wild beast has devoured it »[68]. Time had run out and now Luther was leading a revolutionary reform movement. Failing to heed the warnings of men like Marcellus, the papacy was forced to witness the rending of Christian unity. The Archbishop of Corcyra had not been far from the mark when he sided with his contemporaries in demanding a dedicated clergy and the strict enforcement of ecclesiastical law. Considering the personal weaknesses of Julius II and his general indifference to questions of reform, however, Marcellus' dependence on the papacy to bring about Church renewal was unrealistic. And yet in view of the existing power structures and attitudes in Rome, was not his approach of painting the blackest picture of ecclesiastical corruption in hopes of inspiring Julius with a sense of duty and urgency perhaps after all the only viable way of attacking the problem?

The fifth session of the Council was addressed on February 16, 1513, by John Mary del Monte (1487-1555), the new Archbishop of Siponto, near modern-day Manfredonia on the southern Adriatic coast of Italy. This great honor was conferred on him partly out of respect for his family, partly due to his reputation for learning and eloquence[69].

---

[67] M 761C (John 21:15-17; Psalm 23), 762A (Romans 13:16, Ephesians 4:1-6), 761C (2 Corinthians 11:2; Song of Songs 4:1-16), 762B (Psalm 16:5, 80:13).

[68] Pastor VII, 400.

[69] Born into the Ciocchi family of Roman canon lawyers, John received his early training in the humanities there at Rome under Brandolino and later in civil and canon law at Perugia and Siena under Politi (Catharinus). Helped by the powerful patronage of his uncle Anthony, John was appointed papal chamberlain on his return to Rome and at twenty-three years of age named Archbishop of Siponto. Created Cardinal in 1536 in appreciation for his honest labors as a Curial canonist, he was placed by Paul III on his Reform Commission and in 1545 was appointed the papal legate who opened the first session of the Council of Trent and presided over it. Elected pope in 1550 he took the name Julius III, reconvened the Council, personally saw to the reform of the cardinals, curia, and clergy, confirmed the Jesuits, and temporarily reunited

IV

A tall, powerful youth of peasant features and sanguine temper, John displayed his knowledge of pagan and Christian antiquity in his speech before the Council Fathers. His theme, the restoration of justice, seems to have been taken from the *Divinae Institutiones* of Lactantius, the Christian Cicero [70]. But where the ancient apologist attempted to baptize pagan myths and metaphors, the Renaissance prelate openly ridiculed the imagery, but preserved the theme. With Lactantius he claimed that the evils of society will be remedied only with the restoration of justice which is the origin and font of all virtues. Both agreed that justice involves the sincere worship of God which demands the observance of the moral law and that justice is the greatest bond among men. Justice which is seen by both as almost extinct must be the first virtue restored since it inspires men to embrace fidelity, kindness, piety, severity, and integrity and to flee impiety, pride, perfidy, lust, avarice, anger, ambition, the desire for ruling and the neglect of religious worship [71].

Justice cannot easily be preserved unless unity and peace are joined to it. And such an intimate union exists between peace and unity that one cannot perdure without the other. Unity can be achieved only if everything is submitted to one will. The Sacred Scriptures are in agreement that unity is to be found in one God, one Christ, one Church, one faith, and one chair founded by the Lord's voice upon the firmest rock. Peace vanishes when men take what belongs to another, violating justice, and bringing on the horrors of war. With justice re-

---

England to the Faith. Confer: ONUPHRIUS PANVINIUS, *De Julii III vita ante pontificatum*, Venice 1557, reprinted in *Concilii Tridentini Diariorum*, ed. S. Merkle, Freiburg 1911, II, 146-147; EDWARD MCSHANE, *Julius III, Pope*: New Catholic Encyclopedia VIII, 54; PASTOR XIII, 45-48, 158-182; VI, 434.

[70] PANVINIUS, op. cit., 147; Del Monte in one passage (M 779A) even borrows words and phrases directly from Lactantius: e. g. Del Monte: « Quod si, ut non nulli praedicant, finxere quondam poetae, post Saturni tempora, cum sensissent justitiam a rebus humanis abesse, offensam vitiis hominum recessisse a terra in caelumque migrasse ... » Lactantius: « Hi [poetae] plane intellexerunt abesse hanc a rebus humanis eamque finxerunt offensam vitiis hominum cessisse terra in caelumque migrasse. » (Firmianus Lactantius, *Divinae Institutiones*, lib. V, c. 5, l. 2 in *L. Caeli Firmiani Lactanti Opera Omnia, Pars I*, edited by Brandt CSEL, Vol. 19, 413.) Lactantius was considered a « Christian classic » and some of his works were included in the curriculum of a good humanistic training (P. KRISTELLER, *Renaissance Thought: the Classic, Scholastic and Humanist Strains*, New York 1955, 81.) Before 1500 eleven editions of his works were already in print (E. AMMAN, *Lactance*: DThC VIII-I, 2443). It is no wonder that Del Monte should be familiar with him.

[71] M 779A-B, 778A-C; Lactantius, *Divinae Institutiones* V, 6-7, VI, 10; (CSEL 19, 416-421, 514-519).

vived and unity preserved, we must look then to Christ for peace [72].

The specific evils of the times which demand reform del Monte describes with passing reference: insubordination, a sacrilegious desire of dominion, avarice and thievery, bribery in papal elections, violations of laws and oaths, the Moslem threat, the beginnings of heresy and schism, and the disturbances of wicked and depraved men. These evils need not continue [73].

The best solution to the problems is a council. Ancient secular history attests to the importance of consulting together and what is more fitting than that all the Fathers of the Church come together to find a remedy? Julius was wise in seeking their counsel, not to say their authority and labors, for the reform of the Church [74].

Del Monte's speech resembles more an academic exercise in rhetoric than an urgent call to reform. For the most part this young lawyer spent his time and energies eulogizing the legal abstraction justice while ignoring the problem of how to bring justice down out of the clouds. No homework seems to have been done on identifying the nature and extent of moral decay or on discovering practical ways of remedying these evils. Philosophic analysis and the thousand-year old writings of the Latin Fathers assured him that the restoration of justice must be the central concern of Renaissance reform. The only time he left the safe world of generalizations was when he prudently condemned simony in papal elections. Against this evil the conscience-stricken and dying Julius II had prepared a bull for confirmation by the conciliar Fathers at this session.

On April 27, 1513, the new pope, Leo X, reconvened the Fifth Lateran, having announced his intention of carrying out the ends proposed for it by Julius [75]. Since two of the four ends concerned reformation and an expedition against the Moslems, it is not surprising that Leo chose for speaker at the sixth session a bishop from a reformed diocese under siege by the Turks, Simon Kožičić Begnius, Bishop of Modrus in Dalmatia (1500-1536 †) [76].

---

[72] M 779B-D, 780C-E, 781B-C.
[73] M 777B-E, 781B.
[74] M 776D-777C.
[75] M 783A-B.
[76] Born at Jadera in Dalmatia of a Hungarian family famed for its military exploits, Begnius pursued studies in the humanities, philosophy, and theology, gained skill in oratory, and developed a lasting interest in history. He wrote histories of the Roman Empire, of the papacy, and of ancient Spalato. Appointed bishop of Modrus in 1500 he cooperated with Zanni in the reform of

While Simon's speech before the Council is a commentary on the speaker with its many references to historical happenings and the recent Moslem menace, it is also a stern commentary on the conditions of the Church. Although dealing in generalities, it does propose a realistic approach to reformation.

Simon uses two scriptural images in describing the Church — that of a city and that of a woman. The Roman Church, all embracing, supreme, and the source of our faith, is Jerusalem. As such it should be the city of perfect beauty and the joy of the whole world. As a woman, it is variously called spouse, sister, lover, and beloved of Christ. It is also the daughter of Sion whose beauty consists in chastity and innocence. These images are drawn from both the Old and New Testaments [77].

This daughter of Sion has lost almost all her innocence and purity. She is wasting away and scarcely any faith, piety, or religion remains in her. The fervor of former times has grown cold. Her enemies enter her sanctuaries and desecrate her altars. Even her priests despise God. Nor is there a law, command, or judgment which is not perverted. Evils befall the Church because men have neglected Christ, they have turned their faces from the mirror of divine judgment, they speak soothing words in deceit, they look to their own powers and skills, their efforts and virtues to achieve salvation, not trusting completely in God who alone draws men to beatitude [78].

In this passage Begnius may have been taking issue with some of the exaggerated speculations of such Nominalist theologians as Occam, d'Ailly, and Biel who theorized on the part man plays in his own salvation *ex puris naturalibus*. Whether, like the Luther of 1515, he too drew his inspiration from St. Augustine's *De spiritu et littera* is not easily ascertained. From his orthodox statement on the operation of grace, though, it can be assumed that Simon was not in agreement with the neo-Pelagian temper of his times. Also difficult to determine is whether and to what extent Begnius attributed the other evils here mentioned

---

his diocese. Besides addressing the Fifth Lateran, he was appointed by Leo X to the conciliar commission on reform. He failed to attend the last six sessions of the Council and returned to his diocese which was overrun by the Turks in 1527. Confer: FARLATUS, *Illyrici Sacri* IV (1769) 110-112; III (1765) 425, 432; Fr. BULIC, *Begni (Simeón)*: DHGE VII, 451; M 794C-797E, esp. 795A and 797A. His speech before Leo X on November 5, 1516 treating the desolation of Dalmatia under the sword of the Turks is recorded in *Opuscula Varia ad Conc. Latera.*, fol. 139r-144r.

[77] M 803B-C, 804C-D.
[78] M 803C-D, 798E-799A.

to the rest of Europe or only to his own diocese where reform had at least begun.

Simon envisions reform as coming from above, be it by way of pope, council, bishops, or even secular ruler. Although he does not suggest any secular action at this time, he does, as one proud of his Hungarian heritage, praise Sigismund, Holy Roman Emperor and King of Hungary who a century earlier had saved the Church by his undaunted labors. God Himself, he claims, raised him up and strengthened him with His spirit in order that he might reform the Church where the churchmen had failed. The precedent has thus been established by God [79].

The exact function of the pope in this present reformation is left vague. He is the savior of the daughter of Sion, the expected one, Leo, the lion from the tribe of Juda. He is to take up weapons to defend his spouse and to vindicate her tabernacle which has been polluted by impious hands. This reform of the Church he is to carry out in conjunction with the council [80].

That a general council can enjoy great authority and even instill fear into a pope by its censures is seen by the Council of Basel which Eugene in vain opposed and finally approved. To be in conformity with the decrees of Nicea, however, an assembly needs to be convoked and approved by the pontiff. In the present Lateran Council at least Simon assigns to Leo the position of leadership. All the same, Simon's views on papal supremacy are not so certain as Cajetan's [81].

To the Fifth Lateran Council Simon seems to entrust primarily the task of restoring « the fallen Church ». The Fathers of the Council must exercise care, effort, and prudence and be willing to undergo anything arduous or fear-inspiring to bring about this reformation. The norms that must guide them in this task are the « great efforts and vigilance of our predecessors, the *institutiones* of the evangelical law, and the actions of Christ our law-maker ». These provide « a certain archetype and exemplar » on which to model all of one's life [82].

Toward the end of his speech Simon maps out a program of reform for the Fathers to follow. Let them first rid the

---

[79] M 800C-D.
[80] M 803E-804B.
[81] M 800E-801A, 804B.
[82] M 804B, 799D: « Nobis vero majorum nostrorum studio atque vigiliis tantopere consultum est, nobis ex evangelicae legis institutionibus, et Christi legislatoris nostri actionibus, totius vitae norma ita praescripta est, ut illinc veluti ex archetypo quodam et exemplari, quid fugere, quidve sequi debeat ... »

IV

Church of interior discord and domestic destruction, then with charity and the zeal of their pastoral office overwhelm the open enemy of schism. Let them check incontinence and restore equity and justice, « the preservative and foundation of things human and divine ». With the weapons of charity and power, and the scales of mercy and severity may they encourage the good, check the evil, strengthen the strong, raise up those things fallen, reduce injustices to equity, and seek that which is of Christ and not their own. In another place he exhorts them to eliminate the slightest corruption, to correct what has erred, and to recall to the common use of the good those *instituta* which have fallen into disuse by the efforts of evil men. Peace is also needed; for it we were born; however, let us regain first what we have lost to the Turks. In these ways will the holy Church be restored to her integrity and beauty [83].

Simon is quite explicit on where the reform should begin — *a capite ad pedem*. He exhorts his fellow bishops to be models of virtue, to let their good works shine before men, to show charity to the needy, to stop contending with one another, and to beware lest by St. Augustine's standards they be judged as wolves and incontinent men. Before seeking to reform others, they must cleanse their interior dwellings of evil thoughts and dispose their exterior appearances prudently — only then will they effectively guide others. Among other motives which should inspire the bishops in this work of reform is that of the example set by their predecessors. Their devotion, their fasts, their tears, their prayers, their willingness to undergo the greatest sufferings, even to the shedding of their blood to preserve the Church uncorrupted should be a constant source of inspiration to the Fathers. Such appeals as this to the example of the forefathers may have been influenced by the teachings of the *Devotio Moderna* [84].

While Simon's speech failed to raise a crusade, recall « golden peace », or reform what was deformed, it was remarkable in that it called for reformation by a return to Christ and a renewal of pastoral concern. Thus, the Christ of the Gospels must become the model of conduct and His bride the Church the constant concern of His clergy. Begnius begged his brother bishops to begin by reforming themselves, by giving good example to the faithful, by caring for their flocks. Unfortunately,

---

[83] M 804C-E, 799E.
[84] M 803B, 799E-800A, 805B, 799C-D, 803D; cf. Thomas a Kempis, *Imitation of Christ*, Book I, Chapter 18.

the Bishop of Modrus depended almost exclusively on the example of the saints to inspire and effect such a reform.

On June 17, 1513, at the bidding of Lorenzo Pucci, who was in charge of the papal Datary, Balthassar del Rio († 1540) addressed the seventh session of the Council [85]. His ability as an orator, demonstrated earlier in a speech given before Julius II on Our Lord's passion, and his great interest in the defense of Christendom won for him this honor of addressing the Fathers [86].

The burden of del Rio's speech is a plea for a crusade against the Turks. As a Spaniard he took the opportunity to praise Ferdinand V for his victories over the Moslems, even dedicating his speech to him. He also mentioned the Moslem raid on the march of Arbonos and warned that the Lateran Basilica itself was in danger of being put to the torch by the Turks. In calling on Leo to save Christendom he mentioned in passing the role and powers of the pontiff [87].

In del Rio's ecclesiology the pope is the vicar of Christ on earth, the successor of Peter, the good shepherd whom his own sheep follow and who should recall other sheep into the fold. He is also high priest and king of kings who possesses both a spiritual and a temporal sword. He is to establish peace among Christian princes, rally them about him, and lead them against the Turks in order to free the Christians and force the Moslems into the fold [88].

The Council acknowledges Leo's leadership, del Rio asserted, and it proclaims in the words of the psalm: « You are he who restores my heritage to me » (Ps. 16: 5). Under the lead and

---

[85] Of Spanish birth, Del Rio seems to have taken his studies and taught at Mondoñedo in northwestern Spain during which time he developed an enthusiasm for the study of Platonic philosophy. He became accomplished in Latin rhetoric and in the Castilian literary style. As a cleric he left his native Palencia for Rome where Leo X appointed him archdeacon of Cesena, apostolic protonotary, and secret chamberlain. The Spaniard Jaime Cardinal Serra employed him as his secretary and as his assistant at the Conclave of 1513. He held many benefices and the offices of canon and archdeacon of Seville and of the Church of St. James of the Spaniards in Rome, titular bishop of Scala in Calabria (1515), and governor of Rome (1530). He was chosen by the Conclave of 1522 to announce to Adrian Dedel his election to the papacy. He died at Rome in 1540. Confer: M 658C, 809D, 819C-820C; Pastor IX, 27; A. Renedo Martino, *Escritores Palentinos*, Madrid 1919, II, 346-347; Hergenroether, *Regesta Leonis X, 1513*, N° 3186, 5933, 5978; Ferdinand Ughellus, *Italia Sacra sive episcopis Italiae et insularum adjacentium*, Venice 1721, VII, 338; J. Sanchez Biedma, *Rio (D. Baltasar del)*: Biografia Eclesiastica Completa, ed. Basilio S. Castellanos de Losada, Madrid 1864, XXII, 146.

[86] M 820A-C.
[87] M 819D, 822D-E, 824D-E.
[88] M 827A.

guidance of the pope the Christian religion revives, and as it has but one shepherd may there be but one flock [89].

This speech, then, ignores the theme of reform. The recent gains of the Moslems are not even interpreted as a punishment from God for having neglected reform. Should del Rio have taken up the plea for Church renovation it is safe to assume that the pope would be seen as playing a major, if not primary, role in the restoration.

On December 19, 1513, the eighth session of the Council was addressed by a Knight of St. John of Jerusalem, John Baptist de Gargiis [90]. Such an honor was granted the Knights, it would seem, out of gratitude for their services to the Holy See and with a view to providing them with a forum for pleading their cause which was in imminent danger. The Knights, who were named official protectors of the Council, feared for their island fortress of Rhodes which was under the threat of an invasion by Bajazet the Turk [91]. While the main thrust of his talk before the Council was an explanation of the vocation of a soldier and an appeal for aid in the defense of Rhodes, de Gargiis also touched on the topic of reform.

De Gargiis shared Chrysostom's view of the scope of reform [92]. Since Christian society was one, the morals of both ecclesiastical and civil life were to be the objects of the Council's reforming zeal. The Christian Republic reaches to the Moslem frontier and is governed both by the Christian princes and by the heads of the churches — both of which groups strive to obey the pope. The Church is called the Christian religion, mother, the single spouse of God, the true and holy bride of Leo. Its essential characteristics are nowhere defined [93].

The Medici pope Leo is for de Gargiis the heavenly-sent doctor (*medicus*) who will restore the Christian religion to its

---

[89] M 827A.

[90] De Gargiis (spelt variously: Gargha, Gange, Gargia) was from Siena. He entered the Order of the Knights in his youth and served in Rome under Caretto. He may have been a chaplain since he complained that he was unable to serve the Order with his body. He failed to take part in the great defense of Rhodes in 1480 or later in 1522. Skilled in oratory, he was appointed by Caretto's vicar in Rome and helped by Julius Cardinal Medici (later Clement VII) to prepare this speech and deliver it before the Council. Confer: M 850D, 831D, 660D, 850E-851E; Pastor VIII, 388; Abbé de Vertot, *Histoire des Chevaliers Hospitaliers de S. Jean de Jerusalem*, new augmented edition, Paris 1778, VII, 427-442.

[91] De Vertot, *Histoire des Chevaliers* III, 187-191. On the generally high spiritual level of the Order at the time, cf. 167-202.

[92] G. B. Ladner, *The Idea of Reform: Its Impact on Christian Thought and Action in the Age of the Fathers*, Cambridge (Mass.) 1959, 140-141.

[93] M 855E, 854B, 853C-D, 856C, 857C, 857E.

pristine health. He is also the giver of peace, defender of justice, good shepherd, and vicar of God who leads all onto the right path and by whose authority the council now seeks to help the Christian people [94].

It is to the Council, whose Fathers are « the shining stars » and « firm supports of the Christian religion » and « the chief leaders of the army of Christ », that de Gargiis primarily looks for reformation [95]. As the synods of the past produced the remedies for the evils of their day, so too should this Council first examine and then provide the required immunizing medication. The forces of impiety, passion, ambition, and anger have presently broken down the bounds of reason and honor, and every kind of crime has crept into the world. Unimpeded by proper punishments weakened wills have become attached to their sins. Divine precepts are disobeyed, Church customs scorned, and the morals and discipline of our forefathers spurned [96]. It is up to the Council to correct these evils, to help a fallen Church, to restore to it the glory of its liberty, and to admonish its members to live more religiously. Although de Gargiis never identified by name those who scorned pious customs and the traditional precepts, he may have been referring to men like Erasmus who found favor with the new pope [97].

Evils face Christendom on its frontiers. Those who live under the shadow of the Sultan are defecting from the Faith either out of fear of the scimitar or because of the fallen and neglected condition of the Church. Religion and Empire are

---

[94] M 853C-D, 854D, 857C. In a speech « in obedientia praestanda » of March 6, 1514 de Gargiis addressed the pope in sacred consistory with words of rhetoric likewise as strong: « Te itaque eius nomine Leo X. Pont. Max. verum Iesu Christi Vicarium: legitimumque Petri successorem: ac Romanum Pontificem, gregisque Domini indubitatum Pastorem agnoscimus, adoramus, ac quam maxima posuimus devotione veneramur: devotaque subiectione profitemur: ac tibi tanquam vero Christi Vicario puram, veram, immaculatamque filialem obedientiam reverenter exhibemus. » *Opuscula Varia ad Conc.*, fol. 258ᵛ.
[95] M 852B, 854E.
[96] M 853D-854A: « Ad quam rem sola synodus haec erit veluti quoddam Mithridaticum antidotum. In synodis quoniam solita plerumque est mater ecclesiae salubria remedia providere, si quando nocendi cupiditas, ulciscendi crudelitas, implacabilis animus ac feritas rebellandi suo in populo oriebatur. Nunc impius lucri furor, ac effrenis cupido, iraque praeceps atque immanis libido, quae succensas agit mentes, honestatis fines effregerant, et omnis denique scelerum labes in mundum irrepserat. Mores vero et instituta majorum pro lege tenenda, spreta jacebant: praevaricatores divinarum legum, et ecclesiasticarum consuetudinum contemptores impune cervicibus elatis incedebant. Abusus vero et depravata voluntas, ubi semel coeperant, in dies duriores efficiebantur; et animus sceleribus adstrictus non facile ab eis develli poterat. Quae omnia ab hac sanctissima synodo sincero examine pendetur. »
[97] M 856D, 854E; Pastor VIII, 253-255.

intimately linked. In times past the Christian princes sought first the kingdom of God and their own realms increased. Now they spurn conserving and defending religion, and instead of a crusade, they war among themselves. God's wrath is upon us. « Be not surprised therefore if such misfortunes have befallen Christian affairs » [98]. Let Leo with the help of this synod see to the reform of the Church, appease God, unite the Christian princes, and push back the frontiers of Christendom. « Under your reign, truly, the golden age will begin, and justice, having descended from heaven, will return to the earth » [99].

De Gargiis' speech provides us with a valuable insight into a military man's approach to the problem of reform. The restoration of religion he linked with a military victory over the Moslems. His reform appeals were directed exclusively to the chief officials of the Church, while his proposed assault on evil consisted essentially in the enforcement of law and the punishment of offenders. As a professional defender of the establishment he accurately recognized in society an element of hostility toward the traditional modes of piety, but he was a bit quick in drawing an immediate connection between this and immoral conduct.

While the Council he addressed failed to restore Christianity and his prediction of the golden age of Lactantius never came true, the knight's pleas for aid for Rhodes were, however, heard by Leo who sent three well-armed galleys there and by Francis I who dispatched almost a score of vessels. Dissension in the Sultan's household, though, prohibited an attack at that time. Dissension and jealousy among the Christian princes later would frustrate the Council's efforts to raise a crusade, and within eight years both Rhodes and Belgrade would fall to the Turks [100].

The ninth session of the Council which gave its formal and final approval to the Great Reform Bull was addressed on May 5, 1514, by Anthony Pucci (1485-1544) [101]. His unquestioned

---

[98] M 857D, 856C-D.

[99] M 857C-D, 854C.

[100] DE VERTOT, *Histoire des Chevaliers* III, 190, 198; PASTOR VII, 213-252; IX, 154-174.

[101] Born at Florence into a branch of the Medici family, Pucci was destined from his youth for an ecclesiastical career. He studied at Pisa in the humanities and then went on to the study of law, philosophy, and theology. His knowledge of Sacred Scriptures was profound and he drew large audiences when as canon of the cathedral of Florence he would preach from them. Called to Rome by his uncle Cardinal Lorenzo, he was soon appointed by his relative Leo X as one of the seven members of the apostolic camera (fiscal department) and in this capacity as a member also of the conciliar reform commission. Later he was promoted to bishop of Pistoia (1518); papal ambassador to

ability as an orator and the fact he was related to the right people obtained this honor for him. In addition, his experience on the conciliar reform commission provided him with an unusual knowledge of the problems and their possible solutions [102]. Not only was his speech one of the longest and most replete in places with scriptural references, but it was also explicit in its recommendations on renovation. For Pucci, the reform of the Church would be one of morals, not doctrine.

His notion of the Church resembles that of Cajetan. The Christian Republic and the Church are not identified in his mind. God has granted the pope all power in heaven and on earth, and although princes wield the temporal sword, the pope can interpose his authority to establish peace and determine civil law on behalf of the common good. The Church is also seen as the heavenly Jerusalem, but it is the marital metaphor which Pucci favors, and develops more than Cajetan [103].

The Church stems from God's promise to Abraham that his offspring will be as numerous as the sands on the seashore. Christ fulfilled His Father's pledge by providing for Himself with the last outpouring of His Blood a single bride. He bathed her in the water and Blood which came from His side, cleansing her of every stain and enriching her with a treasure of knowledge and wisdom. This bride He then took to Himself in an indissoluble union consummated both in heaven and on earth. This union can never be broken, neither by death nor by divorce. From this union His bride begets children, so that she becomes the common mother of all. The beauty and splendor of this bride comes from her mystical body and from the humanity of her spouse. At present, however, she is robed in sorrow, reduced to rags, and streaked by ashes and tears. Her home is almost deserted, her vineyard produces thorns, her gardens are in ruin, and her children despise her. From the pope, her gentle spouse, she looks for succor [104].

Switzerland, France, and Spain; Cardinal; and finally High Penitentiary. Under his leadership the clergy of Pistoia are reported to have been reformed. He is known to have engaged in spying for his patron Lorenzo Medici and was accused both of questionable financial transactions in gaining his high curial post and of resisting until his death the efforts of Contarini and Carrafa to reform the Grand Penitentiary. Confer: UGHELLUS, *Italia Sacra* III (1717), 308-309; PASTOR VII, 82-83, 227, 158, n.; VIII, 392, 50, 108; JEDIN, *History of Council of Trent* I, 421, 423, n., 434-435; LITTA, *Famiglie Celebri Italiane*, Vol. 28, Milan 1869, Dispensa 158; HURTER, 1455-1456, N° 668.

[102] M 887A-B; HEFELE-LECLERCQ VIII-I, 411-412.
[103] M 891B, 893C-D, 897D, 892E, 895E.
[104] M 888E-890B, 890E, 895E-896B.

IV

The supreme pontiff is the one, true, and legitimate vicar of Christ and God. His powers stretch from heaven to earth and his duties include « this one outstanding and salvific work of Christian censorship »[105]. In fulfilling this task Pucci exhorts him: « Restore to a pristine reverence for faith, hope, and charity, under the directing guidance of your discipline, first this City, so that judgment may proceed from the house of the lord, and then the world »[106]. The pope is the principal agent of this reformation, a *reformatio in capite et in membris*, and the future of Christendom is in his hands.

Pucci points to two principal sources of motivation for Pope Leo: emulation and fear of judgment. Let him strive to imitate Julius who began this reform council and his predecessors in the papacy who carried councils to very fruitful conclusions. Let him realize that he is being watched and judged not only by all Christians, but also by God. How happy it will be for him at the Last Judgment if this synod produces salvific effects[107]. With truly prophetic vision, Pucci proclaimed:

> Woe, I say, to all the faithful of Christ, if your allow such a rare opportunity for future good, if, what indeed must not even be thought, you allow this opportunity to slip by with no results.[108] Unless you will have carried this out, it is to be feared that the judgment of divine wrath threatens all Christians.[109]

The Council, that « special palace of the Holy Spirit », must assist Leo in this great work of reform. Let the Fathers bring every thought, ounce of attention, counsel, industry, and labor to bear on this so necessary and salvific reformation of morals. Through the efforts of this synod may the dispersed sheep be gathered, the various weaknesses and illnesses be diagnosed and remedies be applied, the truth of the whole Christian law become more clearly known to the mind, more gently and suasively insinuated, and more firmly grasped[110].

Pucci analyzes all levels of society which the Pope and Council are to reform. Evils he lists in detail and at times he prescribes a particular remedy.

---

[105] M 892B, C-D: « hoc unum praeclarissimum ac saluberrium Christianae censurae opus ... »

[106] M 897D: « Urbem primum, ut judicium incipiat a domo domini: inde orbem disciplinae tuae censura in pristinum fidei, spei, caritatisque cultum restitue. » Confer: 1 Peter 4:17.

[107] M 891C, 892A, 891D.

[108] M 892D.

[109] M 891B.

[110] M 891D, 896C.

IV

Among Christians in general Pucci finds innumerable evils: impiety with regard to the divine mysteries of the faith which are examined out of criminal curiosity, derided lightly, or haughtily despised; blasphemies are uttered against God and the saints; the sacred shepherds are slandered; contempt is had for holy censorship; the divine things are subjected to seizure and stolen; and men are guilty of usury, dishonor, hatred, revenge, assaults, murders, and license [111].

The serious irreverence and contempt for the Church which Pucci found in his analysis could be blamed in part on the curiosity and irreverent speculation on the sacred mysteries engaged in by the theologians of the day. His attack also seems to be directed against certain humanistic views which doubted the value of sacraments, ceremonies, and the mediatorship of Christ and the priesthood. Such humanists, according to one interpretation, found wisdom enough in the Ancients and deified reason, looking for a rational explanation of the mysteries of Faith [112].

The secular leaders of Christendom, its most noble members, are, Pucci claimed, destroying the Christian republic by their mutual slaughter. Peace is gone, demoniacal rage has led tens of thousands of Christians to their death and has ravaged the land. To correct this evil, let the pope send his legates and nuncios to the princes and interpose his authority to bring peace [113].

The religious orders, whose peculiar evils are ignorance, ambition, avarice, concern for temporal things, and dissensions, are a source of scandal to the faithful. The Observantine movement Pucci criticized for having introduced divisions so that *frater* is but a name. And even the Observants themselves are torn by contentions and schisms. Let there be one and the same interpretation and observance of evangelical religious discipline. Let there be but one head, body, spirit, obedience, and charity among the followers of founders of the various religious orders [114]. Pucci's plea for a reform of the religious but echoed months and years of behind-the-scene efforts of the conciliar Fathers

---

[111] M 893E-894A.

[112] H. A. ENNO VAN GELDER, *The Two Reformations in the Sixteenth Century: A Study of the Religious Aspects and Consequences of Renaissance and Humanism*, The Hague 1961, 74; for an opposing view that the humanists were fundamentally Christian, confer: KRISTELLER, *Renaissance Thought* I, 70-91.

[113] M 892E-893D.

[114] M 894B-E.

to find a solution to this pressing problem, a solution which would be promulgated in the next session.

The clerical order of the Church has been neglected and is in need of reform. The prescription of the ancient canons must be brought to bear against those clerics guilty of impiety, betrayal, lying, false accusation of their brethren, envy, disturbing the peace, usurping the sacred dignities, adultery, obscenity, cruelty, vindictiveness, usury, profit-seeking. Such clerics should not be promoted to the priesthood and those who are already priests should be either deposed or suspended. The pristine canons, the sacred writings, and the wisdom of the Fathers support such censures [115].

Pucci accused the bishops of his day of being more interested in the rewards of their office than in its duties, of dispersing rather than gathering the sheep. Let the bishops be instead models of modesty, sobriety, wisdom, justice, rectitude, graciousness. By the candor of their lives and the teaching of doctrine and with the help of grace they will pass these sterling qualities on to the faithful [116].

The influential college of cardinals is spared Pucci's criticism. These men are the moderators and divine consultors of the Christian faith, the electors of popes and center of the Church, the pivotal points (*cardines*) of the world and the firm columns by which the temple will remain immobile till the end of time. Their function is to supply for whatever is lacking in *humanis studiis*, in religion, and in the clerical order by their discussion, censure and decrees. Let them provide for the rooting out of heresy, the discipline of morals, the unity of religious obedience, the regulations on clerical garb, the sacred rites, the complex collation of priestly offices, the care of souls, the residence of pastors, the visitation of dioceses, the annual gathering of episcopal synods, and the frequent convocation of councils of metropolitans. Let the cardinals see to the dignities and duties of their office, neglect not the salvation of souls, but recall the awful judgment seat of Christ [117].

Pope Leo should spend on the cause of reform as much time as « certain people » give to the gathering of honors and fortunes and to the quest for leisure, as much as « many » give to *humana studia*, to the snatching of pleasures, and to the rest

---

[115] M 895A-C.
[116] M 896A-C.
[117] M 896C-897A.

of body and soul. Moved by God's favors toward him let him take up the cause of reform [118].

In pathetic yet prophetic words Pucci pleaded with the pope and bishops:

> For unless at this very time of the Council, unless through you, unless under so great a bishop and pastor of our souls we will have recovered our reputation which has been almost totally lost, and will have held on to salvation itself which hangs upon a meagre and last hope, there is nothing else left in which we can take refuge and hope. [119]

God's judgment and wrath are otherwise at hand.

Pucci's speech is noteworthy for its emphasis on the pastoral. Although the cardinals and pope were spared explicit criticism while the lower clergy and bishops were taken to task for their failings, no member of the ministry was exempted from his exhortations to perform the respective duties of his pastoral office. Frequently cited as central to the clergy's concerns was « this one outstanding and salvific work of Christian *censurae* ». The revival of such disciplinary action which insures the observance of laws and the moral quality of the ministry would not be an easy task since censorship was neglected by certain of the clergy and contemned by others of the laity. Pucci's pastoral theme, concern for censuring, other specific reform recommendations, and the stylistic structure of his speech bear certain similarities to the *Libellus* of Giustiniani and Quirini which will be treated later [120]. Since these similarities may be coincidental or too insignificant in particulars to merit a judgment of inspiration, Pucci's speech can also be seen as a summary of the reform commission's considerations to date.

In view of the inside information at Pucci's disposal as a member of this conciliar reform commission, his speech is also noteworthy for the reform measures he proposed but which were not included in the Council's decrees, especially in the Great Reform Bull up for approval at this session. Ignored in the bull were any conciliar decrees which would reunite the religious orders by ending the division between conventual and observants, provide for some kind of codification of the canon law governing the clergy, force pastors to reside in their parishes, and oblige

---
[118] M 890E-891B, 897A-E.
[119] M 897A.
[120] The « Libellus » is treated on pages 221-227.

bishops to instruct their flocks. The absence of these measures is all the more noteworthy since his speech summarizes many of the decrees adopted by the Council.

Pucci's pessimism deserves a final word of comment. His forebodings for the future, it would seem, were closely related to the outcome of the Council. Were these inspired by a realization that the Council had passed over for the most part the pastoral care of the faithful to spend its efforts insuring the privileges and moral image of the clergy; or were they a mere rhetorical device of threatening woes unless the bull up for consideration be approved? Since its passage at that stage was well assured, the former reason seems a more adequate explanation.

The tenth session of the Council, held on May 4, 1515, was addressed by the aged Archbishop of Patras, Stephen Teglatius († 1515)[121]. In poor health, with but several months at most left to his seventy-some year life, Stephen took for his theme Psalm 48 which he claimed contained creation, redemption, reformation, and consummation — all salvation history — within it. Although he kept insisting that he would be brief and by-pass material which he had prepared, his speech was the longest of the Council and full of vague apocalyptic references[122].

The notion of *ecclesia* found in this speech is complex since the word is used in different contexts. From the beginning, before time began, the Word of God, in accordance with a decree of the Trinity, brought forth an immaculate, Eternal Bride, the joyful mother of the just — both angelic and human. Among the angels, those who remained faithful to God constitute the just, Lucifer the unjust. Among men, idolaters make up the Church of the impious while those who give true worship to God constitute the Church of the just. The *ecclesia* among men is divided into that of heaven ruled by prelates and that of earth ruled by princes. The Roman Church, holy, immaculate, and City of God is mother, queen and single ruler of all. The pope,

---

[121] Teglatius seems to have been born in Venice and trained in the humanities and theology. Although appointed to the Archbishoprics of Patras in Achaia and of Antibar in present-day Albania (1475), then transferred from Antibar to Altino in the Venetian Republic (1485), he seems to have resided in Rome where he was an assistant of the Papal Chapel and where he wrote a speech *in materia fidei* and some learned yet poetic Latin commentaries on the Song of Songs. He attended the first to third, ninth and tenth sessions of the Lateran Council, being listed among the papal assistants of Julius II at the first three sessions. Confer: FARLATUS, *Illyrici Sacri* VII (1817) 96-97; G. CAPPELLETTI, *Le Chiese d'Italia*, Venice 1853, IX, 605; HURTER, 1138, N° 1.

[122] M 917A-B, E, 919B.

Christ's vicar, by a primeval and natural right of Christ the eternal Priest and in accord with the decree of the Father, holds all power over things spiritual and temporal. Constantine recognized this when he conceded the Empire to Pope Sylvester and received his scepter back again from the pope. St. Bernard also asserted this universal power. At the end of time there will be but one flock under this chief shepherd and the angelic and human *ecclesia* will become one in Christ [123].

Teglatius' theology of reform is intimately related to his theology of history, the key to which is a theory of the « two Sabbaths ». The first Sabbath, linked to the divine acts of creation and redemption, is the time of the building of the city of the great King, the founding of the Church. Christ established his Church through the agency of the fishermen, the apostles, especially Peter, whose confession of Christ's divinity was the foundation of the Church. During this period of the building of the Church, Christ established the kingdom of heaven of the Roman Church in the very city of Rome and provided that the shedding of the martyrs' blood would be for the support of the apostolic see and of him who canonically held it. As the persecution of the Emperors resulted in a strengthening and growth of the Church, and the later persecution of the heretics was for the exaltation of the Catholic faith, so too now is the persecution of the Moslems for the reformation of the Church, for the day of the Second Sabbath [124].

Evils have come into the world because men have forgotten the greatness of God. Lucifer and Adam, the pagan rulers of the Gentiles and of the Romans have forgotten God and done evil. In Stephen's own day men again extol themselves above the knowledge of God. The jurists and Averroists create confusion about the truth of the holy church, thus symbolizing the wisdom of this world and of Satan. The Moslems represent the knowledge of flesh. The words of the Philosophers (except those of Plato who acquired his wisdom from the Hebrews) are but a confusion of tongues, a Babylon. Thus the jurists, Moslems and Averroists refuse Christ praise and extol their own wisdom against His. If men would embrace the wisdom of God, a true reformation of the whole world would quickly occur [125].

---

[123] M 918D-E, 919A, 923B, 919C, 924C, 923E-914A, 924D, 923A, 919A; St. Bernard of Clairvaux, *De consideratione libri quinque ad Eugenium III*, Lib. IV, c. III, 7 (PL 182, 776-777).
[124] M 918C, 919A, D, 921A, 922C-D, 925A.
[125] M 923A-924C, 921A-C, 920D.

IV

At present sin flourishes, church officials from cardinals and bishops to curial officials and rectors have forgotten Christ's glory and His justice, have committed so many crimes and infractions of law, are without charity and the fear of God, transgress the limits set by the holy fathers and feast on the people of Christ. The times, indeed, are evil: charity is extinct and virtue corrupted. Depravity, pride, avarice, concern for earthly goods and neglect of the flock — such are the crimes of the clergy. On account of the sins of the clergy and laity which flourish in Stephen's time God has sent the scourge of the Turks to wake us from our evil slumber [126].

From the present persecution by the Turks Christ will bring about good for the Second Sabbath. This seventh period of history is the « sacrament » of the great reformation of the city of God and of the whole world. Christ will soon come in spirit, and with the help of the Holy Spirit will bring about this reformation through the human agency of the « spiritual hunters », the Fathers of the Council. Let the Fathers, therefore, awake from their evil sleep and await Christ who, in a second conversion of the world, will revive the decaying clerical state, for establishing the seventh period of the Church. He will also bring to life again the religious and lay states, and by recalling them to an observance of the Catholic faith and apostolic doctrine, He will lead men back to the unity of one fold by obedience to their mother the Roman Church. The Moslems will also be converted on this Second Sabbath and the whole world will be reconciled with God [127].

For the present, however, the day of divine vengeance is at hand unless the Council, under Leo's command, preach penance for the sins of the Christian people and provide by its decrees a true reformation of things temporal and spiritual. Let the pope take heed, for God has visited his judgment on the other patriarchs of the Church for their disobedience. Let those obstinately evil rulers of the Church and of the remaining Christian people beware, for God will require from the pastors an accounting for their flock which has been dispersed in the calamitous and unfortunate time of their wicked rule, and which has been torn by disobedience from the nourishing breasts of holy Church. Those who unworthily governed his Church while thousands of thousands were lost to the flock must face the judgment of God. Let the Fathers of the Council heed these warnings.

---

[126] M 924C-D, 926E-927A, 925C.
[127] M 922D, 918C, 919A, 921A-B, 919D, 922D-923A, 920A.

Let the prelates embrace mother Church, pray, fast, give alms, hold vigils, and distribute the fragments of apostolic doctrine in their churches [128].

For one who seems to have resided seldom (if ever) in his own sees, Teglatius was rather harsh on those who neglected their pastoral duties. With the wisdom of life's eleventh hour, he seems to have gained pastoral perspective while losing his powers of analysis to an apocalyptic monism. Whether or not they fitted, Teglatius forced all his facts into the framework of an evil slumber followed by the Second Sabbath. Without producing supporting evidence, he proclaimed charity extinct and God's glory forgotten. Such unlikely candidates as jurists, Moslems, and Averroists were identified with the evil forces of the world, flesh, and devil. Centuries of millenial imagery were paraded before his listeners and related to the events of the day. The result was a vague, almost mystical, mixture of chiliastic myths.

The theme of the two Sabbaths which the aged Teglatius used is a very ancient one going back to Old Testament imagery and to the beginnings of Patristic literature. His scheme of salvation history seems to have borrowed a number of elements from the common treasury of millenarian theology, especially from the writings of Bernard and possibly from those of Joachim of Fiore. The themes of two sabbaths and of seven stages of the world are found in Ambrose and Augustine and also in Joachim. The tripartite division of history he seems to have borrowed from Bernard, with one addition. He agrees with the Abbot of Clairvaux that the Church has suffered from the persecutions of the Roman emperors, then from the attacks of heretics, and finally in his day from internal moral decay — the « evil slumber ». He goes beyond Bernard, though, in seeing the Moslems as sent by God to wake the Church from her evil sleep. Possible echoes of Joachim may be found in his references to a seventh age, to the conversion of the Moslems on this great Sabbath, and to the assimilation of all mankind into the Church at the end of time. Stephen's « spiritual hunters » who will usher in the Second Sabbath resemble Joachim's « spiritual men » who characterize the last age. The role Teglatius assigns the Holy Spirit in bringing about this last period of history also seems to echo the Calabrian Abbot [129].

---

[128] M 927A, 928B, 926B, 926C-D, 927E-928A, 928E.
[129] LADNER, *The Idea of Reform* 27-29, 222-238; St. Bernard of Clairvaux, *Parabola* IV, 3-7 (PL, 183, 768-770); *Sermones in Cantica*, XXXIII, 8-16, (Ibid.,

While the acts of the Council record no speech as being given at the eleventh session December 12, 1516, it is known that shortly before the close of the Council, the Count John Francis Pico della Mirandola (1469-1533) addressed the Fathers with a speech on reform [130]. This address provides us with interesting insights into the reform ideas of a leading layman and disciple of Savonarola.

The notion of the Church found in this speech follows in the tradition of St. Thomas Aquinas as shared by Savonarola: the structure and sacraments are left unchallenged and the roles of pope, cardinals, and bishops are described in pastoral and juridical terms. Pico also envisioned the Church as part of the Christian Republic which is ruled by princes and by cardinals and over which God's vicar, the Pope, has primary responsibility. This Christian Republic, he claimed, has already fallen and is about to decay [131].

Evils infect all levels of society, but blame lies heavily on the clergy whom the unlearned laity imitate. Instead of being examples of piety and virtue, the clergy are sources of scandal and corruption. Both bishops and priests are guilty of luxury, lust, laziness, dissipation, ambition, greed, squandering of their

---

955-959); MORTON W. BLOOMFIELD, *Joachim of Flora: A Critical Survey of His Canon, Teachings, Sources, Biography, and Influence*: Traditio 13 (1957) 264-266, 297, 307; GORDON LEFF, *Heresy in the Later Middle Ages: the Relation of Heterodoxy to Dissent c. 1250-c. 1450*, New York 1967, I, 69-75.

[130] Nephew of the noted John Pico, John Francis Pico spent his youth in the study of the humanities, philosophy, and theology. He frequented Savonarola's Convent of San Marco in Florence where he deepened his piety, continued his learning, and won the admiration of the leading literary men of his day who also frequented the convent. The loyalty he developed there for Savonarola and his followers was deep and lasting: he argued against the prophet's excommunication, aided his hounded disciples, and even wrote a sympathetic biography during the early days of the Council. His other writings included numerous letters to famous people, biographies, poems, and works on philosophy and theology. He was befriended by such popes as Julius II who personally led the army which reinstated him in his castle and by Leo who chose him to address the Council. Victim of a struggle for power within his family, he was murdered together with his son. Confer: F. BONNARD, *Pic de la Mirandole, Jean-François*: DThC XII, 1607; SIMONDE-SISMONDI, *Mirandole (Jean-François III, Pic de la)*: Biographie universelle, ancienne et moderne, Paris 1821, XXIX, 125-126; F. GILBERT, *Cristianesimo, Umanesimo e la Bolla 'Apostolici Regiminis' del 1513*: Riv. Storica Italiana 79 (1967) 980-983; E. GARIN, *Italian Humanism: Philosophy and Civic Life in the Renaissance*, Oxford 1965, 133-135; PASTOR V, 215-216; VIII, 250; R. RIDOLFI, *The Life of Girolamo Savonarola*, New York 1959, 127, 203, 221, 298, 304; HURTER 1226-1227, N° 577; HEFELE-LECLERCQ VIII-I, 420, 425-426.

[131] M. M. GORCE, *Savonarole, Jérôme*: DThC XIV, 1222-1223; John Francis Pico de Mirandola, «Oratio de Reformandis Moribus ad Leonem Decimum Pontificem Maximum, et Concilium Lateranen.,» in W. ROSCOE, *The Life and Pontificate of Leo the Tenth*, London 1806, VI, 66-69, 76.

money, misusing Church funds, accumulating benefices, and allowing religion to degenerate into superstition. Men of little or no theological training and of low moral repute are raised to even high ecclesiastical office. It is no wonder that all society is in need of reform [132].

The basic reform remedy Pico prescribed was not the making of new laws but the enforcing of old ones. If the decrees of the ancient Fathers against these vices and the unwritten prescriptions of the natural law were observed, the Christian Republic would be conserved and grow [133].

Since the example of leaders is the pivotal factor in this reformation, let certain minimal standards safeguard the conduct of the clergy. The priests need not have the extraordinary virtue of the saint or be men of great learning, but at least let them not be public sinners and unable to read their prayers. To remedy this ignorance and credulity there must be a renovation of clerical formation and style of life. Let the clergy devote themselves to the study of those editions of the Sacred Scriptures which have been purged of errors arising from the evil of the times and from the carelessness of libraries. May similar help be given the priests by revisions of the daily office and of the sacred liturgy and by a sorting out of apocryphal fables from true historical narrative. This reformation of the clerical order must be accompanied by a moral restoration of secular rulers. Let simplicity replace cunning, purity corruption, liberality licence, thrift greed, and peace discord. Not only will the Christian Republic be renewed by such measures, but the good example of sound morals will convert the Moslems whom miracles, military might, and legal prescriptions have been unable to win thus far to Christendom [134].

The chief agents of this reformation of Christendom are the cardinals and bishops gathered in Council, and especially the pope. All the people hopefully look to their leaders and earnestly beg for a renovation of the Christian Republic. Let the bishops be for the faithful living laws which will lead them to the norm of piety and of true discipline. Let the cardinals watch over the *instituta* and the decrees of the ancient Fathers. The pope, however, for Pico must be the chief force behind reform. His example of industry and innocence of life must be combined with a concern for others' salvation. To heal and cure the sick

---
[132] ROSCOE 67-71, 74.
[133] ROSCOE 66-68, 75.
[134] ROSCOE 66-68, 72-77.

Christian society, let him first exhort men by the example of his life to a love of virtue and, should that fail, instill in them a fear of punishments. The force of justice, rigor, severity, and punishments must be joined to his kind and easy-going ways. Churchmen must, therefore, be models of virtue and stern enforcers of law [135].

The evils of the times are warnings from God to reform. If the pope, the principal agent of reform, fails to enforce the law, it is to be feared that God Himself will with fire and sword cut off the diseased members. Unless God is placated with improved morals and prayers, Churchmen will drink from the bitter and sorrowful cup offered them by the « perfidious deserters of our religion » [136].

The shadow of Savonarola spread over the Council as Pico spoke. Calamities were promised the Church if it failed to do penance. The evils of high Churchmen were boldly denounced and the pope was solemnly reminded of his duties. A change in morals, not in ecclesiastical structure, was demanded. The clergy were to esteem learning and to study carefully the sacred scriptures. Pico, however, was more pessimistic than Savonarola. Although both saw everywhere moral decay and approaching punishment from heaven, the friar assured his listeners of an era of reform to follow the destruction, while the layman hesitated and merely hoped for a future period of peace. Like his master, the disciple would live to see his words go unheeded and would also die a violent death looking at a crucifix of his rejected Savior [137].

Pico's speech is variously evaluated. By some he is accused of dealing in generalities and of offering no practical remedies [138]. By another he is praised for his frankness, realistic approach to reformation, and prophetic vision [139]. Yet another saw in his speech a « most precise and most serious » demand for reform which turned into a program of action a century of concern over the problem. This demand was a severe summons to religion as a discipline of science and of life, as a school of serious and integral human formation — the attempts of a humanist in the traditions of Savonarola and of his uncle John Pico della Mi-

---

[135] ROSCOE 66-69, 74-76.
[136] ROSCOE 68.
[137] SIMONDE-SISMONDI, *Mirandole* 126.
[138] HEFELE-LECLERCQ VIII-I, 541.
[139] PASTOR VII, 5-6; VIII, 406-407.

randola [140]. Whatever else may be said it must be admitted that with the clear vision of a prophet John Francis had foreseen some sort of schism in the Church and a prime cause of it in the failure of Leo to take seriously the grave responsibilities of his office. Would that the high priest had listened to the layman!

The twelfth and last session of the Council held on March 16, 1517 was addressed by Maximus Brunus Corvinus († 1522) [141]. This honor was conferred on him, he claimed, out of appreciation for the thirty years of labors and sufferings spent in the service of the Holy See. His speech at this session on the origins and authority of Councils, on the mystery of Christ and the benefit of the priesthood, and on doctrine and virtue was of considerable length until abridged by a commission at the pope's command. Only the last part of this speech treats reform [142].

The tenor of the times, he claimed, is evil. Men have forgotten the debt of gratitude they owe to Christ and the clergy, and are unmoved by justice, piety, or God. Indeed, the light of piety is being extinguished and the vengeful wrath of God provoked. Men seek the wisdom of astrologers and of certain philosophers which is vain and superstitious. The true way to wisdom is through Christ and his gospels. He established priests and bishops as the supports of his Church and charged them to preach the « good news » to all creation. With the aid of sacred scriptures, the clergy have established doctrine and virtue and destroyed vice, schism, and heresy. Thanks to their great efforts over the past years, this council has been a success. [143] In his closing words, Corvinus assessed the achievements of the Fifth Lateran: the Church has recovered what belongs to her, she has regained a dignity with authority. The Christian Republic, once again submitting to this authority, finds itself

---

[140] E. GARIN, *La Culture Filosofica del Rinascimento Italiano*, Florence 1961, 181-182.

[141] Of Neapolitan birth and humanistic training, Corvinus won the friendship of such men of letters as Sannazaro. He became a cleric of the Knights of St. John of Rhodes and was promoted to the episcopacy of Isernia (near Campobasso in central Italy). Dedicated to the service of the papacy, he was sent as nuntio to Venice and Naples but seems to have suffered from calumny and imprisonment. At the Fifth Lateran Council he was both faithful in attendance and active at the formal sessions and general congregations. Confer: UGHELLUS, *Italia Sacra* VI (1659), 505; *Hierarchia Catholica medii et recentioris aevi* III, 214; PASTOR VIII, 202-204; M 977E, 938B, 849E-850A, 993C-E, 994B.

[142] M 993C, 994B; E. RODOCANACHI, *Histoire de Rome: le pontificat de Leon X, 1513-1521*, Paris 1931, 148; SANUDO, XXII, 394.

[143] M 997B-999B.

in the repossession of peace, piety, justice, and the holy way of life pointed out by Christ Jesus.[144] Such a glowing assessment of the Council's achievements would be disproved before the year was out and the schism predicted by Pico would reveal the weak foundations for such optimism.

Before concluding this treatment of reform concepts found in the official acts of the Council, a few words might be said on the conciliar decrees. Although these do not come strictly under the heading of reform proposals, they do contain certain general statements on the nature of reform and deserve at least a passing reference.

In these decrees of the Council the pope is clearly pictured as the principal agent of reform. His pastoral office obliges him to care for the flock and to serve his subjects by protecting Church liberty, acting as conciliator, and suppressing scandals. He will achieve this later by making sure that his flock follows Christian discipline and leads a correct way of life. He is to insure that the Word of God is properly preached and that the erring are led back to the path of truth. His special care is the Curia. Julius established a commission to study its practices and to make recommendations. Leo who had been a member of that commission now seeks to bring the work of reform to a successful conclusion.[145]

The evils which infect the Church are serious. Almost every level of Christianity has seriously departed from the ancient ways and customs due to the difficulties of the times, continued negligence, and human frailty. The source of present curial corruption is none other than Sixtus IV, the uncle of Julius II. Satan has also been busy with his deceits and snares, sowing errors in the field of the Lord and watering them with avarice and ambition. Due to the present « security in sinning », it is to be feared that many may actually fall into these errors. Philosophy and poetry already contain them and they are preached from the pulpit and published in books.[146] The precise nature of these doctrinal abberations, however, is never stated.

The solution to these evils is basically a return to the ancient and just ways of the holy Fathers. Let those canons fallen into disuse be reaffirmed and a pristine observance restored. Errors

---

[144] M 999C: « ut et sua sibi reddatur ecclesia, et ut ecclesiae dignitas, dignitati auctoritas, auctoritati Christiana reipublica, Christianae vero reipublicae pax, justitia, pietas, et ipsa Jesu Christi sacra et sancta institutio restituatur. »
[145] M 847D, 907D, 971A-B, 944A, 912C, 846A-B.
[146] M 847D, 875A, 846B, 771D, 847E, 842A-B, 912D-E, 944E-945B; *Bull. Rom.*, Leo X, V, Preamble, p. 571, N° 11, 576, N° 23, 583, N° 30, 590-592, N° 36, 595.

are to be vanquished by the study of theology or canon law and greater episcopal control over the pulpit and press.[147] A restored episcopacy together with a reformed Roman Curia were the principal goals of the program of a return to former juridical structures implicit in many of the decrees. Although these normative structures were not those of Christian antiquity, they were probably those which characterized the pre-Renaissance Church, and perhaps even the pre-Gregorian Church due to the decrees' concern to restore certain local authority and their references to the ancient and primeval practices of the holy Fathers.

While the conciliar speakers dealt in pastoral and rhetorical generalities and called for a sweeping reform of the Church, the decrees gave only passing attention to reform theory, covered only certain areas of Church life with their precepts, and went into legal detail. Except for their repeated references to the role of Satan and the problem of errors, these conciliar decrees envisioned reform along many of the same general lines as the speakers. It is doubtful, however, if these speakers had much, if any, influence on their composition. Even the comments of Pucci seem to have merely reflected what was already contained in the reform bull. To find the source of the reform thought which is embodied in the conciliar decrees, one must, therefore, look outside the official acts of the Council.

A unique source for the concepts of reform at Lateran V is a collection of fragmentary comments made outside the Council's halls and seemingly during meetings of the sacred consistory, the general and particular congregations of the Council, and its reform commissions[148]. The speaker was Raphael Cardinal Riario, Dean of the Sacred College, head of the Apostolic Camera, member of the conciliar reform commission, and a personal adviser of the pope[149]. The duties of his offices, he claimed,

---

[147] Ibid., Preamble; M 885B, 847E.

[148] At least four manuscript editions of these « voti consistorialia » can be found in the Vatican Library: Archiva Varia Politicorum: *Miscellanea*, Arm. II, Tom. 19, fol. 293r-306v and Tom. 21, fol. 40r-56v in the Secret Archives; and *Cod. Vat. lat.* 12146, fol. 1r-22r and Mss. Chigiana I. III. 89, fol. 44r-55v in the Manuscript Collection. Because of its greater legibility and care for fidelity, the Chigi text has been here used. A transcription of it may be found in the Appendices at the end of this article.

[149] Born 1460/61 at Savona in Liguria, adopting the family name of his mother, he was nephew of Peter Cardinal Riario and relative of Sixtus IV by whom he was raised to the cardinalate (1477) while studying at Pisa. During the celebration of this promotion at Florence, some of his relatives took part in the Piazzi conspiracy against the Medici; the innocence of youth and his presence at the altar, however, saved him from the fury of the Florentines.

demanded that he give his opinions on a number of reform proposals and that he exhort and keep asking the Council Fathers to fulfill their offices and tasks in this work of reform. He professed that he had always desired a reform in the Church but confessed that this desire was imperfect, and that in spite of his good intentions he was not up to the task. He claimed though that he had refused no labor nor neglected any duty which pertained to a cardinal member of the reform commission or to any other work. His wealth of experience and information plus his frankness and at times sarcasm in stating his opinions add an important dimension to an understanding of the reform thought of Lateran V.

Riario made only indirect references to the nature of the Church. He compared its present condition to that of a sick body and referred to the Roman Curia as the head of all the world. Due to its dignity this Curia should be the norm and rule of the Christian religion. References to the Church he generally cushioned in legal and regal terminology while his strongly papal conception of the Church is evidenced in his descriptions of the office and duties of the pope. The Roman pontiff is pastor of the flock and should provide for it personally when its needs are not adequately cared for by his subordinates. At present there is nothing more fitting for him to do than maintain the Curia and his subjects in a good condition and way of life and reform for the better whatever has deviated, leading it back to its proper state. God has given the present pope the

He received from Sixtus numerous benefices and in 1483 the office of Camerarius (Treasurer). A skilled diplomat, he was also a friend and patron of humanists. In hopes of receiving political favors for his family, he supported the election of Alexander VI. Although considered one of the more worldly cardinals, he was appointed to the aborted reform commission established by Alexander during his short-lived repentance on the occasion of the violent death of one of his favorites. When the pope turned against Riario's family, he fled to his see of Tréguier in France, returning in triumph to Rome (1503) on the death of Alexander. He was soon numbered among the very few cardinal advisers of his close relative, Julius II, becoming Dean of the Sacred College (1511), and being appointed by Julius as « moderator » of the Lateran Council. Leo X, whose election he opposed, made him member of the conciliar reform commission and grand chancellor of the University of Rome. Involved in a plot to poison Leo (1517), he was 'tried', stripped of his ecclesiastical dignities, and forced to pay a huge ransom. Later reinstated to the cardinalate, he retired to Naples where he died (1521). Confer: CIACONIUS, *Vitae et res gesta Pontificum Romanorum et S. R. E. Cardinalium*, ed. A. Oldoinus, Rome 1677, III, 70-76; UGHELLUS, *Italia Sacra* I, 77-78; M. E. COSENZA, *Biographical and Bibliographical Dictionary of the Italian Humanists and of the World of Classical Scholarship in Italy, 1300-1800*, Boston 1962, IV, 3037; E. RODOCANACHI, *Histoire de Rome: Le Pontificat de Jules II 1503-1513*, 1928, 37, 137, 179; L. MORÉRI, *Le Grand Dictionnaire Historique*, Paris 1759, IX, 171; PASTOR V, 362, 354, 515.

desire and determination to begin this reform and the zeal to bring it to a successful conclusion with the help of the Council, no matter what sinister interpretations may have been placed on his predecessor's good intentions. The pope should not just remain on the level of desiring reform, but actually busy himself with achieving it. Leo has in fact done just that. He has ordered that reform begin with the pope himself and with his palace. To make sure that this work was carried out as quickly as possible, Leo was personally present at and presided over all the meetings of the congregation treating this reform. Being well informed, he removed difficulties, checked delays, and confirmed its work with his wisdom and authority. In spite of these efforts taken by the pope, Riario felt that the bull reforming the curial officials, while befitting its end, lacked the rigor required by the situation. Referring to the process used in formulating a different reform measure, Riario, pointed out that the material had been carefully compiled and annotated by cardinal deputies and much discussed and debated in several congregations and in a sacred consistory held in the presence of the pope. Suggestions on modifications made by prelates were to be referred to the pope who would determine what is best. The ultimate decisions on reform would, therefore, seem to have been in the hands of the pope with his cardinals advising. The Council's function was to confirm publicly what they had decided. Addressing the pope and cardinals, Riario asserted:

But in this work of reform, which depends entirely on our will and judgment, we are able to be censured vehemently if, either through contempt or through our negligence, it [i.e., the *institutum majorum*] has fallen into a worse condition; or rather, if, as it is slipping down, we have no concern to replace and restore it with all our strength.[150]

Riario's thinking on the function and importance of a council centered on the specific goals set for Lateran V. He asserted that no one should seek or give occasion for seeking a council, but that once one was legitimately convoked there is nothing more necessary, expedient, and glorious than a general Council. If for no other reason the convoking of the present Council was justified by the practice of the ancient Fathers whereby councils were used to repair what was broken and strengthen what was still solid whenever the Church was split by schism. This Lateran Council must likewise condemn the Pisan Schism and ratify the actions of the pope. Adhesion to the Council is one way of

---

[150] Confer the final words of the speech in Appendix N. 6.

showing devotion to His Holiness. The rumors that he was trying to avoid a Council are unfounded; a postponement of its sessions is due rather to the difficulties which bishops are experiencing in travelling through war-torn territory. Riario did not seem enthusiastic about having the Council involved in establishing political peace between Christian princes. Rather, he felt that the Council was keeping more to the traditions of the Fathers when it busied itself with questions of faith. Among the many things which were proposed for the Council's consideration « almost nothing is more necessary and opportune », he asserted, than a « reformation of morals and Church discipline ».

Since Leo has been careful to celebrate the Council according to the precepts and practices of the ancient Fathers both with regards to its ceremonies and substance, he has ordered that the question of reform be treated in general and particular congregations. Part of the members of the particular congregations were to be elected by the Council Fathers and they were to follow their dictates of prudence and conscience in their discussions. In this way the pope will have good advice as to what to treat in the formal sessions of the Council. Riario, therefore, envisioned Lateran V as an effective means of strengthening papal authority and of achieving goals set by the pope.

The evils which should command the attention of pope and Council are schism and moral decay. The schismatic cardinals have inflicted a wound on the Church and their continued absence is against the law, scandalous, productive of bad fruit, and more likely to cause destruction than achieve laudible ends. Their Pisan Synod is a source of murmurings and detractions against the Holy See. The affairs of the Church continue to collapse into greater confusion. This is due to the fact that much has been said over the past years about reform, but little put into practice. Indeed, the question of reform has always been imperfectly dismissed and not without serious scandal. Our present condition is like that of a person who can be cured of his illness only with great difficulty, if at all, since he neglected to seek a remedy when the disease first appeared. Evidence of this illness is to be found in the morals and practices of the Roman Curia which have undoubtedly deviated much from the ways of our ancient Fathers.

For Riario the required reform consisted primarily in restoring that best norm of moral life and Church discipline of our ancestors in the Faith, the ancient Fathers. Their footsteps are our guides to a good and praiseworthy life in the Church of God. The goal of such a reform is the honor of God and the conservation and growth of the state of the pope and clergy in honor and of the ecclesiastical state in morals and life. Indeed, nothing is more fitting for conserving, securing, and increasing our interests and those of the whole state of the Holy Roman Church than a reform in the Church and Roman Curia. It is the means for restoring authority to the Church, for preserving the honor of the Holy See, and for adding dignity to every ecclesiastical order. Such a reform of the Curia will edify those under us and free us from the many detractions and murmurings of those living beyond the Alps and in foreign nations. The good will of foreign nations depends on our giving them the satisfaction of a true reform. According to the expressed desires of Leo, this reformation should begin with the pope and his own palace. Once the curial officials have been « modified », reforming efforts should be extended to morals. The grace of God has and must continue to sustain this work of renovation. While those charged with preparing the reform materials are the various conciliar congregations, the ultimate responsibility for content and execution of this reformation is in the hands of the cardinals and pope.

These remarks of Riario add several important practical dimensions to the concepts of reform found thus far in the official conciliar speeches and decrees. Implied in much he said was a view of reformation as a tool of papal politics aimed at checking the complaints, murmurings, and erosion of good will toward Rome found among the non-Italian nations, especially those beyond the Alps. By a return to the curial practices of the ancient Fathers, Riario hoped to remove the causes of much dissatisfaction. His emphasis, unfortunately, was more on modifying curial procedures and seeing to it that the outward deportment of Church officials tended to promote the honor, dignity, and authority of the Holy See than on demanding an interior renovation and conversion of the heart to Christ. While agreeing with the other speakers on the central rôle of the pope in the reformation process, he played down the importance of the bishops, emphasized the significant rôle and responsibility of the cardinals, and openly complained of the weakness of those measures which were the first products of Leo's reforming zeal.

To what extent this Dean of the Sacred College and leading curial official represented the views of his fellow cardinals or reflected the desires of the reigning pontiffs is difficult to discern.

It is clear that he was dissatisfied with the current curial procedures and feared that the cardinals charged with formulating reform were not convinced of the seriousness of their task. Under Julius who feared the evils of the Pisan Schism, Riario stressed restoring Church authority; under Leo who ended the schism and urged reform, he emphasized renovating Church morals and returning to the practices of the ancient Fathers. It does not seem, however, that Riario merely bent with the present wind. The initial reform efforts of Leo he prophetically criticized as lacking the rigor required to put a stop to continued complaints beyond the Alps. Granted this expressed desire for reform, why were the efforts of so powerful a cardinal not more productive of results within the congregations, commission, and consistories? Are Leo and his fellow curial cardinals solely to be blamed? Or was he perhaps a victim of his own « reform rhetoric » whereby he could sincerely and publicly denounce the evils of the times as did everyone else and yet recognize no contradiction in the fact that he himself was one of the major contributors to the present sad state of affairs and had no real desire to see things properly changed? Unfortunately, the necessary documents have not as yet been discovered to answer these important questions.

In addition to the official acts of the Council and the comments of the Cardinal Dean there also exist a few other sources on conciliar reform thought. In preparation for Lateran V a number of Spanish bishops gathered together in synod and also individually submitted their suggestions to His Catholic Majesty Ferdinand. During the time of the Council two Venetian Camalodese hermits recorded their recommendations in a memorandum to Leo X. These Spanish and Italian proposals were in general more detailed and practical than the suggestions of the conciliar speeches.

On November 16, 1511, a Mass was offered at Burgos to celebrate the adhesion of the Spanish lands to the coming Council. The papal nuncio announced that the Lateran Synod had been convoked for the union of all Christians and for the reform of the Church with regard to customs and whatever else will help bring about this renovation. Soon after these words the Bishop of Oviedo, Villa-Quiran, spoke in the name of the King as-

---

[151] Juan Pascual de Rebenga, Bishop of Burgos, was born of poor parents in 1442. He entered the Dominicans, studied theology at Bologna, and returned to Spain where he was elected vicar general of his congregation and by his learning and personal holiness helped in the reform of the Dominicans there.

serting that His Majesty was very pleased with Julius' solicitude and care for the good government and reform of Holy Church and that the King offered to send whatever prelates and material resources (soldiers and money) the pope may desire. The Bishop of Oviedo, subsequently preached a sermon based on the Gospel of the Mass [152].

Unlike the recorded comments of some of his fellow bishops, Villa-Quiran [153] gave but lip-service to the theme of reform and launched into a theoretical description of the Church and pope. The Church which needs its health restored and certain things reformed is our holy Mother, the Spouse of Christ born from his side on the cross, united with him forever in matrimony, a bride without spot or wrinkle. This bride was commended to St. Peter and his canonically elected successors as « quasi grooms » to govern, preserve, administer, and pray for her. These Roman pontiffs are vicars of Christ, the shepherds of his flock, the heads of his Church, and captains of his army. This Roman Church is the mother of our faith and doctrine, and the giver of law and head of the spiritual government of Christianity. Because of our sins the Church now suffers the fourfold persecution of tyrants, heretics, false brethren, and the Anti-Christ, Louis, King of France. Although these persecutions will

---

Nominated Bishop of Burgos on September 16, 1495, he was confirmed in that office in 1496 and took possession of his see in 1497. As bishop he employed visitations, exhortations, ordinances, and the power of personal example to reform the clergy and provide for the religious instruction of the faithful. He also restored churches, founded a model monestary, and distributed the revenues of his office to the poor. In spite of his age he travelled to Rome to attend the opening and first two sessions of the Lateran Council in hopes of supporting the pope, re-establishing ecclesiastical discipline, and reforming Church practices, especially those of the Roman Court. While awaiting the third session, he took ill and died on July 19, 1512. Confer: S. BIEDNA, *Pascual de Fontecasto*: Biografia Eclesiastica Completa, Madrid 1863, 16, 879-884; S. RUIZ, *Burgos*: DHGE 10, 1339; J. QUETIF and J. ECHARD, *F. Paschalis de la Fuensanta*: Scriptores Ordinis Praedicatorum Recensiti, Paris 1721, II, 25-26.

[152] J. M. DOUSSINAGUE, *Fernando el Catholico y el Cisma de Pisa*, Madrid 1946, II, 505-507.

[153] Ibid., 508-512; Valerian Alphonsus Ordoñez de Villaquirán came from Zamora in northern Spain. Licensed in theology he was made bishop of Ciudad Rodrigo on September 24, 1501 and transferred to Oviedo on December 22, 1508. He is said to have written « De la Translación del Cuerpo de S. Ildefonso y milagros sucedidos » and wrote a gloss on the popular poem « Al dolor de mi cuydado ». Due to his theological learning he was one of the few recommended by the Bishop of Cordova and the bishops of that province to represent Spain at the Lateran Council. He died, however, at Burgos on August 12, 1512 and was buried in the monestary of the Franciscan sisters he had built at Zamora. Confer: Nicholas Antonius Hispalensis, *Bibliotheca Hispana Nova*, Matriti 1788, II, 320-321; F. PÉREZ, *Ciudad Rodrigo*: DHGE 12, 1016; J. S. DIAZ, *Bibliografia de la Literatura Hispanica* III-I, Madrid 1963, 409, N° 2840 (121); DOUSSINAGUE, *Fernando y el Cisma* II, 523.

strengthen the Church's virtue, she does not know at present where to find a remedy for her sufferings. Let Ferdinand defend her from injury with the resources of his Kingdom.

A month later when the bishops of Castile convened a synod at Burgos, they drew up for the King a program of reform. Their proposals urged among other things a reformation of the papacy and decentralization of its power. Let the pope begin by reforming himself and assuring an end to simony in papal elections. He should be limited in the number and kind of men he can appoint as cardinals and these men should be given power to convoke and hold a Council every five years. In the coming Council let there be a guarantee of liberty and freedom from fear. Canon law should be thoroughly revised, its regulations regarding benefices strictly enforced, and unjustifiable papal dispensations not tolerated. In fact, the Council should confirm the right of local ordinaries to resist illegitimate dispensations. Even the practice of dispensing from university examinations must be abolished. Appointments of abbots and priors should be left to the choice of the religious order itself and not made by the pope. Benefices which are dependent on local ordinaries should be given to men whose ability has been proven by an examination. With regard to those benefices which involve pastoral duties, no dispensation from residency requirements should be allowed [154]. While providing thus for the remedy of certain diocesan abuses, the Bishops of Burgos had directed their attention primarily at the Roman administrative level where reform would consist in legal constraints on the power of the papacy. By confirming such restrictions, the Council would remove abuses and strengthen the authority of local authorities.

There also exists from this time an unidentified set of reform proposals written in Spanish [155]. Its author looked favorably on the proper use of papal power but was strongly critical

---

[154] Ibid., 521-522; DÖLLINGER, Beiträge III, 201-203; a French translation of these proposals can be found in HEFELE-LECLERCQ VIII-I, 307-309.

[155] DOUSSINAGUE, Fernando y el Cisma II, 530-532; DÖLLINGER, Beiträge III, 203-208; a French rendition of these proposals which leaves out uncomplimentary references to the French can be found in HEFELE-LECLERCQ VIII-I, 309-313. Seemingly on the basis of an edition which ends with the words: « Del obispo de Burgos. », Doussinague identified the author of this proposal as Juan Pascual, Bishop of Burgos (1497-1512). The Döllinger and Hefele-Leclercq edition concludes: « Bien sera hable algo en el concilio sobre los patronazgos de las montanas para el senamiento de sus consciencias de los mesmos patronos y los obispos de Burgos. » Lacking any clear indication as to authorship, they left these proposals unidentified.

* (See Addenda)

of certain « sins » of the city and Curia of Rome. His pastoral zeal for reform extended beyond the problems of the clergy to embrace those of the religious and laity alike. Papal authority, except when used simoniacally, is not questioned in his proposals; rather, his concern is to see that only worthy men exercise it, and that it be used to confirm the Council's reform measures. The Roman Curia is censured for granting scandalous dispensations, engaging in simony, and manipulating for its financial advantage the system of expectives, provisions, and collation of benefices. The city of Rome he condemned not only for its corrupt Curia, but also for tolerating pagan rites and superstitions and for protecting Jews. A stricter enforcement of the laws regarding clerical celibacy, residence, the ordination of canons, and the prohibition of conflicting benefices in the same cathedral is also urged. Religious are to lose many of their privileges and their positions of precedence determined. Spanish monasteries are to be freed from French control. The laity are to be protected from excessive tithes and released from the obligation under pain of sin of fasting, observing holydays, and making their Easter duty. They in turn are to guarantee clerical liberty, refrain from pre-empting Church benefices, and stop fighting among themselves.

These proposals embraced a wide variety of Church discipline. The reformation which they envisioned depended much on the correction of curial practices and the enforcement of the canons on all levels of the Church. Certain of its suggestions were actually incorporated into the instructions of the Spanish ambassadors to the Council and in the final decrees of Lateran V.

A long and detailed set of reform measures was proposed by the Archbishop of Seville, Diego de Deza, a leading Churchman, theologian, and reformer of Spain [156]. Intent on analyzing

---

[156] Diego de Deza was born 1443 or 1444 of noble parents at Toro (Zamora) where sixteen years later he entered the Dominicans. Studying under Pedro Jimenez de Prexamo and Pedro de Osma at the University of Salamanca where he earned his doctoral degree in 1480, de Deza also taught there, then at Calvea, and finally returned to Salamanca, succeeding to the chair of de Osma. An eminent theologian, he wrote numerous works in defense of St. Thomas Aquinas and is numbered among the first representatives of the new theology in sixteenth century Spain. He tutored Don Juan from 1486 until 1494 when he officiated at the wedding of the heir apparent. After 1497 he was confessor to Ferdinand and Isabella, their Grand Almoner (1499), Chancellor of Castile, and Grand Inquisitor for Leon, Castile, and Aragon (1498-1506). At court he was a devoted protector of Christopher Columbus. He held a series of ecclesiastical dignities, culminating at the time of his death in Primate of Spain: Zamora (1494), Salamanca (1494), Jaen (1498), Palencia (1500), Seville (1504), and Toledo († 1523). As bishop he zealously cared for the faith and morals of

evils and prescribing their appropriate remedies, this Dominican prelate of wide experience and deep erudition did not delay in describing the nature of the Church or its offices. Claiming that the source of many evils was the division of Church law into canons, conciliar constitutions, and common law, with resulting confusion by way of contradictions, dispensations, and privileges, de Deza urged that the Church's disciplinary rules be all reduced to common law and that all dispensations from it be suppressed by the pope. If this could not be effected, the Archbishop urged a series of specific reforms. The vast majority of these are aimed at correcting abuses in the Roman Curia [157].

Papal practices of appointing to Church offices and of bestowing benefices came under sharp criticism. At present almost all Spanish benefices depend upon Rome. Under the recent popes beginning with Sixtus IV, Rome has despoiled vacant metropolitan and diocesan cathedrals of their wealth, leaving little revenue to the successor for meeting the annate and dispensation fees. Cathedral canons have been bestowed on unworthy men, the uneducated, and even children, much to the detriment of the diocese. In order to reward their servants, popes have granted parochial benefices to men who do not reside there. They continue to enjoy its revenues while not providing for the pastoral needs of the faithful. Religious must no longer be made bishops since they act against their superiors and demand large stipends. Seculars, on the other hand, should not be put in charge of the administration of religious houses since they absorb the revenues and allow religious observance to decline. The system of reservations, prolonged expectations, and incompatible benefices should be revoked. It is not unknown that Rome fraudulently confers benefices in secret and initiates litigation over benefices without the proper citations. Curial officials drag these cases out interminably to the advantage of certain cardinals and prelates, to the neglect of pastoral care in the benefice in question, and to the dispossession of the poor clerics for whom the benefices were designed. Before a

---

his flock; converted many Moors by his kindness; published books of liturgical prayers, homilies, and pastoral advice; and held diocean reform synods at Salamanca, Palencia, and Seville. The famous decrees of these synods reflect a real concern for the spiritual well-being of his clergy and faithful. Confer: G. M. COLOMBAS, *Deza (Diego de)*: DHGE 14, 372-373; QUETIF-ECHARD, *F. Didacus de Deca*: Scriptores O. P. Recensiti II, 51-52; A. COTERALO Y VALLEDOR, *Fray Diego de Deza. Ensayo biografico*, Madrid 1905; HEFELE-LECLERCQ VIII-I, 219, 383-388; HURTER 1213-1215, N° 571.

[157] DOUSSINAGUE, *Fernando y el Cisma* II, 532-538.

man can be deposed from his benefice, let a citation be made publicly in his own diocese. The trial should be held there and be decided according to common law. Without consulting the pope or the persons involved or even giving a reason, certain cardinals have taken bequests made to hospitals and taken control of the benefices of chaplaincies and of hospitals for lepers. The pope should stop such practices and see that the canons are observed.

The system of papal dispensations and privileges is another area for reform. Because of dispensations from residency requirements the sacraments go unadministered and the divine worship neglected. Let this pastoral obligation be enforced and if the cleric resides outside his benefice, let him not receive its revenues. Religious whom Rome has dispensed from their rules and allows to live outside their houses are living the « good life » and evading local authorities with the help of papal papers and apostolic judges. Such dispensations must be stopped and bishops empowered to force these men to reside in their religious houses. There are certain members of the secular clergy who, lacking ability and the necessary qualifications, were granted by Rome, contrary to the canons, papal letters which obliged the local bishops to ordain them. Once they have become priests, they lead scandalous lives while eluding diocesan discipline. Let the pope not grant such letters or only with the approval of the local bishop. The papal privilege of the « portable altar » should be suspended since many Spaniards are scandalized by the celebration of Mass in a home. Nobles should be allowed the privilege only if the local bishop agrees. Papal permission to wear the military garment should not be granted to men who are not Knights. So lax has the Curia become in granting special favors that almost no one goes to Rome and returns without dispensations of one kind or other.

The quality and conduct of certain papal officials leaves much to be desired. Claiming direct dependence on the pope, a number of bishops, protonotaries, and exempt religious escape censures for their evil example. These exemptions should be invalid outside Rome and religious houses. Many apostolic judges are ignorant of the canons, open to bribes, and ready to decide a case contrary to the opinion of the local ordinary and civil authorities. Papal notaries have also been shown to lack ability and be all too ready to dispense illegitimacy. Considerable confusion has been created by other apostolic officials with power to intervene in benefices. Such abuses point to a need for the serious enforcement of the canons, the removal of offenders, and a greater local control over the appointment and conduct of these officials.

The pope's help was asked to remedy a number of local problems. Certain lax religious orders in Spain ought to be reformed by the pope. A papal bull should be issued enforcing the wearing of clerical garb and demanding that those tonsured receive orders or lose their privileges. Benefices must not be given to the sons of priests or of heretics due to the scandal caused. That practice must be suppressed whereby many churches function as banks by using tithe money that was intended to benefit the churches. And let the pope grant bishops the power to have rowdy criminals removed from the church sanctuary where they have taken refuge from the law.

Deza's program of reform centered around Church law. He had suggested that common law govern all ecclesiastical discipline, but sensing that this would not be approved, he recommended certain specific measures. These were directed at correcting serious abuses perpetrated by the Roman Curia and at having the system of papal privileges and dispensations severely curtailed. To achieve this he called upon the pope to abandon the practices of his recent predecessors and to adopt a program of reform which would increase local authority. Ordinaries were to see that the law was enforced and that only worthy men be appointed to Church office. These recommendations were not an exercise in ecclesiological speculation but sprang from his years of experience as an important Church administrator. He prided himself in the success of his reform measures as bishop of Palencia and urged that some of these be adopted primarily by the Spanish Church, but also by the Universal Church soon to be gathered in Council under the pope.

In his letters to the royal court of December and January of 1511-12 [158], Sancho de Azeves, Bishop of Astorga [159], treated in detail the agents of conciliar reform, but said little of its content. The evil which commanded his attention was the wound of schism which has been inflicted on our Mother, the one, holy,

---

[158] Ibid., 523-528.
[159] Sancho de Azeves was born at Valtanas, became doctor « in decreto », archpriest of Rojas, archdeacon of Talaver (a chapter of Toledo), a « capellan mayor » of the Kingdom of Castile, and president of the Chancellery of Granada. He was named bishop of Astorga on December 4, 1500, first entered his see on July 1, 1512, and seems never to have resided there, although he enforced residency requirements for the priests of the chapter. He died at Valladolid on April 21, 1515. Confer: V. MARTÍNEZ, Azeves (Sancho de): DHGE 5, 1355.

apostolic Church . The ends proposed for the Council are indeed just, and its ways of achieving this reform should be in accordance with the canons. The Council is like a body and its members should be varied and numerous. The pope is its head, the cardinals its arms and legs. The other proper parts of the body are the patriarchs, archbishops, and bishops. In addition, there can be present abbots with episcopal jurisdiction and princes with their ambassadors as Constance advises and the material may demand. The pope, however, is rumored also content if religious, theologians, canonists, lawyers, and knights attend. Although the King has authority to decide which bishops may go, Azeves urged that as many as possible attend in order to provide the Council with strength and wise counsel. By their office bishops are successors of the apostles, the soul of the Church, princes of the earth, and have special angels to guide and illumine them. The King, however, should see that only those go who are qualified: men of virtue, wisdom, experience, holiness of life, and with a desire for the good of the Republic. Let the advice of the Council of Constance be the King's guide in these matters. Azeves, indeed, looked with favor on the coming Council, for its success he prayed daily. Although he himself could not go, he wanted his fellow bishops to be there in large number, since where there are many wise men and much counsel, there also is salvation for the world. It would thus seem that the conciliar bishops should have a principal part at least in the discussions on reform measures, if not also in their formulation.

The Patriarch of Alexandria, Alonso de Fonseca [160], had little to suggest for the Council [161]. Negatively, he asserted that the Council has no need to clarify Church teaching. No heresy is able to shake the faith since it is deeply ingrained in the people, while Church doctrines are well founded on the declarations of the holy doctors which contain all the necessary remedies.

---

[160] Alonso II de Fonseca was born at Salamanca where he studied as a youth. He pursued further studies in Italy and earned there the degree of doctor of canon and civil law. Returning to Spain he was made dean of the Cathedral of Seville, and in 1460 he succeeded his uncle Alonso I as Archbishop of Santiago, in which office he was confirmed by the King in 1481. As Archbishop he encountered lay opposition and became deeply involved in the politics of the day. Grown tired of political maneuverings, he resigned that office in 1506 and was promoted to the Patriarchate of Alexandria. His son later succeeded him as Alonso III of Santiago. He died on March 12, 1512 before the Council opened. Confer: *Fonseca (Alonso II de)*: Enciclopedia Universal Ilustrada Europeo-Americana 24, 313-314.

[161] DOUSSINAGUE, *Fernando y el Cisma* II, 528-529.

Should the Council treat the problem of Church reform, it could well investigate the customs and style of life of prelates and other ecclesiastics. He also recommended that the Spanish representatives to the Council be prepared to talk intelligently and convincingly on this problem and on any others presented. He himself would be unable to attend since within weeks of writing these suggestions and before the Council opened, de Fonseca died.

At the beginning of 1512, Ferdinand the Catholic drew up a list of instructions for his ambassadors to the Lateran Council [162]. He praised the celebration of such councils as the cause of great good while their neglect was the source of serious harm. According to the canons, these synods should seek an end to any heresies and schism, interpret divine precepts, determine questions of faith, and reform the Church in its head and members. Pope Julius and Lateran V should set out to destroy schism and heresies. They should also seek to clear up the inheritance of confusion left by Constance and Basel due to the opposition of Martin V and Eugenius IV to their decrees. Let Julius formally revoke at the coming Council those decrees of Constance and Basel, such as « Sacrosanct », which place the Council over the pope in matters touching faith, reform, and the removal of schism. In their place, let a new decree be published which declares that the vicar of Christ is over the Council except in cases of heresy and the election of two or more popes. Since the frequent celebration of councils is of such benefit to the Church, let another constitution be issued ratifying *Frequens* of Constance and commanding that a council be called every ten or fifteen years. In his concern for rescuing certain salutary decrees of Constance and Basel, Ferdinand seems to have shared Azeves' high esteem for these former conciliar accomplishments.

The evil which ranked high on Ferdinand's list of things to be reformed by Lateran V was that of buying and selling Church offices: the papacy, cardinalates, bishoprics, canonries, and other benefices. To put an end to the great scandal of certain papal elections, let a new constitution be published forbidding cardinals to bring money to the conclave. Since cardinals are the foundation on which the gate of the Church is guided and sustained, let the pope at Council forbid that this office be sold for money. Rather, let appointments to it be made according to the canons and those just and holy decrees

---
[162] Ibid. II, 538-543.

of Basel which Lateran should re-issue. The practice at Rome of publicly selling bishoprics, canonries, and other benefices must be stopped. This is an offense against God and man, and a cause of confusion and scandal in the Church of God. Let the Council promulgate that those pertinent canons governing appointments be observed, especially those of Martin V in the Council of Constance. The time honored rights of royal patrons to nominate men for office and approve those appointed should also be affirmed by the Council. This attention given by Ferdinand to correcting simoniacal practices resembles a similar care shown by the episcopal Synod of Burgos and by the « Del obispo de Burgos » memorial.

The King also urged that certain practices of the Roman Curia be abolished. Papal reservations *in pectore* ought to be stopped. The revenues of vacant offices should go to the successor and not to Rome. Money should not be taken from the diocese, nor the expectives of Castile given away, nor benefices bestowed on foreigners. The Council ought also provide for the proper upkeep of churches and monasteries. Let two cathedral canonries be set aside, one for a theologian, the other for a canonist. A bull should assure that only qualified men are appointed and that these hold but one canonry. This concern of Ferdinand for cathedral canonries and for the revenues of vacant sees seems to echo that found in the proposals of Diego de Deza.

The memorial went on to instruct the royal ambassadors on a number of other proposals. Ecclesiastical courts were to impose the full sanctions of the canons on criminal clerics. Foreigners, especially Frenchmen, were no longer to have control of the administration and finance of Spanish religious houses — a nationalistic sentiment also found in the « Del obispo de Burgos » memorial. Rich monasteries ought to be subject to royal taxes, their revenues limited, and some of their lands sold to the laity. Local ordinaries should be given the authority to dispense from the marital impediment of consanguinity. Knights should be dispensed from their vow of chastity. And if the King of France continues to disturb the peace, occupy a portion of the Papal States, and force me to divert my men and money from the holy crusade against the Moors, he should be tried and deposed, and his vassals absolved of their oaths of loyalty.

In general, Ferdinand's plan of reform was aimed at strengthening the authority of the pope and remedying the abuses of the Roman Curia. Papal power, however, was to be constrained by the rights of royal patrons and the precepts of the canons. By having certain decrees of Constance and Basel revoked or re-issued, Ferdinand hoped to achieve these two ends simultaneously: papal authority would be strengthened by clarifying its relation to a council while curial practices would be more firmly circumscribed by having a number of former conciliar reform canons reaffirmed [163].

Similar in some of its recommendations [164], but more comprehensive than the proposals of the Spanish memoranda, was the lengthy *Libellus ad Leonem X. Pontificem Maximum* by two Venetian Camaldolese hermits, Blessed Paul (Thomas) Giustiniani (1476-1528) [165] and Peter (Vincent) Quirini († 1514) [166]. Over

---

[163] It is interesting to note that as Louis of France hoped to use the Pisan Synod as a political tool in his struggle with the Papal States, so too now did Ferdinand of Spain see Lateran V as a means for censuring his French opponent, freeing Spanish benefices from foreign control, and confirming his rights of patronage. Ironically, the Council wound up rewarding France and not Spain. By its bull *Primitiva illa Ecclesia* Lateran V confirmed His Christian Majesty in some of the very privileges Ferdinand wanted guaranteed for himself in Spain.

[164] Unlike the other conciliar sources on reform is a literary work by the humanist Raphael Brandolinus, addressed to Dominic Cardinal Grimaus, and entitled « Oratio ad Lateranense concilium excogita. » Although it touches on reform, its chief concern is with praising Leo X, narrating the history of the past councils, and commenting on the politics of the day. Confer: *Cod. Ottob. lat.* 813, fols. 1-61 in the Vatican Library.

[165] Born into the Venetian aristocracy, he attended in 1492 at the University of Padua lectures in Aristotelian philosophy and theology, but his interests were with poetry. An illness (1504-05) turned his thoughts to the philosophic humanism of Seneca and Cicero. Realizing eventually that all wisdom comes from the Scriptures and consists in an intimate knowledge of God, he attempted a life of prayerful seclusion and study. On the isle of Murano (1506) he gathered about him a group of highly-educated, like-minded aristocratic youths (G. B. Egnazio, G. Contarini, V. Quirini, etc.) who engaged themselves in prayer, study, and teaching. He failed in his attempt to lead such a life alone in the Holy Land (1507) and returned to Murano. Becoming convinced of the need of a hermit's habit and public renunciation of the world, he entered the Camaldolese of St. Romuald near Arezzo (1510) and made his solemn profession (1512). Together with Quirini he led a reform movement which attacked problems arising from the coenobites by urging complete seclusion, from lax observance by imposing a very strict observance, and from the curia of the generalate by introducing a republican-style decentralization and the convocation of reform chapters. He also revised the rule and established new hermitages in Italy. He was supported in his work by Leo X, Adrian VI, Clement VII, Caraffa, and St. Cajetan of Thiene. His writings, dating from 1506 on, include commentaries on Scripture and the Fathers, treatises on prayer, and a number of ascetical tracts on conversion, perfection, obedience, and charity. Confer: E. MASSA, *Giustiniani, Paolo*: Bibliotheca Sanctorum VII, 2-9; JEDIN, *History of Council of Trent* I, 129, 147, 377; PASTOR X, 454-455, 400; GILBERT, *Cristianesimo, Umanesimo e la Bolla*, 976-990.

[166] Born of noble family, Quirini gained wide experience of the world by serving in various civic offices and as ambassador to numerous princes of

one-hundred columns long [167], this memorial is the fruit of years spent by a scholarly recluse and an experienced diplomat in a life of prayer and study. It provides us with the reforming views of hermit humanists who have steeped themselves in Sacred Scripture and the writings of the Fathers and who have a certain objective distance from the evils, intrigues, and ambitions which afflicted the Churchmen of their day.

Their work treats five topics: the office and powers of the pope, the conversion of non-Christians, the crusade against the Moslems, the healing of schisms within Christendom, and the reform of all Christians subject to the Roman Pontiff [168]. The sections on the role of the papacy and on the reform of the Church are of central concern.

Christendom, now in its last period of history, has lost that kind of piety, purity, and simplicity which we read about in the first beginnings of the Faith. The evils which presently infect the Christian body politic are traceable to two major sources: the avarice and ambition of secular princes and the ignorance, superstitions and disobedience of the faithful. The first root evil is to be remedied by the pope's sending cardinal legates to the Christian princes for establishing a peace that is based on justice [169]. The care of the second set of evils is much more complicated.

Ignorance has given birth to many errors and false opinions about the true faith and to many practices against Christian piety. The laity, however, can not trust themselves to the leadership of the clergy since they too are blind. Scarcely one or two percent of religious understand Latin and those who do, spend their time reading non-religious works. To solve this problem clerical studies must be revised so as to emphasize Sacred Scripture, the ancient Fathers, and the canons and de-

---

his time. He was famed also as a linguist, having mastery of Hebrew, Greek, Latin, and the vernacular. These language skills he later applied to a study of Scripture and produced translations of the Book of Job and the Song of Songs. Leaving a promising career behind he joined Giustiniani first on the isle of Murano and then at the hermitage of Arezzo. He was one of the leading reform spirits within the Camaldolese and enjoyed a reputation for sanctity. Shortly after he had jointly composed the « Libellus », Leo X called him from his seclusion with the intention of raising him publicly to the cardinalate, but Quirini died at Rome in 1514 before receiving the red hat. Confer: MORONI, *Dizionario di Erudizione Storico-Ecclesiastica* XLI, 141-142; VI, 295.

[167] Paul Giustiniani and Peter Quirini, *Libellus ad Leonem X. Pontificem Maximum*: Annales Camaldulenses Ordines Sancti Benedicti edited by John-Benedict MITTARELLI and Anselm COSTADONI, vol. IX, 612-719, (Venice 1773).
[168] *Libellus* 614.
[169] *Libellus* 670-674.

crees of the Church. Nor should anyone be admitted to sacred orders unless he can read and understand them [170]. These writings in addition to the ten commandments, articles of Faith, and Epistles and Gospels translated into the vernacular should be the basis of sermons preached to the laity. Canon law is to be revised so that it can be « purely and sincerely understood and interpreted » [171].

Superstition equally infects the ranks of clergy and laity alike. The great supply of books on the divining arts and their authors should be condemned by the pope, the books destroyed, and those practicing black arts burnt alive or sent into perpetual exile if not repentant. The sick should be forbidden to go to those « doctors » with their cures and charms. Religious superstitions such as patron saints and miraculous pictures carried in procession to obtain rain or fertility should be discontinued. Superstitions which come from ignorance would be partially corrected if the people understood the scriptures, divine offices, and church canons [172].

Failure to observe the rules of one's own state in life is the last major source of evils among the Christian peoples. In detail these diseases are described and their remedies carefully prescribed for each clerical rank in the Church.

Reform must begin *in capite* with the pope himself since « the ecclesiastical hierarchical order is such that, should he who holds the highest place grow weak through illness, all the lower orders will of necessity become sickly » [173]. According to this hierarchical model the pope is ultimately responsible for the whole world since he has the plentitude of power and it is his responsibility to see to it that the lower orders fulfill their duties. If he is negligent in this, he shares in their sins. It is primarily by the example of his life and by his teaching that he is to lead others to fulfill their duties. Laws and statutes are also to be employed in bringing about this reformation. The

---

[170] This attack on the theological ignorance of their day was closely allied to Giustiniani's reforming efforts within the Camaldolese. The preservation of learning by a life of study and writing was considered by him as part of the hermit's vocation. The widespread ignorance in the Church, then, must in part be blamed on those hermits who have neglected the life of learning. Confer: MASSA, *Giustiniani* 8.

[171] *Libellus* 675-682.

[172] *Libellus* 680-688.

[173] *Libellus* 698: « Sic enim in hac ecclesiastica hierarchia ordo se habet, ut illo, qui supremam sedem tenet, languescente, inferiores omnes ordines aegrotare necesse sit ... »

CONCEPTS OF REFORM

pope is to see that these are « guarded and observed inviolably » and abuses punished with « firm and unbreakable sanction »[174].

The primary concern of the pope should be with his own household — the Roman Curia and the Cardinals, since only he is superior to and responsible for them. Let not the difficulty of extirpating abuses grown into customs or the constant contradiction he will probably be called on to suffer deflect him from a reform of the Roman Curia. Let him also look to the future and, disregarding the blandishments and deceptions of his advisers, appoint only men outstanding in conduct and learning to high ecclesiastical office. The conduct of cardinals is to be investigated and abuses condemned since God will hold the pope responsible for the slightest unbecoming behavior of his brothers and right-hand men. In particular, the loose morals of curial officials must not be tolerated lest the pope invite on himself the punishment of Eli. As a remedy for avarice the two Camaldolese suggested that cardinals hold no benefices, but enjoy pensions which the pope is to examine very carefully each year[175].

The cardinals in their turn have primary responsibility for the archbishops and bishops. These are described as being guilty of ignorance, superstition, ambition, avarice, pride, incontinence — of not having embraced « the divine precepts and discipline of sacred scripture ». The remedy for this situation is to be found first in a system of promotion. The pope must see to it that only men of proven worth, of integrity of life, holiness of conduct, and of knowledge of the divine scriptures be appointed to episcopacies. Such offices are not to be bestowed as favors for princes or prizes of importuning office seekers. Each year or at least every three years bishops holding offices are to render an account of their ministry to the cardinals, knowing that they are threatened with the privation of their dignities and even life imprisonment if they do not visit the flock entrusted to them and teach it by word and example how to live properly. Yearly reports to Rome are not sufficient. Their dioceses are to be visited personally by cardinals who will inquire of clergy and laity alike whether the bishops have performed their duty. If negligent, they are to be corrected or deprived of their dignities[176].

The lower clergy, the priests, is the primary concern of the bishops. Due to ignorance, vice, or the distraction of business

---
[174] *Libellus* 617, 699, 691-692, 713, 695.
[175] *Libellus* 699, 711-712, 717, 694-696, 707.
[176] *Libellus* 696-697.

often unbefitting their sacerdotal office the diocesan clergy neglect the souls entrusted to them or even corrupt them by their own defects. Many of the poorer clergy have descended « to every illicit art and to a way of life as vile as you may wish to imagine ». To remedy this, care must be taken first of all that candidates for minor orders be examined and only those of good birth, proper upbringing, outstanding in talent and morals, and instructed in letters be approved. Only men of proven virtue and learning are to assume the sacerdotal office. Once ordained, they are to be visited by their bishop who is to correct, admonish, and urge them on to greater effort [177].

Easiest among all the groups to reform will be the religious since they cannot spurn papal correction. Those orders which are guilty of heresy, superstition, and devil worship should be destroyed by the pope. Monks should be forbidden to leave their monastery, talk at liberty with laity, or speak and write so as to calumniate their monastery or order. Diversity within the same order should be ended. Conventuals should observe their rule more strictly and the distinction of Conventual and Observant dropped. For those who live under the same rule, differences of food, dress, and occupations should be eliminated and uniformity established. The two major agents of reform will be chapters whose reform decrees the pope should bind with the fulness of Apostolic power and bishops to whom religious orders are to be subject and who should personally visit monasteries. Once the religious have been reformed, the laity will follow suit since they imitate them [178].

Occasions for sin should be removed from religious and laity alike. Thus, swearing should be strictly restricted, gambling forbidden, Lenten fast and abstinence no longer binding under pain of mortal sin, use of excommunication against delinquent debtors forbidden, and loose women relegated to the back of the church and to the corners of the city lest Rome continue as a stinking brothel [179].

The present sorry state of the Church is due to only one thing — the omission of Councils. These are the chief and absolutely necessary vehicle of reform and should be convoked frequently: General Councils every five years, provincial and diocesean synods and general chapters of religious orders often. Only by these gatherings can the Church of God learn from its

---

[177] *Libellus* 697-698.
[178] *Libellus* 689-690, 699-703.
[179] *Libellus* 704-707.

experience and rising from its present wretched state preserve for long its proper strength and beauty. Let the Lateran Council under the leadership of Leo bring about the reform of Christendom [180].

Fairly accurate in its assessment of the evils infecting the Church, optimistic and constructive in its outlook, comprehensive, practical in its recommendation of remedies, yet avoiding a demand for a radical change in the doctrine and structure of the Church of its day, the *Libellus* of Giustiniani and Quirini has been called « both the widest and the boldest of all the many reform programmes drawn up since the conciliar era » [181].

In a sense this memorial was but a mirror of their lives. Their ascetical practices as hermits had taught them the importance of understanding and embracing the divine precepts and discipline of the Sacred Scriptures. Their analysis of the present conditions of the Church revealed widespread ignorance and negligence of the Christian message — problems which they had encountered to a lesser degree in the reform of their order. Their remedy for these evils centered in a Church-wide system of mutual consultation and joint decision making: councils, synods, and chapters. Among the Camaldolese they had made the local chapter their principal vehicle of reform, and this had proved a great success. Their earlier experience in public affairs and then in renovating a religious order had helped them to assess conditions and recommend reforms but it should also have taught them caution. An easy-going Renaissance pope and an assembly of largely similar churchmen were not the most likely candidates for initiating a sweeping reform which would begin with themselves. If the papacy did not embrace with enthusiasm their proposals, it did, nonetheless, reward their trust in its benevolence and power. Leo, for one, blessed their work among the Camaldolese and conferred on them honors.

From the preceding detailed analysis of the various opinions and proposals represented at the Fifth Lateran, a picture slowly emerges of substantial agreement on the need for reform, although this theme is expressed in various ways.

These proponents of reform theory present certain marked similarities. Almost all were Italian by birth or else made Italy their second home as did del Rio and Celadoni. Begnius, who was of Hungarian extraction but lived in Venetian Dalmatia, and certain bishops of Ferdinand's lands, which included parts

---
[180] *Libellus* 707-709.
[181] JEDIN I, 128.

of Italy, are the only possible exceptions. In general the speakers were men of learning, well acquainted with conditions in Rome, and except for King Ferdinand and the nobleman Pico della Mirandola all were clerics. The majority of the conciliar speakers had practical pastoral experience and were known for their preaching talents. The first three speakers, de Deza, and the two Camaldolese monks had distinguished themselves in the cause of reform. Although the ages of the speakers spanned almost fifty years' difference, their average was in the forties or fifties.

Their proposals reflect a basic conservatism, fear of novelty, and strong papalism. The institutional structure and traditional practices are seldom if ever called into question, while some of the reformers seem to have reacted strongly against the « irreverent » attitudes of certain humanists: poets and philosophers. Classical imagery is seldom used, although references are sometimes made to events of historical antiquity. The basic sources are the Sacred Scriptures and the Fathers. The most quoted texts from the Bible come from the Psalms, Song of Songs, Apocalypse, and St. Paul. Only Cajetan engages in obvious scholastic argumentation. The other speakers draw on the writings of the Fathers: Augustine's moral exhortations, Lactantius' theme of the restoration of justice, and Bernard's theory of the two swords. Also cited are Leo, Gregory, Jerome and Ambrose. In general, the speeches see the times as very evil, yet look optimistically to the future. From the eighth session on, however, there comes more and more into prominence a sense of foreboding and fear that God will punish the Church if the Council fails to effect reform.

The nature of the Church was expressed in hierarchical, juridical, pastoral and scriptural terms. The Church was seen as possessing definite clerical and lay orders and among the clergy the various offices of pope, bishop and priest. No one challenged this. In Zanni, Pucci and Pico there is a marked emphasis on the juridical aspect of the Church — the hierarchy making and enforcing laws of conduct. The memorials of the Spanish and of Giustiniani and Quirini share this emphasis on the juridical. A favorite image reflecting a pastoral orientation is that of the shepherd, his flock, and the threat of ravening wolves. Another metaphor employed is that of the New Jerusalem, the *civitas perfecta* where the gathering of the faithful live in peace and unity. The notion of a mystical body is variously expressed. In Cajetan it is an intimate and loving union among the faithful while in Zanni it carries a heavy juridical charge. The favorite image of the Church by far is that of the bride of Christ. Viterbo, Marcellus, Pucci, and Villa-Quiran cast their whole appeal for reform in a vivid portrayal of an abandoned, filthy, and miserable bride who cries for help. Pucci goes so far as to tell all salvation history in terms of the origins, life, vicissitudes, and glorification of the bride. In all these descriptions, except for Cajetan's, the question of the essential nature of the Church is never taken into hand and treated. Various speakers, however, do touch on the holiness of the Church.

While Cajetan, for one, distinguished between the essential holiness of the Church and the fallen morals of its members, a number of other speakers seem to have questioned the essential holiness. Villa-Quiran and Cajetan asserted that Christ remained in the Church and preserved it free from all filth and contagion. Viterbo on the contrary held that Christ has abandoned His Bride, that the Church is now extinct and dead but not totally destroyed since He can return and restore her to life. Marcellus similiarly asserted that the Church is derelict, abandoned, in dire need of being cleansed of her filth. Charity is extinct in the Church, Teglatius lamented, and all her laws are violated. Begnius claimed that she has lost almost all her innocence and chastity and that scarcely any religion and faith remain in her. The two Camaldolese also depicted this loss of pristine piety, purity, and simplicity. The majority of the speakers, however, never called this essential holiness into question.

Some of Council Fathers espoused a papal conception of **Christian society,** which they expressed in terms of the traditional theory of the two swords. Del Rio and Teglatius held extreme versions of this, Stephen claiming that the pope held the temporal sword by a primeval right of Christ the King whose vicar is the pope. Constantine was supposed to have recognized this and surrendered his scepter to Sylvester, receiving it back from him in trust. A moderate version of the theory was held by Pucci who assigns the temporal sword to princes while allowing the pope the right and power to intervene when necessary. In his speech Cajetan claimed that the temporal sword was shared by princes and the pope (as ruler of the Papal States) and that only the spiritual sword is properly his own.

The role of the pope in the work of reform was variously described. In its most extreme statement Marcellus held that he was a second God on earth and on him depended the reformation of the Church. The *Libellus ad Leonem* came close to this in asserting a plentitude of papal power even over non-Christians and in envisioning reform as emanating primarily from the pope. The Spanish memorials seem to have accepted a theoretical fulness of papal power over even local ecclesiastical affairs. They bitterly complained, nonetheless, of its abuses and pleaded with the pope to cleanse his own curia, grant greater authority to bishops and the royal patron, and enforce Church law. Pico also saw the pope as the chief force in reform by his personal example of virtue and his pastoral care for the enforcement of discipline. For Zanni he was the essential and practically sole agent of reform. « Farnese » described the pope as teacher, judge, lord, and pastor of all souls, while ascribing to the Council the function of supporting and assisting him. He is to accomplish the work of reform, according to Celadoni, in his role as teacher and collaborator with the bishops. Viterbo and Begnius assigned to the pontiff the power of convoking a council to carry out the work of reform, but left vague his relationship to it. In spite of individual variations the consensus of the authors of the proposals was that the pope held chief juridical authority in the Church and was a principal agent of reform. Only Riario, who knew well the inside power structure of the Council, pointed to the importance of the cardinals as sharers with the pope in the prime responsibility for formulating reform.

Some of the speakers gave special primacy to the Council in the work of reform. The Bishops at Burgos, Viterbo, de Gargiis, and Pucci envisioned the pope as giving his necessary authority to the synod and helping it achieve its ends, but the actual task of reform remaining with the Fathers. Julius himself publicly laid responsibility for reform at the feet of the Conciliar Fathers, although he seems to have limited their function to that of merely offering advice. Celadoni and del Monte singled out mutual consultation as being the key characteristic of a council. The bishops, therefore, were not to be passive puppets in the hands of an all-powerful pontiff. « Farnese » called the Council the most efficacious remedy for evils and urged its members to lend their assistance and authority to the pope. Even the papalist Cajetan espoused some to these sentiments, although he tended to see the Fifth Lateran as a tool for undoing the Pisan Synod.

Most of the proponents of conciliar reform singled out what they considered the basic evil afflicting the Church. For Viterbo and Celadoni it was the failure to hold frequent councils. This omission can jeopardize faith and has led to moral decline. The two Camaldolese shared this sentiment and claimed that avarice and ignorance and non-observance of divine precepts were the effects of such negligence. Cajetan pointed to the evil of schism while Zanni added to this the ambition of princes. Selfishness in all its forms was excoriated by Marcellus. Teglatius blamed every evil on a forgetfulness of the grandeur of God, while Begnius laid the blame on a neglect of Christ and trust in one's own powers. Pico pointed to a failure to enforce laws. Disregard for the ancient and honorable practices of our ancestors was singled out by Riario. The habits of the Roman Curia were indicted by the Spaniards, while de Deza cited their legal pretext in the confusion of Church law. On at least one evil the speakers were in general agreement — clerical neglect of the pastoral office.

Implicit in what some speakers condemned was a rebuke to certain humanistic attitudes found among patrons of pagan antiquity and even in the writings of such professedly Christian authors as Erasmus. Viterbo complained of those who boldly speak and write against piety and hold religion up to the derision of the rabble. Religious objects, the sacraments, church authority, and the teachings of the saints are neglected and scorned. Indignantly attacked by de Gargiis were those who spurn pious customs and the *instituta* of their forefathers. Pucci found among Christians irreverence for the divine mysteries which are examined curiously, derided lightly, and haughtily despised. While the actual existence and extent of such phenomena in the rhetorical world of Renaissance polemics is open to question, the burden of responsibility for such attitudes and actions certainly does not lie wholly with the patrons and disciples of humanistic learning. Rather, it may have been an unfortunate by-product of an intelligent, awakened awareness of what constituted the essentials of Christianity and what were merely historical and even superstitious accretions.

References to heresy and error must be approached with a similar reserve since reform rhetoric gives no solid basis for assuming that doctrinal deviations were entrenched and widespread. A few « new » heresies may have been implicit in Begnius' passing reference to those (neo-Pelagians) who seek salvation by wit and virtue and in the condemnations of four reform bulls. Denials of the individuality and immortality of the human soul and assertions of the « double truth » were roundly denounced. Concern was also shown for errors found in the study of the pagan poets and philosophers. Bishops were to see that misinterpretations of the Sacred Scriptures were not preached from the pulpit or untruths touching religion printed in books. These before mentioned errors which Satan has sowed in the field of the Lord are never identified with precision nor do they seem in general to have reached the level of theological speculation and exposition. When heresies are pin-pointed they are found to consist in no doctrinal innovations of very recent origin, but rather in resolute remnants of Waldensian and Hussite teachings or perhaps in a reassertion of the conciliar thesis implicit in the « heresy » of the Pisan Schism.

The speakers also found fault with secular rulers whose ambition and greed have brought death, destruction, and continued disturbances to the Christian Republic, and have thus destroyed peace and justice, the preconditions of reform. De Gargiis claimed that the princes' neglect of religion has brought numerous misfortunes on Christendom and is responsible for the shrinking frontiers in the East. Viterbo, on the other hand, criticized a temporal ruler for taking too much interest in religion. Constantine, he claimed, by conferring wealth and favor on the Church unwittingly undid its pristine rigor and fervor. All secular rulers are not, however, seen as injuring the cause of religion. The Spaniard del Rio praised Ferdinand for his exploits against the Moslems and the Hungarian Begnius saw in the Emperor Sigismund a heaven-sent savior of religion. The fact, though, that Europe, and especially Italy, had been for the last thirty years one huge battlefield was thoroughly denounced by almost all the speakers and the blame for it laid against secular princes. So angered was Ferdinand of Spain by the recent campaign of Louis XII in Italy that he suggested that he be deposed.

Various remedies were identified by the speakers as being the single key factor in a program of reform. Marcellus recognized peace as the necessary precondition of any reform while del Monte went deeper in showing that peace and any reformation depended on a restoration of justice. The acknowledgment of God's grandeur and the submission to His wisdom demanded by Teglatius also pointed to a notion of justice. « Farnese » called for a conversion of the heart to Christ. In the speech of Corvinus reformation is closely related with the preaching of Sacred Scripture, while in that of Viterbo, de Gargiis, and Giustiniani and Quirini reform hinges on the frequent holding of councils.

The majority of the speakers saw law as the cornerstone of reform. A strengthening of ecclesiastical law and its sanctions was advocated by Cajetan. Celadoni urged the making and enforcing of conciliar decrees. Riario and Zanni, and perhaps also « Farnese » and Corvinus, looked to a whole-hearted observance of the *instituta* of the ancient Fathers, while Begnius saw the *institutiones* of the evangelical law and the action of Christ the Law-Maker as the norms of reform. Imitation of a model pope who enforces both old and new legislation was the theme of Marcellus. Pico differed from him only in emphasis — let the pope enforce old legislation since new is not needed. Pucci also emphasized the observance of the pristine canons but for him the papal duty narrows down to one of correction or censure by instruction. A thorough-going reform of canon law was advocated by the *Libellus ad Leonem. X*, the Bishops at Burgos, and especially de Deza. The notion of reformation by legislation of conduct was generally accepted by the Council and embodied in its decrees.

The plea for a *reformatio in capite* was explicitly urged by a few speakers. Popes Julius and Leo are depicted as wanting the reform to begin with their own palace and curia — from the City to the world. The demand of Pucci and of the Bishops at Burgos that judgment begin in the house of the Lord and then spread to the world was perhaps its most forceful expression. The notion that if the pope were a model of virtue others would soon follow suit found its strongest advocate in Marcellus. The two Camaldolese hermits urged that reform begin *in capite*, with the pope and cardinals. The Roman Curia was also singled out by Riario and the Spanish bishops, especially de Deza. The episcopal order was the object of the reforming zeal of men like Viterbo, Begnius, and also Pucci. Pico clearly saw the necessity of a reform which began with the clergy. This theme is also implicit in most of the other speeches.

The fundamental concept of reform found in these speeches is not one of aggiornamento, of up-dating or adapting to the times. Even the new laws which are to be enacted have as their intent a return to a former and allegedly more perfect state. This basic orientation backward is evident in the vocabulary of reform: restore, revive, recall, return, remove, reform, correct, cleanse, and emend.

The object of this reformation was neither ecclesiastical structure nor traditional doctrine. The only speakers seriously concerned with points of theology were Cajetan who urged a strongly papal understanding of the Church and Begnius who feared that faith was under attack by neo-Pelagian tendencies in the Church. Even these two speakers, however, joined with the other speakers in making morals the object of reform.

This reform of morals was in general seen as a return to and observance of church law. This Roman legal mentality underlies the exhortations for a restoration of justice found in Marcellus, del Monte, and even Begnius. This approach to problem-solving by an application of law is evident in the almost unanimous plea for observance of existing church law and for new legislation to check the evils of the times.

The norms which were to govern this new legislation were the decrees of former Councils, previous canons and laws, the *instituta*, and the teachings of the forefathers. This legal mentality seemed locked within its system, tradition bound and basically conservative.

Even the three speakers who pointed to Christian antiquity as the norm of reform looked upon themselves and acted as conservatives. Viterbo demanded that men, not the *res sacra*, be changed. This Augustinian carried his principle of a return to the past to its logical conclusions, not stopping with the recent centuries of legislation. His plea was for a return to the ancient, pristine, and *nativitatum*, to the sources and to the fervor and faith and piety of the past and for a life based on evangelical law and the actions of Christ. Pucci wanted the Bride of Christ restored to the beauty and purity she possessed when Christ brought her forth on the Cross. He also described this reformation as a restoration of the pristine reverence for faith, hope, and charity. Although the two Camaldolese pointed to the past, their practical proposals reflected no attempt to imitate the patterns of life of primitive Christianity. These reformers remained in vague generalities and never described in detail what they envisioned as being the essential aspects of either Christian antiquity or a contemporary life in conformity with it.

While most speakers stayed with the conventional reform imagery of a tended flock and of a restoration of morals, of a fallen Church, and of beauty to the Bride, Teglatius emphasized an apocalyptic second Sabbath, a chiliastic second conversion of the world which was closely indentified with neither the past nor present condition of affairs although the hierarchical Church and its teachings seem to remain.

Millenarianism was implicit in the cries for a restoration of justice. Del Monte closely paralleled Lactantius in his treatment of justice but mentioned not a Golden Age. De Gargiis, however, explicitly predicted its advent while Viterbo used the theme extensively. Giustiniani and Quirini also felt that the Church was in its last days.

Fear of impending divine punishment on the Church for its sins is found in the majority of the speakers, from the first to the last, but especially from the eighth session on. In three of these speeches the Moslems were seen as the agents of God's wrath. Viterbo feared a take-over of Christendom by them as a punishment. The advance of the Moslems was interpreted by de Gargiis as a punishment for the Christian princes' neglect of religion. Teglatius saw the Turks as a heaven-sent scourge to waken Christendom from its evil slumber and feared that divine vengeance was close at hand if the Church was not immediately reformed. Celadoni and Corvinus warned that God's anger was provoked by the present evils. If the Council failed to reform the Church, Pucci predicted, God's wrath would fall on all Christians. Pico prophecized the same, foreseeing a schism in Christendom. Cajetan also seemed to have some premonitions of future discords if the Fifth Lateran failed to reform the Church. When Riario actually saw the inadequate final formulations of one of the first reform measures, he prophetically repeated his warning of continued serious discontent among the foreign nations and especially beyond the Alps.

Was Lateran V really the failure its contemporaries and historians have billed it? And if so, where precisely were its inadequacies? In the absence of empirical data, was the Council forced to fall back on the exaggerations of reform rhetoric and thus misconceive the needs of the Church? Were more juridical decrees the best answer to the almost unanimous demand for a strict enforcement of existing Church law and for exemplary conduct on the part of the clergy? Did there exist a serious disparity between these demands made on the floor of the Council and what came to be incorporated in its final decrees? The Council did provide fine-sounding decrees on the appointment and conduct of the clergy and listed in detail what sanctions would befall those who spurned Church law — why then is the Council judged a failure? Was it perhaps taken up with the external aspects of Christianity to the neglect of inspiring a more interior type of religion, or was the Council perhaps so pre-occupied with the legacy of juridical machinery that it failed to recognize and find constructive ways of channeling a widespread and serious movement toward a more intense spiritual life? If the Lateran Council was in fact on target in its understanding of the needs of the Church and in its provision for these needs by conciliar reform decrees, it failed at least in its formulation of these decrees. Too many loop-holes were strategically inserted into these decrees by Curial figures, while the execution of this reform was left in the hands of an easy-going pope and unscrupulous administrative office. But even if the conciliar Fathers could have foreseen this faulty execution of their reform measures, what could they have done? The machinery of the Council was closely controlled by the popes and College of Cardinals, and these men felt no real urgency or need for a thoroughgoing reform. The highest official echelons of Renaissance Catholicism, it would seem, had grown accustomed to and even dependent on the continuance of abuses. Although the Fifth Lateran Council recognized the evils and tried to correct them there was perhaps little in the practical order it could do to effect reform. Is the following appraisal of a contemporary of the Council also the final judgment of History?

The Church is in need of reform — which is not the duty of one man, the pope, or of many cardinals (as the most recent council has proven both points), but of the whole world, even of God alone. But the time of this reform is known to Him alone who founded the times.[182]

Thus spoke Martin Luther who eight months after the close of the Council heralded the Reformation.

---

[182] *D. Martin Luthers Werke: Kritische Gesamtausgabe*, Weimar 1883, I, 627: « Ecclesia indiget reformatione, quod non est unius hominis Pontificis nec multorum Cardinalium officium, sicut probavit utrumque novissimum concilium, sed totius orbis immo solius Dei. Tempus autem huius reformationis novit solus ille qui condidit tempora. »

CONCEPTS OF REFORM 237

1. Speech of Julius II [1]

Mss. Chigiani I. III. 89: *Consistorialia Raph. Riarii*, Tom. II.: *De Concilio*, fols. 44r-46r.

Cogitantibus nobis saepe numero, Venerabiles fratres et dilecti filii, etiam dum in minoribus agebamus, quid potissimum esset, quod maxime pertineret ad dignitatem et existimationem huius Sanctae Sedis, et ad commodum et utilitatem totius ordinis nostri ecclesiastici, profecto nihil prius, neque etiam maius veniebat in mentem, quamque de celebratione concilii. Et quum circa hoc desiderium et sententiam semper versati simus, tamen multo magis in eadem confirmati sumus, posteaque, Deo annuente, non nostris meritis, quae scimus quam sint tenuia et exigua, sed ex sua gratia et bonitate ascendimus ad hunc apicem Apostolatus; et licet non potuerimus ob multiplicia impedimenta complere opere et effectu id, quod animo conceperamus, nunquam tamen postposuimus audire vocem Isaiae inclamantem auribus nostris: Ini consilium, coge concilium. Benedictus igitur dominus Deus noster, qui collatus in excelso solio suo, non deserens vota bonarum mentium, interposuit (ut videtis) aliquam parvam moram desiderio nostro, tamen non abstulit facultatem perficiendi. Ecce enim ope Dei adiuti, convenimus in medio Ecclesiae suae sanctae, ubi in Spiritu Sancto legitime congregati, debemus cum omni sinceritate cordis et puritate mentis vacare et intendere ad bonum commune et ad publicam utilitatem. Videtis enim Dominicum agrum obsitum et repletum zizaniis, et malis herbis; videtis universum orbem Christianum vexari, et exardescere armis et bellis; non ignoratis etiam, Turcos saevissimos hostes fidei nostrae redigisse prope in angulum res nostras, neque continere adhuc cruentas et sacrilegas manus, et adhuc aspirare ad has miseras reliquias; et propterea studendum est, ut eo authore, a quo omnia bona proveniunt, ager ipse reducatur ad veram culturam, et quantum humano consilio provideri potest, omnia redigantur ad pacem et tranquillitatem christianorum et unitatem ecclesiae suae sanctae, ut tandem pro tutela ipsius fidei christianae, in qua omnes renati sumus, et sine qua non possumus salvari, possimus suscipere sanctissimam expeditionem contra communes hostes, et illorum pravis conatibus obviare.

---

[1] This document contains a speech given in the name of Julius II to the opening session of the Fifth Lateran Council May 3, 1512. The central section of the speech is recorded in M (667B-D) and Harduin (1574E-1575B) as having been read to the Council by Alexander Cardinal Farnese. It was not presented personally by the pope due to his illness, lack of preparation, and the advice of the cardinals consulted by Paris de Grassis (RAYNALDUS, 1512, N° 34, 38). The text of the speech here recorded reveals a repetitious style and lack of organization. The presence of this and the following document in a collection of fragments identified as *Consistorialia Raph. Riarii* (Mss. Chigiani, I. III. 89) and as *Voti del Cardinale Riario in Concilio Lateranensi* (Archiva Varia Politicorum, *Miscellanea*, Arm. II, Tom. 21) may be explained either by the fact that Riario, who was Dean of the Sacred College, celebrated the Mass after which the discourses were delivered or by his possible participation in their composition — he was a relative and intimate adviser of Julius.
This and the following documents, with the exception of the 3rd, are briefly treated by E. Guglia in his article *Studien zur Geschichte des V. Laterankonzils. Neue Folge*: Sitzungsberichte 152, III, 2-8.

Interea hortamur Fraternitates Vestras, quae vocatae sunt in partem solicitudinis, ut velint iuvare communem pastorem, non solum orationibus, et ieiuniis, verum etiam solertia, industria et integritate consiliorum, ut omnes gentes intelligant, nihil esse omissum per nos et hanc sanctam synodum, quod pertineat ad unitatem ecclesiae, ad augmentum religionis nostrae, ad salutem et incolumitatem plebis christianae, et demum ad recuperationem dominici sepulchri et aliorum locorum sacrorum e manibus infidelium, sperantes, quod Deus, qui tribuit nobis voluntatem et propositum bene agendi, sit et pro sua benignitate concessurus facultatem, et potestatem prosequendi et perficiendi.

[What immediately follows is not printed here since this central section of the speech is already published in the official acts.]

Inter multa beneficia quae Dominus noster Deus quotidie in nos confert, potissimum adnumerandum existimo, quod haec nostra tempora dignatus sit insignire celebratione huius sacri Concilii, quo nihil magis pertinere potest ad unitatem fidei Catholicae, ad exaltationem christianae religionis, ad bonorum omnium quietem et pacem, et ad fidei nostrae hostium confusionem atque depressionem.

Nam quum non solum disciplina ecclesiastica, sed omnis humanae vitae institutio collabefactata, a recta itineris orbita longe deflexerit, atque in omni ordine aetatis et hominum magna iactura morum sit facta.

Sperare possumus, quod per hanc Sanctam Synodum in Spiritu Sancto legitime congregatam redibimus ad normam et regulam, retrahemur a noxiis itineribus, eradicabuntur mali mores, plantabuntur boni, praevalebunt virtutum semina, et ager Domini sentibus ac malis herbis depuratus proferet fructus tanto uberiores, quanto excultus fuerit cura et studio diligentiori.

2. Speech on the purposes of the Council [2]

Mss. Chigiani I. III. 89: *Consistorialia Raph. Riarii*, Tom. II.: *De Concilio*, fols. 46r-47r.

Quum igitur S.mus D. N. Julius PP. II, cui Deus, et Salvator noster iudicium, magisterium et dominium in terra tribuit super cunctis fidelibus, et omnium animarum curam commisit, in hac celeberrima Lateranensi basilica concilium legitime congregaverit: vos omnes, R.mi D. et caeteri Patres amplissimi, nomine Suae Sanctitatis per mutuam charitatem perque viscera Domini nostri Jesu Christi exhortor, ut Dominum prae oculis habentes ad commune bonum, et in primis ad laudem et honorem divini nominis intendamus; ut heresibus extinctis, sedatis intestinis Christianorum bellis, et intestinis prope malis et vitiis, quibus obsessi sumus, repressis, contra fidei hostes non minus utilia et neces-

---

[2] Due to its introduction and comments on the declared purposes of the Council, this speech would seem to have followed immediately the address read in the name of Julius on May 3, 1512. References to the pope, cardinals, and certain Fathers as being present, to « this famous Lateran Basilica », and to « this sacred Synod » point to a formal session of the Council. The speaker would seem to have been Alexander Cardinal Farnese, head of the cardinal deacons and later Paul III, who had just read Julius' speech to the opening session (M 667B-D; RAYNALDUS, 1512, N° 39).

saria quam optata sumantur arma, et interea, iuxta Apostoli praeceptum malum e medio nostrum tollentes et veritatem facientes, in charitate crescamus in illo, qui est caput Christus, ex quo totum corpus compactum augumentum corporis facit in aedificationem sui in charitate.

Abiiciamus itaque opera tenebrarum, et ad eum, qui est vera lux, nos convertentes, ita res nostras disponamus, et ita opera nostra bona luceant coram hominibus, ut, quemadmodum ipse Apostolus iubet, simus sine offensione et Judeis et Graecis et ecclesiae Dei; in quo glorificabitur pater noster, qui in coelis est, et nos eius gloria perfruemur, qui sua gratia et misericordia per unigenitum eius filium D. N. Jesum Christum nos redimere dignatus est.

Inter omnia beneficia, quae potuissemus expectare aut etiam desiderare a divina bonitate, potissimum adnumerari potest, quod tribuerit Sanctitati Vestrae facultatem et occasionem celebrandi hoc sacrum concilium, prout eadem semper exoptavit, dum esset in minoribus, et non minus etiam posteaquam pervenit ad apicem apostolatus.

Nam ultra quod accedat ad maximum ornamentum horum temporum nostrorum, erit etiam efficacissimum remedium ad emendationem morum, et ad restaurationem bonorum institutorum antiquorum. Quorum non potest dici, quin sit facta maxima dissolutio et labefactatio, praesertim in toto et universo ordine ecclesiastico.

Accedit etiam ad hoc, quod Sanctitas Vestra, suffulta authoritate et assistentia huius sanctae Synodi et divina gratia opitulante, poterit commodius et liberius vacare compositioni bellorum et discordiarum, quae vigent inter hos principes Christianos.

Quibus sedatis, licebit etiam tanto melius intendere et vacare circa expeditionem contra infideles. Quod certe nihil poterit esse utilius et magis necessarium reipublicae Christianae neque etiam gloriosius Sanctitati Vestrae.

3. Section of Cajetan's Speech [3]

Vatican Library, Rac. I. IV. 2107: *Opuscula varia ad Concilium Lateranense V*, fols. 62r-63v.

Habetis patres: quid de Pisana synodo communiter constituendum sit, nunc de nostra Laterana et de sensu animi mei pauca dicam.

---

[3] This section of Cajetan's speech is missing from certain editions of the acts of the Council and should be inserted into Harduin, IX, 1622 and Mansi, XXXII, 726B8 changing the « locutus sum » of Mansi to « constituendum sit » and continuing with « nunc de nostra Laterana ... » This omission was not made in *Opuscula Omnia Thomae de Vio Caietani*, no editor given, Venice 1588, 191-192. Its deletion from the official acts may be explained by a mistake in the printed binder's signature for this section which read « B3 » instead of « C3 ». The first printings of this speech (Romae: Impressa apud sanctum Eustachium per Ioannem Beplin. Alemanum de Argentina, no date given) contain this error and as a result this section was placed out of order (e. g.: Vatican Library, Rac. I. IV. 1734 numbers this section as fol. 7 and 8, instead of 12 and 13, and as fol. 21 and 22, instead of 26 and 27). This mistake in the signature was later recognized and corrected in ink with the proper rearrangement being made (e. g.: Rac. I. IV. 2107, fols. 62 and 63). It seems that Anthony del Monte must have had an uncorrected and perhaps defective

IV

Cum ecclesia pisana de caelo non descenderit, uti iam vidimus, et alteram ex propositis descendisse necessarium sit (hoc enim posuimus paulo ante) patet, ecclesiam nostram, quam Lateran. synodus perfecta referet, divinam illam esse civitatem, quae habet sanctitatem propriam pacisque abundantiam et aeternae novitatis azimos et sinceritatis panis, quaeque cum uno summo unius Christi vicarii principatu de caelo descendit. Haec tametsi magno nobis esse debeant argumento, Concilium nostrum rectum, sanctum atque legitimum esse, huc accedit tamen: primum quod Concilium hoc a Romano Pont. indictum inchoatumque est, deinde quod praeclara nostrorum maiorum Concilia non imitatur modo, sed eorum etiam multa apostolici splendoris praesentia exsuperat, quodque eidem postremo, propterea quia praesentia hac illustratur, dominus promittit, spiritum veritatis omnem illi veritatem esse patefacturum. Quae quum ita sint, nequaquam illis assentior, patres, qui solo Concilii nomine audito, rem sanctam et utilem continuo arbitrentur effectam esse. Propterea, quod qui aptius et callidius fallere consueverunt, ii pravis rebus honesta vocabula praetendere sunt soliti. Et tamen Concilium illud probo, quod suis partibus omnibus absolutum perfectumque est, quodque illa habet, quae et necessaria Conciliis sunt et a sacrosanctis requiruntur atque expectantur. Expectantur autem multa hoc tempore et requiruntur, atque haec potissimum, ecclesiae videlicet reformatio,[4] morum prolabentium restitutio, exorti iam scismatis oppressio, conversio infidelium, revocatio hereticorum, roboratio optimarum legum atque sanctionum, quae ad salutem universae fidei Christianae pertineant, atque illa etiam, quae passim depravata et deformata cernimus, ut ecclesiasticae dignitates benemeritis tribuantur, virtutes praemiis honorentur, vitia aut severe puniantur aut saltem ab honoribus et praemiis arceantur. Hoc enim nostrum Lateranense Concilium, quod pia origine et ab autore suo sancte et legitime inchoatum est, si ad proprium quoque et cognatum finem corrigendi atque emendandi, quae detorta sunt, pertenderit, nulla erit ratio, quare, qui contradicere aut ullo pacto opponere se voluerint, temerarii, amentes, scelerati insuper et nepharii homines non merito existimentur. Quare si Concilium hoc nostrum eum finem exitumque habere desideratis, quem sanctissima semper florentissimaque Concilia habuerunt, de iis, patres, quae iam dixi, providendum est diligenter, atque de hoc celeriter omni cura diligentiaque constituendum, quod neque hodierno die dissimulare possum neque silentio ullo pacto praeterire. Lactantur enim voces, quae etiam ad aures meas perveniunt, percussum pastorem, oves dispersas, Pisanam synodum, summo Pont. et in terris deo, potestate autoritateque interdixisse. Maximis ecclesiam, patres, et dissensionibus involvi, et novis quibusdam vexari et perturbari malis iam pridem vidimus, sed haec tanta tam exitiosa, tot periculosa haberi consilia a patribus illis, quis, queso, unquam putavisset? Nunc quicquid est, quantum ad vos delatum dedecus et facinus admissum sit, videtis, memoria tenetis, patres; legistis enim quamplurima,

---

edition of this speech when he set about editing the official acts of the Council (M 650E-651A). This section is missing from his Rome, 1521 edition; confer: fol. 36r. The omission would not then have been a deliberate attempt to eliminate from Cajetan's speech the only section in which he criticized the evils in the Church.

[4] The 1588 edition of this speech substitutes here « informatio » for « reformatio ». Cf. *Opuscula Omnia Thomae de Vio Caietani* 191.

quid aliquando viri clarissimi et sapientissimi in Calcedonensi synodo, contra Ephesinam secundam et illius principem Dyoscorum, quid in Constantinopolitana, quae octava fuisse dicitur, contra Fotium omnium discordiarum fautorem decreverunt, propterea quod Ephesinus caetus graviter erraverit, Dyoscorus in Leonem urbis episcopum sententiam scripserit; Fotius autem non solum absque Romani Pontificis autoritate Concilium congregaverit, quod quidem alienum est ab homine Christiano, sed in Nicolaum etiam summum Pont. anathema protulerit. Quemadmodum igitur conventus Pisanus Fotium et Dyoscorum secutus est delinquendo, ita vos consulendo atque animadvertendo celeriter synodum Calcedonensem illamque Constantinopolitanam imitemini. Incumbite, patres, ad ovium gregem, ad pastoris autoritatem salutemque ecclesiarum omnium respicite. Providete quod ipsum et facile factu est et fieri debet; providete, patres, ne quis talia post hac unquam non modo perpetrare, sed ne cogitare quidem aut desiderare possit. Verum ne sanctissimo Concilio nostro in tot adversis rebus, ad communem salutem et conservandam et amplificandam, legitima praesidia desint, quin id potius, quod o(mn)ium votis expetitur desideriisque postulatur, ad debitum finem perveniat, ad te convertor, Iuli Pontifex Maxime, quod ea abs te peto, quae tuae virtutis, tuae dignitatis, tuae potestatis propria sunt. Antea enim, cum in singulis rebus insistebamus, alios ordines ecclesiae inferiores sumus allocuti; nunc de summa rerum dicturi breviter, summum principem et caput omnium appellamus. Te itaque, pater beatissime, obsecro atque obtestor; tua enim post Deum maxima est potestas, tuum est imperium, tua reipub. gubernatio, Christianae fidei defensio; obsecro, inquam, et obtestor, hoc omni studio cures atque effitias: ut haec synodus Lateranensis per te congregata, quem admodum ecclesia, quam refert, de caelo descendit, uti Ioannes vidit, ita cum illa rursus ascendat in caelum. Hoc enim universi totis devotisque animis depraecamur. Assequetur autem hoc te volente teque imperante, si tu ipse, pater sancte, omnipotentis Dei, cuius vices in terris non solum honore dignitatis, sed etiam studio voluntatis gerere debes, si ipsius Dei potentiam, perfectionem sapientiamque imitaberis.

4. Advice on Postponing the Council [5]

Mss. Chigiana I. III. 89: *Consistorialia Raph. Riarii*, Tom. II.: *De Concilio*, fols. 54v-55v.

Possumus optime meminisse, quod ab initio, quo fuit indictum tempus Concilii, omnes viderunt et consideraruntur illud idem, quod nunc videmus et palpamus, videlicet tempus statutum esse nimis breve et

---

[5] The occasion for these comments of Riario would seem to have been the reception by the pope of a letter from Ladislas of Hungary stating the reasons why his representative, Thomas Cardinal Bakocz, was unable to make it to Rome by April 19, the date fixed for the opening of the Council by a bull of July 18, 1511. Julius seems to have followed Riario's advice and on April 17th published a bull prorouging the opening of the Council until May 1st (Raynaldus, 1512, N° 28). The confusion and uncertainties caused by this postponement may have caused Saint John Fisher of Rochester and others of the English delegation to decide not to attend (H. C. PORTER, *Erasmus and Cam-*

nimis angustum; omnia tamen fuerunt facta ad bonum finem et cum optimo consilio et proposito, praesertim ad evitandum murmurationes et calumnias istorum depositorum; sed ille idem respectus, qui movit Sanctitatem Vestram, videtur esse etiam nunc maximopere attendendus, ne scilicet incurramus in detractiones illorum, a quibus voluimus ab initio praecavere.

Rationes allatae per Serenissimum Dominum Regem Ungariae sine dubio sunt efficacissimae, et quae possint afferri et allegari ab omnibus aliis cum optima ratione. Nemo est enim, qui non videat, esse pene impossibile, quod praelati ultramontani et ultramarini, ac alii volentes interesse, possint intra breve spatium componere res suas et praeparare ea, quae sunt necessaria ad aggrediendum et conficiendum iter tam longum et insuetum, praesertim vigentibus istis bellis, quae detinent omnes vias et omnes aditus clausos et occupatos.

Accedit praeterea, quod tempus indictum incidit in eam partem anni, quae est valde suspecta et periculosa, ac etiam valde formidolosa ultramontanis, quibus est impressum et persuasum, aerem romanum esse noxium et valde insalubrem, et propter frequentiam peregrinorum effici pestilentem. Omnes iste rationes et multae aliae possent facile persuadere et inducere Sanctitatem Vestram ad faciendum hanc prorogationem.

Et licet omnia ista sint multum efficatia et urgentia, conditio tamen temporum et qualitas rei, de qua agitur, exigit, ut etiam multum respiciatur et habeatur ratio ad ea, quae possent obiicere illi depositi, quos credibile est, esse semper paratos et intentos ad sinistre interpretandum omnia gesta Sanctitatis Vestrae quantumvis rationabilia, neque praetermissuros aliquid, in quo videant posse laedere et maculare famam et nomen Sanctitatis Vestrae, insimulando et accusando eam illusionis et simulationis; et quod Sanctitas Vestra velit prorogare hoc tempus, non ex necessitate aut aliqua alia bona ratione, sed potius ex mente et animo evitandi et effugiendi hoc concilium.

Quamobrem his omnibus bene consideratis et multis aliis, quae causa brevitatis omisi, ego essem in sententia, quod multum expediret in hac re sumere et tenere aliquam mediam viam, videlicet, ut Sanctitas Sua daret aliquod initium Concilio suo, et teneret saltem duas aut tres sessiones, in quibus poterit, factis prius debitis et solemnibus cerimoniis, declarare et decernere ipsum Concilium et consessum esse authoritate sua legitime, in Spiritu Sancto congregatum, approbando et ratificando omnia gesta per Vestram Beatitudinem; deinde damnare et anatematizare conciliabulum sive conventiculam illorum depositorum, annullando et infringendo omnia acta per eos; postea, si videbitur expedire, poterit supersedere et prorogare tempus concilii sui sub optimis et rationabilibus causis, sed potissimum propter paucitatem debentium interesse, qui non

---

bridge: *The Cambridge Letters of Erasmus*, Toronto 1963, 142). In any event, such postponements actually did provide the enemies of Julius II with an opportunity to malign him (e. g., confer: « Julius II. Exclusus. A Dialogue, » produced on the stage at Paris, 1514 and printed in J. A. FROUDE, *The Life and Letters of Erasmus*, New York 1896, 149-168, esp. 157). Riario's arguments and suggestions here recorded reveal a pre-occupation with defeating the Pisan Schism and Julius' detractors. This fragment, however, does not give a basis for determining whether the intimate adviser of Julius initially considered the Lateran Council as a mere tool of papal politics or as a real reform Council which could tackle the problem of renovation only after the pope's position had been strengthened and his enemies silenced.

potuerunt accedere propter causas alligatas et maxime propter bella vigentia. Et hoc modo Sanctitas Vestra firmabit et roborabit res suas et authoritatem suam, et adimet illis omnem saltem coloratam materiam detrahendi et obloquendi de Sanctitate Vestra.

5. Expressions of Joy over the Emperor's Good Will Toward the Council and Pope [6]

Mss. Chigiana I. III. 89: *Consistorialia Raph. Riarii*, Tom. II.: *De Concilio*, fols. 51r-51v.

Suscepimus omnes, pro ut merito potuimus et debuimus, singulare gaudium et laetitiam, quum Reverendissimus Dominus Gurgensis nomine Caesareae Maiestatis consensit et adhesit sacro sancto huic Lateranensi concilio, et illius sessioni personaliter interfuit et assedit. Nunc autem possumus dicere, ex his litteris modo recitatis longe magis auctum esse et cumulatum gaudium nostrum, et omnem laetitiam esse congeminatam, quum videamus Caesaream Maiestatem non modo persistere et perseverare in hoc suo bono et devoto animo erga Sanctitatem Vestram et erga commune bonum et utilitatem Sanctae Romanae Ecclesiae, sed ex sua propria voluntate et ex optimo suo instituto, quotidie magis accendi et propensiorem fieri ad omnem dignitatem, commodum et utile ipsius Ecclesiae. Et licet non aliter, quam id, quod modo reperimus in effectu, liceret sperare et expectare ab eius imperiali bonitate et animi magnitudine (semper enim patuit eius optimus animus, et zelus erga Sanctam Sedem Apostolicam), est tamen maximopere laetandum et gaudendum, quod id ipsum modo per has litteras attestetur Maiestas Sua cum omni significatione caritatis et observantiae. Et profecto non est dubitandum, quin quotidie meliora et maiora de se studia et officia sit praestiturus. Quam obrem non video nunc aliud esse dicendum, nisi quod existimo esse valde condecens et conveniens, ut Sanctitas Vestra benigne et gratiose sibi respondeat et rescribat, agendo in primis gratias pro tanto eius officio et observantia erga Sanctam Sedem Apostolicam, deinde etiam exortando Maiestatem Suam ad perseverandum, prout indubitanter credibile est esse facturam, et demum offerendo sibi omnia, quae in eius gratificationem per Sanctitatem Vestram et per universum Sacrum Collegium agi et fieri poterunt.

---

[6] The comments recorded here seem to have been occasioned by the reading of a letter from the Emperor Maximilian before a meeting of the Sacred College. The emphasis on joy over the assistance in person of the Emperor's ambassador Matthew Cardinal Lang at the Council would seem to point to his presence at the third session, December 3, 1512, when he read in the name of the Emperor a declaration which terminated any remaining relations of the Empire with the Pisan Synod and announced its complete adhesion to the Lateran Council. When Lang returned to Rome at the end of the following year he was shown much deference at the meetings of cardinals on December 9th and 17th and personally attended the eighth session on the 19th. A letter to Maximilian dated December 28th mentioned Gurk's visit while exhorting the Emperor to fight the Turks (*Regesta Leonis X*, 1513, N° 5971; Raynaldus, 1513, N° 101-103). It is difficult to determine if this was the letter Riario exhorted the pope to write or whether it was some letter to have been written by Julius nearly a year earlier.

IV

6. An Address to the Pope and Cardinals [7]

Mss. Chigiani I. III. 89: *Consistorialia Raph. Riarii*, Tom. II.: *De Concilio*, fols. 47r-49v.

Haec materia conciliorum, licet semper habita fuerit magni momenti et digna multo respectu et consideratione, nunc tamen merito potest et debet videri non solum magna et difficilis, sed etiam molesta et gravis: tum propter multa, tum propter modum, quem servant hi Reverendissimi Domini absentes, qui (sic dictum cum bona eorum venia) potuissent et debuissent melius omnia considerare et maturius agere, et non incedere per hanc viam, quae omnium iudicio reputatur potius scandalosa, et aliena ab ordine iuris et honestatis quam legitima et iuridica, ita ut possit facilius afferre aliquod incendium, et parere aliquos malos fructus, quam ut respiciat illos optimos et laudabiles fines, propter quos fuerunt ordinata et instituta concilia a veteribus illis et sanctissimis Patribus predecessoribus nostris.

Quum igitur (ut dixi) haec materia, tam per se, quam propter circumstantias suas, sit ardua et difficilis, fateor vires meas esse longe minores, et inferiores, quam ut possint sufficere ponderi, et magnitudini ipsius rei.

Sed ut pro officio ac debito meo, ac etiam pro more et consuetudine huius loci breviter dicam pauca, quae mihi occurrunt recens.

Considerans saepius mecum ipse, quanti momenti semper extiterit, quantumque etiam prosit tum ad aedificationem subditorum, tum etiam ad liberandum nos ipsos a multis detractionibus et murmurationibus,

---

[7] Riario addressed his remarks at times to a group of Cardinals and at another to the pope. He sought from them wise counsel and a will to carry out the work of reform for which they were wholly responsible.

Although unidentified the pope would seem to be Leo X. He is praised for his continuous desires for reform, for giving a beginning to the work of reform (establishing a commission?), and for his concern that the Council's reform plans be brought to a successful conclusion. In a bull read at the sixth session, Leo expressed thoughts similar to those recorded here in Riario's remarks (RAYNALDUS, 1513, N° 24). Julius, however, did not look to the Council for new reform measures, in spite of the fact he had established a reform commission (ibid. N° 27; HEFELE-LECLERCQ, VIII-I, 340, n. 2). The only reform measures decreed by the Council under his reign were reaffirmations of his 1505 prohibition against simony in papal elections (M 768A-772B) and of his apostolic letters of March 30, 1512 which, he asserted, had in general already reformed the Curia (M 753A-B, 772E; RAYNALDUS, 1512, N° 30; JEDIN, *Council of Trent* I, 127). An interest in the cause of reform ascribed to the pope and an exhortation to initiate that renovation in the Curia which, Riario asserted, continues to grow more corrupt would make more sense if Leo were the one addressed.

References to the « custom of the place » and to the presence of cardinals seem to indicate a consistory or cardinal congregation. This speech was given before the June 17th, 1513 retraction of the Pisan cardinals due to Riario's complaints of the way in which they were absent. As yet the material to be treated and the time and order for treating its divisions were not determined, and so Riario's remarks would seem to point to some initial meeting of cardinals on the question of reform during the Spring of 1513. The summaries of his address to the general congregation of May 13 do not contain the same points treated here (RAYNALDUS, 1513, N° 27; M 794D-E).

ut in Ecclesia Dei bene et laudabiliter vivatur: Deus novit quod semper fui cupidus et studiosus videndi aliquam bonam reformationem in Ecclesia et in Romana curia, quae merito habetur et est caput totius orbis, et debet esse norma, et regula totius Christianae religionis.

Et quemadmodum detinuit me semper hoc desiderium, ita nunc maximopere gaudeo, quod S^{mus} D. N., qui etiam illud idem semper concupivit, maneat in firmissimo proposito exequendi, et quod iam caeperit dare hoc felicissimum et sanctissimum initium.

Quo nihil a Sanctitate Sua posset fieri salutarius, tum ad conservationem et ad securitatem, tum ad augumentum rerum nostrarum et totius status Sanctae Romanae Ecclesiae, tum etiam ad praecidendum prefatas murmurationes, et detrectationes. Et quod videtur esse maxime necessarium ad restituendum et conservandum Ecclesiam in eam sanctam et venerabilem authoritatem, quae iure, et merito debetur.

Unum tamen mihi est molestissimum, et maximopere doleo, quod scilicet non sum eius meriti et earum qualitatum, qui possim et debeam censeri idoneus et sufficiens ponderi et magnitudini tantae rei.

Spero tamen, quod bona mens et bona intentio, quae in omni re plurimum valere solet, adiuvabit imperfectum desiderium meum, et in illis, in quibus ego defecero, supplebit doctrina, et prudentia Dominationum Vestrarum Reverendissimarum.

Et interea omnipotens Deus, qui dedit S.^{mo} D. N. mentem et animum incipiendi, dabit etiam bonum medium, et (ut aiunt) meliorem finem, et exitum captis et rebus nostris; et ita precanda est Maiestas Sua quod nobis concedat pro infinita bonitate, et clementia sua.

Sed ut veniamus ad substantiam rei, omissis superfluis verbis et circumstantiis:

Haec materia habet diversa capita et multiplicia: et primo, iudicio meo, videndum super quibus sit agendum; deinde a quo capite incipi debeat, et quando incipiendum sit a S.^{mo} D. N. et eius palatio, ut Sanctitas Sua dixit esse faciendum, bene est. Quando etiam videatur aliunde incipiendum, tam de hoc, quamque de aliis rebus remitto me iudicio et sententiae Sanctitatis Suae, ac etiam Dominationum Vestrarum Reverendissimarum.

Ex omnibus rebus, quae spectant ad Summos Pontifices, meo iudicio nulla potest iudicari convenientior, et quae pro dignitate et officio eorum magis sit secundum Deum et homines, quam retinere curiam et subditos eorum in bono statu et in bona forma vivendi, si in ea esse comperti fuerint, aut saltem si ab ea fuerit deviatum, providere, ut omnia reformentur in melius et reducantur ad eum statum, qui merito probari et laudari possit.

A multis hinc annis fuit pluries et multipliciter tractatum de hac reformatione, et tamen nihil unquam fuit demandatum exequutioni, ex quo postea factum est, ut omnia semper venerint in maiorem deteriorationem.

Et ita accidit nobis veluti corpori aegroto et male affecto, quod, quia a principio morbi non curatur, ad id postmodum deducitur, ut necesse sit, vel quod pereat et periclitetur, vel cum difficultate curetur et reducatur ad sanitatem.

Quam obrem, attenta qualitate et conditione temporum, et attentis moribus huius curiae, qui certe non potest dici, quin multum deviaverint et recesserint ab institutis antiquorum patrum nostrorum:

Ego sum in voto, quod Sanctitas Vestra omnino debeat incumbere et vacare huic reformationi, et ab ea non desistere, donec non fuerit deducta ad aliquem bonum et laudabilem exitum.

Quod erit res non tantum laudabilis apud homines, quantum etiam meritoria apud Deum. Et ulterius praecidetur, et auferetur materia obloquendi et obtrectandi contra nos, praesertim apud ultramontanos et nationes externas; et tanto magis, quod quum saepius (ut dixi) de hac reformatione fuerit agitatum, semper res fuit dimissa imperfecta, et non sine scandalo et murmuratione illorum, qui videntur quaerere et quodammodo emere causas et occasiones detrahendi.

Sunt multa agenda in celebratione huius sacri Concilii, quae omnia videri et possunt et debent magni ponderis et momenti. Sed inter caetera, agendum est de aliqua reformatione morum et disciplinae Ecclesiasticae, quae, licet fortasse videatur esse minoris momenti quam sint caetera alia, tamen si voluerimus omnia haec bene perpendere et considerare, reperiemus fere nihil esse magis necessarium et magis opportunum. Quum nihil sit, quod possit addere huic Sanctae Sedi et universo ordini Ecclesiastico plus auctoritatis et plus dignitatis, quam optima quaedam vivendi norma et disciplina, in qua maiores nostri censuerunt fundandam et stabiliendam omnem hanc ditionem Ecclesiasticam quam retinemus. Ex quo satis admoneri debemus, ut illorum vestigia subsequentes, nullo modo praeterire aut negligere debeamus huiusmodi reformationem. Ad quod etiam tanto magis excitari debemus, quod in caeteris rebus, quae sunt partim in potestate nostra, et partim in potestate aliena, quando non sequantur illi successus, quos volumus et optamus, possumus aliquo modo excusari; verum in hac reformatione, quae penitus pendet et voluntate et arbitrio nostro, possumus vehementer reprehendi, si vel per contemptum vel per negligentiam nostram in deterius prolapsum, immo si prolabatur, non curabimus totis viribus restituere, ac restaurare. Quam obrem, ...

7. Speech to Reform Commission [8]

Mss. Chigiana I. III. 89: *Consistorialia Raph. Riarii*, Tom. II.: *De Concilio*, fols. 49v-50v.

Reverendissimi Domini mei, et vos caeteri Reverendi Patres, audivimus omnes tenorem et continentiam huius cedulae; et propterea non est opus, ut multa dicantur, nisi quod tenor et continentia ipsius est ex omni parte probabilis et laudabilis. Et certe omnia contenta in ea

---

[8] This speech of Riario is directed to the members of the reform commission to which Leo appointed him on June 3, 1513 (HEFELE-LECLERCQ VIII-I, 402). The occasion may have been one of the first sessions of the commission held in the apostolic palace in early June (M 797E, 816C-817A). His references to beginning the work of reform with a « modification of the officials of the Roman Curia » would suggest an early stage of the commission's work and place the discourse before December 13, 1513 when a bull was published reforming these officials (« Pastoralis officii divina providentia, » *Bull. Rom.*, Leo X, V, pp. 571-601, confer esp. N° 2, 571). The *cedula* to which Riario referred may have been a proposal on how to proceed with the work of reform or have contained specific reform recommendations.

tendunt ad optimum et sanctissimum illum finem, quem omnes debent expetere et desiderare pro conservatione honoris huius sanctae Sedis et universi ordinis Ecclesiastici. In quo certe S.mus D. N. est dignus aeterna laude et commendatione; quum in omnibus rebus ostendat se habere optimum zelum, et optimum animum in perseverantia et continuatione huius sacri concilii, et ostendat illam integerrimam mentem et illum sanctissimum effectum, quem ab initio nobis concepimus et persuasimus de Sanctitate Sua in prosecutione ipsius concilii, donec fuerint absoluta omnia, propter quae ipsum Concilium incaeptum et institutum fuit: et quoniam materiae, et causae ipsius sunt variae, et diversae, S.mus D. N. voluit eas dividere et partiri pro faciliori et meliori absolutione: proptereaque voluit nobis iniungere hoc onus reformationis, quod, licet fortasse non videatur ita magni momenti, tamen si voluerimus bene et mature omnia considerare, reperiemus hanc unam causam reformationis esse ex maximis et potissimis, quae faciunt ad dignitatem et decentiam Sedis Apostolicae et etiam ad satisfactionem omnium nationum.

Haec autem reformatio habet duo principalia capita: unum, quod spectat ad disciplinam morum, alterum ad modificationem officialium Romanae Curiae. Et quoniam hoc ultimum, videlicet de officialibus, videtur esse maxime necessarium, pro retinendis animis exterarum nationum bene dispositis et aedificatis, debemus credere, quod non sine optimo iudicio felicis recordationis Julius et deinde modernus S.mus D. N. statuerunt ab eo tanquam magis necessario incipiendum esse, ut manifeste appareat, et pro indubitato ab omnibus teneatur, quod, illo capite absoluto, deveniendum sit ad reformationem morum, et ad omnia alia, quae fuerint tam ad ornamentum ordinis Ecclesiastici, quam etiam ad decentiam Sanctae Sedis Apostolicae.

8. Recommendation to the Pope Concerning Absent Cardinals [9]

Mss. Chigiani I. III. 89: *Consistorialia Raph. Riarii*, Tom. II.: *De Concilio*, fols. 50v-51r.

Sanctitas Vestra audivit tenorem huius minutae, quae ita loquitur, et est ita clara per se ipsa, ut quicquid in huiuscemodi re ego vellem loqui, posset censeri potius ad superfluitatem, vel etiam ad fastidium,

---

[9] In this fragment Riario urged the pope to accept a proposal for healing the wound inflicted by certain absent cardinals. The cardinals referred to were more likely Carvajal and Briçonnet, two leaders of the Pisan Schism. Indications as to the occasion and contents of the *minutae* are not given. Later references to reasons for celebrating a general council would suggest that Riario's comments were made around the time of the convocation of the Council and that the draft copy proposed something to do either with calling the Council or with condemning the Pisan cardinals.

His remarks about discussions preceding the composition of the proposal and his description of it as the best remedy for healing the schism might, on the other hand, point to an event of June, 1513. Prolonged discussions were held in that month over how to reconcile officially the now repentant cardinals (HEFELE-LECLERCQ VIII-I, 406). The Sacred College was almost unanimously in favor of granting them pardon if they confessed their fault and

quam ad necessitatem; praesertim quum interfuerim discussioni, et compositioni ipsius. Quam obrem non video per me esse aliud dicendum nisi comprobare id, quod in praefata minuta continetur; et certe quantum ego cognosco, non poterat reperiri efficacius et salutarius remedium ad infirmitatem et vulnus, quod intulerunt isti Domini Cardinales absentes.

Hoc unum tamen non omittam, quod dato, quod nemo petiisset concilium, vel etiam dedisset aliquam occasionem ad illud petendum, tamen Sanctitas Vestra nihil posset agere, quod esset sibi gloriosius, et quod esset magis necessarium et expediens ordini Ecclesiastico et universae Reipublicae Christianae, quam celebrare temporibus suis unum generale Concilium. Et si non propter aliud, saltem servando laudabili et veteri instituto Sanctissimorum Patrum antiquorum. Ex eo enim sequetur, quod, si aliqua sunt confracta et male coherentia, resarcientur, et illa, quae sunt sana et firma, consolidabuntur et roborabuntur, cum maxima laude et amplificatione nominis Sanctitatis Vestrae et cum ingenti meritorum gratia apud Deum omnipotentem:

9. Remarks Before a General Congregation [10]

Mss. Chigiana I. III. 89: *Consistorialia Raph. Riarii*, Tom. II.: *De Concilio*, fols. 51v-54r.

S.mus D. N., pro sua singulari sapientia et bonitate undequaque circumspiciens et considerans ad omnia ea, quae spectant ad bonum publicum, ad auctoritatem Sanctae Sedis Apostolicae, et denique ad sta-

---

sought forgiveness. A commission of cardinals, however, deferred the ultimate decision to Leo (PASTOR VII, 54-59). These fragmentary remarks of Riario may, therefore, have been occasioned by such recommendations and the *minutae* may have contained a formula of abjuration to be read by them in public on June 27th (RAYNALDUS, 1513, N° 44). Two other documents contained in this collection of « Consistorialia » should be read in conjunction with this fragment: « De Privationibus » (fol. 57-71) in which Riario speaks of a « remedy » for the schism and « De Restitutione » (fol. 72-76) in which he urges that the absent Cardinals be restored to their former ranks provided they confess their fault.

[10] Due to his references to material prepared by the faith commission as being as yet unapproved by the Council and to his mention of material on reform which was prepared under the careful guidance of the pope, the general congregation which Riario here addressed would seem to have been that of December 17, 1513. This met in the upper chapel of the apostolic palace two days before the eighth session in order to review the work of the three conciliar commissions (M 819C). He directed his remarks first to his fellow cardinals, then to the prelates « who live in the midst of the City under the eyes of the Curia », and finally to Pope Leo. The *cedula* which he described as having been prepared by the congregation on reform, reviewed by the cardinals, and destined to be read at the coming session was probably the bull « In apostolici culminis » (M 845D-846E). This bull repeated the norms for reform of « Pastoralis officii » and added to it certain severe sanctions.

The fragmentary remarks recorded here confirm what is known from other sources on the way in which the reform documents were prepared. At the command of Leo the prelates chose from their ranks delegates for membership in the reform commission (M 794C-E; RAYNALDUS, 1513, N° 26, 27). To this commission Leo added certain Fathers who were present at the meetings of the

tum et augumentum universalis nostrae religionis; et in primis cupiens prosequi et complere celebrationem huius sacratissimi Concilii Lateranensis, iuxta institutiones et laudabiles consuetudines antiquorum patrum, voluit ac ordinavit debere fieri aliquas particulares congregationes, in quibus nonnulla particularia tractentur, omnia tamen pertinentia ad beneficium, et substantiam ipsius Concilii. Novissime autem iussit cogi et celebrari hanc ipsam generalem congregationem, ut coram omnibus exponi et referri posset de his, quae sunt acta et tractata in praefatis congregationibus particularibus. Quamobrem, ut breviter referam ea, quae sunt acta in congregatione, videlicet de reformatione, ad quam ego sum deputatus, una cum Reverendissimis Dominis placuit, ut deberet fieri quaedam cedula, prout est facta, et ea postmodum deberet legi in prima celebranda sessione ipsius Concilii. Vestrae igitur Dominationes poterunt videre et intelligere tenorem et continentiam ipsius; et quando ita placeat, ego, et sic etiam spero, immo firmiter teneo de caeteris deputatis, non sum recusaturus ullum laborem, nec omissurus quicquam, quod pertineat ad studium et diligentiam boni et officiosissimi Cardinalis; et non solum ad hanc materiam, sed etiam ad omnia alia, ad quae parvitas, et tenuitas ingenii, et virium mearum extendi poterit.

Scimus Reverendi Patres, non esse opus, neque oportere recensere ac repetere paternitatibus vestris rationes et causas, quae moverunt mentem et animum S.^{mi} D. N. ad indictionem et celebrationem huius sacri Lateranensis Concilii, in Spiritu Sancto per Suam Beatitudinem legitime congregati. Quum omnia sint notissima, non solum Paternitatibus Vestris, quae vivunt in media Urbe et in oculis (ut dixerim) curiae, sed cunctis etiam Principibus, et populis tam intra quam extra Italiam. Et propterea non curabo circa haec superflua aliter immorari. Solum superest, ut intelligant Paternitates Vestrae, quod S.^{mus} D. N., assidua meditatione invigilans more boni et providi pastoris super curam gregis sibi commissi, et super statum et bonum publicum Ecclesiae Sanctae Dei; ob idque cupiens et volens, mediante ope et gratia Sancti Spiritus, prosequi et perficere saluberrimum opus et sanctissimum ipsius Sacri Concilii; et intendens progredi, et incedere secundum antiquas patrum institutiones, tam circa cerimonialia, quam circa substantialia, ut omnia scilicet et eo decentius et maiori cum robore et dignitate ordinentur et disponantur;

---

particular congregations (M 796B, 816C-817A; HEFELE-LECLERCQ VIII-I, 402-403, 411-413). These congregations met frequently, often with Leo present (M 797E, 819C; *Bull. Rom.*, Leo X, V, N° 2). The cardinals reviewed the material together in private (the secret consistory of *Bull. Rom.*, Leo X, V, N° 2).

Brought into new light by this fragment are the rôles played by Leo X and Riario in the workings of the reform commission. The pope is described as being intent on following the conciliar procedures of the ancient Fathers, as assuring that the reform measures for the curial officials be drawn up rapidly, as being well-informed and present at « all » of the discussions on reform, and as using his know-how and authority to eliminate delays and difficulties. Riario asserted that he himself was concerned with carrying out his own duties in preparing this material on reform and that his efforts extended to as many other things as possible. While praising the first product of Leo's reform zeal as being conducive to a « proper and fitting end », he also criticized it for lacking that rigor which was required and expected by the Ultramontane and certain other nations. This comment raises the question as to whether in Riario's mind the difficulties which Leo eliminated came from both the curial and reformer groups and that Leo struck a middle course or from primarily the reformers and that the pope initially nullified their efforts.

quo meliori fuerint directa consilio, statuit ac iussit, fieri electionem ac deputationem de personis paternitatum vestrarum, ut, habita de his decenti et convenienti ratione, tanquam de bonis et fructuosis palmitibus in Ecclesia Sancta Dei, debeant intelligere, et una cum caeteris Patribus cogitare et decernere de iis, quae in occurrentibus sessionibus fuerint tractanda et deliberanda:

Vestrarum igitur partium vestraeque bonitatis erit, iuxta datam vobis a Domino Deo prudentiam, ad ea tantum intendere, ac mentem et animum dirigere, quae secundum Deum et conscientiam vestram visa fuerint magis conducere et expedire ad laudem et honorem Divinae Maiestatis et ad conservationem et augmentum felicissimi status S.^{mi} D. N. et totius religionis Christianae, nec non ad reformationem totius cleri et Ecclesiastici status in moribus et in vita, et demum ad pacem, quietem et unionem Christianorum Principum et fidelium omnium populorum. Ad quae omnia, licet non sit dubitandum, quin Paternitates Vestrae per se ipse sint dispositae et animatae, ego tamen pro debito et officio meo non cessabo eas rogare et exhortari, ut operibus et ministerio adimpleant illud ipsum, quod S.^{mus} D. N. et ego et caeteri Patres Sacri Collegii sibi proposuerunt et conceperunt de prudentia, probitate, studio, et officio Paternitatum Vestrarum. Quibus adimpletis firmiter sperare et tenere poterimus, quod Deus in omnibus actionibus nostris sit futurus nobiscum, et interveniente eius gratia, res nostrae et Ecclesiae Suae Sanctae sint quotidie de bono in melius processurae.

Causae, quas Sanctitas Vestra commisit tractandas et examinandas Reverendissimis Dominis deputatis, iure et merito requirebant maturitatem et spatium temporis; quod certe ex omnibus semper fuit habitum et reputatum maxime necessarium ad electionem bonorum consiliorum. Et ego usque ab initio memini me dicere et affirmare, quod impossibile esset tantam rem posse confici et absolvi intra breve illud spatium, quod habebamus. Immo quantum ad materiam huius reformationis, nisi Sanctitas Vestra omnibus interfuisset et praefuisset, cum tota hac ipsa dilatione, quam habuimus, vix pervenissemus ad medium itineris, quo tendebamus. Nam Sanctitas Vestra sua sapientia et authoritate substulit et amovit omnes difficultates, quae potuissent quoquo modo rem impedire et remorari, ita ut cum Dei auxilio omnia sint redacta ad satis condecentem et convenientem finem; de quibus, quum omnibus (ut dixi) interfuerit Sanctitas Vestra et de omnibus habeat meliorem informationem quam ego, non curabo aliter esse molestus Sanctitati Vestrae in recensendo et replicando. Hi etiam Reverendissimi Domini ex lectione ipsa omnia intelligent plenius ac melius quam ex me ipso. Unum tamen non omittam dicere: quod, licet fortasse res non sint deductae ad omnem illum rigorem, qui potuisset expeti et requiri, tamen sunt amota et sublata e medio illa, quae potuissent exhibere causam querelarum ultramontanis et caeteris nationibus.

De hac materia rerum, quae pertinent ad fidem, quantum meum iudicium se extendit, hi Reverendissimi Domini omnia sunt prosecuti cum maxima maturitate, prudentia et doctrina; et certe est res dignissima, et quae accedit ad maximam dignitatem huius Sacri Concilii. Videtur enim redolere ac referre spetiem et formam conciliorum illorum veterum et bonorum patrum, in quibus non de contentionibus, non de bellis, neque de aliis huiuscemodi rebus, sed tantummodo de his, quae pertinebant ad fidem ac religionem, agebatur. Quamobrem non video quid aliud sit dicendum, nisi ea omnia, quantum ad me attinet, approbare et laudare et supplicare Sanctitati Vestrae, ut in acta publica ad perpetuam memoriam, cum assensu Sacri Concilii, referri et redigi faciat.

10. An Invitation to Discuss Certain *Capitula* [11]

Mss. Chigiana I. III. 89: *Consistorialia Raph. Riarii*, Tom. II.: *De Concilio*, fols. 54r-54v.

Posteaquam S.mus D. N. absolvit negocium et reformationem officialium; quod certe fuit opus valde utile et laudabile, nunc sedulo invigilans pro cura et debito sui pastoralis officii, et pro innata eius prudentia et bonitate ad reliqua, quae, divina ope assistente, et ad ornamentum et utilitatem huius curiae pertinere posse videantur, commisit nobis, ut deberemus ostendere et communicare cum Paternitatibus Vestris haec capitula et has reformationes, quae novissime per Reverendissimos Dominos deputatos fuerunt cum summa prudentia et circumspectione adnotata et compilata; et de quibus coram Sanctitate Sua in sacro consistorio et in compluribus congregationibus, saepius ac mature discussum et agitatum fuit. Itaque Paternitates Vestrae poterunt videre et intelligere, et si cuique vestrum videbitur aliquid addendum vel minuendum, poterint libere loqui et ferre iudicium et sententiam suam. De quibus omnibus nos referemus S.mo D. N., qui decernet et determinabit, prout melius et oportunius visum fuerit Sanctitati Suae. Interea mihi nihil aliud superest ad dicendum, nisi exhortari Paternitates Vestras, ad quod tamen propria sponte animatos esse non dubito, ut ad id tantum habeant mentem et oculos, quod in primis ad laudem omnipotentis Dei, et deinde ad bonum commune et universale pertinere diiudicaverint.

---

[11] Although this fragment would seem to form a literary unit with what went before, it is not clear that these comments were addressed to the general congregation of December, 1513. In this section Riario referred to « haec capitula et has reformationes » and not to the « cedula et materia » of the earlier section. The prelates he exhorted to a free and spontaneous debate over the proposals and promised to pass on their suggestions to the pope. This comment poses two problems. If the occasion were the December congregation, there would be no need to inform Leo on the minutes of the meeting since he seems to have been present at it. If such a discussion took place at that meeting as here urged, the complaints of the bishops two days later that they knew not the contents of the reform proposals become difficult to explain (M 846B-847A; RAYNALDUS, 513, N° 97).

A more likely candidate for the occasion of these remarks is the meeting of a special commission held on May 1, 1514 to iron out the voiced objections of the prelates to some of the proposed contents in the bull « Supernae dispositionis arbitrio » to be approved at the ninth session five days later (M 848C-850D). References in this fragment to recent modifications made by cardinals and to the holding of numerous congregations may echo what was described in Leo's bull convoking the general congregation of April 29th (M 848B).

11.* Praise of Leo X for Adding to Those Twenty-four Deputies Elected by the Council Men of His Own Choosing[12]

BAV Ms. Chis. I.III.89: *Consistorialia Raph. Riarii*, Tomus II: *De dignis promotionibus*, fols. 139^v-140^r.

Beatissime Pater, ut translatio et exempla trahantur a minoribus rebus ad maiora et digniora, Sanctitas Vestra sapientissime fecit imitari bonos imperatores et bonos duces exercituum, qui aliquando in locum deffficientium militum, multoties etiam, ut ad omnes casus habeant paratiores et ualidiores uires, consueuerunt mittere supplementum et habere nouos delectus. Hoc dico quia pridie in illa congregatione Lateranensi, quae de mandato Sanctitatis Vestrae fuit celebrata, fuerunt per tacita suffragia siue palluctas designati illi uiginti quattuor praelati de quibus eadem intellexit; et licet quod numerus et qualitas et merita personarum existimari debeant sufficientia ad omnia quantumuis grauia et ardua rite et recte peragenda, tamen Sanctitas Vestra sapientissime cogitauit uelle addere istos de quibus modo proposuit, quorum doctrina, prudentia, usus, bonitas, et caeterae optimae et laudabiles partes sunt notae et exploratissimae apud omnes. Ex quo fit ut, quum illi sint existimandi dignissimi per se, ipsi multo tamen (efficiantur) [Ms.: efficiuntur] digniores ex hac electione et (iudicio) [Ms.: iuditio] Sanctitatis Vestrae, de quo et ipsi immortaliter debent [139^v/140^r] et obligantur Sanctitati Vestrae; et nos etiam debemus multum gaudere, quum de illorum prudentia sic probata per Sanctitatem Vestram possimus multum sperare et multum nobis repromittere in consultationibus habendis de quibuscunque rebus pro tempore accidentibus. Quamobrem et caetera.

---

[12] In my transcription of the documents in appendices 11*, 12*, and 13*, I have preserved the orthography of the original, but I have silently expanded abbreviations, represented the e-cedilla as ae, and have normalized paragraphing, punctuation, and capitalization according to modern taste and convenience. I have enclosed in square brackets letters and words to be omitted, while parentheses have been used to surround letters and words required by the sense of the passage. I am most grateful to Professor Frank A.C. Mantello for having checked my transcription and for having made valuable suggestions for improvement. Any deficiencies are my sole responsibility.

The occasion for Riario's comments recorded here in appendix 11* would appear to be a meeting of the sacred consistory soon after (pridie) the general congregation assembled under Riario's presidency in the Hall of Councils of the Lateran Palace on Friday 13 May 1513 at which the ninety conciliar fathers chose twenty-four representatives to sit on Lateran V's deputations (M 794C-95B). On June 3rd Leo divided these representatives among three deputations and added to each deputation eight cardinals, two other bishops (often a non-Italian and a curialist), and two generals of religious orders (M 796A-97D). On October 26th he subdivided the reform deputation and added numerous curial officials (Hergenröther, *Conciliengeschichte*, VIII, 810-12).

CONCEPTS OF REFORM 253*

12.* Praise of Leo X for Wanting the Council to Achieve Its Ends[13]

BAV, Ms. Chis. I.III.89: *Consistorialia Raph. Riarii*, Tomus II: *De rebus comunibus*, fol. 116[r.]

Beatissime Pater, uidetur esse non solum rationabile et consentaneum, uerum etiam maxime naturale, ut omnia appetant et progrediantur ad certum aliquem finem. Et cum fines sint varij et diuersi, certe illi sunt magis expetendi qui sunt maioris momenti et ex quibus uberiores et meliores fructus possunt expectari. Sed quia ad ipsos fines non potest perueniri neque illi possunt attingi sine opera et ministerio hominum, meo iudicio Sanctitas Vestra optime ac sanctissime facit uelle preficere hoc sanctissimum opus concilij; quod sperandum est non fuisse inceptum sine diuina ope et Spiritus Sancti afflatu et cooperatione.

13.* Praise of Leo X's Prorogation of the Next Session[14]

BAV, Ms. Chis. I.III.89: *Consistorialia Raph. Riarii*, Tomus II: *De causis mature expediendis*, fol. 106[v.]

Beatissime Pater, non immerito solet dici quod ad electionem bonorum consiliorum potissime requiratur spatium et maturitas temporis, quod certe cum magna laude et commendatione sua uidemus seruari a Sanctitate Vestra, prout proxime fecit de prorogatione huius instantis sessionis, quae profecto fuit valde utilis et necessaria. Et ego memini me dixisse et affirmasse quod intra tam breve spatium erat impossibile posse confici et absolui materiam et negotium reformationis; immo quantum experti sumus cum toto hoc spatio quod habuimus, uix peruenissemus ad medium itineris quo tendebamus, nisi Sanctitas Vestra interfuisset, et sua sapientia et authoritate praefuisset ac rexisset, et moderata esset haec omnia quae sunt facta.

---

[13]In this excerpt Riario points out the need for human effort in addition to divine assistance for the Council to achieve its goals, and he praises the pope for wanting the Council to be a success. In his brief speech at the sixth session of the Lateran Council on 23 April 1513, Leo X announced his intention to continue the Council until universal peace and concord were established among Christians (M 657DE, 788DE). In his other consistorial comments (see above pp. 245, 247, 249-50), Riario speaks of Leo X's determination that the Council also attain its goal of church reform.

[14]These comments addressed by Riario to Leo X are a paraphrasing and reworking of a section of the speech published above (see p. 250). What is here added is a reference to the prorogation of the impending session by the pope which allowed the deputation to complete its work in time. On 15 December 1513 Leo prorogued the eighth session scheduled for Friday December 16th to meet instead on Monday the 19th because the deputations had not yet completed their work (M 818B-19C). On December 13th the papal bull *Pastoralis officii* reforming the officials and fees of the curia had been issued (*Bullarum ... Taurinensis editio*, V [Torino 1860], 571-601), but the Council was then called upon to confirm the penalties for violations of its measures (M 846B-D). On December 17th a general congregation of the three conciliar deputations was held in the upper chapel of the papal palace (M 819C). This meeting was the probable occasion for Riario's comments here recorded.

IV

ADDENDA AND CORRIGENDA

- p. 169, n.15: *'Reformer:* Augustiniana 12 (1962) 225-253; and his *The Registers of Giles of Viterbo*: ibid. 142-160;' should read *'Reformer:* Analecta Augustiniana 25 (1962) 225-253; and his *The Registers of Giles of Viterbo*: Augustiniana 12 (1962) 142-160;'.
- p. 214, n.155, add to end of note: For further information on Juan Pascual, see on page 212, n. [155 cont.] and Joaquin Luis ORTEGA MARTÍN, 'Un reformador pretridentino: Don Pascual de Ampudia, obispo de Burgos (1496-1512),' *Anthologica Annua* 19 (Rome 1972), 185-556.

V

The Proposals for an Episcopal College at Lateran V

A renewed episcopacy was central to the concerns of many reformers in the early sixteenth century. While most of these writers demanded a reform of episcopal morals and a fulfillment of pastoral duties, the bishops themselves tended to see reform in terms of a restoration of their juridical rights. The papal triumph over conciliarism a half-century earlier and subsequent developments in church policy were often at the expense of the bishops. Concordats were negotiated between popes and secular rulers giving the laity greater control over local churches. Religious orders received what was known as a *mare magnum* of papal privileges and exemptions from episcopal control. In keeping with their pretensions to an oligarchic share in Church government, the curial cardinals acquired commensurate privileges for themselves and their staffs, conferred benefices in others' dioceses, and with their great wealth proceeded to employ impoverished but ambitious absentee bishops as their secretaries and servants. The stern opposition of the pope and cardinals frustrated any attempt to convene a general council in which the bishops could have sought to restore their diminished dignity and authority.[1] When in his struggle

---

[1] For an introduction to these issues, see: Hubert JEDIN, A History of the Council of Trent, I, trans. Ernest GRAF, St. Louis 1957, 5-165 and his Zur Entwicklung des Kirchenbegriffs im 16. Jahrhundert (1955), reprinted in: Kirche des Glaubens, Kirche der Geschichte, II: Konzil und Kirchenreform, Freiburg im Br. 1966, 7-16; Paul BROUTIN, L'évêque dans la tradition pastorale du xve siècle: Adaptation française de "Das Bischofsideal der katholischen Reformation" par Hu-

to free Italy of foreign domination Julius II (1503-13) was forced to contend with a French diversionary tactic which became the schismatic Council of Pisa (1511-12) and decided to "drive out a nail with a nail" by calling his own Lateran Council (1512-17), the bishops of Christendom were offered at last a forum in which to seek remedies for their afflictions.[2]

One of the problems which the bishops had to solve was their lack of representation in a Roman curia where their rivals enjoyed a recognized system of cardinal protectors and curial procurators. Under Julius II the interests of temporal rulers were officially entrusted to cardinals who promoted the nomination to benefices in a particular country of candidates sponsored by its ruler and assisted that ruler in obtaining various other favors from the papacy.[3] On a lower level

---

bert JEDIN, Bruges 1953, 11-43, reissued in an enlarged Italian version as Hubert JEDIN and Giuseppe ALBERIGO, Il tipo ideale di vescovo secondo la reforma cattolica, trans. E. DURINI and G. COLOMBI, Brescia 1986, 11-24: Alaphridus DE BONHOME, Jurisdiction des évêques et exemption des réguliers selon le projet de bulle de Paul III *Superni dispositione consilii* (Decembre 1540-Janvier 1542), in: Revue de droit canonique 15 (1965) 97-183, 214-39, 331-49; *Ibid.*, 16 (1966), 3-21; Francis OAKLEY, Council Over Pope? Toward a Provisional Ecclesiology, New York 1969, Chp. II, esp. 62-68; Barbara McClung HALLMAN, Italian Cardinals, Reform and the Church as Property (= UCLA Center for Medieval and Renaissance Studies 22), Berkeley/Los Angeles/London 1985, 102-04 (cardinal's collation rights in others' dioceses); Cristoforo MARCELLO (ed.), The Caeremoniale Romanum of Agostino Patrizi Piccolomini, Venice 1516, reprinted Ridgewood, N.J. 1965, Lib. III, cap. xiii, fol. CXXII^r; and Giuseppe CATALANI, Sacrarum caeremoniarum sive rituum ecclesiasticorum sanctae Romanae ecclesiae libri tres, II Roma 1751, 337-39. My study Episcopal Reform at the Fifth Lateran Council (1512-1517), a doctoral dissertation in the Department of History, Harvard University, Cambridge, Mass. 1976, examines these issues at length.

[2] The most recent study of the Lateran Council is that by Olivier DE LA BROSSE in the collaborative work Latran V et Trente by Olivier DE LA BROSSE, Joseph LECLER, Henri HOLSTEIN, and Charles LEFEBVRE (=Histoire des conciles oecuméniques 10) Paris 1975, with an up-to-date bibliography on pages 471-73, and my Paride de Grassi's Diary of the Fifth Lateran Council, in: AHC 14 (1982) 370-460, here 373-87.

[3] To be effective cardinal protectors had to reside at the center of ecclesiastical power. Rulers preferred to have a cardinal from their own country be their nation's protector (e.g., Christopher Bainbridge for England), but were not hesitant to enlist the services of influential Italians when their native cardinal(s) did not reside in Rome (thus, Federico Sanseverino and Giulio dei Medici repre-

were national procurators, often conationals who held a curial position in Rome. They were charged with furthering the ruler's political and ecclesiastical interests amid the intricacies of Roman bureaucracy.[4] Both of these agents were rewarded for their services by gifts, fees, and even ecclesiastical provision to a benefice in the nation they represented. For centuries religious had enjoyed the official protection of cardinals specially designated for each of the monastic and mendicant orders.[5] These religious were also represented in the Roman curia by a procurator or *commissarius* of their own order and choosing.[6] The most powerful of the bishops' rivals, the cardinals, were well represented in the Roman curia since they often headed a number of its more important bureaux and advised the pope in the Sacred Consistory. If episcopal interests, when they conflicted with their rivals', were to be adequately represented in Rome, the bishops would need an organized common front and procurators of their own. While the papal court already had an episcopal association known as the college of assistants to the papal throne, its functions

---

sented France) or their nation was without its own cardinal (thus, Achilles de Grassi for Poland-Lithuania). See Josef WODKA, Zur Geschichte der nationalen Protektorate der Kardinäle an der römischen Kurie (= Publikationen des österreichischen historischen Instituts in Rom IV-I) Innsbruck 1938, 32-33, 35, 44, 98,114; William E. WILKIE, The Cardinal Protectors of England: Rome and the Tudors Before Reformation, Cambridge 1974, 6-7, 45; Sacrorum conciliorum nova et amplissima collectio, G.D. MANSI, *et alii* (edd.), XXXII (1438-1549), reprinted Paris 1902, cols. 878 A-C, 880 A-B — hereafter this volume is cited as MANSI; and Paride DE GRASSI, Diarium Leonis, Bibliotheca Apostolica Vaticana (= BAV), Ms. Vat. Lat. 12275, fol. 58^{r-v} (A. de Grassi as protector of Poland).

[4] E.g., Thomas Nudry for Scotland and Zutfeld von Wardenburg for Denmark — see The Letters of James the Fourth 1505-1513, ed. Robert Kerr HANNEY, Edinburgh 1953, 266, 334 and Regesta Diplomatica Historiae Danicae, ed. a Societate Regiae Scientiarum Danicae, Series 2, I-II (1488-1536) Copenhagen 1889, nr. 10,059, p. 1199.

[5] Extensive studies of this office are provided by BERNARDINO DA SIENA, Il cardinale protettore negli istituti religiosi, specialemente negli ordini Francescani, Firenze 1940, and Stephen L. FORTE, The Cardinal-Protector of the Dominican Order (= Institutum Historicum Fratrum Praedicatorum Romae ad S. Sabinae, Dissertationes Historicae XV) Roma 1959.

[6] E.g., Innocenzo M. TAURISANO, Hierarchia Ordinis Praedicatorum, rev. ed, Roma 1916, 97-98 and Luke WADDING, Annales Minorum seu Trium Ordinum, rev. by Joseph Maria FONSECA DA EVORA, Quaracchi 1933, XV 519, 539.

were limited to the liturgy and did not extend into the area of Church government.

This college of papal assistants has been briefly described in the writings of papal masters of ceremonies.[7] Efforts to trace its origins have succeeded only in placing it prior to the pontificate of Eugenius IV (1431-47). By the late fifteenth century its membership often exceeded the customary ten. In addition to representatives from each of the three episcopal orders(bishops, archbishops, and any patriarch residing in Rome), this college traditionally included the papal sacristan and master of ceremonies and the governor of Rome, provided they were bishops. Before his coronation, the new pontiff would appoint a new college of papal assistants and would later on add members to it at his own discretion or at the urgings of cardinals or influential laymen. He usually chose his assistants from among the more eminent prelates of the Roman curia who were mostly Italians.[8] Under Julius II this office was conferred not so much as a reward for virtue or outstanding service to the Church, but as an acknowledgment of one's noble birth and as a favor.[9] A fee of ten golden ducats was paid upon appointment and members shared in the stipends given for services performed.[10] In dignity these papal assistants ranked between the

---

[7] The Caeremoniale Romanum, a treatise on the rituals of the papal court compiled in 1488 by the master of ceremonies Agostino Patrizi (Piccolomini), was first published during the Lateran Council by Cristoforo Marcello. The Venetian edition of 1516 has been reprinted as The Caeremoniale Romanum, Ridgewood, N.J. 1965. The diaries of Paride de Grassi, master of ceremonies both for the popes Julius II and Leo X and for the Lateran Council, are soon to be published in a critical edition by Marc DYKMANS. Dykmans has already published large sections of that diary relating to the Fifth Lateran Council as Le cinquième Concile du Latran d'après le Diaire de Paris de Grassi, in: AHC 14 (1982) 271-369 – hereafter cited as DE GRASSI, Diarium (DYKMANS, ed.). My references to material in de Grassi's diary not yet edited are to the manuscript copies in the Bibliotheca Apostolica Vaticana: Vat. Lat. 12414 is hereafter cited as DE GRASSI, Diarium Julii and Vat. Lat. 12275 as DE GRASSI, Diarium Leonis.

[8] CATALANI, Sacrarum Caeremoniarum, 4, 363; PATRIZI, Caeremoniale Romanum, fols. CXXXI^v-CXXII^r; DE GRASSI, Diarium Julii, fol. 192^r, Leonis, fol. 21^{r-v}; Johann BURCHARD, Diarium sive rerum urbanarum commentarii I ed. L. THUSANE, Paris 1883, 90.

[9] DE GRASSI, Diarium, Vat. Lat. 12413, fol. 319^v.

[10] DE GRASSI, Diarium Julii, fol. 124^{r-v}; PATRIZI, Caeremoniale Romanum, fol. CXXII^r.

cardinals and archbishops, and while Julius II merely planned on elevating some of its members to the cardinalate, Leo appointed as cardinals a large number of those in his college.[11] These bishops functioned as assistants to the pope during solemn liturgical functions: holding the lectionary and candles and following him about in a semicircular formation. On the Sundays of Advent and Lent, they were called upon to lead the principal Eucharistic celebration in the papal chapel.[12] Because this college was already an accepted feature of the papal court, it is not surprising that discussions during the Council on establishing at Rome a permanent organization to represent the interests of bishops throughout the Church would include the possibility merely of expanding the functions of these papal assistants.

---

[11] The rolls of the Lateran Council list the *Patriarchae et assistentes papae* between the *Diaconi cardinales* and *Archiepiscopi* – see MANSI 677CD, 707D-08A, 728B-D, 743E-44B, etc. – For a list of some of the papal assistants named by Julius II, see: DE GRASSI, Diarium, Vat. Lat. 12413: Angelo Leonini (fol. 192^v), Fernando de Herrera (319^v); Diarium Julii: Orlando del Caretto (fol. 118^r), Gian Vincenzo Carafa (124^{r-v}), Stefano de Taleazis (126^r), Francesco Gustaferro (144^v), Francesco Pisauro (144^v), Alfonso Carafa (144^v), Federigo Fregoso (145^r), Bernardo Zanni (192^r), Giuliano Cibò (237^r), Francesco de Rovere (MANSI, 677D). The men appointed as assistants by Leo X during the time of the Council are recorded in DE GRASSI, Diarium Leonis: Gianvincenzo Tedeschini-Piccolomini – card. (fol. 21^r), Francesco de Conti dei Domicelli – card. (21^r), Federigo Fregoso – card. (21^r), Roberto Latino Orsini – resigned to marry (21^r), Scaramuzia Trivulzio – card. (21^r), Giambattista Pallavicini – card. (21^r), Gianfrancesco de Rovere – died ca. 1516 (21^r), Pompejo Colonna – card. (21^r), Lorenzo Pucci – card. (21^r), Gabriele Masciolo – sacristan (21^r), Giulio de' Medici – card. (43^r), Angelo Leonini – died 1517 (74^v), Andrea de Valle – card. (75^r), Giuliano Soderini – Florentine rival family (75^r), Domenico Giacobazzi – card. (97^v), Alessandro Guasco – died 1517 (110^r), Bernardo Rossi – card. (122^r), Francisco Bobadilla – Spaniard (132^r), Paride de Grassi – master of ceremonies (151^r), and Aloisio Rossi – card. (191^v). – The remarkable number of papal assistants who were later raised to the cardinalate is probably related to a decision of Leo to promote his most promising curialists and relatives to this honor. Given the role assigned these assistants in the revised proposal for an episcopal college (see below footnote 19) and the possible leadership they had in promoting episcopal demands (MANSI, 850CD; DE GRASSI, Diarium Leonis, fol. 117^r), it would not be surprising if Leo eliminated their potentially dangerous leadership role among the bishops by promoting them to the cardinalate – not unlike his ending of French opposition by rewarding Francis I with the Concordat of Bologna.

[12] CATALANI, Sacrarum Caeremoniarum, 326-64.

While papal theologians were generally ready to find reasons for opposing such an association of episcopal representatives, respected exponents for all sides of the conciliarist question propounded at Rome ideas which would provide a theological basis for granting bishops an on-going voice in the government of the Church. The group least in sympathy with such ideas would have included those curialists responsible for the wording of conciliar documents which tended to depict bishops as mere deputies of the pope.[13] Other curialists like the conciliarists Giovanni Gozzadini (1477-1517) and Girolamo Massaino sought a check on abuses of the pope's power: Gozzadini by assigning an *ad hoc* regulative function to general councils[14] and Massaino by claiming that Christ himself provided a remedy for tyranny by giving his Church a mixed constitution. To a monarchial position of honor in the Church granted by a Byzantine emperor to the patriarch of Rome, Christ has so annexed an episcopal aristocracy that the pope cannot rule the Church without the consent of his brother bishops who are equal to him in the powers of both orders and jurisdiction.[15] Yet another curialist, a moderate conciliarist and eminent canonist, Domenico Giacobazzi (1444-1527/28), claimed that bishops were successors to the office and powers of the Apostles and by reason of their episcopal dignity enjoyed jurisdiction in the

---

[13] E.g., MANSI 970E-71C, 990C. As an example of theological argumentation against granting bishops a common voice in the government of the Church, see Karl Joseph von HEFELE and Joseph HERGENRÖTHER, Conciliengeschichte nach den Quellen bearbeitet, VIII Freiburg im Br. 1887, 848-49 – hereafter this volume is cited as HEFELE-HERGENRÖTHER. See also the positions of Cypriano Benet, Giovanni Francesco Poggio, Antonio Trombetta, Alberto Pasquali, and Isidoro Isolani who propounded papalist ideas at the time of the Lateran Council. Their writings are analyzed in Ulrich HORST, Zwischen Konziliarismus und Reformation: Studien zur Ekklesiologie im Dominikanerorden (=Dissertationes Historicae XXII) Roma 1985, 55-115.

[14] JEDIN, Giovanni Gozzadini, ein Konziliarist am Hofe Julius' II, in: Kirche des Glaubens II 68-69; and Remigius BÄUMER, Nachwirkungen des konziliaren Gedankens in der Theologie und Kanonistik des frühen 16. Jahrhunderts (=RST 100), Münster 1971, 22-25, 71-73, 254-57.

[15] Girolamo MASSAINO, De conciliis, BAV, Regin. Lat. 392, fol. 260^v-61^r, 268^r-270^r, 272^v-73^r, 275^{r-v}, and my study, Girolamo Massaino: Another Conciliarist at the Papal Court, Julius II to Adrian VI, in : Studies in Catholic History in Honor of John Tracy Ellis, ed. Nelson H. MINNICH *et alii*, Wilmington, Del. 1985, 520-65, here 537-52.

universal Church which together they represented.[16] Even so ardent an advocate of the papacy as the Dominican master general and speculative theologian, Tommaso de Vio (1469-1534), accepted the traditional theory contained in the *Ecclesiastical Hierarchies* of Dionysius the Pseudo-Areopagite which placed bishops together at the summit of the Church's earthly structure.[17] He also argued that bishops were the successors of the Apostles and their office was of divine institution.[18] Thus, while the official doctrine on the episcopacy tended to reduce it to an appendage of the papacy, serious and varied theological reflection at Rome acknowledged a greater dignity and authority in the episcopal office.

The events and factors which shaped the schemes for an episcopal organization at Rome can be traced only in part due to a paucity of source materials.[19] The bishops' initial proposal probably never ema-

---

[16] Domenico GIACOBAZZI de Faceschi, De concilio tractatus, ed. Cristoforo GIACOBAZZI, Roma 1538, 85C-86B. The best introductory study of Giacobazzi is that by Josef KLOTZNER, Kardinal Dominikus Jacobazzi und sein Konzilswerk: ein Beitrag zur Geschichte der konziliaren Idee, Brixen 1947.

[17] Sancti Thomae Aquinatis doctoris angelici opera omnia iussu impensaque Leonis XIII. P.M. edita. Secunda secundae Summae Theologiae cum commentariis Thomae de Vio Caietani ordinis praedicatorum, cura et studio fratrum eiusdem ordinis, Roma 1899, X 465 or Pars II-II, quaestio 184, articulus 8, capitulum 7. Years later (1529) Cajetan questioned the identification of Dionysius the Areopagite with the author of the Ecclesiastical Hierarchy – see Anton BODEN, Das Wesen der Kirche nach Kardinal Cajetan: ein Beitrag zur Ekklesiologie in Zeitalter der Reformation, Trier 1971, 43.

[18] Tommaso DE VIO, De comparatione autoritatis papae et concilii cum apologia eiusdem tractatus, ed. Vincent M. Jacques POLLET, (=Scripta Theologica 1) Roma 1936, nr. 33, 39, 52, 200, 560-61, 586, pp. 27-29, 34, 97, 244-45, 253. For a study of the context and ideas contained in these texts, see Olivier DE LA BROSSE; La Pape e le Concile: La comparaison de leur pouvoirs à la veille de la Réforme, Paris 1965.

[19] The official acts of the Council published in 1521 and reprinted by Mansi make not direct mention of the proposal for an episcopal college. The diary of Paride de Grassi not only sketches the events surrounding the proposal, but also supplies a copy of its revision (Diarium [DYKMANS, ed.] Nr. 1185: 7, pp. 360-61; excerpts from this diary are reprinted by Odorico RAINALDI in his continuation of Cesare BARONIO's Annales ecclesiastici, rev. and ed. Giovanni Domenico MANSI and Augustin THEINER, XXXI Paris 1880, ad annum 1516, nr. 1-3 – hereafter this volume is cited as RAINALDI).- Among the few conciliar working papers known to have survived are an unsigned rebuttal of the bishops' first proposal

nated from the conciliar reform deputation since it was dominated by cardinals, curialists, and religious.[20] On 15 January 1514 this deputation was charged with receiving in writing all suggestions for reform and judging whether they deserved further consideration. At a general congregation on April 19th preparatory to the ninth session, many bishops protested that their wishes were being ignored. François Hamon and Giovanni Antonio Scotti appealed directly to the pope to

---

and an annotated revision of that proposal in the form of a supplication from the bishops addressed to the pope by their deputies (HEFELE-HERGENRÖTHER 845-53, App. H and J). – While the names of the deputies who probably authored the revised proposal remain unknown, internal evidence suggests that the writer of the rebuttal was an absentee (probably curial) bishop residing at Rome (*quod nos in civitatibus nostris non concederemus. . . . nimis multi episcopi nostris sumptibus in Urbe residemus*) and of Italian nationality since he gave examples from an Italian perspective of civil authority (*Marchiones et Comites Regi Ducibusque subjecti*) and of what were the foreign nations (*Germani . . . Galli . . . Hispani*) – HEFELE-HERGENRÖTHER 847-51. Francis OAKLEY claims that this document emanated from the cardinals – perhaps, but its author was a bishop – see his Conciliarism at the Fifth Lateran Council? Church History 41 (1972), 457, n. 29, 459, n. 43. The rebuttal which is printed as Appendix J, HEFELE-HERGENRÖTHER 847-53 has been by another hand mistakenly entitled on the cover sheet: *Quaedam tractata inter cardinales et episcopos pro XII sessione Lateranensis Concilii*, a title more appropriately belonging to Appendix K. The original copy of this rebuttal is in the Archivo Segreto Vaticano, Armadi I-XVIII, nr. 3017. – The identity of the person who annotated the revised proposal is unknown. He made each meeting of the college hinge on previous papal consent and judged unnecessary an extended listing of the college's officials and their functions, reducing them to brief phrases, and made their existence dependent on the pope's prior approval and the needs of the college. He also reported that the pope was willing at the proper time to satisfy the prelates by appointing new papal assistants. These comments suggest that the annotator was privy to discussions in the pope's entourage prior to a rejection of the proposal. (See HEFELE-HERGENRÖTHER 845-46).

[20] As constituted on 3 June 1513 the reform deputation consisted of eight cardinals, two curial bishops, and two generals of religious orders all appointed by Leo X and eight bishops elected by their peers (MANSI 796A, D-97B). By 16 October 1513 the membership had been notably altered by the loss of one reforming cardinal and two elected bishops and the addition by the pope of three cardinals, another curial bishop, and numerous lesser curial officials (HEFELE-HERGENRÖTHER 810-12). The official deputation remained in the control of the pope and cardinals – see Eugen GUGLIA, Studien zur Geschichte des V. Laterancocils. (1512-1517.), in: Sitzungsberichte der philosophisch-historischen Classe der kaiserlichen Akademie der Wissenschaften, Wien 140 (1899), X 22-33.

The Proposals for an Episcopal College at Lateran V 221

consider the bishops' petitions.[21] In order to woo episcopal support for his own programs, Leo urged the bishops to back the measures scheduled for a vote at the coming session and promised in return to hold a special session for a favorable hearing of their requests. After many meetings and much discussion the bishops drew up a common set of petitions which focused on two issues: an end to the exemptions of religious and the establishment at Rome of a permanent episcopal organization to defend and promote their interests. They also elected from their number deputies of every nation and profession to present their petitions to the pope and cardinals.[22] Given an espousal of theological concepts supportive of an episcopal voice in Church government and their earlier election as deputies of their fellow bishops, it is reasonable to suspect two men of having been closely associated with the proposal: Domenico Giacobazzi (1444-1527/28), the eminent canonist, and Alexios Celadenus (1451-1517), the Greek homelist at the third session.[23] Which models influenced the plans for an episcopal organization is a question open to speculation. The lived experience of the Council itself with its special congregations of bishops, election of deputies from every nation, and taste of effective episcopal power could have provided the stimulus and outlines for a permanent association of bishops at Rome. Confraternities founded to promote the various interests of their members are also suggested

---

[21] MANSI 847C-E, 849B-50C. The acts of the Council record only that there were petitions (*petitiones praelatorum* 849D, *petitiones eorum* 850A) and do not describe their contents.

[22] DE GRASSI, Diarium (DYKMANS, ed.) Nrs. 1116:3, 1185:1, pp. 355-56, 359-60, or RAINALDI, 1516, nr. 1.

[23] Recent studies of Celadenus are those by Franz BABINGER, Alessio Celidonio und seine Türkendenkschrift, in: Beiträge zur Südosteuropa-Forschung: Anlässlich des 1. Internationalen Balkanologenkongresses in Sofia, 26. VIII-1.IX.1966, München 1966, 326-30, John M. MCMANAMON, The Ideal Renaissance Pope: Funeral Oratory from the Papal Court, in: AHP 14 (1976) 54-59, 61-70, H.J. KISSLING, Celidonio, Alessio, in: Dizionario biografico degli italiani 23 (Rome 1979) 421-23; John MONFASANI, Alexius Celadenus and Ottaviano Ubaldini: An Epilogue to Bessarion's Relationship with the Court of Urbino, in: Bibliothèque d'Humanisme et Renaissance 46 (1984) 95-110; and my forthcoming, Alexios Celadenus: A Disciple of Bessarion in Renaissance Italy. Celadenus' views on bishops are found in his conciliar oration (MANSI 738A-E). His election and that of Giacobazzi as episcopal deputies are recorded in the Council's acts (MANSI, 850D).

as possible models for it.[24] The choice of its minor offices does not seem to have been borrowed from any particular group or society, but followed the functions assigned to the episcopal organization and used terms then in common parlance.[25] When Leo X was about to schedule the session promised the bishops, he inquired about their deliberations and petitions. On learning of the care which went into the preparation of their requests, he was initially inclined to grant them.[26]

While the original proposal for the episcopal organization has not survived, its major elements can be reconstructed from references to it in contemporary documents. The terms used for it are *confraternitas, sodalitium,* and *societas,* Latin words which in addition to their

---

[24] E.g., MANSI 847D, 848B, 850C, 898B, D, etc.; RAINALDI 1516, nr. 1. A century earlier, Pierre d'Ailly recorded a somewhat similar proposal, but much more threatening to the existence of the college of cardinals – see below footnote 33. The existence of many guilds and confraternities in Rome established to promote the material, social, and spiritual concerns of their members could in part also have helped inspire bishops to found the college as a similiar organization of their own, as de Grassi suggests. His references to it as a confraternity and its assumption of the traditional task of such organizations of performing works of piety in addition to promoting its members' interests both seem to indicate that confraternities and guilds served in some way as models for the episcopal college. The rival college of the cardinals with its direct access to the pope and members who represented various national interests more likely also served as an inspiration and pattern for the bishops' – see below footnotes 25-28.

[25] Offices like advocate, deputy, procurator, scribe, syndic, and treasurer were not honorific, but to each was assigned a function. Similar officials and functions can be found in contemporary Roman confraternities and guilds – see Antonio MARTINI, Arti mestieri e fede nella Roma dei papi, (=Roma cristiana 13) Bologna 1965, 55-60, 140-48, Anna ESPOSITO, Le 'Confraternite' del Gonfalone (secoli XIV-XV), in: Le confraternite romane: esperienza religiosa, società, committenza artistica; Colloquio della Fondazione Caetani, Roma, 14-15 maggio 1982, Luigi FIORANI (ed.) (=Ricerche per la storia religiosa di Roma 5) Roma 1984, 91-136, here 110 (Cap. vii); and the constitutions of the Confraternity of Divine Love, esp. chps. 2-8, which probably guided the Roman group at the time of the Council and are reproduced in Pietro TACCHI VENTURI, Storia della Compagnia di Gesù in Italia, rev. ed. I-II Roma 1950, 26-30. Officials with such titles could, of course, also be found in the bureaucracies of the Roman commune and papal curia.

[26] DE GRASSI, Diarium (DYKMANS, ed.) Nr. 1185:2, p. 360, or RAINALDI 1516, nr. 1.

more obvious English derivatives can also be fittingly translated by the expression college of bishops.[27] This college is likened to the confraternities formed by many laymen of various trades.[28] The functions assigned to it come under the general headings of caring for the defense and promotion of episcopal interests and undertaking works of piety. The college is to represent through its deputies the bishops of Christendom who are assumed to be residing in their own dioceses. These deputies are charged with procuring the rights of diocesan bishops – no mention is made of curial bishops – and with defending bishops who find themselves oppressed and their rights violated, whether by their ecclesiastical superiors such as archbishops or by civil rulers, even kings. As planned, all episcopal business having to do with Rome would be channeled through the fraternity and its deputies.[29]

Three organizational components are evident in this college. At the head are three or four presidents, probably of different nationalities: French, German, Spanish, and Italian. These men preside over a college of deputies or *consodales*, bishops called to Rome and resid-

---

[27] DE GRASSI described it as *consocietas episcoporum, confraternitas episcoporum*, and *societas* – see Diarium (DYKMANS, ed.), Nr. 1185:1-2, p. 360, and RAINALDI 1516, nr. 1. The rebuttal of the first proposal referred to it as a *fraternitas* and *sodalitium*, its members as *fraternales* and *consodales* – see HEFELE-HERGENRÖTHER 847-53. Because this organization was to have a voice in the government of the Church, terms like "confraternity" and "society" seem too weak as translations. The English expression "episcopal college" is more appropriate, even though the Second Vatican Council has given it a slightly different technical meaning by including curial cardinals and several heads of religious orders in the Synod of Bishops and making its existence periodic instead of permanent – see The Documents of Vatican II, ed. Walter M. ABBOTT, translation ed. Joseph GALLAGHER, New York 1966, 399-403, 720-24.

[28] In the early sixteenth century, guilds and confraternities at Rome were very popular – see MARTINI, Arti mestiere, 148, 156, 164, 173; and Peter PARTNER, Renaissance Rome 1500-1559: A Portrait of a Society, Berkeley 1976, 102-06. The episcopal college as proposed would have had too important a function in the government of the Church to have been seriously considered just another confraternity in Rome. By calling it a confraternity instead of a college, its proponents may have hoped to make it seem less innovative and threatening and to avoid those comparisons between it and the college of cardinals which could have only hurt their chances of getting it approved.

[29] HEFELE-HERGENRÖTHER 847-53 for App. J with its twelve-point rebuttal, see nrs. 2, 4, 8.

ing there at the expense of the college in order to represent the hierarchy of their respective countries. The college is to have its own procurators or agents in the Roman curia just as religious and civil rulers have theirs. These procurators are to be informed on the affairs of the country in which particular problems concerning a bishop occurred. A practical way of matching the problems with local expertise is to assign special procurators for each nationality. It is apparently suggested that such a system of representatives and procurators will incline the diocesan bishops to render prompter obedience to the Roman pontiff. While such a college would be a new institution for Rome, the proposal apparently also points out that the times have changed and justify such an innovation.[30]

The arguments against this college presented in a rebuttal were both theoretical and practical. The proposal was considered incompatible with the role of the pope as universal bishop and with the intimate relation between him and local bishops which prevents these discrete "members of the pontiff" from forming a fraternity. On pragmatic grounds the college is equally indefensible. Given the concern for bishops shown by such powerful persons as the pope, cardinals, and procurator of the fisc and the protective ordinances of canon law and conciliar decrees, such a college is unnecessary. If these are unable to defend episcopal interests, what hope is there that a college could be any more effective? It would be ignored by the bishops' opponents and lack proper funding. In addition, it would limit a bishop's freedom of action in Rome, encourage a spirit of rebellion, and accentuate national divisions. Besides, this college which the bishops want for themselves they are unwilling to grant to the clergy in their own dioceses.[31] What answer, if any, the bishops made to these criticisms of their proposal is unknown.

Leo X submitted the plans for an episcopal college to the cardinals for their sincere and considered opinion. They reported that the pope, college of cardinals, current Church law, and recent decrees of the Lateran Council met more adequately the needs of the bishops than did a college. The cardinals also seem to have underscored the useless multiplication of colleges at Rome since the episcopal order was already represented by papal assistants who were of the pope's

---

[30] *Ibid.* nrs. 2-5, 8, 9.
[31] *Ibid.* nrs. 1-12, esp. 1-4.

own choosing, understood the needs of their fellow bishops, and could relay to the pope whatever pleased these prelates. One of the bishops suspected the real reason for the cardinals' opposition was fear of the moral reform such a college might initiate.[32] What they probably feared more was the implicit challenge to their power and influence posed by such a college.[33]

As a new pope Leo X felt especially bound by the wishes of the cardinals and hence withdrew his promised support of the bishops' proposal, declaring their reasons insufficient to merit such a college. He also admitted to them that his own opposition was based on that of the cardinals and he would therefore in no way grant the prelates any kind of confraternity. To emphasize this opposition, he imposed a perpetual silence on further discussions.[34]

The bishops were not ready to take no for an answer. In a congregation of their own, over three-quarters of them voted to pursue the matter further. Avoiding this time any mention of a society or confraternity, the bishops took up the expressed objection of the cardinals and recast their proposal for an episcopal college so that it centered around the papal assistants. They drew up their proposal in the form

---

[32] HEFELE-HERGENRÖTHER 852; DE GRASSI, Diarium (DYKMANS, ed.) Nr. 1185:2, p. 360, or RAINALDI 1516, nr. 1,2; the recent decrees of the Lateran Council, here cited, which addressed the needs of the bishops were probably certain provisions of *Supernae dispositionis arbitrio* (MANSI 878A) and of *Regimini universalis ecclesiae* (MANSI 907D-12A).

[33] HEFELE-HERGENRÖTHER 851-52, App. J, nrs. 4 and 9 refer to the colleges as a potential source of rebellion and spirit of contradiction. The opponents of the episcopal college may also have recognized that this college could over time supplant the college of cardinals, for while the hierarchical order of cardinals is a mere invention of man, the episcopal order was instituted by Christ. As Pierre d'Ailly, a century earlier, noted: *Ideo fuit quorundam opinio, quam tamen non approbo, quod expediret Ecclesiae Papam habere loco cardinalium aliquos praelatos de diversis regnis et provinciis eidem pro consilio assistentes, et quod ille cardinalium status, tanquam male stabilis, caderet.* – see D'AILLY, Tractatus de materia concilii generalis (1402/03), in: Francis OAKLEY, The Political Thought of Pierre d'Ailly. The Voluntarist Tradition (=Yale Historical Publications, Miscellany 81), New Haven 1964, 328. There is no record that secular rulers or religious were consulted on the proposal for an episcopal college, nor have their opinions, if expressed, been found by scholars.

[34] DE GRASSI, Diarium (DYKMANS, ed.). Nr. 1185:2, p. 360, or RAINALDI 1516, nr. 1; HEFELE-HERGENRÖTHER 853.

of a supplication and deputized a new delegation of prelates to present it to the pontiff and, if necessary, to persuade the cardinals that "their petitions were just, honest, and tending toward virtue."[35] While the sources do not give the identity of these deputies, they seem to indicate that these events occurred during the wintry months of 1515-16 while Leo and the papal court were away from Rome visiting Bologna and Florence and that the supplication was presented in spring or summer of 1516.[36]

The bishops tried to make the proposals in their supplication seem as little threatening as possible by assuring the pontiff of his firm control over their college. By agreeing that its composition be identical with that of the papal assistants, the bishops entrusted the pope with naming the defenders and promoters of the episcopal order. The supplication also sought the pontiff's explicit permission each time the college met with other curial bishops or made any ordinances regarding works of piety or regulating such episcopal affairs as the collection of money and appointment of secretaries, lawyers, and

---

[35] DE GRASSI, (DYKMANS, ed.) Nr. 1185:3, p. 360, or RAINALDI 1516, nr. 1.

[36] De Grassi fails to identify these deputies. The official acts of the Council record two times when the bishops elected their own representatives who are named: on 14 May 1513 they chose twenty-four men to sit on three deputations of the Council (MANSI 794C-95B, 796A-97E) and on 30 April 1514 they elected eight to work out a compromise with the cardinals on the text of the Great Reform Bull (MANSI 850CD). Of this latter group, half were currently papal assistants: Giovanni Vincenzo Tedeschini-Piccolomini, Roberto Latino Orsini, Domenico Giacobazzi, and Pompejo Colonna (see above footnote 11). Some of these men may have been among the deputies elected by their fellow bishops to present their petitions to the pontiff and cardinals. Given Leo's threat to keep proroguing the Council from one October to the next should the bishops refuse to drop their demand for a college (DE GRASSI, Diarium [DYKMANS, ed.], Nr. 1185:4, p. 360, or RAINALDI 1516, nr. 1), the pope's rejection of their supplication probably occurred just prior to or after Leo's postponement on 5 June 1516 of the eleventh session from early June to October of 1516 (DE GRASSI, Diarium Leonis, 174^r). The absence from Rome of Leo and his entourage to vacation in Viterbo, meet Francis I at Bologna, and settle affairs in Florence, from 1 October 1515 to 28 February 1516, may have provided the bishops remaining in Rome the free atmosphere in which to pursue their plans (DE GRASSI, Diarium Leonis, 143^v-168^r).

procurators. It begged the pope who is the head and prince of all the bishops to cherish them and be their primary protector.[37]

In spite of this cautious courting of papal approval, the plan for an episcopal college contained the seeds of autonomy. Mere lip service was paid to one of bishops' chief rivals, the cardinals, who were entreated to be their perpetual protectors. One of the primary purposes of the college was to eliminate the need for depending on cardinals or others' procurators for defending and promoting specifically episcopal interests. Indeed, the proposal implicitly excluded from its affairs the influences of cardinals, religious, and temporal rulers. The original draft would have empowered the college to assemble when it felt necessary – a later hand made this conditional on the pope's approval. The college could also elect from among its members those who would be more specifically charged with defending and promoting the interests of the bishops and could elect other officials (syndics, procurators, or advocates) to do the same. In addition, the college was to have its own chancellery and treasury with powers to issue official correspondence, appoint a treasurer, and collect money to promote the needs of bishops. The supplication ended with the suggestion that an episcopal college, in order to serve the purposes for which it is established, needed members others than the current body of papal assistants who were almost all Italians and engaged in curial affairs. It urged the pope either to deputize some other prelates who were well-informed on episcopal affairs to collaborate with these papal assistants or to add to the college of papal assistants bishops of diverse foreign languages who were free to work together with other assistants on episcopal matters.[38]

---

[37] HEFELE-HERGENRÖTHER 845-46; a slightly variant version of this supplication without the marginalia in another hand is given by DE GRASSI, in his Diarium (DYKMANS, ed.) Nr. 1185:7, pp. 360-61.

[38] *Ibid.* In response to this last petition, an annotation recorded that pope Leo was ready to satisfy the prelates' desire by adding to the number of papal assistants when it seemed expedient and in the accustomed manner, some other prelates whom he thought suitable for this task. The only non-Italian Leo appointed as papal assistant during the time of the Council was Francisco Bobadilla, the youthful bishop of Salamanca, named on Chritmas Day of 1514(DE GRASSI, Diarium Leonis, 132ʳ). It is doubtful that the papal assistants functioned later as liaison agents for their fellow bishops.

In spite of the bishops' efforts to meet the objections of the cardinals, Leo firmly rejected their revised proposal, claiming he could not go against the continuing opposition of the cardinals. He added a warning: if the bishops persisted in demanding an episcopal college, he would not only hold no further sessions, proroguing them from October of one year to October of the next, but would ignore the bishops' other request for a modification and elimination of the privileges granted to religious, thus confirming their present exemptions from episcopal jurisdiction.[39]

Apart from Odorico Rainaldi (1595-1671) and Karl Hergenröther (1824-90) who published documents related to the college, only three historians have given serious consideration to the college: Mandell Creighton (1843-1901), Ludwig von Pastor (1845-1928), and Francis Oakley (1931-   ). In each case they have devoted about two and a half pages to the topic.[40] Their interpretations of the college and issues surrounding the proposals deserve a closer examination.

An exclusively Italian inspiration and support for the college was asserted by Creighton and implied by Oakley.[41] This is based in part on the mistaken impression that the Council's membership was composed almost, if not totally, "only of Italian prelates." A careful study of the conciliar rolls for the period during which the proposal for a college was advanced reveals that about forty foreign bishops were in attendance. That support for the college was not "confined to a few Italian bishops who were present in Rome" is indicated by a report

---

[39] DE GRASSI, Diarium (DYKMANS, ed.), Nr. 1185:4, p. 360, or RAINALDI 1516, nr. 1.

[40] Mandell CREIGHTON, A History of the Papacy from the Great Schism to the Sack of Rome, V London 1897, 260-63 – hereafter this volume is cited as CREIGHTON; Ludwig von PASTOR, The History of the Popes from the Close of the Middle Ages, VIII, 2nd ed., trans. Ralph Francis KERR, St. Louis 1923, 400-02 – hereafter this volume is cited as PASTOR; Francis OAKLEY, Conciliarism at the Fifth Lateran Council? in: Church History 41 (1972), 456-59 – hereafter cited as OAKLEY. In his The Western Church in the Later Middle Ages, Ithaca 1979, 77, OAKLEY suggests that the proposal had "a whiff of 'episcopalism' about it...."

[41] CREIGHTON: "the Council consisted only of Italian prelates...."(260); "the movement was very partial, and was confined to a few Italian bishops who were present in Rome...."(262) OAKLEY: "When one recalls the degree to which the council was composed of Italian prelates...."(459) and his reference to Döllinger's description of the Council as Leo's "italienisches Taschenkonzil" (459, n. 36).

that the proposal was drawn up at meetings of bishops from every nation and that over three-quarters of the bishops gathered at a special congregation voted to continue pressing their petitions once the pope and cardinals had initially rejected them. Even if support for the college were substantial among Italian curial bishops, it must also be pointed out that one of these same bishops probably composed the detailed rebuttal of the proposed college. The Council's acts record the support for the bishops' petitions given by the foreigners Hamon and Celadenus.[42] Sympathy outside of Italy for a collegial approach to the defense of episcopal interests is suggested by the contemporary Spanish synod at Burgos, English convocation at London, French assemblies at Tours and Lyon, German meetings of prince-bishops at diets, and Maronite collegial government by the patriarch and his bishops.[43] Backing for the proposal was not limited to Italy.

The chronology of the events has not been properly traced by Pastor and Oakley. Given the on-going conflict between bishops and religious up to the very eve of the eleventh session, Oakley has erred in placing the contest over the college "after their bitter struggle."[44] The unrest of the bishops first registered at the eighth session and their petitions which surfaced before the ninth probably indicate an

---

[42] Nelson H. MINNICH, The Participants at the Fifth Lateran Council, in: AHP 12 (1974) 157-206, here 181-96; MANSI 849CD, 850D.

[43] TARSICIO DE AZCONA, La elección y reforma del episcopado español en tiempo de los reyes católicos, Madrid 1960, 303; José M. DOUSSINAGUE, Fernando el católico y el cisma de Pisa, Madrid 1946, 521 - 23; Frederic SEEBOHM, The Oxford Reformers: John Colet, Erasmus, and Thomas More: Being a History of Their Fellowship, London ³1911, 223-24; Karl Joseph von HEFELE and Joseph HERGENRÖTHER, Histoire des conciles d'après les documents originaux, trans. and rev. Henri LECLERCQ, VIII-I, Paris 1917, 275-84; R.G.D. LAFFAN, The Empire under Maximilian I, in: The Renaissance 1493-1520, ed. Denys HAY, Vol. I of The New Cambridge Modern History, ed. G.N. CLARK et al., London 1957, 194-95, 215-16; Petro B.T. BILANIUK, The Fifth Lateran Council (1512-1517) and the Eastern Churches, Toronto 1975, 173; MANSI 1006E-08E.

[44] OAKLEY: "After their bitter struggle with the regular clergy on the matter of monastic privileges and exemptions, the bishops were clearly impressed with the need to close their own ranks if they were to protect their common interests." (457).

earlier origin for the proposal than that implied by Oakley.[45] The absence of any reference to the papal assistants in the surviving rebuttal of the original proposal argues against the claim made by Pastor and implied by Oakley that the cardinals' opposition and papal imposition of silence recorded in that rebuttal were subsequent to the revisions focusing on the papal assistants.[46] The papal threat to keep postponing subsequent sessions of the council and to maintain intact the privileges of religious should the bishops not drop their proposal came not from Leo's refusal to approve their first plan for a college, as stated by Pastor and Oakley,[47] but only after the pope's rejection of their revised version when it had become clear that his imposed silence was ineffective and more subtle tactics were needed. What these corrections in chronology indicate is that the efforts of the bishops to secure their college were simultaneous with their opposition to the privileges of religious, continued unabated for almost two year, and were not deterred by papal demands that they desist. The bishops at Lateran V were not docile.

An attempt by Creighton to reduce the conflict to "little more than a struggle of one party in the Curia against another"[48] does not square with either proposal. The first wanted the college to consist of representatives from various nations who would reside in Rome. It apparently made no mention of curial bishops. The second was constructed around curial prelates in the hope that by adopting the papal assistants as the core of the college, it would seem less threatening and thereby become more acceptable to the pope. Because these assistants were almost all Italians and employed at the curia, the bishops asked that foreign bishops not involved in curial affairs be added to the college. The bishops at Lateran were not concerned with an in-

---

[45] OAKLEY: "The proposal . . . forced itself on the attention of the curia in the months that elapsed between the tenth and eleventh sessions of the council (May 14, 1515 to December 19, 1516)." (457); RAINALDI 1513, nr. 97.

[46] OAKLEY cites arguments made against the first proposal and claims, "therefore . . . a 'perpetual silence' was imposed on the whole idea" (458); PASTOR also claims these same arguments were lodged against the second proposal centering on the papal assistants (401-02).

[47] After discussing the first proposal for the college, PASTOR claims Leo X threatened to postpone the next session if the bishops continued to press their demand (401); OAKLEY makes the same claim (457).

[48] CREIGHTON 262.

The Proposals for an Episcopal College at Lateran V 231

ternal curial power struggle, but with protecting the rights of the whole episcopate.

Although historians agree that the search for a practical solution to grievances lay behind the proposed college, they differ on the nature of these complaints. Creighton pointed to the bishops' need for a remedy against current oppression by cardinals, excessive exemptions for religious, and impaired episcopal jurisdictional rights.[49] Pastor and Oakley emphasized the religious as the opponents and implicitly behind them the papacy which granted their privileges.[50] Once the pope and cardinals indicated their stern opposition to an episcopal college, it is hard to believe, as claimed by Creighton, that the bishops remained "most probably ignorant of its real importance."[51] Pastor held that the cardinals and pope were quick to recognize the threat to centralized papal power implicit in the proposal.[52] When treating the motivations of the bishops, Oakley was inclined to play down the role theological considerations may have had in winning their support for the college.[53] The absence of a theological justification for the college in the extant revision of the proposal would support his contention. And yet men as disparate as Massaino, Giacobazzi, and de Vio were all propounding in Rome ideas supportive of such a college. The practical yet theological lessons learned at the Council regarding the power of bishops in determining Church policy may well have influenced their proposal. That bishops had become aware of the dignity of their office is suggested in their reluctance to remove their

---

[49] CREIGHTON: "They resented the overgrown power of the Cardinals, they wished to reduce the monks to obedience, and to re-establish their own jurisdiction." (261).

[50] PASTOR: "The confraternity ... was directed in the first instance against the regular clergy." (400) OAKLEY: "What moved them, above all, was their dismay at the damage done to their jurisdictional authority by the privileges extended to the regular clergy...." (458).

[51] CREIGHTON 261.

[52] PASTOR: "But how easily might this have developed by an inevitable sequence into a sort of oligarchical constitution.... was foreseen by the Curia...." (400) and "The danger of the situation did not escape the Pope; the Cardinals were against the scheme from the beginning...." (401).

[53] OAKLEY: "Theological considerations played little direct role in rallying the bishops to the idea." (458).

mitres and pay reverence to Leo X at the eleventh session.[54] Were they objecting, as Gozzadini and Massaino had before them, to the abuse of papal power which in the case of the bishops protected their opponents, the cardinals and religious? As Oakley has suggested, the bishops gathered in Rome recognized an imbalance of power in the ecclesiastical organism and were groping for a remedy in the principle and practice of episcopal collegiality.[55] Their failure to rectify this situation did not end the matter. More radical solutions were soon to be adopted in Protestant Europe. It took four and a half centuries and three councils later before Rome would again take up a similar proposal and this time officially accept the principle of episcopal collegiality with its embodiment in the Synod of Bishops.

The struggle at Lateran V for an episcopal college was probably not without a more immediate consequence. Those who attended this Council were not likely to forget the difficulties the papacy had in managing discontented bishops. If such was the case for a council meeting in Rome at which were present numerous Italian and curial bishops, how much greater problems could not the pope expect a few years later from "a free Christian council in German lands" demanded by Luther and his followers? Earlier in their careers Clement VII, Paul III, Julius III, and Paul IV had all attended the Lateran Council as bishops.[56] If they were reluctant to call a council or exercised great care in seeing that it was properly controlled, an explanation for this caution can at least in part be found in their personal experiences of Lateran V.

---

[54] DE GRASSI, Diarium (DYKMANS, ed.), Nr. 1206:7-8, p. 363: *Pontifice in solio sedente, mandavimus paramenta omnium recipi, et sandalia pontifici imponi, et papa legit ut alias. Deinde secuta est omnium mitratorum reverentia, licet aliqui voluissent illam postponi, presertim prelatorum, asserentes prelatos non debere esse nisi in capis, et non prestare reverentiam, sed fuit prestita, ut dixi.*

[55] OAKLEY 459.

[56] MINNICH, Participants at the Fifth Lateran Council, 184-90, nrs. 80, 139, 244, 261.

INDEX*

Acciaiuoli,Roberto: II 112, 122,125,132,136
Accolti,Pietro de: II 90, 111,121,127,168,195*;III 266
Ailly,Pierre d': IV 186;V 222, 225
Albergati,Alberto: II 102
Albert,Amanieu d': II 139,179
Albonesi,Teseo Ambrogio degli: I 166
Aleandro,Girolamo: II 116
Alexander VI,pope: II 60,67, 70,77,86,89;IV 173,175,208
Alexandre,Noël: I 157
Algimunt,Paweł: I 170
Alidosi,Francesco: II 67,68
Alverina,Jean de: II 141
Amadeo de Marseille: II 138
Amboise,Georges d': II 64,66,69
Ambrose,St.: II 158;IV 201,228
Ampudia,Pascual de: see Rebenga
Anne of Brittany: II 96,116,179
Annocque,Jacques: II 280
Antonini da Viterbo, Egidio: IV 168-71,173,177,180,229-35
Aquinas,St. Thomas: IV 202,215
Aragona,Luigi d': II 92,97-98
Ariosto,Ludovico: II 93,97
Arius: IV 169
Armellini,Francesco: II 180,184
Arzelier,Jean: II 141
Augustine,St.: IV 186,188,201, 228
Azeves,Sancho de: IV 218

Babenberg,Daniel: I 173
Baglioni,Ercole: II 103
Bainbridge,Christopher: II 91, 104,107;V 214
Bajazet: IV 190
Bakócz,Tamás Erdödi: I 160;II 84-87,98;IV 241
Bannissis,Jacobus de: II 280
Bargelini,Ovidio: II 102
Bejna Kožićić, Šimun: IV 185-88,227,229-34
Bellarmino,Roberto: I 157
Bembo,Pietro: I 167;III 266
Benet,Cypriano: V 218
Bentivogli,family: II 76,78-79,84-86,88,90,92,97, 100-01,112
Bentivoglio,Annibale II: II 76,100,102
Bentivoglio,Antongaleazzo: II 100
Bentivoglio,Costantino: II 103
Bentivoglio,Ercole: II 102
Bentivoglio,Ermes: II 100
Bentivolgio,Giovanni II: II 101
Bernard,St.: IV 199,201,228
Bernardi,Giovanni: II 143
Bessarion,Janos: IV 179
Biel,Gabriel: IV 186
Binius,Severinus: I 168-69
Blankenfeld,Johann von: I 167
Bobadilla,Francisco: V 217,227
Bongiovanni,Giambattista: II 140
Boniface VIII,pope: II 118,128, 160
Bonomi,Pietro: III 270
Borgia,Cesare: II 60,70,78,81
Borgia,Lucrezia: II 76,77
Borja,Francisco de:II 139
Bottigella,Girolamo: II 82
Boullioud,Symphorien: II 139-40,171
Brandolini,Raffaelo "Lippo": IV 183,222
Briçonnet,Denys: II 82,110,138, 140,152,163
Briçonnet,Guillaume: II 82,94, 110,124,133,138,147,152-53,163;IV 247
Burgo,Andrea dal: II 83-84;III 274
Buṭrus Būlus: I 174

Cajetan (Tommaso de Vio):II 116;IV 175-78,228-31,233, 235,239;V 219,231
Calchagnin,Giovanni Francesco: II 190
Campofregoso,Alessandro: II 67,141
Campofregoso,Ottaviano: II 141,143,171-72
Canossa,Luigi de: II 117,138, 178
Capodivacca,Antonio: III 271
Capponi,Guglielmo: I 176
Capranica,Niccolo: II 78
Caraccioli,Marino: II 137,193*; III 261
Carafa,Alfonso: V 217
Carafa,Giampietro: see Paul IV,

*The list of over 400 participants at the Fifth Council of the Lateran found on pages 181-196 of article I has not been incorporated into this index.

pope
Carafa,Gianvincenzo: V 217
Caretto,Carlo Domenico del: II 88-89,104,120,178
Caretto,Fabrizio del: II 86;IV 190
Caretto,Orlando del: V 217
Carles,Geoffrey: II 89,91
Carondelet,Ferry de: II 81
Carvajal,Bernardino López de: I 163,166,174,176;II 78,81,83, 94,103,105-10,115-16,118, 124,126,130,138,140,146,153, 155,163;III 265,268-70,276; IV 247
Castellesi,Adriano: II 98,150
Castro,Fernando de: I 158,165
Catharinus (Politi),Ambrosius (Lancellotto de'): IV 183
Celadenus (Celadoni),Alexios: I 163;II 90;IV 179-80,227,230, 233,235;V 221,229
Charles V,emperor: II 65-66,71, 94,135;III 262,282
Cheminart,Jean: II 178
Chrysostom,St. John: IV 190
Cibò,Giovanni Battista: I 172
Cibò,Giuliano: V 217
Cibò,Innocenzo: I 163
Claudi,Michele: I 170
Clemens of Kolossi: I 171
Clement V,pope: II 118,128,160
Clement VII,pope: I 175;II 89-90,111,127-28,132-33,178, 182,184;III 266;IV 190;V 214,217,232
Clermont-Lodève,François Guilhelm de: II 78,80,88,138
Coimbra,Henrique Alvari de: I 172
Coleti,Nicola: I 170
Colonna,Fabrizio: II 90,92-93,104
Colonna,Pompejo: V 217,226
Colonna,Prospero:II 93
Columbus,Christopher: IV 215
Conchillos,Jaime de: II 64,72-73
Constantine I,emperor: IV 169, 171,199,229,232
Contarini,Gasparo: IV 193
Conti dei Domicelli,Francesco de': V 217
Contreras,Bernardino de: I 164; II 143,145
Contugii,Geremia: I 169
Cornaro,Marco: II 100,105
Corte,Giannotto: II 89
Corvino,Massimo Bruno: II 78;IV 205,232-33,235
Cospi,Angelo: II 103
Cossart,Gabriel: I 170

Crabbe,Pierre: I 168-69
Creighton,Mandell: I 158;V 228, 230-31

Decio,Filippo: II 82,105;III 264
Delfino,Pietro: I 167
Deza, Diego de: IV 215,221,233
Dioscorus: IV 178,241
Doria,Eduardo: II 143
Dorotheos II: I 174
Dovizi da Bibbiena,Bernardo: II 97,181,194*
Dronius,Ludovico: II 169
Duvet,Jean: II 143
Du Vivier,Edouard: II 143

Erasmus,Desiderius: I 159;IV 172,191,231,242
Estaing,Antoine d': II 139-40, 171
Este,Alfonso d': II 62,65,67-69,71,73-74,77-80,83,85-86, 88,90-93,97-100,103,128,138, 166,180-81,185,187;III 277-78
Este,Ercole d': III 276
Este,Ferrante d': II 93
Este,Fresco d': II 77
Este,Giulio d': II 93
Este, Ippolito d': II 98-99,117,162,180,182,185-87,190
Eugenius IV,pope: IV 187;V 216
Eylac,Johannes de: I 173

Faella,Ludovico: II 83;III 271
Falcem,Petrus: I 173
Fantuzzi,family: II 99,102
Fantuzzi,Bonifatio: II 102
Fantuzzi,gonfaloniere: II 92
Farnese,Alessandro: II 98,121, 127,195*;IV 237-38
Fedrigo de Portugal: II 109-110
Fernando,king of Aragon: I 158; II 61,64-68,71-72,75,77,83, 84-85,88,91,104,109,114-15, 134-35,139,175;III 272;IV 189,212,214-15,220-21,228, 232
Ferreri,Giovanni: II 147-48
Ferreri,Zaccaria: I 176;II 82, 94,119,140,146-47;III 275
Ficino,Marsilio: IV 168
Fieschi,Agostino: I 172
Fieschi,Lorenzo de: I 165
Fieschi (Flisco),Niccolò: II 92,98,115,120
Filonardi,Ennio: II 144,197*
Fisher,St. John: I 159;IV 241
Flores,Antonio: I 163
Flores,Pedro: I 158; II 144

Foix,Gaston de: II 85
Foix,Germaine de: II 175
Fonseca,Alonso II de: IV 219
Fonseca,Juan Rodrigo: II 110
Forbin,Louis de: II 104,115,
    117,121,127,134,136-38,143-
    45,161,194*;III 265-66
Forman,Andrew: I 163;II 64-65,
    73-74,77-78,80,82
Francis I,king of France: II
    100,110,133,145,152,175;IV
    192;V 226
Fregoso,Federigo: V 217
Fregoso,Ottaviano: II 114
Fresne,Jean du: II 140,171
Fürst,Viet von: II 66;III 274

Gabbionetta,Alessandro: II 64,
    65
Gannay,Jean de: II 161
Garampi,Giuseppe: I 178
Gargiis,Giovanni Battista de:
    IV 190,230-32,235
Gentile,Andrea: II 183
Geraldino,Alessandro Girolamo:
    I 164
Gheri,Goro: II 197*
Giacobazzi,Domenico: V 217-18,
    221,226,231
Giberti,Gian Matteo: II 184
Gigli,Silvestro: I 164;II 193*
Giustiniani, Leonardo qu.
    Lorenzo qu. Bernardo: II 182
Giustiniani, Bl. Paolo
    (Tommaso): IV 222,228,231-
    35
Gonzaga,Ercole: II 98
Gonzaga,Federico II: II 78
Gonzaga,Gianfrancesco: II 92
Gonzaga,Giovanni: II 64
Gouffier de Boisy,Adrian de: II
    197*
Gozzadini,Giovanni: V 218,232
Grassi,Achille de: II 90,103;V
    215
Grassi,Agamemnon de: II 102
Grassi,Paride de: I 158,167,
    170;II 72,74,88,91,104,106,
    108,137;III 261,271,280;IV
    163,165,169,181,237;V 216-
    17,219,222-23,226
Gregorovius,Ferdinand: I 158
Gregory I,pope St.: IV 228
Griffi,Andrea: II 101
Griffo,Pietro: II 180,186
Grimani,Domenico: II 100;IV 222
Guasco,Alessandro: II 78;V 217
Guglia,Eugen: I 168
Guibé,Robert de: II 76-77,85-
    87,96,104,115,117,120,131-
    32,138;III 265-66
Guicciardini,Francesco: II 74

Guillard,Louis: II 149
Gustaferro,Francesco: V 217

Halwin,François de: II 139,171
Hamon,François: II 117;III 266;
    V 220,229
Hapsburg, Ferdinand von: II 135
Hardouin,Jean: I 169-70
Hautbois,Charles de: II 149-50
Hefele,Karl Joseph: I 158
Henry VIII,king of England: I
    161;II 85,88,104,114,124,
    134,150,153
Hergenröther,Karl: V 228
Herrera,Fernando de: V 217
Hus,Jan: IV 178

Inghirami,Tommaso: II 137;III
    261,270,280
Ilyās ibn Ibrāhīm: I 166
Ilyās ibn Zarzūr al-Ḥadatī: I
    166
Isolani,Isidoro: V 218
Isuales,Pedro: II 72

James IV,king of Scotland: II
    64,94
Jedin,Hubert: I 159
Jerome,St.: IV 171,174,228
Joachim of Flora: II 94;IV 169,
    201
John XXII,pope: II 129
Juana,queen of Castilla: II 175
Julius II,pope: I 159-62,168,
    175;II 60-107 passim,112,
    116,118-19,123-24,126,128-
    29,132,139,145,147-48,151,
    153-54,156,159,166,169,187;
    III 261-64,270-71,277-78,
    287;IV 164-65,167,172-73,
    175,181,183,185,189-90,194,
    208,233,237-38,241-43;V 214,
    216
Julius III,pope: I 175;IV 183-
    85,230,232,234-35;V 232

Labbe,Philippe: I 169-70
Lactantius: IV 184,192,228,235
Ladislas,king of Hungary: IV
    241-42
Lalexa,Martinus: I 172
Lang von Wellenburg,Matthäus: I
    160,163;II 62,64-65,69,71-
    73,75,83,95,110,112,114,135-
    36,138,193*,197*;III 263,
    267,270-72,279,281,287,243
Lascaris,Janus: II 116
Łaski,Jan: I 160
Laureliis,Lorenzo de: II 108
Lebna Dengel (David),emperor of
    Ethiopia: I 174
Lefranc,Jean: 1 169

LeLamiens, Jean: II 140,171
Leo X,pope: I 160,162,165-66,
　168,175;II 72,85,87-89,91,
　97-100,103-54 passim,161,
　168,170-71,175,179-81,185,
　193*,197*;III 261,265-66,
　281-83;IV 165,167,185,187,
　189-90,192,194,196,208-10,
　233,244,246,248-49,251,252*,
　253*;V 217,220,222,226-27,
　232
Leonini,Angelo: II 77-80,82,88-
　89,117;V 217
Lessart,Guiscard (de Beysard):
　II 141
Loaysa,Juan de: I 165
Longwy,Claude de: II 141
Louis XI,king of France: II
　152,179
Louis XII,king of France: I
　161;II 62-91 passim,94-96,
　101,104,111,113,115-137
　passim,146,148-49,152-53,
　159-61,165,167,177-79,194*;
　III 261-64,266,270-74,277,
　281,283,285-87,289;IV 174,
　213,221,232
Luther,Martin: IV 178,181,183,
　186,236;V 232
Luxembourg,Philippe de: II 96,
　139
Luxemburg,Sigismund von: IV
　187,232

Machiavelli,Niccolò: I 173;II
　67
Malabaila,Vasino: II 140,145
Malvetti,Lorenzo Battista: II
　101,103
Malvezzi,Matteo: II 102
Mansi,Giovanni Domenico: I 158,
　170
Marcello,Cristoforo: IV 181-
　83,229,231-34;V 216
Marck,Erard de la: II 91
Marescotti,Ercole: II 103
Mârqos,patriarch of Ethiopia:
　I 174
Marsupina,Francesco: II 88
Masciolo,Gabriele: V 217
Massaino,Girolamo: V 218,231-32
Massimo,Domenico: II 120
Maximilian I,emperor: I 160;II
　62-76 passim,79,82-84,95,
　104,109,112-15,127,134-38,
　149-50,153,183;III 261,263-
　64,267-73,275-76,278,280-81;
　IV 174,243
Mazzocchi,Jacopo: I 168-69
Medici,Giovanni dei: see Leo X,
　pope
Medici,Giuliano dei: II 99,103,
　121,134-35,194*;III 267,281
Medici,Giulio dei: see Clement
　VII, pope
Medici,Lorenzo dei: II 110
Merino,Esteban Gabriel: I 163
Middelburg,Paulus van: I 163
Monte,Antonio Maria Ciochi del:
　I 165,168-70;II 90,92,104,
　109,121,127-28,143,145,193*,
　195*;III 266,282;IV 183,239
Monte,Giammaria del: see Julius
　III,pope
More,St. Thomas: IV 172
Morone,Girolamo: I 166,176;II
　140,142,174;III 280
Mota,Pedro Ruiz de la: III 274
Musuros,Markos: I 163;II 116

Neideck,Georg von: II 83
Niccolò da Este: II 186
Neuhaus,Nikolas von: III 274
Nogarola,Girolamo de: II 83;III
　271,274
Nory,Guillaume de: II 140,171
Nostromars: II 143
Nudry,Thomas: V 215

Oakley,Francis: V 220,228-32
Ockham,William of: IV 186
Oldenburg,Hans von,king of
　Denmark: II 94
Oliz,Pierre: II 149
Orsini,Gian Giordano: II 76,104
Orsini,Roberto Latino: V 217,
　226
Ostrorog,Stanislaw: I 176

Pallavicini,Giambattista: V 217
Pandolfino,Francesco: II 132,
　178
Paolo da Lodi: II 84
Pasquali,Alberto: V 218
Pastor,Ludwig von: I 169;V 228-
　31
Patrizi (Piccolomini),Agostino:
　V 216
Paul II,pope: II 71
Paul III,pope: I 175;V 232
Paul IV,pope: I 175;IV 193;V
　232
Pecunia,Tommaso: II 143
Pepoli,Alessandro: II 102
Perusco,Mario de: II 113,142
Petrucci,Alfonso: II 110
Philip IV (the Fair),king of
　France: II 118,161
Photinus: IV 169
Photius: IV 178,241
Piccolomini,Girolamo: I 170
Pico della Mirandola,
　Gianfrancesco: I 167;III
　277;IV 202-04,228,230-31,

233,235
Pio,Alberto: I 166;II 67-68,97,
    104,113,120,135-37,150,180,
    185,192,193*,197*;III 261-
    62,268-73,276-83
Pio,Enea: II 184
Pio,Giberto: III 276
Pio,Marco: III 276
Pisauro,Francesco: V 217
Pistoia,Sebastiano da: II 130-
    31,138,162
Plato: IV 199
Poggio,Giovanni Francesco: V
    218
Pomponazzi,Pietro: IV 178
Poncher,Étienne: II 64-65,68,
    73-75,117,161,179;III 271
Portinari,Pigello: II 83
Poupet,Jean de: II 139,171
Prie,René de: II 124,138-39,
    147,153,163
Pucci,Antonio: IV 192,194-98,
    207,228-31,233-35
Pucci,Lorenzo: II 127-28,175,
    178,187,190;IV 189,192; V
    217

Quentel,Jean: I 168,169
Quesvel,Pierre: II 141
Quirini,Pietro (Vicenzo): IV
    222,228,231,232-35

Radvilas,Albert: I 170
Rainaldi,Odorico: V 228
Rangoni,Guido: II 183
Raphael: II 106
Rebenga,Pascual (Juan) de
    Ampudia (de la Fuentesanta)
    de: I 158,167
Reby,Jean de: II 81
Regis,Thomas: I 164
Remolines,Francisco: I 163;II
    104,135,193*
Riario,Girolamo: II 77
Riario,Raffaello: I 159;II 72,
    98,104,153,155;IV 167,207-
    12,230-31,233,235,237,241,
    243-44,246-449,251,252*,253*
Rio,Baltasar del: IV 189,227,
    229,232
Robertet,Charles: II 132-33
Robertet,Florimond: II 132,179
Rohan,François de: II 147-48
Rohan-Guéménée,Pierre de: II
    84
Rossi,Bernardo: V 217
Rossi,Luigi de: II 179;V 217
Rovere,Antonio Giuppo della:
    II 134;III 270,278-79,281
Rovere,Francesco della: V 217
Rovere,Francesco Maria della:
    II 62,67,92

Rovere,Gianfrancesco della: V
    217
Rovere,Leonardo Grosso della:
    II 92,121,151,193*
Rovere,Sisto di Franciotti
    della: II 104,106
Rucellai (Oricellarius),
    Joannes: I 174

Sabellius: IV 169
Sachus,Jacobus: II 134
Sacierges,Pierre de: II 119
Sadoleto,Jacopo: IV 169
Salviati,Giorgio Benigno (Juraj
    Dragišić): I 163
Salviati,Jacopo: I 173
Sanseverino,Alessandro: II 111
Sanseverino,Federigo: I 176;II
    81,103,105-08,110,115-18,
    120-21,124,126-27,130,132,
    134,137-38,140,146,153,155,
    161,163,194*;III 265-66;V
    214
Sanseverino,Galeazzo: II 132,
    161-62
Sanseverino,Roberto: II 161
Saint André,Martin de: II 149
Saraceno,Gherardo: II 186
Savonarola,Girolamo: IV 202,204
Schinner,Matthäus: I 163;II
    104,107,111,144,197*
Schulz von Lowenburg,Bernhard:
    I 164;II 143,145
Scotti,Giovani Antonio: V 220
Sepulveda,Juan Ginés de: I 158
Serra,Jaime: I 163;II 91
Seurre,Antoine: II 171
Seyssel,Claude de: I 166;II 84,
    95-96,118-37 passim,142,161-
    62,172,177,194*,197*;III
    261,265-66,280
Sforza,family: II 114,134
Sforza,Francesco: II 137;III
    270
Sforza,Massimiliano,duke of
    Milan:I 166;II 93-96,109,
    137,141-42,144,171,173-74,
    197*;III 261
Simeon ibn Dāwūd ibn Ḥassān al-
    Hadaṭī: I 166
Sixtus IV,pope: II 77;IV 206-
    07,216
Soderini,Francesco: II 94,98,
    109,121
Soderini,Giuliano: V 217
Stölli,Johannes: I 173
Sylvester,pope St.: IV 199,229

Taleazzi,Stefano: IV 198,229,
    231-32,234-35;V 217
Tedeschini-Piccolomini,
    Gianvincenzo: V 217,226

Teodorici,Gian Battista de: II 81
Tillières,Jean le Veneur: II 139,171
Torella,Gaspar: I 158
Tornabuoni,Giuliano: I 173
Tournon,Claude de: II 119
Tournon,Gaspar de: II 141
Treio,Francesco de: II 81
Trémouille,Louis de la: II 96
Trithemius (Johann Heidenberg): III 274
Trivulzio,Antonio: II 145-46
Trivulzio,Giangiacomo de: II 66,76-77
Trivulzio,Scaramuzia: V 217
Trombetta,Antonio: V 218

Ulfsson,Jakob: I 164
Urrea,Felipe de: I 164
Urrea,Pedro de: I 172

Valle,Andrea de: V 217
Valois,Claude de: II 66
Vettori,Francesco: I 173;II 131-32

Vich,Jeronimo de: I 158;II 64-66,68-69,72-74,81,92,135, 196*;III 281
Vigerio,Marco: II 90,92,98,121, 128,195*
Villalva,Juan: I 163
Villa-Quiran,Valerian Alphonsus Ordoñez de: IV 213,229

Wardenburg,Zutfeldus von: I 164;V 215
Wolsey,Thomas: II 150

Yūsuf al-Hūri: I 166

Zancha,Ambrogio: II 81
Zanni,Bernardo II: IV 173-75, 228-31,231;V 217

INDEX OF MANUSCRIPTS

Brussels
Archives Générales du Royaume de Belgique
 Grand Conseil de Malines,Nr.143: II 94, 149

Florence
Archivio di Stato
 Archivio Mediceo avanti il Principato,Filza 105,nr.34: II 122, 135. Filza 107,nr.27: II 138. Filza 113,nr.94: II 99. Filza 147,nr.34: II 122,135
 Dieci di Balia,Carteggi Missive Legazioni Commissarie,Nr.40: II 112,122,126,131
 Dieci di Balia,Carteggi, Responsive,Nr.117: II 97,112-13,121-23,125,134.Nr.118: II 75,117,123,125-26,131-33,135-36, 138-39,142
 Dieci di Balia,Legazione e Commissarie, Instruzione e Lettere Missive,Nr.40: II 134. Nr.41: II 137
 Otto di Pratica, Carteggi,Serie Responsive 1471-1533, Registro Carteceo,Nr.11: II 113
 Signori,Carteggi,Responsive Originale,Filza Carteceo, Nr.33: II 89. Nr. 35: II 102
 Signori,Dieci di Balia,Otto di Pratica,Legazione e Commissarie,Missive e Responsive,Nr.55: II 133, 150,153,178
 Strozziane,Carte,Prima Serie,Filza 8: II 110
 Torrigiani,Manoscritti, Filza III,Inserta XIV Leone X e Ferrara,Nrs. 1-10: II 100,180,182, 185,187,190

Lille
Archives départmentales du Nord
 Coté B 1462,nr.18060: II 124,162
 Coté B 18859,nr.30846: II 116,121
 Coté B 18861,nr.31067: II 137;III 280
 Coté B 18863,nr.31164: III 269

Paris
Archives Nationales
 L329 nr.1: II 128,165
Bibliothèque Nationale
 Dupuy 86: III 264,272
 Dupuy 261: II 114,117;III 265
 Dupuy 262: II 114
 Fond Ancien Français 2930: III 265
 Fond Ancien Français 2933: II 117,161
 Fond Ancien Français 2964: II 121
 Fond Ancien Français 3087: II 62,118,159
 Fond Ancien Français 5501: III 264

Philadelphia
University of Pennsylvania, Van Pelt Library, Rare Book Collection,Henry Charles Lea Library
 Ms. 414: II 193*,197*

Rome
Archivio di Stato
 Archivio del Collegio dei Notari Capitolini,vol. 1914: II 101
Biblioteca Angelica
 Ms. 1888: I 172

Vatican City
Archivio Segreto Vaticano
 Arch.Miscel.,Acta Consist. 3: II 79,81,89,97,137
 Arm. I,nr.43: II 97
 Arm. II,vol.21: IV 237
 Arm. I-XVIII,nr.2621: II 135. nr.3017: V 220
 Arm. XXXIX,vol.30: II 101, 109-11,151. vol.31: II 110. vol.36: II 110-11, 148
 Arm. XL,vol.2: II 100
 Arm.XLIV,vol.5: II 98-99, 139,171-73
 Arm.LXIV,vol.5: II 102,109
 Fondo Camerale,Introitus et exitus,nr.551: II 89
 Reg.Vat.956: II 88,128,166

Reg.Vat.967: II 78
Reg.Vat.984: II 62,128,166
Reg.Vat.999: II 102
Reg.Vat.1004: II 129,151
Reg.Vat.1005: II 129,169
Reg.Vat.1010: II 129,151,169
Reg.Vat.1026: II 151
Reg.Vat.1035: II 129,151
Reg.Vat.1093: II 110,151
Reg.Vat.1194: II 110
Reg.Vat.1197: II 110
Reg.Vat.1198: II 110,111,139
Reg.Vat.1204: II 175
Reg.Vat.1205: II 111
Reg.Vat.1206: II 111
Reg.Vat.1207: II 111
Biblioteca Apostolica Vaticana
  Barb.Lat.3552: II 120
  Chigi,I.III.89: II 79,105,
    155;IV 238,241,243-44,
    246-47,251,252*,253*
  Chigi,L.III.60: III 269,283,
    285
  Regin.Lat.392: V 218
  Vat.Lat.6232: II 85,94,96,
    104
  Vat.Lat.12208: II 153
  Vat.Lat.12269: IV 169
  Vat.Lat.12275: II 102,117;
    III 266,280;V 215-16
  Vat.Lat.12413: V 216-17
  Vat.Lat.12414: III 272; V
    216

Vienna
Haus-,Hof- und Staatsarchiv
  Maximiliana,box 24,III:
    II 64-65,77;III 263-
    64,272,275,278
  Maximiliana,box 25,I: II 68;
    III 264,275,278.
  Maximiliana,box 25,III: II
    68;III 272,275,278
  Maximiliana,box 25,IV: II
    81;III 264
  Maximiliana,box 26,II: II 82
  Maximiliana,box 26,III: II
    82,86;III 275
  Maximiliana,box 26,IV: II
    82-83,85
  Maximiliana,box 27,II: II 86
  Maximiliana,box 27,IV: II 95
  Maximiliana,box 28,II: II 95
  Maximiliana,box 28,V: II 96
  Maximiliana,box 29,II: II
    115
  Maximiliana,box 29,III: II
    110,112-15,117,120,135;
    III 268
  Maximiliana,box 29,IV: II
    109-10,113,115,126,135,
    150;III 268-69,278,281
  Maximiliana,box 30,I: II
    122;III 279
  Maximiliana,box 30,II: II
    75,109,111-13,122,131,
    134-35,150;III 279,281
  Maximiliana,box 30,III: II
    75,113,115,138;III 267,
    278-79
  Maximiliana,box 31,I: III
    267,269,279,281
  Maximiliana,box 31,II: II
    100
  Maximiliana,box 32,II: II
    138
  Maximiliana,box 42,II: II
    110
Österreichische National-
  bibliothek
  cod.12589: II 76